# EX MACHINA
## BOOK TWO

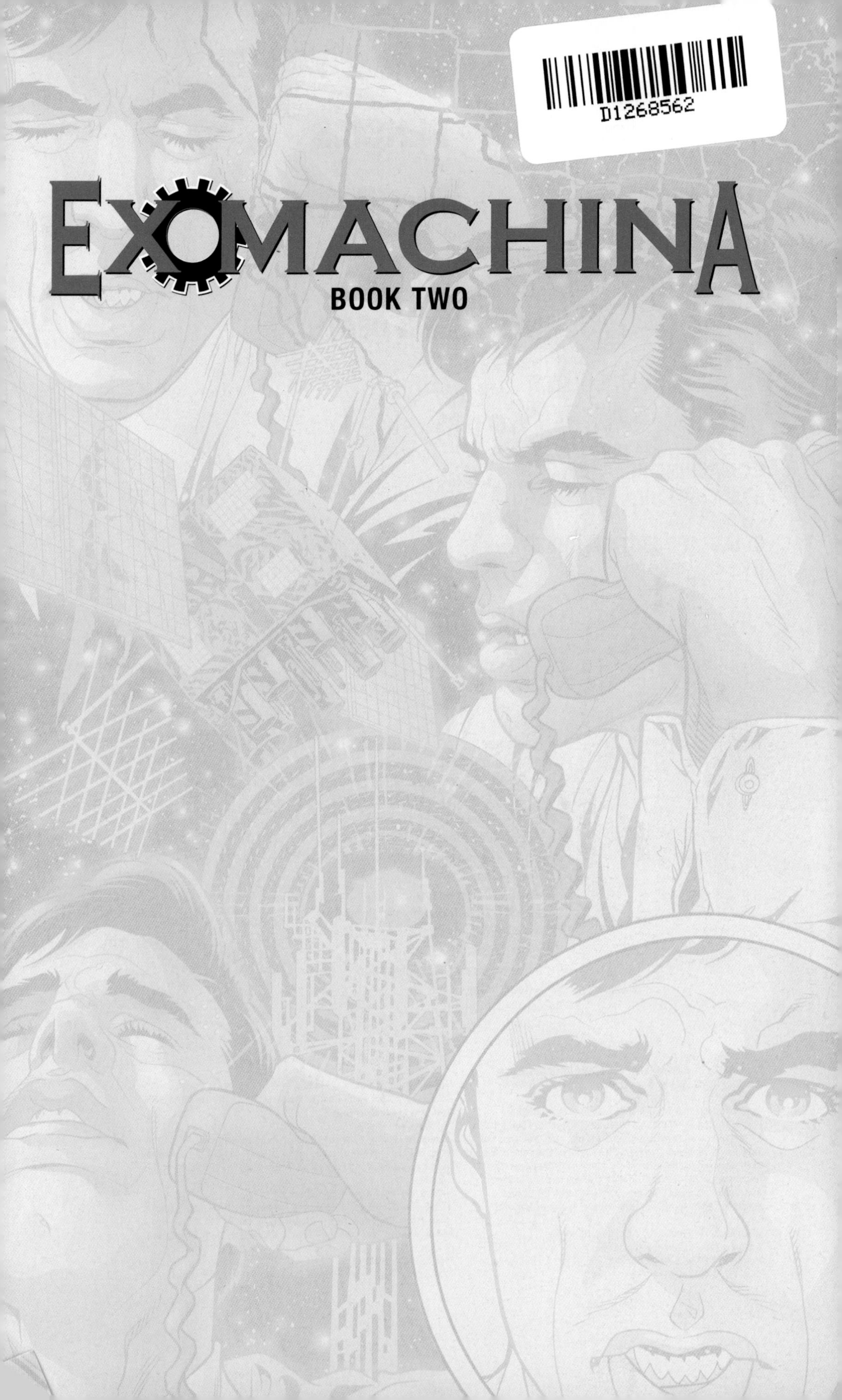

# BRIAN K. VAUGHAN: WRITER
# TONY HARRIS: PENCILS

## CHRIS SPROUSE: PENCILS (LIFE & DEATH)
## TOM FEISTER: INKS

## KARL STORY: INKS (LIFE & DEATH)

## JD METTLER: COLORS
## JARED K. FLETCHER: LETTERS

### EX MACHINA CREATED
### BY VAUGHAN AND HARRIS

### COLLECTED EDITION COVER
### BY TONY HARRIS

| | |
|---|---|
| Ben Abernathy | Editor – Original Series |
| Robbin Brosterman | Design Director – Books |
| | |
| Shelly Bond | Executive Editor – Vertigo |
| Hank Kanalz | Senior VP – Vertigo and Integrated Publishing |
| | |
| Diane Nelson | President |
| Dan DiDio and Jim Lee | Co-Publishers |
| Geoff Johns | Chief Creative Officer |
| John Rood | Executive VP – Sales, Marketing and Business Development |
| Amy Genkins | Senior VP – Business and Legal Affairs |
| Nairi Gardiner | Senior VP – Finance |
| Jeff Boison | VP – Publishing Planning |
| Mark Chiarello | VP – Art Direction and Design |
| John Cunningham | VP – Marketing |
| Terri Cunningham | VP – Editorial Administration |
| Alison Gill | Senior VP – Manufacturing and Operations |
| Jay Kogan | VP – Business and Legal Affairs, Publishing |
| Jack Mahan | VP – Business Affairs, Talent |
| Nick Napolitano | VP – Manufacturing Administration |
| Sue Pohja | VP – Book Sales |
| Courtney Simmons | Senior VP – Publicity |
| Bob Wayne | Senior VP – Sales |

EX MACHINA BOOK TWO
Published by DC Comics. Copyright © 2014 Brian K. Vaughan
and Tony Harris. All Rights Reserved.

Originally published in single magazine form by WildStorm
Productions as EX MACHINA #12-20, EX MACHINA SPECIALS 1-2,
EX MACHINA: TAG Copyright © 2005, 2006 Brian K. Vaughan and
Tony Harris. All Rights Reserved. All characters, their distinctive
likenesses and related elements featured in this publication are
trademarks of DC Comics. The stories, characters and incidents
featured in this publication are entirely fictional. DC Comics
does not read or accept unsolicited ideas, stories or artwork.

DC Comics, 1700 Broadway, New York, NY 10019
A Warner Bros. Entertainment Company.
Printed by RR Donnelley, Salem, VA, USA. 4/18/14. First Printing.
ISBN 978-1-4012-4691-4

Library of Congress Cataloging-in-Publication Data

Vaughan, Brian K., author.
  Ex Machina. Book Two / Brian K. Vaughan ; illustrated by Tony Harris ;
illustrated by Chris Sprouse.
    pages cm
  Summary: "Former superhero Mitchell Hundred becomes the elected
Mayor of New York City after the events of 9/11, combatting corruption
and supervillains from both sides of the costume." — Provided by
publisher.
  ISBN 978-1-4012-4691-4 (paperback)
  1. Mayors—Comic books, strips, etc. 2. Superheroes—Comic books,
strips, etc. 3. New York (N.Y.)—Comic books, strips, etc. 4. Graphic
novels. I. Harris, Tony, 1969- illustrator. II. Sprouse, Chris, illustrator.
III. Title.
  PN6728.E98V353 2014
  741.5'973—dc23
                                    2014000396

SUSTAINABLE
FORESTRY
INITIATIVE
Certified Chain of Custody
At Least 20% Certified Forest Content
www.sfiprogram.org
SFI-01042
APPLIES TO TEXT STOCK ONLY

We're not terribly good at this sort of thing but we thought we should do it…because even though we have never met him, we are in love with Brian K. Vaughan. And we have been from the moment we picked up the first issue of Y: THE LAST MAN and started giggling when everything with a Y-chromosome suddenly exploded like a cat in a microwave—giggling not in a disturbing, sociopathic way, but in a completely delighted way as the sheer audaciousness of a new story-teller startled us awake from the sleepwalking world of comics where "fresh" and "original" are usually synonyms for "costume change." We left the comic shop that day with little hearts in our eyes…and ever since, we have faithfully bought every comic with Brian K. Vaughan's name on it.

However, as Sappho suggested, what is once sweet often turns bitter.

We had, on occasion, talked about the fact that if a real super hero existed he or she would be a shoo-in for any political election. Let's face it, California elected someone just because he used to pretend he was a super hero. The moral quagmire of politics seemed to us an ideal world to set a new kind of super hero story. We kept the idea safe in our back pocket, figuring there were only a handful of writers who would dare defy one of the Establishment's favorite creeds: thou shalt not mix Art and Politics.

So, without any inkling whatsoever, we picked up the first issue of EX MACHINA and immediately the valentine-colored eyes with which we usually read a Brian K. Vaughan comic turned a Hulk-shaded green. How does one describe the feeling a writer has when they discover one of their ideas in the arms of another? Shock. Outrage. Panic. Lots of huffing and puffing followed by a slow deflation into resignation with mumbled, begrudging respect designed to mask petty, bitter jealousy.

It took a while for us to be big enough to buy the second issue but we're glad we did. The book is absolutely terrific. Tony Harris and Tom Feister's clean-lined, expressive artwork seamlessly weaves the "real" world of politics into the normal fabric of comics. And as for Brian's impeccable storytelling, well, what can we say? We love him.

- The Wachowski Brothers

These insanely talented filmmakers are responsible for bringing you such diverse hits as the *Matrix* trilogy, *V for Vendetta* and *Speed Racer*.

# CHAPTER 1 FACT v. FICTION

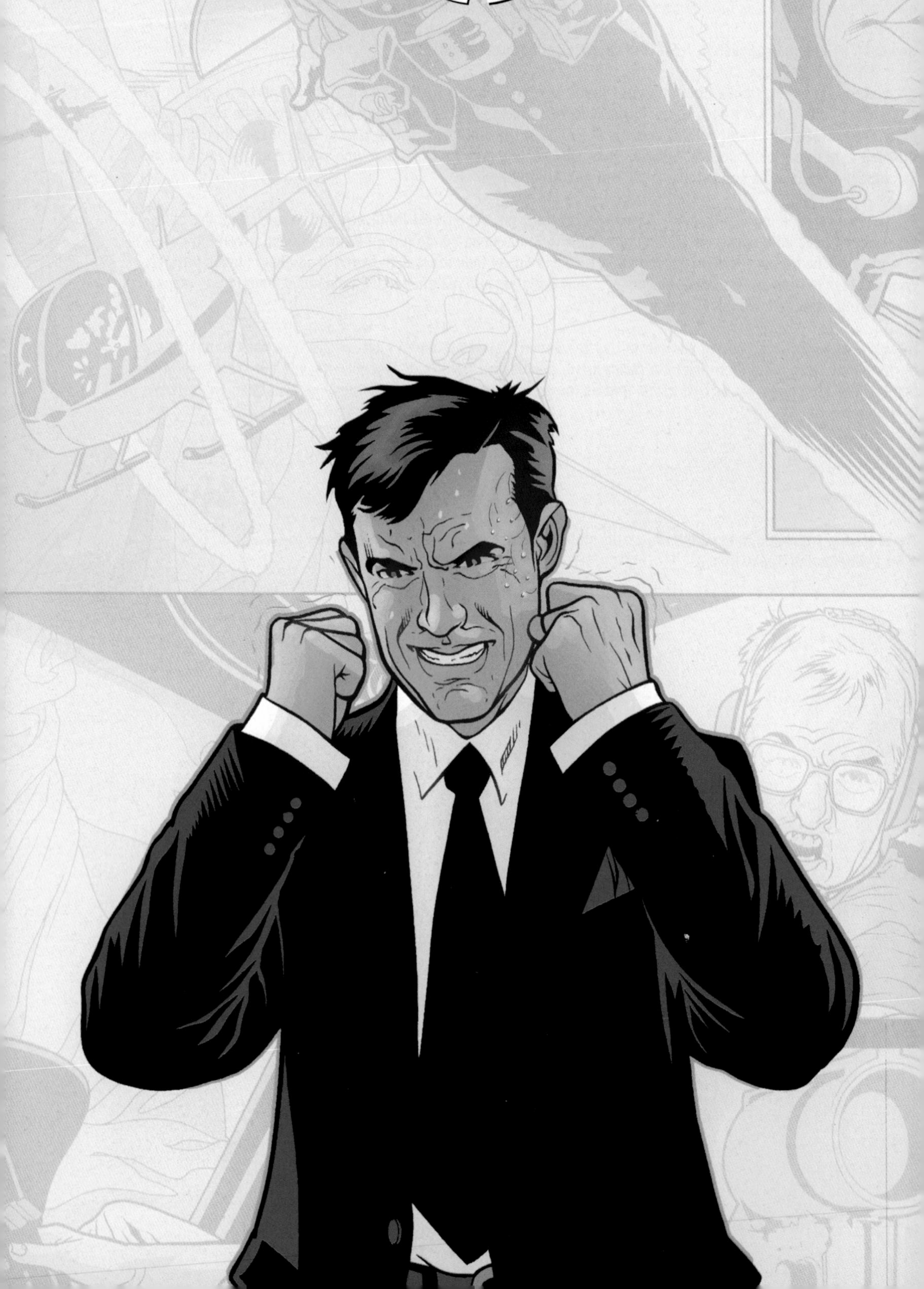

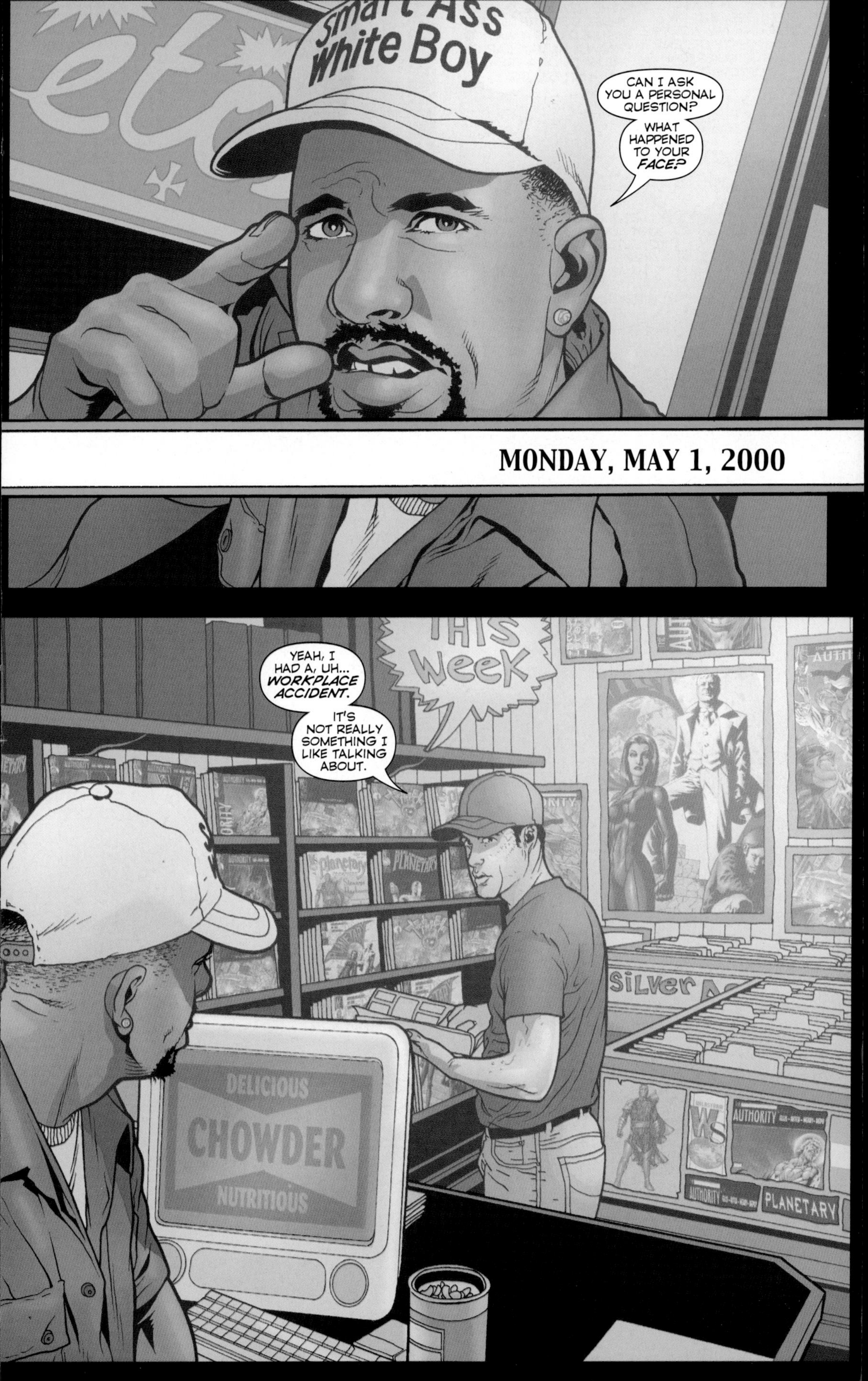
Smart Ass White Boy
CAN I ASK YOU A PERSONAL QUESTION?
WHAT HAPPENED TO YOUR *FACE?*
MONDAY, MAY 1, 2000
THIS week
YEAH, I HAD A, UH... *WORKPLACE ACCIDENT.*
IT'S NOT REALLY SOMETHING I LIKE TALKING ABOUT.
DELICIOUS
CHOWDER
NUTRITIOUS
PLANETARY

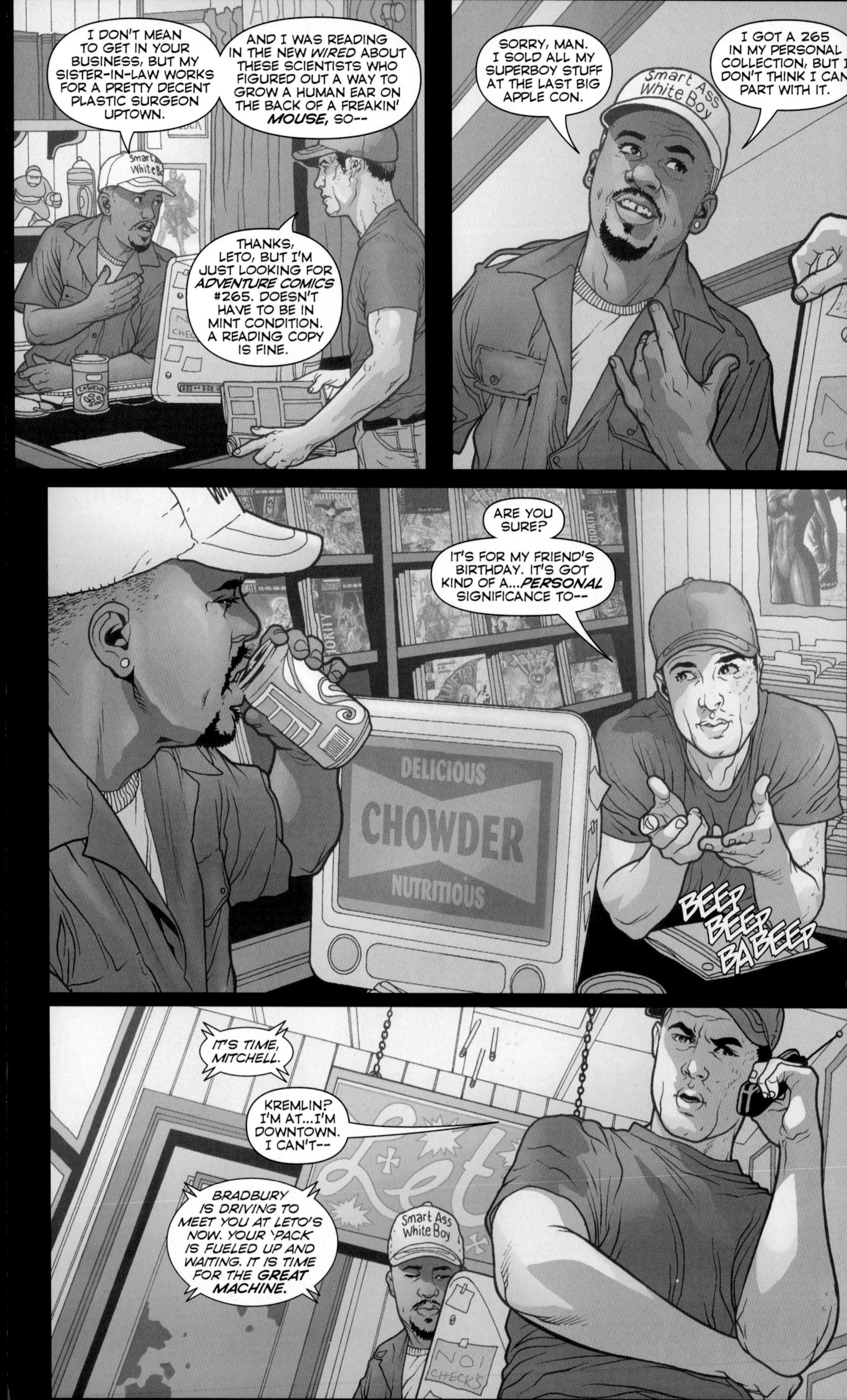
I DON'T MEAN TO GET IN YOUR BUSINESS, BUT MY SISTER-IN-LAW WORKS FOR A PRETTY DECENT PLASTIC SURGEON UPTOWN.
AND I WAS READING IN THE NEW *WIRED* ABOUT THESE SCIENTISTS WHO FIGURED OUT A WAY TO GROW A HUMAN EAR ON THE BACK OF A FREAKIN' ***MOUSE,*** SO--
THANKS, LETO, BUT I'M JUST LOOKING FOR *ADVENTURE COMICS* #265. DOESN'T HAVE TO BE IN MINT CONDITION. A READING COPY IS FINE.
SORRY, MAN. I SOLD ALL MY SUPERBOY STUFF AT THE LAST BIG APPLE CON.
Smart Ass White Boy
I GOT A 265 IN MY PERSONAL COLLECTION, BUT I DON'T THINK I CAN PART WITH IT.
ARE YOU SURE?
IT'S FOR MY FRIEND'S BIRTHDAY. IT'S GOT KIND OF A...***PERSONAL*** SIGNIFICANCE TO--
DELICIOUS
CHOWDER
NUTRITIOUS
BEEP BEEP BABEEP
*IT'S TIME, MITCHELL.*
KREMLIN? I'M AT...I'M DOWNTOWN. I CAN'T--
*BRADBURY IS DRIVING TO MEET YOU AT LETO'S NOW. YOUR 'PACK IS FUELED UP AND WAITING. IT IS TIME FOR THE **GREAT MACHINE.***
Smart Ass White Boy
NO CHECKS

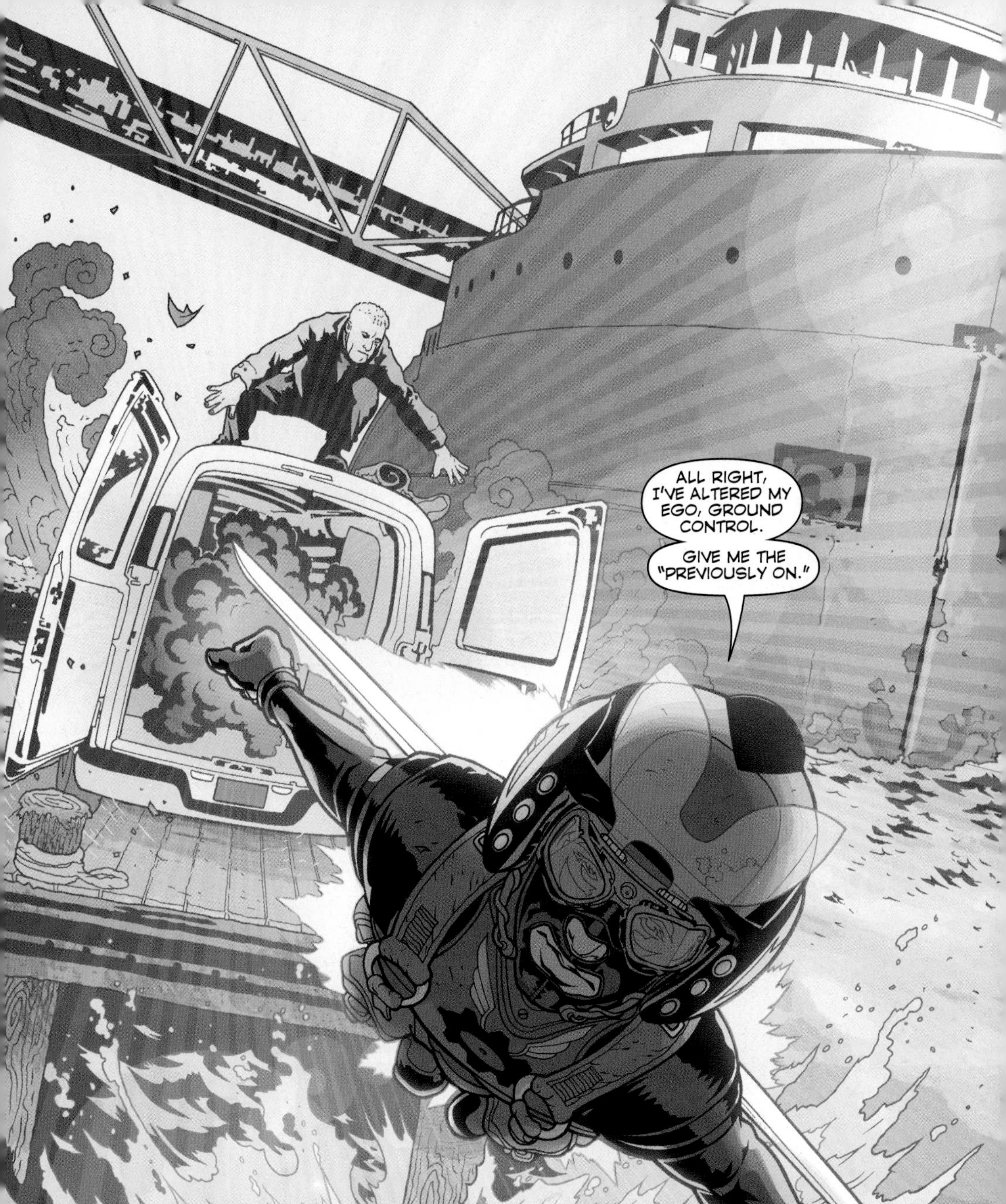
ALL RIGHT, I'VE ALTERED MY EGO, GROUND CONTROL.
GIVE ME THE "PREVIOUSLY ON."

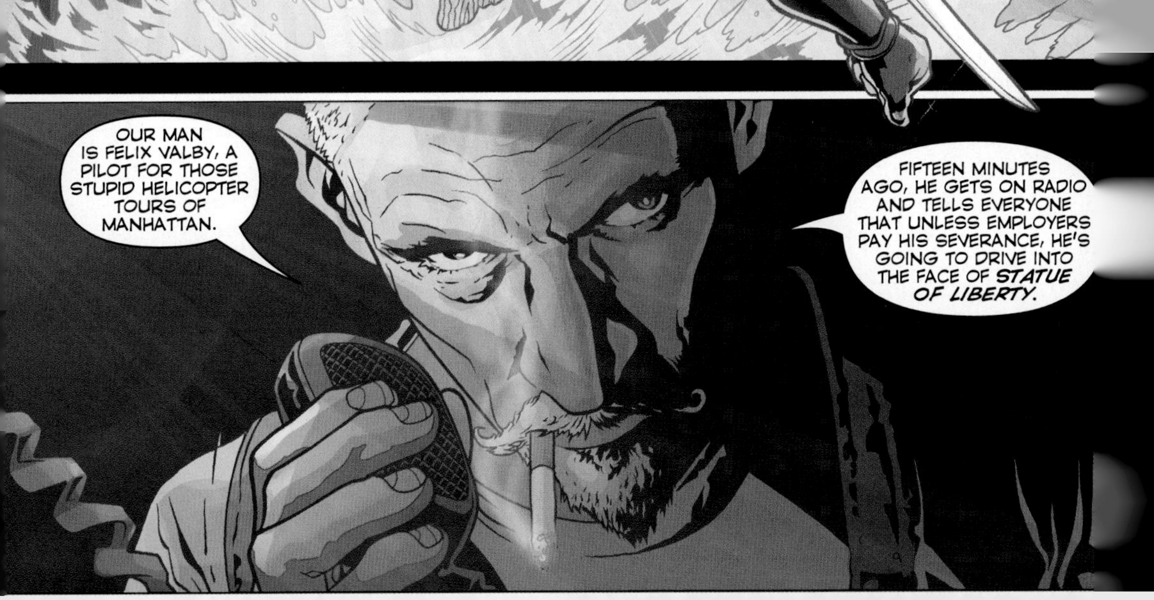
OUR MAN IS FELIX VALBY, A PILOT FOR THOSE STUPID HELICOPTER TOURS OF MANHATTAN.
FIFTEEN MINUTES AGO, HE GETS ON RADIO AND TELLS EVERYONE THAT UNLESS EMPLOYERS PAY HIS SEVERANCE, HE'S GOING TO DRIVE INTO THE FACE OF ***STATUE OF LIBERTY***.

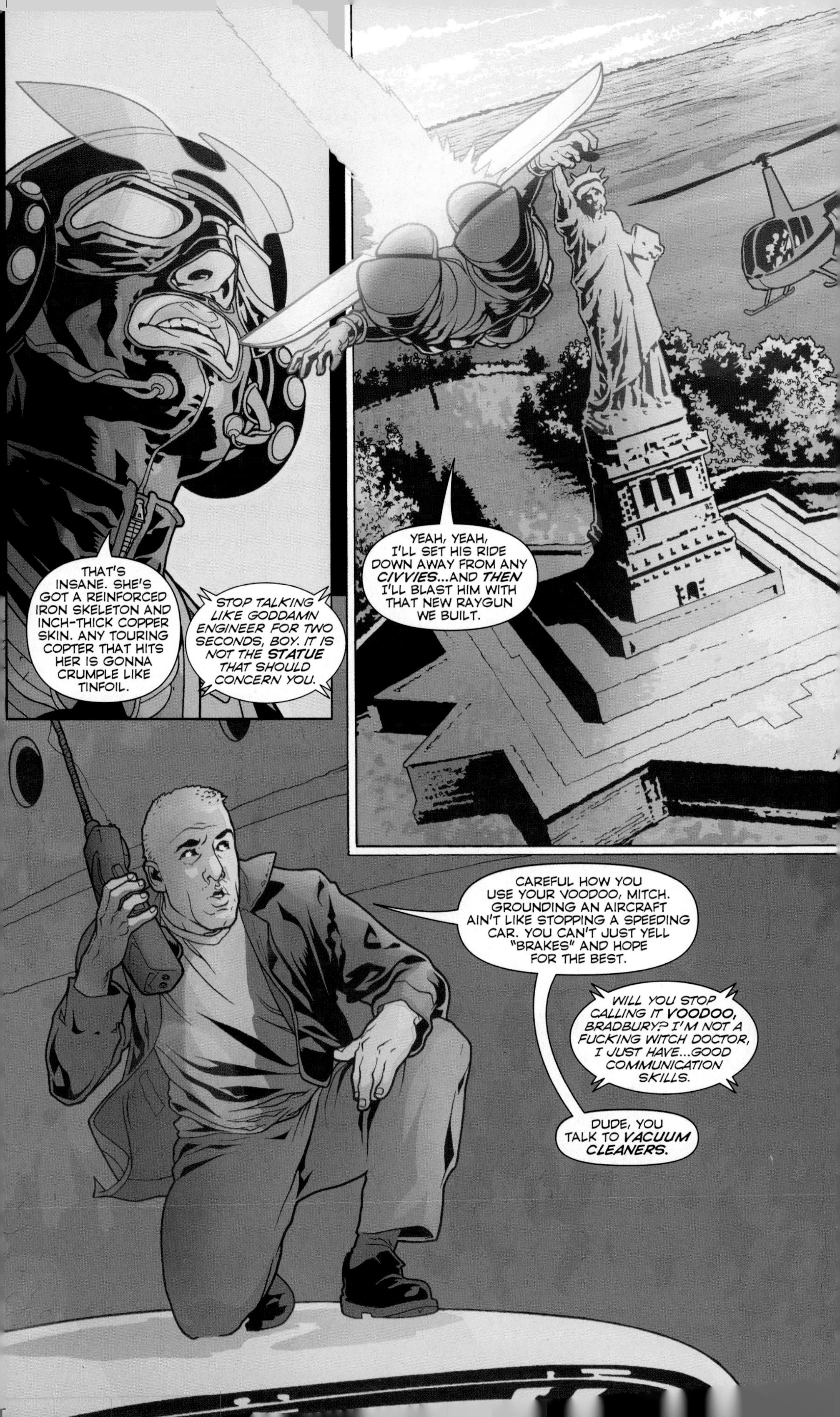
THAT'S INSANE. SHE'S GOT A REINFORCED IRON SKELETON AND INCH-THICK COPPER SKIN. ANY TOURING COPTER THAT HITS HER IS GONNA CRUMPLE LIKE TINFOIL.
STOP TALKING LIKE GODDAMN ENGINEER FOR TWO SECONDS, BOY. IT IS NOT THE STATUE THAT SHOULD CONCERN YOU.
YEAH, YEAH, I'LL SET HIS RIDE DOWN AWAY FROM ANY CIVVIES...AND THEN I'LL BLAST HIM WITH THAT NEW RAYGUN WE BUILT.
CAREFUL HOW YOU USE YOUR VOODOO, MITCH. GROUNDING AN AIRCRAFT AIN'T LIKE STOPPING A SPEEDING CAR. YOU CAN'T JUST YELL "BRAKES" AND HOPE FOR THE BEST.
WILL YOU STOP CALLING IT VOODOO, BRADBURY? I'M NOT A FUCKING WITCH DOCTOR, I JUST HAVE...GOOD COMMUNICATION SKILLS.
DUDE, YOU TALK TO VACUUM CLEANERS.

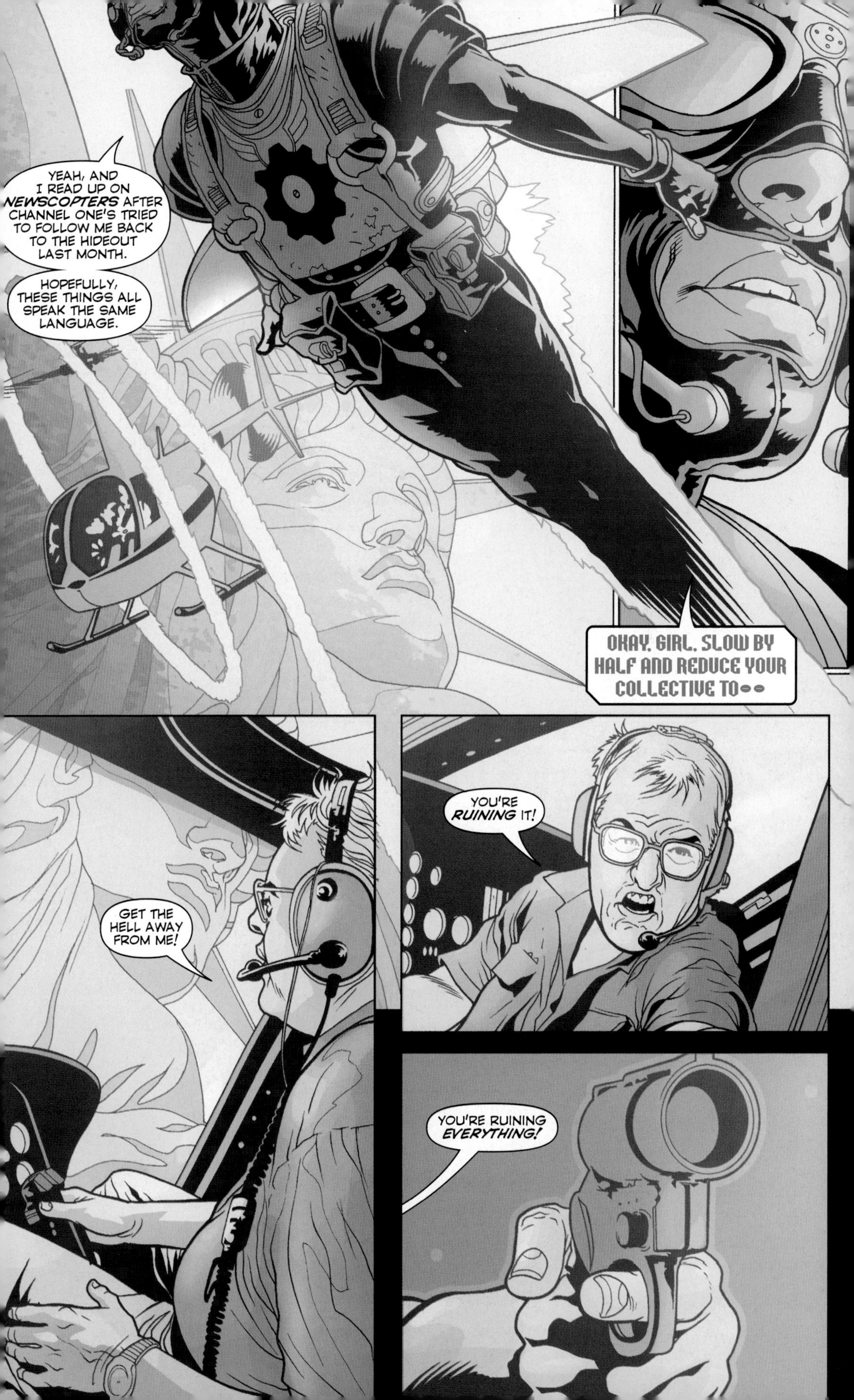
YEAH, AND I READ UP ON NEWSCOPTERS AFTER CHANNEL ONE'S TRIED TO FOLLOW ME BACK TO THE HIDEOUT LAST MONTH.
HOPEFULLY, THESE THINGS ALL SPEAK THE SAME LANGUAGE.
OKAY, GIRL, SLOW BY HALF AND REDUCE YOUR COLLECTIVE TO--
GET THE HELL AWAY FROM ME!
YOU'RE RUINING IT!
YOU'RE RUINING EVERYTHING!

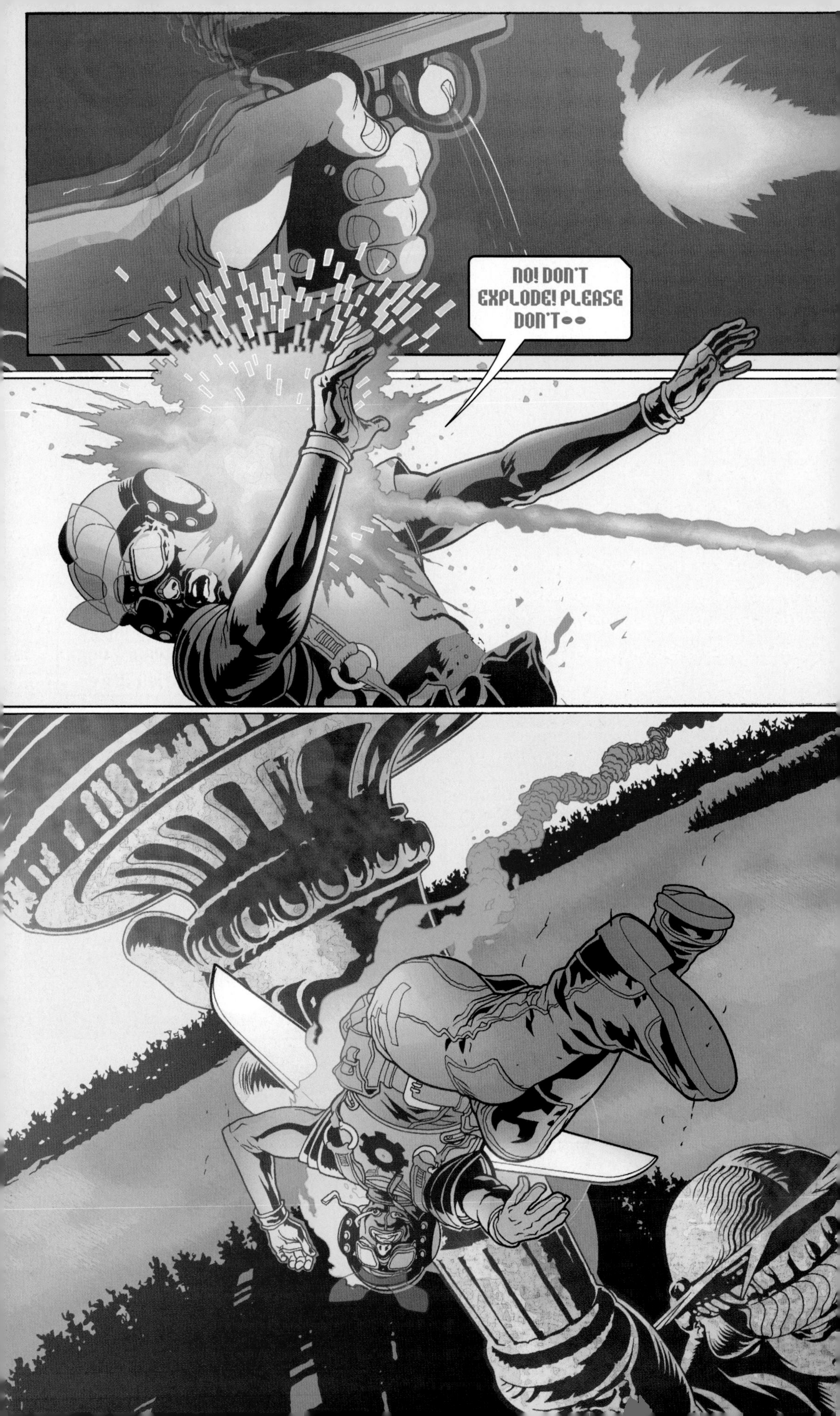
NO! DON'T EXPLODE! PLEASE DON'T--

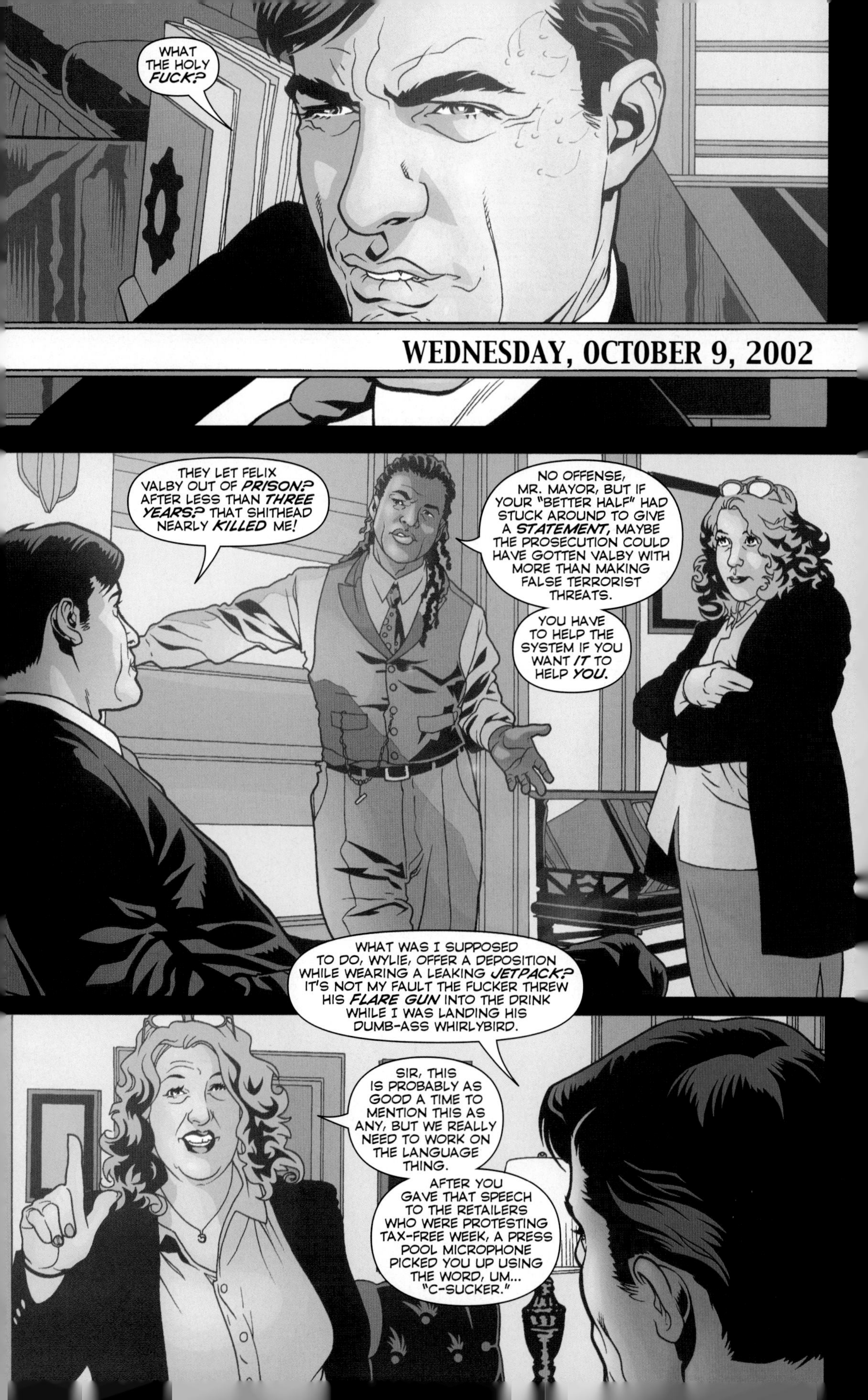
WHAT THE HOLY FUCK?
WEDNESDAY, OCTOBER 9, 2002
THEY LET FELIX VALBY OUT OF PRISON? AFTER LESS THAN THREE YEARS? THAT SHITHEAD NEARLY KILLED ME!
NO OFFENSE, MR. MAYOR, BUT IF YOUR "BETTER HALF" HAD STUCK AROUND TO GIVE A STATEMENT, MAYBE THE PROSECUTION COULD HAVE GOTTEN VALBY WITH MORE THAN MAKING FALSE TERRORIST THREATS.
YOU HAVE TO HELP THE SYSTEM IF YOU WANT IT TO HELP YOU.
WHAT WAS I SUPPOSED TO DO, WYLIE, OFFER A DEPOSITION WHILE WEARING A LEAKING JETPACK? IT'S NOT MY FAULT THE FUCKER THREW HIS FLARE GUN INTO THE DRINK WHILE I WAS LANDING HIS DUMB-ASS WHIRLYBIRD.
SIR, THIS IS PROBABLY AS GOOD A TIME TO MENTION THIS AS ANY, BUT WE REALLY NEED TO WORK ON THE LANGUAGE THING.
AFTER YOU GAVE THAT SPEECH TO THE RETAILERS WHO WERE PROTESTING TAX-FREE WEEK, A PRESS POOL MICROPHONE PICKED YOU UP USING THE WORD, UM... "C-SUCKER."

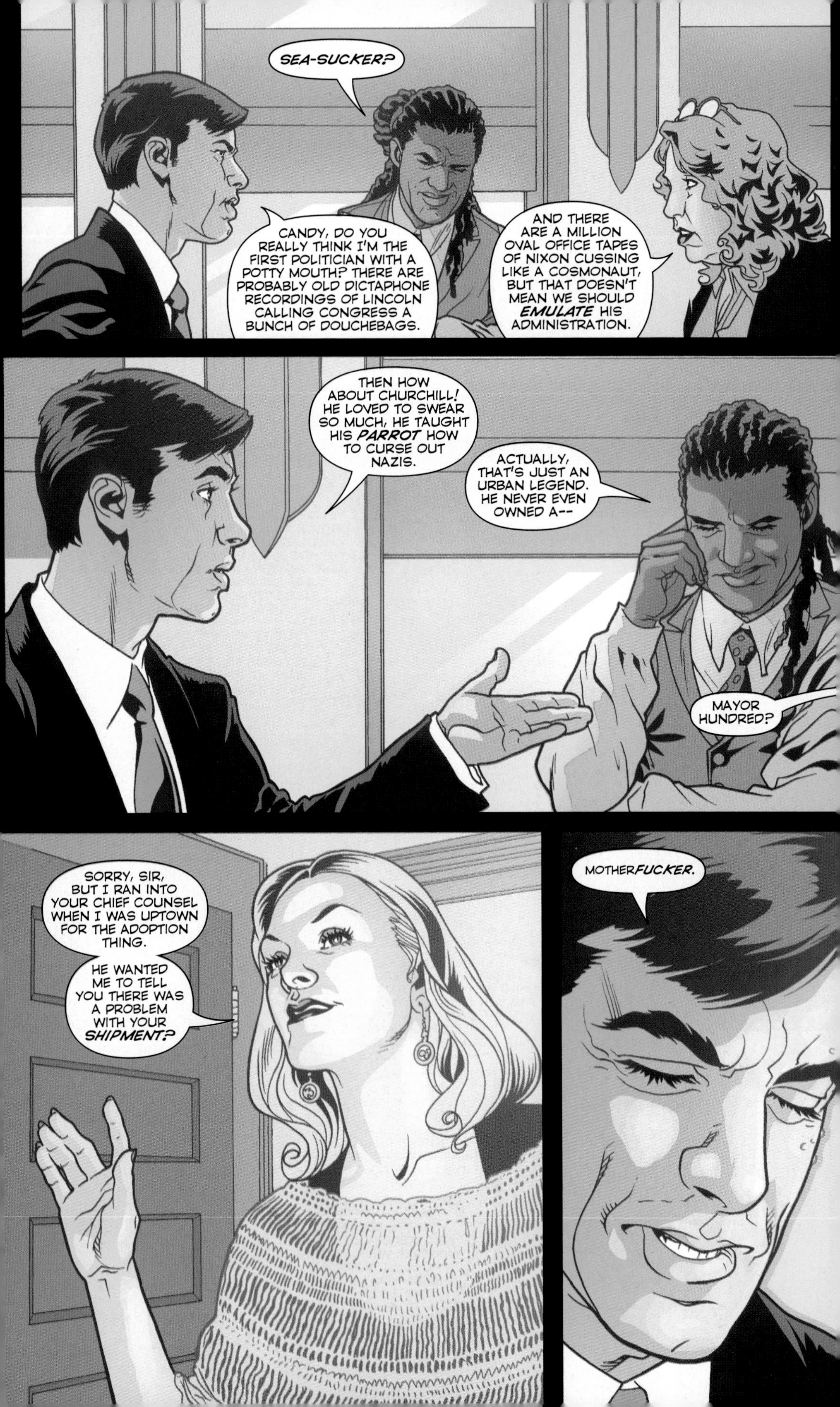
SEA-SUCKER?
CANDY, DO YOU REALLY THINK I'M THE FIRST POLITICIAN WITH A POTTY MOUTH? THERE ARE PROBABLY OLD DICTAPHONE RECORDINGS OF LINCOLN CALLING CONGRESS A BUNCH OF DOUCHEBAGS.
AND THERE ARE A MILLION OVAL OFFICE TAPES OF NIXON CUSSING LIKE A COSMONAUT, BUT THAT DOESN'T MEAN WE SHOULD EMULATE HIS ADMINISTRATION.
THEN HOW ABOUT CHURCHILL! HE LOVED TO SWEAR SO MUCH, HE TAUGHT HIS PARROT HOW TO CURSE OUT NAZIS.
ACTUALLY, THAT'S JUST AN URBAN LEGEND. HE NEVER EVEN OWNED A--
MAYOR HUNDRED?
SORRY, SIR, BUT I RAN INTO YOUR CHIEF COUNSEL WHEN I WAS UPTOWN FOR THE ADOPTION THING.
HE WANTED ME TO TELL YOU THERE WAS A PROBLEM WITH YOUR SHIPMENT?
MOTHERFUCKER.

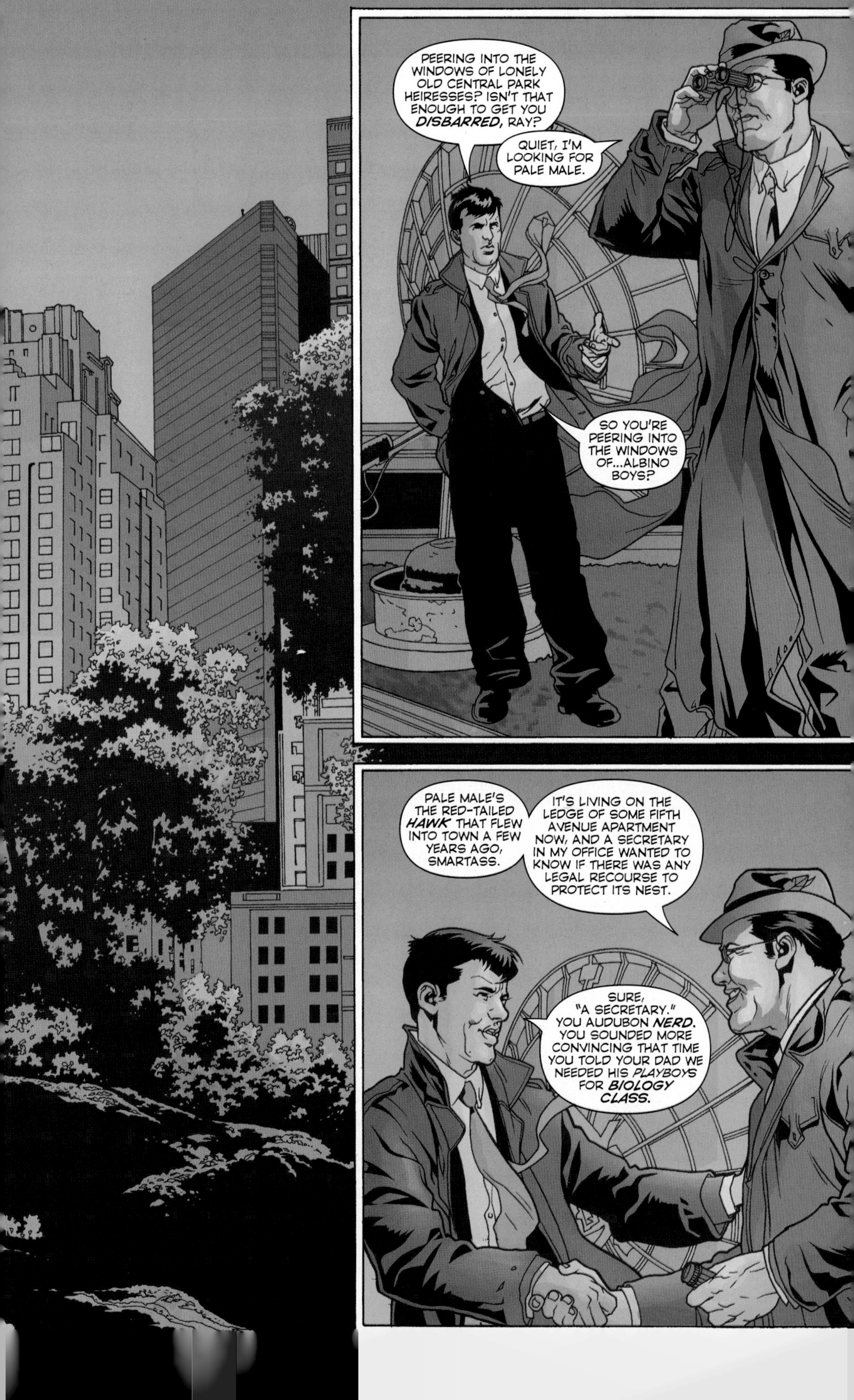
PEERING INTO THE WINDOWS OF LONELY OLD CENTRAL PARK HEIRESSES? ISN'T THAT ENOUGH TO GET YOU DISBARRED, RAY?
QUIET, I'M LOOKING FOR PALE MALE.
SO YOU'RE PEERING INTO THE WINDOWS OF...ALBINO BOYS?
PALE MALE'S THE RED-TAILED HAWK THAT FLEW INTO TOWN A FEW YEARS AGO, SMARTASS.
IT'S LIVING ON THE LEDGE OF SOME FIFTH AVENUE APARTMENT NOW, AND A SECRETARY IN MY OFFICE WANTED TO KNOW IF THERE WAS ANY LEGAL RECOURSE TO PROTECT ITS NEST.
SURE, "A SECRETARY." YOU AUDUBON NERD. YOU SOUNDED MORE CONVINCING THAT TIME YOU TOLD YOUR DAD WE NEEDED HIS PLAYBOYS FOR BIOLOGY CLASS.

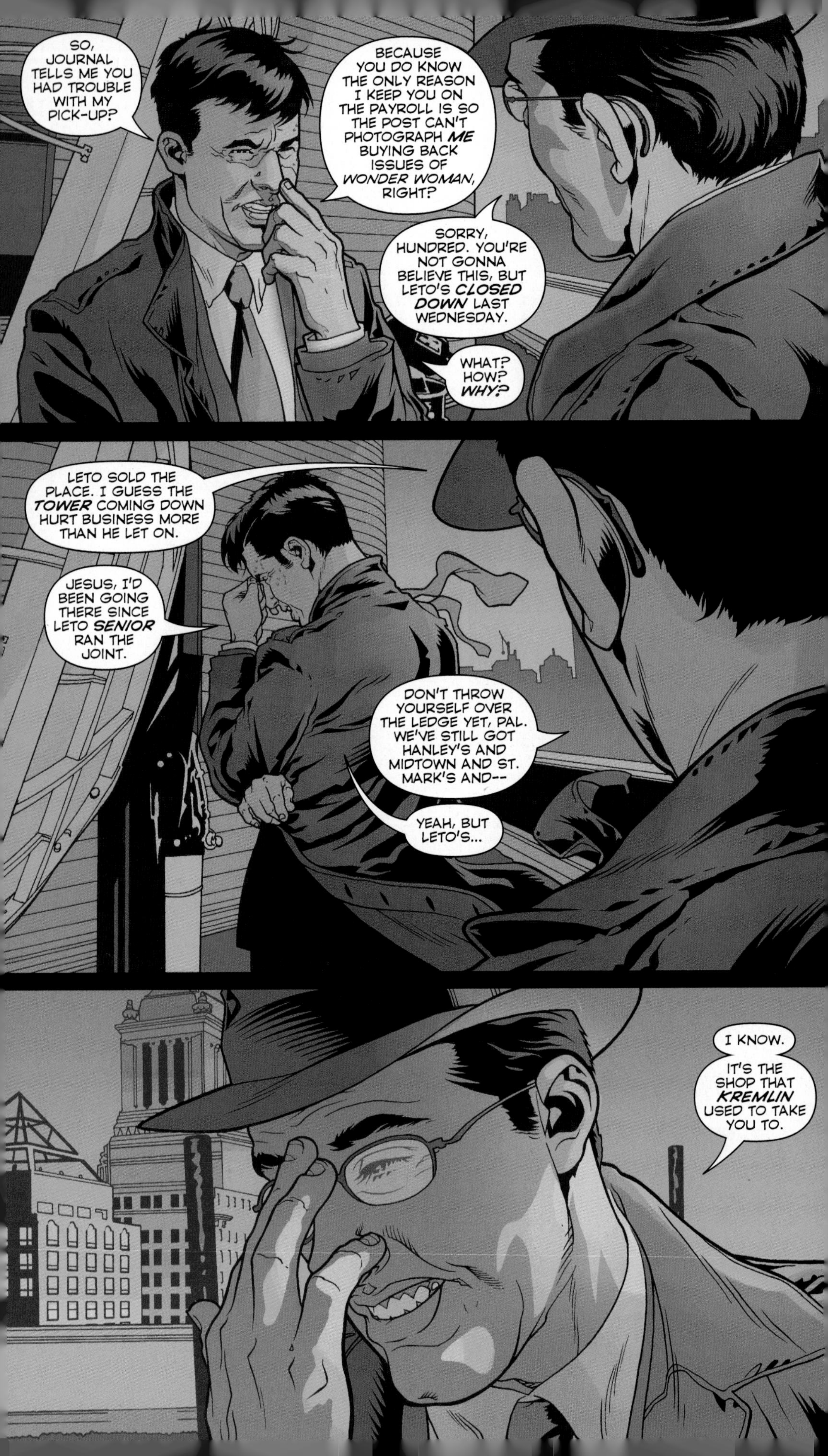
SO, JOURNAL TELLS ME YOU HAD TROUBLE WITH MY PICK-UP?
BECAUSE YOU DO KNOW THE ONLY REASON I KEEP YOU ON THE PAYROLL IS SO THE POST CAN'T PHOTOGRAPH *ME* BUYING BACK ISSUES OF *WONDER WOMAN*, RIGHT?
SORRY, HUNDRED. YOU'RE NOT GONNA BELIEVE THIS, BUT LETO'S *CLOSED DOWN* LAST WEDNESDAY.
WHAT? HOW? *WHY?*
LETO SOLD THE PLACE. I GUESS THE *TOWER* COMING DOWN HURT BUSINESS MORE THAN HE LET ON.
JESUS, I'D BEEN GOING THERE SINCE LETO *SENIOR* RAN THE JOINT.
DON'T THROW YOURSELF OVER THE LEDGE YET, PAL. WE'VE STILL GOT HANLEY'S AND MIDTOWN AND ST. MARK'S AND--
YEAH, BUT LETO'S...
I KNOW.
IT'S THE SHOP THAT *KREMLIN* USED TO TAKE YOU TO.

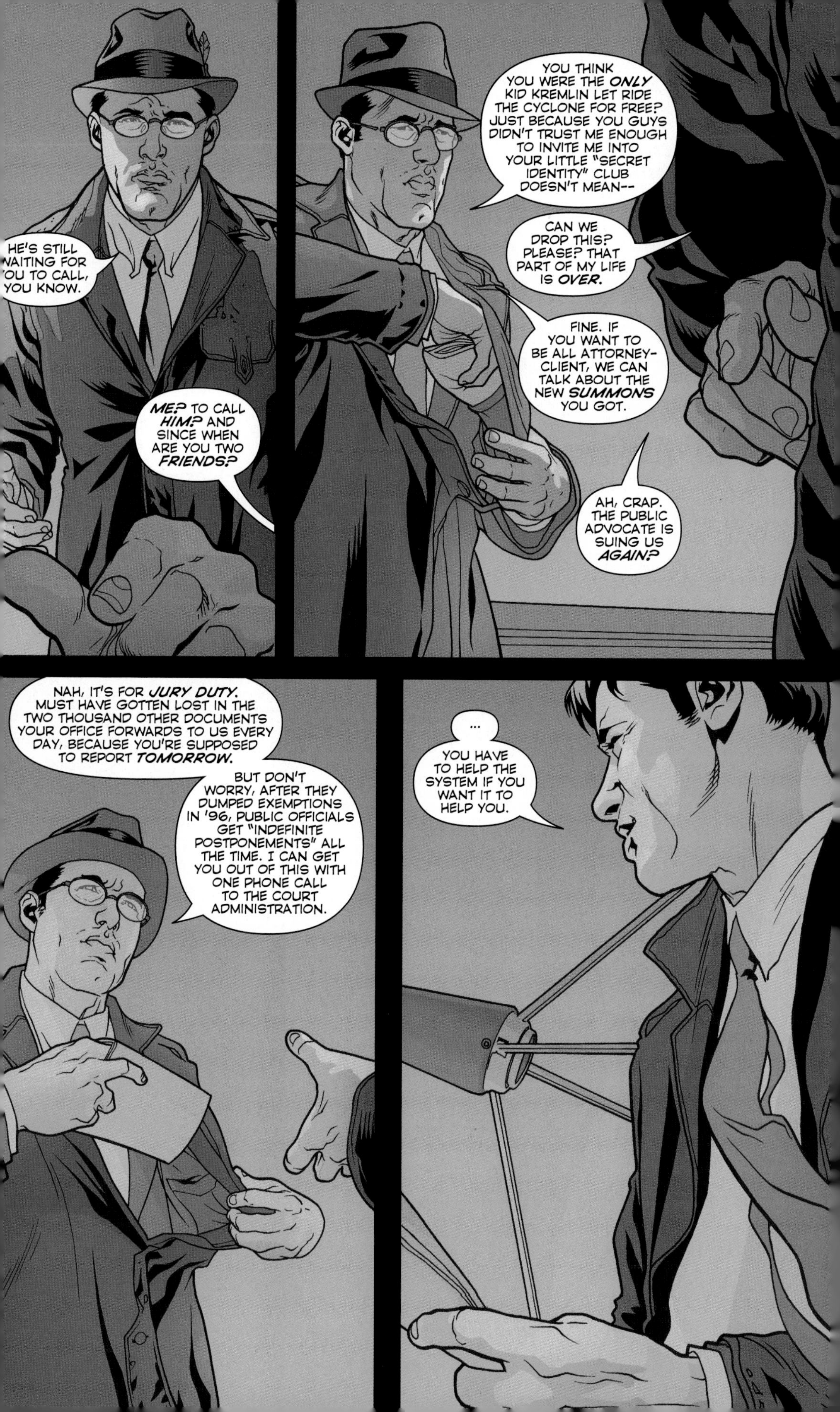
HE'S STILL WAITING FOR YOU TO CALL, YOU KNOW.
ME? TO CALL HIM? AND SINCE WHEN ARE YOU TWO FRIENDS?
YOU THINK YOU WERE THE ONLY KID KREMLIN LET RIDE THE CYCLONE FOR FREE? JUST BECAUSE YOU GUYS DIDN'T TRUST ME ENOUGH TO INVITE ME INTO YOUR LITTLE "SECRET IDENTITY" CLUB DOESN'T MEAN--
CAN WE DROP THIS? PLEASE? THAT PART OF MY LIFE IS OVER.
FINE. IF YOU WANT TO BE ALL ATTORNEY-CLIENT, WE CAN TALK ABOUT THE NEW SUMMONS YOU GOT.
AH, CRAP. THE PUBLIC ADVOCATE IS SUING US AGAIN?
NAH, IT'S FOR JURY DUTY. MUST HAVE GOTTEN LOST IN THE TWO THOUSAND OTHER DOCUMENTS YOUR OFFICE FORWARDS TO US EVERY DAY, BECAUSE YOU'RE SUPPOSED TO REPORT TOMORROW.
BUT DON'T WORRY, AFTER THEY DUMPED EXEMPTIONS IN '96, PUBLIC OFFICIALS GET "INDEFINITE POSTPONEMENTS" ALL THE TIME. I CAN GET YOU OUT OF THIS WITH ONE PHONE CALL TO THE COURT ADMINISTRATION.
...
YOU HAVE TO HELP THE SYSTEM IF YOU WANT IT TO HELP YOU.

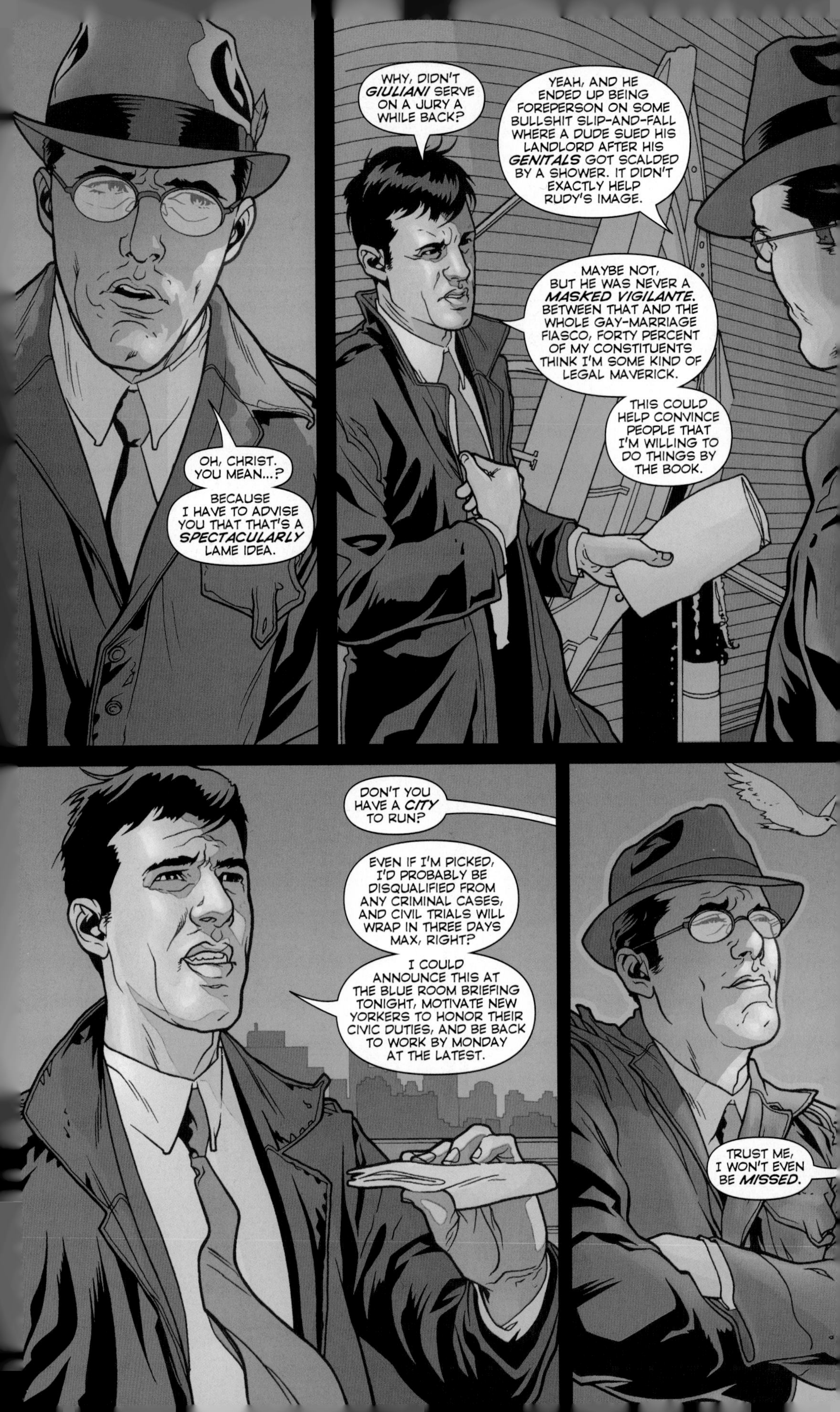
WHY, DIDN'T *GIULIANI* SERVE ON A JURY A WHILE BACK?
YEAH, AND HE ENDED UP BEING FOREPERSON ON SOME BULLSHIT SLIP-AND-FALL WHERE A DUDE SUED HIS LANDLORD AFTER HIS *GENITALS* GOT SCALDED BY A SHOWER. IT DIDN'T EXACTLY HELP RUDY'S IMAGE.
MAYBE NOT, BUT HE WAS NEVER A ***MASKED VIGILANTE***. BETWEEN THAT AND THE WHOLE GAY-MARRIAGE FIASCO, FORTY PERCENT OF MY CONSTITUENTS THINK I'M SOME KIND OF LEGAL MAVERICK.
THIS COULD HELP CONVINCE PEOPLE THAT I'M WILLING TO DO THINGS BY THE BOOK.
OH, CHRIST. YOU MEAN...?
BECAUSE I HAVE TO ADVISE YOU THAT THAT'S A ***SPECTACULARLY*** LAME IDEA.
DON'T YOU HAVE A *CITY* TO RUN?
EVEN IF I'M PICKED, I'D PROBABLY BE DISQUALIFIED FROM ANY CRIMINAL CASES, AND CIVIL TRIALS WILL WRAP IN THREE DAYS MAX, RIGHT?
I COULD ANNOUNCE THIS AT THE BLUE ROOM BRIEFING TONIGHT, MOTIVATE NEW YORKERS TO HONOR THEIR CIVIC DUTIES, AND BE BACK TO WORK BY MONDAY AT THE LATEST.
TRUST ME, I WON'T EVEN BE ***MISSED***.

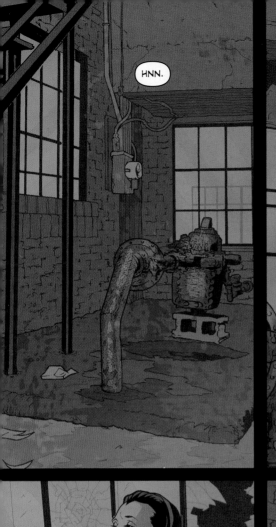

HNN.

HNN. *HNN.* YOU... YOU COME YET?

NOT... NOT YET.

THIS...THIS IS GONNA SOUND SORTA PSYCHO, BUT IF I GIVE YOU ANOTHER EIGHTY, CAN I...CAN I *CHOKE* YOU A LITTLE BIT?

I WON'T STRANGLE YOU OR ANYTHING BUT--

SHIT, MAN, FOR ANOTHER EIGHTY YOU CAN CUT MY DAMN HEAD OFF.

GOD, THANK YOU. THIS IS SO HOT. THIS IS SO FUCKING--

GET YOUR HANDS ⸮KZZT⸮ OFF OF HER.

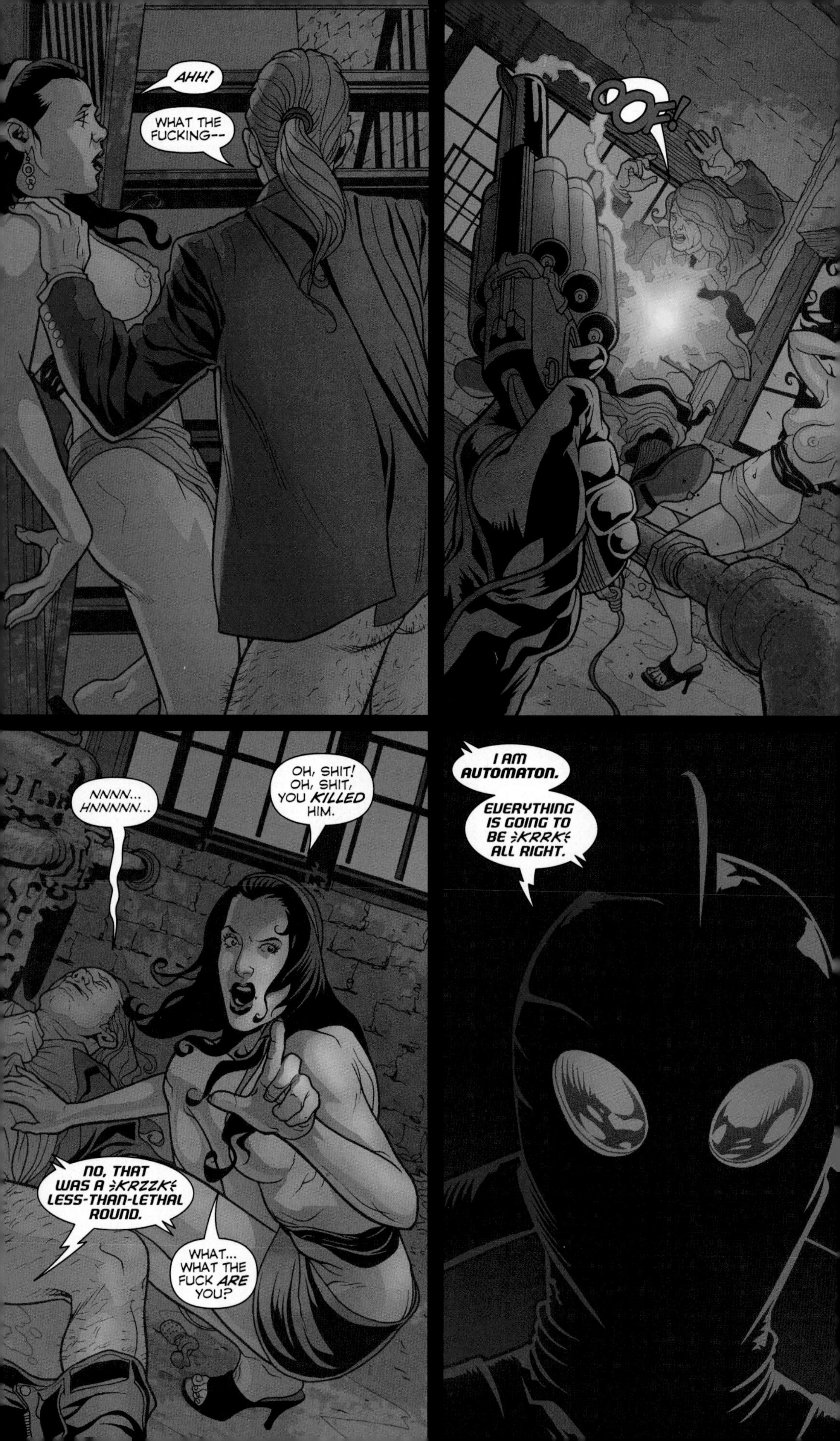
AHH!
WHAT THE FUCKING--
OOF!
NNNN... HNNNNN...
OH, SHIT! OH, SHIT, YOU *KILLED* HIM.
NO, THAT WAS A ⋟KRZZK⋞ LESS-THAN-LETHAL ROUND.
WHAT... WHAT THE FUCK *ARE* YOU?
I AM AUTOMATON.
EVERYTHING IS GOING TO BE ⋟KRRK⋞ ALL RIGHT.

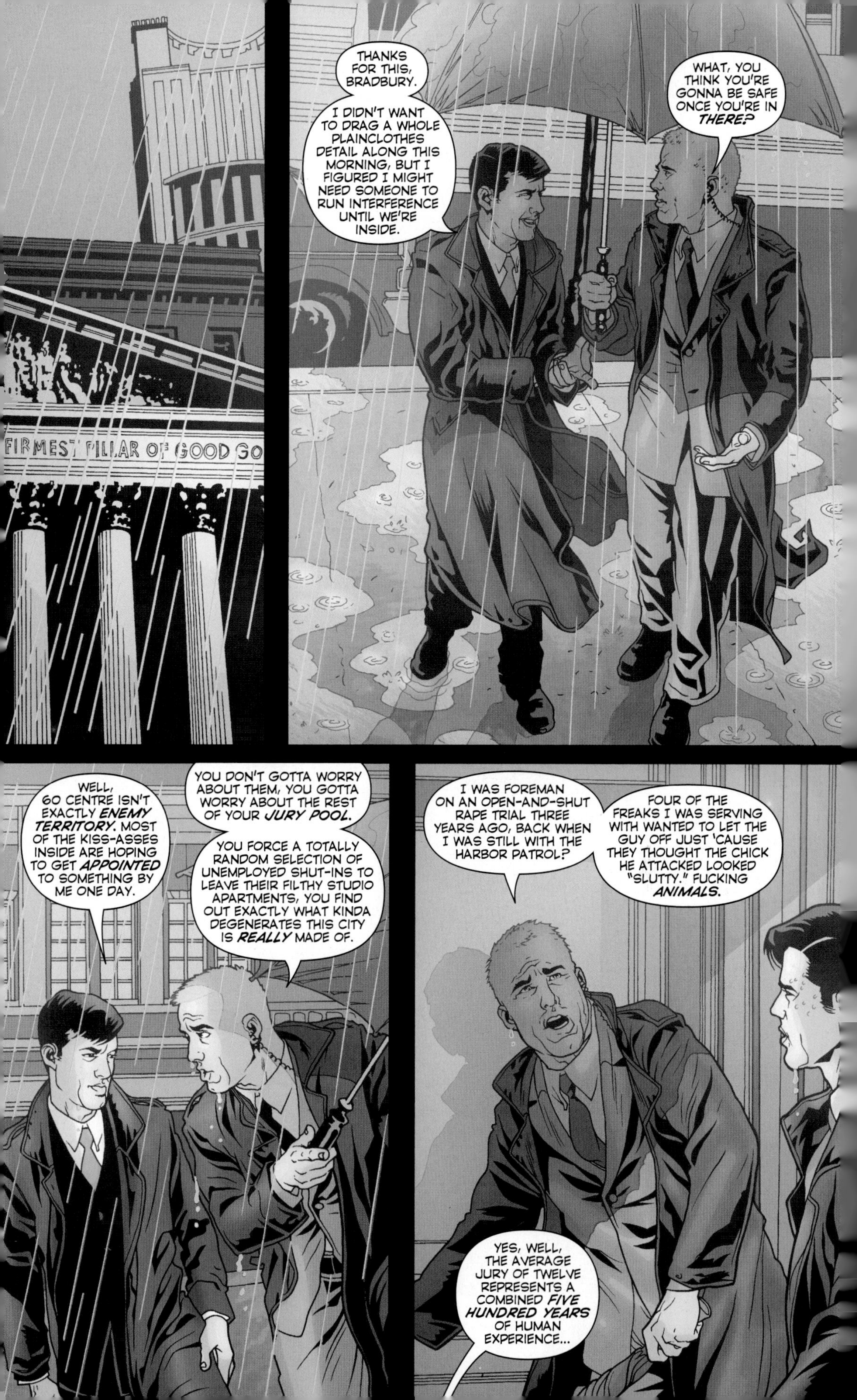
FIRMEST PILLAR OF GOOD GO
THANKS FOR THIS, BRADBURY.
I DIDN'T WANT TO DRAG A WHOLE PLAINCLOTHES DETAIL ALONG THIS MORNING, BUT I FIGURED I MIGHT NEED SOMEONE TO RUN INTERFERENCE UNTIL WE'RE INSIDE.
WHAT, YOU THINK YOU'RE GONNA BE SAFE ONCE YOU'RE IN *THERE?*
WELL, 60 CENTRE ISN'T EXACTLY *ENEMY TERRITORY.* MOST OF THE KISS-ASSES INSIDE ARE HOPING TO GET *APPOINTED* TO SOMETHING BY ME ONE DAY.
YOU DON'T GOTTA WORRY ABOUT THEM, YOU GOTTA WORRY ABOUT THE REST OF YOUR *JURY POOL.*
YOU FORCE A TOTALLY RANDOM SELECTION OF UNEMPLOYED SHUT-INS TO LEAVE THEIR FILTHY STUDIO APARTMENTS, YOU FIND OUT EXACTLY WHAT KINDA DEGENERATES THIS CITY IS *REALLY* MADE OF.
I WAS FOREMAN ON AN OPEN-AND-SHUT RAPE TRIAL THREE YEARS AGO, BACK WHEN I WAS STILL WITH THE HARBOR PATROL?
FOUR OF THE FREAKS I WAS SERVING WITH WANTED TO LET THE GUY OFF JUST 'CAUSE THEY THOUGHT THE CHICK HE ATTACKED LOOKED "SLUTTY." FUCKING *ANIMALS.*
YES, WELL, THE AVERAGE JURY OF TWELVE REPRESENTS A COMBINED *FIVE HUNDRED YEARS* OF HUMAN EXPERIENCE...

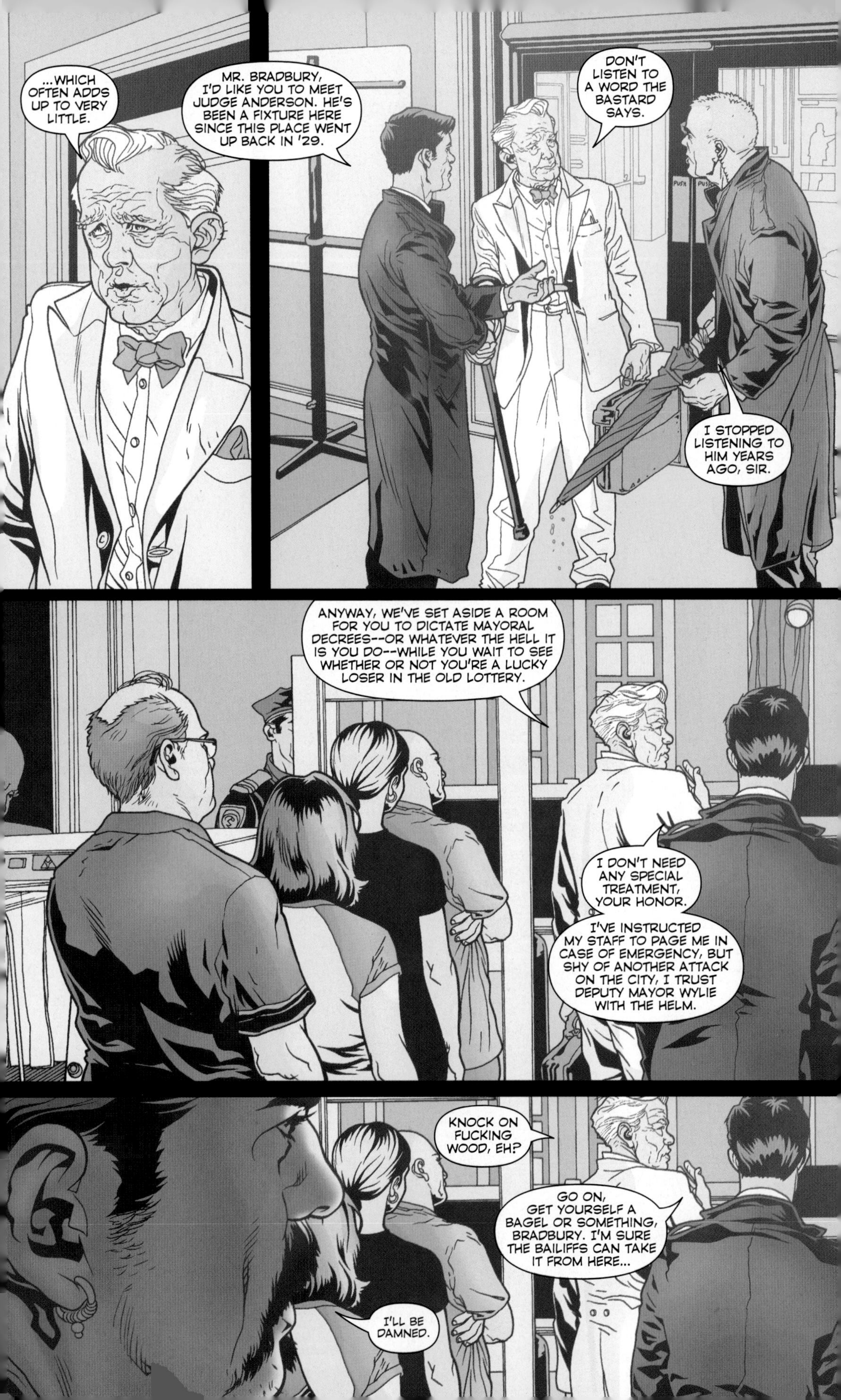
...WHICH OFTEN ADDS UP TO VERY LITTLE.
MR. BRADBURY, I'D LIKE YOU TO MEET JUDGE ANDERSON. HE'S BEEN A FIXTURE HERE SINCE THIS PLACE WENT UP BACK IN '29.
DON'T LISTEN TO A WORD THE BASTARD SAYS.
PUSH
I STOPPED LISTENING TO HIM YEARS AGO, SIR.
ANYWAY, WE'VE SET ASIDE A ROOM FOR YOU TO DICTATE MAYORAL DECREES--OR WHATEVER THE HELL IT IS YOU DO--WHILE YOU WAIT TO SEE WHETHER OR NOT YOU'RE A LUCKY LOSER IN THE OLD LOTTERY.
I DON'T NEED ANY SPECIAL TREATMENT, YOUR HONOR.
I'VE INSTRUCTED MY STAFF TO PAGE ME IN CASE OF EMERGENCY, BUT SHY OF ANOTHER ATTACK ON THE CITY, I TRUST DEPUTY MAYOR WYLIE WITH THE HELM.
KNOCK ON FUCKING WOOD, EH?
GO ON, GET YOURSELF A BAGEL OR SOMETHING, BRADBURY. I'M SURE THE BAILIFFS CAN TAKE IT FROM HERE...
I'LL BE DAMNED.

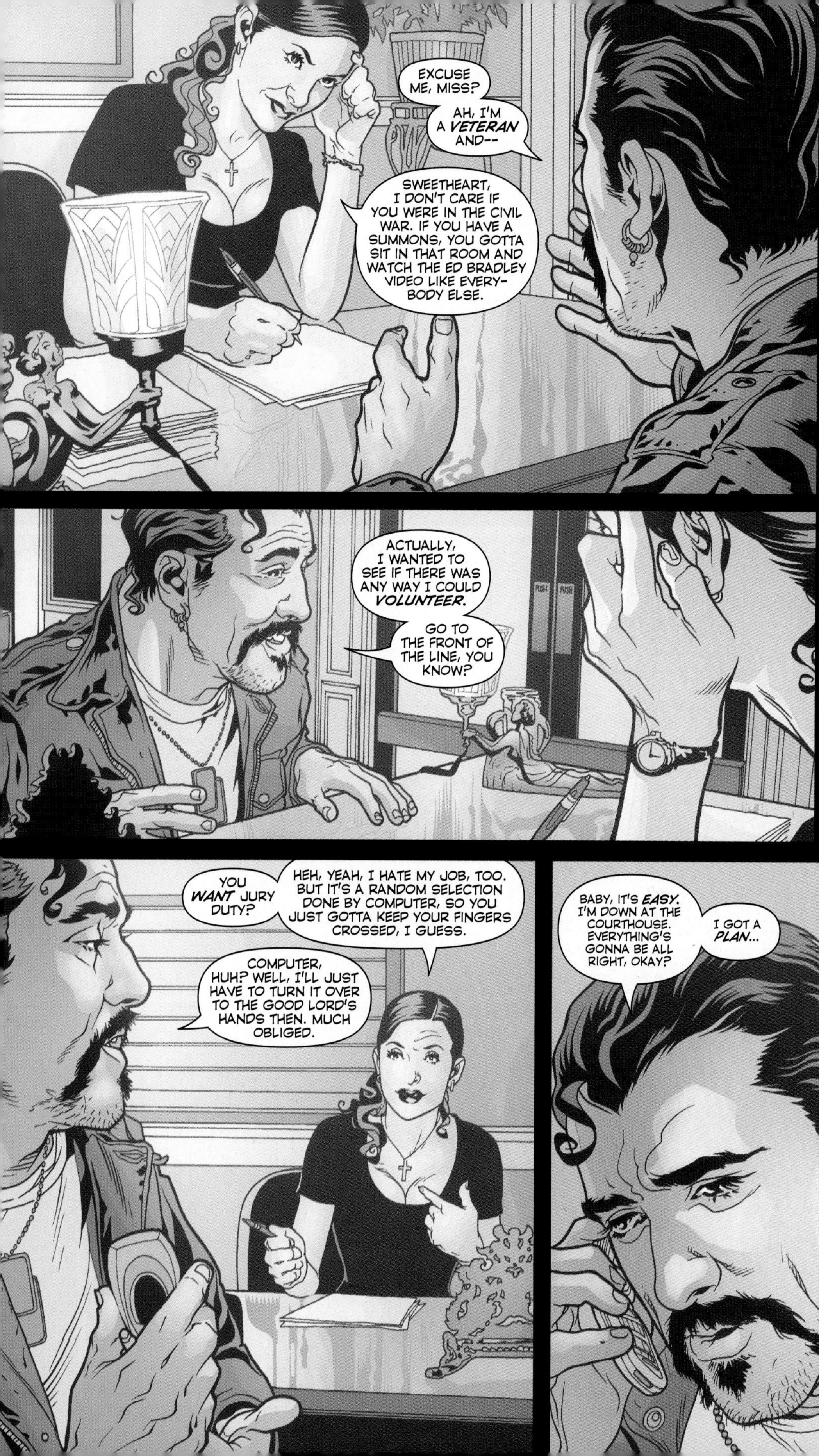
EXCUSE ME, MISS?
AH, I'M A VETERAN AND--
SWEETHEART, I DON'T CARE IF YOU WERE IN THE CIVIL WAR. IF YOU HAVE A SUMMONS, YOU GOTTA SIT IN THAT ROOM AND WATCH THE ED BRADLEY VIDEO LIKE EVERY-BODY ELSE.
ACTUALLY, I WANTED TO SEE IF THERE WAS ANY WAY I COULD VOLUNTEER.
GO TO THE FRONT OF THE LINE, YOU KNOW?
PUSH
PUSH
YOU WANT JURY DUTY?
HEH, YEAH, I HATE MY JOB, TOO. BUT IT'S A RANDOM SELECTION DONE BY COMPUTER, SO YOU JUST GOTTA KEEP YOUR FINGERS CROSSED, I GUESS.
COMPUTER, HUH? WELL, I'LL JUST HAVE TO TURN IT OVER TO THE GOOD LORD'S HANDS THEN. MUCH OBLIGED.
BABY, IT'S EASY. I'M DOWN AT THE COURTHOUSE. EVERYTHING'S GONNA BE ALL RIGHT, OKAY?
I GOT A PLAN...

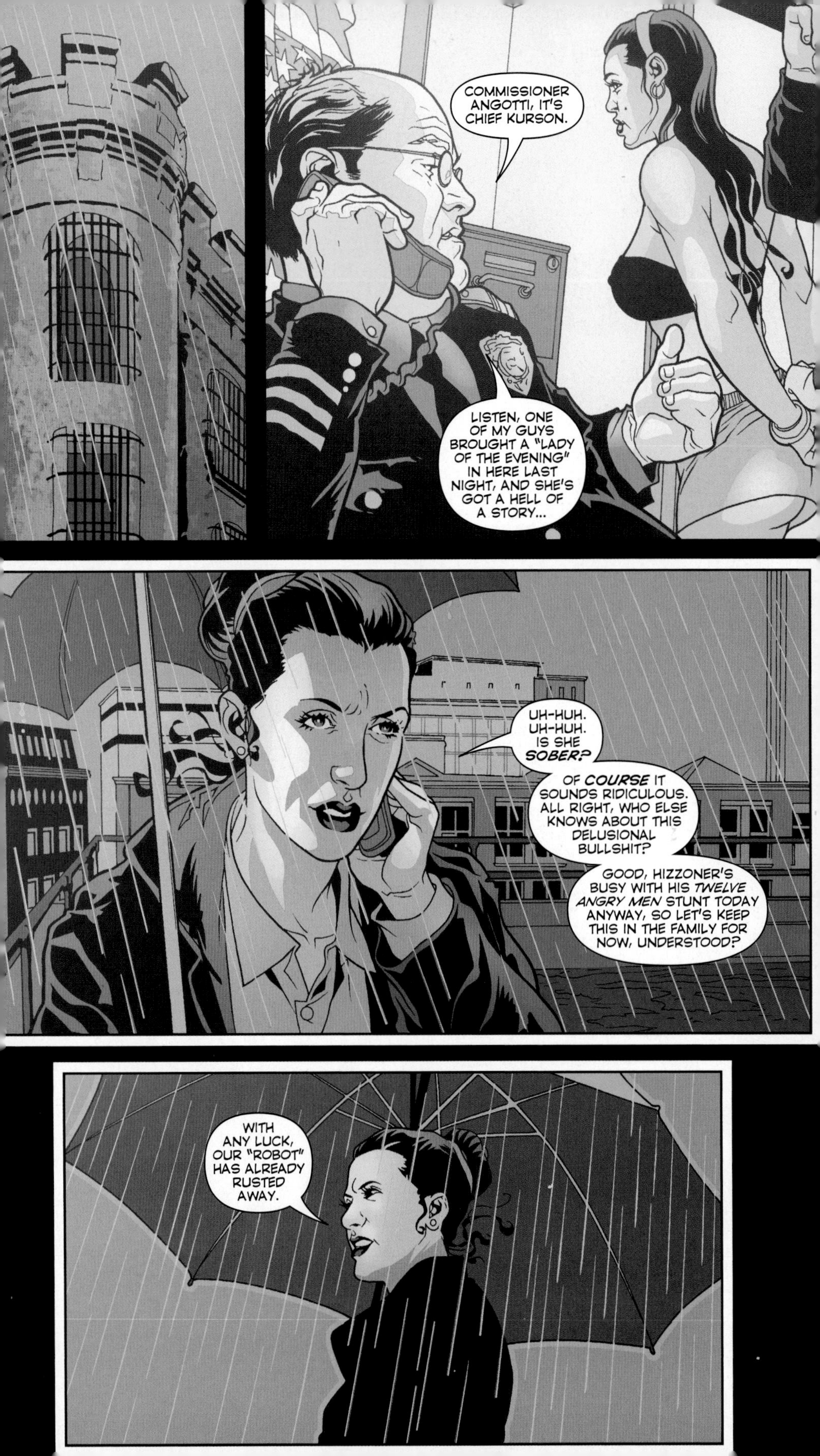
COMMISSIONER ANGOTTI, IT'S CHIEF KURSON.
LISTEN, ONE OF MY GUYS BROUGHT A "LADY OF THE EVENING" IN HERE LAST NIGHT, AND SHE'S GOT A HELL OF A STORY...
UH-HUH. UH-HUH. IS SHE *SOBER?*
OF *COURSE* IT SOUNDS RIDICULOUS. ALL RIGHT, WHO ELSE KNOWS ABOUT THIS DELUSIONAL BULLSHIT?
GOOD, HIZZONER'S BUSY WITH HIS *TWELVE ANGRY MEN* STUNT TODAY ANYWAY, SO LET'S KEEP THIS IN THE FAMILY FOR NOW, UNDERSTOOD?
WITH ANY LUCK, OUR "ROBOT" HAS ALREADY RUSTED AWAY.

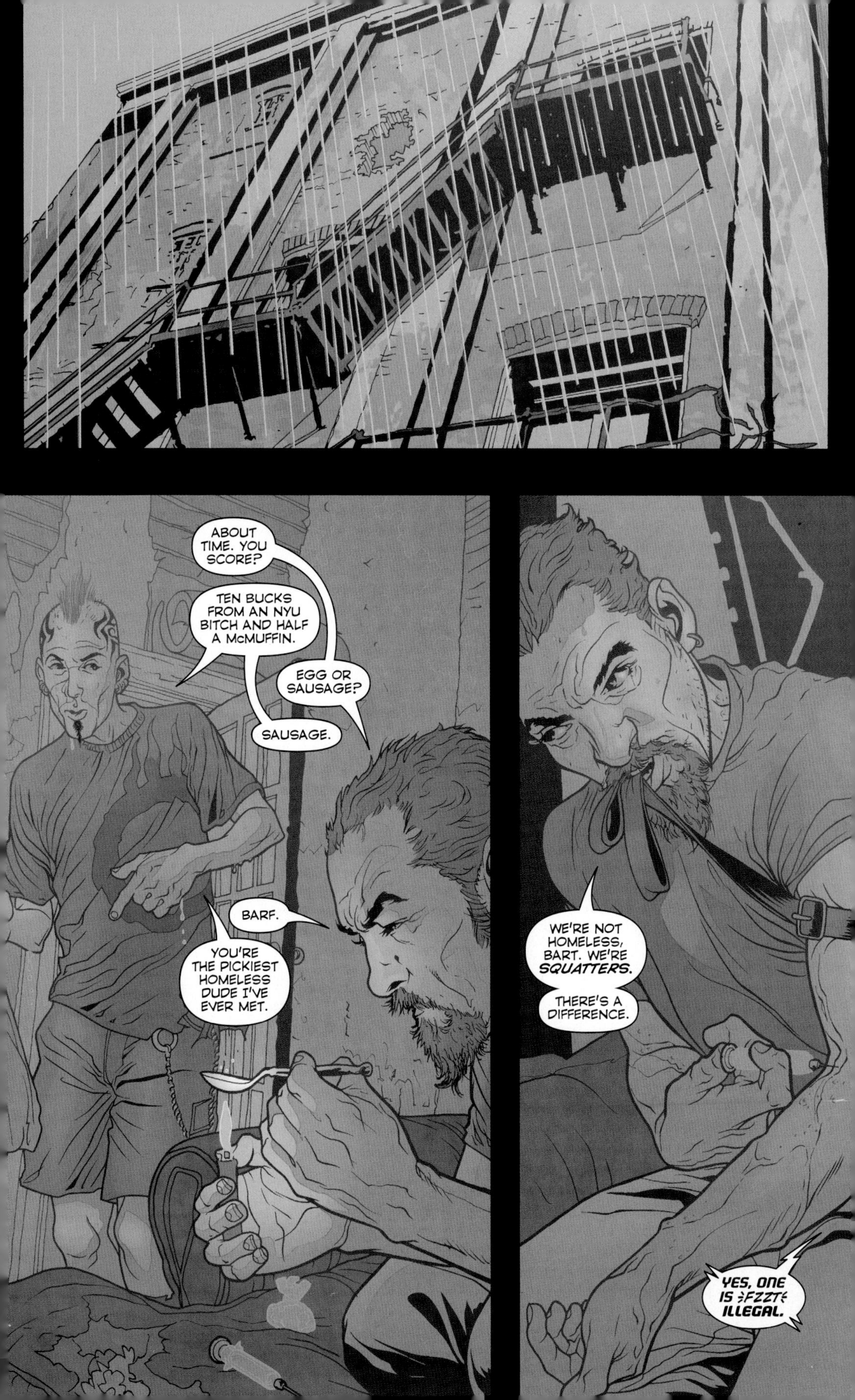
ABOUT TIME. YOU SCORE?
TEN BUCKS FROM AN NYU BITCH AND HALF A McMUFFIN.
EGG OR SAUSAGE?
SAUSAGE.
BARF.
YOU'RE THE PICKIEST HOMELESS DUDE I'VE EVER MET.
WE'RE NOT HOMELESS, BART. WE'RE *SQUATTERS*.
THERE'S A DIFFERENCE.
YES, ONE IS FZZT ILLEGAL.

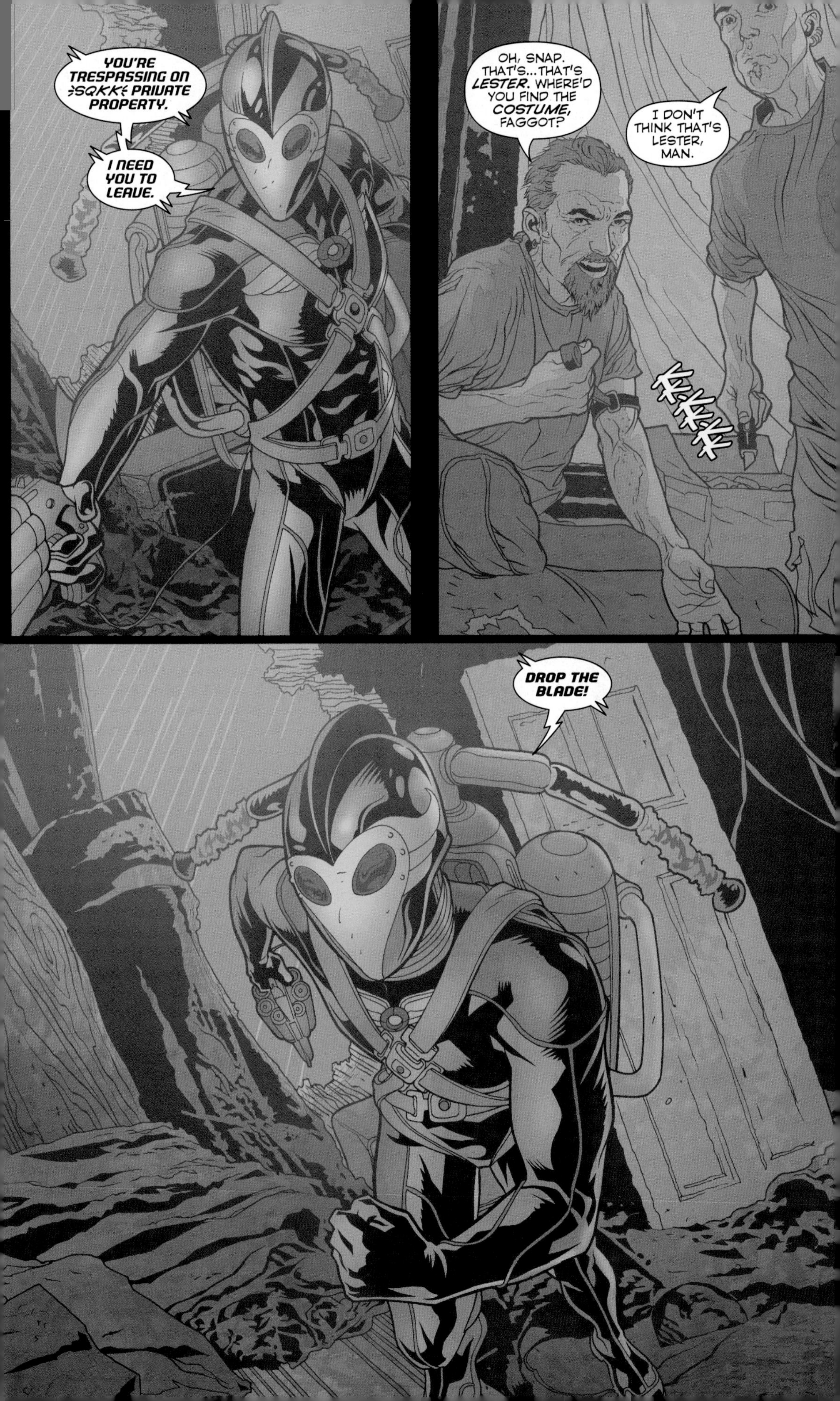
YOU'RE TRESPASSING ON ⚡SQKK⚡ PRIVATE PROPERTY.
I NEED YOU TO LEAVE.
OH, SNAP. THAT'S...THAT'S LESTER. WHERE'D YOU FIND THE COSTUME, FAGGOT?
I DON'T THINK THAT'S LESTER, MAN.
KLIK-KLIK-KLIK
DROP THE BLADE!

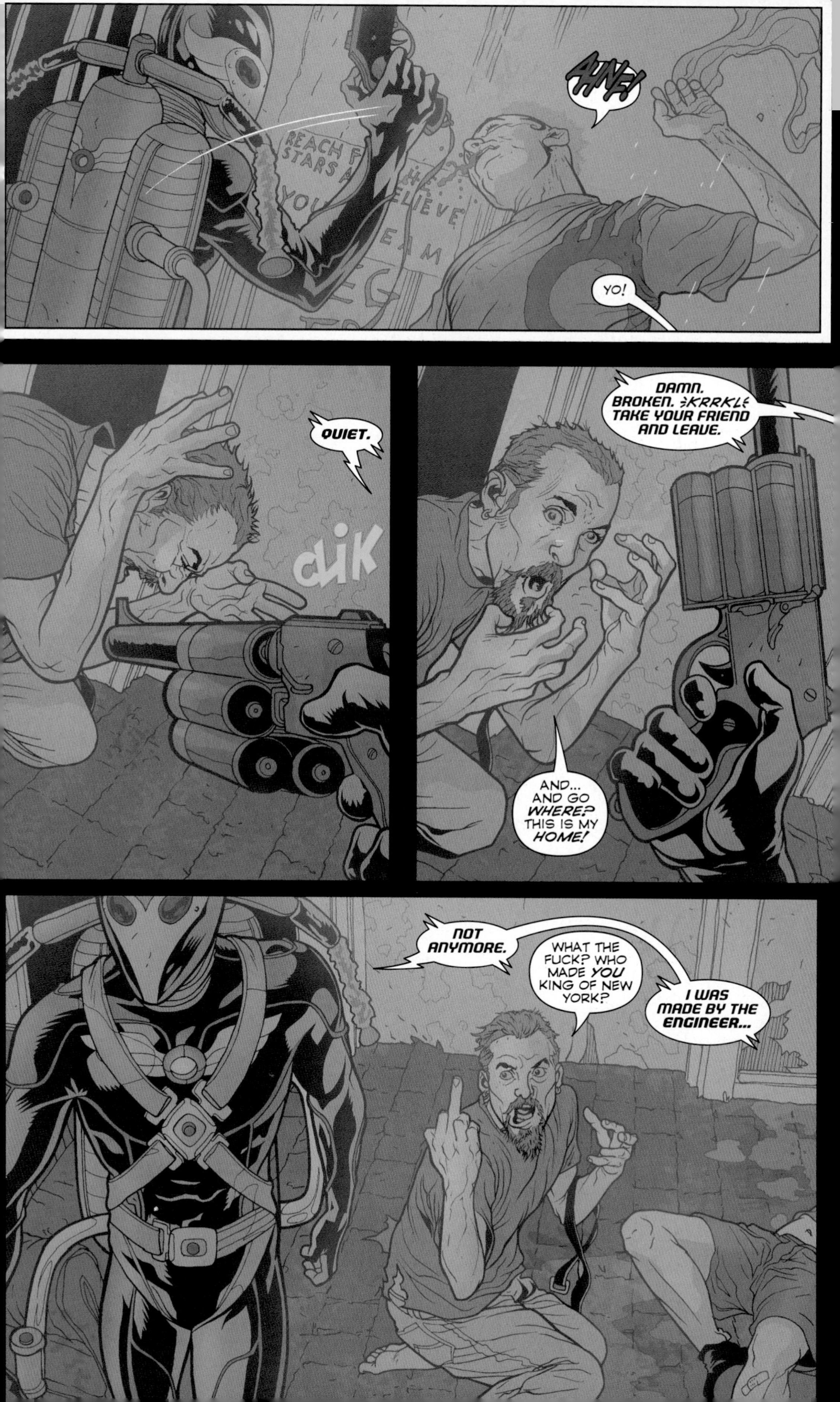
AUNF!
YO!
QUIET.
CLIK
DAMN. BROKEN. KRRKL TAKE YOUR FRIEND AND LEAVE.
AND... AND GO *WHERE?* THIS IS MY *HOME!*
NOT ANYMORE.
WHAT THE FUCK? WHO MADE *YOU* KING OF NEW YORK?
I WAS MADE BY THE ENGINEER...

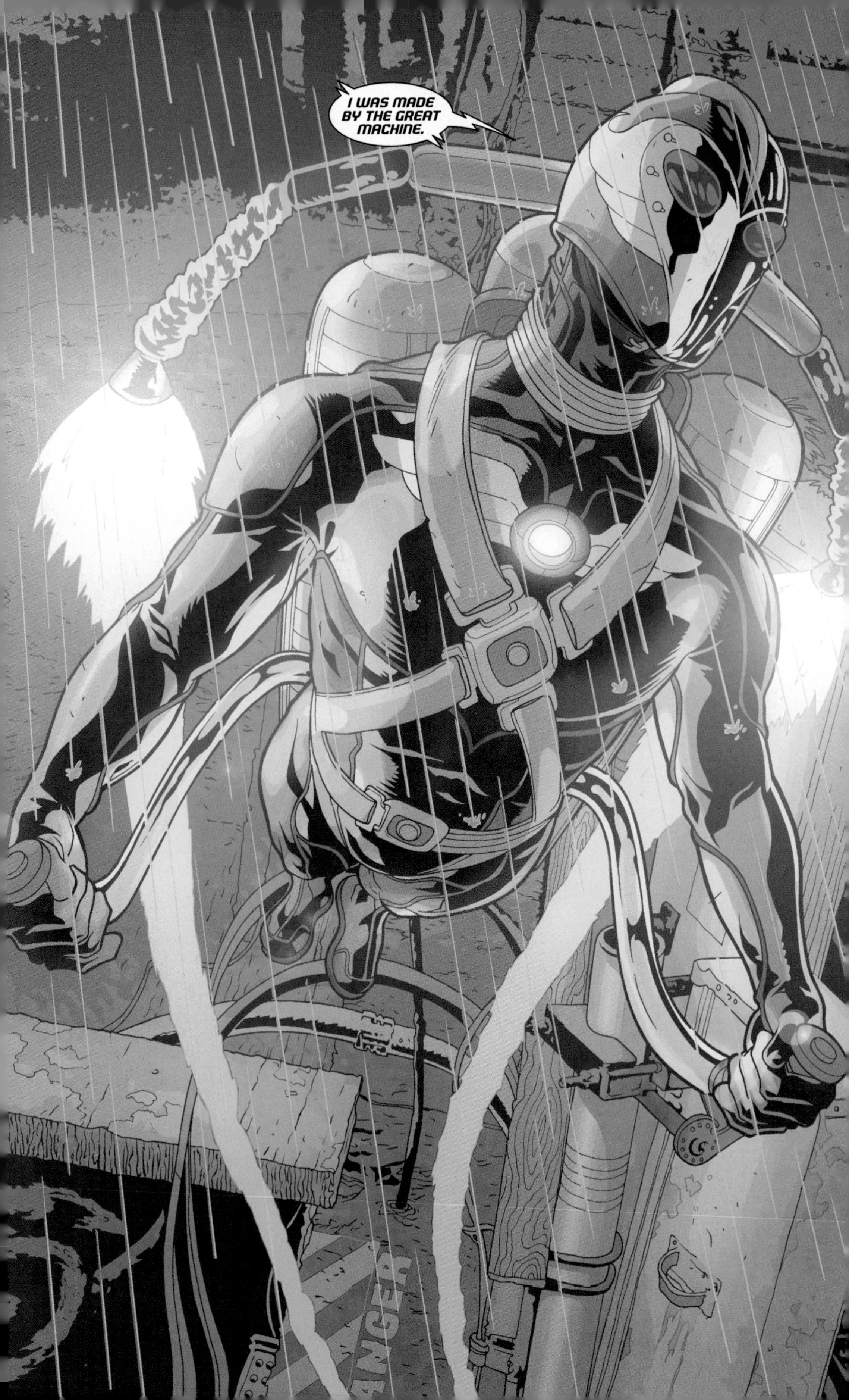
I WAS MADE BY THE GREAT MACHINE.

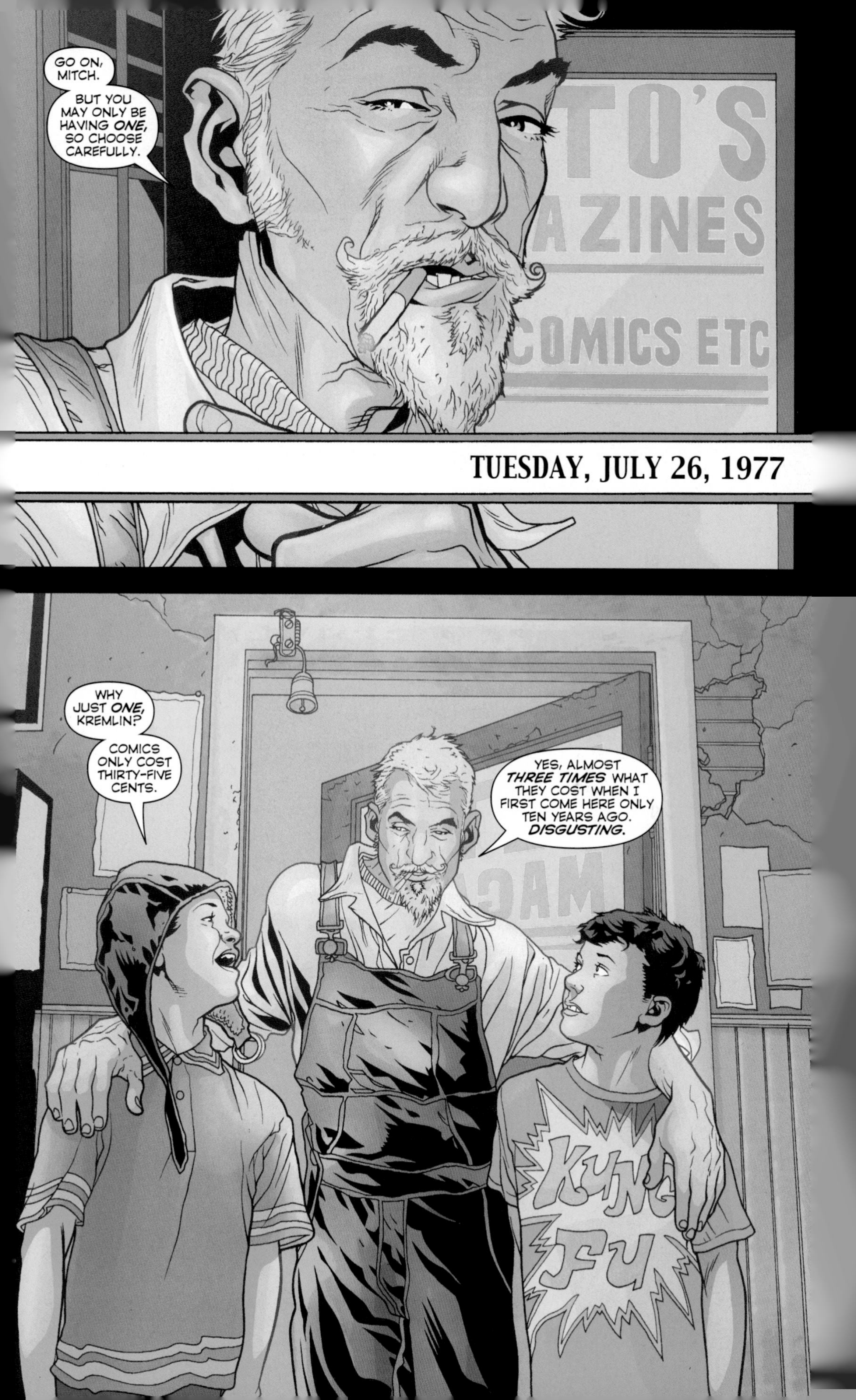
GO ON, MITCH.
BUT YOU MAY ONLY BE HAVING *ONE,* SO CHOOSE CAREFULLY.
COMICS ETC
TUESDAY, JULY 26, 1977
WHY JUST *ONE,* KREMLIN?
COMICS ONLY COST THIRTY-FIVE CENTS.
YES, ALMOST *THREE TIMES* WHAT THEY COST WHEN I FIRST COME HERE ONLY TEN YEARS AGO. *DISGUSTING.*
KUNG FU

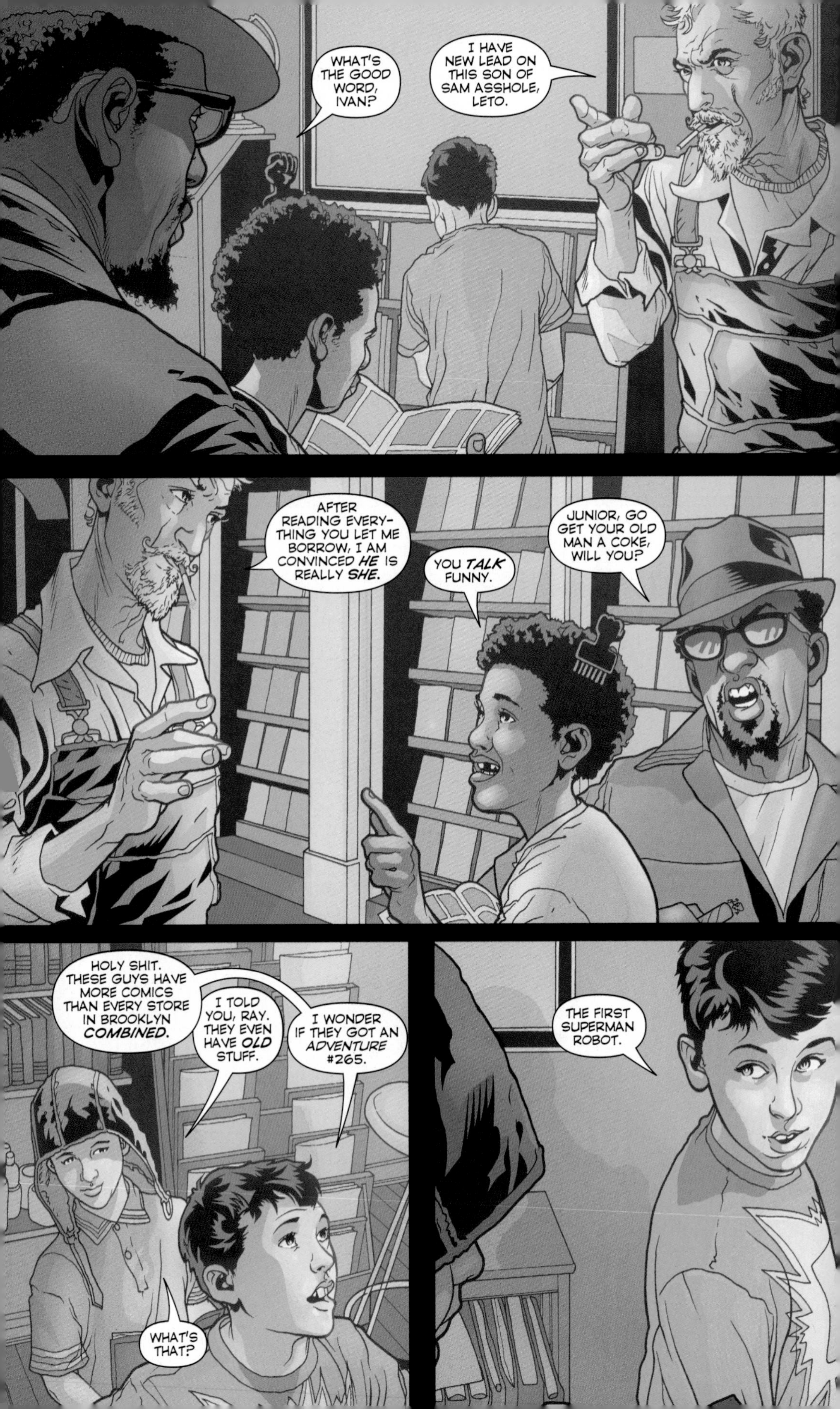
WHAT'S THE GOOD WORD, IVAN?
I HAVE NEW LEAD ON THIS SON OF SAM ASSHOLE, LETO.
AFTER READING EVERY-THING YOU LET ME BORROW, I AM CONVINCED *HE* IS REALLY *SHE*.
YOU *TALK* FUNNY.
JUNIOR, GO GET YOUR OLD MAN A COKE, WILL YOU?
HOLY SHIT. THESE GUYS HAVE MORE COMICS THAN EVERY STORE IN BROOKLYN *COMBINED*.
I TOLD YOU, RAY. THEY EVEN HAVE *OLD* STUFF.
I WONDER IF THEY GOT AN *ADVENTURE* #265.
WHAT'S THAT?
THE FIRST SUPERMAN ROBOT.

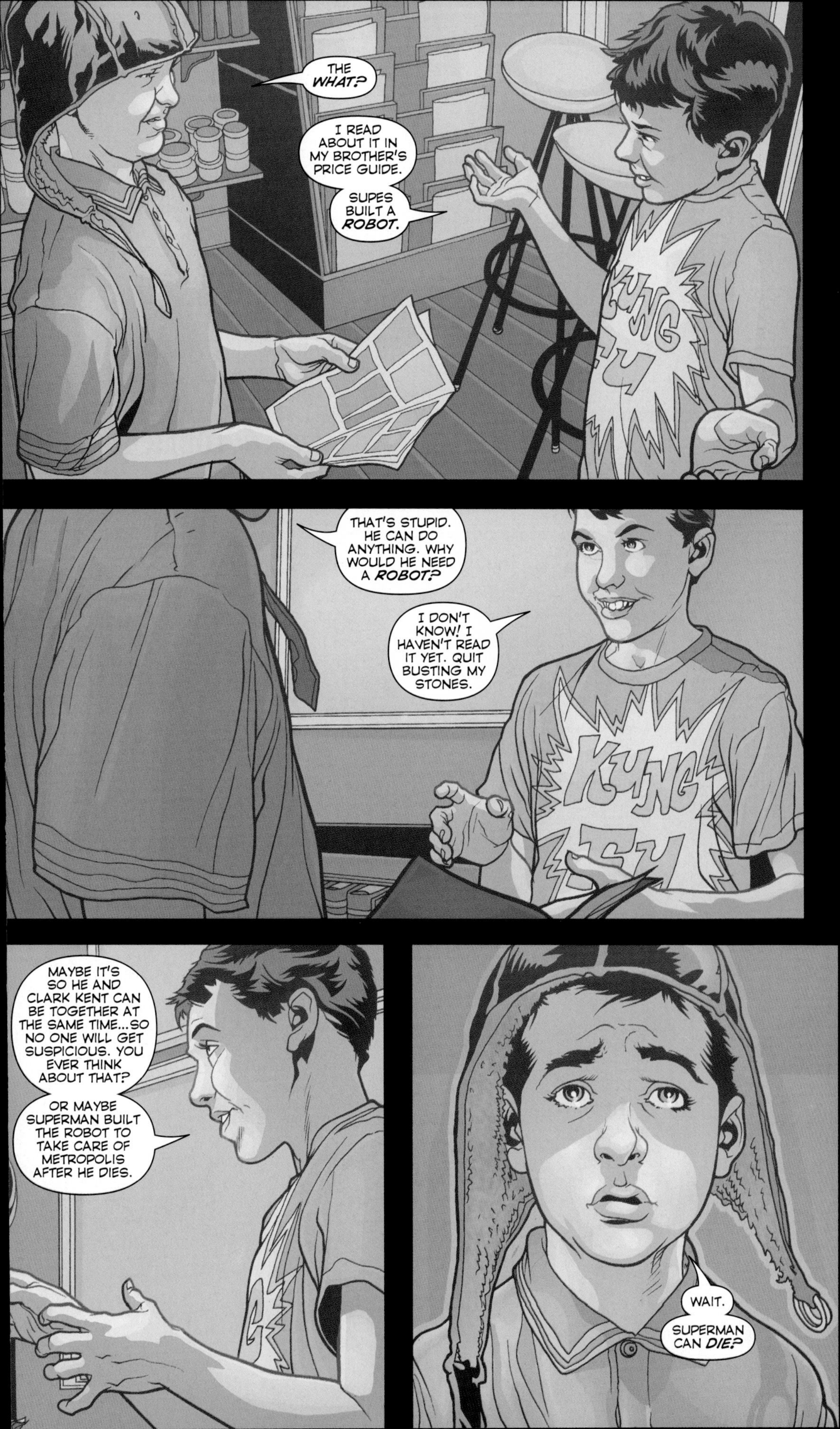

THE *WHAT?*
I READ ABOUT IT IN MY BROTHER'S PRICE GUIDE.
SUPES BUILT A ***ROBOT***.
THAT'S STUPID. HE CAN DO ANYTHING. WHY WOULD HE NEED A ***ROBOT?***
I DON'T KNOW*!* I HAVEN'T READ IT YET. QUIT BUSTING MY STONES.
MAYBE IT'S SO HE AND CLARK KENT CAN BE TOGETHER AT THE SAME TIME...SO NO ONE WILL GET SUSPICIOUS. YOU EVER THINK ABOUT THAT?
OR MAYBE SUPERMAN BUILT THE ROBOT TO TAKE CARE OF METROPOLIS AFTER HE DIES.
WAIT.
SUPERMAN CAN ***DIE?***

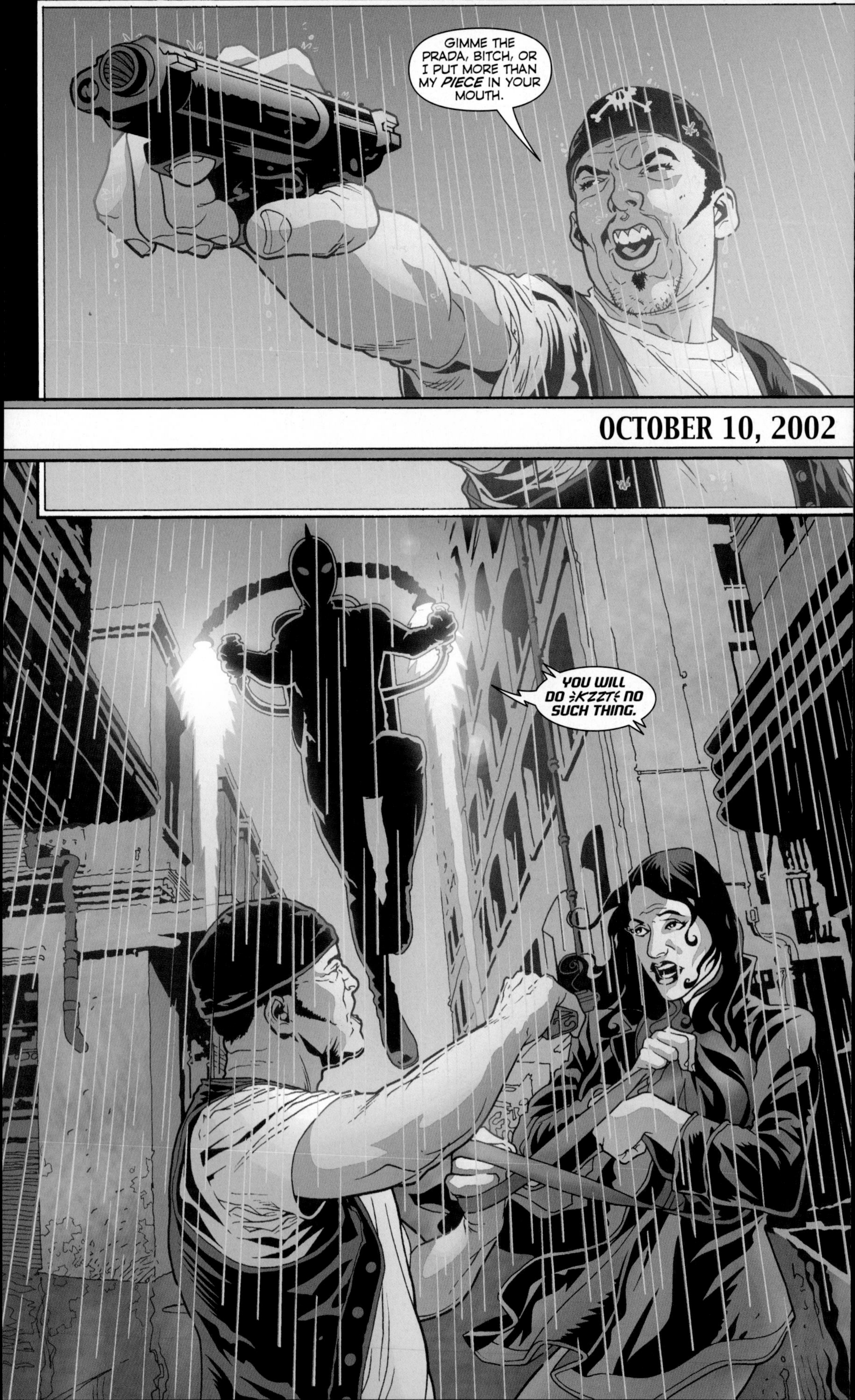
GIMME THE PRADA, BITCH, OR I PUT MORE THAN MY *PIECE* IN YOUR MOUTH.
OCTOBER 10, 2002
*YOU WILL DO KZZT NO SUCH THING.*

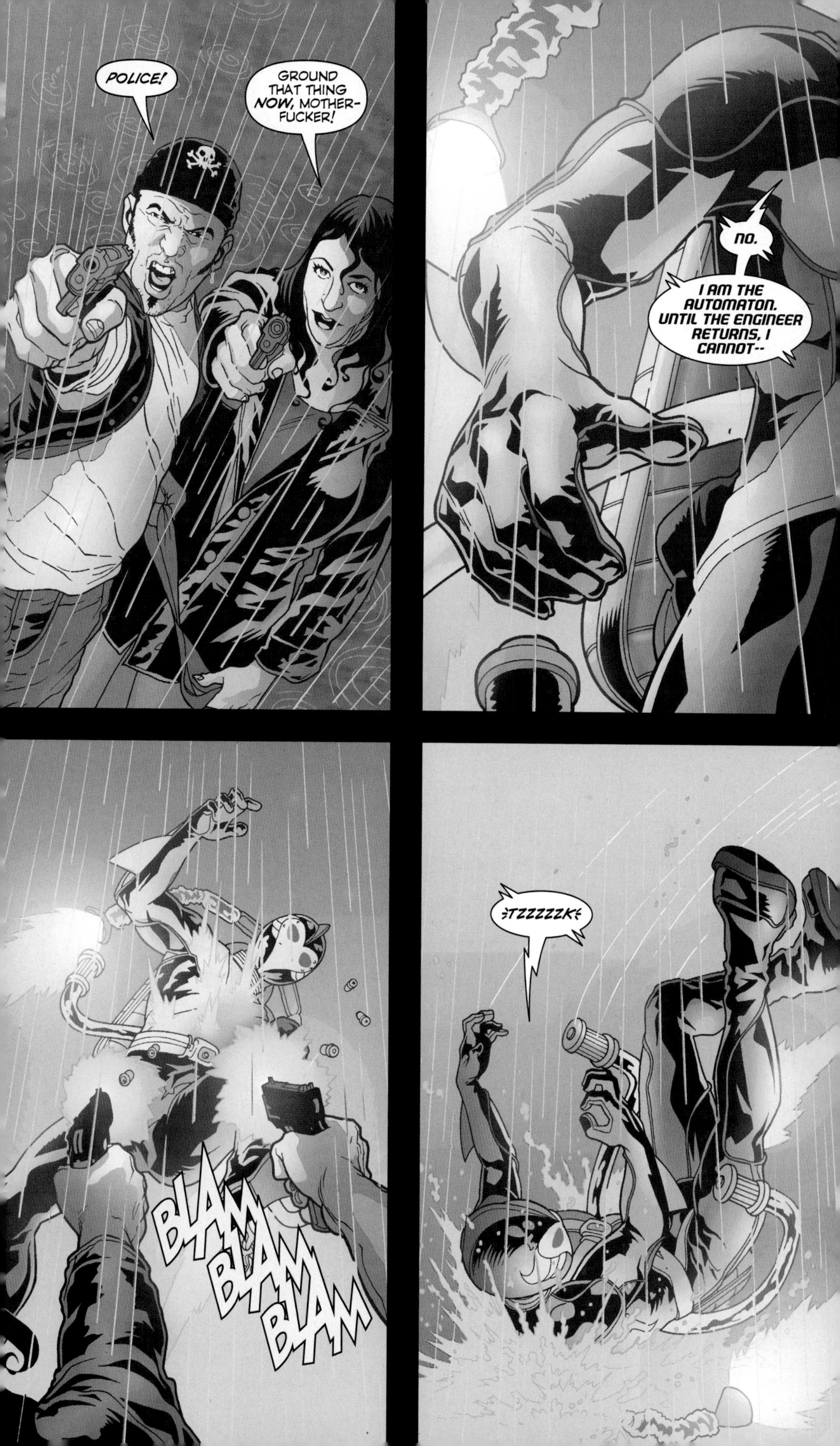
POLICE!
GROUND THAT THING NOW, MOTHER-FUCKER!
NO.
I AM THE AUTOMATON. UNTIL THE ENGINEER RETURNS, I CANNOT--
BLAM BLAM BLAM
TZZZZZK

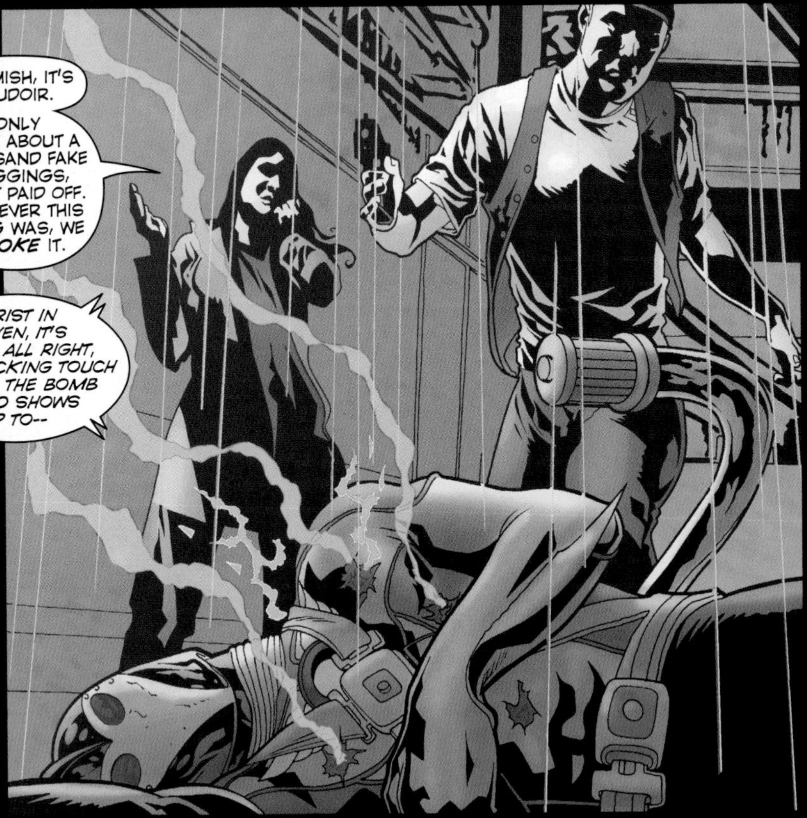
COMMISH, IT'S BOUDOIR.
ONLY TOOK ABOUT A THOUSAND FAKE MUGGINGS, BUT IT PAID OFF. WHATEVER THIS THING WAS, WE BROKE IT.
CHRIST IN HEAVEN, IT'S REAL? ALL RIGHT, DON'T FUCKING TOUCH IT UNTIL THE BOMB SQUAD SHOWS UP TO--

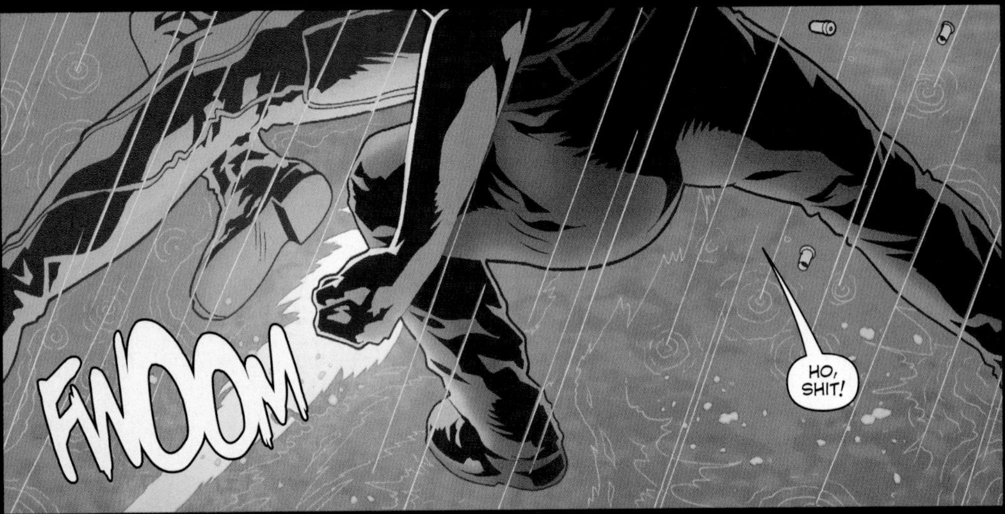
FWOOM
HO, SHIT!

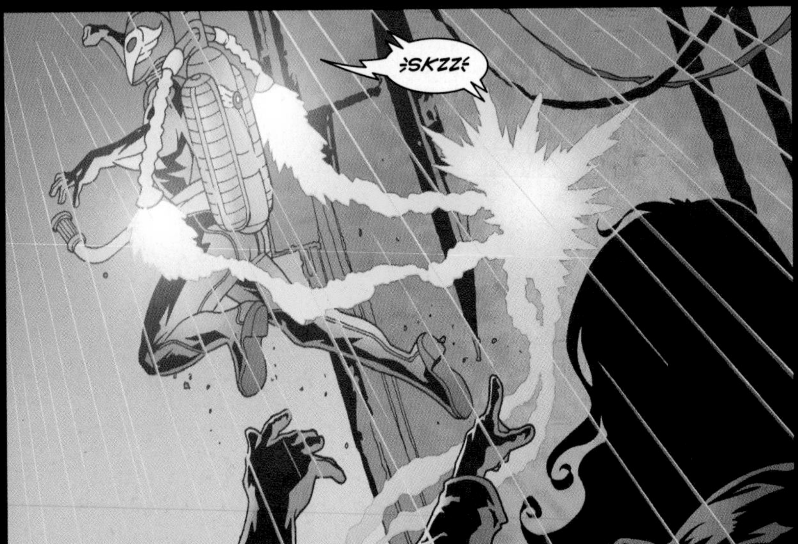
SKZZ

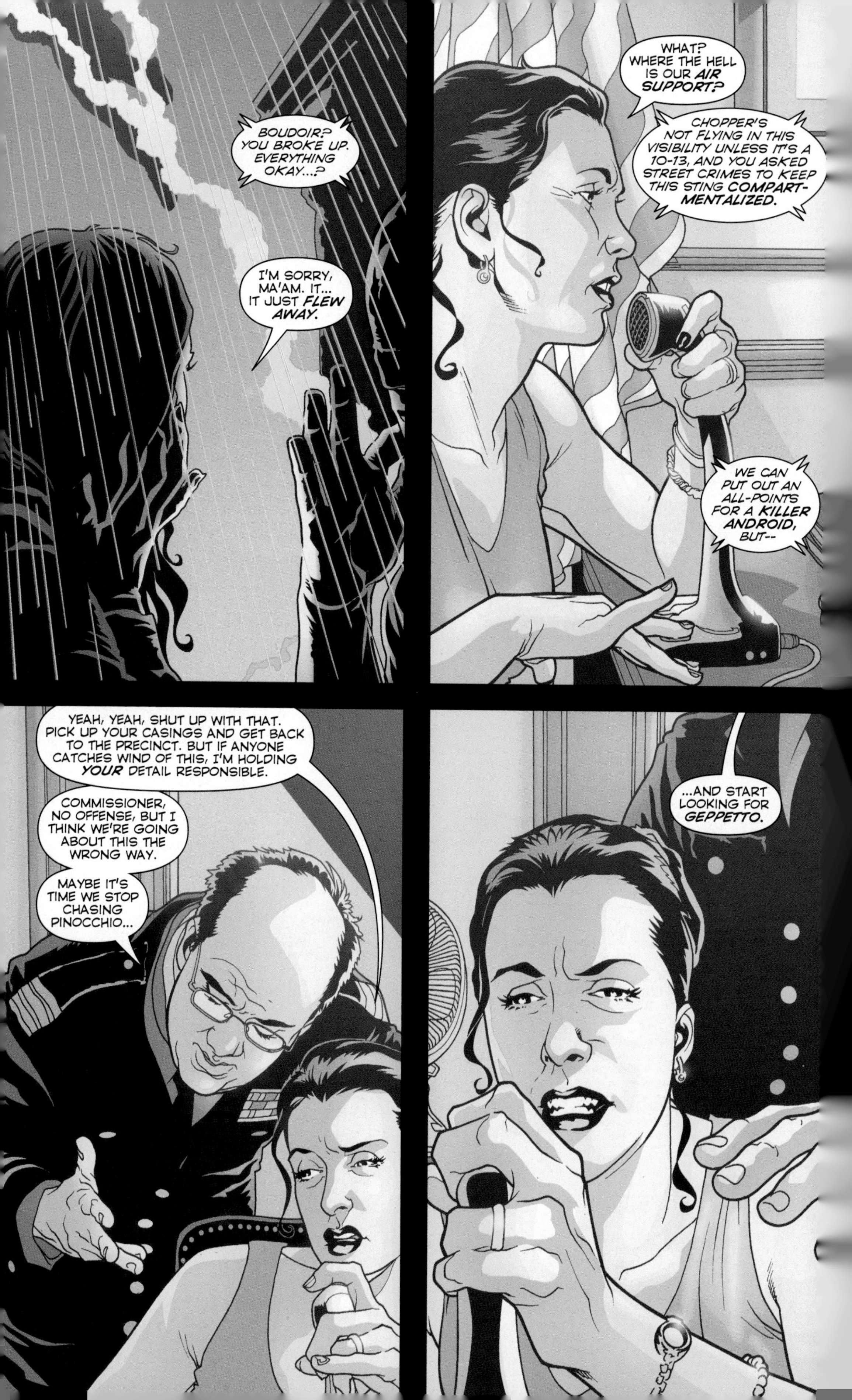
BOUDOIR? YOU BROKE UP. EVERYTHING OKAY...?
I'M SORRY, MA'AM. IT... IT JUST FLEW AWAY.
WHAT? WHERE THE HELL IS OUR AIR SUPPORT?
CHOPPER'S NOT FLYING IN THIS VISIBILITY UNLESS IT'S A 10-13, AND YOU ASKED STREET CRIMES TO KEEP THIS STING COMPARTMENTALIZED.
WE CAN PUT OUT AN ALL-POINTS FOR A KILLER ANDROID, BUT--
YEAH, YEAH, SHUT UP WITH THAT. PICK UP YOUR CASINGS AND GET BACK TO THE PRECINCT. BUT IF ANYONE CATCHES WIND OF THIS, I'M HOLDING YOUR DETAIL RESPONSIBLE.
COMMISSIONER, NO OFFENSE, BUT I THINK WE'RE GOING ABOUT THIS THE WRONG WAY.
MAYBE IT'S TIME WE STOP CHASING PINOCCHIO...
...AND START LOOKING FOR GEPPETTO.

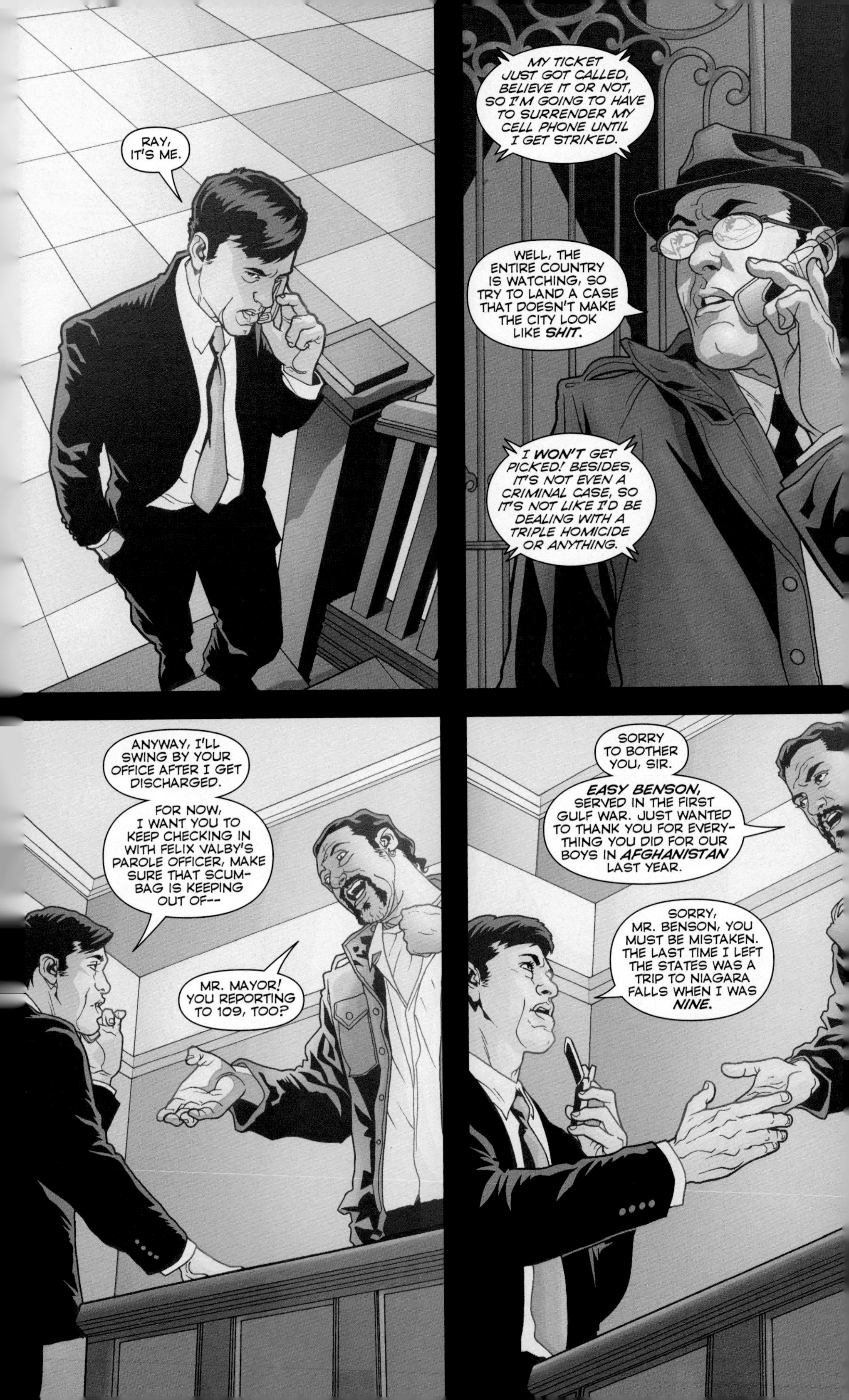
RAY, IT'S ME.
MY TICKET JUST GOT CALLED, BELIEVE IT OR NOT, SO I'M GOING TO HAVE TO SURRENDER MY CELL PHONE UNTIL I GET STRIKED.
WELL, THE ENTIRE COUNTRY IS WATCHING, SO TRY TO LAND A CASE THAT DOESN'T MAKE THE CITY LOOK LIKE SHIT.
I WON'T GET PICKED! BESIDES, IT'S NOT EVEN A CRIMINAL CASE, SO IT'S NOT LIKE I'D BE DEALING WITH A TRIPLE HOMICIDE OR ANYTHING.
ANYWAY, I'LL SWING BY YOUR OFFICE AFTER I GET DISCHARGED.
FOR NOW, I WANT YOU TO KEEP CHECKING IN WITH FELIX VALBY'S PAROLE OFFICER, MAKE SURE THAT SCUM-BAG IS KEEPING OUT OF--
MR. MAYOR! YOU REPORTING TO 109, TOO?
SORRY TO BOTHER YOU, SIR.
EASY BENSON, SERVED IN THE FIRST GULF WAR. JUST WANTED TO THANK YOU FOR EVERY-THING YOU DID FOR OUR BOYS IN AFGHANISTAN LAST YEAR.
SORRY, MR. BENSON, YOU MUST BE MISTAKEN. THE LAST TIME I LEFT THE STATES WAS A TRIP TO NIAGARA FALLS WHEN I WAS NINE.

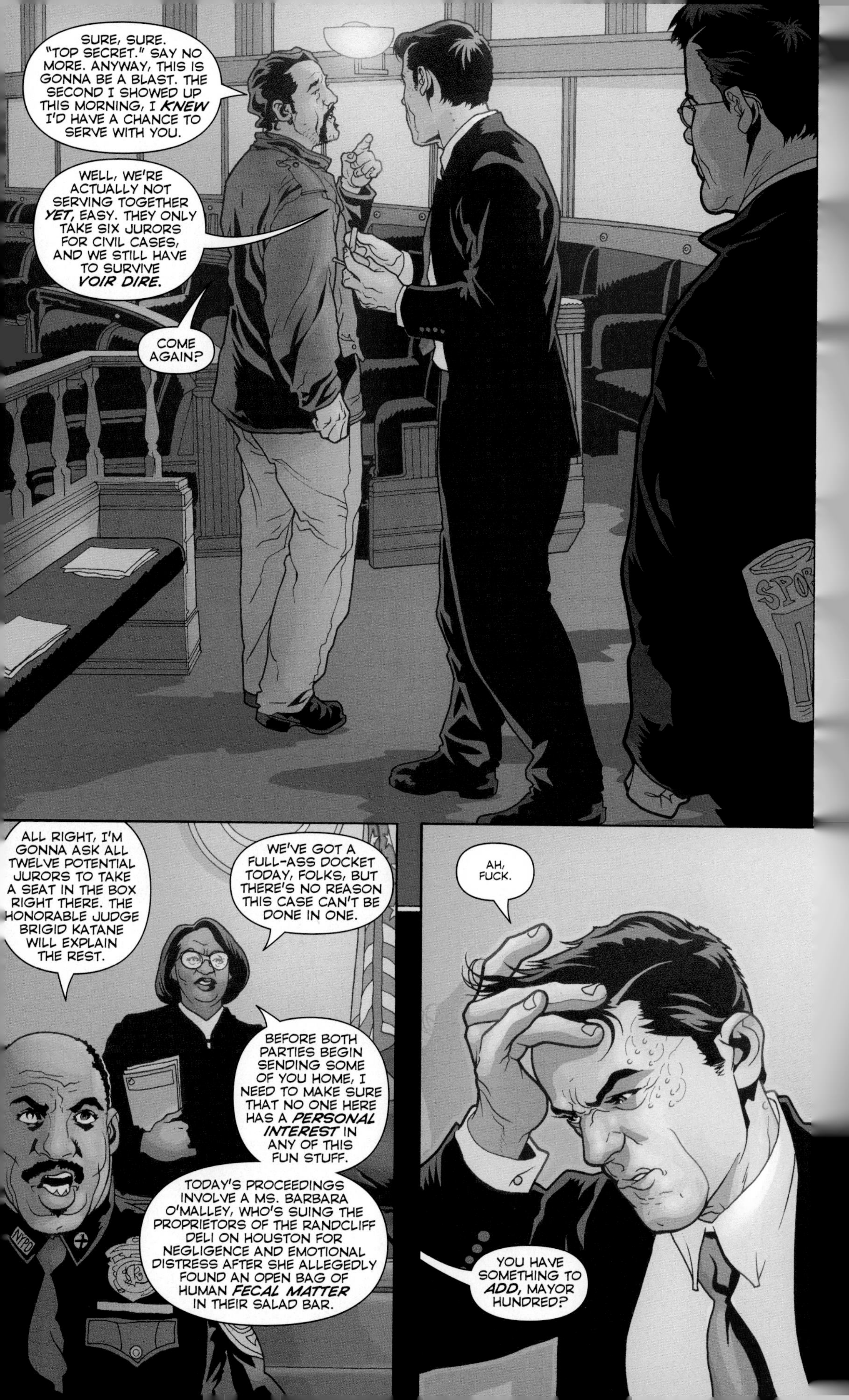
SURE, SURE. "TOP SECRET." SAY NO MORE. ANYWAY, THIS IS GONNA BE A BLAST. THE SECOND I SHOWED UP THIS MORNING, I KNEW I'D HAVE A CHANCE TO SERVE WITH YOU.
WELL, WE'RE ACTUALLY NOT SERVING TOGETHER YET, EASY. THEY ONLY TAKE SIX JURORS FOR CIVIL CASES, AND WE STILL HAVE TO SURVIVE VOIR DIRE.
COME AGAIN?
ALL RIGHT, I'M GONNA ASK ALL TWELVE POTENTIAL JURORS TO TAKE A SEAT IN THE BOX RIGHT THERE. THE HONORABLE JUDGE BRIGID KATANE WILL EXPLAIN THE REST.
WE'VE GOT A FULL-ASS DOCKET TODAY, FOLKS, BUT THERE'S NO REASON THIS CASE CAN'T BE DONE IN ONE.
BEFORE BOTH PARTIES BEGIN SENDING SOME OF YOU HOME, I NEED TO MAKE SURE THAT NO ONE HERE HAS A PERSONAL INTEREST IN ANY OF THIS FUN STUFF.
TODAY'S PROCEEDINGS INVOLVE A MS. BARBARA O'MALLEY, WHO'S SUING THE PROPRIETORS OF THE RANDCLIFF DELI ON HOUSTON FOR NEGLIGENCE AND EMOTIONAL DISTRESS AFTER SHE ALLEGEDLY FOUND AN OPEN BAG OF HUMAN FECAL MATTER IN THEIR SALAD BAR.
AH, FUCK.
YOU HAVE SOMETHING TO ADD, MAYOR HUNDRED?

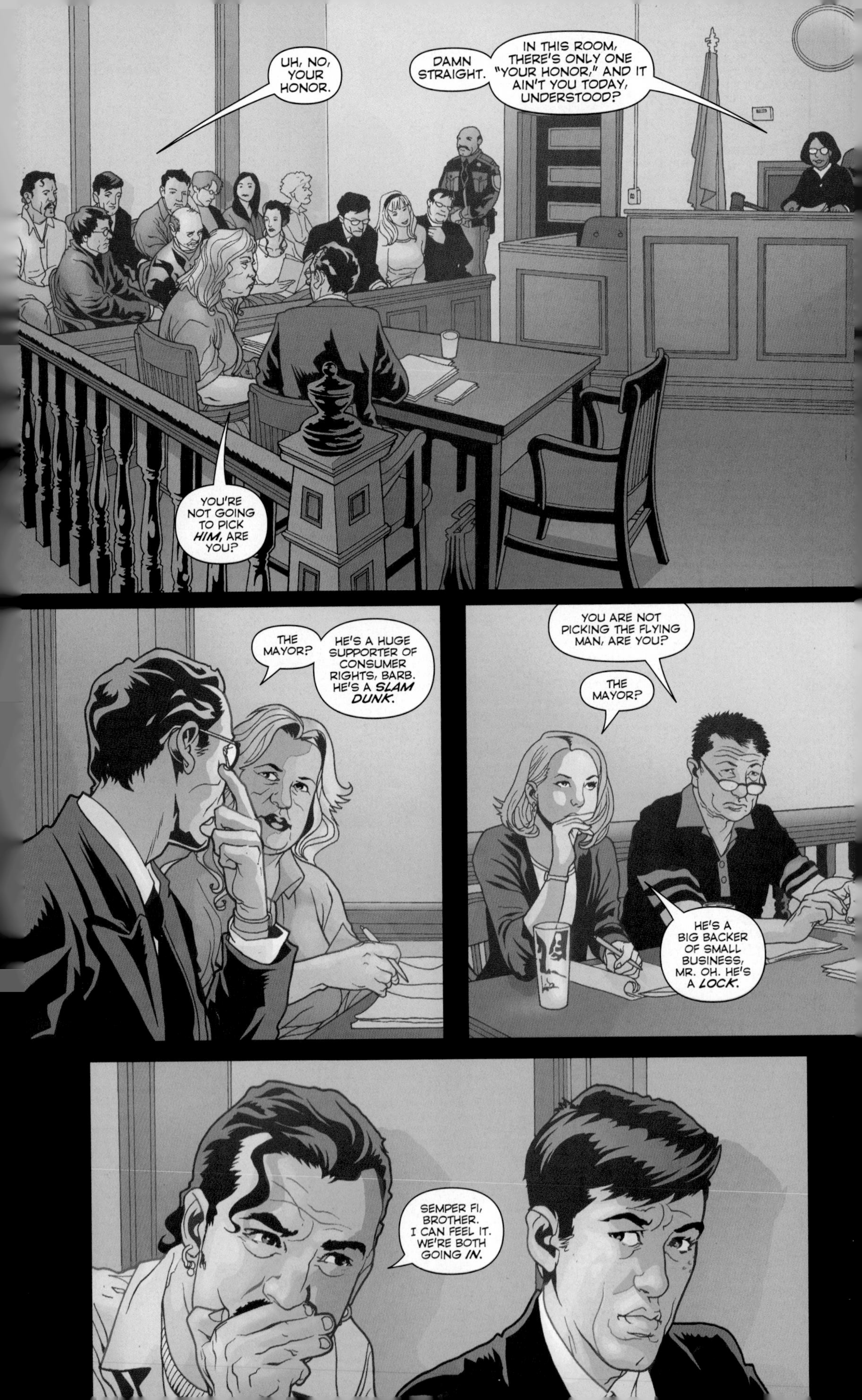

UH, NO, YOUR HONOR.
DAMN STRAIGHT.
IN THIS ROOM, THERE'S ONLY ONE "YOUR HONOR," AND IT AIN'T YOU TODAY, UNDERSTOOD?
YOU'RE NOT GOING TO PICK HIM, ARE YOU?
THE MAYOR?
HE'S A HUGE SUPPORTER OF CONSUMER RIGHTS, BARB. HE'S A SLAM DUNK.
YOU ARE NOT PICKING THE FLYING MAN, ARE YOU?
THE MAYOR?
HE'S A BIG BACKER OF SMALL BUSINESS, MR. OH. HE'S A LOCK.
SEMPER FI, BROTHER. I CAN FEEL IT. WE'RE BOTH GOING IN.

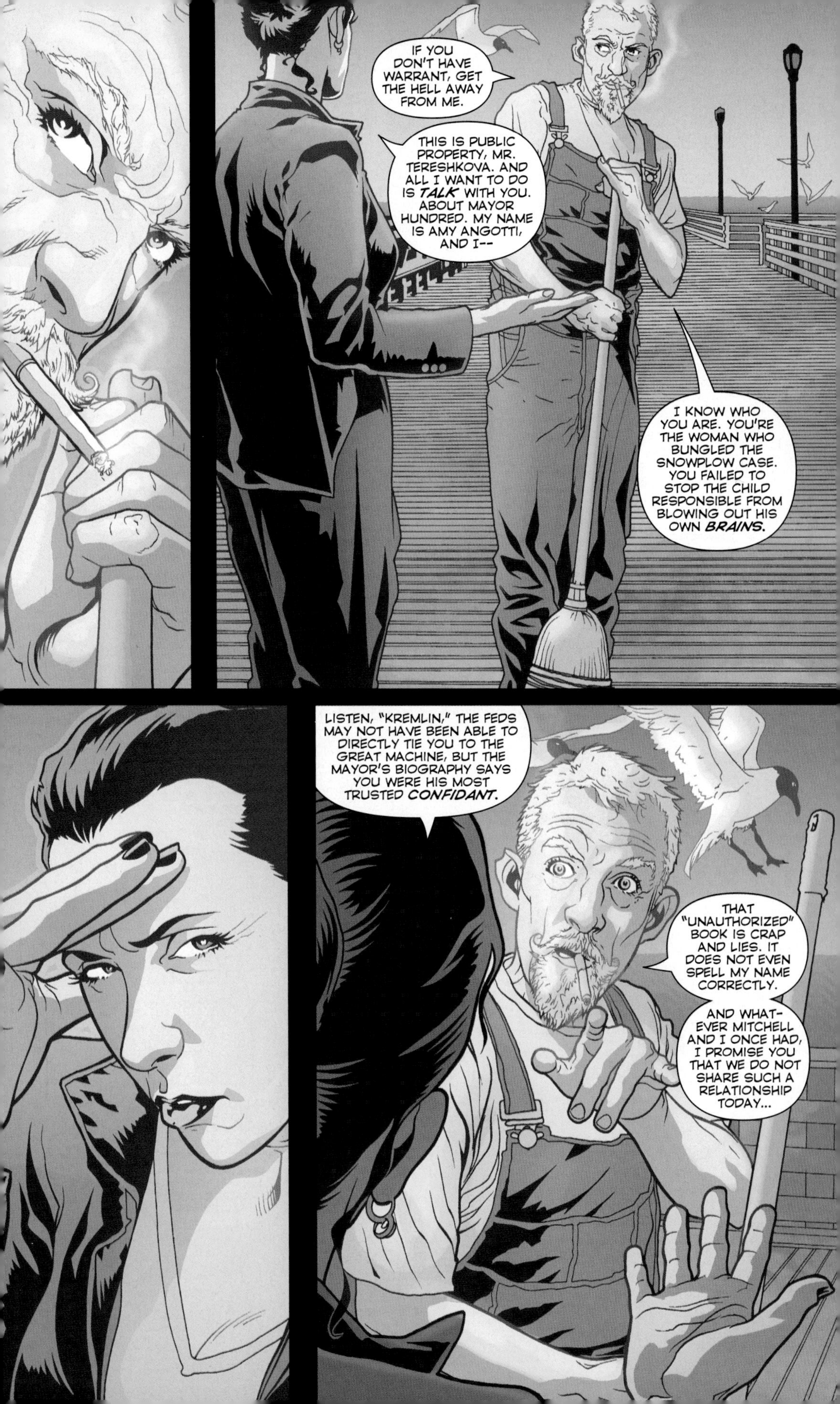

IF YOU DON'T HAVE WARRANT, GET THE HELL AWAY FROM ME.
THIS IS PUBLIC PROPERTY, MR. TERESHKOVA. AND ALL I WANT TO DO IS *TALK* WITH YOU. ABOUT MAYOR HUNDRED. MY NAME IS AMY ANGOTTI, AND I--
I KNOW WHO YOU ARE. YOU'RE THE WOMAN WHO BUNGLED THE SNOWPLOW CASE. YOU FAILED TO STOP THE CHILD RESPONSIBLE FROM BLOWING OUT HIS OWN *BRAINS*.
LISTEN, "KREMLIN," THE FEDS MAY NOT HAVE BEEN ABLE TO DIRECTLY TIE YOU TO THE GREAT MACHINE, BUT THE MAYOR'S BIOGRAPHY SAYS YOU WERE HIS MOST TRUSTED *CONFIDANT*.
THAT "UNAUTHORIZED" BOOK IS CRAP AND LIES. IT DOES NOT EVEN SPELL MY NAME CORRECTLY.
AND WHATEVER MITCHELL AND I ONCE HAD, I PROMISE YOU THAT WE DO NOT SHARE SUCH A RELATIONSHIP TODAY...

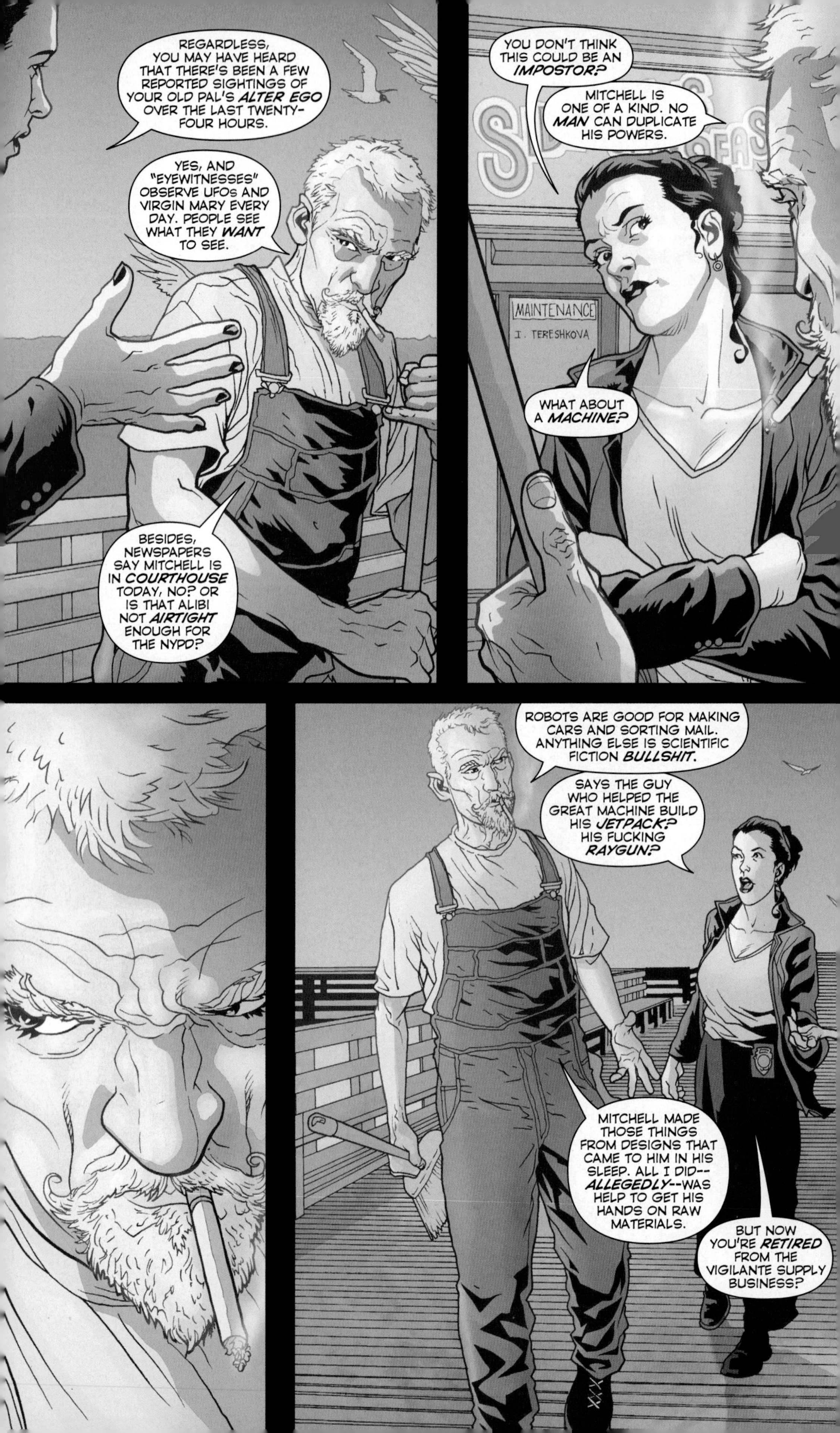
REGARDLESS, YOU MAY HAVE HEARD THAT THERE'S BEEN A FEW REPORTED SIGHTINGS OF YOUR OLD PAL'S ALTER EGO OVER THE LAST TWENTY-FOUR HOURS.
YES, AND "EYEWITNESSES" OBSERVE UFOs AND VIRGIN MARY EVERY DAY. PEOPLE SEE WHAT THEY WANT TO SEE.
BESIDES, NEWSPAPERS SAY MITCHELL IS IN COURTHOUSE TODAY, NO? OR IS THAT ALIBI NOT AIRTIGHT ENOUGH FOR THE NYPD?
YOU DON'T THINK THIS COULD BE AN IMPOSTOR?
MITCHELL IS ONE OF A KIND. NO MAN CAN DUPLICATE HIS POWERS.
MAINTENANCE
I. TERESHKOVA
WHAT ABOUT A MACHINE?
ROBOTS ARE GOOD FOR MAKING CARS AND SORTING MAIL. ANYTHING ELSE IS SCIENTIFIC FICTION BULLSHIT.
SAYS THE GUY WHO HELPED THE GREAT MACHINE BUILD HIS JETPACK? HIS FUCKING RAYGUN?
MITCHELL MADE THOSE THINGS FROM DESIGNS THAT CAME TO HIM IN HIS SLEEP. ALL I DID--ALLEGEDLY--WAS HELP TO GET HIS HANDS ON RAW MATERIALS.
BUT NOW YOU'RE RETIRED FROM THE VIGILANTE SUPPLY BUSINESS?

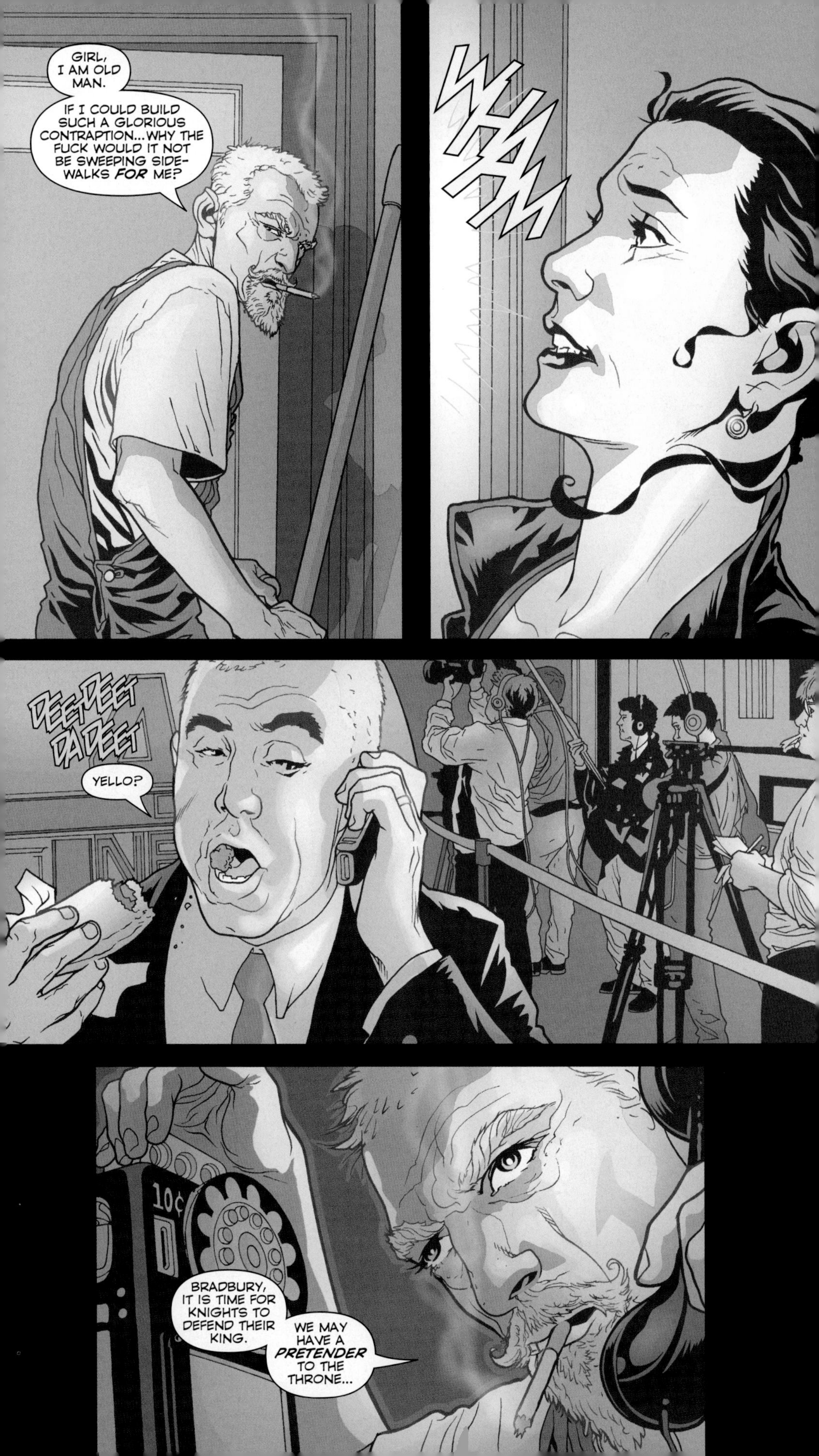
GIRL, I AM OLD MAN.
IF I COULD BUILD SUCH A GLORIOUS CONTRAPTION...WHY THE FUCK WOULD IT NOT BE SWEEPING SIDE-WALKS *FOR* ME?
WHAM
DEET-DEET DA DEET
YELLO?
10¢
BRADBURY, IT IS TIME FOR KNIGHTS TO DEFEND THEIR KING.
WE MAY HAVE A *PRETENDER* TO THE THRONE...

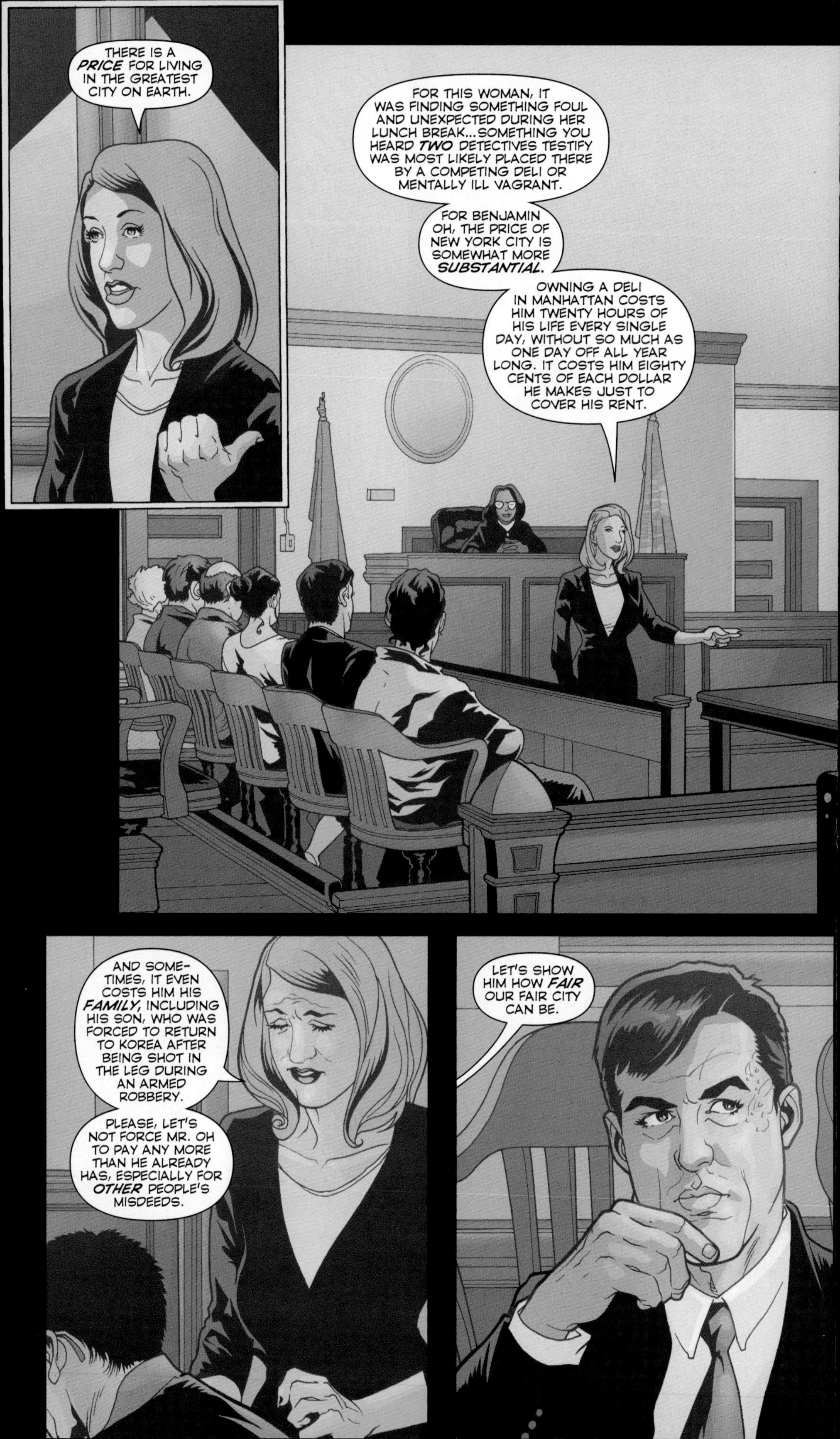
THERE IS A *PRICE* FOR LIVING IN THE GREATEST CITY ON EARTH.
FOR THIS WOMAN, IT WAS FINDING SOMETHING FOUL AND UNEXPECTED DURING HER LUNCH BREAK...SOMETHING YOU HEARD *TWO* DETECTIVES TESTIFY WAS MOST LIKELY PLACED THERE BY A COMPETING DELI OR MENTALLY ILL VAGRANT.
FOR BENJAMIN OH, THE PRICE OF NEW YORK CITY IS SOMEWHAT MORE *SUBSTANTIAL*.
OWNING A DELI IN MANHATTAN COSTS HIM TWENTY HOURS OF HIS LIFE EVERY SINGLE DAY, WITHOUT SO MUCH AS ONE DAY OFF ALL YEAR LONG. IT COSTS HIM EIGHTY CENTS OF EACH DOLLAR HE MAKES JUST TO COVER HIS RENT.
AND SOME-TIMES, IT EVEN COSTS HIM HIS *FAMILY,* INCLUDING HIS SON, WHO WAS FORCED TO RETURN TO KOREA AFTER BEING SHOT IN THE LEG DURING AN ARMED ROBBERY.
PLEASE, LET'S NOT FORCE MR. OH TO PAY ANY MORE THAN HE ALREADY HAS, ESPECIALLY FOR *OTHER* PEOPLE'S MISDEEDS.
LET'S SHOW HIM HOW *FAIR* OUR FAIR CITY CAN BE.

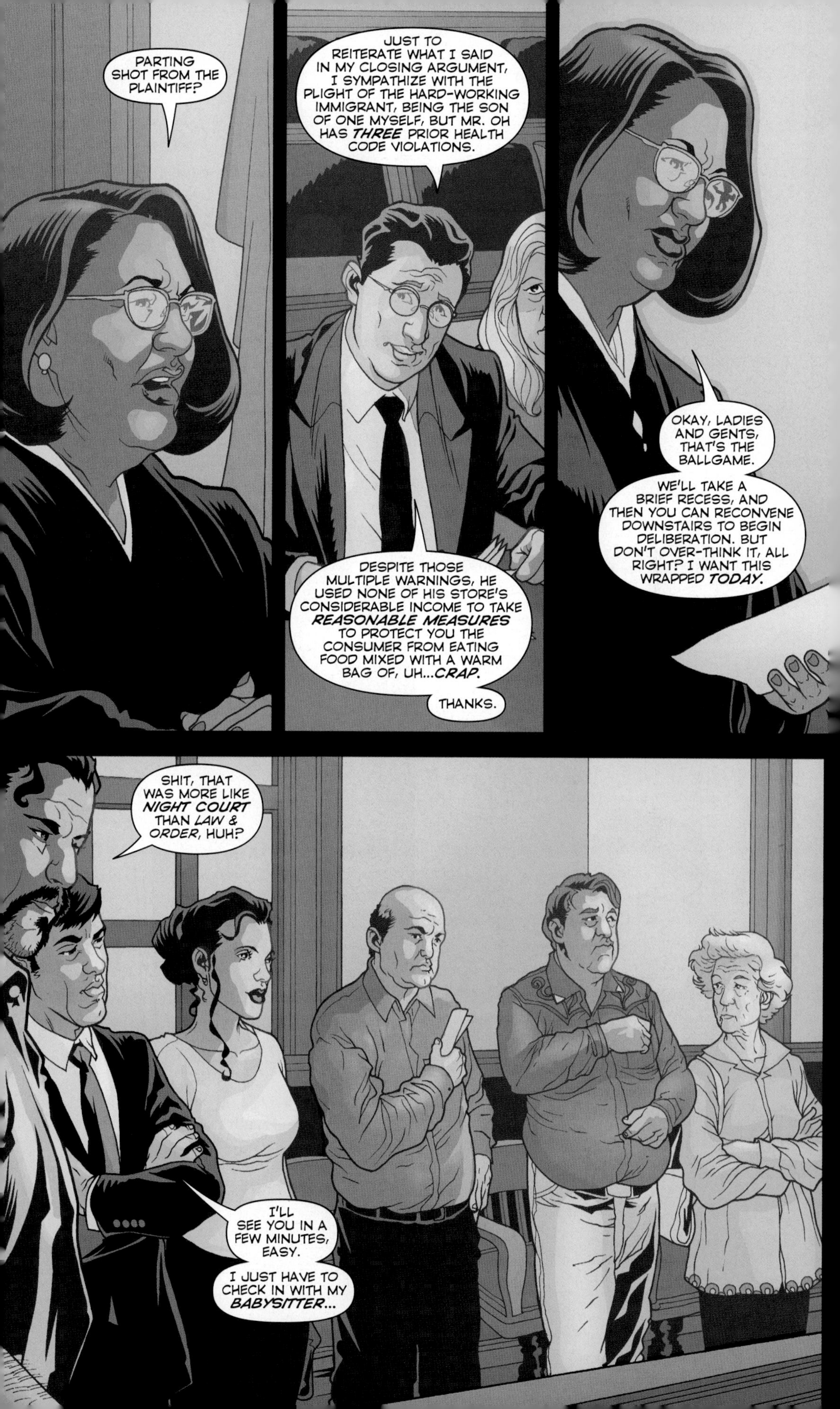
PARTING SHOT FROM THE PLAINTIFF?
JUST TO REITERATE WHAT I SAID IN MY CLOSING ARGUMENT, I SYMPATHIZE WITH THE PLIGHT OF THE HARD-WORKING IMMIGRANT, BEING THE SON OF ONE MYSELF, BUT MR. OH HAS *THREE* PRIOR HEALTH CODE VIOLATIONS.
DESPITE THOSE MULTIPLE WARNINGS, HE USED NONE OF HIS STORE'S CONSIDERABLE INCOME TO TAKE *REASONABLE MEASURES* TO PROTECT YOU THE CONSUMER FROM EATING FOOD MIXED WITH A WARM BAG OF, UH...*CRAP*.
THANKS.
OKAY, LADIES AND GENTS, THAT'S THE BALLGAME.
WE'LL TAKE A BRIEF RECESS, AND THEN YOU CAN RECONVENE DOWNSTAIRS TO BEGIN DELIBERATION. BUT DON'T OVER-THINK IT, ALL RIGHT? I WANT THIS WRAPPED *TODAY*.
SHIT, THAT WAS MORE LIKE *NIGHT COURT* THAN *LAW & ORDER*, HUH?
I'LL SEE YOU IN A FEW MINUTES, EASY.
I JUST HAVE TO CHECK IN WITH MY *BABYSITTER*...

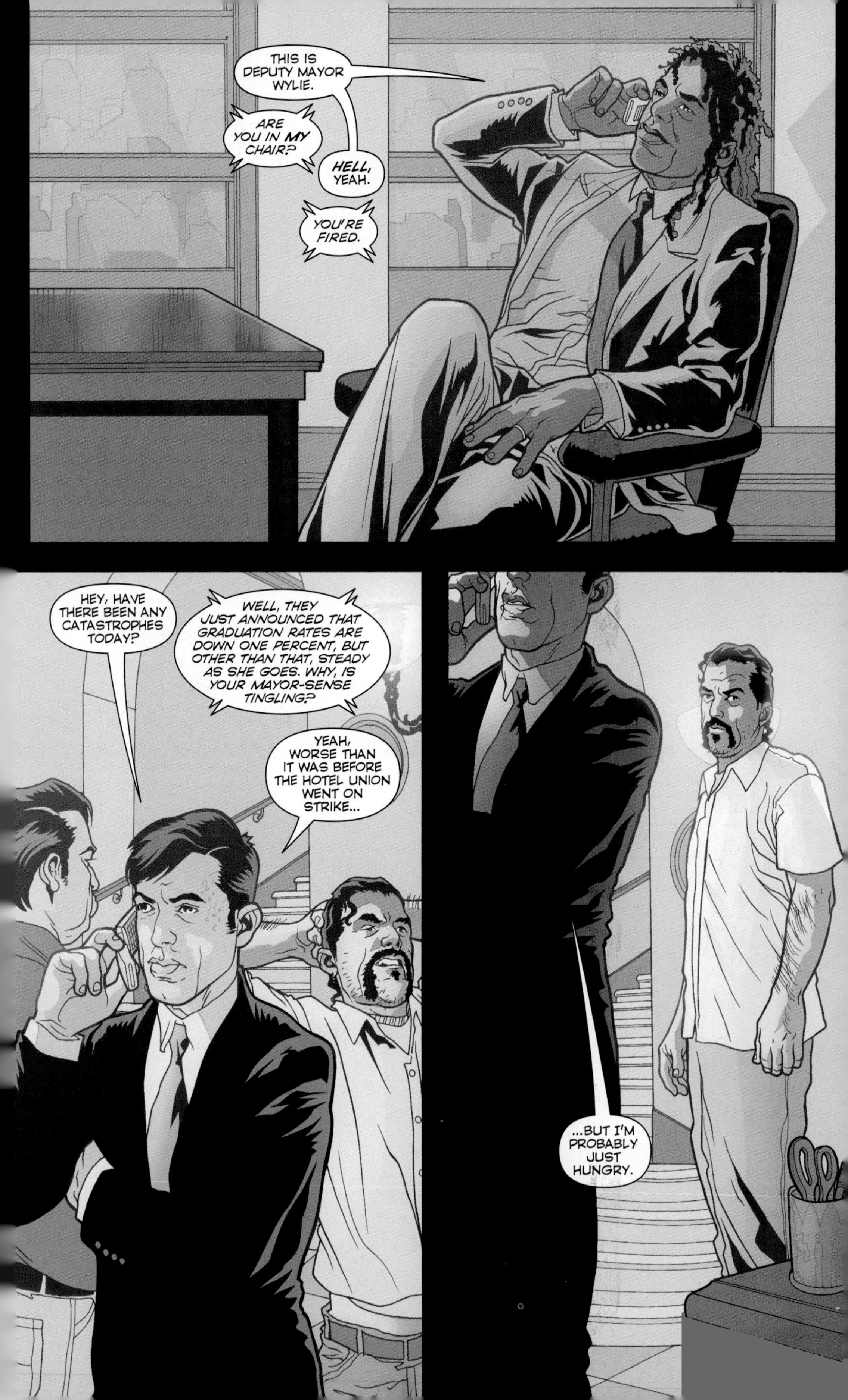
THIS IS DEPUTY MAYOR WYLIE.
ARE YOU IN MY CHAIR?
HELL, YEAH.
YOU'RE FIRED.
HEY, HAVE THERE BEEN ANY CATASTROPHES TODAY?
WELL, THEY JUST ANNOUNCED THAT GRADUATION RATES ARE DOWN ONE PERCENT, BUT OTHER THAN THAT, STEADY AS SHE GOES. WHY, IS YOUR MAYOR-SENSE TINGLING?
YEAH, WORSE THAN IT WAS BEFORE THE HOTEL UNION WENT ON STRIKE...
...BUT I'M PROBABLY JUST HUNGRY.

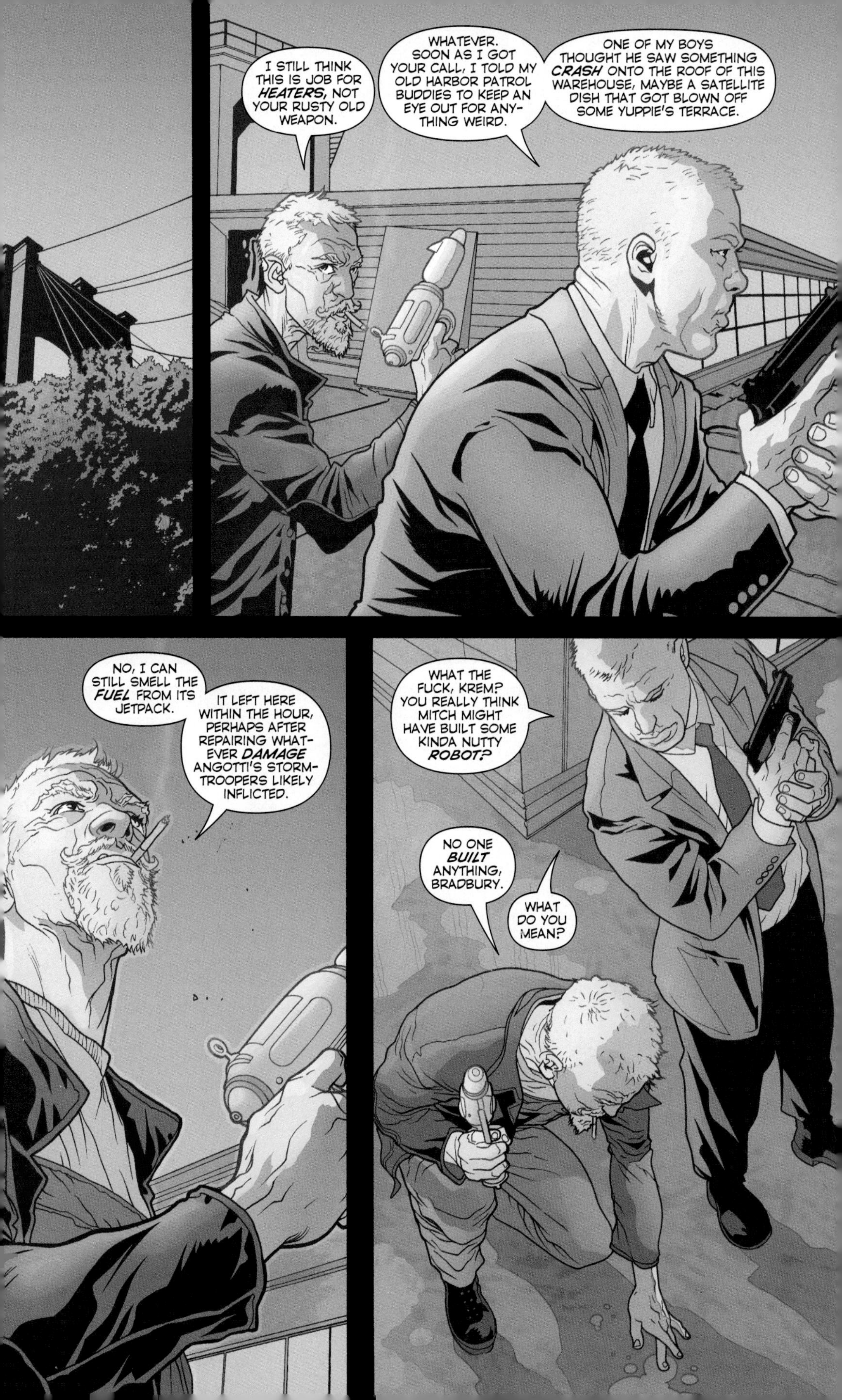
I STILL THINK THIS IS JOB FOR *HEATERS,* NOT YOUR RUSTY OLD WEAPON.
WHATEVER. SOON AS I GOT YOUR CALL, I TOLD MY OLD HARBOR PATROL BUDDIES TO KEEP AN EYE OUT FOR ANY-THING WEIRD.
ONE OF MY BOYS THOUGHT HE SAW SOMETHING *CRASH* ONTO THE ROOF OF THIS WAREHOUSE, MAYBE A SATELLITE DISH THAT GOT BLOWN OFF SOME YUPPIE'S TERRACE.
NO, I CAN STILL SMELL THE *FUEL* FROM ITS JETPACK.
IT LEFT HERE WITHIN THE HOUR, PERHAPS AFTER REPAIRING WHAT-EVER *DAMAGE* ANGOTTI'S STORM-TROOPERS LIKELY INFLICTED.
WHAT THE FUCK, KREM? YOU REALLY THINK MITCH MIGHT HAVE BUILT SOME KINDA NUTTY *ROBOT?*
NO ONE *BUILT* ANYTHING, BRADBURY.
WHAT DO YOU MEAN?

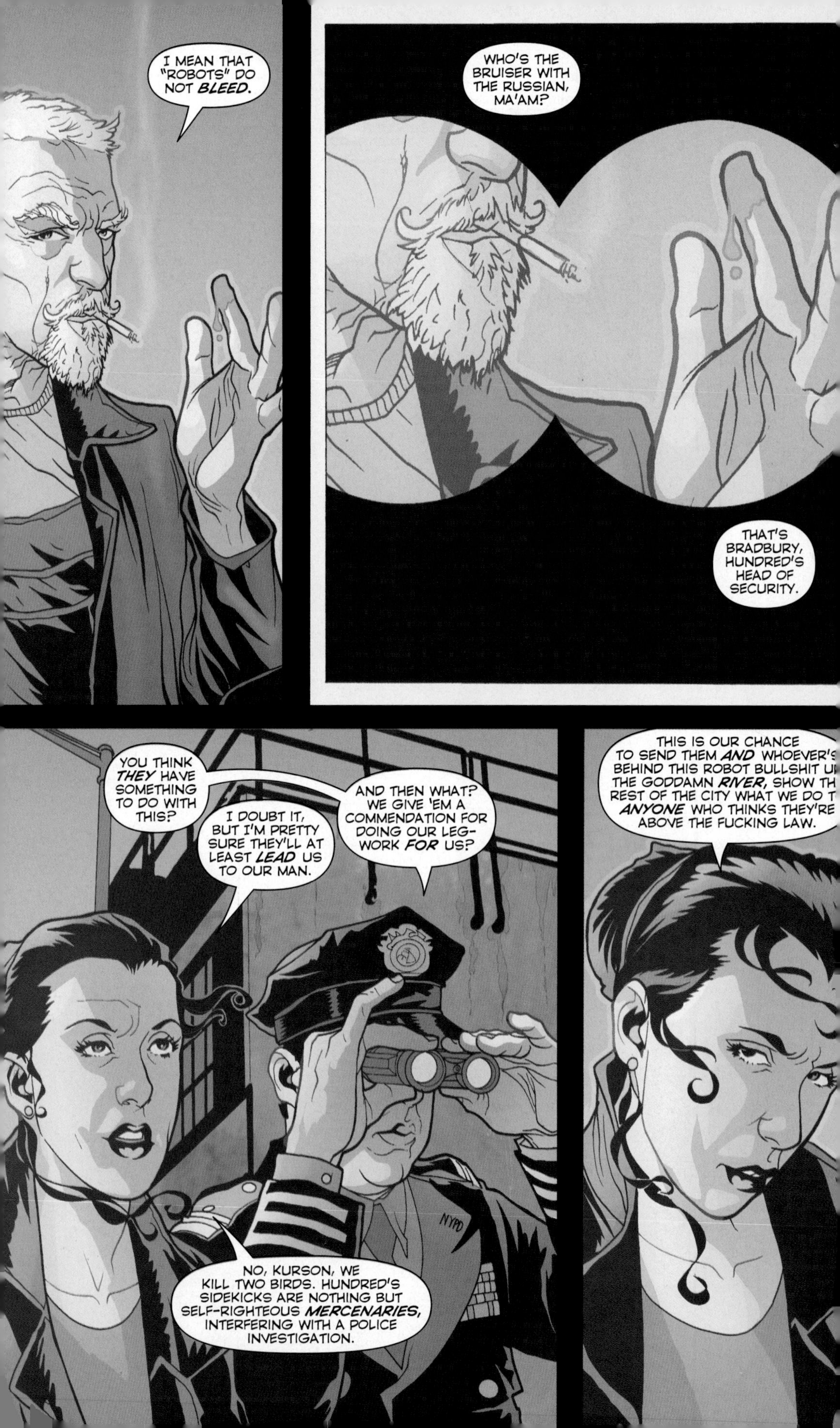
I MEAN THAT "ROBOTS" DO NOT BLEED.
WHO'S THE BRUISER WITH THE RUSSIAN, MA'AM?
THAT'S BRADBURY, HUNDRED'S HEAD OF SECURITY.
YOU THINK THEY HAVE SOMETHING TO DO WITH THIS?
I DOUBT IT, BUT I'M PRETTY SURE THEY'LL AT LEAST LEAD US TO OUR MAN.
AND THEN WHAT? WE GIVE 'EM A COMMENDATION FOR DOING OUR LEG-WORK FOR US?
NO, KURSON, WE KILL TWO BIRDS. HUNDRED'S SIDEKICKS ARE NOTHING BUT SELF-RIGHTEOUS MERCENARIES, INTERFERING WITH A POLICE INVESTIGATION.
NYPD
THIS IS OUR CHANCE TO SEND THEM AND WHOEVER'S BEHIND THIS ROBOT BULLSHIT UP THE GODDAMN RIVER, SHOW THE REST OF THE CITY WHAT WE DO TO ANYONE WHO THINKS THEY'RE ABOVE THE FUCKING LAW.

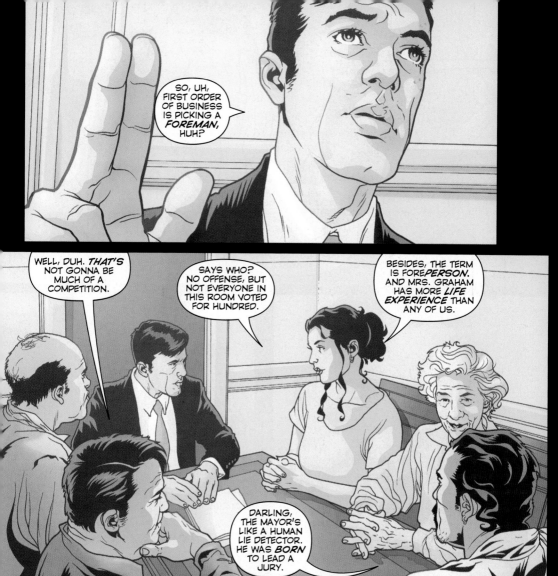

SO, UH, FIRST ORDER OF BUSINESS IS PICKING A *FOREMAN*, HUH?

WELL, DUH. *THAT'S* NOT GONNA BE MUCH OF A COMPETITION.

SAYS WHO? NO OFFENSE, BUT NOT EVERYONE IN THIS ROOM VOTED FOR HUNDRED.

BESIDES, THE TERM IS FORE*PERSON*. AND MRS. GRAHAM HAS MORE *LIFE EXPERIENCE* THAN ANY OF US.

DARLING, THE MAYOR'S LIKE A HUMAN LIE DETECTOR. HE WAS *BORN* TO LEAD A JURY.

THANK YOU, EASY, I'M NOT A *CYBORG*. NO DIFFERENT THAN ANYONE ELSE HERE.

BULL. YOU CAN COMMUNICATE WITH MACHINES, RIGHT? YOU KNOW IF THERE'S SOMETHING WRONG WITH ONE JUST BY LOOKING AT IT?

ACTUALLY, THE NSA DOESN'T PERMIT ME TO DISCUSS--

WELL, THE *HUMAN BODY* IS A MACHINE, AIN'T IT?

WE'RE ALL JUST THINGS THAT EXTRACT ENERGY FROM FUEL IN ORDER TO...TO PERFORM LITTLE *TASKS*, YEAH?

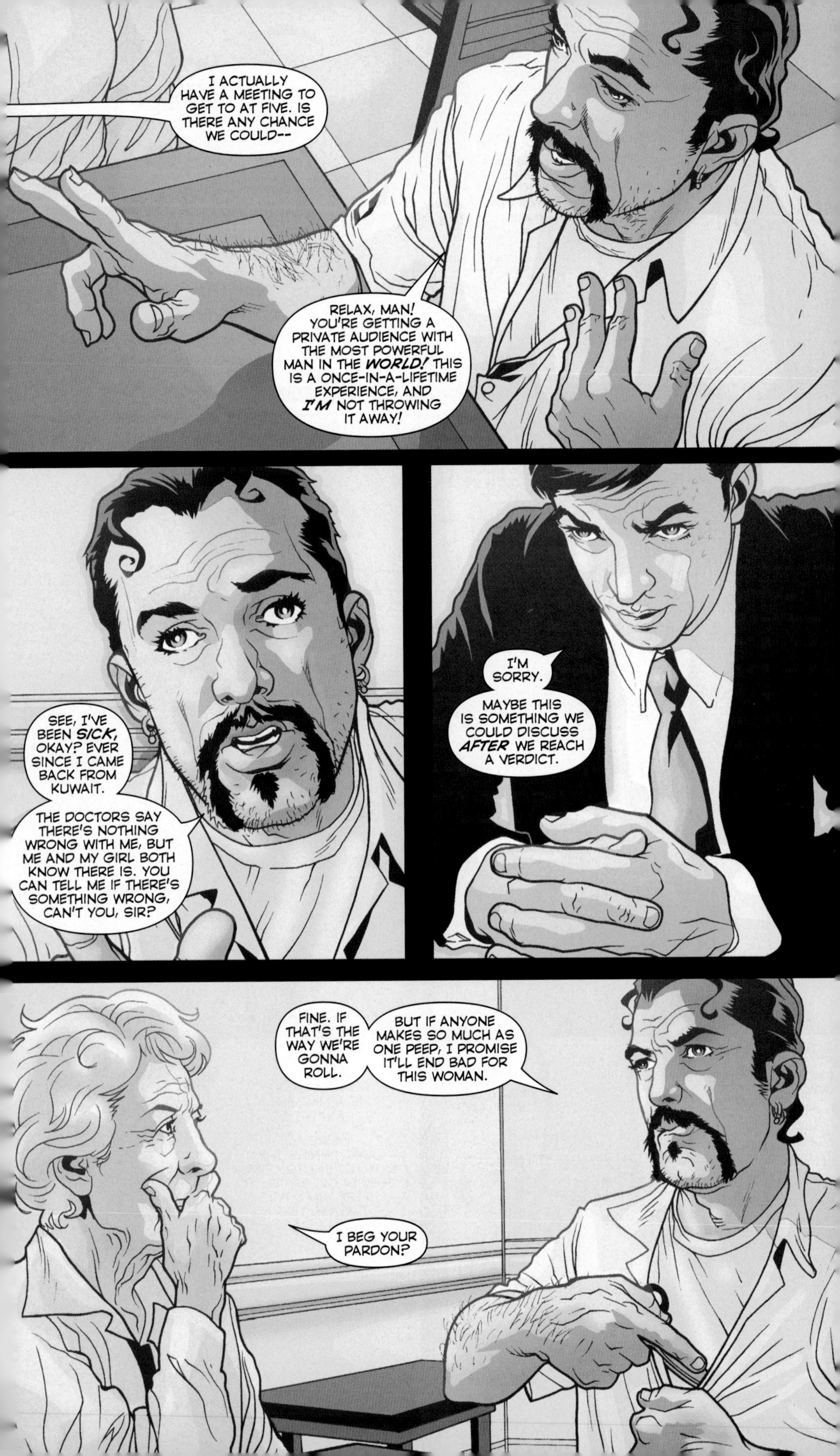
I ACTUALLY HAVE A MEETING TO GET TO AT FIVE. IS THERE ANY CHANCE WE COULD--
RELAX, MAN! YOU'RE GETTING A PRIVATE AUDIENCE WITH THE MOST POWERFUL MAN IN THE WORLD! THIS IS A ONCE-IN-A-LIFETIME EXPERIENCE, AND I'M NOT THROWING IT AWAY!
SEE, I'VE BEEN SICK, OKAY? EVER SINCE I CAME BACK FROM KUWAIT.
THE DOCTORS SAY THERE'S NOTHING WRONG WITH ME, BUT ME AND MY GIRL BOTH KNOW THERE IS. YOU CAN TELL ME IF THERE'S SOMETHING WRONG, CAN'T YOU, SIR?
I'M SORRY.
MAYBE THIS IS SOMETHING WE COULD DISCUSS AFTER WE REACH A VERDICT.
FINE. IF THAT'S THE WAY WE'RE GONNA ROLL.
BUT IF ANYONE MAKES SO MUCH AS ONE PEEP, I PROMISE IT'LL END BAD FOR THIS WOMAN.
I BEG YOUR PARDON?

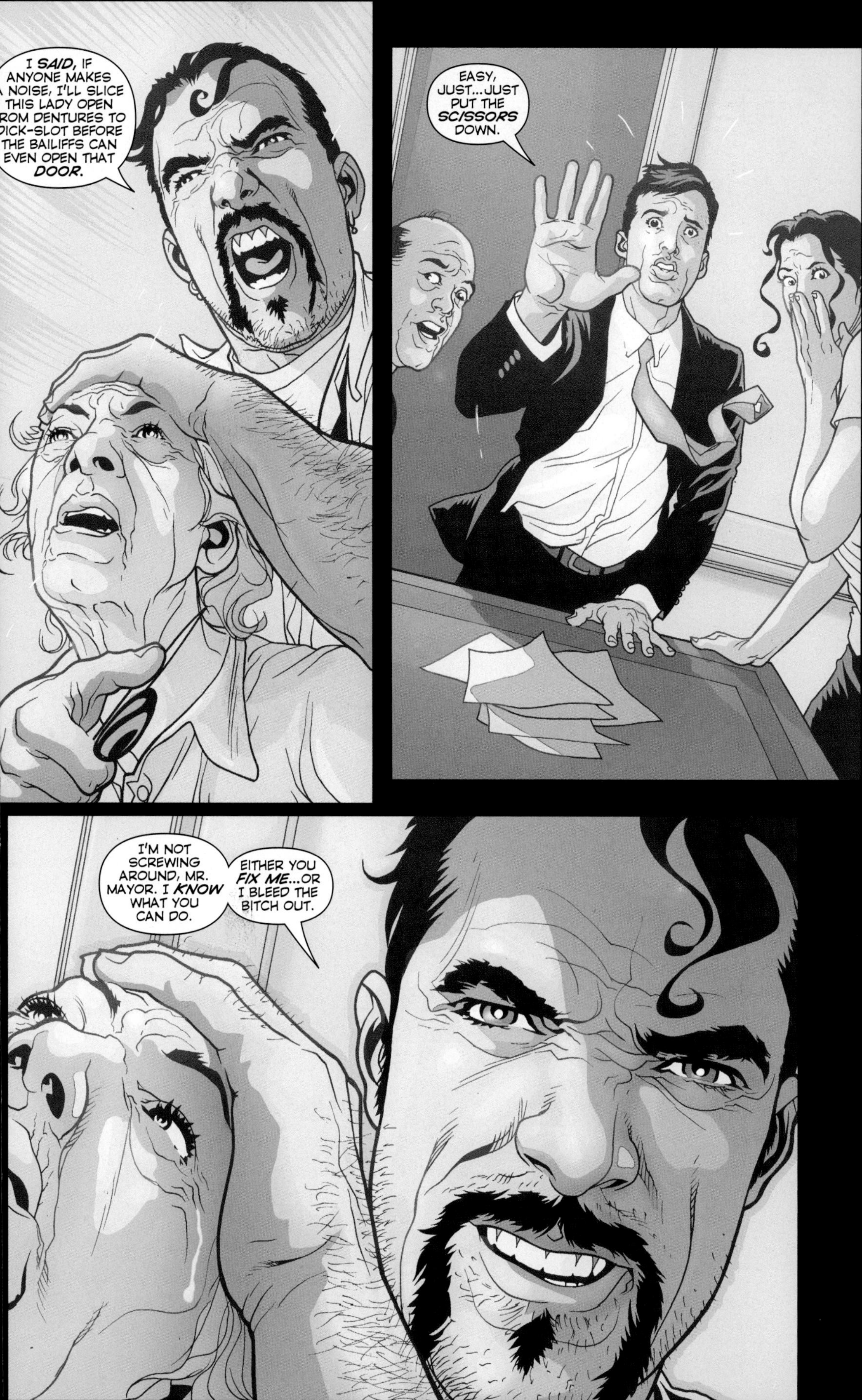
I SAID, IF ANYONE MAKES NOISE, I'LL SLICE THIS LADY OPEN ROM DENTURES TO DICK-SLOT BEFORE THE BAILIFFS CAN EVEN OPEN THAT DOOR.
EASY, JUST...JUST PUT THE SCISSORS DOWN.
I'M NOT SCREWING AROUND, MR. MAYOR. I KNOW WHAT YOU CAN DO.
EITHER YOU FIX ME...OR I BLEED THE BITCH OUT.

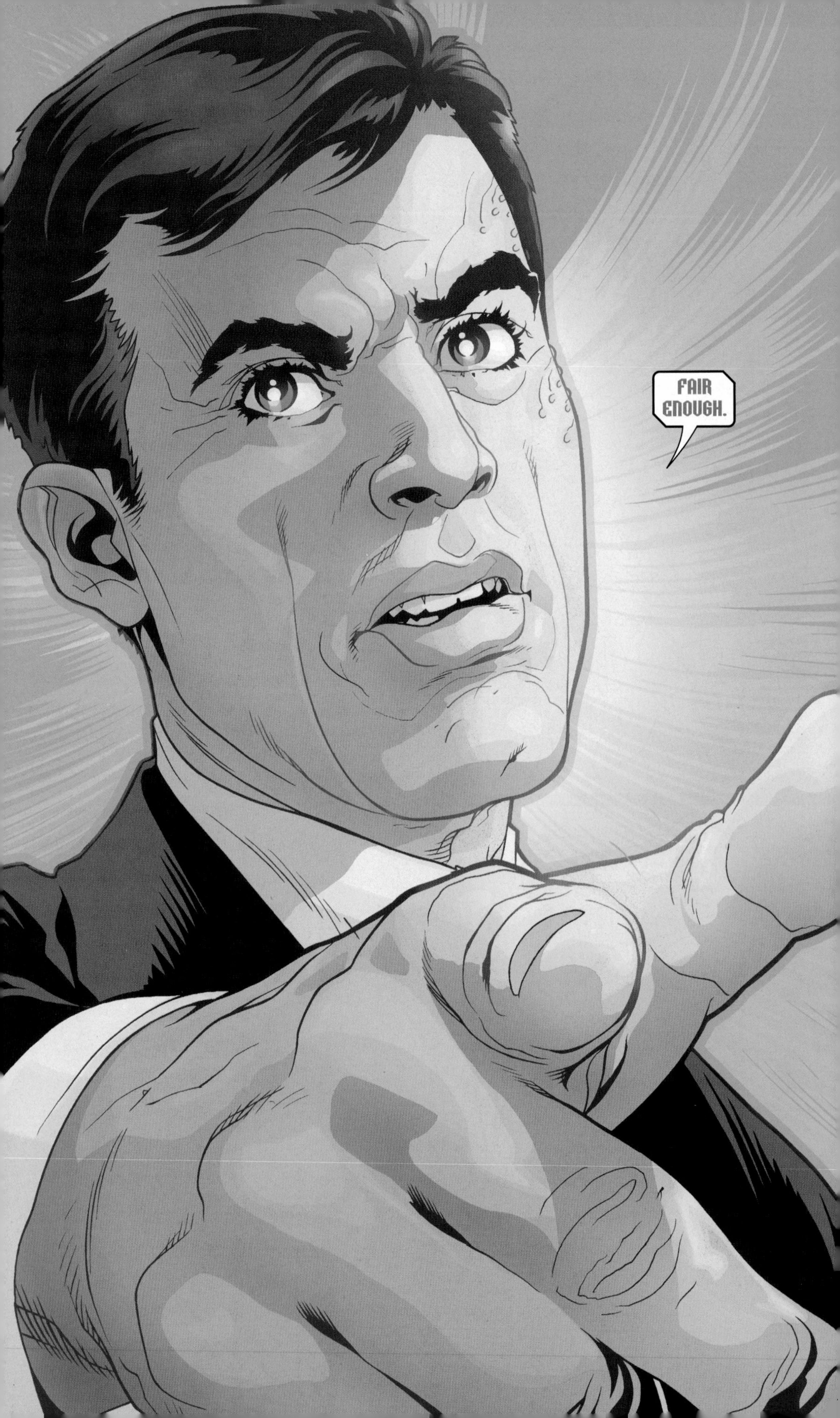
FAIR ENOUGH.

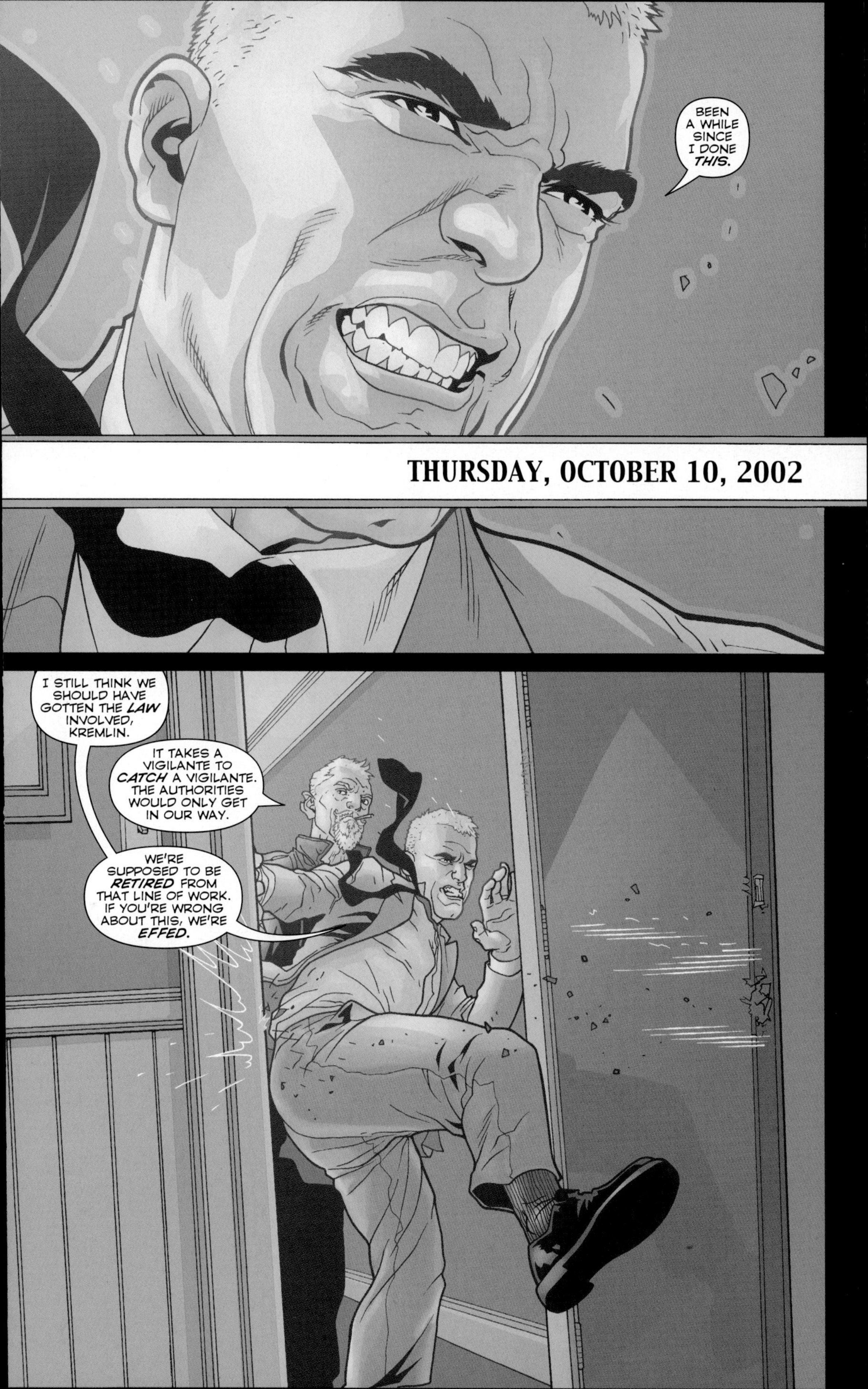
BEEN A WHILE SINCE I DONE *THIS*.
THURSDAY, OCTOBER 10, 2002
I STILL THINK WE SHOULD HAVE GOTTEN THE *LAW* INVOLVED, KREMLIN.
IT TAKES A VIGILANTE TO *CATCH* A VIGILANTE. THE AUTHORITIES WOULD ONLY GET IN OUR WAY.
WE'RE SUPPOSED TO BE *RETIRED* FROM THAT LINE OF WORK. IF YOU'RE WRONG ABOUT THIS, WE'RE *EFFED*.

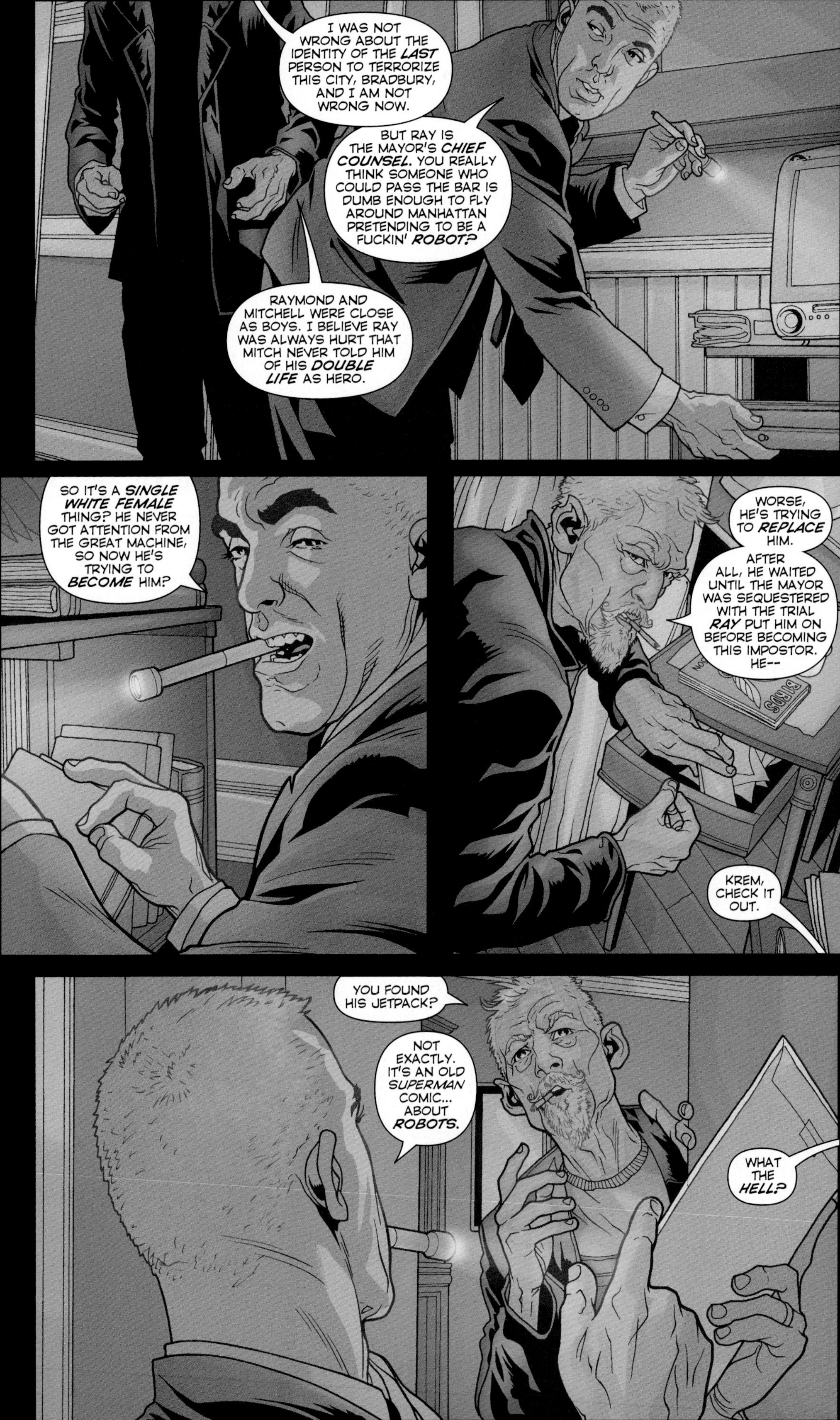
I WAS NOT WRONG ABOUT THE IDENTITY OF THE *LAST* PERSON TO TERRORIZE THIS CITY, BRADBURY, AND I AM NOT WRONG NOW.
BUT RAY IS THE MAYOR'S *CHIEF COUNSEL*. YOU REALLY THINK SOMEONE WHO COULD PASS THE BAR IS DUMB ENOUGH TO FLY AROUND MANHATTAN PRETENDING TO BE A FUCKIN' *ROBOT?*
RAYMOND AND MITCHELL WERE CLOSE AS BOYS. I BELIEVE RAY WAS ALWAYS HURT THAT MITCH NEVER TOLD HIM OF HIS *DOUBLE LIFE* AS HERO.
SO IT'S A *SINGLE WHITE FEMALE* THING? HE NEVER GOT ATTENTION FROM THE GREAT MACHINE, SO NOW HE'S TRYING TO *BECOME* HIM?
WORSE, HE'S TRYING TO *REPLACE* HIM.
AFTER ALL, HE WAITED UNTIL THE MAYOR WAS SEQUESTERED WITH THE TRIAL *RAY* PUT HIM ON BEFORE BECOMING THIS IMPOSTOR. HE--
KREM, CHECK IT OUT.
YOU FOUND HIS JETPACK?
NOT EXACTLY. IT'S AN OLD *SUPERMAN* COMIC... ABOUT *ROBOTS*.
WHAT THE *HELL?*

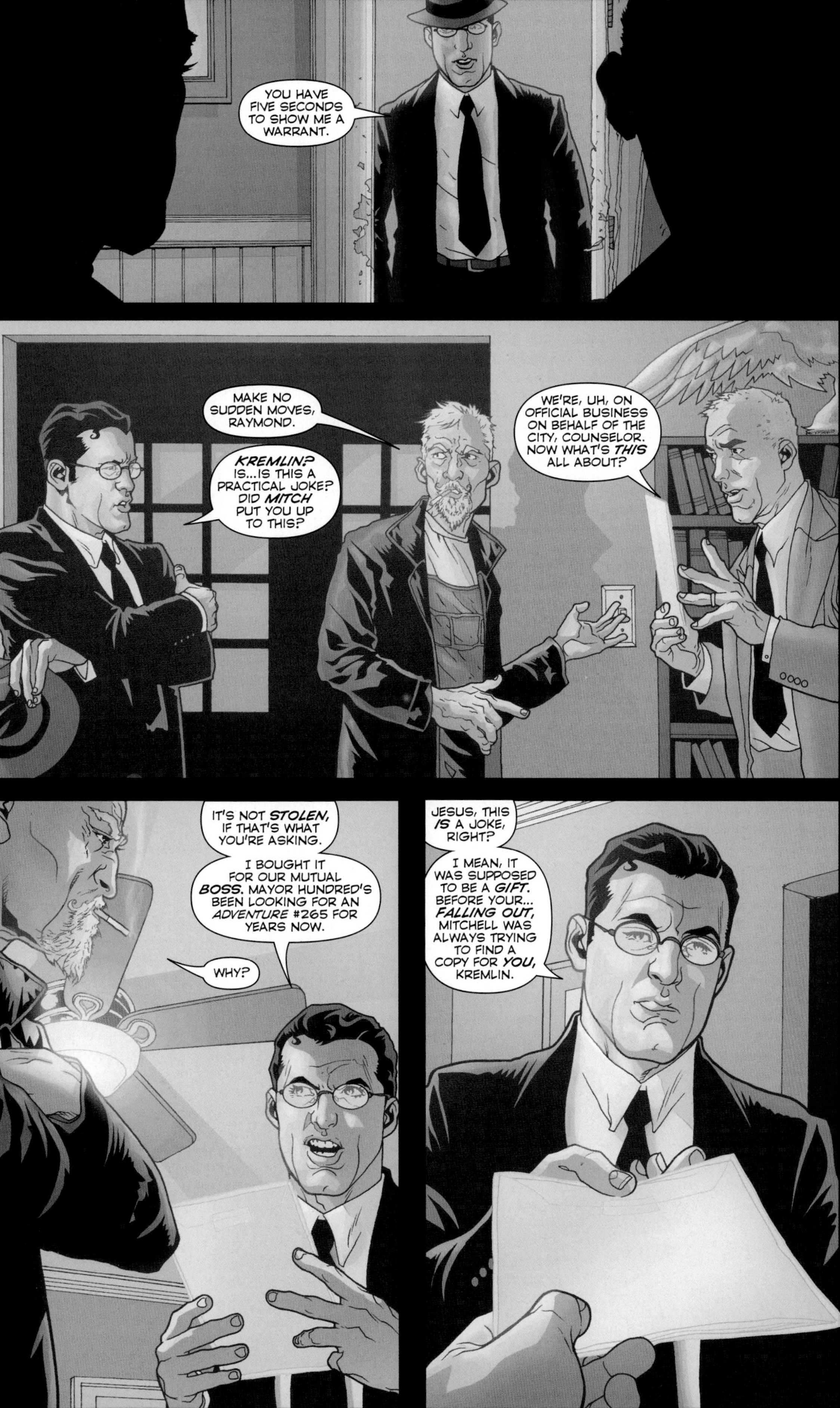
YOU HAVE FIVE SECONDS TO SHOW ME A WARRANT.
MAKE NO SUDDEN MOVES, RAYMOND.
KREMLIN? IS...IS THIS A PRACTICAL JOKE? DID MITCH PUT YOU UP TO THIS?
WE'RE, UH, ON OFFICIAL BUSINESS ON BEHALF OF THE CITY, COUNSELOR. NOW WHAT'S THIS ALL ABOUT?
IT'S NOT STOLEN, IF THAT'S WHAT YOU'RE ASKING.
I BOUGHT IT FOR OUR MUTUAL BOSS. MAYOR HUNDRED'S BEEN LOOKING FOR AN ADVENTURE #265 FOR YEARS NOW.
WHY?
JESUS, THIS IS A JOKE, RIGHT?
I MEAN, IT WAS SUPPOSED TO BE A GIFT. BEFORE YOUR... FALLING OUT, MITCHELL WAS ALWAYS TRYING TO FIND A COPY FOR YOU, KREMLIN.

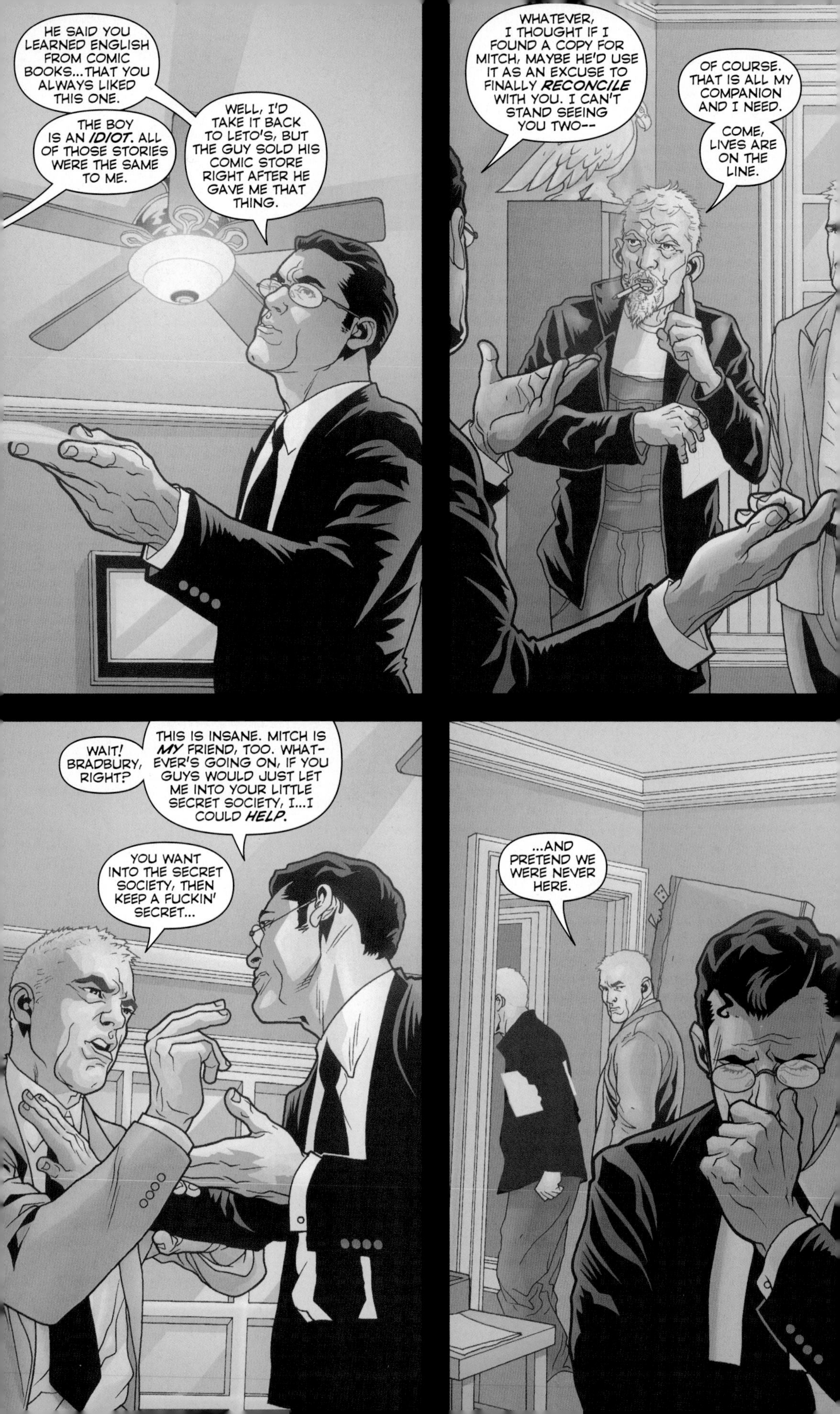

HE SAID YOU LEARNED ENGLISH FROM COMIC BOOKS...THAT YOU ALWAYS LIKED THIS ONE.
THE BOY IS AN *IDIOT*. ALL OF THOSE STORIES WERE THE SAME TO ME.
WELL, I'D TAKE IT BACK TO LETO'S, BUT THE GUY SOLD HIS COMIC STORE RIGHT AFTER HE GAVE ME THAT THING.
WHATEVER, I THOUGHT IF I FOUND A COPY FOR MITCH, MAYBE HE'D USE IT AS AN EXCUSE TO FINALLY *RECONCILE* WITH YOU. I CAN'T STAND SEEING YOU TWO--
OF COURSE. THAT IS ALL MY COMPANION AND I NEED.
COME, LIVES ARE ON THE LINE.
WAIT! BRADBURY, RIGHT?
THIS IS INSANE. MITCH IS *MY* FRIEND, TOO. WHATEVER'S GOING ON, IF YOU GUYS WOULD JUST LET ME INTO YOUR LITTLE SECRET SOCIETY, I...I COULD *HELP*.
YOU WANT INTO THE SECRET SOCIETY, THEN KEEP A FUCKIN' SECRET...
...AND PRETEND WE WERE NEVER HERE.

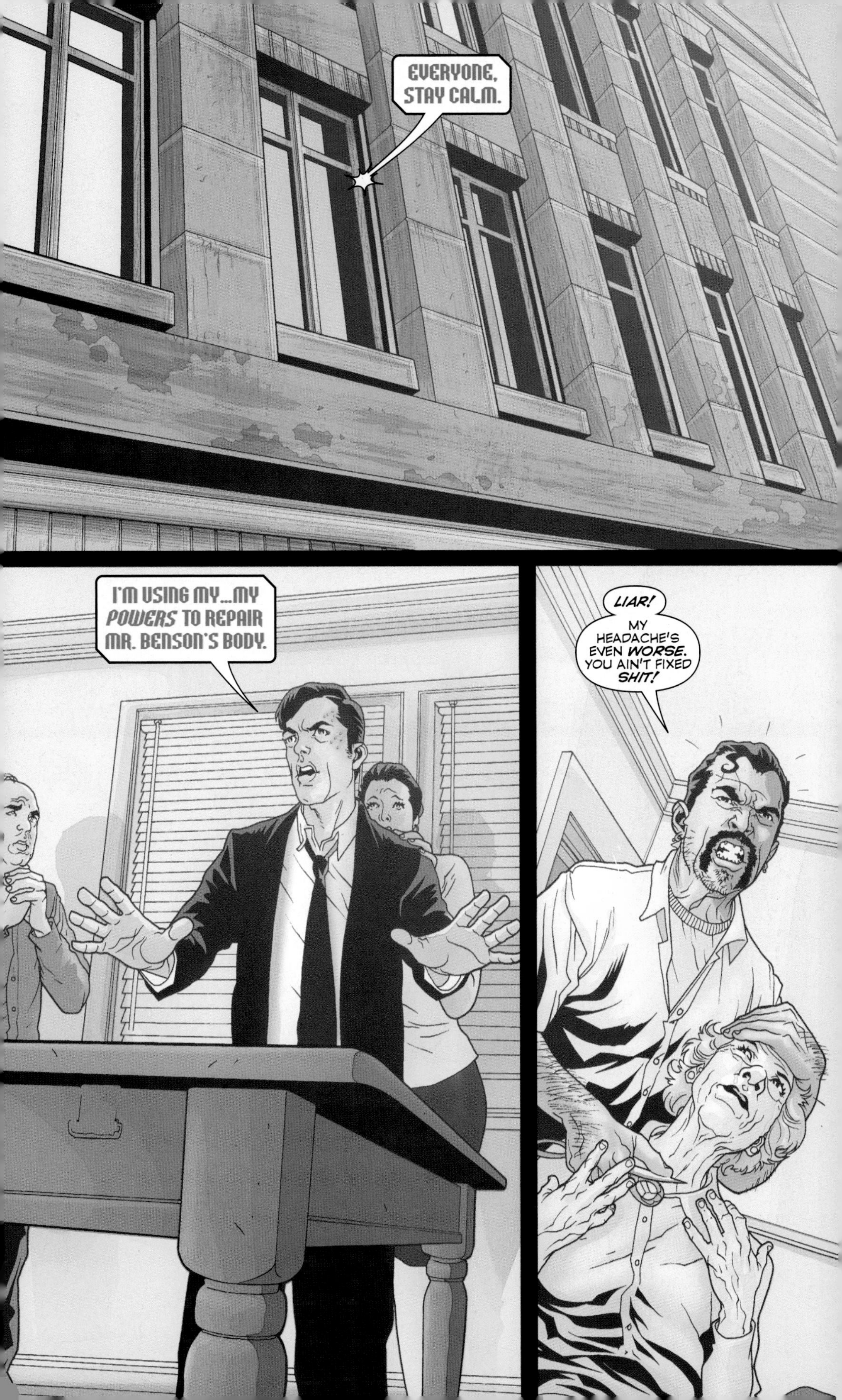
EVERYONE, STAY CALM.
I'M USING MY...MY POWERS TO REPAIR MR. BENSON'S BODY.
LIAR!
MY HEADACHE'S EVEN WORSE. YOU AIN'T FIXED SHIT!

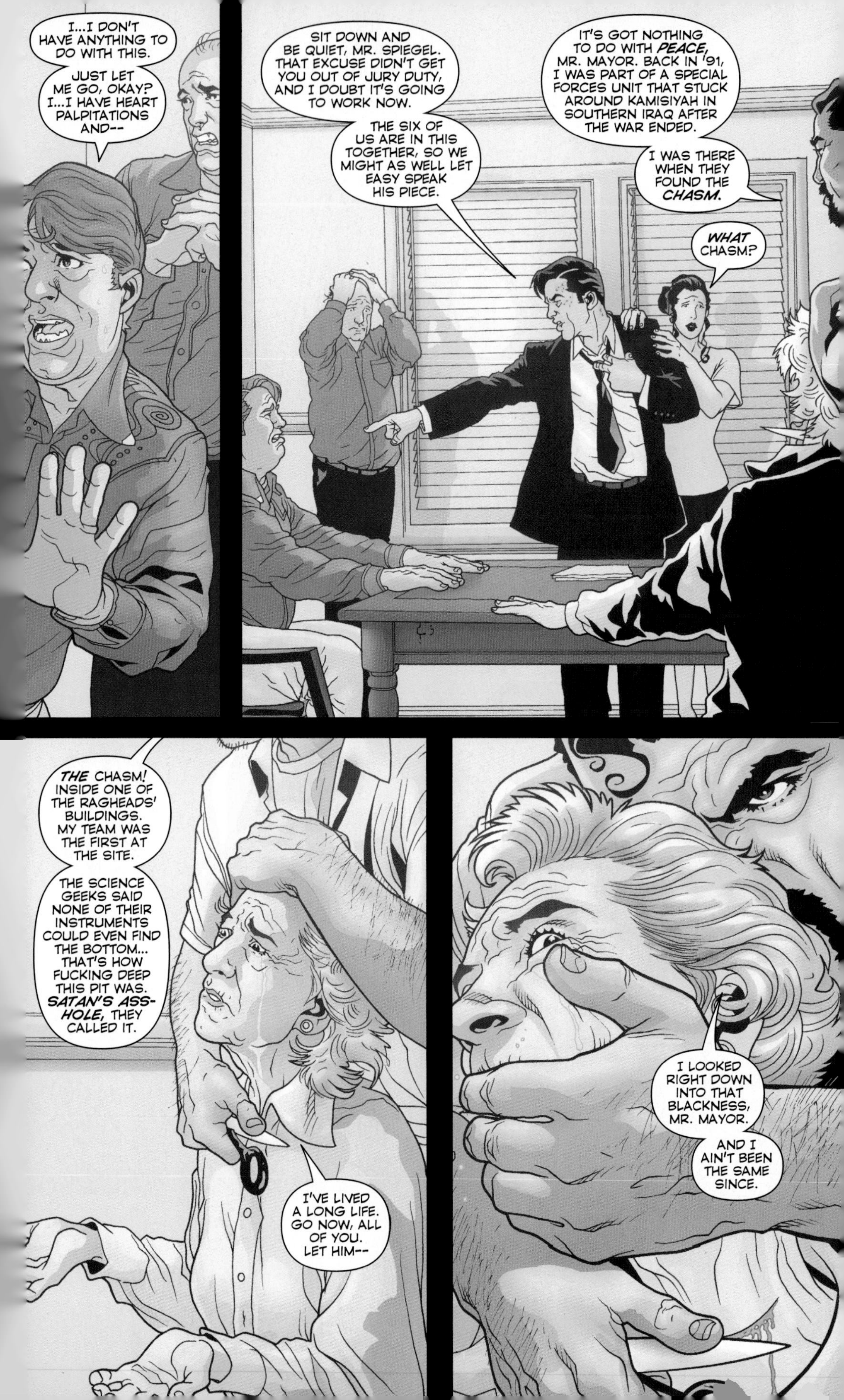
I...I DON'T HAVE ANYTHING TO DO WITH THIS.
JUST LET ME GO, OKAY? I...I HAVE HEART PALPITATIONS AND--
SIT DOWN AND BE QUIET, MR. SPIEGEL. THAT EXCUSE DIDN'T GET YOU OUT OF JURY DUTY, AND I DOUBT IT'S GOING TO WORK NOW.
THE SIX OF US ARE IN THIS TOGETHER, SO WE MIGHT AS WELL LET EASY SPEAK HIS PIECE.
IT'S GOT NOTHING TO DO WITH PEACE, MR. MAYOR. BACK IN '91, I WAS PART OF A SPECIAL FORCES UNIT THAT STUCK AROUND KAMISIYAH IN SOUTHERN IRAQ AFTER THE WAR ENDED.
I WAS THERE WHEN THEY FOUND THE CHASM.
WHAT CHASM?
THE CHASM! INSIDE ONE OF THE RAGHEADS' BUILDINGS. MY TEAM WAS THE FIRST AT THE SITE.
THE SCIENCE GEEKS SAID NONE OF THEIR INSTRUMENTS COULD EVEN FIND THE BOTTOM... THAT'S HOW FUCKING DEEP THIS PIT WAS. SATAN'S ASS-HOLE, THEY CALLED IT.
I'VE LIVED A LONG LIFE. GO NOW, ALL OF YOU. LET HIM--
I LOOKED RIGHT DOWN INTO THAT BLACKNESS, MR. MAYOR.
AND I AIN'T BEEN THE SAME SINCE.

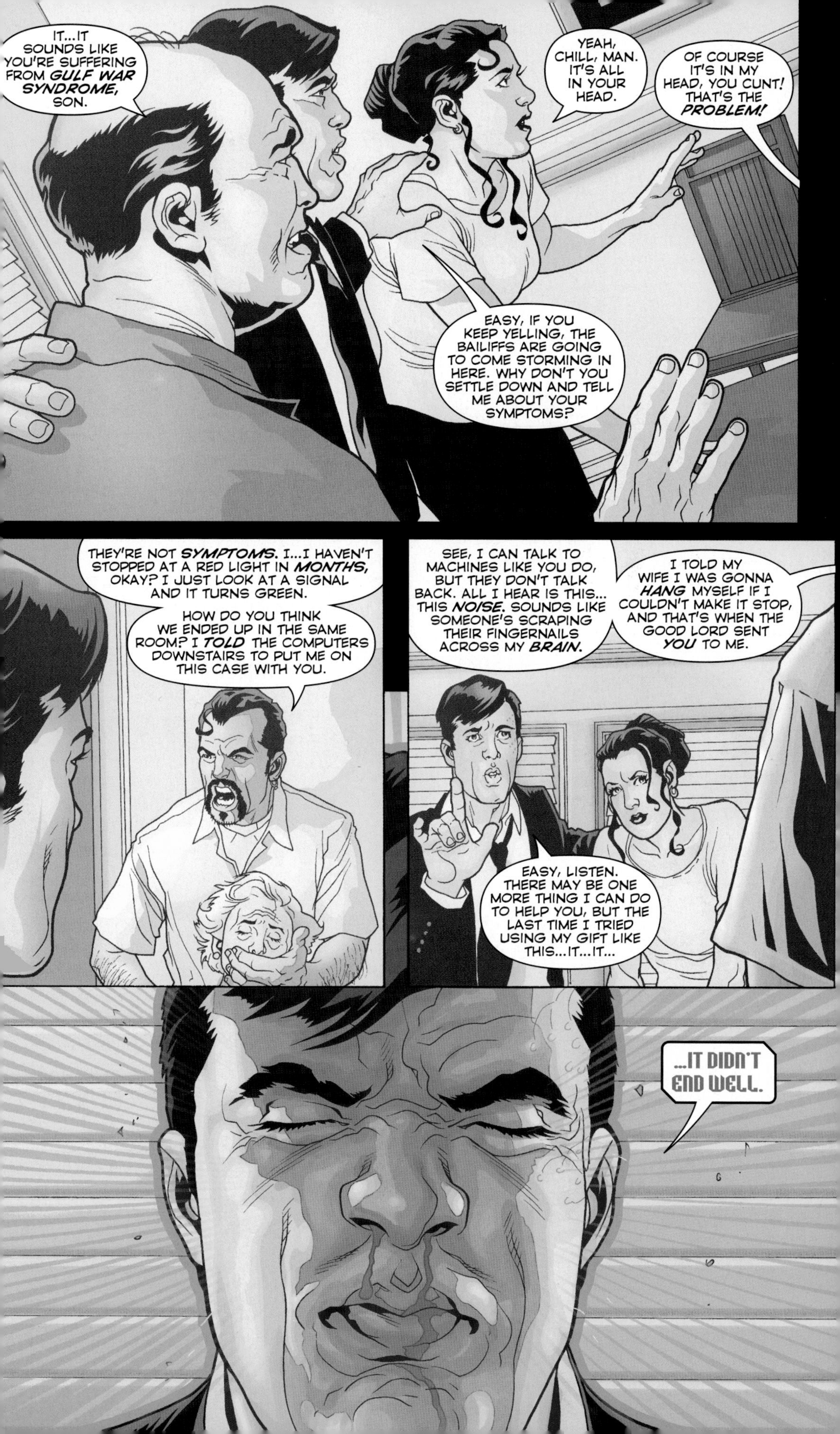
IT...IT SOUNDS LIKE YOU'RE SUFFERING FROM GULF WAR SYNDROME, SON.
YEAH, CHILL, MAN. IT'S ALL IN YOUR HEAD.
OF COURSE IT'S IN MY HEAD, YOU CUNT! THAT'S THE PROBLEM!
EASY, IF YOU KEEP YELLING, THE BAILIFFS ARE GOING TO COME STORMING IN HERE. WHY DON'T YOU SETTLE DOWN AND TELL ME ABOUT YOUR SYMPTOMS?
THEY'RE NOT SYMPTOMS. I...I HAVEN'T STOPPED AT A RED LIGHT IN MONTHS, OKAY? I JUST LOOK AT A SIGNAL AND IT TURNS GREEN.
HOW DO YOU THINK WE ENDED UP IN THE SAME ROOM? I TOLD THE COMPUTERS DOWNSTAIRS TO PUT ME ON THIS CASE WITH YOU.
SEE, I CAN TALK TO MACHINES LIKE YOU DO, BUT THEY DON'T TALK BACK. ALL I HEAR IS THIS... THIS NOISE. SOUNDS LIKE SOMEONE'S SCRAPING THEIR FINGERNAILS ACROSS MY BRAIN.
I TOLD MY WIFE I WAS GONNA HANG MYSELF IF I COULDN'T MAKE IT STOP, AND THAT'S WHEN THE GOOD LORD SENT YOU TO ME.
EASY, LISTEN. THERE MAY BE ONE MORE THING I CAN DO TO HELP YOU, BUT THE LAST TIME I TRIED USING MY GIFT LIKE THIS...IT...IT...
...IT DIDN'T END WELL.

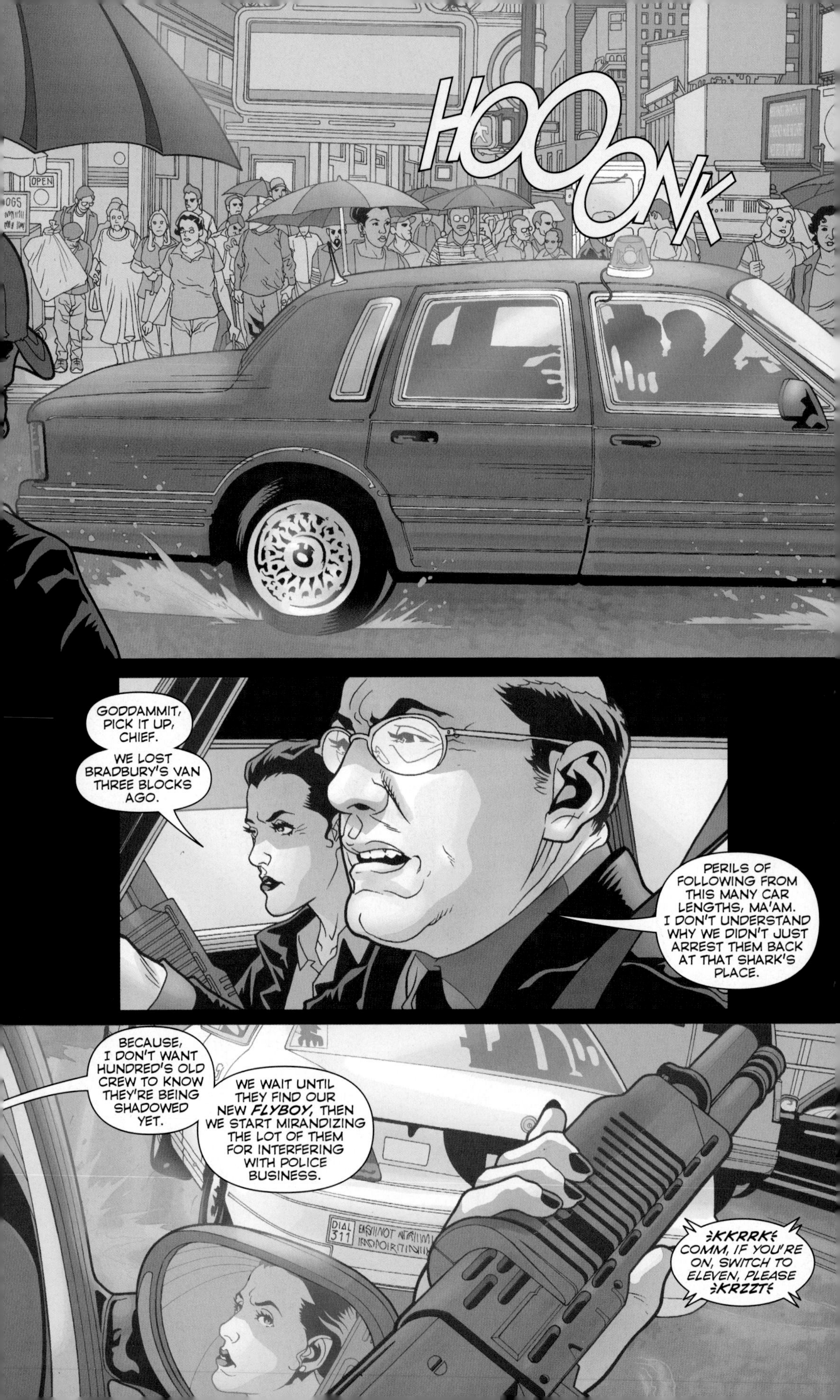

HOOOONK..
OPEN
DIAL 311
GODDAMMIT, PICK IT UP, CHIEF.
WE LOST BRADBURY'S VAN THREE BLOCKS AGO.
PERILS OF FOLLOWING FROM THIS MANY CAR LENGTHS, MA'AM. I DON'T UNDERSTAND WHY WE DIDN'T JUST ARREST THEM BACK AT THAT SHARK'S PLACE.
BECAUSE, I DON'T WANT HUNDRED'S OLD CREW TO KNOW THEY'RE BEING SHADOWED YET.
WE WAIT UNTIL THEY FIND OUR NEW *FLYBOY*, THEN WE START MIRANDIZING THE LOT OF THEM FOR INTERFERING WITH POLICE BUSINESS.
*KKRRK* COMM, IF YOU'RE ON, SWITCH TO ELEVEN, PLEASE *KRZZT*

THIS IS ANGOTTI.

COMMISSIONER, IT'S HOLLIDAY WITH MIDTOWN NORTH. IS THE MAYOR STILL AT THE COURTHOUSE?

I GUESS, BUT I'M NOT HIS FUCKING PERSONAL ASSISTANT. WHY, WHAT'S UP?

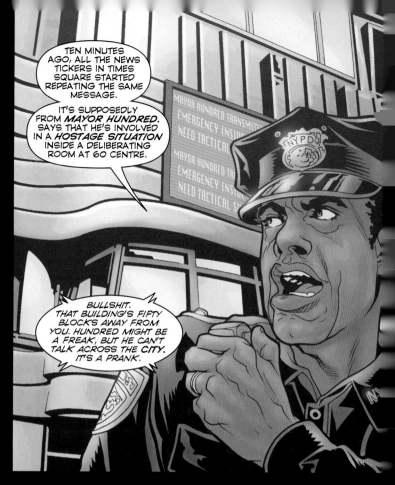

TEN MINUTES AGO, ALL THE NEWS TICKERS IN TIMES SQUARE STARTED REPEATING THE SAME MESSAGE.

IT'S SUPPOSEDLY FROM *MAYOR HUNDRED.* SAYS THAT HE'S INVOLVED IN A *HOSTAGE SITUATION* INSIDE A DELIBERATING ROOM AT 60 CENTRE.

BULLSHIT. THAT BUILDING'S FIFTY BLOCK'S AWAY FROM YOU. HUNDRED MIGHT BE A FREAK, BUT HE CAN'T TALK ACROSS THE CITY. IT'S A PRANK.

I DON'T KNOW, MA'AM. THE TECH WONKS AT ALL THE NEWS DESK'S SAY THOSE SIGNS ARE A CLOSED SYSTEM, SO THEY CAN'T HAVE BEEN *HACKED.*

AND I TRIED CALLING THE MAYOR'S HEAD OF SECURITY, BUT HE'S NOT ANSWERING HIS CELL.

CHRIST. ALL RIGHT, TURN THIS BOAT AROUND, KURSON. WHATEVER HUNDRED'S GOONS ARE UP TO...

...THEY'RE ON THEIR OWN NOW.

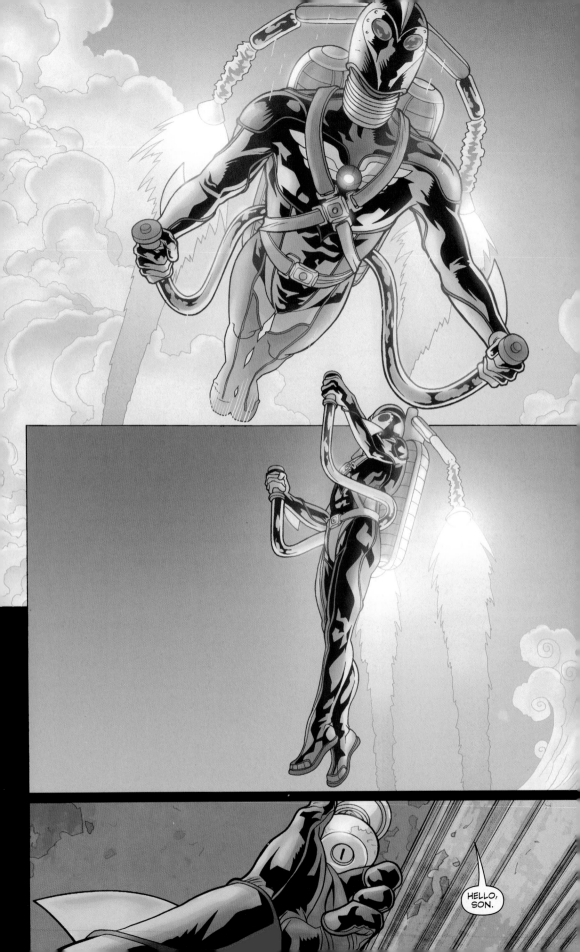

HELLO, SON.

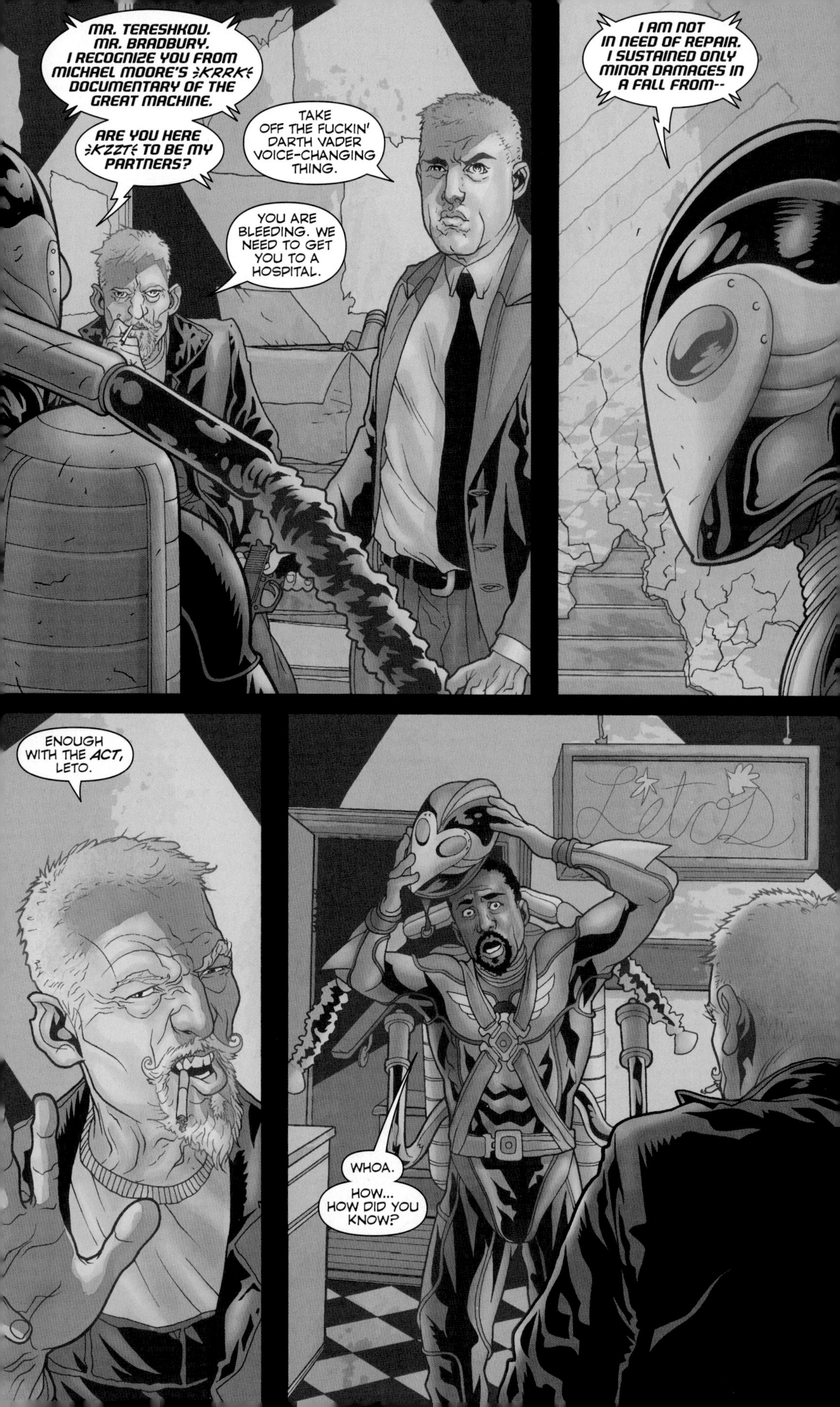
MR. TERESHKOV. MR. BRADBURY. I RECOGNIZE YOU FROM MICHAEL MOORE'S KRRK DOCUMENTARY OF THE GREAT MACHINE.
ARE YOU HERE KZZT TO BE MY PARTNERS?
TAKE OFF THE FUCKIN' DARTH VADER VOICE-CHANGING THING.
YOU ARE BLEEDING. WE NEED TO GET YOU TO A HOSPITAL.
I AM NOT IN NEED OF REPAIR. I SUSTAINED ONLY MINOR DAMAGES IN A FALL FROM--
ENOUGH WITH THE *ACT*, LETO.
WHOA.
HOW... HOW DID YOU KNOW?

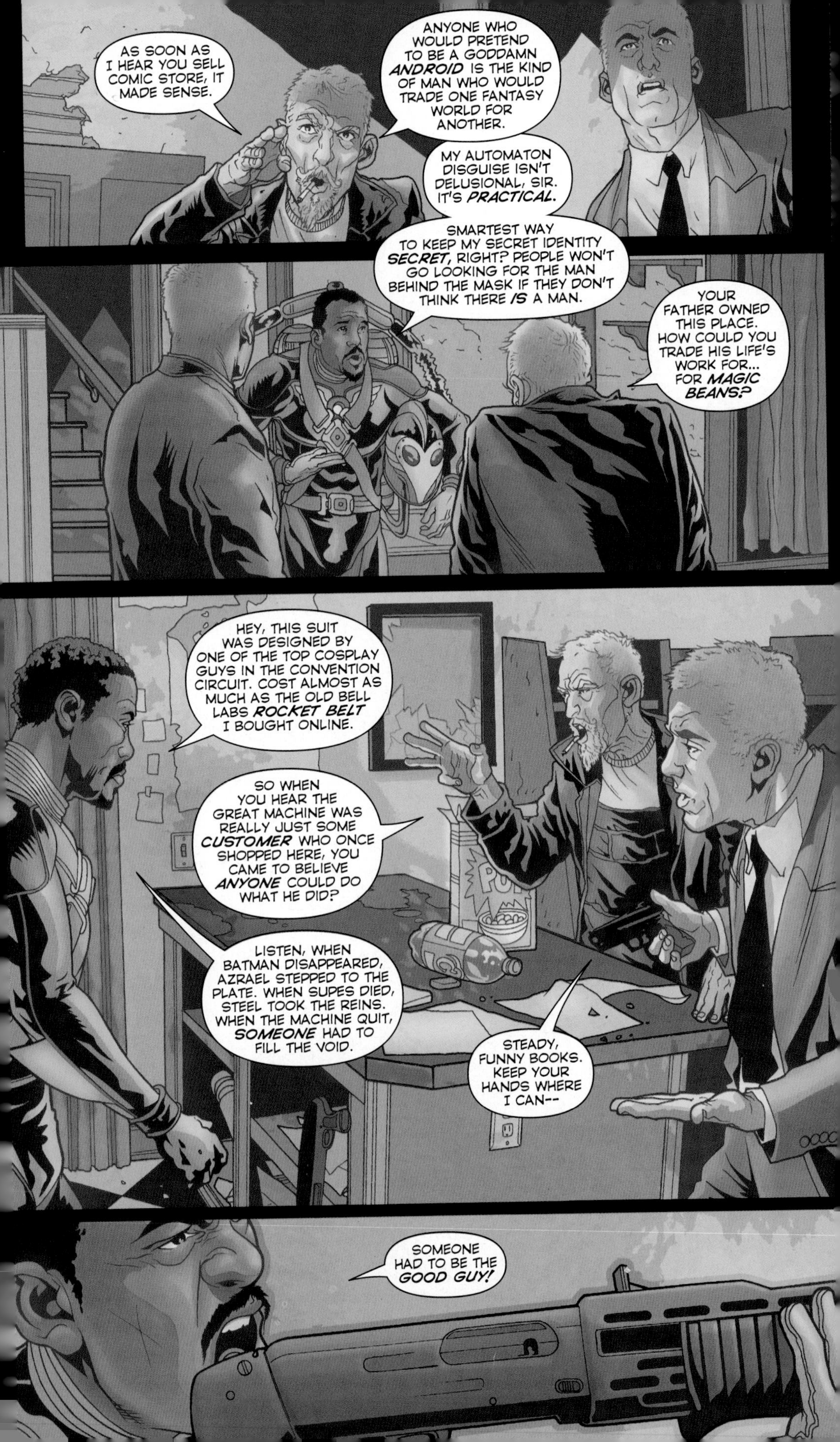
AS SOON AS I HEAR YOU SELL COMIC STORE, IT MADE SENSE.
ANYONE WHO WOULD PRETEND TO BE A GODDAMN ANDROID IS THE KIND OF MAN WHO WOULD TRADE ONE FANTASY WORLD FOR ANOTHER.
MY AUTOMATON DISGUISE ISN'T DELUSIONAL, SIR. IT'S PRACTICAL.
SMARTEST WAY TO KEEP MY SECRET IDENTITY SECRET, RIGHT? PEOPLE WON'T GO LOOKING FOR THE MAN BEHIND THE MASK IF THEY DON'T THINK THERE IS A MAN.
YOUR FATHER OWNED THIS PLACE. HOW COULD YOU TRADE HIS LIFE'S WORK FOR... FOR MAGIC BEANS?
HEY, THIS SUIT WAS DESIGNED BY ONE OF THE TOP COSPLAY GUYS IN THE CONVENTION CIRCUIT. COST ALMOST AS MUCH AS THE OLD BELL LABS ROCKET BELT I BOUGHT ONLINE.
SO WHEN YOU HEAR THE GREAT MACHINE WAS REALLY JUST SOME CUSTOMER WHO ONCE SHOPPED HERE, YOU CAME TO BELIEVE ANYONE COULD DO WHAT HE DID?
LISTEN, WHEN BATMAN DISAPPEARED, AZRAEL STEPPED TO THE PLATE. WHEN SUPES DIED, STEEL TOOK THE REINS. WHEN THE MACHINE QUIT, SOMEONE HAD TO FILL THE VOID.
STEADY, FUNNY BOOKS. KEEP YOUR HANDS WHERE I CAN--
SOMEONE HAD TO BE THE GOOD GUY!

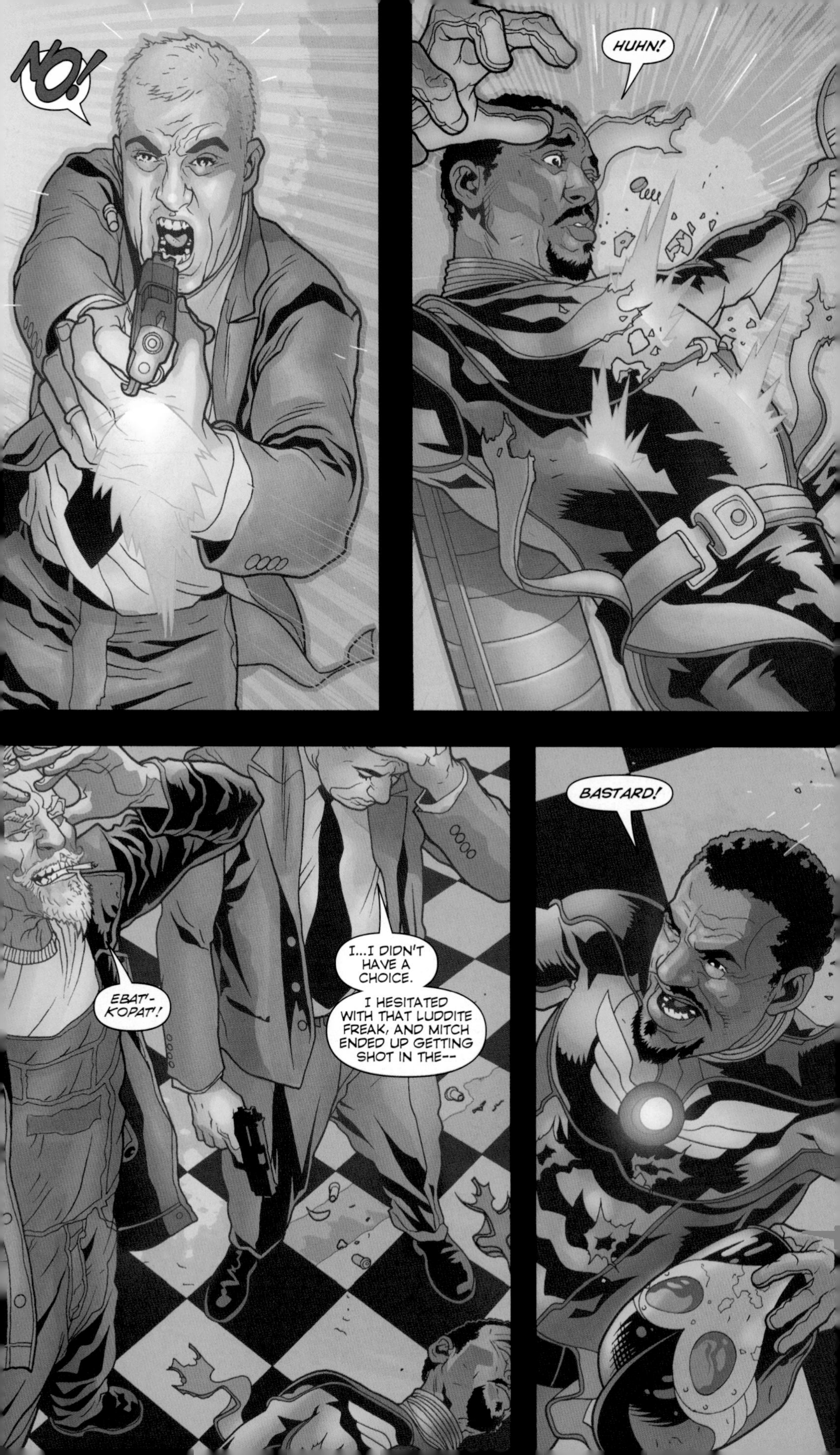
NO!
HUHN!
EBAT'-KOPAT'!
I...I DIDN'T HAVE A CHOICE.
I HESITATED WITH THAT LUDDITE FREAK, AND MITCH ENDED UP GETTING SHOT IN THE--
BASTARD!

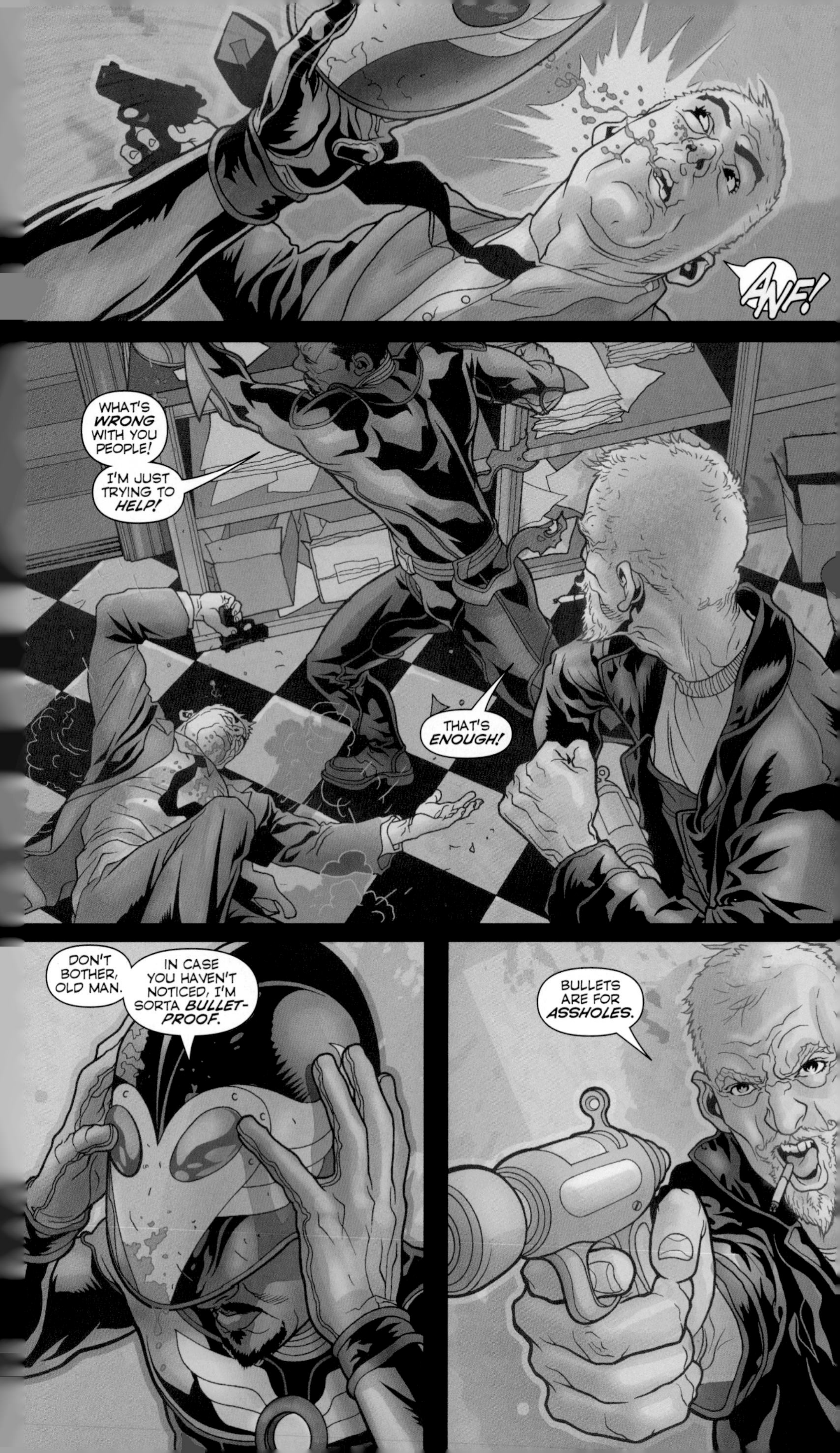
ANF!
WHAT'S WRONG WITH YOU PEOPLE!
I'M JUST TRYING TO HELP!
THAT'S ENOUGH!
DON'T BOTHER, OLD MAN.
IN CASE YOU HAVEN'T NOTICED, I'M SORTA BULLET-PROOF.
BULLETS ARE FOR ASSHOLES.

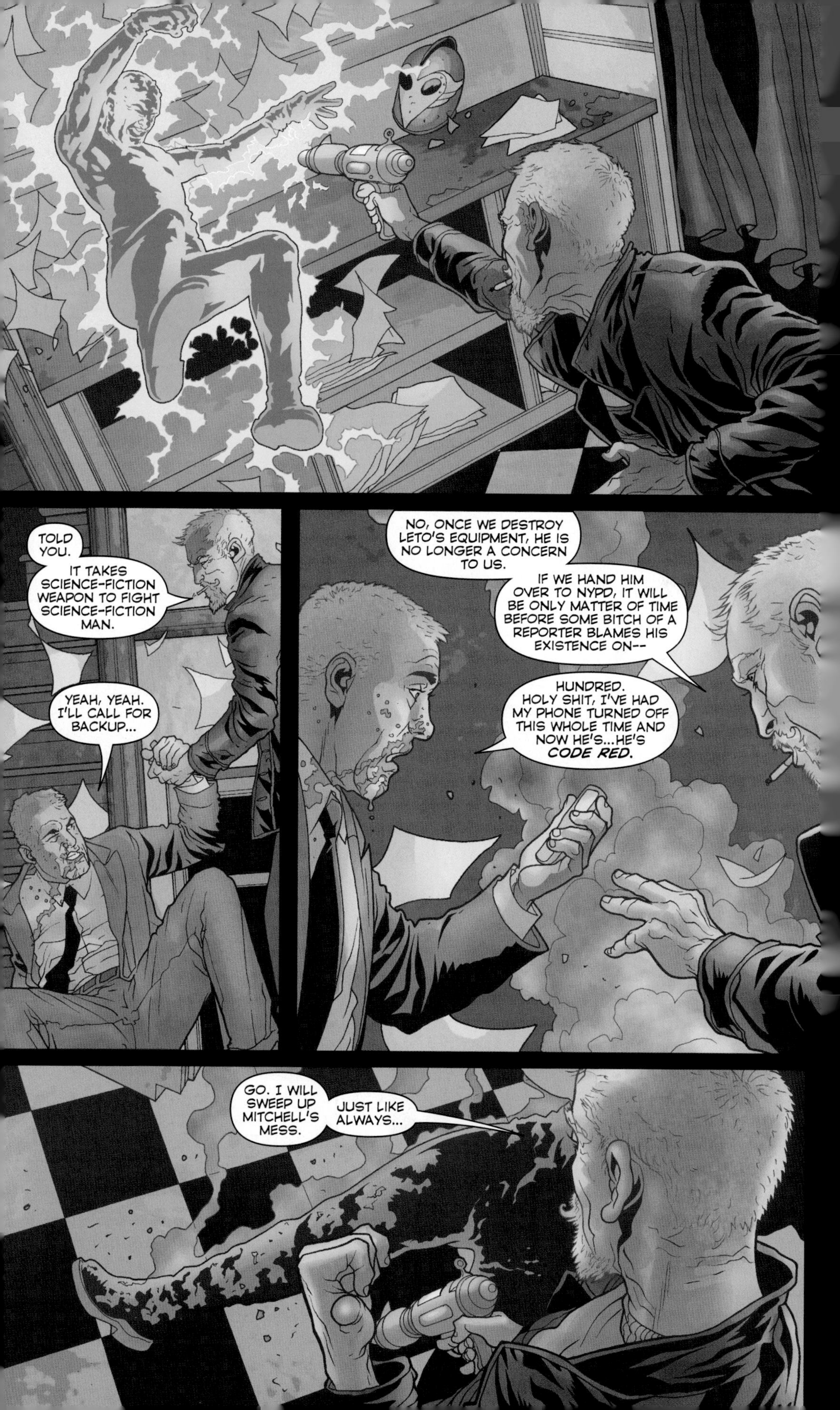
TOLD YOU.
IT TAKES SCIENCE-FICTION WEAPON TO FIGHT SCIENCE-FICTION MAN.
YEAH, YEAH. I'LL CALL FOR BACKUP...
NO, ONCE WE DESTROY LETO'S EQUIPMENT, HE IS NO LONGER A CONCERN TO US.
IF WE HAND HIM OVER TO NYPD, IT WILL BE ONLY MATTER OF TIME BEFORE SOME BITCH OF A REPORTER BLAMES HIS EXISTENCE ON--
HUNDRED. HOLY SHIT, I'VE HAD MY PHONE TURNED OFF THIS WHOLE TIME AND NOW HE'S...HE'S ***CODE RED.***
GO. I WILL SWEEP UP MITCHELL'S MESS.
JUST LIKE ALWAYS...

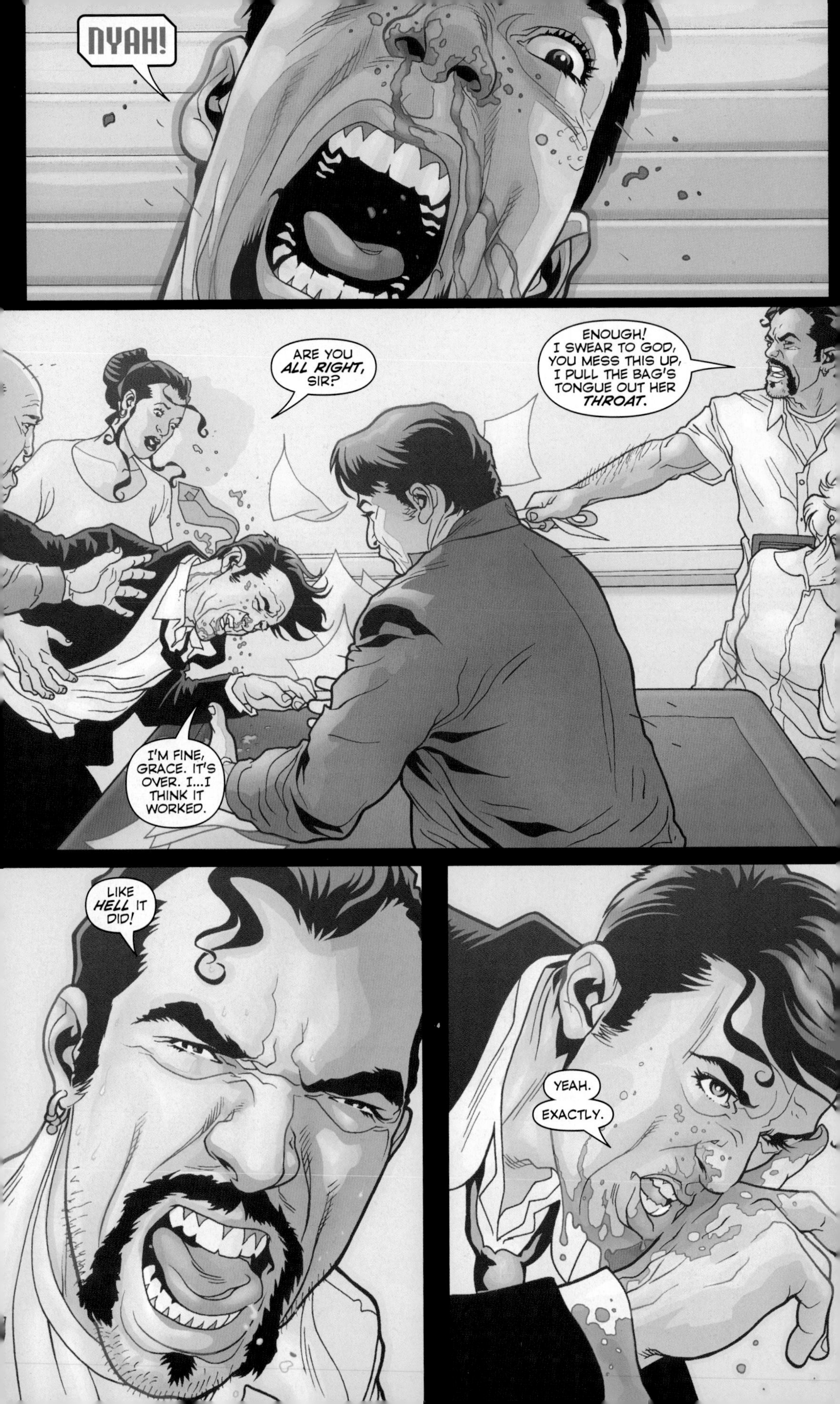
NYAH!
ARE YOU ALL RIGHT, SIR?
ENOUGH! I SWEAR TO GOD, YOU MESS THIS UP, I PULL THE BAG'S TONGUE OUT HER THROAT.
I'M FINE, GRACE. IT'S OVER. I...I THINK IT WORKED.
LIKE HELL IT DID!
YEAH.
EXACTLY.

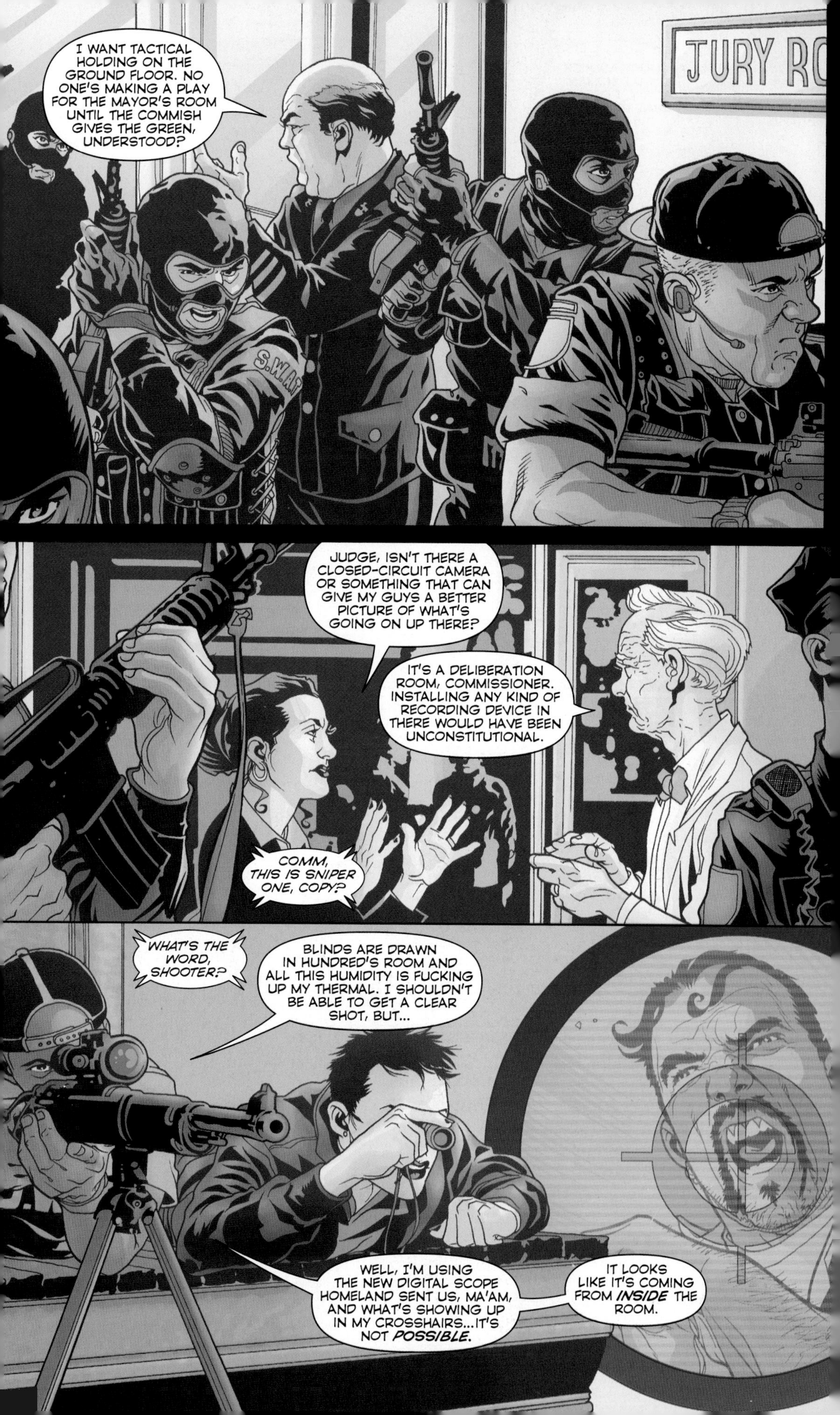
I WANT TACTICAL HOLDING ON THE GROUND FLOOR. NO ONE'S MAKING A PLAY FOR THE MAYOR'S ROOM UNTIL THE COMMISH GIVES THE GREEN, UNDERSTOOD?
JURY RO
S.W.A.T.
JUDGE, ISN'T THERE A CLOSED-CIRCUIT CAMERA OR SOMETHING THAT CAN GIVE MY GUYS A BETTER PICTURE OF WHAT'S GOING ON UP THERE?
IT'S A DELIBERATION ROOM, COMMISSIONER. INSTALLING ANY KIND OF RECORDING DEVICE IN THERE WOULD HAVE BEEN UNCONSTITUTIONAL.
COMM, THIS IS SNIPER ONE, COPY?
WHAT'S THE WORD, SHOOTER?
BLINDS ARE DRAWN IN HUNDRED'S ROOM AND ALL THIS HUMIDITY IS FUCKING UP MY THERMAL. I SHOULDN'T BE ABLE TO GET A CLEAR SHOT, BUT...
WELL, I'M USING THE NEW DIGITAL SCOPE HOMELAND SENT US, MA'AM, AND WHAT'S SHOWING UP IN MY CROSSHAIRS...IT'S NOT *POSSIBLE*.
IT LOOKS LIKE IT'S COMING FROM *INSIDE* THE ROOM.

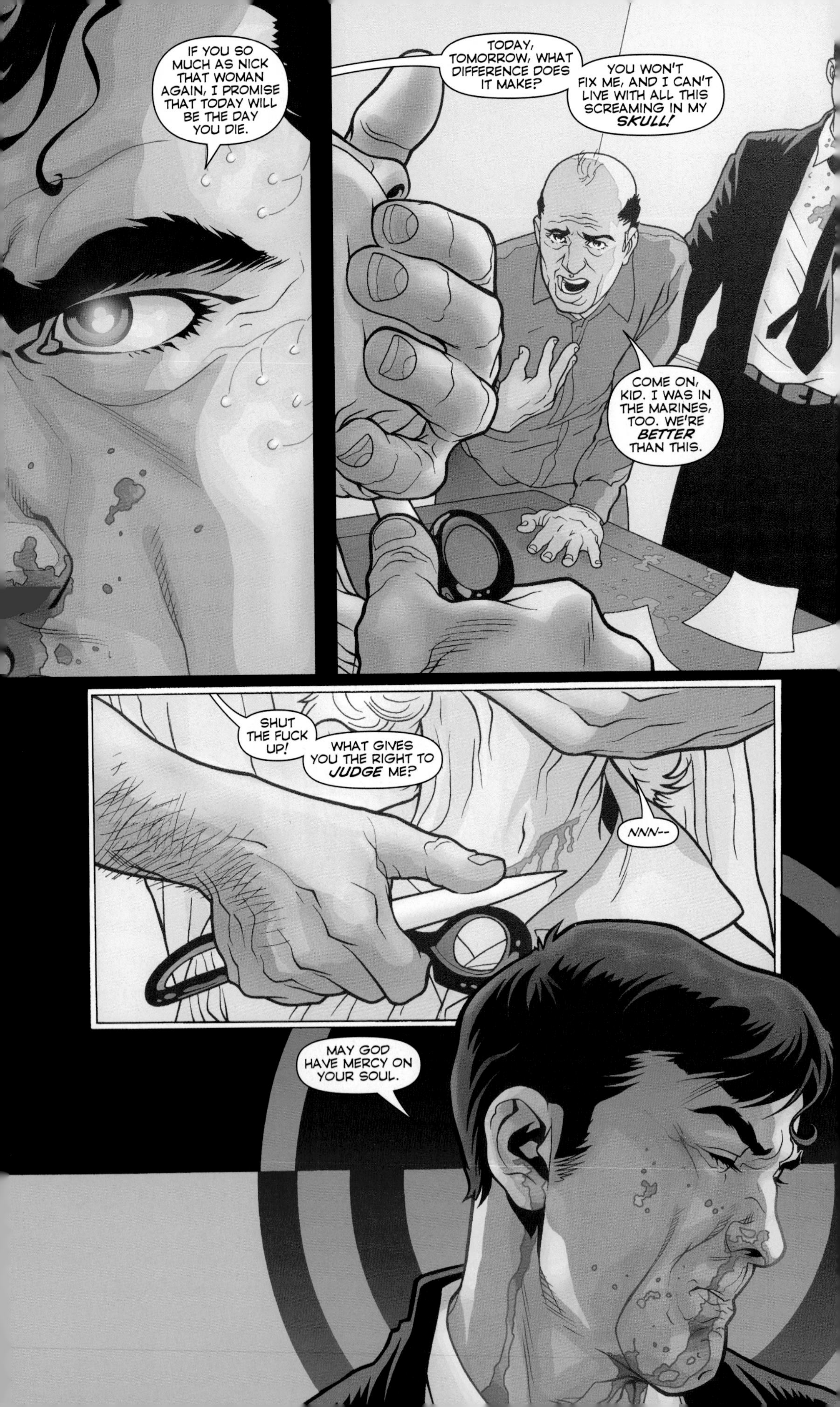
IF YOU SO MUCH AS NICK THAT WOMAN AGAIN, I PROMISE THAT TODAY WILL BE THE DAY YOU DIE.
TODAY, TOMORROW, WHAT DIFFERENCE DOES IT MAKE?
YOU WON'T FIX ME, AND I CAN'T LIVE WITH ALL THIS SCREAMING IN MY SKULL!
COME ON, KID. I WAS IN THE MARINES, TOO. WE'RE BETTER THAN THIS.
SHUT THE FUCK UP!
WHAT GIVES YOU THE RIGHT TO JUDGE ME?
NNN--
MAY GOD HAVE MERCY ON YOUR SOUL.

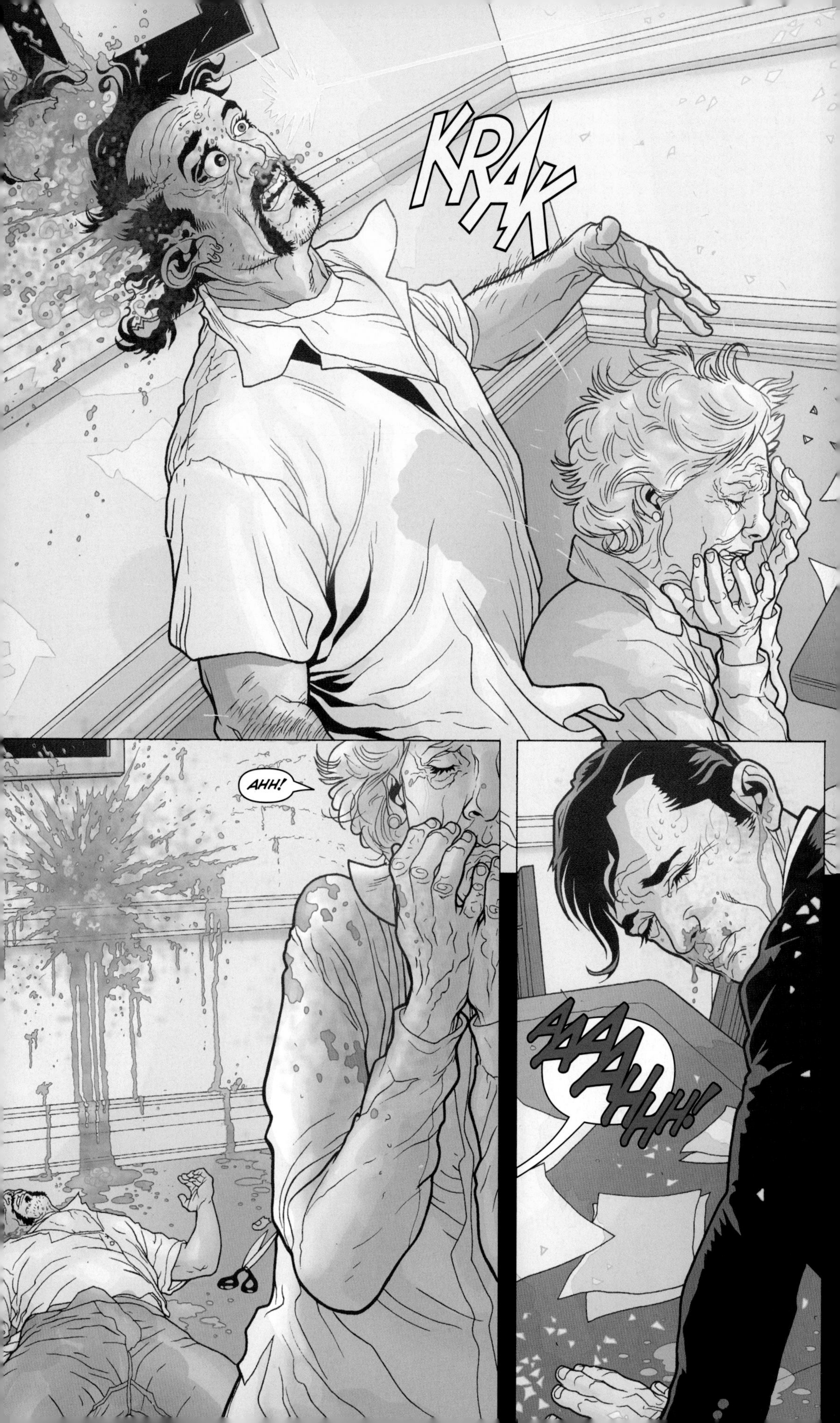
KRAK
AHH!
AAAAHHH!

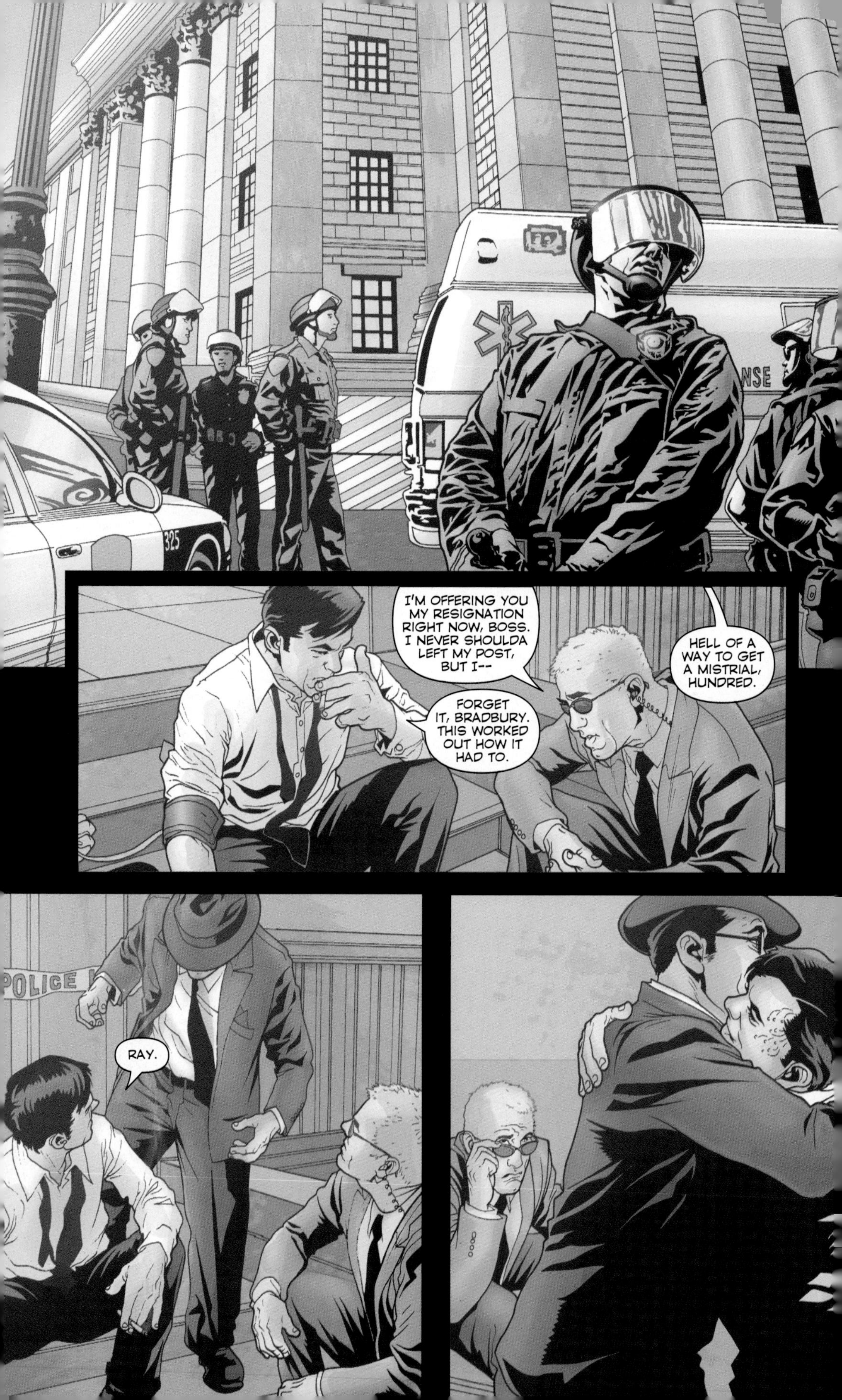
325
NSE
I'M OFFERING YOU MY RESIGNATION RIGHT NOW, BOSS. I NEVER SHOULDA LEFT MY POST, BUT I--
FORGET IT, BRADBURY. THIS WORKED OUT HOW IT HAD TO.
HELL OF A WAY TO GET A MISTRIAL, HUNDRED.
POLICE
RAY.

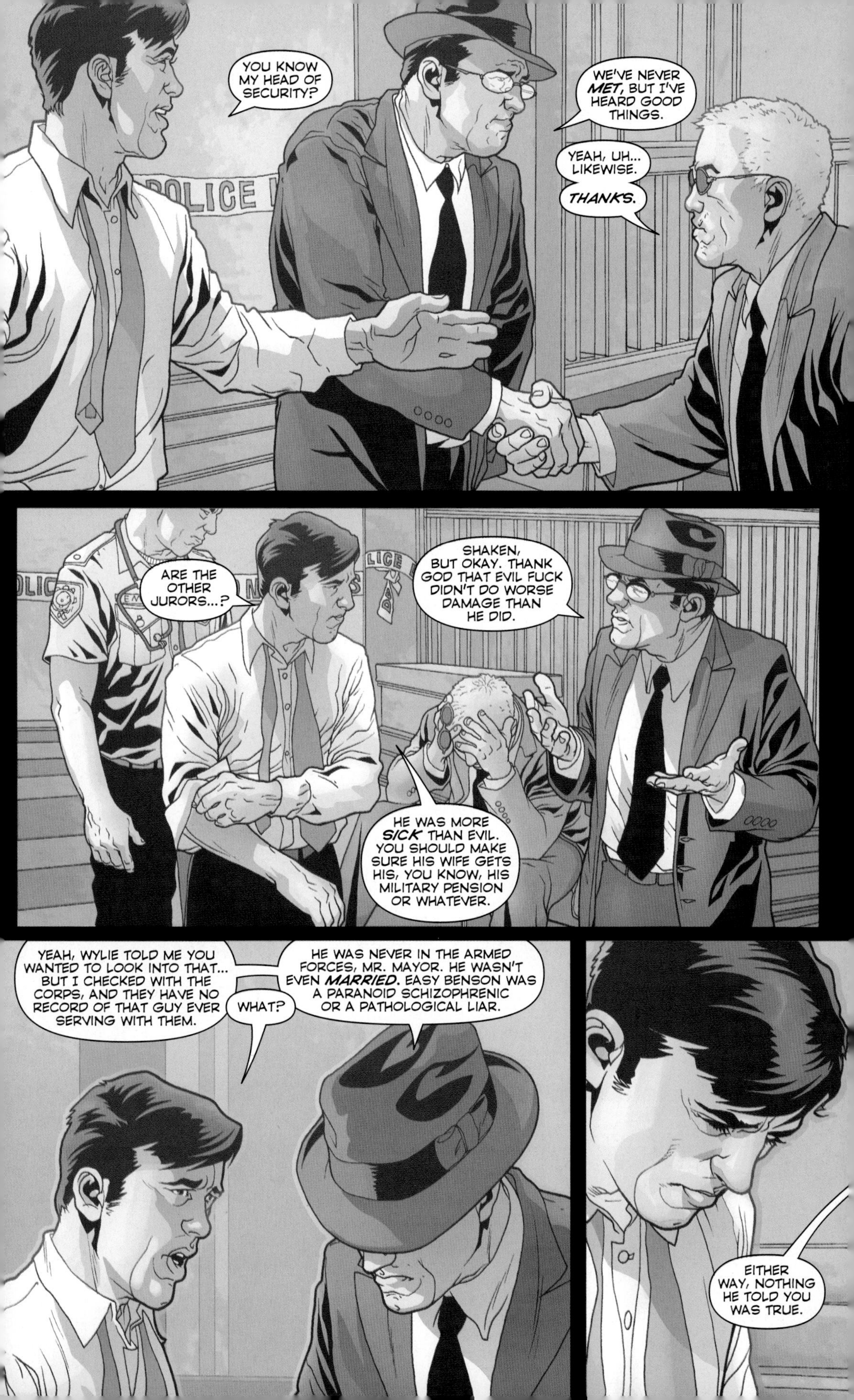
YOU KNOW MY HEAD OF SECURITY?
WE'VE NEVER *MET*, BUT I'VE HEARD GOOD THINGS.
YEAH, UH... LIKEWISE.
*THANKS*.
POLICE
ARE THE OTHER JURORS...?
SHAKEN, BUT OKAY. THANK GOD THAT EVIL FUCK DIDN'T DO WORSE DAMAGE THAN HE DID.
HE WAS MORE *SICK* THAN EVIL. YOU SHOULD MAKE SURE HIS WIFE GETS HIS, YOU KNOW, HIS MILITARY PENSION OR WHATEVER.
YEAH, WYLIE TOLD ME YOU WANTED TO LOOK INTO THAT... BUT I CHECKED WITH THE CORPS, AND THEY HAVE NO RECORD OF THAT GUY EVER SERVING WITH THEM.
WHAT?
HE WAS NEVER IN THE ARMED FORCES, MR. MAYOR. HE WASN'T EVEN *MARRIED*. EASY BENSON WAS A PARANOID SCHIZOPHRENIC OR A PATHOLOGICAL LIAR.
EITHER WAY, NOTHING HE TOLD YOU WAS TRUE.

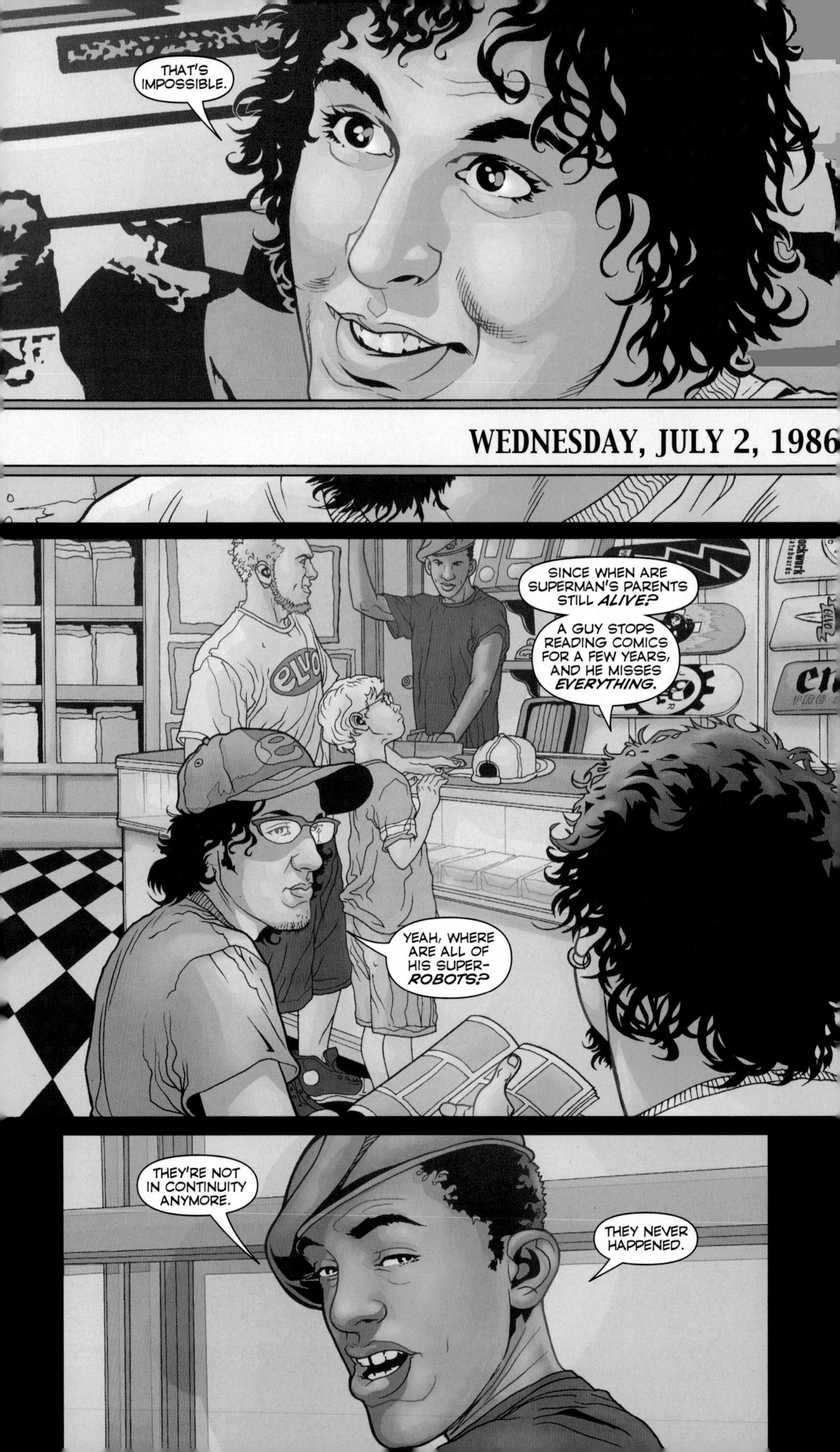
THAT'S IMPOSSIBLE.
WEDNESDAY, JULY 2, 1986
SINCE WHEN ARE SUPERMAN'S PARENTS STILL *ALIVE?*
A GUY STOPS READING COMICS FOR A FEW YEARS, AND HE MISSES *EVERYTHING.*
YEAH, WHERE ARE ALL OF HIS SUPER-*ROBOTS?*
THEY'RE NOT IN CONTINUITY ANYMORE.
THEY NEVER HAPPENED.

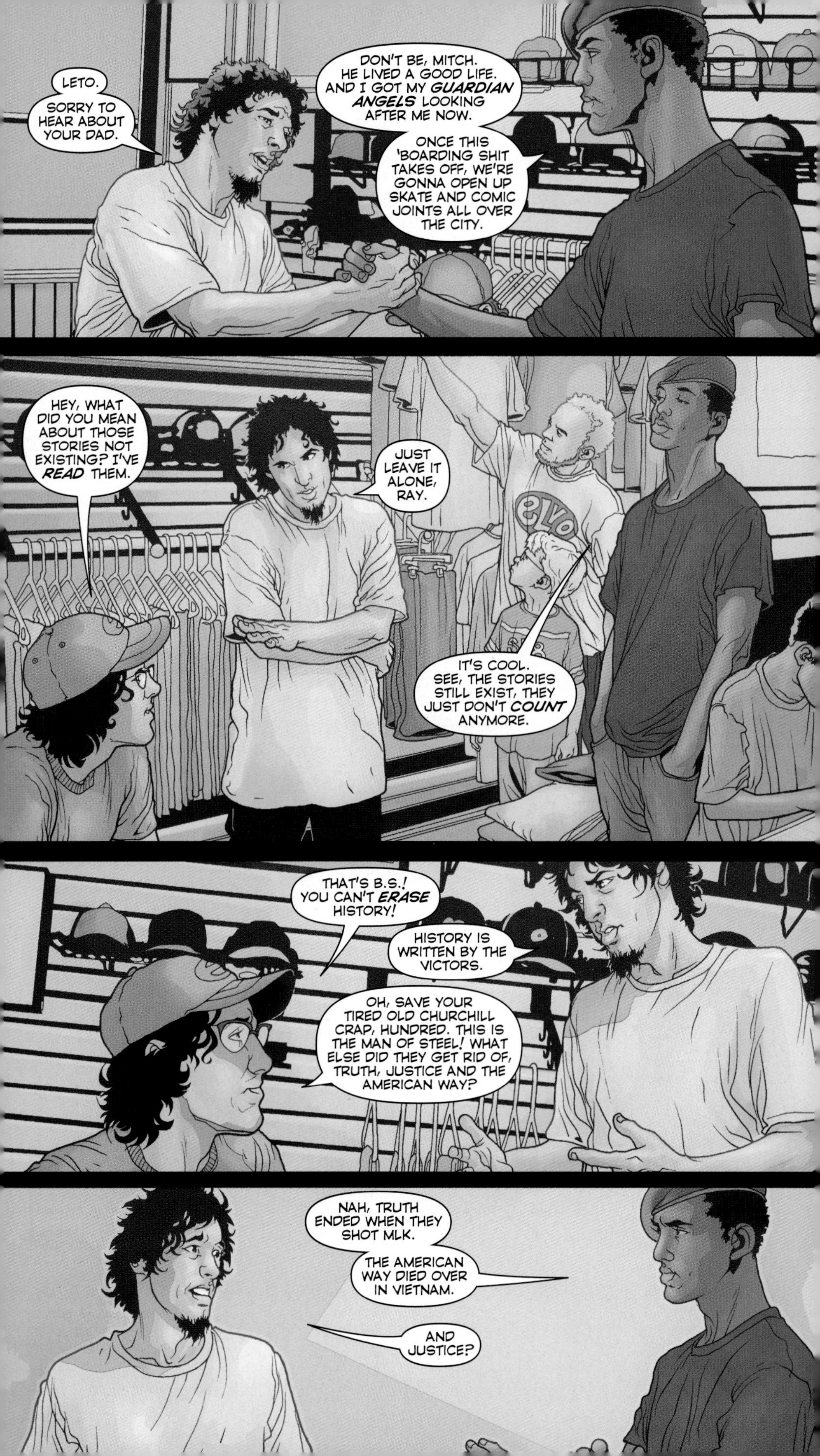
LETO.
SORRY TO HEAR ABOUT YOUR DAD.
DON'T BE, MITCH. HE LIVED A GOOD LIFE. AND I GOT MY GUARDIAN ANGELS LOOKING AFTER ME NOW.
ONCE THIS 'BOARDING SHIT TAKES OFF, WE'RE GONNA OPEN UP SKATE AND COMIC JOINTS ALL OVER THE CITY.
HEY, WHAT DID YOU MEAN ABOUT THOSE STORIES NOT EXISTING? I'VE READ THEM.
JUST LEAVE IT ALONE, RAY.
IT'S COOL. SEE, THE STORIES STILL EXIST, THEY JUST DON'T COUNT ANYMORE.
THAT'S B.S.! YOU CAN'T ERASE HISTORY!
HISTORY IS WRITTEN BY THE VICTORS.
OH, SAVE YOUR TIRED OLD CHURCHILL CRAP, HUNDRED. THIS IS THE MAN OF STEEL! WHAT ELSE DID THEY GET RID OF, TRUTH, JUSTICE AND THE AMERICAN WAY?
NAH, TRUTH ENDED WHEN THEY SHOT MLK.
THE AMERICAN WAY DIED OVER IN VIETNAM.
AND JUSTICE?

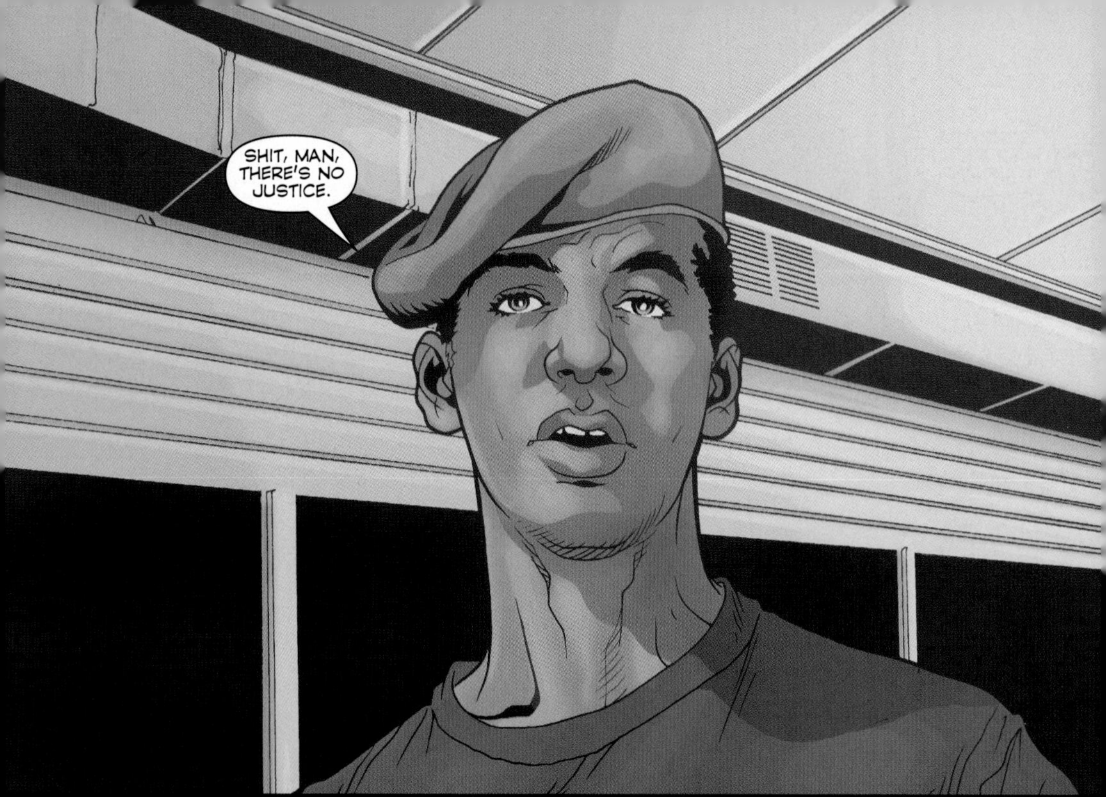
SHIT, MAN, THERE'S NO JUSTICE.

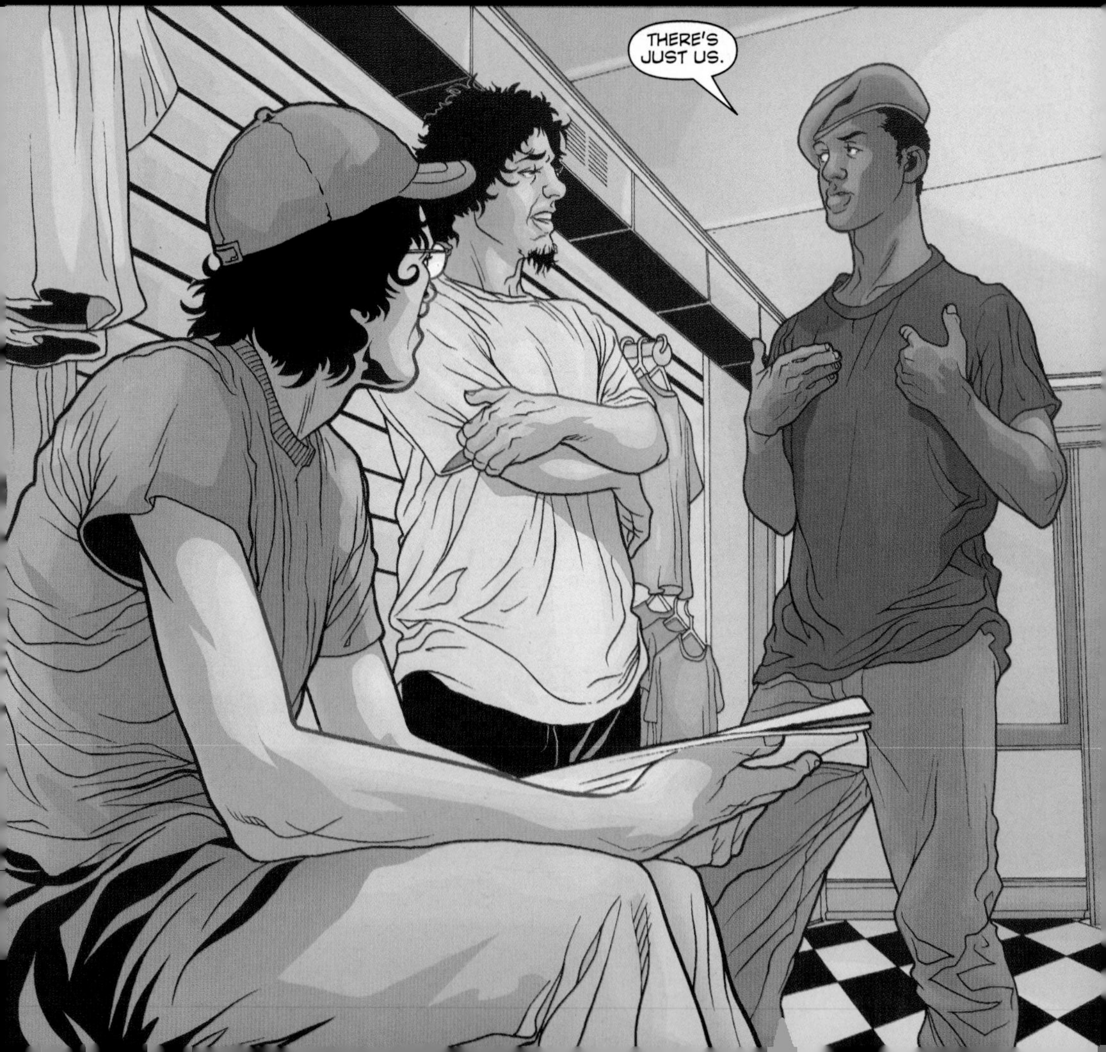
THERE'S JUST US.

# CHAPTER 2 OFF THE GRID

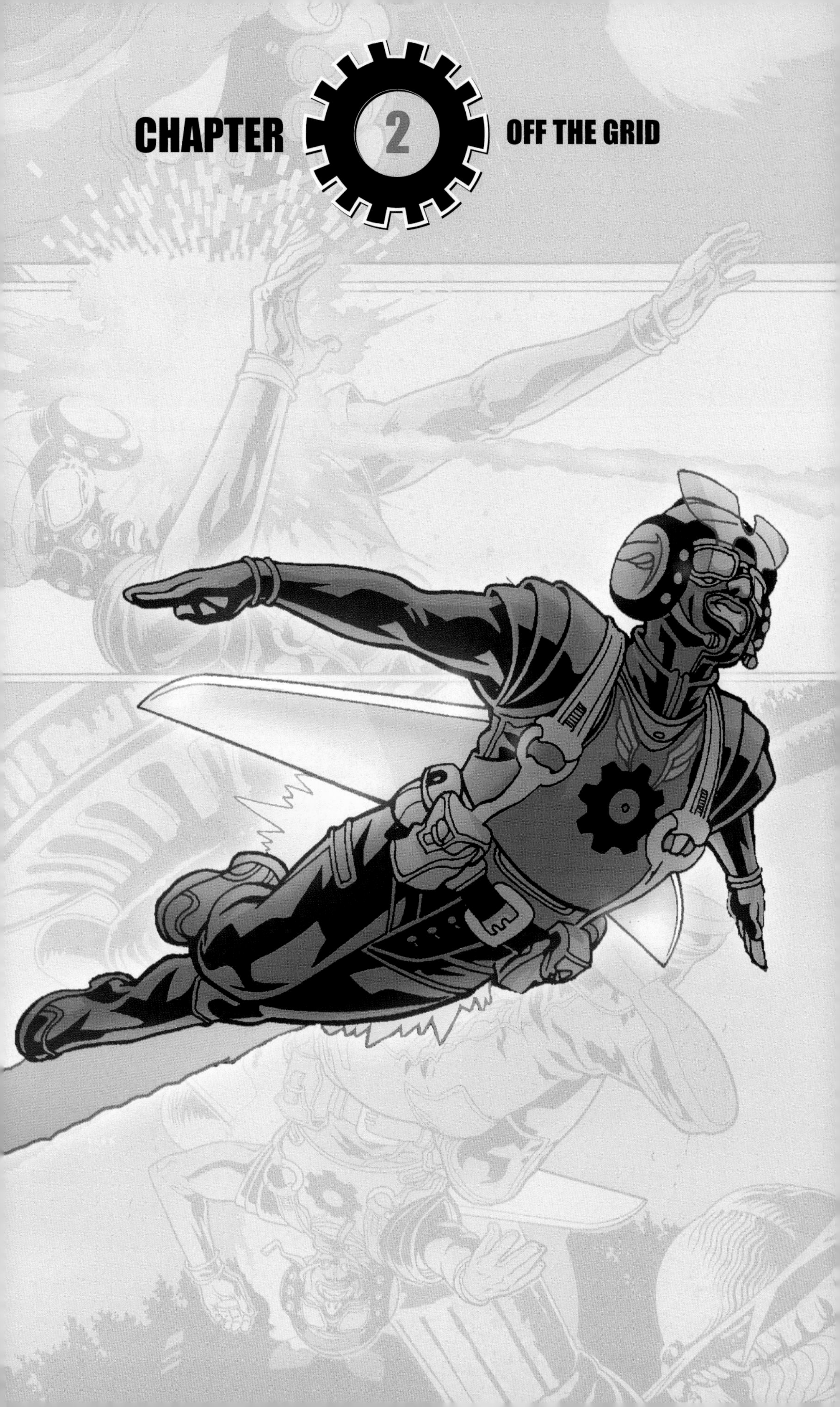

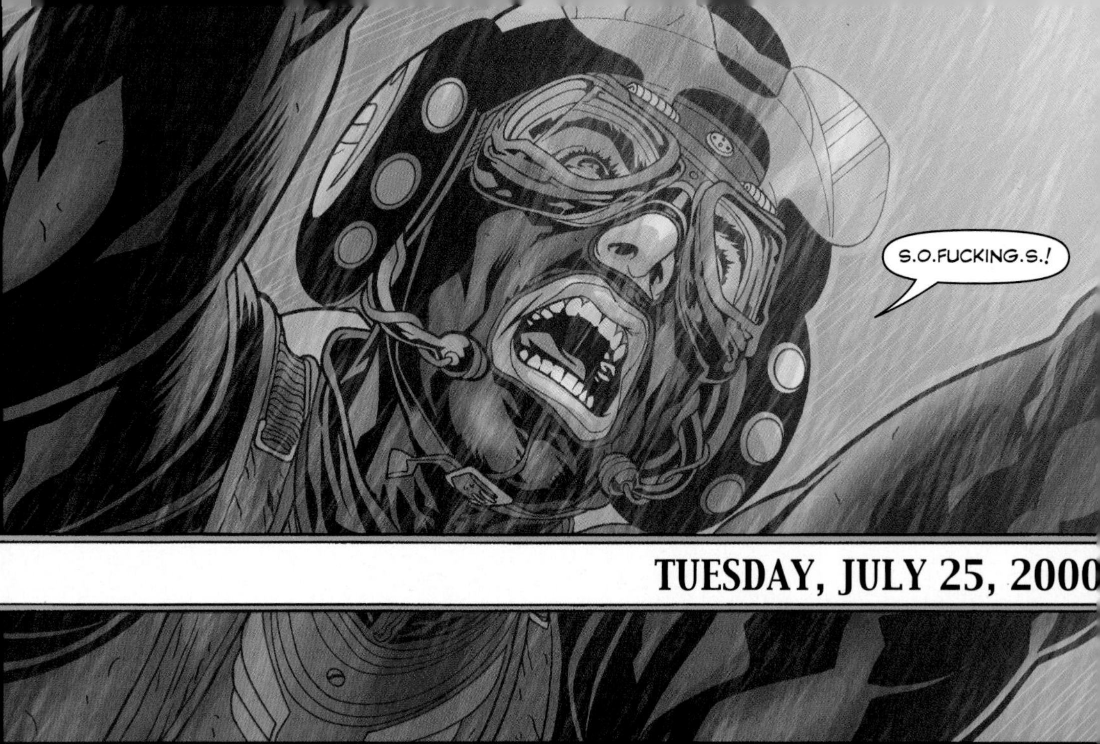
S.O.FUCKING.S.!
TUESDAY, JULY 25, 2000

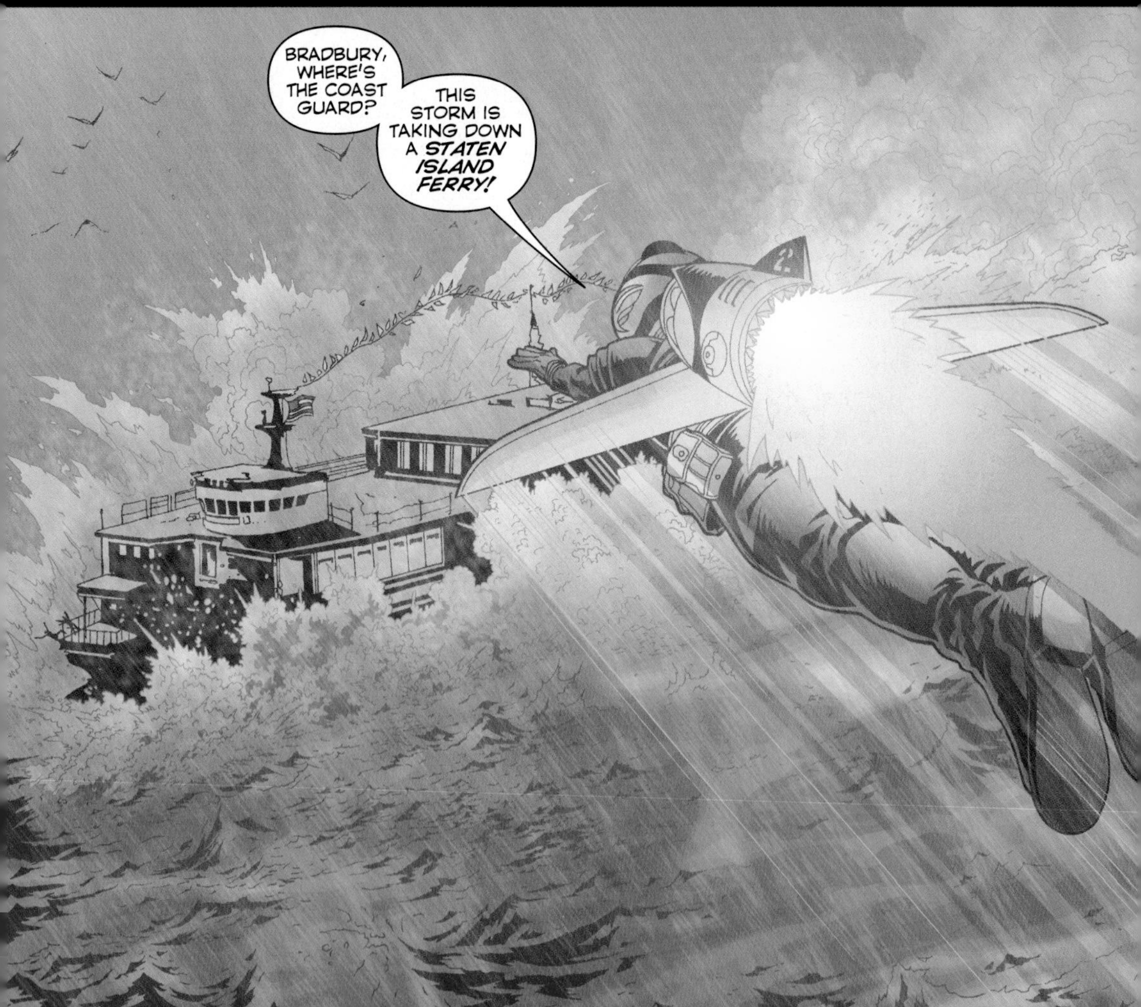
BRADBURY, WHERE'S THE COAST GUARD?
THIS STORM IS TAKING DOWN A STATEN ISLAND FERRY!

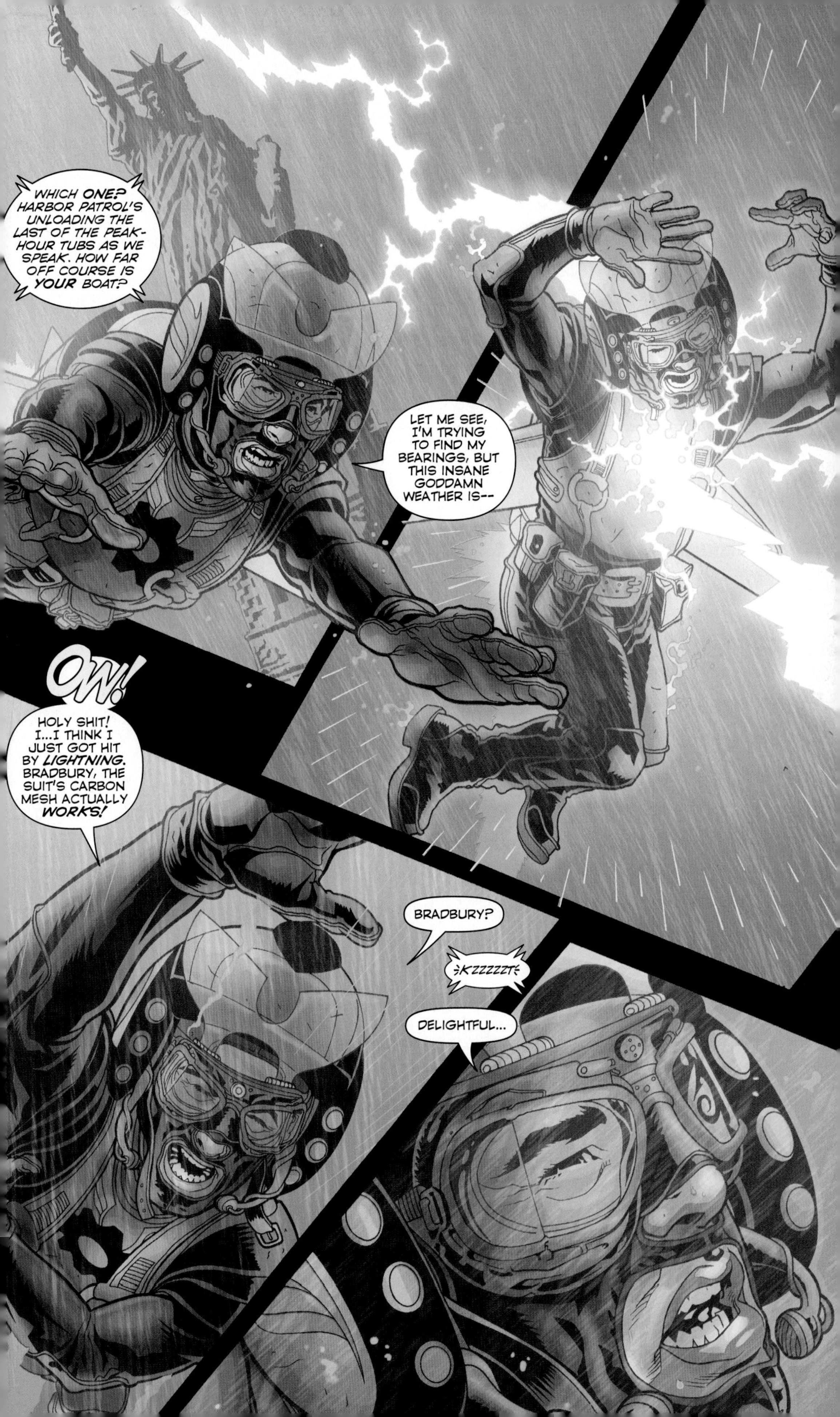
WHICH ONE? HARBOR PATROL'S UNLOADING THE LAST OF THE PEAK-HOUR TUBS AS WE SPEAK. HOW FAR OFF COURSE IS YOUR BOAT?
LET ME SEE, I'M TRYING TO FIND MY BEARINGS, BUT THIS INSANE GODDAMN WEATHER IS--
OW!
HOLY SHIT! I...I THINK I JUST GOT HIT BY LIGHTNING. BRADBURY, THE SUIT'S CARBON MESH ACTUALLY WORKS!
BRADBURY?
KZZZZZT
DELIGHTFUL...

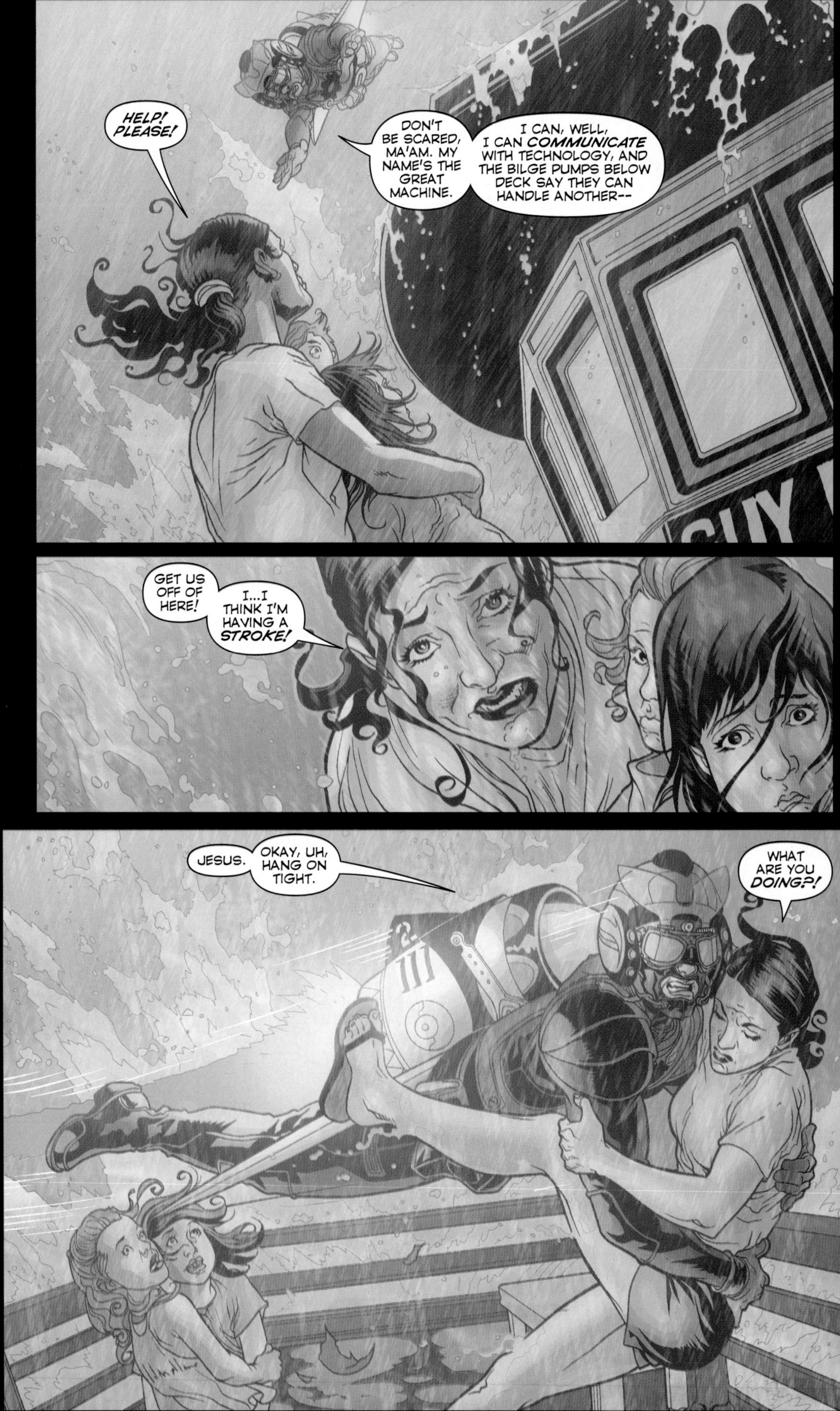
HELP! PLEASE!
DON'T BE SCARED, MA'AM. MY NAME'S THE GREAT MACHINE.
I CAN, WELL, I CAN COMMUNICATE WITH TECHNOLOGY, AND THE BILGE PUMPS BELOW DECK SAY THEY CAN HANDLE ANOTHER--
GET US OFF OF HERE!
I...I THINK I'M HAVING A STROKE!
JESUS.
OKAY, UH, HANG ON TIGHT.
WHAT ARE YOU DOING?!

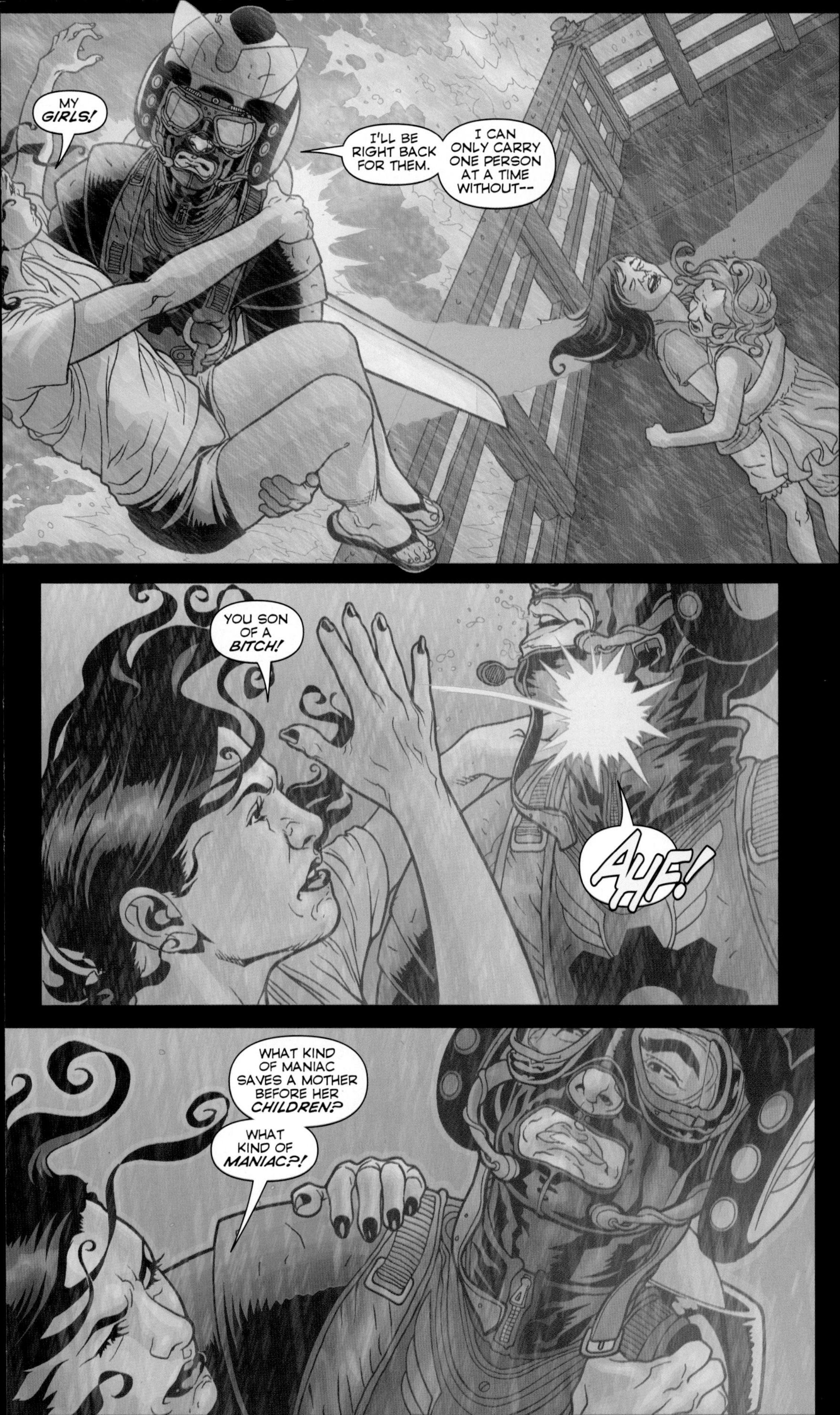
MY GIRLS!
I'LL BE RIGHT BACK FOR THEM.
I CAN ONLY CARRY ONE PERSON AT A TIME WITHOUT--
YOU SON OF A BITCH!
AHF!
WHAT KIND OF MANIAC SAVES A MOTHER BEFORE HER CHILDREN?
WHAT KIND OF MANIAC?!

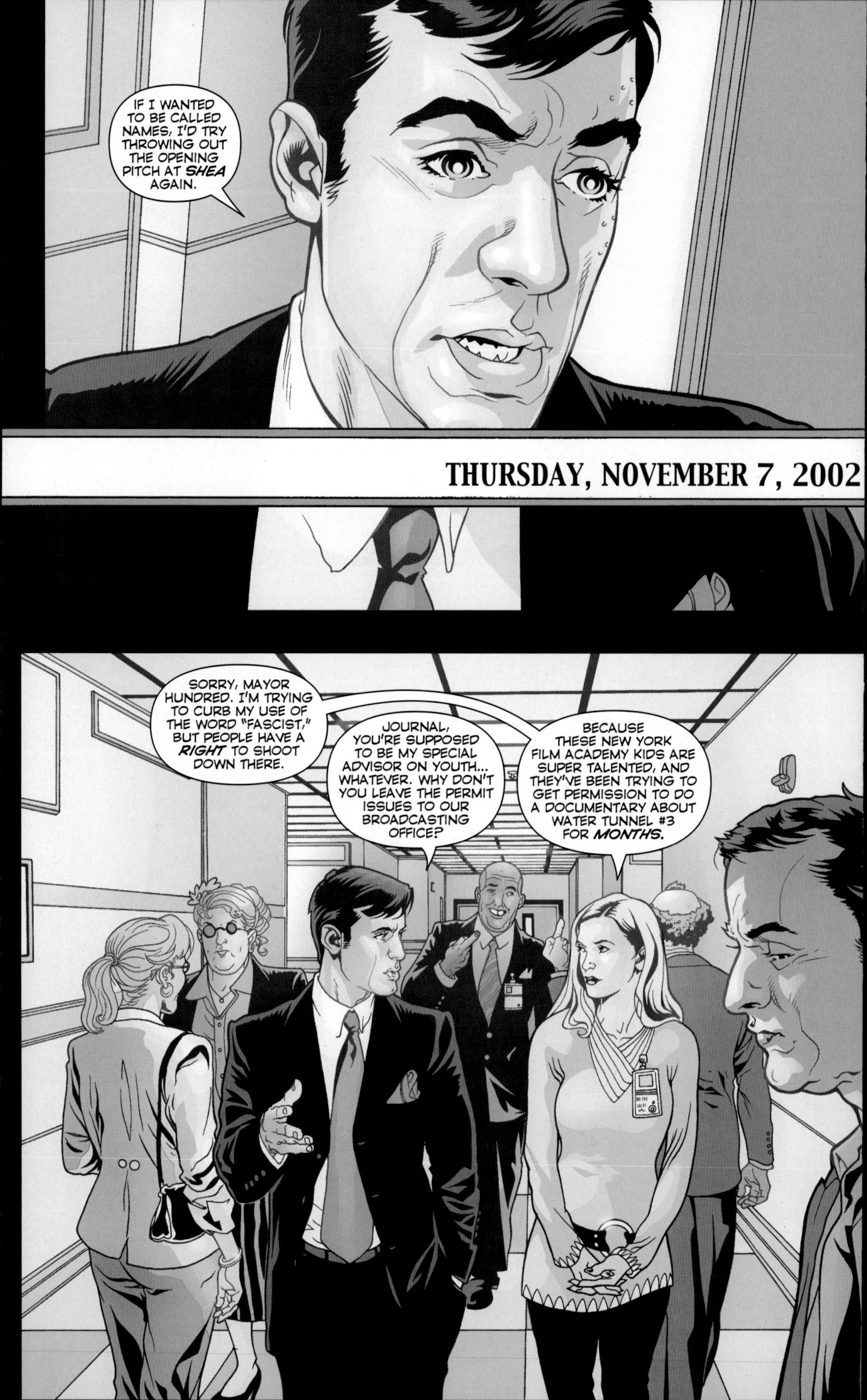
IF I WANTED TO BE CALLED NAMES, I'D TRY THROWING OUT THE OPENING PITCH AT *SHEA* AGAIN.
THURSDAY, NOVEMBER 7, 2002
SORRY, MAYOR HUNDRED. I'M TRYING TO CURB MY USE OF THE WORD "FASCIST," BUT PEOPLE HAVE A *RIGHT* TO SHOOT DOWN THERE.
JOURNAL, YOU'RE SUPPOSED TO BE MY SPECIAL ADVISOR ON YOUTH... WHATEVER. WHY DON'T YOU LEAVE THE PERMIT ISSUES TO OUR BROADCASTING OFFICE?
BECAUSE THESE NEW YORK FILM ACADEMY KIDS ARE SUPER TALENTED, AND THEY'VE BEEN TRYING TO GET PERMISSION TO DO A DOCUMENTARY ABOUT WATER TUNNEL #3 FOR *MONTHS*.

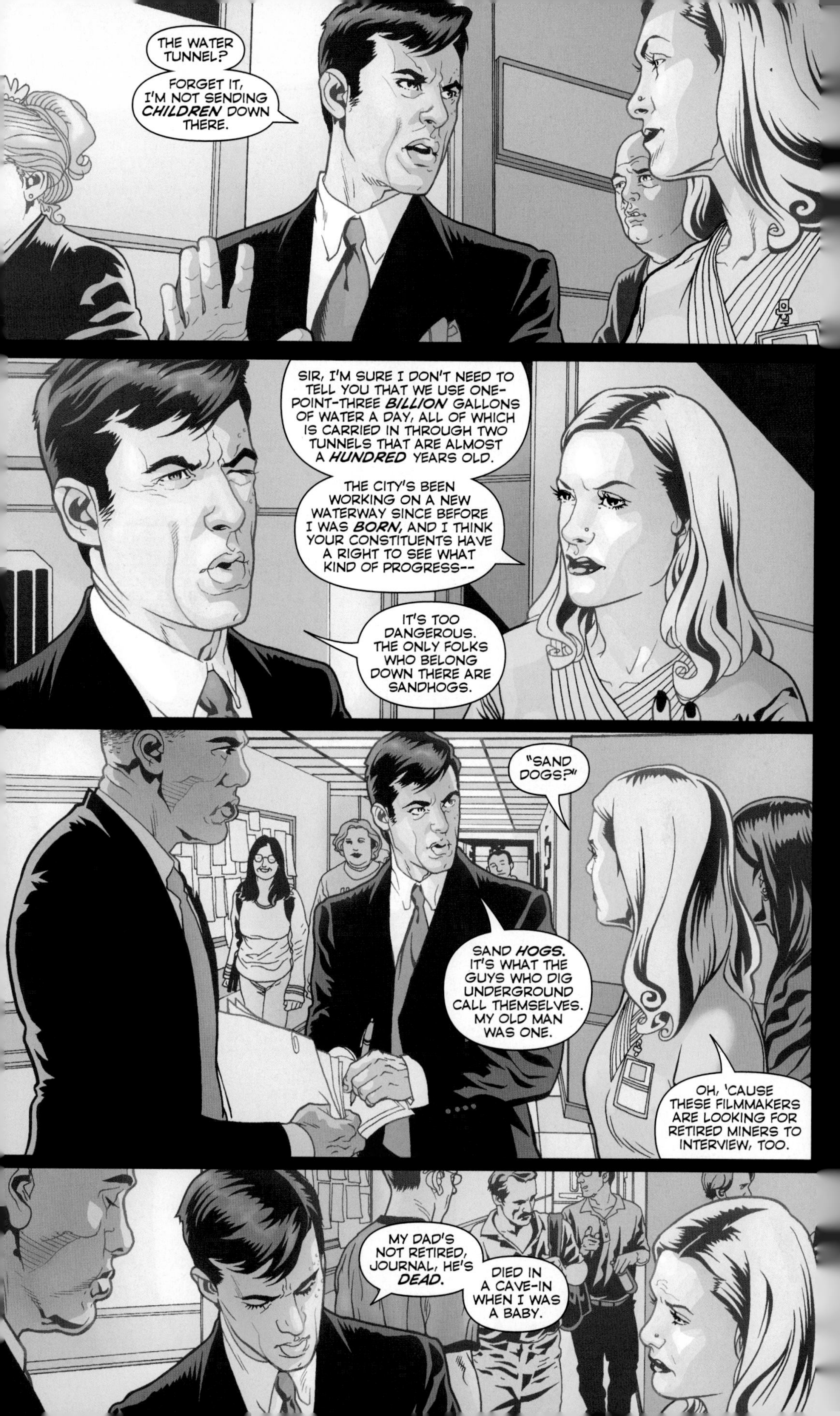
THE WATER TUNNEL?
FORGET IT, I'M NOT SENDING *CHILDREN* DOWN THERE.
SIR, I'M SURE I DON'T NEED TO TELL YOU THAT WE USE ONE-POINT-THREE *BILLION* GALLONS OF WATER A DAY, ALL OF WHICH IS CARRIED IN THROUGH TWO TUNNELS THAT ARE ALMOST A *HUNDRED* YEARS OLD.
THE CITY'S BEEN WORKING ON A NEW WATERWAY SINCE BEFORE I WAS *BORN,* AND I THINK YOUR CONSTITUENTS HAVE A RIGHT TO SEE WHAT KIND OF PROGRESS--
IT'S TOO DANGEROUS. THE ONLY FOLKS WHO BELONG DOWN THERE ARE SANDHOGS.
"SAND DOGS?"
SAND *HOGS.* IT'S WHAT THE GUYS WHO DIG UNDERGROUND CALL THEMSELVES. MY OLD MAN WAS ONE.
OH, 'CAUSE THESE FILMMAKERS ARE LOOKING FOR RETIRED MINERS TO INTERVIEW, TOO.
MY DAD'S NOT RETIRED, JOURNAL, HE'S *DEAD.*
DIED IN A CAVE-IN WHEN I WAS A BABY.

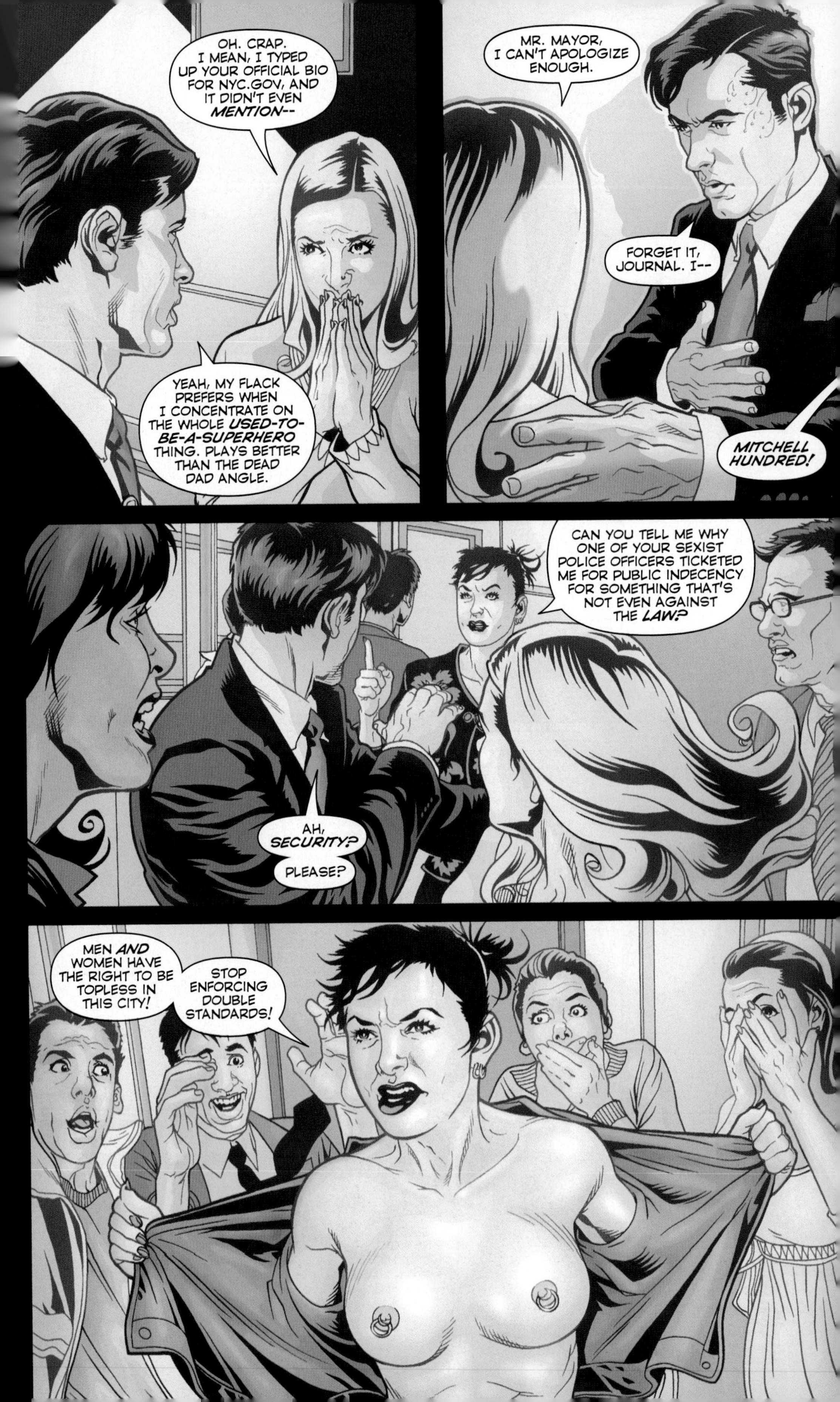
OH. CRAP. I MEAN, I TYPED UP YOUR OFFICIAL BIO FOR NYC.GOV, AND IT DIDN'T EVEN MENTION--
YEAH, MY FLACK PREFERS WHEN I CONCENTRATE ON THE WHOLE USED-TO-BE-A-SUPERHERO THING. PLAYS BETTER THAN THE DEAD DAD ANGLE.
MR. MAYOR, I CAN'T APOLOGIZE ENOUGH.
FORGET IT, JOURNAL. I--
MITCHELL HUNDRED!
CAN YOU TELL ME WHY ONE OF YOUR SEXIST POLICE OFFICERS TICKETED ME FOR PUBLIC INDECENCY FOR SOMETHING THAT'S NOT EVEN AGAINST THE LAW?
AH, SECURITY?
PLEASE?
MEN AND WOMEN HAVE THE RIGHT TO BE TOPLESS IN THIS CITY!
STOP ENFORCING DOUBLE STANDARDS!

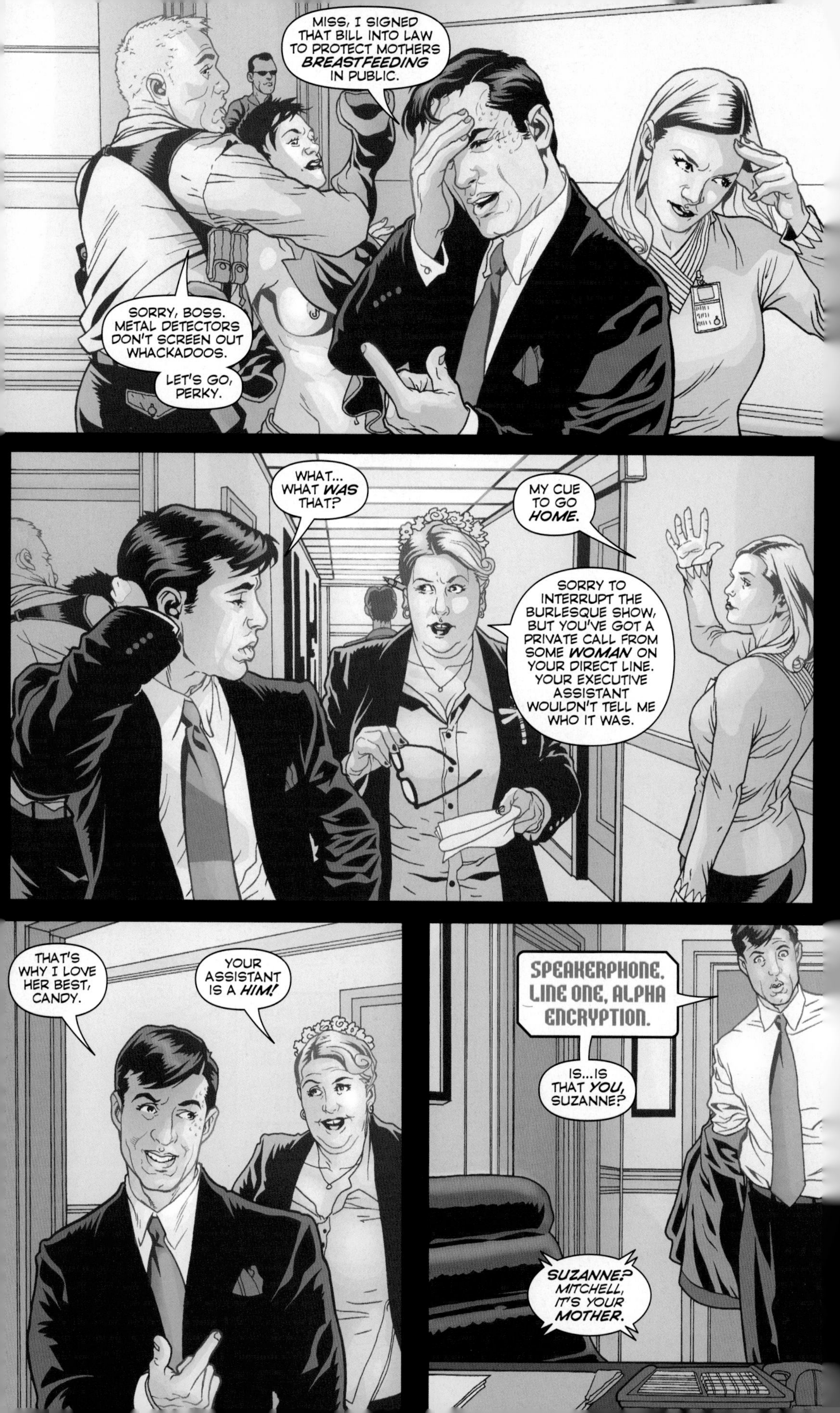
MISS, I SIGNED THAT BILL INTO LAW TO PROTECT MOTHERS *BREASTFEEDING* IN PUBLIC.
SORRY, BOSS. METAL DETECTORS DON'T SCREEN OUT WHACKADOOS.
LET'S GO, PERKY.
WHAT... WHAT *WAS* THAT?
MY CUE TO GO *HOME*.
SORRY TO INTERRUPT THE BURLESQUE SHOW, BUT YOU'VE GOT A PRIVATE CALL FROM SOME *WOMAN* ON YOUR DIRECT LINE. YOUR EXECUTIVE ASSISTANT WOULDN'T TELL ME WHO IT WAS.
THAT'S WHY I LOVE HER BEST, CANDY.
YOUR ASSISTANT IS A *HIM!*
SPEAKERPHONE. LINE ONE, ALPHA ENCRYPTION.
IS...IS THAT *YOU*, SUZANNE?
*SUZANNE? MITCHELL, IT'S YOUR MOTHER.*

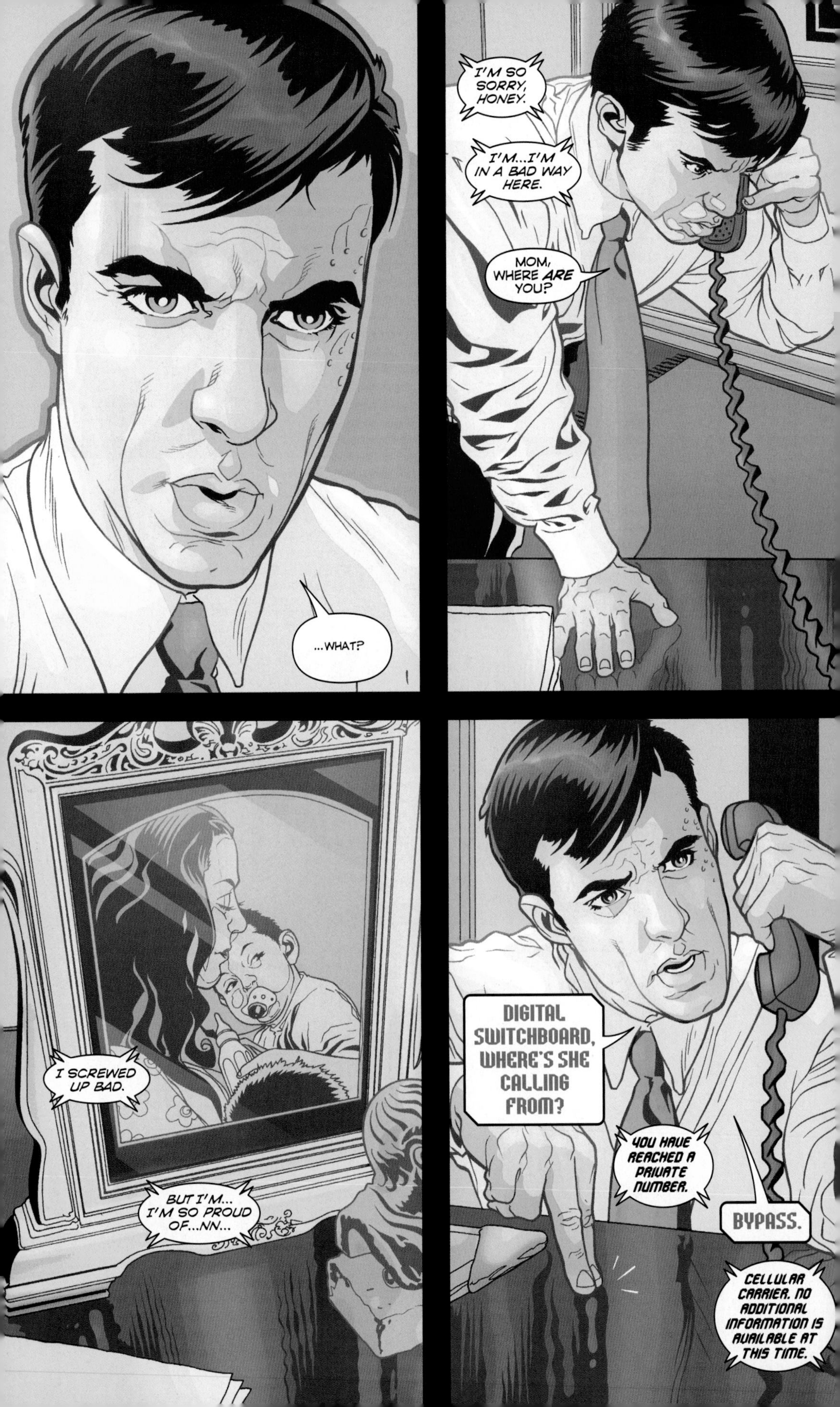
...WHAT?
I'M SO SORRY, HONEY.
I'M...I'M IN A BAD WAY HERE.
MOM, WHERE ARE YOU?
I SCREWED UP BAD.
BUT I'M... I'M SO PROUD OF...NN...
DIGITAL SWITCHBOARD, WHERE'S SHE CALLING FROM?
YOU HAVE REACHED A PRIVATE NUMBER.
BYPASS.
CELLULAR CARRIER. NO ADDITIONAL INFORMATION IS AVAILABLE AT THIS TIME.

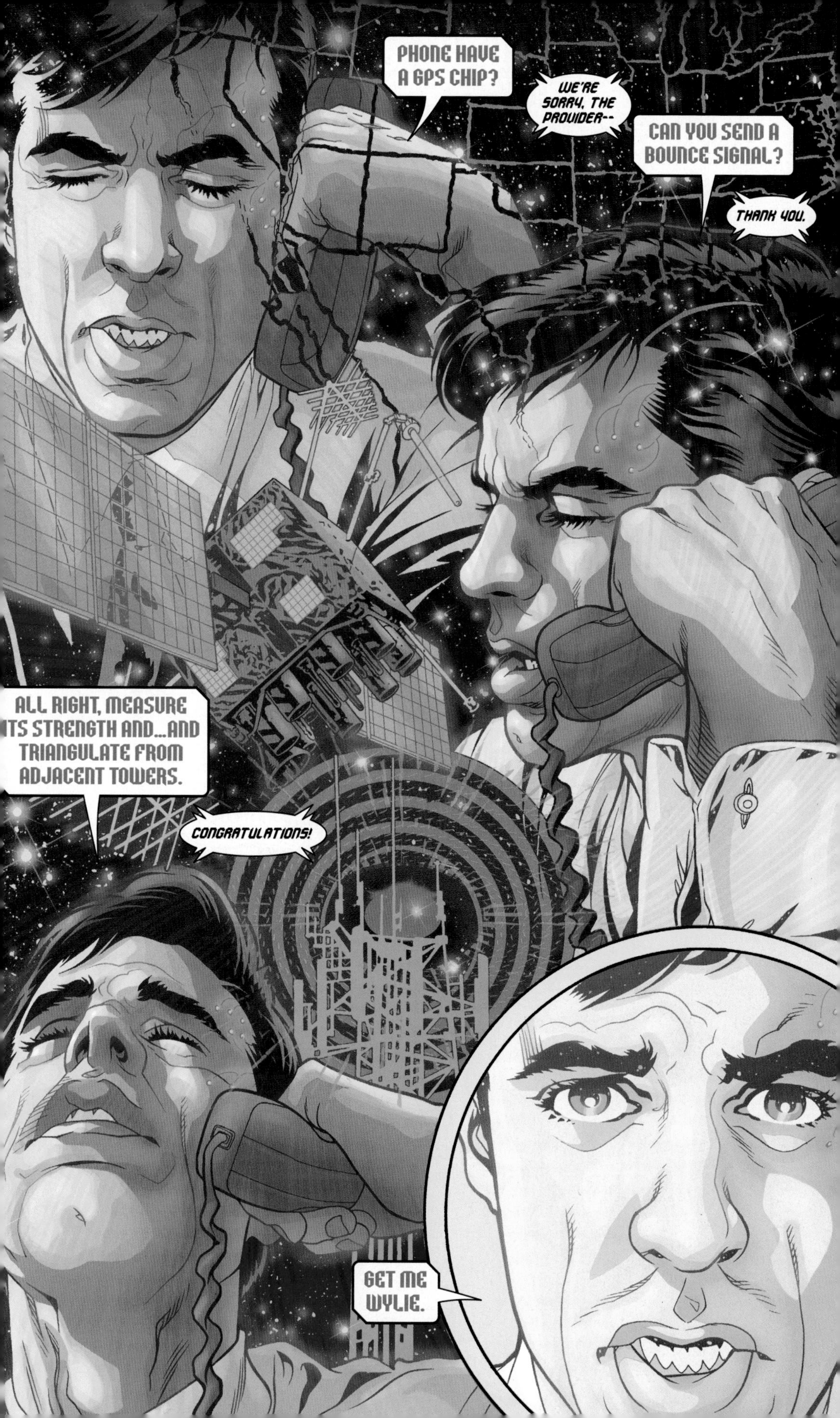

PHONE HAVE A GPS CHIP?
WE'RE SORRY, THE PROVIDER--
CAN YOU SEND A BOUNCE SIGNAL?
THANK YOU.
ALL RIGHT, MEASURE ITS STRENGTH AND...AND TRIANGULATE FROM ADJACENT TOWERS.
CONGRATULATIONS!
GET ME WYLIE.

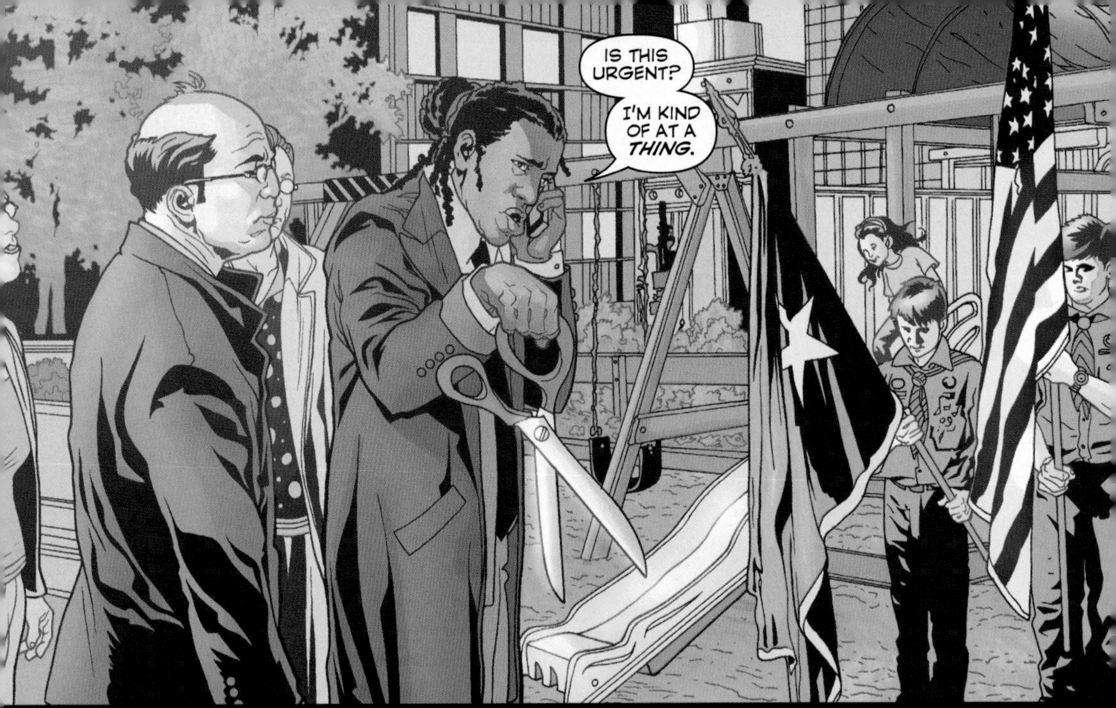
IS THIS URGENT?
I'M KIND OF AT A *THING*.

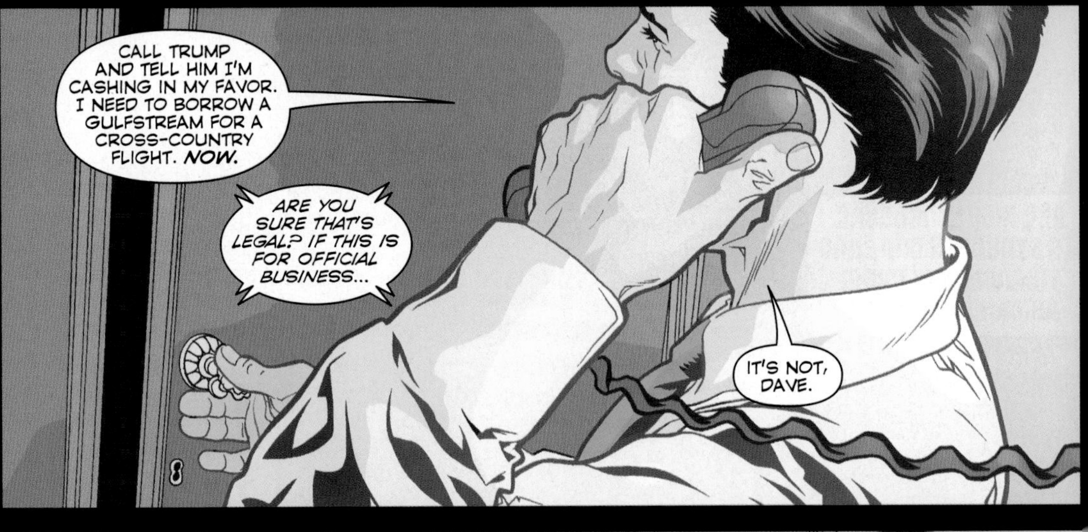
CALL TRUMP AND TELL HIM I'M CASHING IN MY FAVOR. I NEED TO BORROW A GULFSTREAM FOR A CROSS-COUNTRY FLIGHT. *NOW.*
*ARE YOU SURE THAT'S LEGAL? IF THIS IS FOR OFFICIAL BUSINESS...*
IT'S NOT, DAVE.

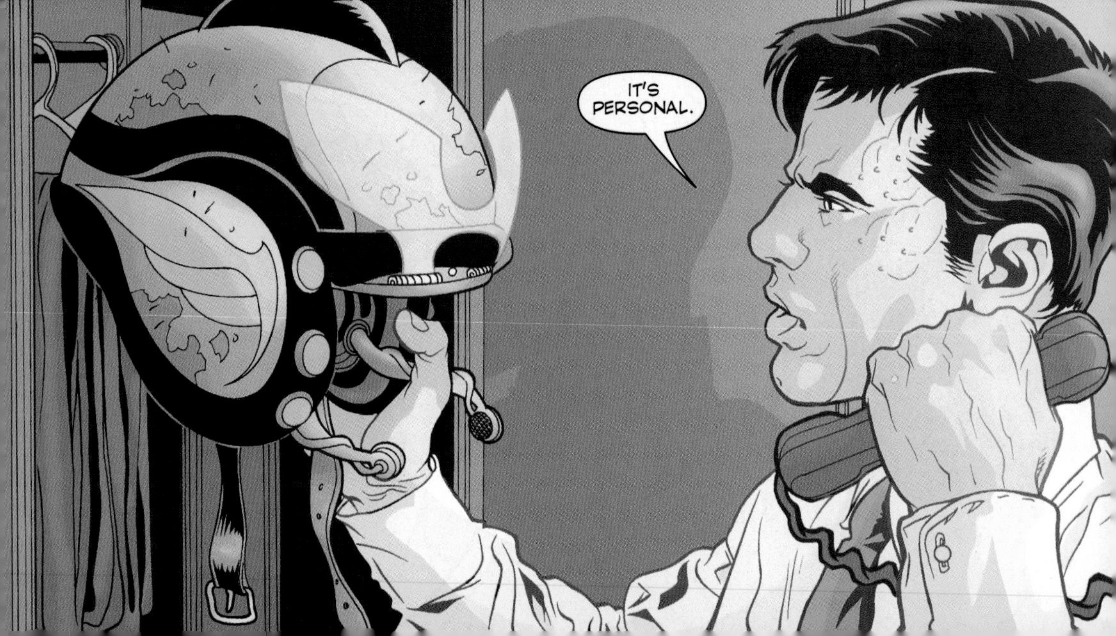
IT'S PERSONAL.

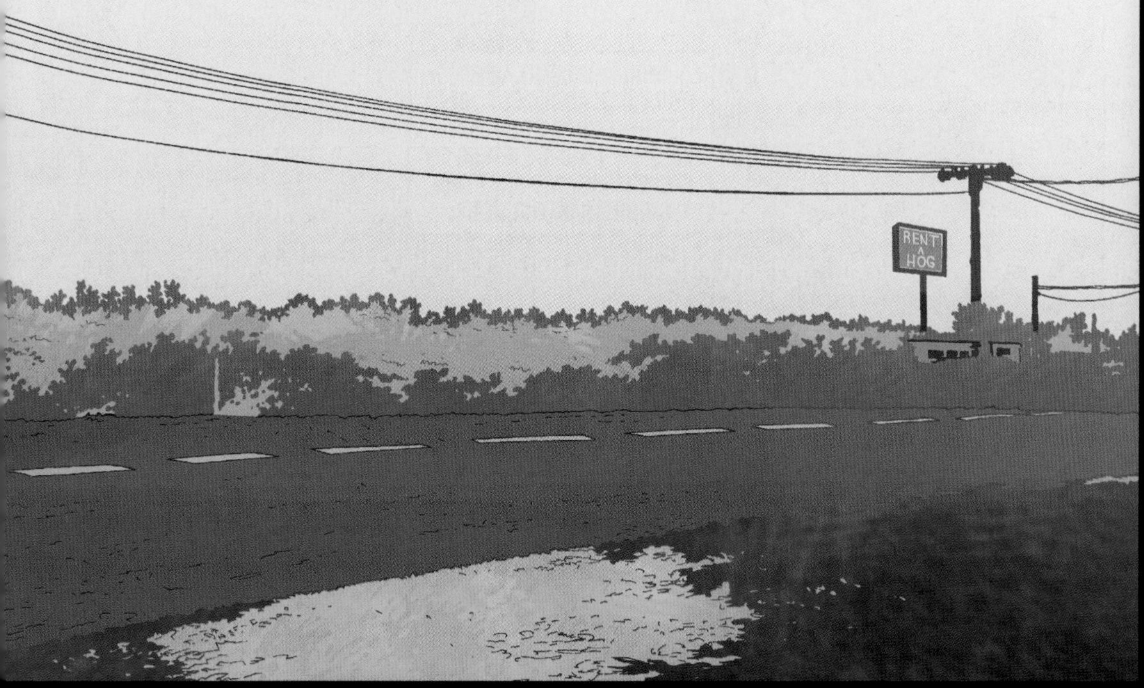
RENT A HOG
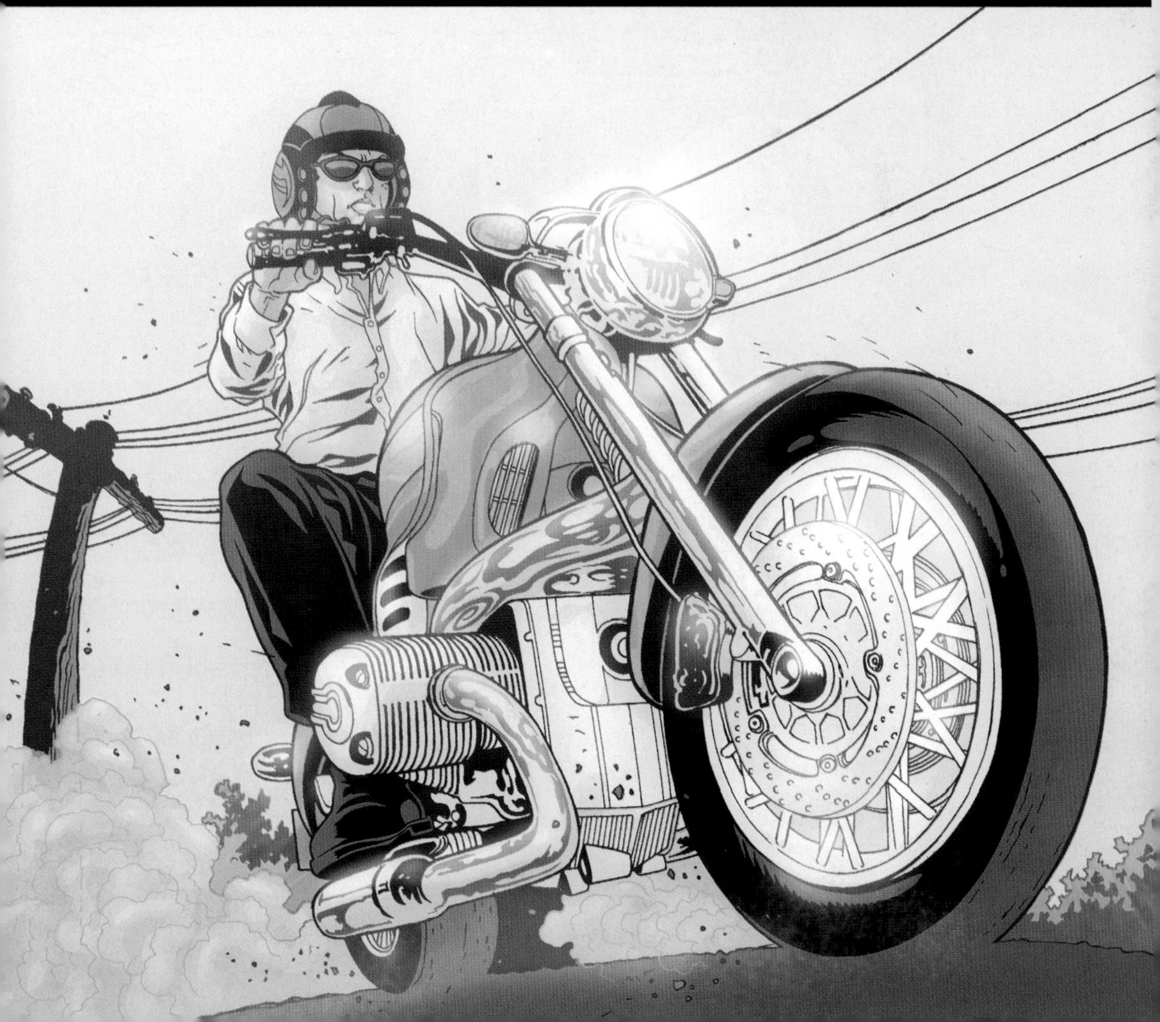

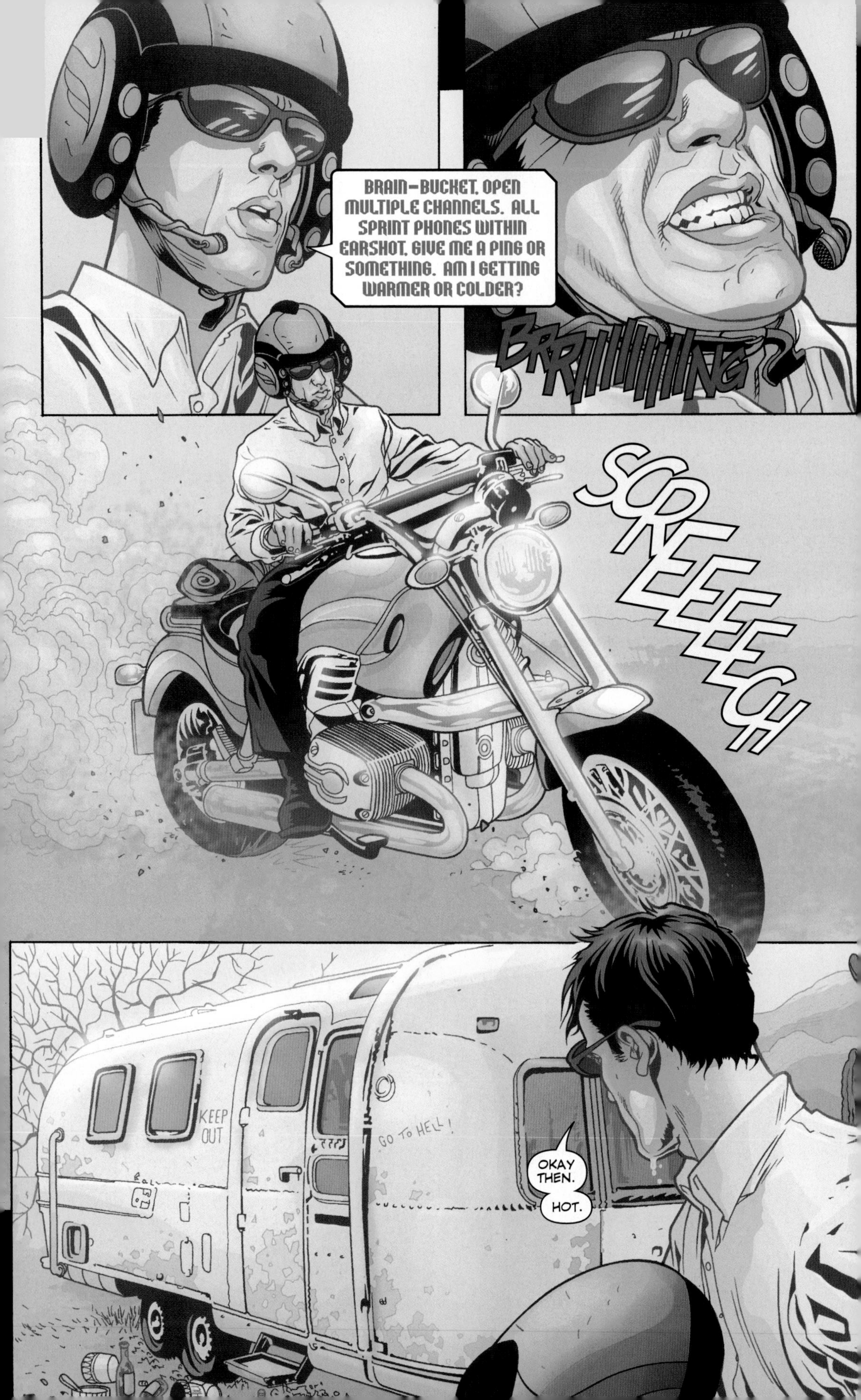
BRAIN-BUCKET, OPEN MULTIPLE CHANNELS. ALL SPRINT PHONES WITHIN EARSHOT, GIVE ME A PING OR SOMETHING. AM I GETTING WARMER OR COLDER?
BRRIIIIIIIIING
SCREEEEECH
KEEP OUT
GO TO HELL!
OKAY THEN.
HOT.

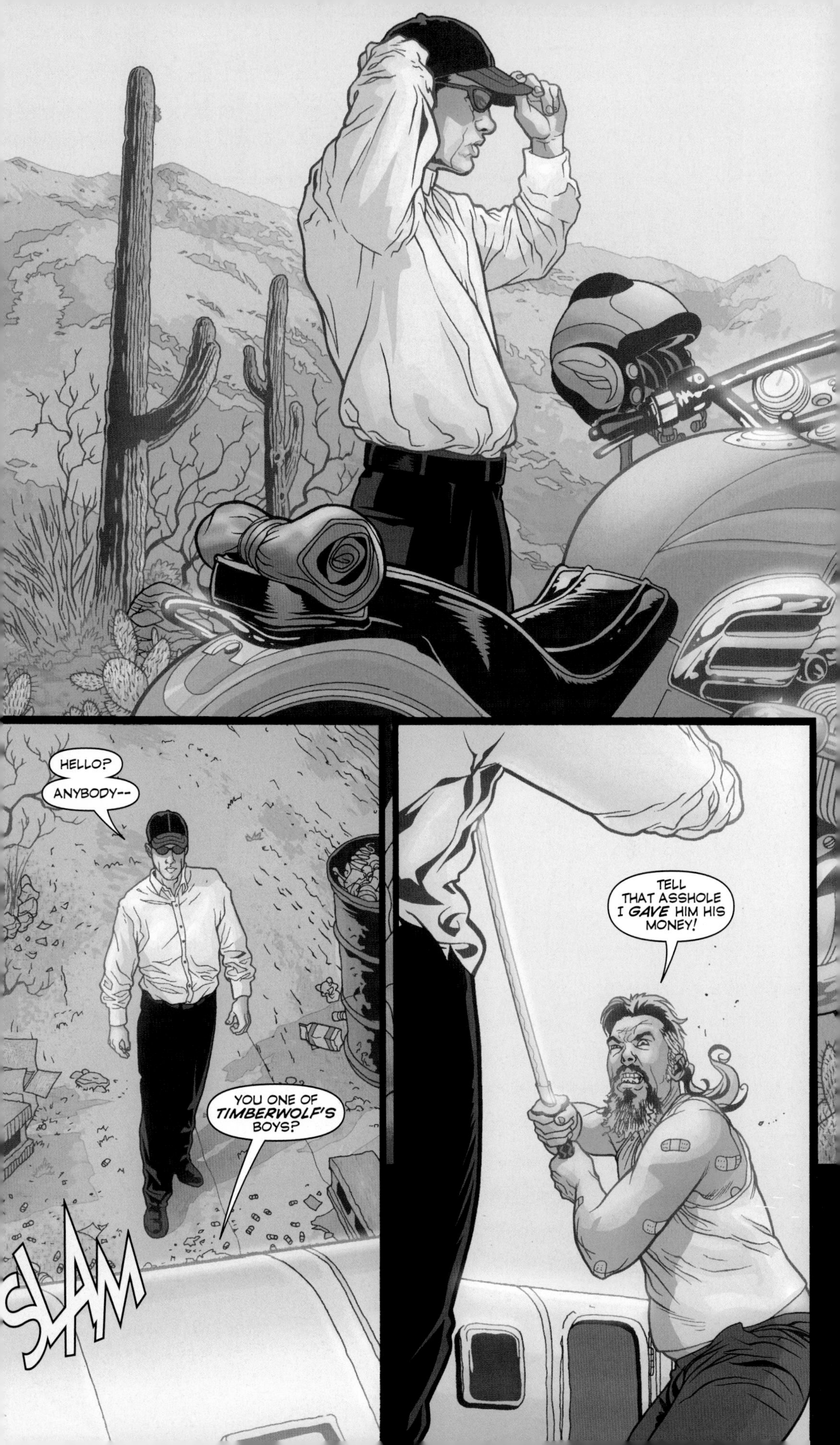
HELLO?
ANYBODY--
YOU ONE OF TIMBERWOLF'S BOYS?
SLAM
TELL THAT ASSHOLE I GAVE HIM HIS MONEY!

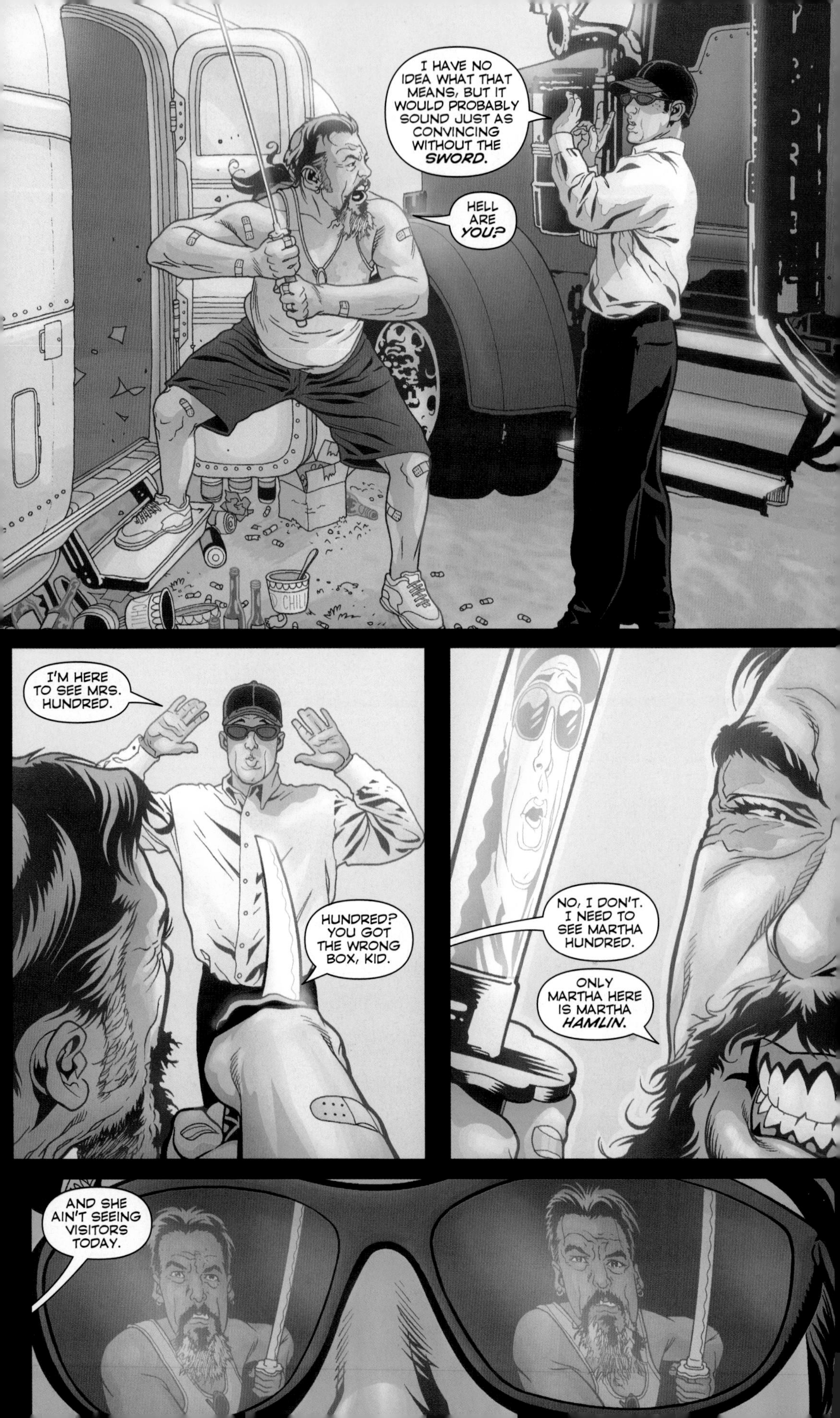
I HAVE NO IDEA WHAT THAT MEANS, BUT IT WOULD PROBABLY SOUND JUST AS CONVINCING WITHOUT THE SWORD.
HELL ARE YOU?
I'M HERE TO SEE MRS. HUNDRED.
HUNDRED? YOU GOT THE WRONG BOX, KID.
NO, I DON'T. I NEED TO SEE MARTHA HUNDRED.
ONLY MARTHA HERE IS MARTHA HAMLIN.
AND SHE AIN'T SEEING VISITORS TODAY.

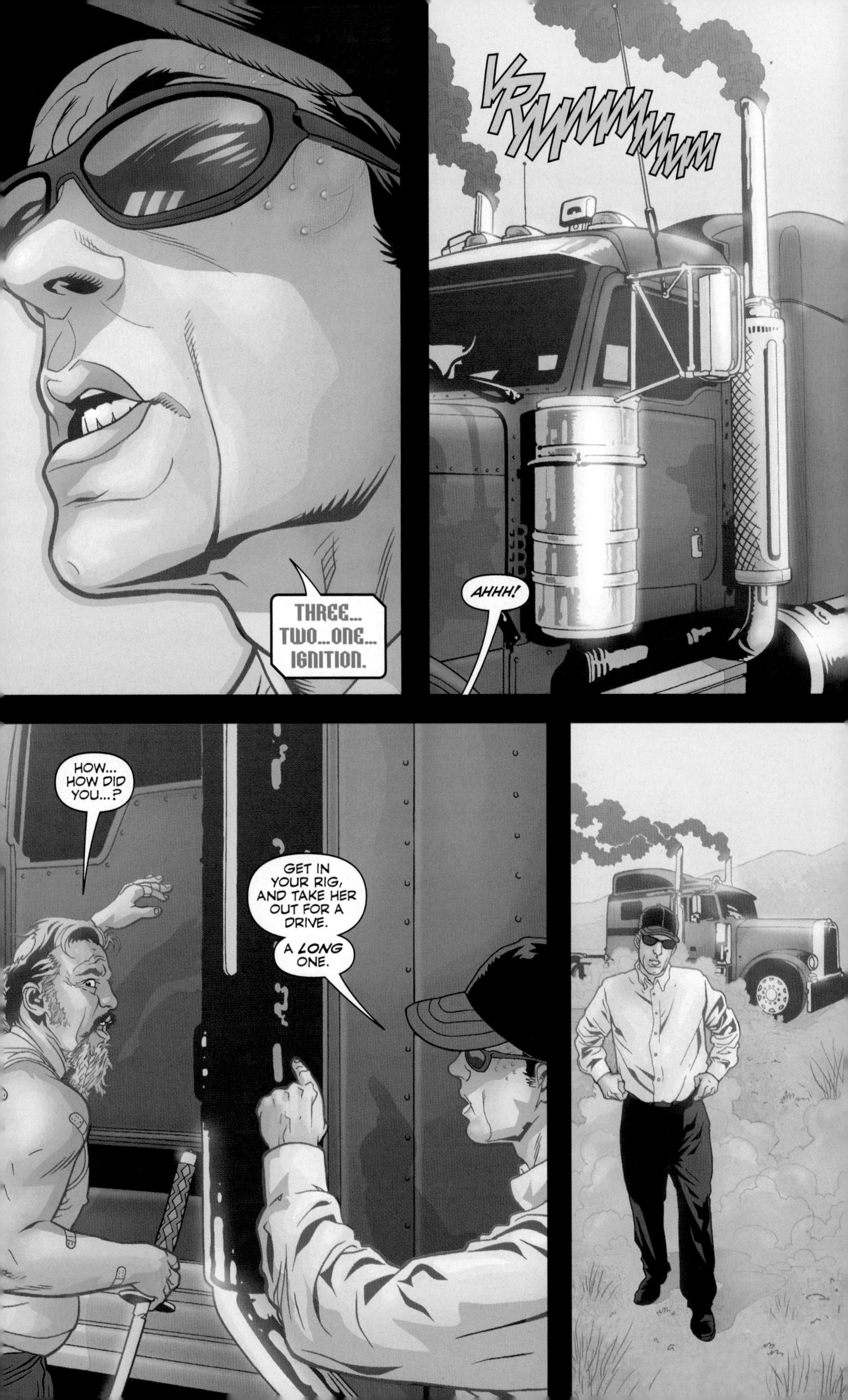
THREE... TWO...ONE... IGNITION.
VRMMMMMMM
AHHH!
HOW... HOW DID YOU...?
GET IN YOUR RIG, AND TAKE HER OUT FOR A DRIVE.
A LONG ONE.

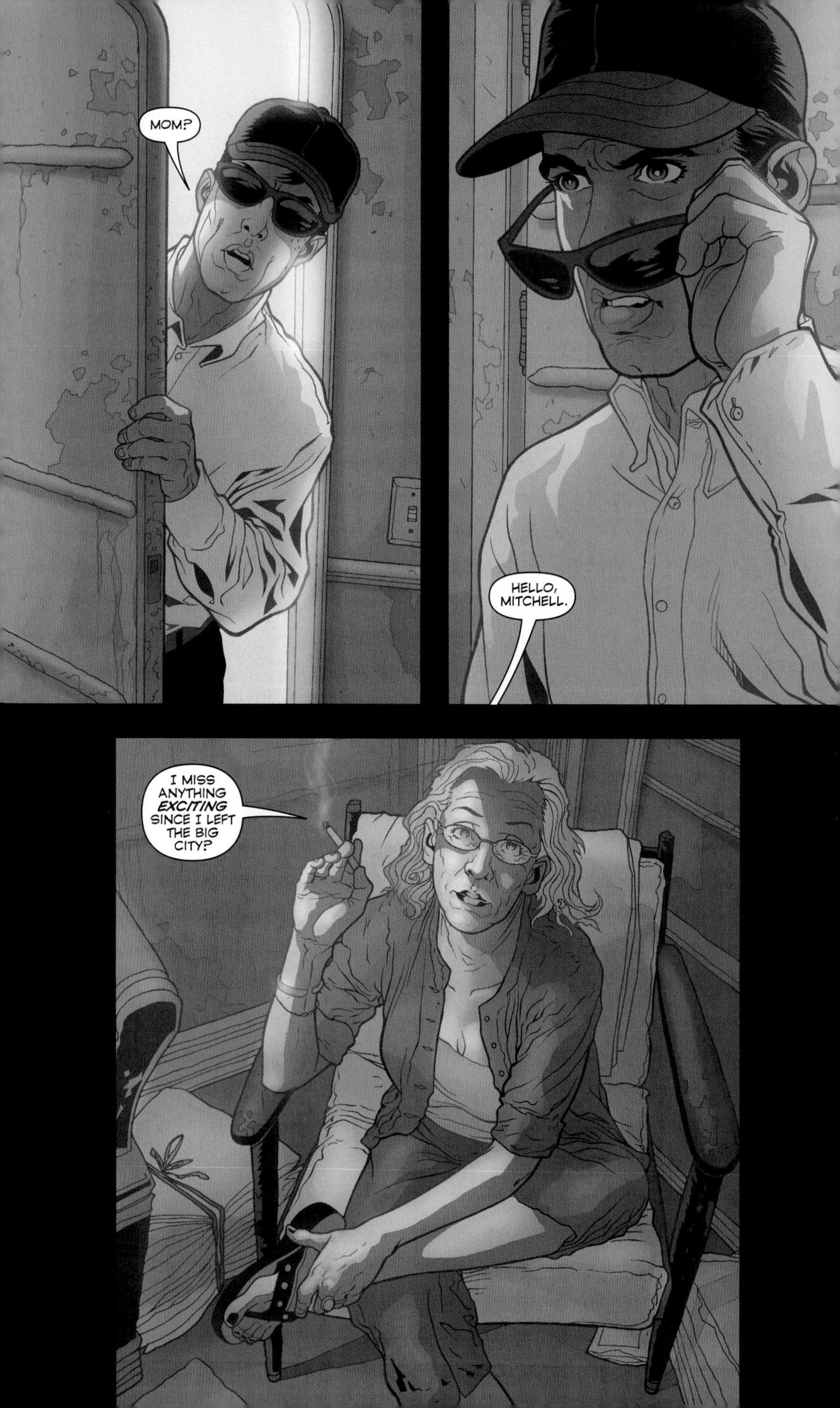
MOM?
HELLO, MITCHELL.
I MISS ANYTHING *EXCITING* SINCE I LEFT THE BIG CITY?

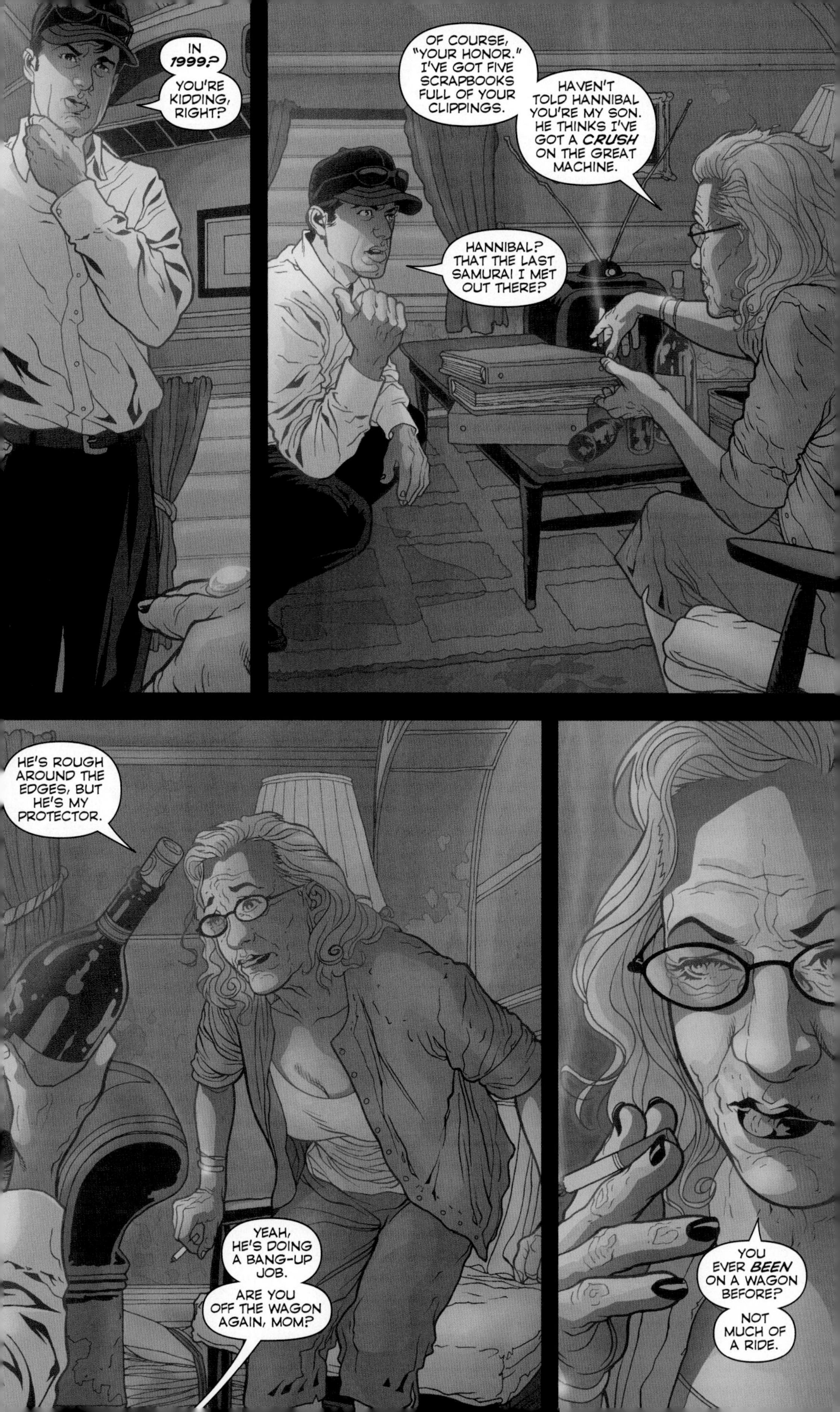
IN *1999?*
YOU'RE KIDDING, RIGHT?
OF COURSE, "YOUR HONOR." I'VE GOT FIVE SCRAPBOOKS FULL OF YOUR CLIPPINGS.
HAVEN'T TOLD HANNIBAL YOU'RE MY SON. HE THINKS I'VE GOT A *CRUSH* ON THE GREAT MACHINE.
HANNIBAL? THAT THE LAST SAMURAI I MET OUT THERE?
HE'S ROUGH AROUND THE EDGES, BUT HE'S MY PROTECTOR.
YEAH, HE'S DOING A BANG-UP JOB.
ARE YOU OFF THE WAGON AGAIN, MOM?
YOU EVER *BEEN* ON A WAGON BEFORE?
NOT MUCH OF A RIDE.

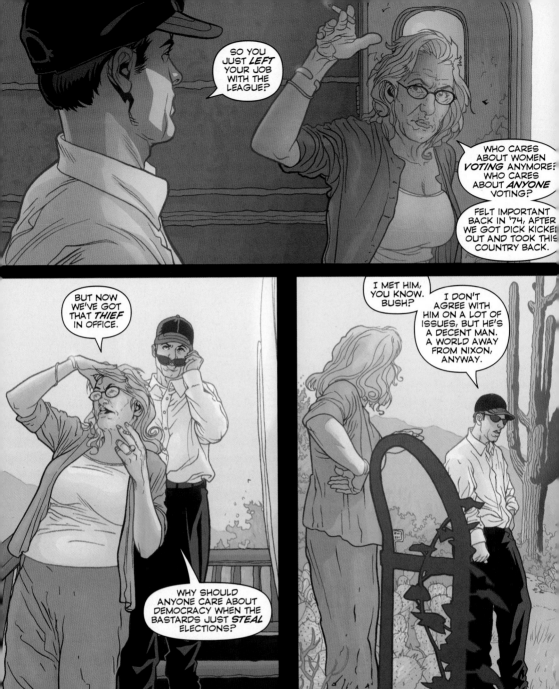

SO YOU JUST *LEFT* YOUR JOB WITH THE LEAGUE?

WHO CARES ABOUT WOMEN *VOTING* ANYMORE? WHO CARES ABOUT *ANYONE* VOTING?

FELT IMPORTANT BACK IN '74, AFTER WE GOT DICK KICKED OUT AND TOOK THIS COUNTRY BACK.

BUT NOW WE'VE GOT THAT *THIEF* IN OFFICE.

WHY SHOULD ANYONE CARE ABOUT DEMOCRACY WHEN THE BASTARDS JUST *STEAL* ELECTIONS?

I MET HIM, YOU KNOW. BUSH?

I DON'T AGREE WITH HIM ON A LOT OF ISSUES, BUT HE'S A DECENT MAN. A WORLD AWAY FROM NIXON, ANYWAY.

...
I NEED A *DRINK*.

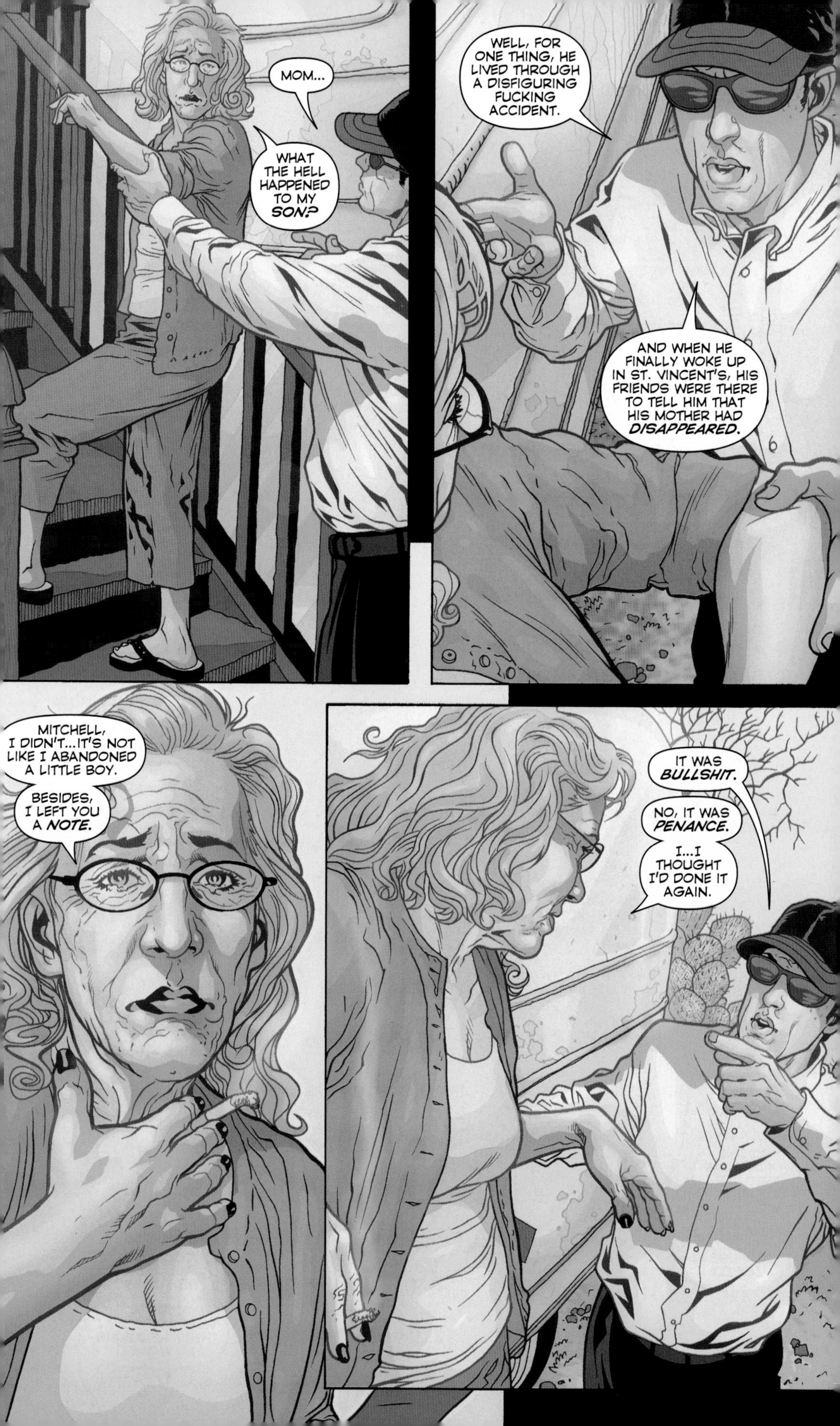
MOM...
WHAT THE HELL HAPPENED TO MY SON?
WELL, FOR ONE THING, HE LIVED THROUGH A DISFIGURING FUCKING ACCIDENT.
AND WHEN HE FINALLY WOKE UP IN ST. VINCENT'S, HIS FRIENDS WERE THERE TO TELL HIM THAT HIS MOTHER HAD DISAPPEARED.
MITCHELL, I DIDN'T...IT'S NOT LIKE I ABANDONED A LITTLE BOY.
BESIDES, I LEFT YOU A NOTE.
IT WAS BULLSHIT.
NO, IT WAS PENANCE.
I...I THOUGHT I'D DONE IT AGAIN.

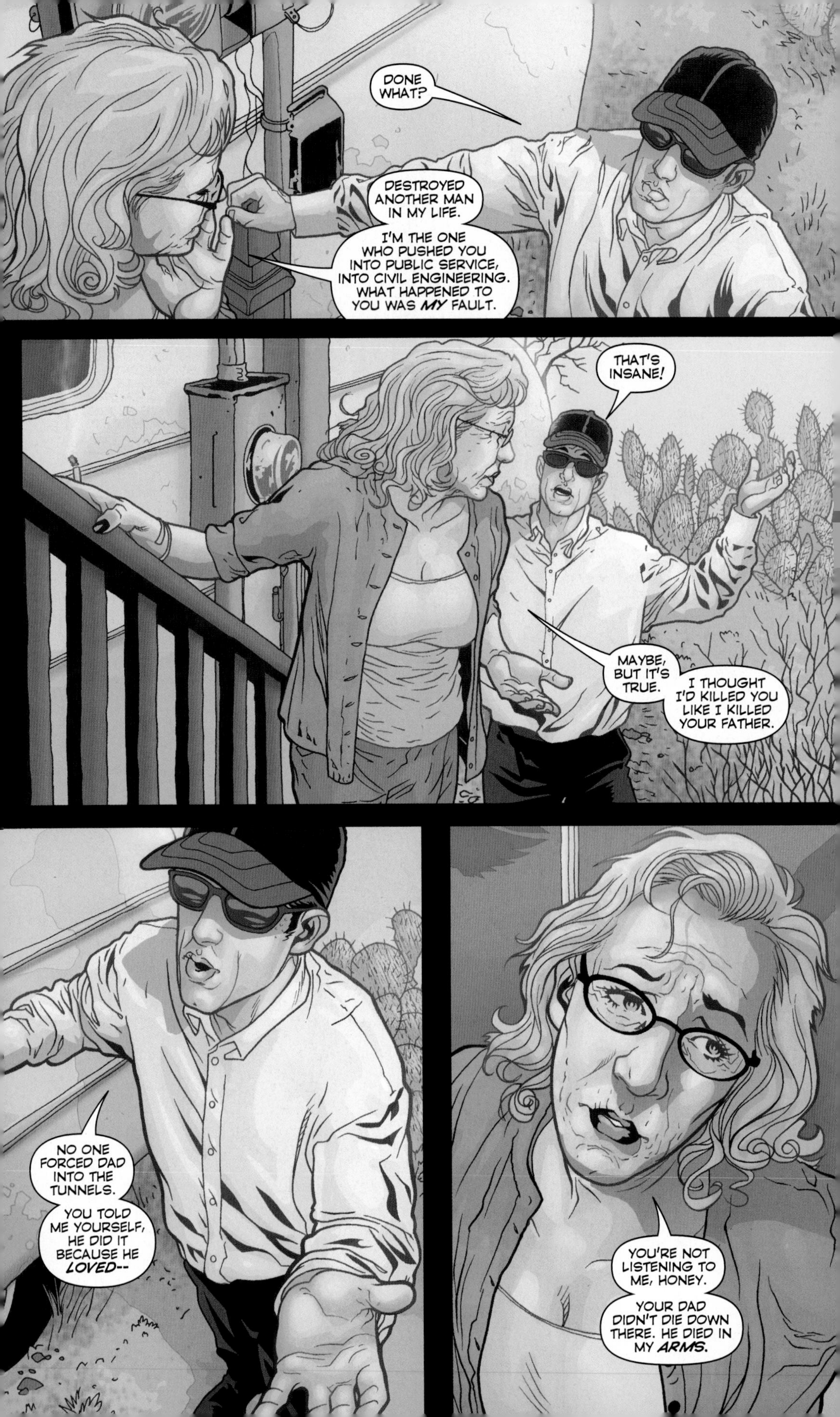
DONE WHAT?
DESTROYED ANOTHER MAN IN MY LIFE.
I'M THE ONE WHO PUSHED YOU INTO PUBLIC SERVICE, INTO CIVIL ENGINEERING. WHAT HAPPENED TO YOU WAS MY FAULT.
THAT'S INSANE!
MAYBE, BUT IT'S TRUE.
I THOUGHT I'D KILLED YOU LIKE I KILLED YOUR FATHER.
NO ONE FORCED DAD INTO THE TUNNELS.
YOU TOLD ME YOURSELF, HE DID IT BECAUSE HE LOVED--
YOU'RE NOT LISTENING TO ME, HONEY.
YOUR DAD DIDN'T DIE DOWN THERE. HE DIED IN MY ARMS.

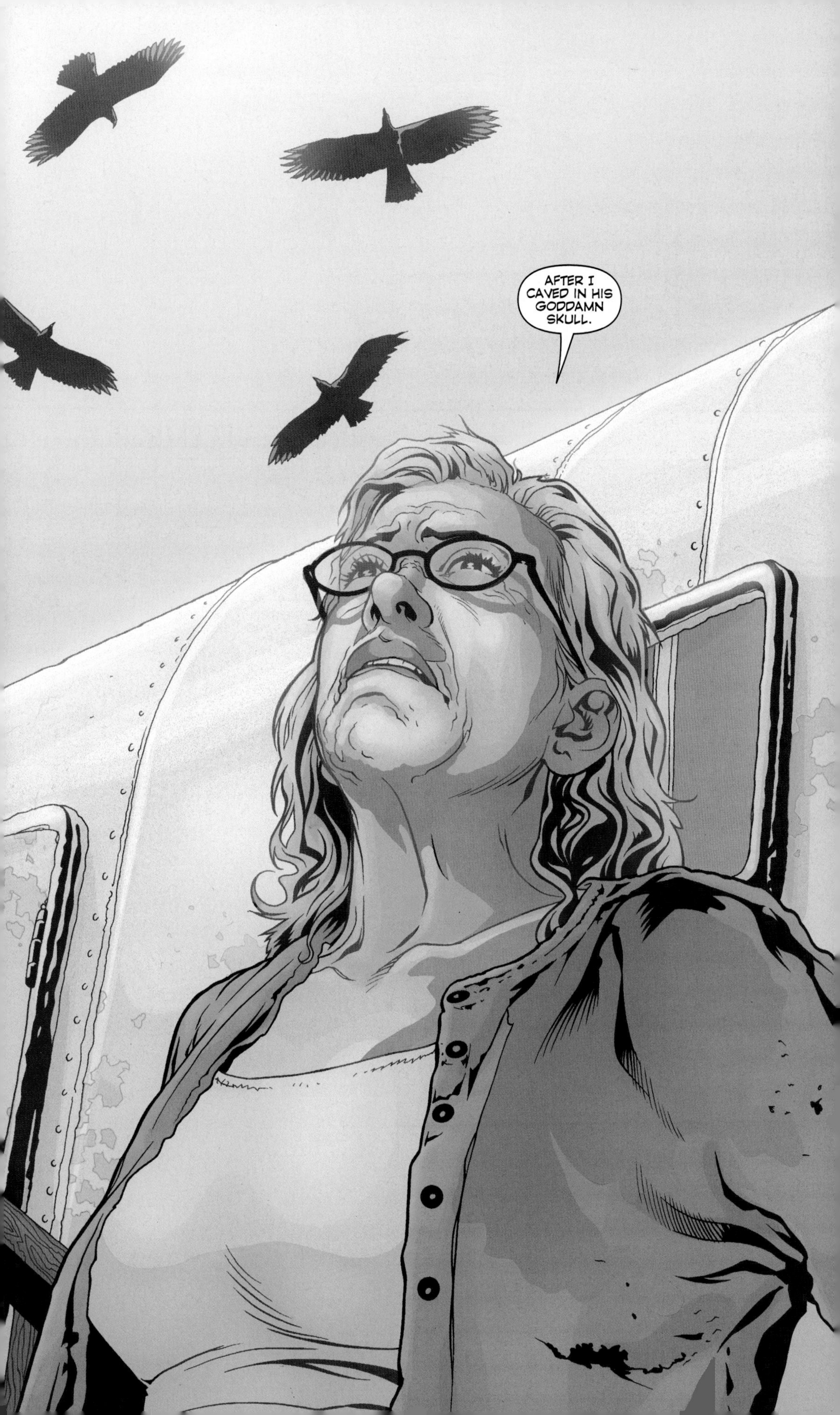
AFTER I CAVED IN HIS GODDAMN SKULL.

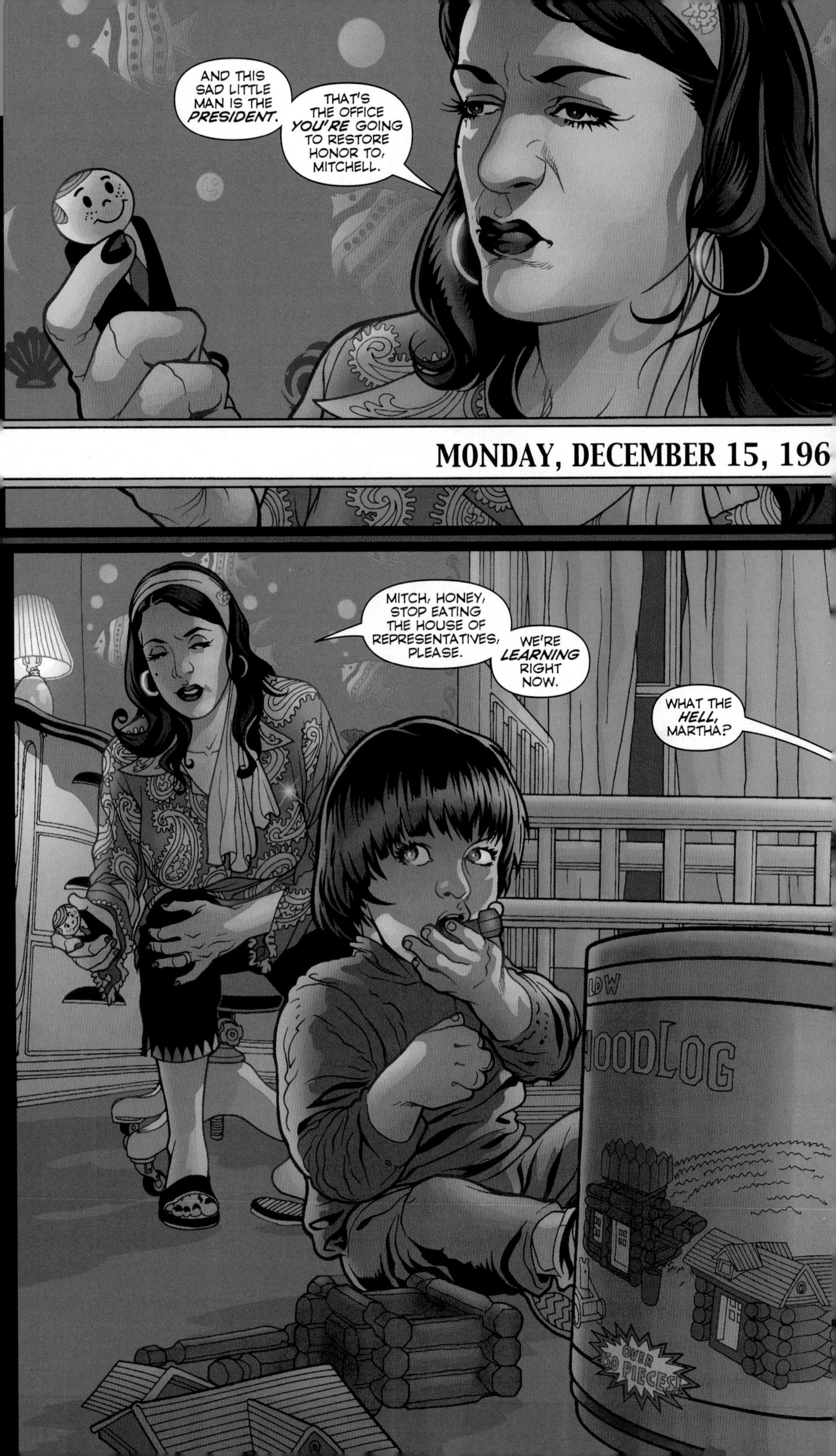
AND THIS SAD LITTLE MAN IS THE PRESIDENT.
THAT'S THE OFFICE YOU'RE GOING TO RESTORE HONOR TO, MITCHELL.
MONDAY, DECEMBER 15, 196
MITCH, HONEY, STOP EATING THE HOUSE OF REPRESENTATIVES, PLEASE.
WE'RE LEARNING RIGHT NOW.
WHAT THE HELL, MARTHA?
LDW
WOODLOG
OVER 150 PIECES!

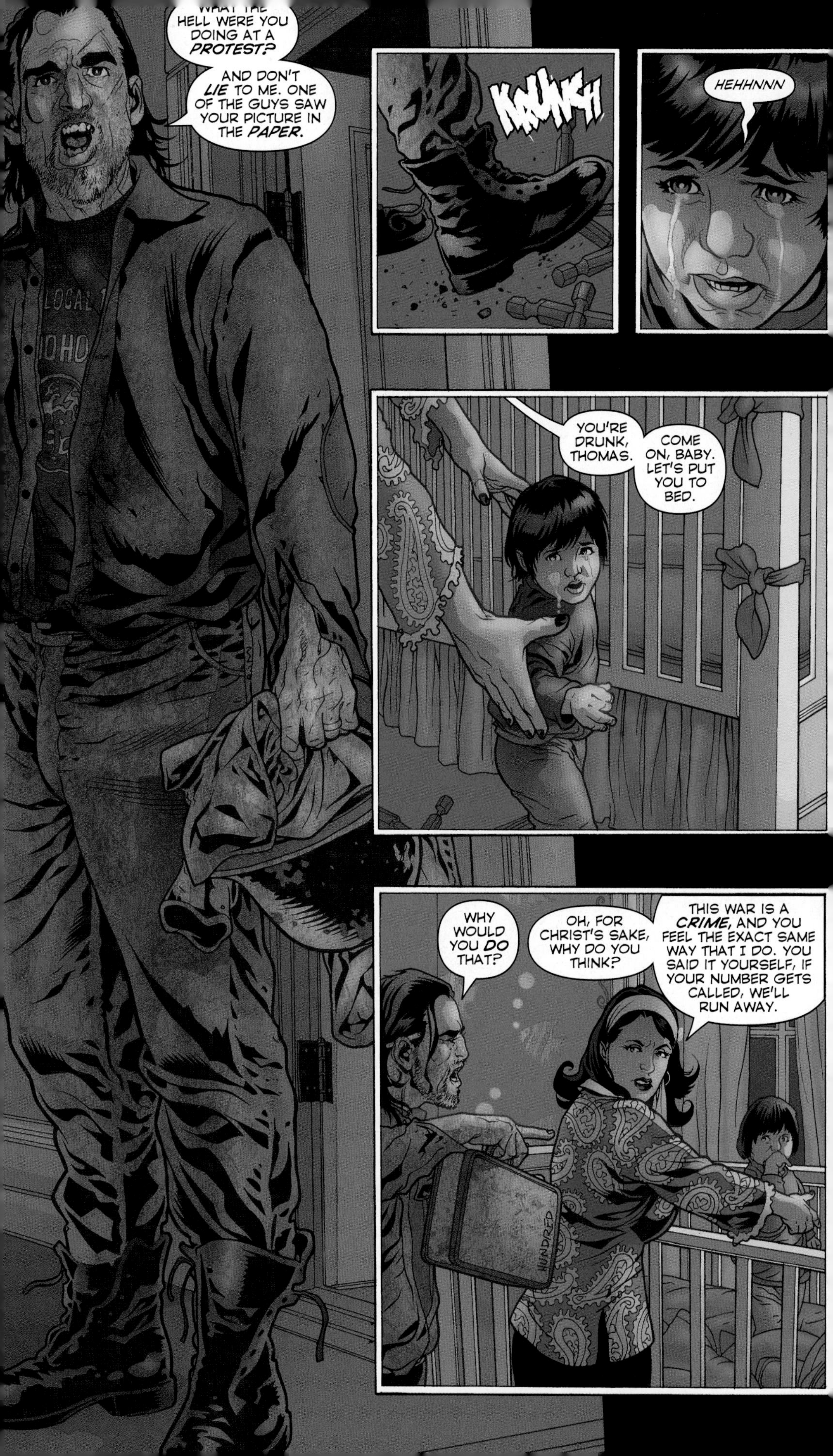
WHAT THE HELL WERE YOU DOING AT A *PROTEST?*
AND DON'T *LIE* TO ME. ONE OF THE GUYS SAW YOUR PICTURE IN THE *PAPER*.
KRUNCH
HEHHHNNN
YOU'RE DRUNK, THOMAS.
COME ON, BABY. LET'S PUT YOU TO BED.
WHY WOULD YOU *DO* THAT?
OH, FOR CHRIST'S SAKE, WHY DO YOU THINK?
THIS WAR IS A *CRIME,* AND YOU FEEL THE EXACT SAME WAY THAT I DO. YOU SAID IT YOURSELF, IF YOUR NUMBER GETS CALLED, WE'LL RUN AWAY.
HUNDRED

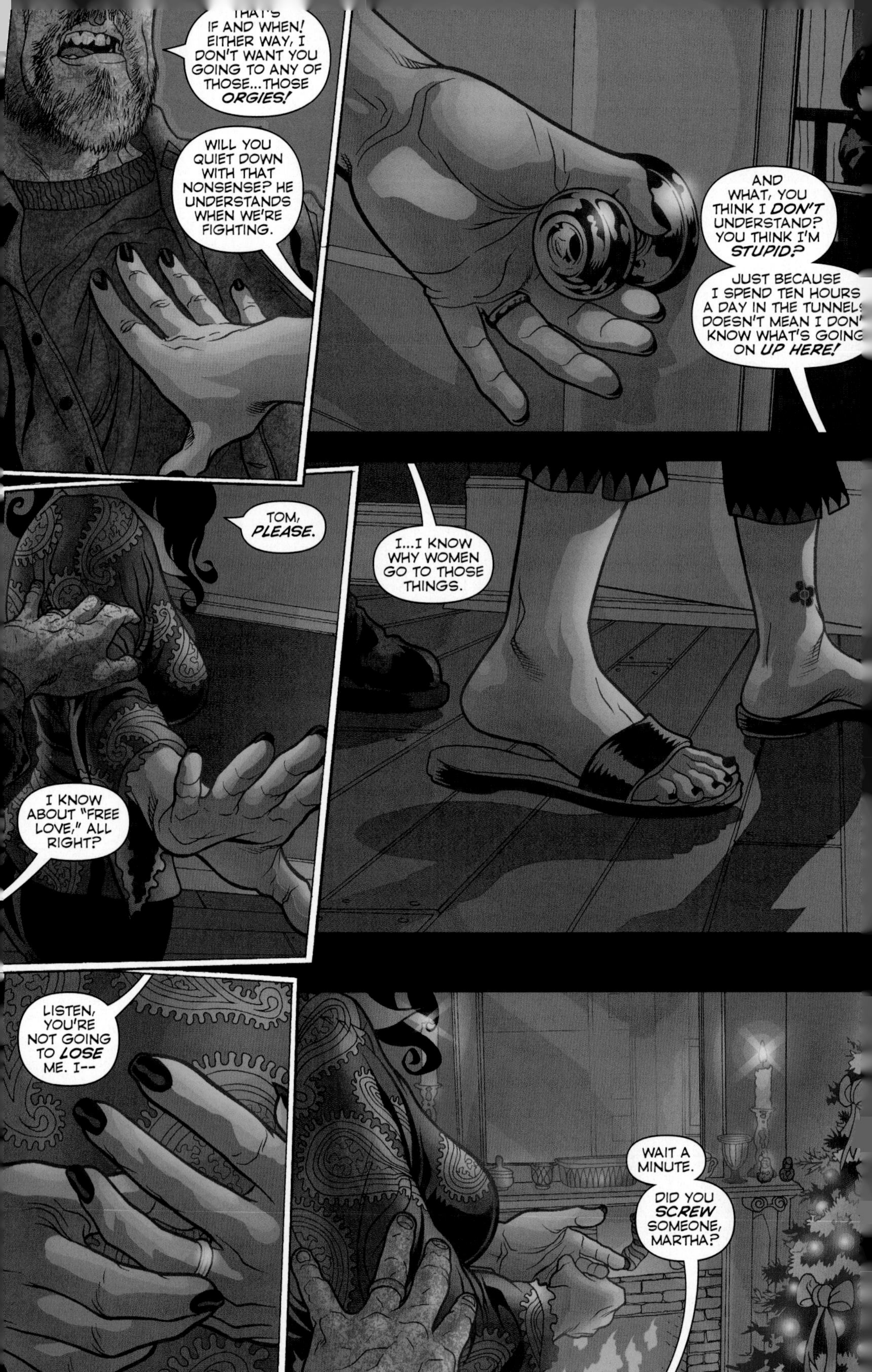
THAT'S IF AND WHEN! EITHER WAY, I DON'T WANT YOU GOING TO ANY OF THOSE...THOSE *ORGIES!*
WILL YOU QUIET DOWN WITH THAT NONSENSE? HE UNDERSTANDS WHEN WE'RE FIGHTING.
AND WHAT, YOU THINK I *DON'T* UNDERSTAND? YOU THINK I'M *STUPID?*
JUST BECAUSE I SPEND TEN HOURS A DAY IN THE TUNNELS DOESN'T MEAN I DON'T KNOW WHAT'S GOING ON *UP HERE!*
TOM, *PLEASE.*
I...I KNOW WHY WOMEN GO TO THOSE THINGS.
I KNOW ABOUT "FREE LOVE," ALL RIGHT?
LISTEN, YOU'RE NOT GOING TO *LOSE* ME. I--
WAIT A MINUTE.
DID YOU *SCREW* SOMEONE, MARTHA?

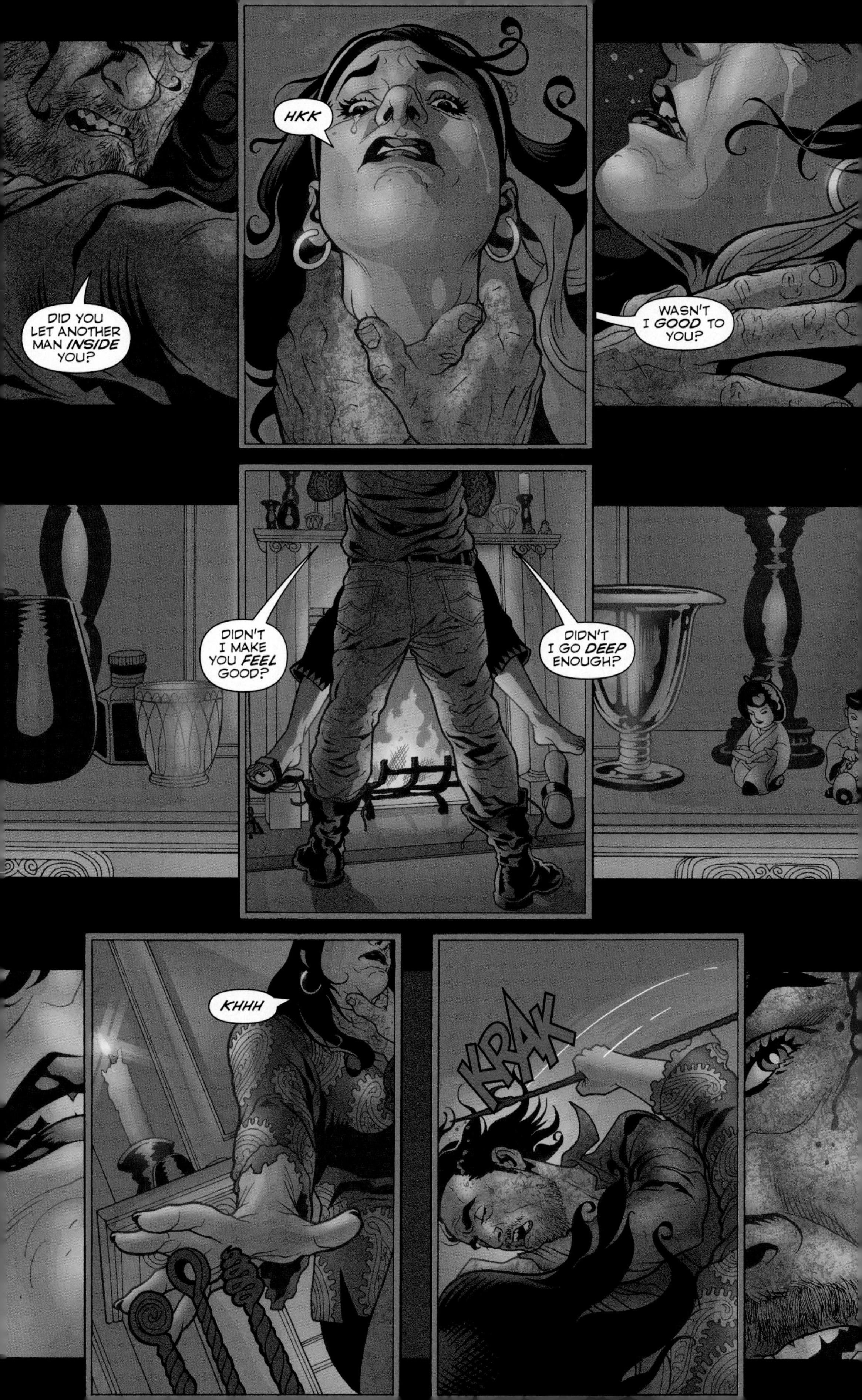
DID YOU LET ANOTHER MAN INSIDE YOU?
HKK
WASN'T I GOOD TO YOU?
DIDN'T I MAKE YOU FEEL GOOD?
DIDN'T I GO DEEP ENOUGH?
KHHH
KRAK

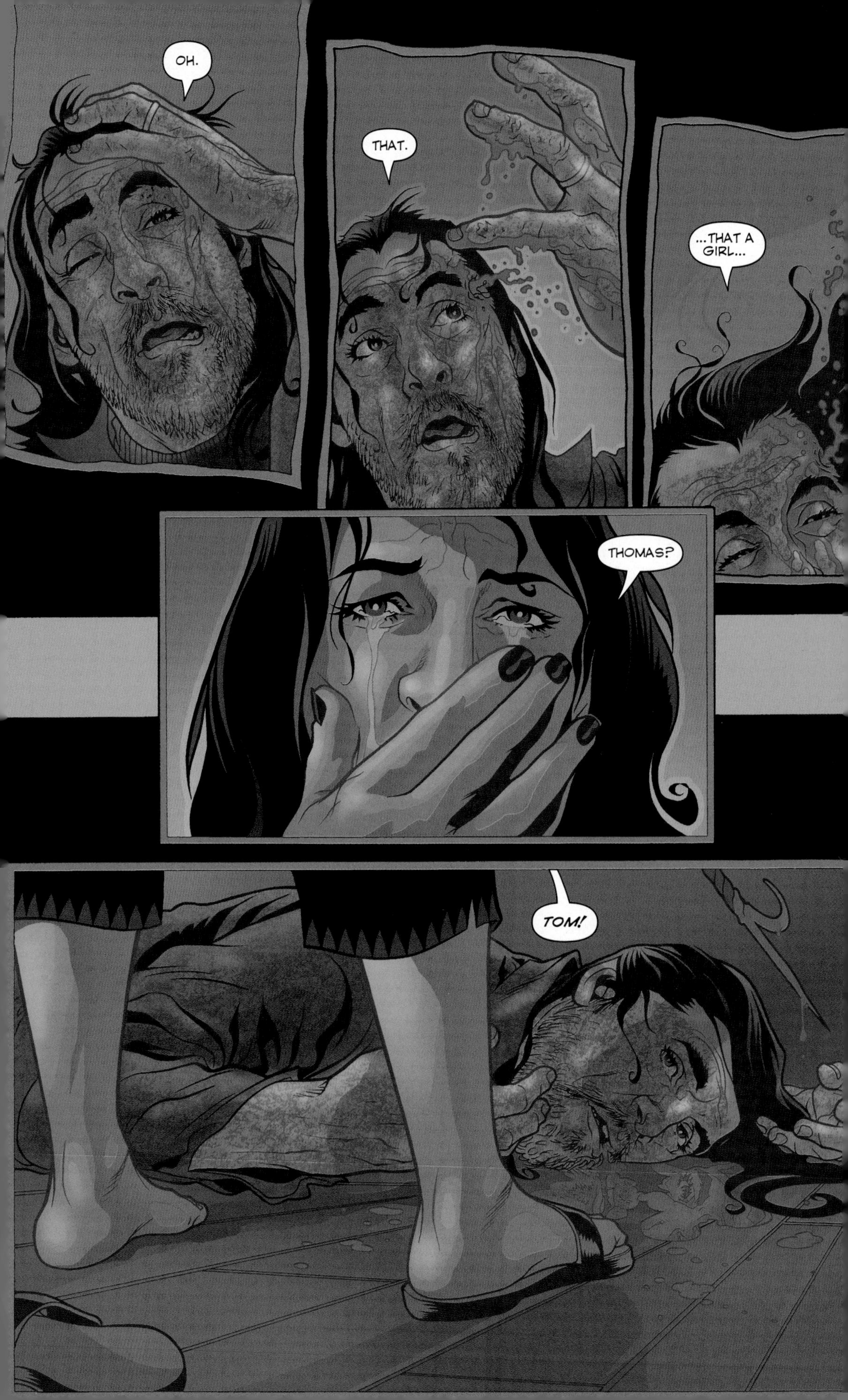
OH.
THAT.
...THAT A GIRL...
THOMAS?
TOM!

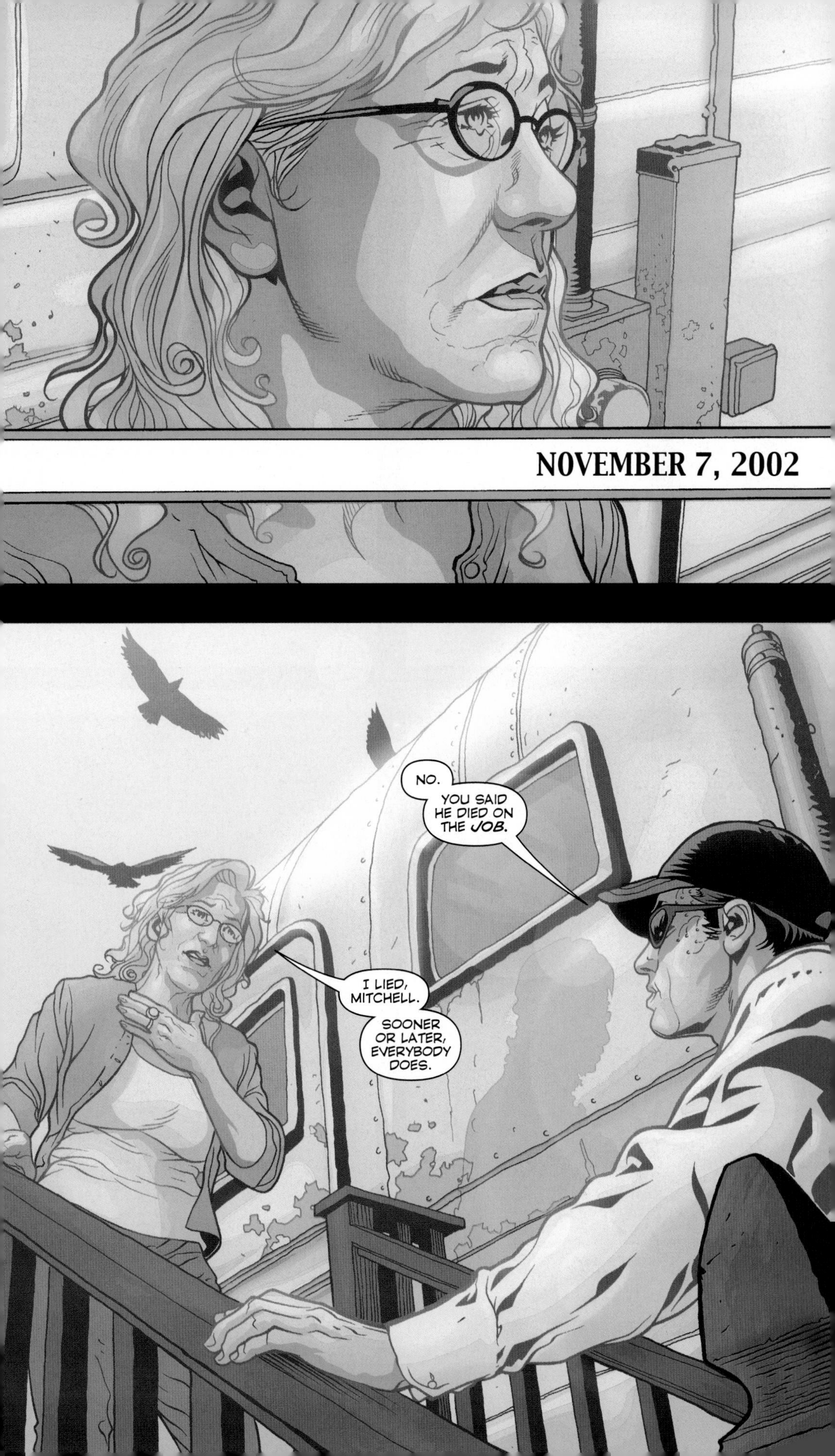
NOVEMBER 7, 2002
NO.
YOU SAID HE DIED ON THE JOB.
I LIED, MITCHELL.
SOONER OR LATER, EVERYBODY DOES.

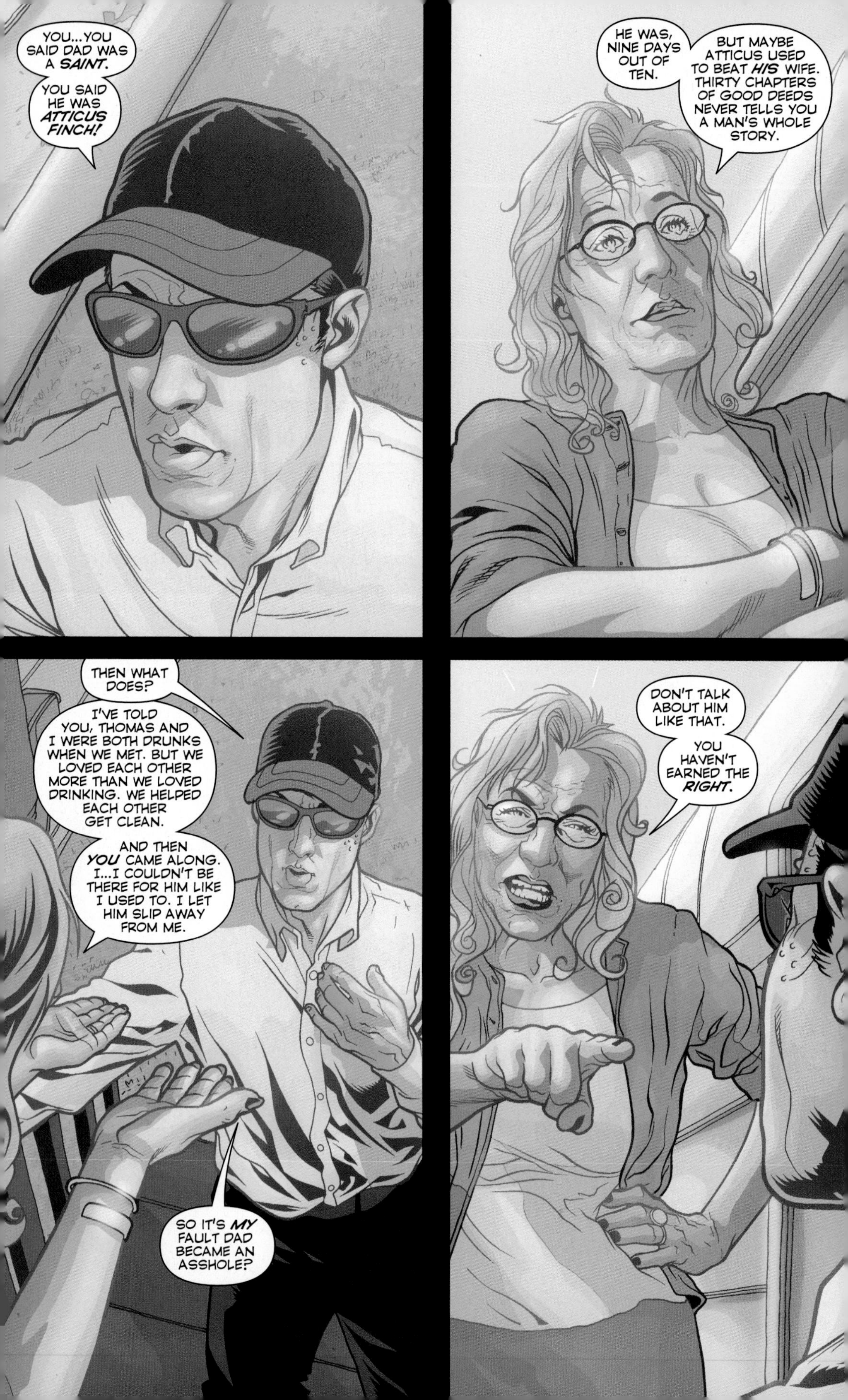
YOU...YOU SAID DAD WAS A *SAINT*.
YOU SAID HE WAS *ATTICUS FINCH!*
HE WAS, NINE DAYS OUT OF TEN.
BUT MAYBE ATTICUS USED TO BEAT *HIS* WIFE. THIRTY CHAPTERS OF GOOD DEEDS NEVER TELLS YOU A MAN'S WHOLE STORY.
THEN WHAT DOES?
I'VE TOLD YOU, THOMAS AND I WERE BOTH DRUNKS WHEN WE MET. BUT WE LOVED EACH OTHER MORE THAN WE LOVED DRINKING. WE HELPED EACH OTHER GET CLEAN.
AND THEN *YOU* CAME ALONG. I...I COULDN'T BE THERE FOR HIM LIKE I USED TO. I LET HIM SLIP AWAY FROM ME.
SO IT'S *MY* FAULT DAD BECAME AN ASSHOLE?
DON'T TALK ABOUT HIM LIKE THAT.
YOU HAVEN'T EARNED THE *RIGHT*.

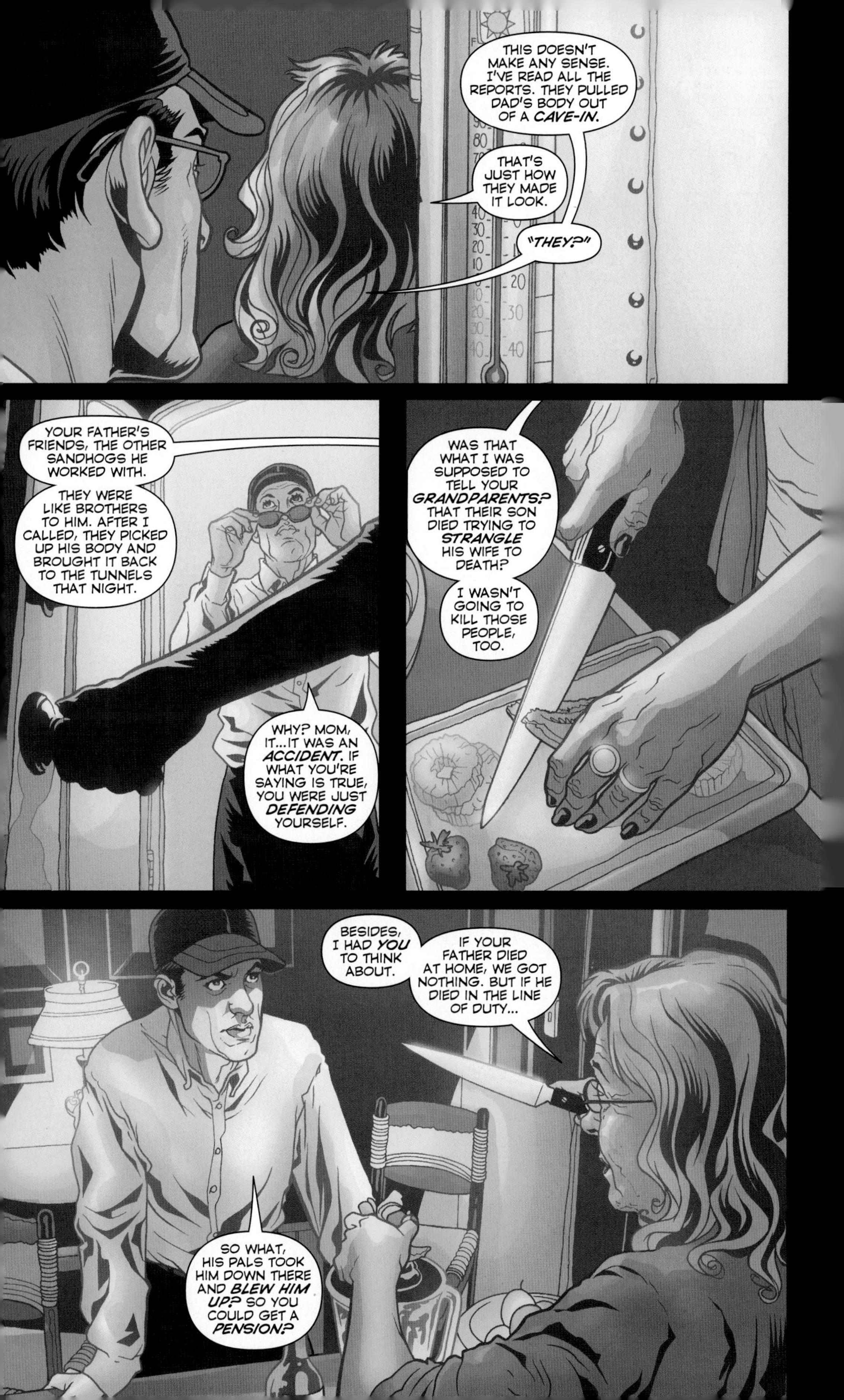
THIS DOESN'T MAKE ANY SENSE. I'VE READ ALL THE REPORTS. THEY PULLED DAD'S BODY OUT OF A CAVE-IN.
THAT'S JUST HOW THEY MADE IT LOOK.
"THEY?"
YOUR FATHER'S FRIENDS, THE OTHER SANDHOGS HE WORKED WITH.
THEY WERE LIKE BROTHERS TO HIM. AFTER I CALLED, THEY PICKED UP HIS BODY AND BROUGHT IT BACK TO THE TUNNELS THAT NIGHT.
WHY? MOM, IT...IT WAS AN ACCIDENT. IF WHAT YOU'RE SAYING WAS TRUE, YOU WERE JUST DEFENDING YOURSELF.
WAS THAT WHAT I WAS SUPPOSED TO TELL YOUR GRANDPARENTS? THAT THEIR SON DIED TRYING TO STRANGLE HIS WIFE TO DEATH?
I WASN'T GOING TO KILL THOSE PEOPLE, TOO.
BESIDES, I HAD YOU TO THINK ABOUT.
IF YOUR FATHER DIED AT HOME, WE GOT NOTHING. BUT IF HE DIED IN THE LINE OF DUTY...
SO WHAT, HIS PALS TOOK HIM DOWN THERE AND BLEW HIM UP? SO YOU COULD GET A PENSION?

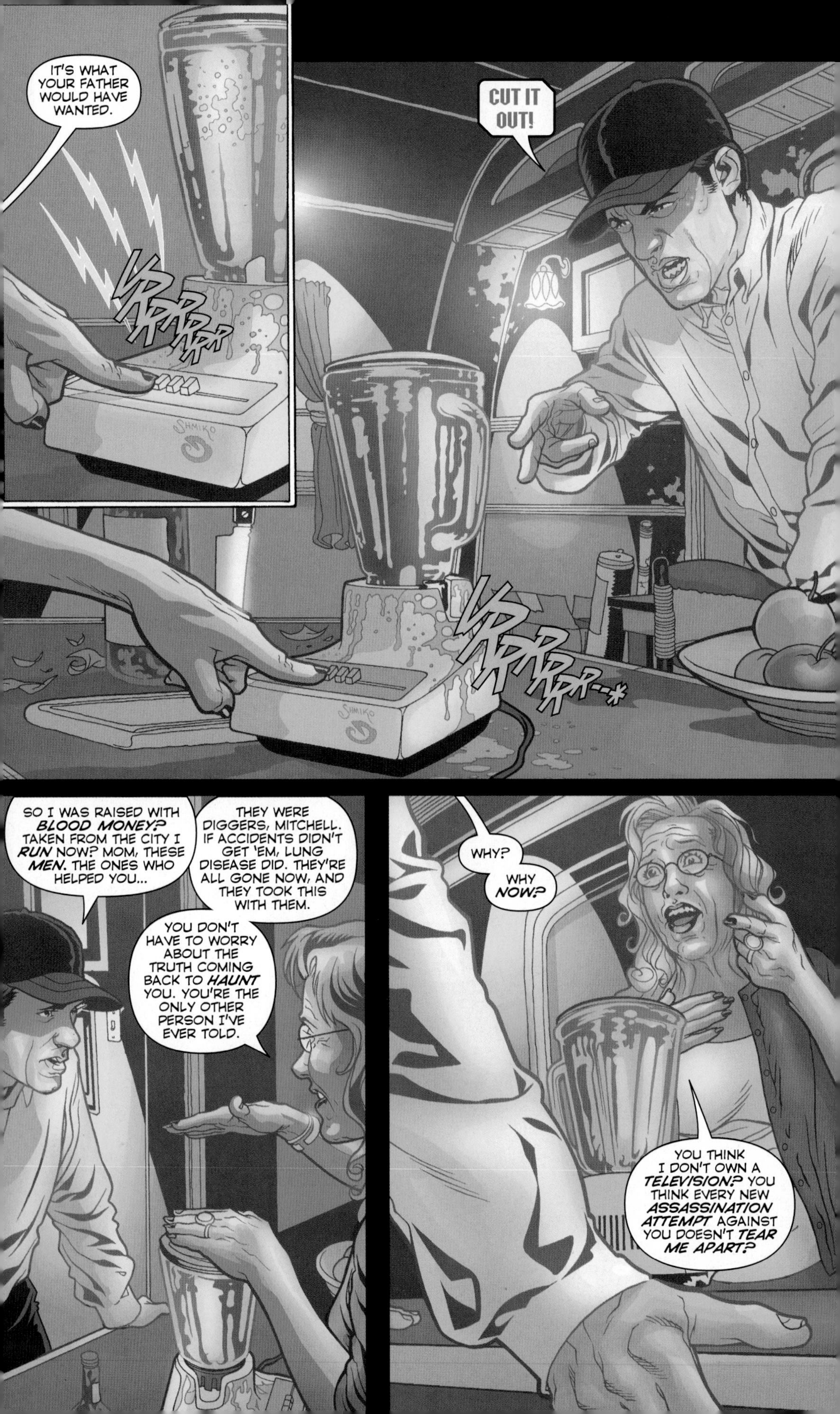
IT'S WHAT YOUR FATHER WOULD HAVE WANTED.
VRRRRRR
SHMIKO
CUT IT OUT!
VRRRRRR--*
SHMIKO
SO I WAS RAISED WITH BLOOD MONEY? TAKEN FROM THE CITY I RUN NOW? MOM, THESE MEN. THE ONES WHO HELPED YOU...
THEY WERE DIGGERS, MITCHELL. IF ACCIDENTS DIDN'T GET 'EM, LUNG DISEASE DID. THEY'RE ALL GONE NOW, AND THEY TOOK THIS WITH THEM.
YOU DON'T HAVE TO WORRY ABOUT THE TRUTH COMING BACK TO HAUNT YOU. YOU'RE THE ONLY OTHER PERSON I'VE EVER TOLD.
WHY?
WHY NOW?
YOU THINK I DON'T OWN A TELEVISION? YOU THINK EVERY NEW ASSASSINATION ATTEMPT AGAINST YOU DOESN'T TEAR ME APART?

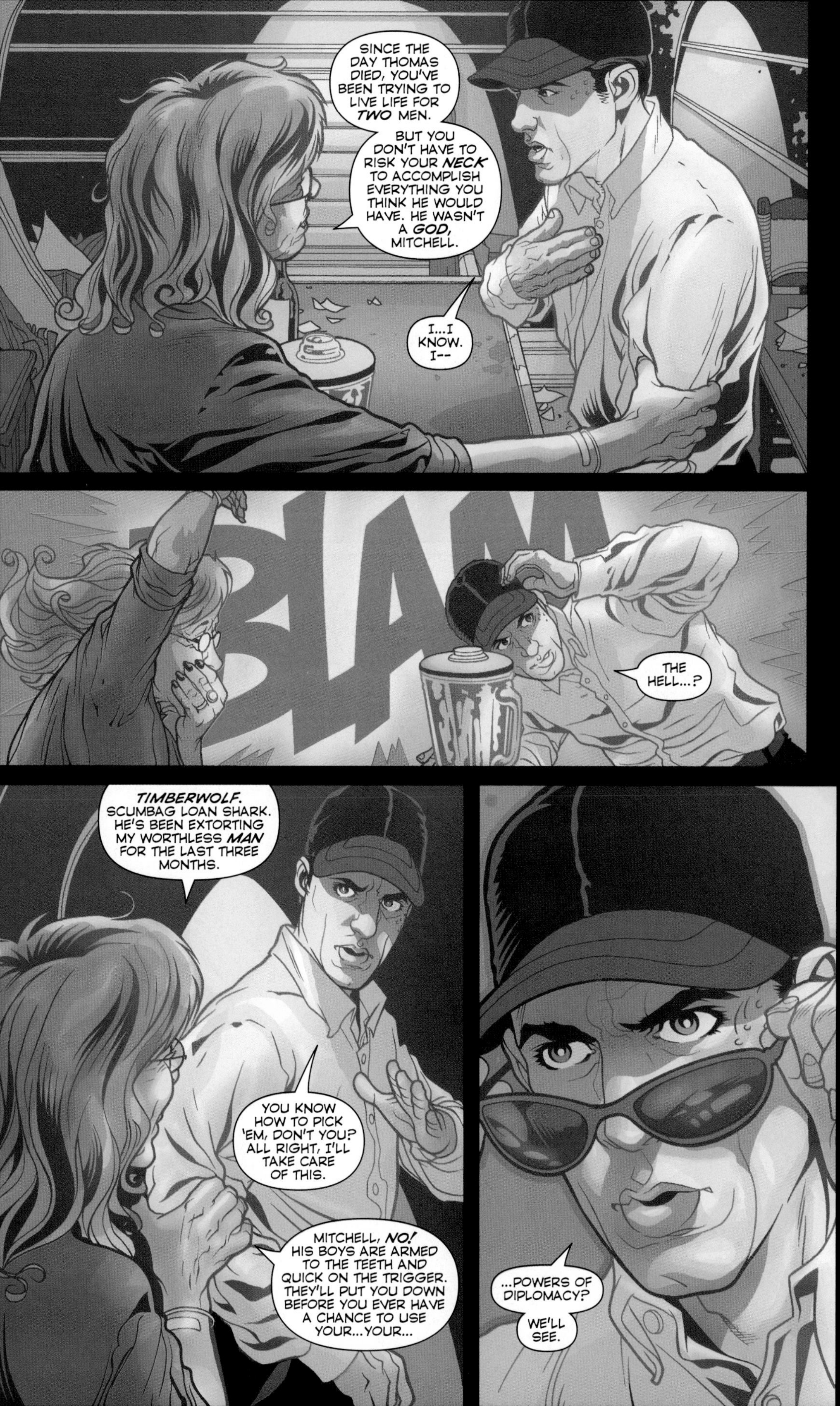
SINCE THE DAY THOMAS DIED, YOU'VE BEEN TRYING TO LIVE LIFE FOR TWO MEN.
BUT YOU DON'T HAVE TO RISK YOUR NECK TO ACCOMPLISH EVERYTHING YOU THINK HE WOULD HAVE. HE WASN'T A GOD, MITCHELL.
I...I KNOW. I--
BLAM
THE HELL...?
TIMBERWOLF. SCUMBAG LOAN SHARK. HE'S BEEN EXTORTING MY WORTHLESS MAN FOR THE LAST THREE MONTHS.
YOU KNOW HOW TO PICK 'EM, DON'T YOU? ALL RIGHT, I'LL TAKE CARE OF THIS.
MITCHELL, NO! HIS BOYS ARE ARMED TO THE TEETH AND QUICK ON THE TRIGGER. THEY'LL PUT YOU DOWN BEFORE YOU EVER HAVE A CHANCE TO USE YOUR...YOUR...
...POWERS OF DIPLOMACY?
WE'LL SEE.

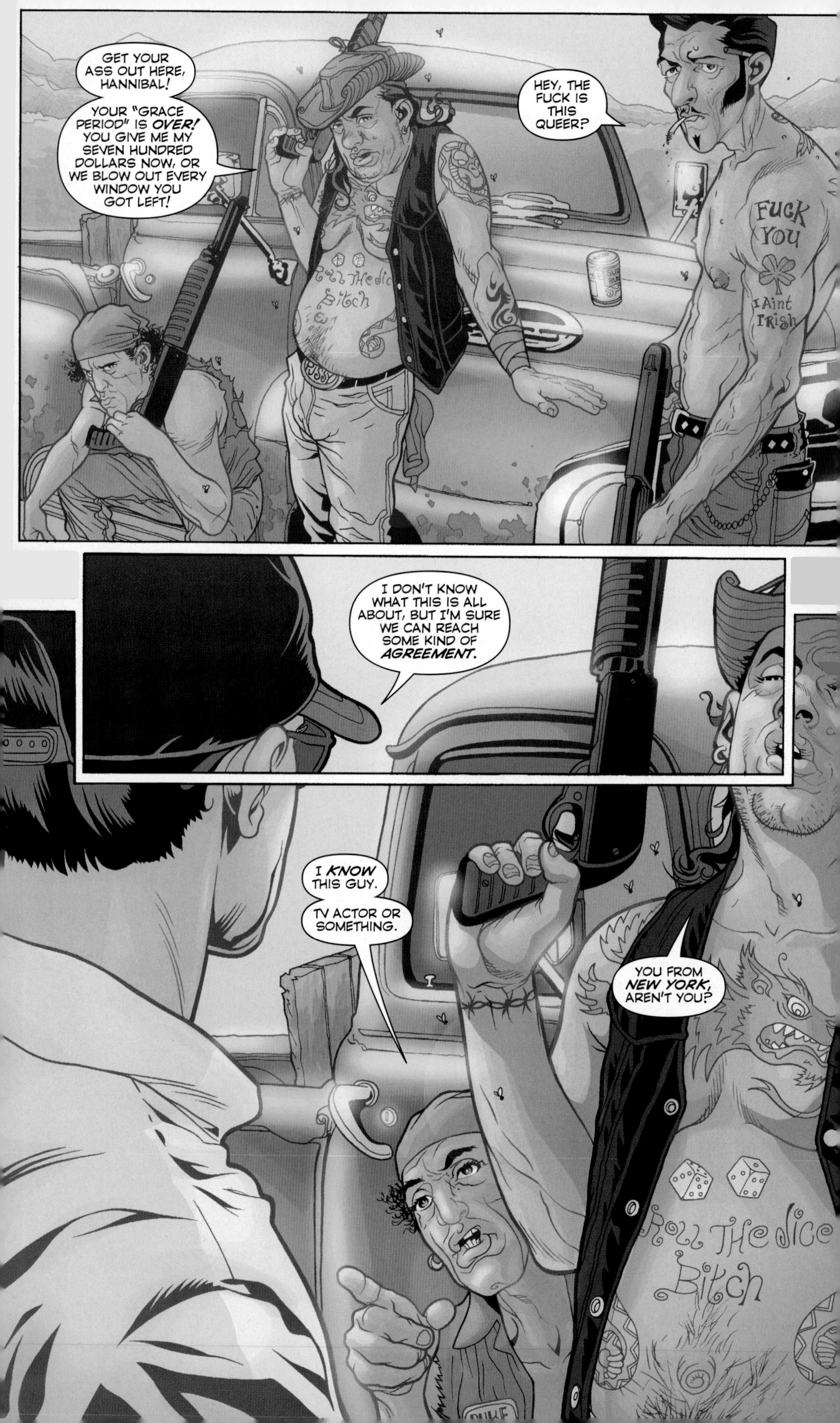
GET YOUR ASS OUT HERE, HANNIBAL!
YOUR "GRACE PERIOD" IS *OVER!* YOU GIVE ME MY SEVEN HUNDRED DOLLARS NOW, OR WE BLOW OUT EVERY WINDOW YOU GOT LEFT!
HEY, THE FUCK IS THIS QUEER?
I DON'T KNOW WHAT THIS IS ALL ABOUT, BUT I'M SURE WE CAN REACH SOME KIND OF *AGREEMENT*.
I *KNOW* THIS GUY.
TV ACTOR OR SOMETHING.
YOU FROM *NEW YORK*, AREN'T YOU?

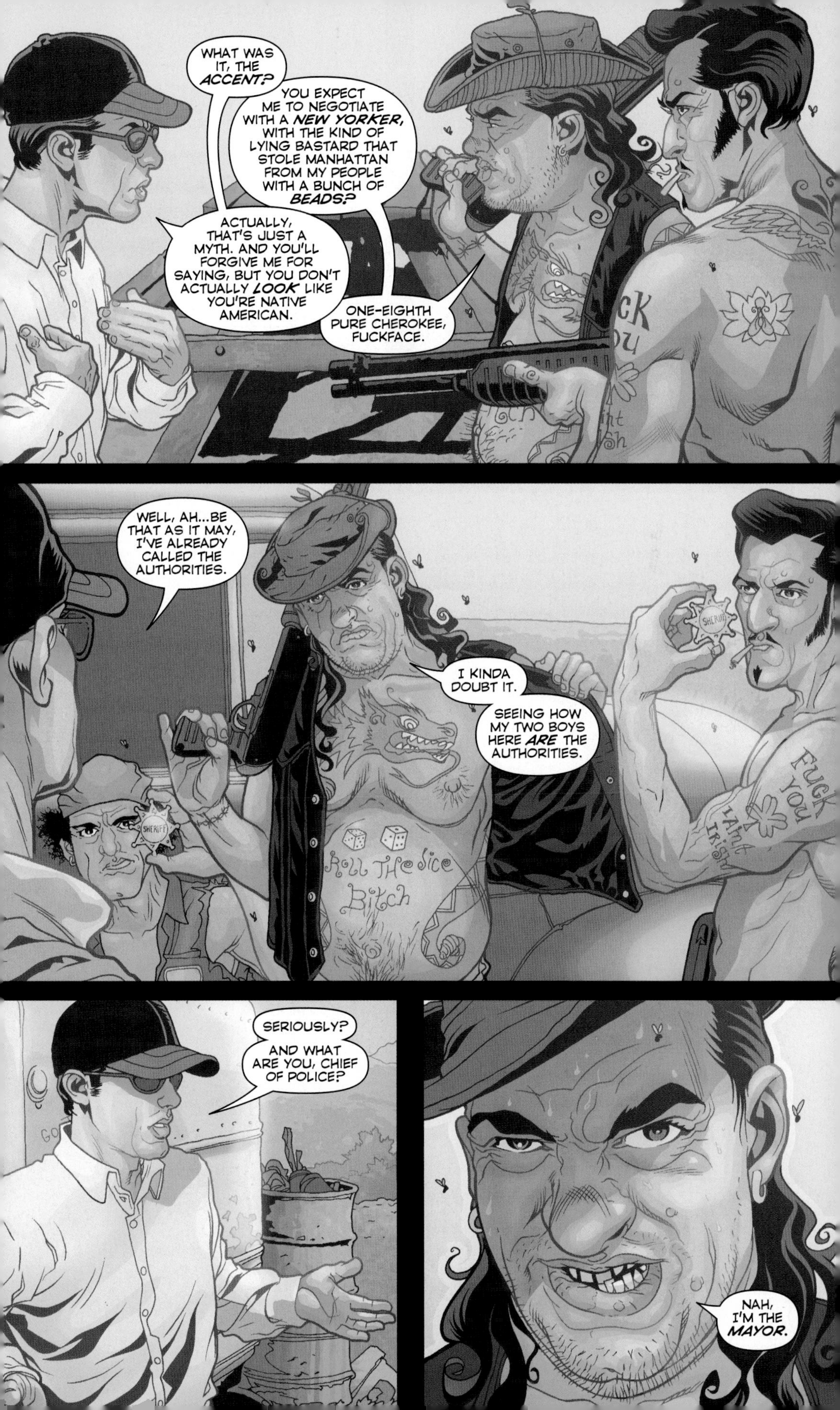
WHAT WAS IT, THE *ACCENT?*
YOU EXPECT ME TO NEGOTIATE WITH A *NEW YORKER,* WITH THE KIND OF LYING BASTARD THAT STOLE MANHATTAN FROM MY PEOPLE WITH A BUNCH OF *BEADS?*
ACTUALLY, THAT'S JUST A MYTH. AND YOU'LL FORGIVE ME FOR SAYING, BUT YOU DON'T ACTUALLY *LOOK* LIKE YOU'RE NATIVE AMERICAN.
ONE-EIGHTH PURE CHEROKEE, FUCKFACE.
WELL, AH...BE THAT AS IT MAY, I'VE ALREADY CALLED THE AUTHORITIES.
SHERIFF
I KINDA DOUBT IT.
SEEING HOW MY TWO BOYS HERE *ARE* THE AUTHORITIES.
SHERIFF
Roll The dice Bitch
FUCK YOU
I Ain't Irish
SERIOUSLY?
AND WHAT ARE YOU, CHIEF OF POLICE?
NAH, I'M THE *MAYOR.*

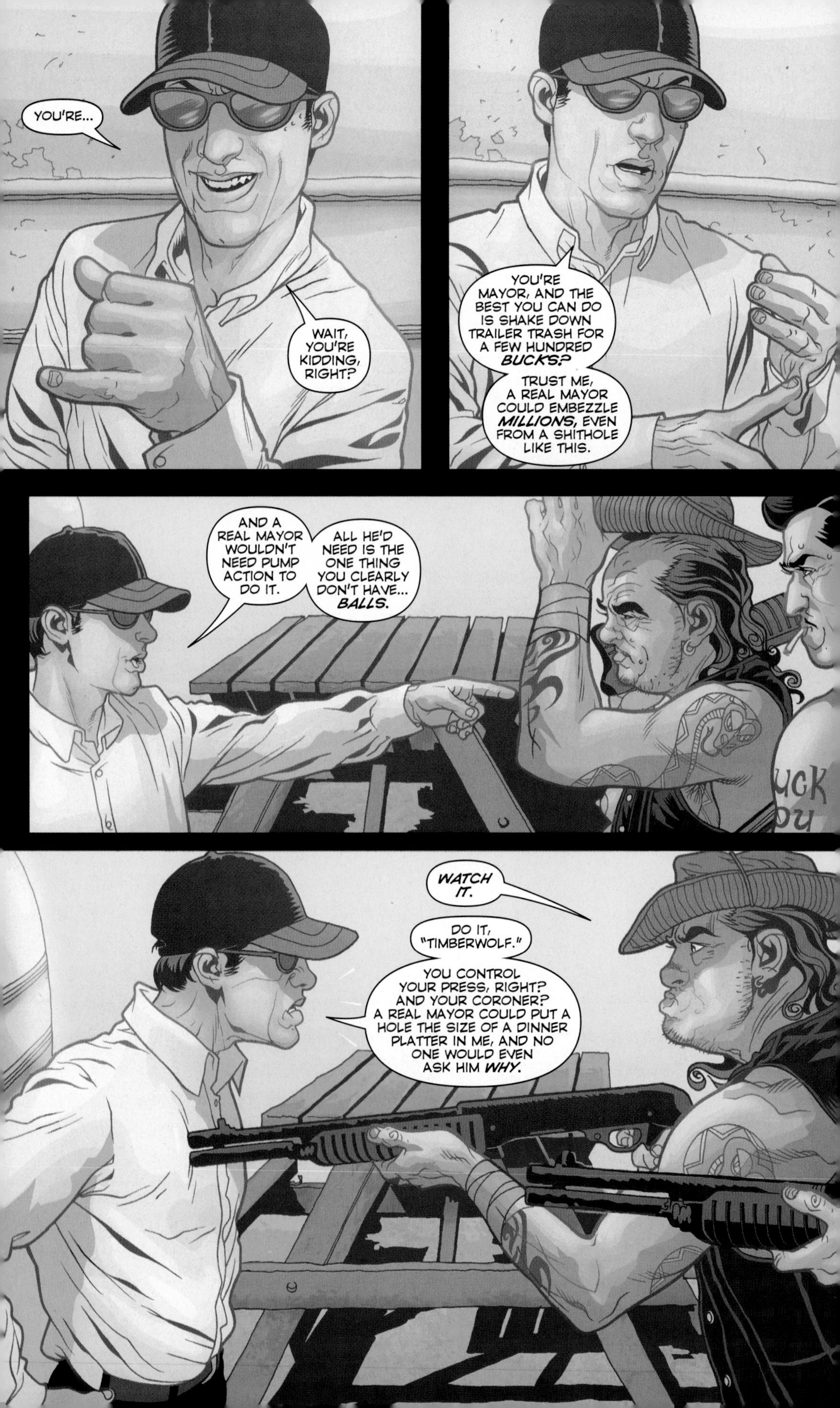
YOU'RE...
WAIT, YOU'RE KIDDING, RIGHT?
YOU'RE MAYOR, AND THE BEST YOU CAN DO IS SHAKE DOWN TRAILER TRASH FOR A FEW HUNDRED BUCKS?
TRUST ME, A REAL MAYOR COULD EMBEZZLE MILLIONS, EVEN FROM A SHITHOLE LIKE THIS.
AND A REAL MAYOR WOULDN'T NEED PUMP ACTION TO DO IT.
ALL HE'D NEED IS THE ONE THING YOU CLEARLY DON'T HAVE... BALLS.
WATCH IT.
DO IT, "TIMBERWOLF."
YOU CONTROL YOUR PRESS, RIGHT? AND YOUR CORONER? A REAL MAYOR COULD PUT A HOLE THE SIZE OF A DINNER PLATTER IN ME, AND NO ONE WOULD EVEN ASK HIM WHY.

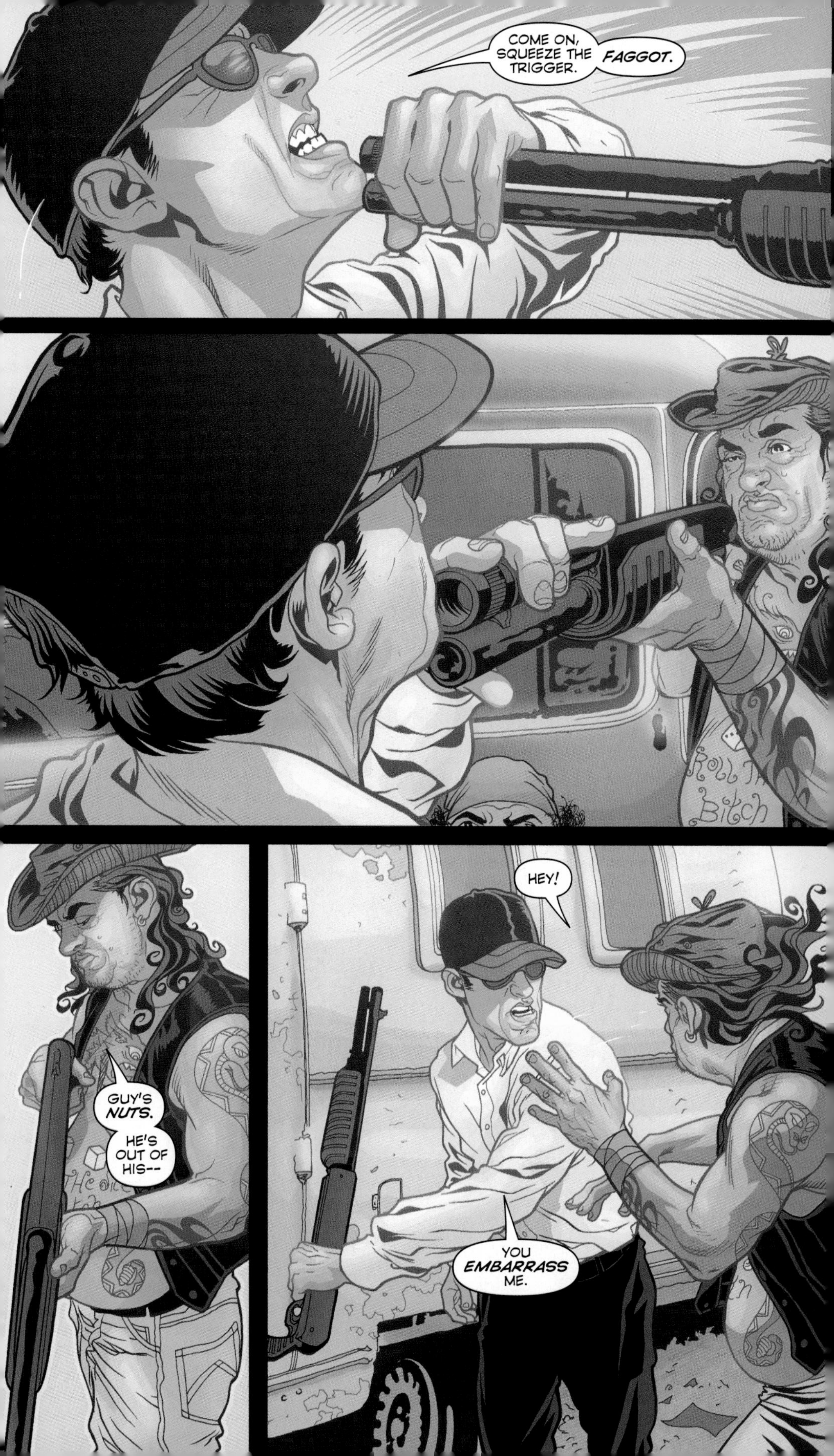

COME ON, SQUEEZE THE TRIGGER.
*FAGGOT.*
GUY'S *NUTS.*
HE'S OUT OF HIS--
HEY!
YOU *EMBARRASS* ME.

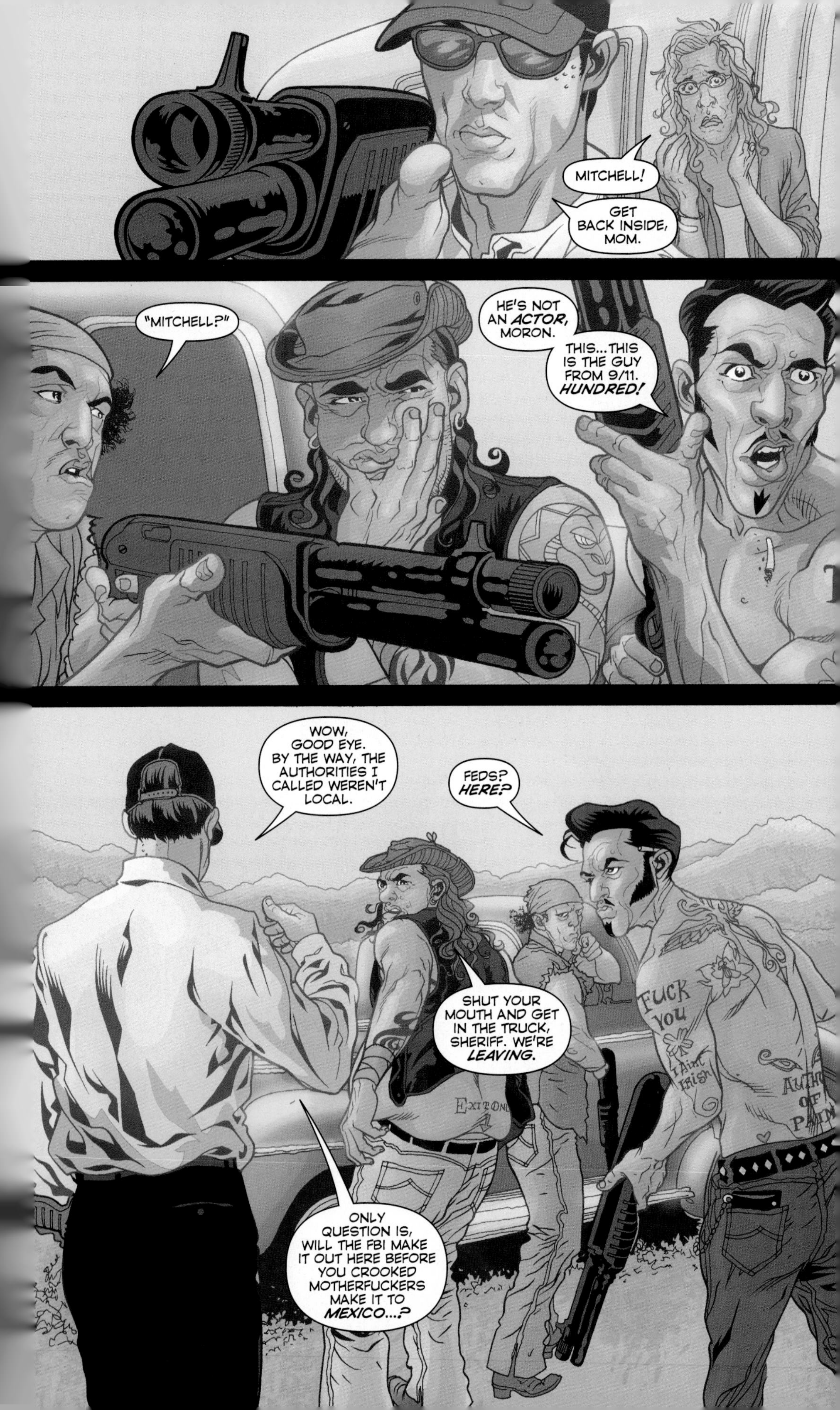

MITCHELL!
GET BACK INSIDE, MOM.
"MITCHELL?"
HE'S NOT AN ACTOR, MORON.
THIS...THIS IS THE GUY FROM 9/11. HUNDRED!
WOW, GOOD EYE. BY THE WAY, THE AUTHORITIES I CALLED WEREN'T LOCAL.
FEDS? HERE?
SHUT YOUR MOUTH AND GET IN THE TRUCK, SHERIFF. WE'RE LEAVING.
ONLY QUESTION IS, WILL THE FBI MAKE IT OUT HERE BEFORE YOU CROOKED MOTHERFUCKERS MAKE IT TO MEXICO...?
FUCK YOU
I Aint Irish

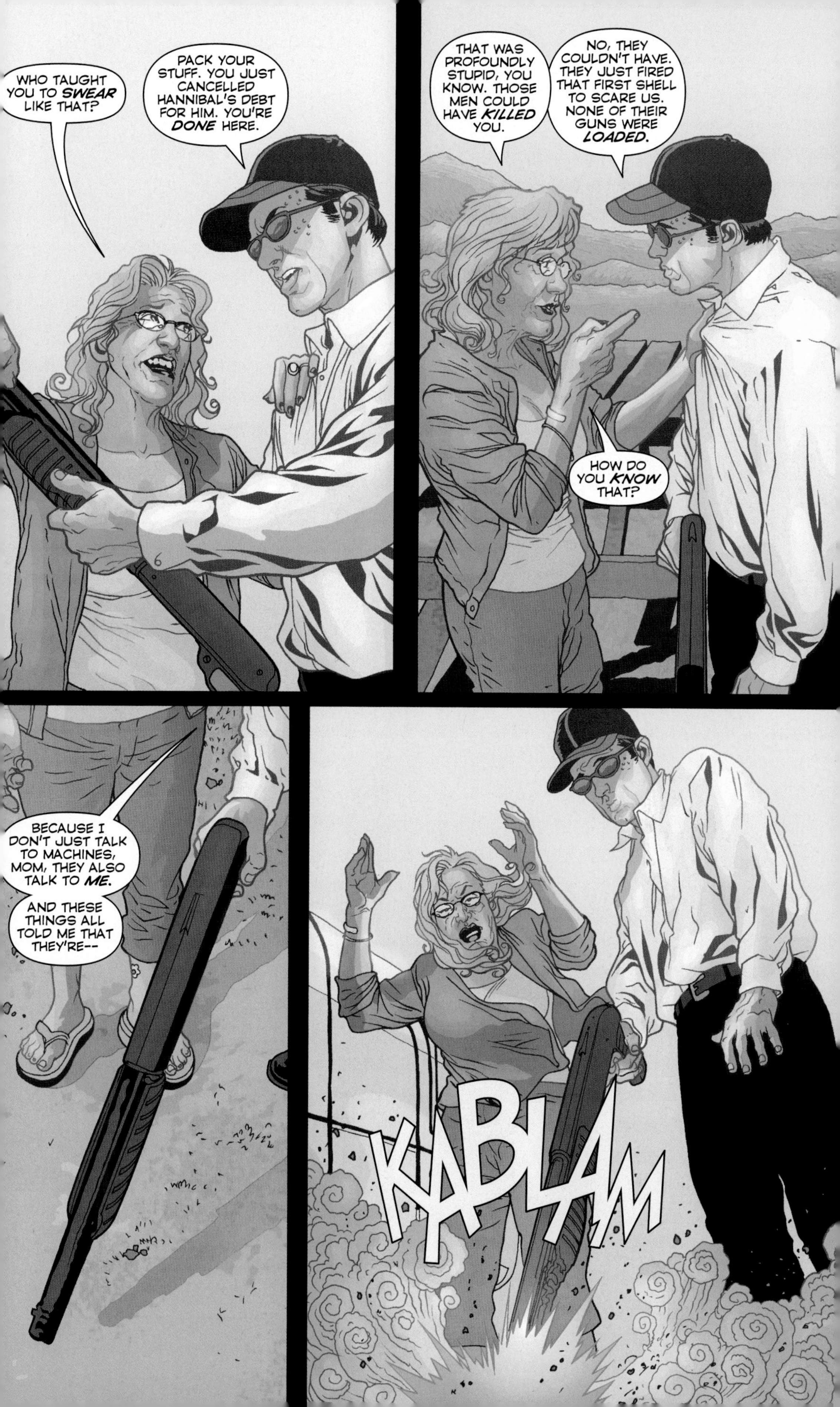
WHO TAUGHT YOU TO SWEAR LIKE THAT?
PACK YOUR STUFF. YOU JUST CANCELLED HANNIBAL'S DEBT FOR HIM. YOU'RE DONE HERE.
THAT WAS PROFOUNDLY STUPID, YOU KNOW. THOSE MEN COULD HAVE KILLED YOU.
NO, THEY COULDN'T HAVE. THEY JUST FIRED THAT FIRST SHELL TO SCARE US. NONE OF THEIR GUNS WERE LOADED.
HOW DO YOU KNOW THAT?
BECAUSE I DON'T JUST TALK TO MACHINES, MOM, THEY ALSO TALK TO ME.
AND THESE THINGS ALL TOLD ME THAT THEY'RE--
KABLAM

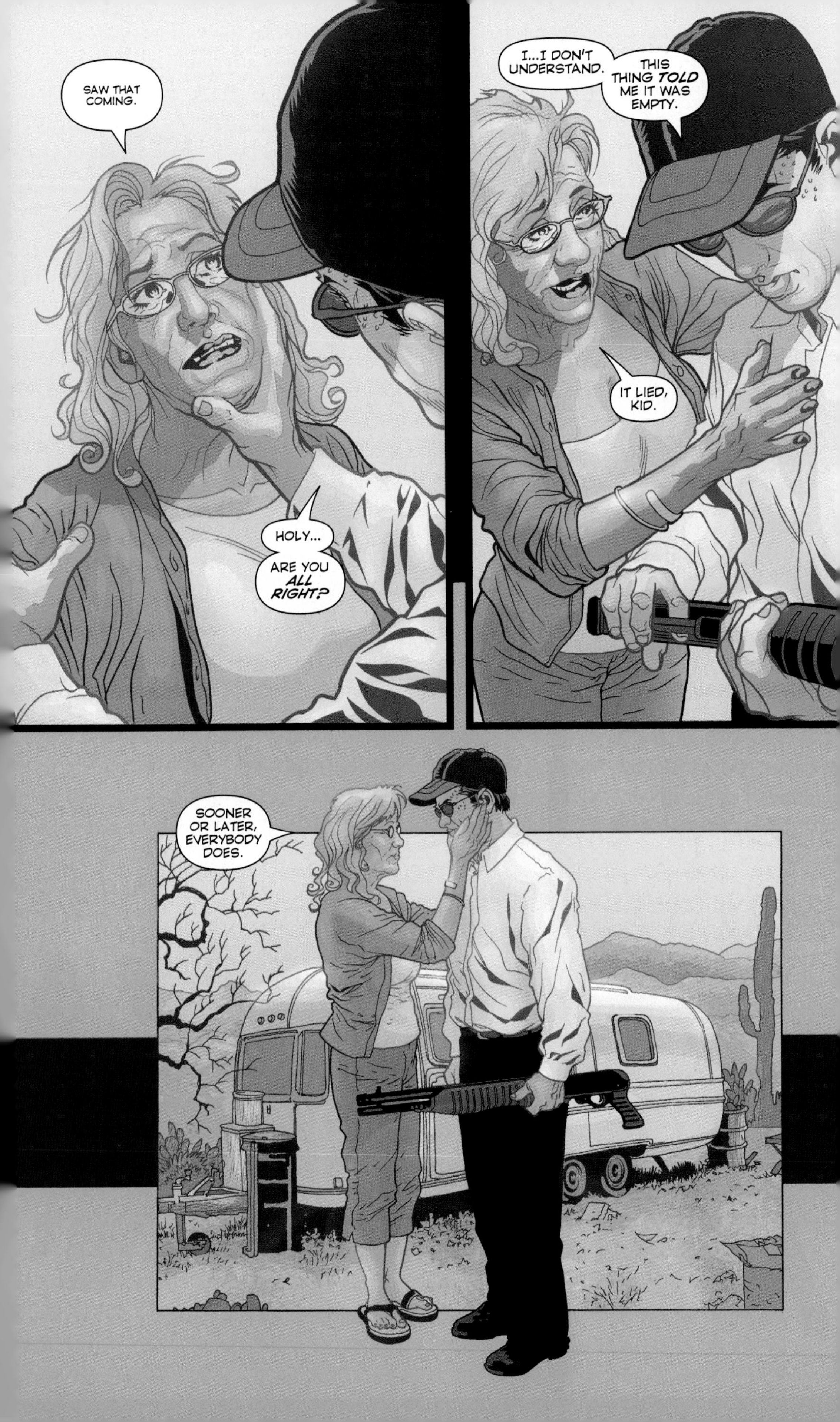
SAW THAT COMING.
HOLY...
ARE YOU ALL RIGHT?
I...I DON'T UNDERSTAND.
THIS THING TOLD ME IT WAS EMPTY.
IT LIED, KID.
SOONER OR LATER, EVERYBODY DOES.

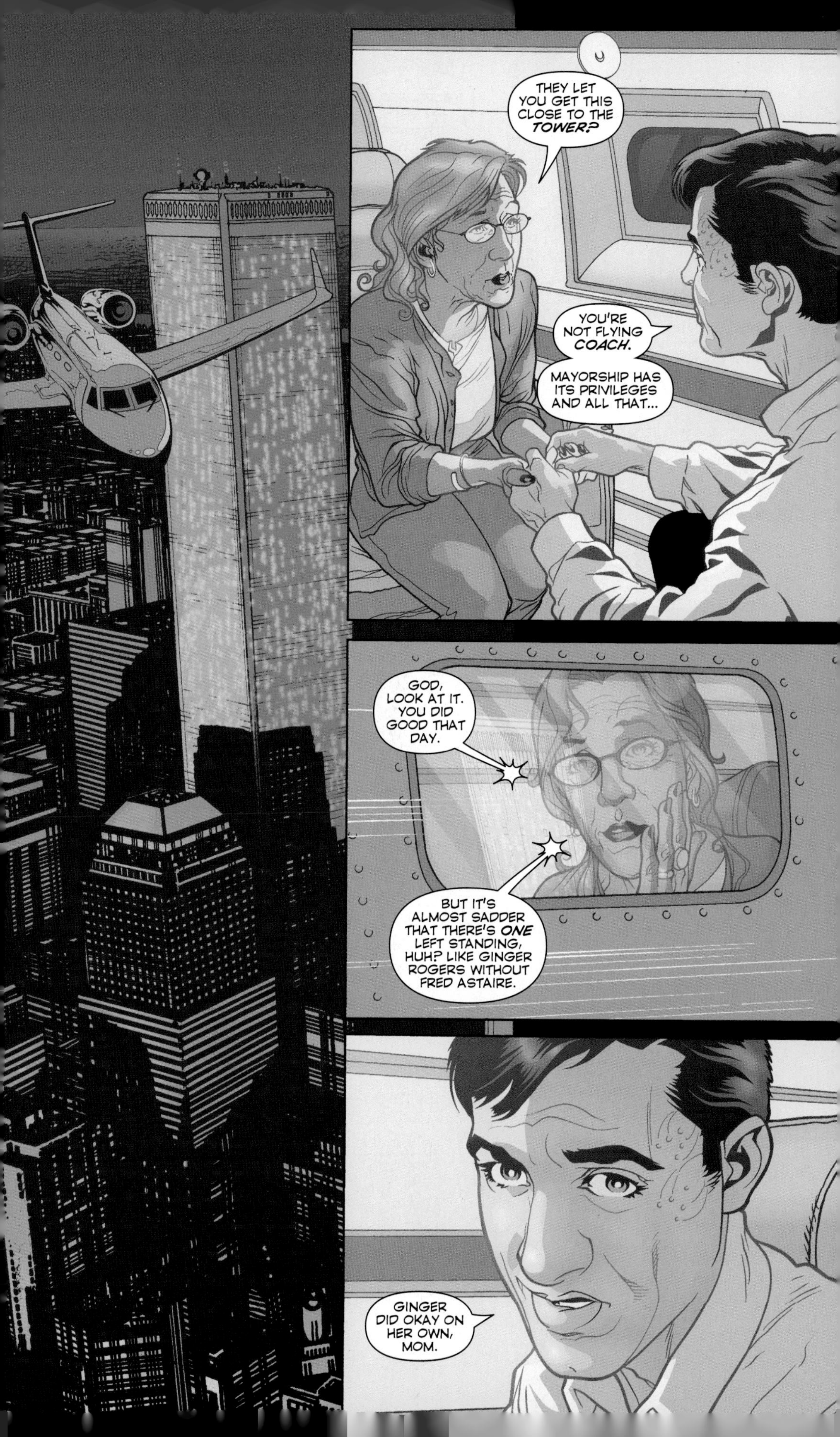
THEY LET YOU GET THIS CLOSE TO THE *TOWER?*
YOU'RE NOT FLYING *COACH*.
MAYORSHIP HAS ITS PRIVILEGES AND ALL THAT...
GOD, LOOK AT IT. YOU DID GOOD THAT DAY.
BUT IT'S ALMOST SADDER THAT THERE'S *ONE* LEFT STANDING, HUH? LIKE GINGER ROGERS WITHOUT FRED ASTAIRE.
GINGER DID OKAY ON HER OWN, MOM.

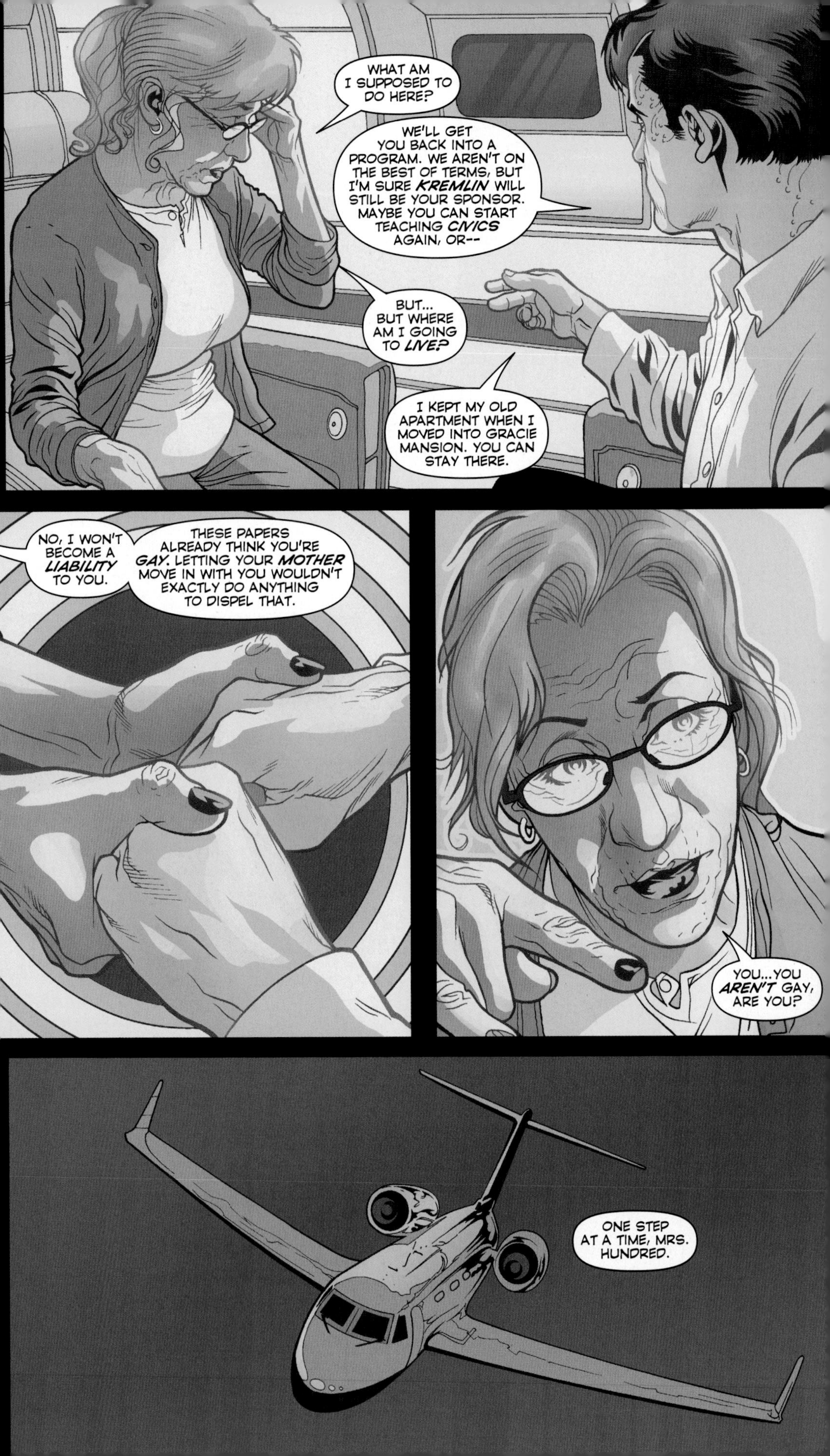
WHAT AM I SUPPOSED TO DO HERE?
WE'LL GET YOU BACK INTO A PROGRAM. WE AREN'T ON THE BEST OF TERMS, BUT I'M SURE *KREMLIN* WILL STILL BE YOUR SPONSOR. MAYBE YOU CAN START TEACHING *CIVICS* AGAIN, OR--
BUT... BUT WHERE AM I GOING TO *LIVE?*
I KEPT MY OLD APARTMENT WHEN I MOVED INTO GRACIE MANSION. YOU CAN STAY THERE.
NO, I WON'T BECOME A *LIABILITY* TO YOU.
THESE PAPERS ALREADY THINK YOU'RE *GAY*. LETTING YOUR *MOTHER* MOVE IN WITH YOU WOULDN'T EXACTLY DO ANYTHING TO DISPEL THAT.
YOU...YOU *AREN'T* GAY, ARE YOU?
ONE STEP AT A TIME, MRS. HUNDRED.

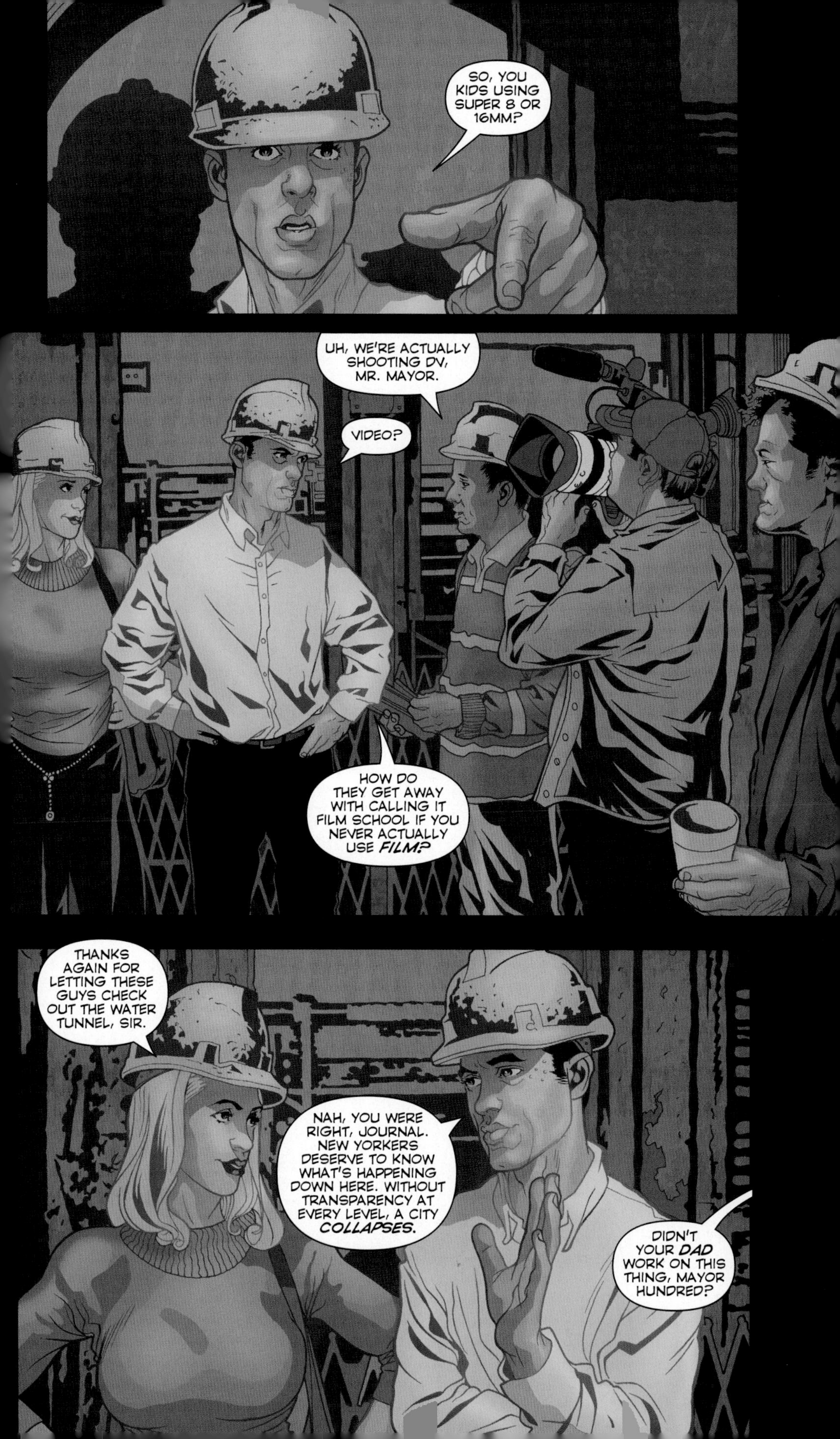
SO, YOU KIDS USING SUPER 8 OR 16MM?
UH, WE'RE ACTUALLY SHOOTING DV, MR. MAYOR.
VIDEO?
HOW DO THEY GET AWAY WITH CALLING IT FILM SCHOOL IF YOU NEVER ACTUALLY USE *FILM?*
THANKS AGAIN FOR LETTING THESE GUYS CHECK OUT THE WATER TUNNEL, SIR.
NAH, YOU WERE RIGHT, JOURNAL. NEW YORKERS DESERVE TO KNOW WHAT'S HAPPENING DOWN HERE. WITHOUT TRANSPARENCY AT EVERY LEVEL, A CITY *COLLAPSES.*
DIDN'T YOUR *DAD* WORK ON THIS THING, MAYOR HUNDRED?

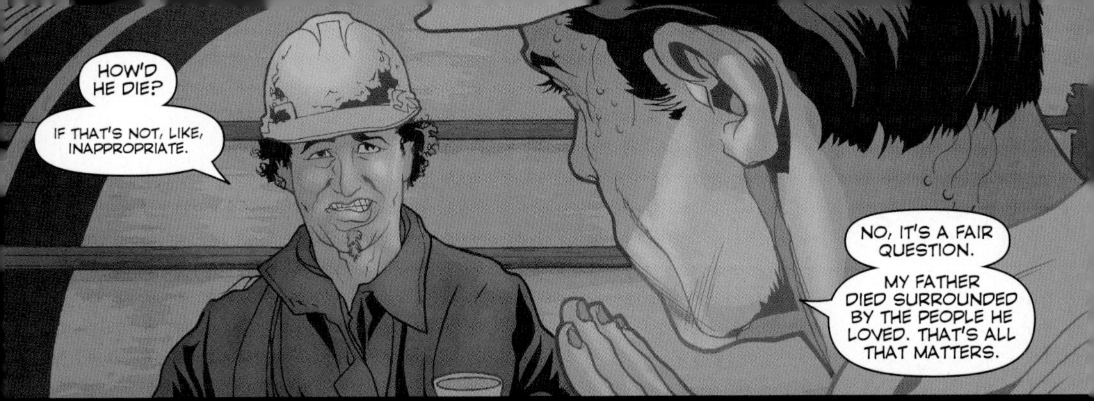
HOW'D HE DIE?
IF THAT'S NOT, LIKE, INAPPROPRIATE.
NO, IT'S A FAIR QUESTION.
MY FATHER DIED SURROUNDED BY THE PEOPLE HE LOVED. THAT'S ALL THAT MATTERS.

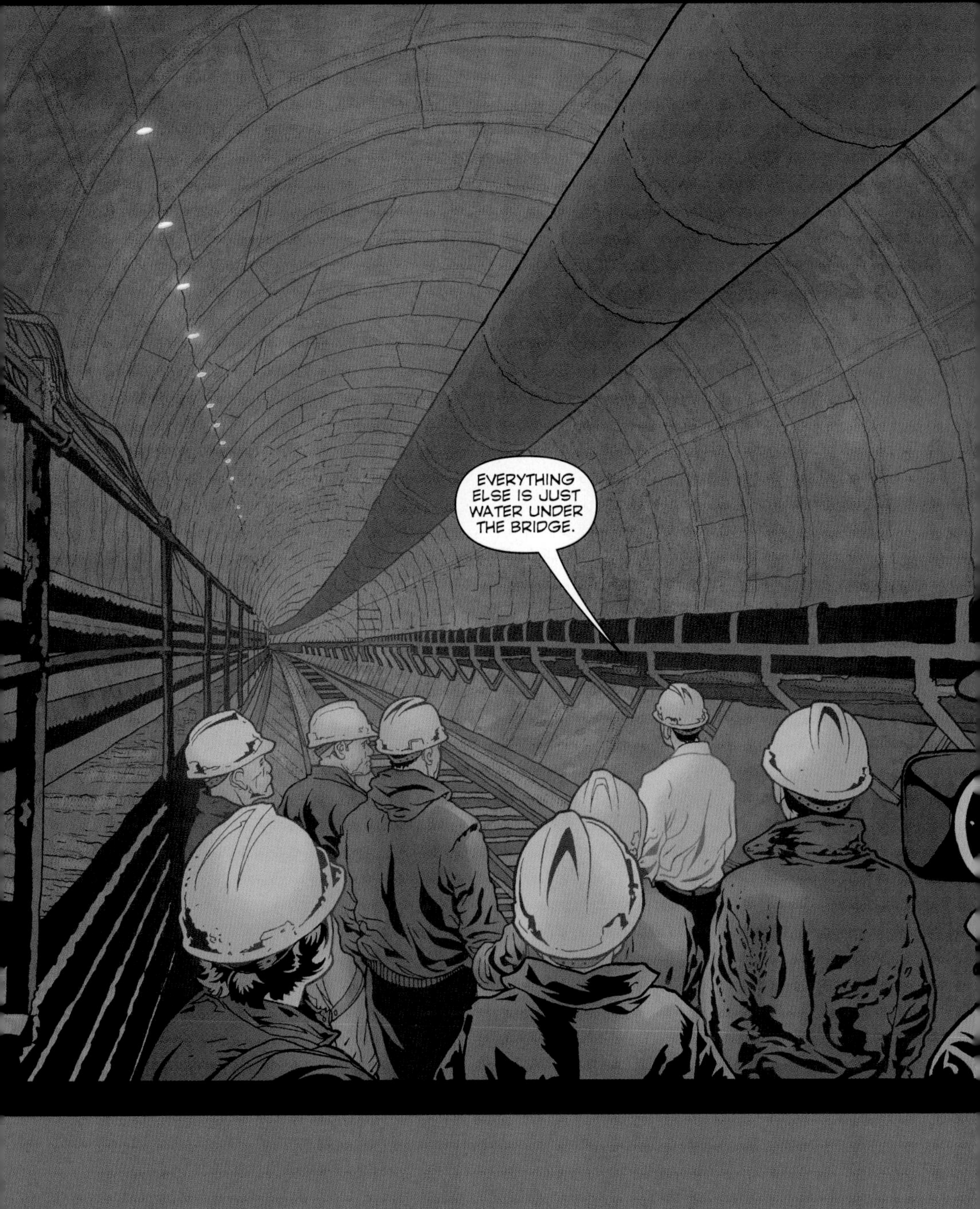
EVERYTHING ELSE IS JUST WATER UNDER THE BRIDGE.

# CHAPTER 3 MARCH TO WAR

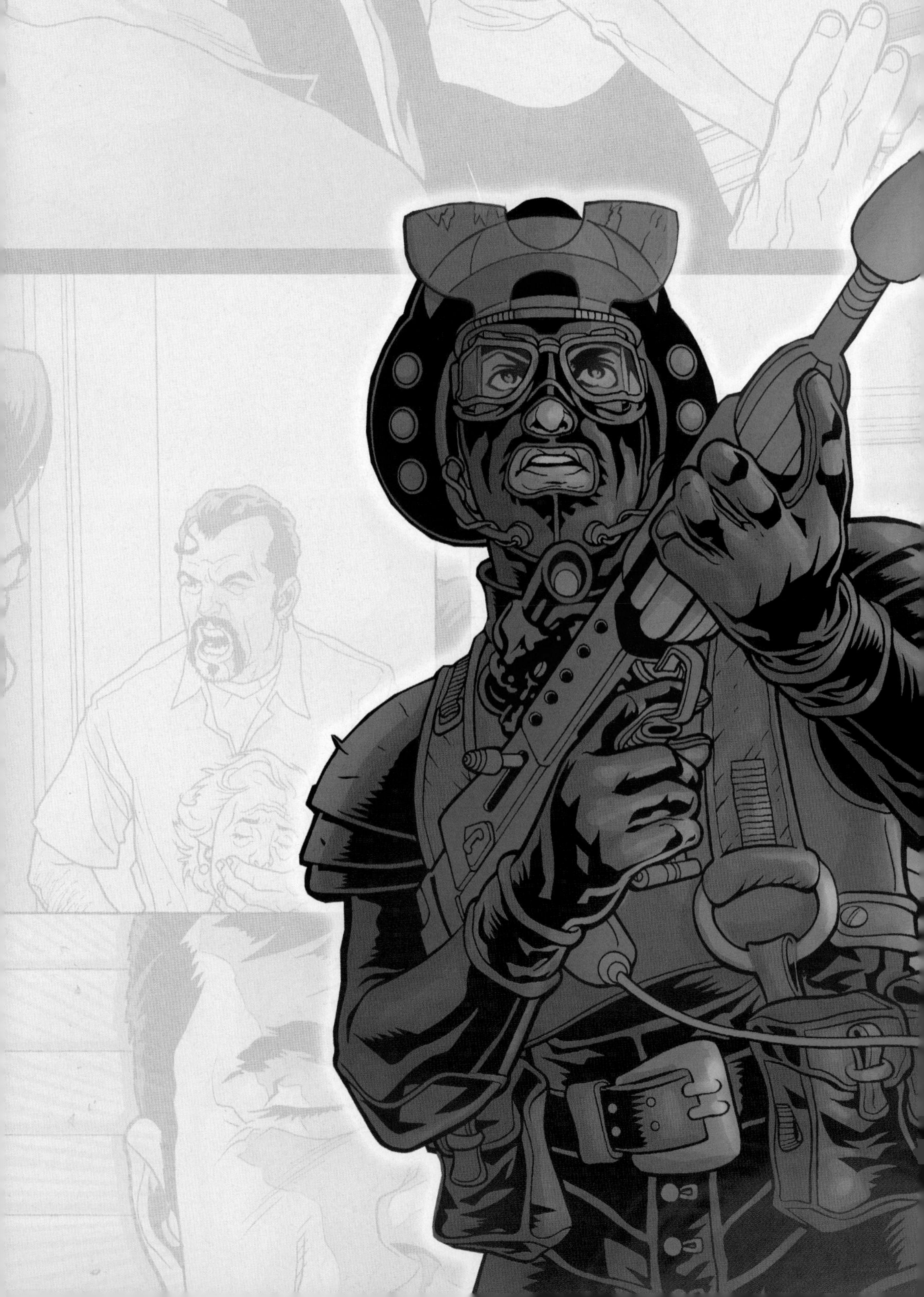

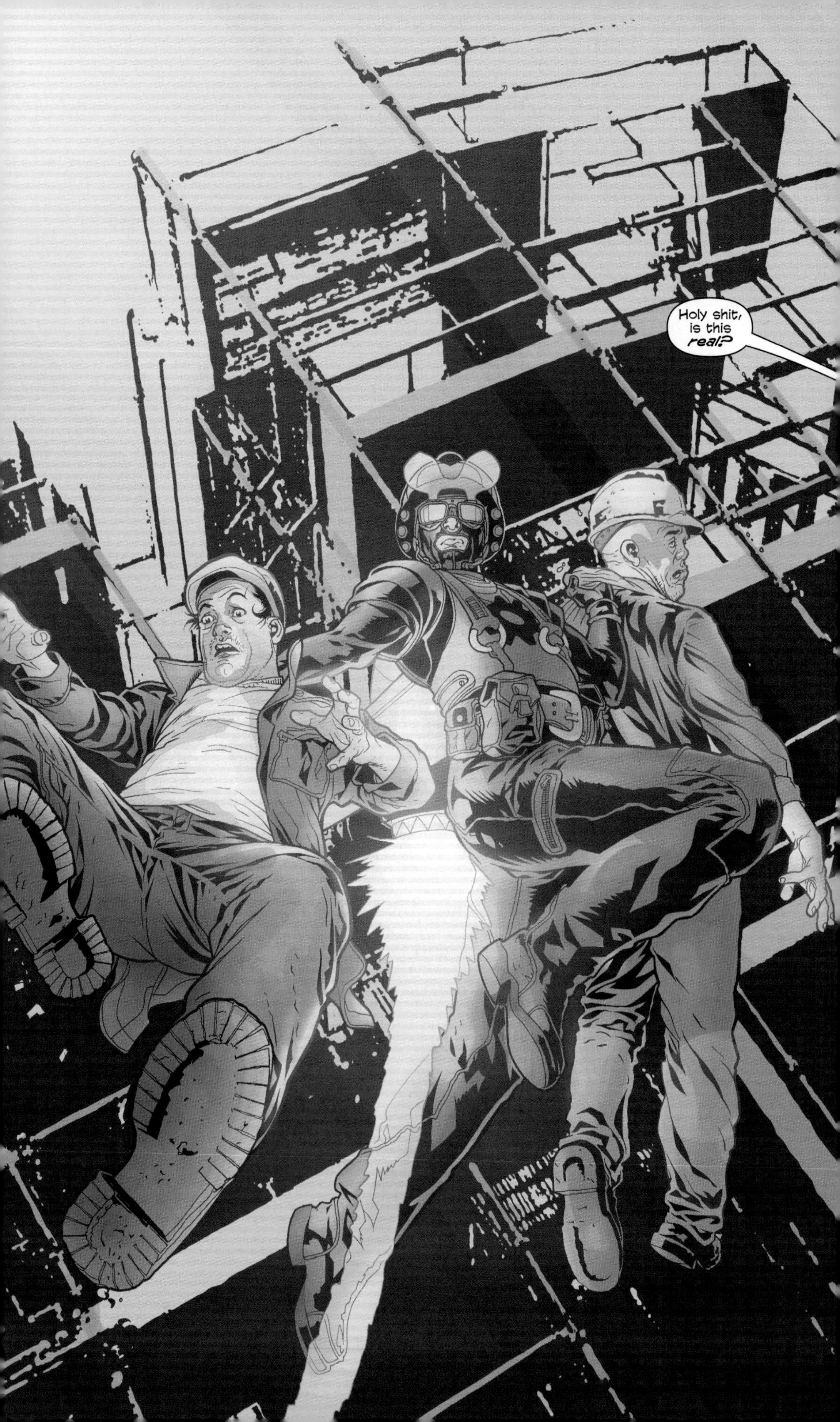
Holy shit, is this *real?*

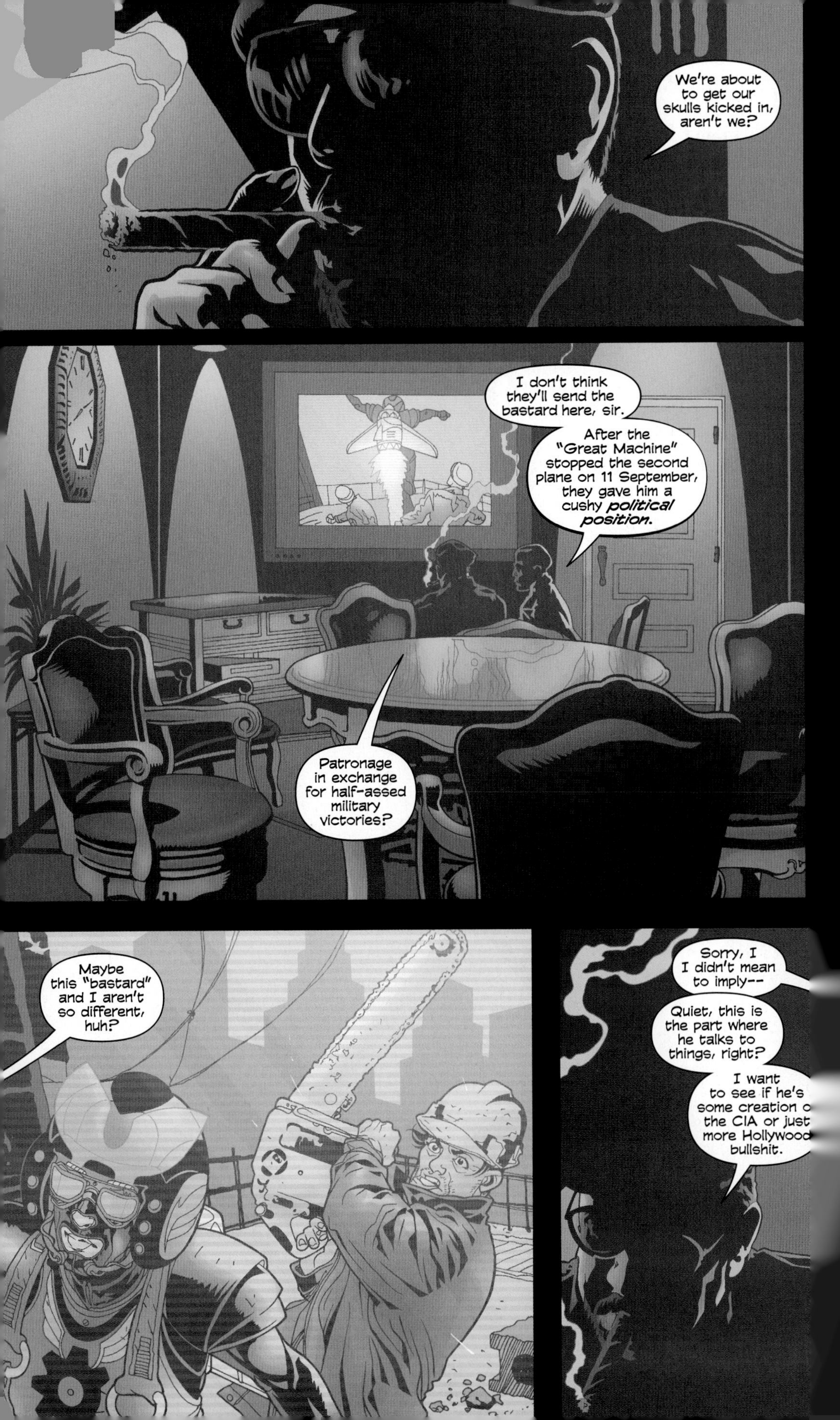
We're about to get our skulls kicked in, aren't we?
I don't think they'll send the bastard here, sir.
After the "Great Machine" stopped the second plane on 11 September, they gave him a cushy *political position.*
Patronage in exchange for half-assed military victories?
Maybe this "bastard" and I aren't so different, huh?
Sorry, I I didn't mean to imply--
Quiet, this is the part where he talks to things, right?
I want to see if he's some creation o the CIA or just more Hollywood bullshit.

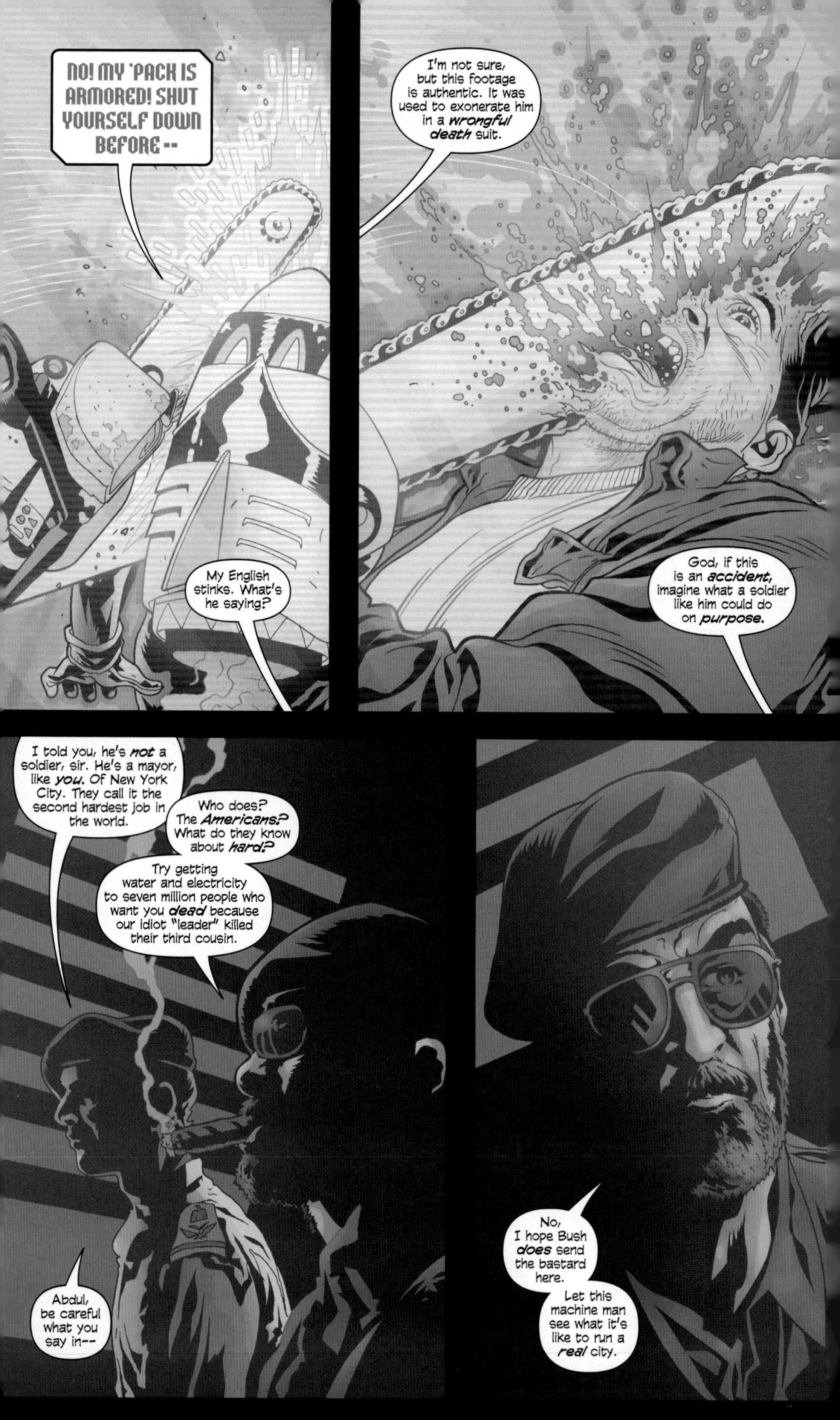
NO! MY 'PACK IS ARMORED! SHUT YOURSELF DOWN BEFORE --
I'm not sure, but this footage is authentic. It was used to exonerate him in a wrongful death suit.
My English stinks. What's he saying?
God, if this is an accident, imagine what a soldier like him could do on purpose.
I told you, he's not a soldier, sir. He's a mayor, like you. Of New York City. They call it the second hardest job in the world.
Who does? The Americans? What do they know about hard?
Try getting water and electricity to seven million people who want you dead because our idiot "leader" killed their third cousin.
Abdul, be careful what you say in--
No, I hope Bush does send the bastard here.
Let this machine man see what it's like to run a real city.

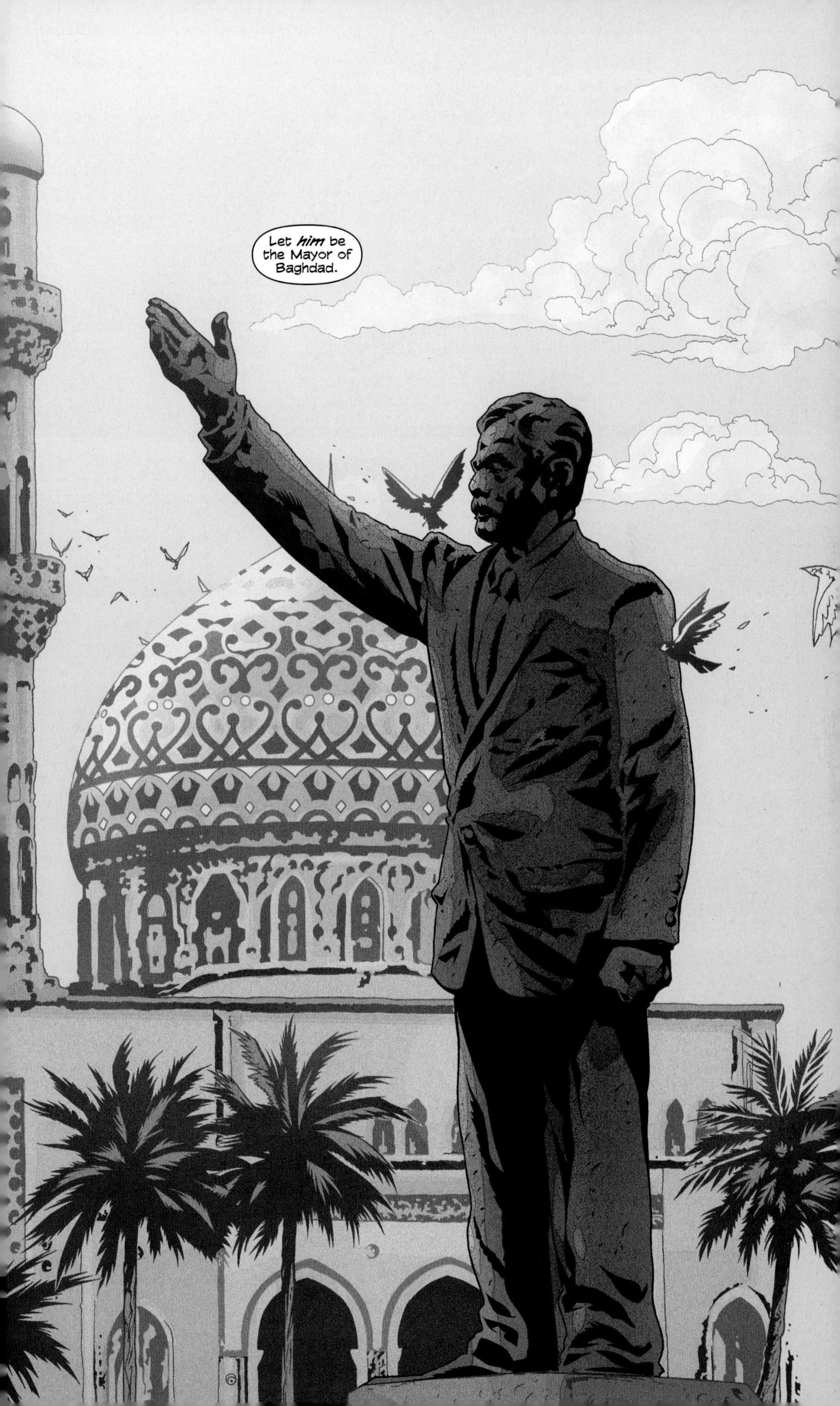
Let *him* be the Mayor of Baghdad.

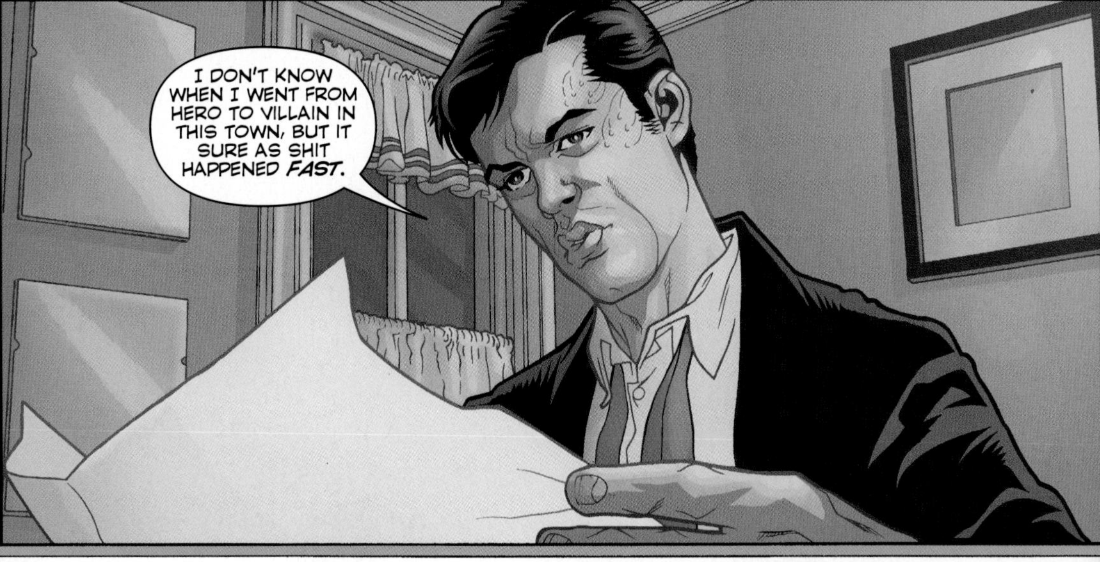
I DON'T KNOW WHEN I WENT FROM HERO TO VILLAIN IN THIS TOWN, BUT IT SURE AS SHIT HAPPENED FAST.

FRIDAY, FEBRUARY 14, 2003

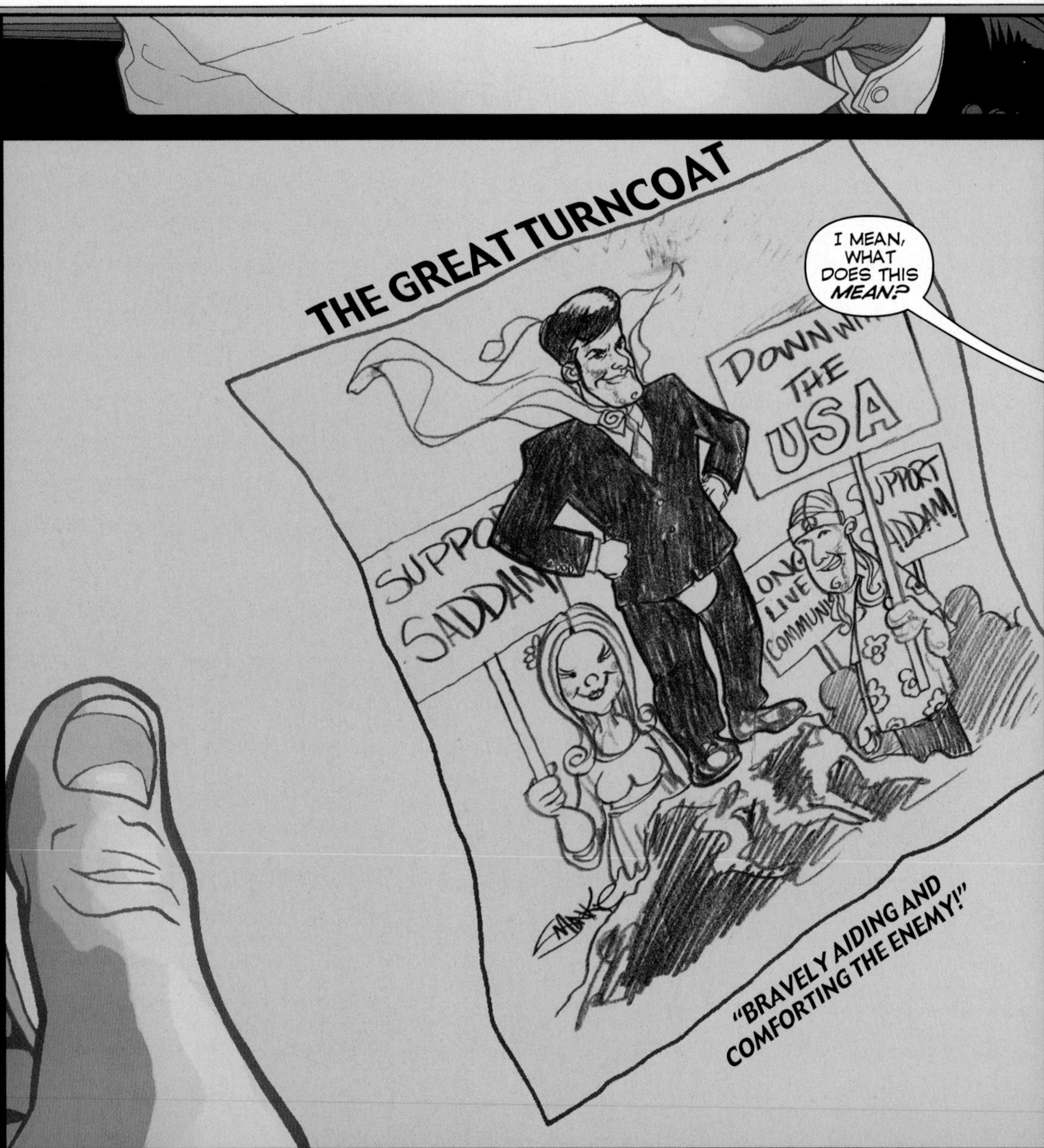
THE GREAT TURNCOAT
I MEAN, WHAT DOES THIS MEAN?
DOWN WI
THE USA
SUPPORT SADDAM!
SUPPO
SADDAM
LONG LIVE COMMUNI
"BRAVELY AIDING AND COMFORTING THE ENEMY!"

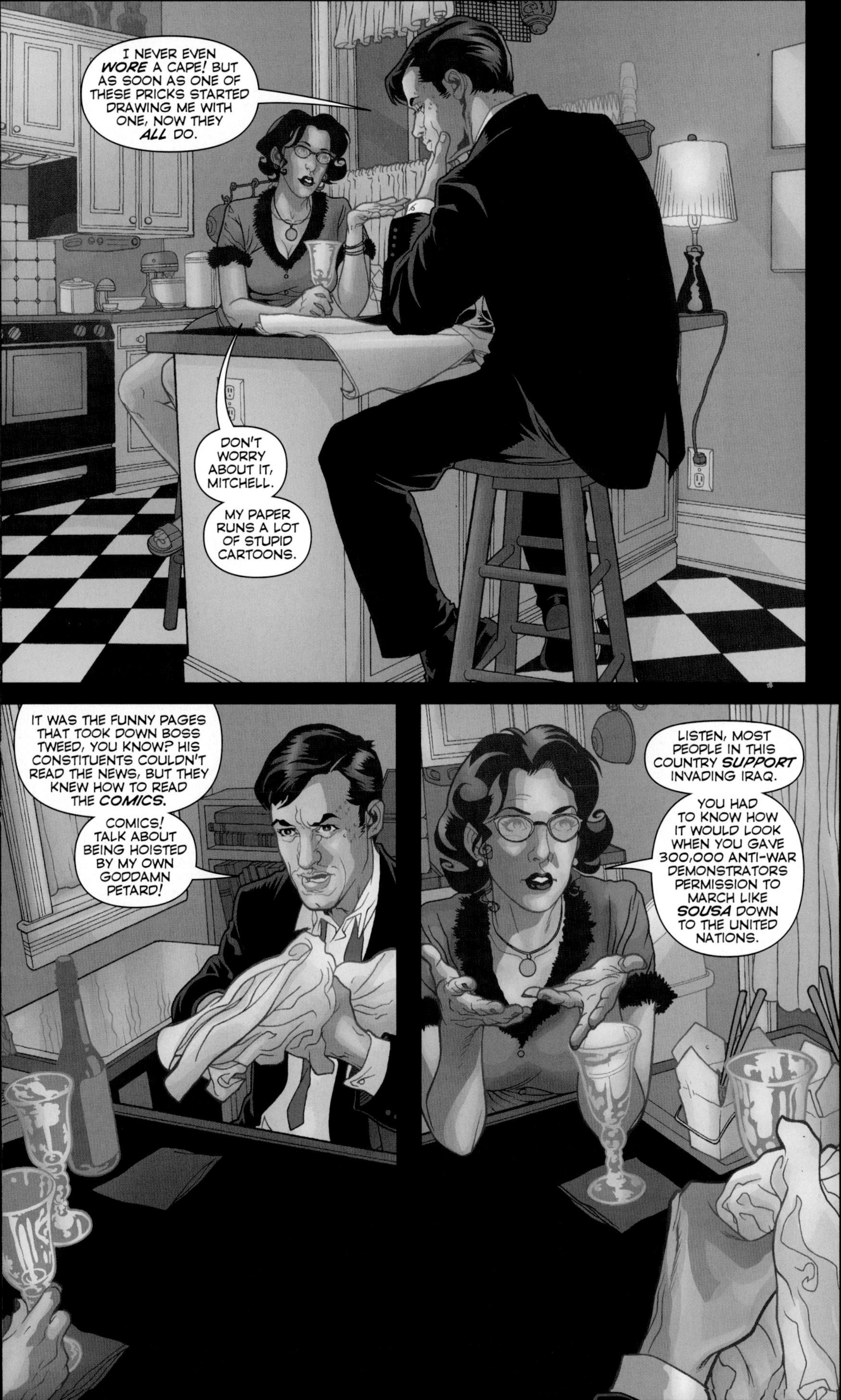

I NEVER EVEN WORE A CAPE! BUT AS SOON AS ONE OF THESE PRICKS STARTED DRAWING ME WITH ONE, NOW THEY ALL DO.
DON'T WORRY ABOUT IT, MITCHELL.
MY PAPER RUNS A LOT OF STUPID CARTOONS.
IT WAS THE FUNNY PAGES THAT TOOK DOWN BOSS TWEED, YOU KNOW? HIS CONSTITUENTS COULDN'T READ THE NEWS, BUT THEY KNEW HOW TO READ THE COMICS.
COMICS! TALK ABOUT BEING HOISTED BY MY OWN GODDAMN PETARD!
LISTEN, MOST PEOPLE IN THIS COUNTRY SUPPORT INVADING IRAQ.
YOU HAD TO KNOW HOW IT WOULD LOOK WHEN YOU GAVE 300,000 ANTI-WAR DEMONSTRATORS PERMISSION TO MARCH LIKE SOUSA DOWN TO THE UNITED NATIONS.

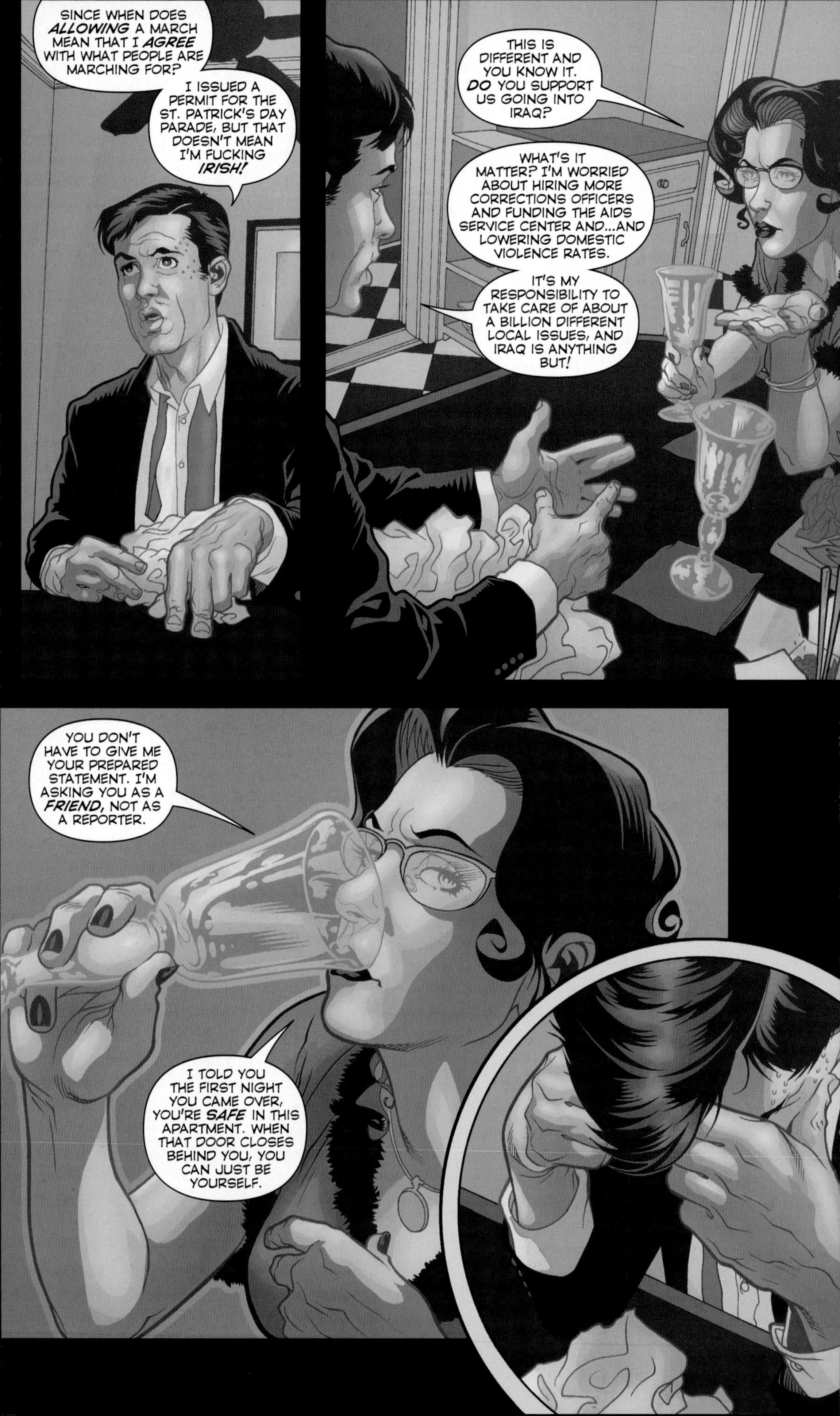
SINCE WHEN DOES ALLOWING A MARCH MEAN THAT I AGREE WITH WHAT PEOPLE ARE MARCHING FOR?
I ISSUED A PERMIT FOR THE ST. PATRICK'S DAY PARADE, BUT THAT DOESN'T MEAN I'M FUCKING IRISH!
THIS IS DIFFERENT AND YOU KNOW IT. DO YOU SUPPORT US GOING INTO IRAQ?
WHAT'S IT MATTER? I'M WORRIED ABOUT HIRING MORE CORRECTIONS OFFICERS AND FUNDING THE AIDS SERVICE CENTER AND...AND LOWERING DOMESTIC VIOLENCE RATES.
IT'S MY RESPONSIBILITY TO TAKE CARE OF ABOUT A BILLION DIFFERENT LOCAL ISSUES, AND IRAQ IS ANYTHING BUT!
YOU DON'T HAVE TO GIVE ME YOUR PREPARED STATEMENT. I'M ASKING YOU AS A FRIEND, NOT AS A REPORTER.
I TOLD YOU THE FIRST NIGHT YOU CAME OVER, YOU'RE SAFE IN THIS APARTMENT. WHEN THAT DOOR CLOSES BEHIND YOU, YOU CAN JUST BE YOURSELF.

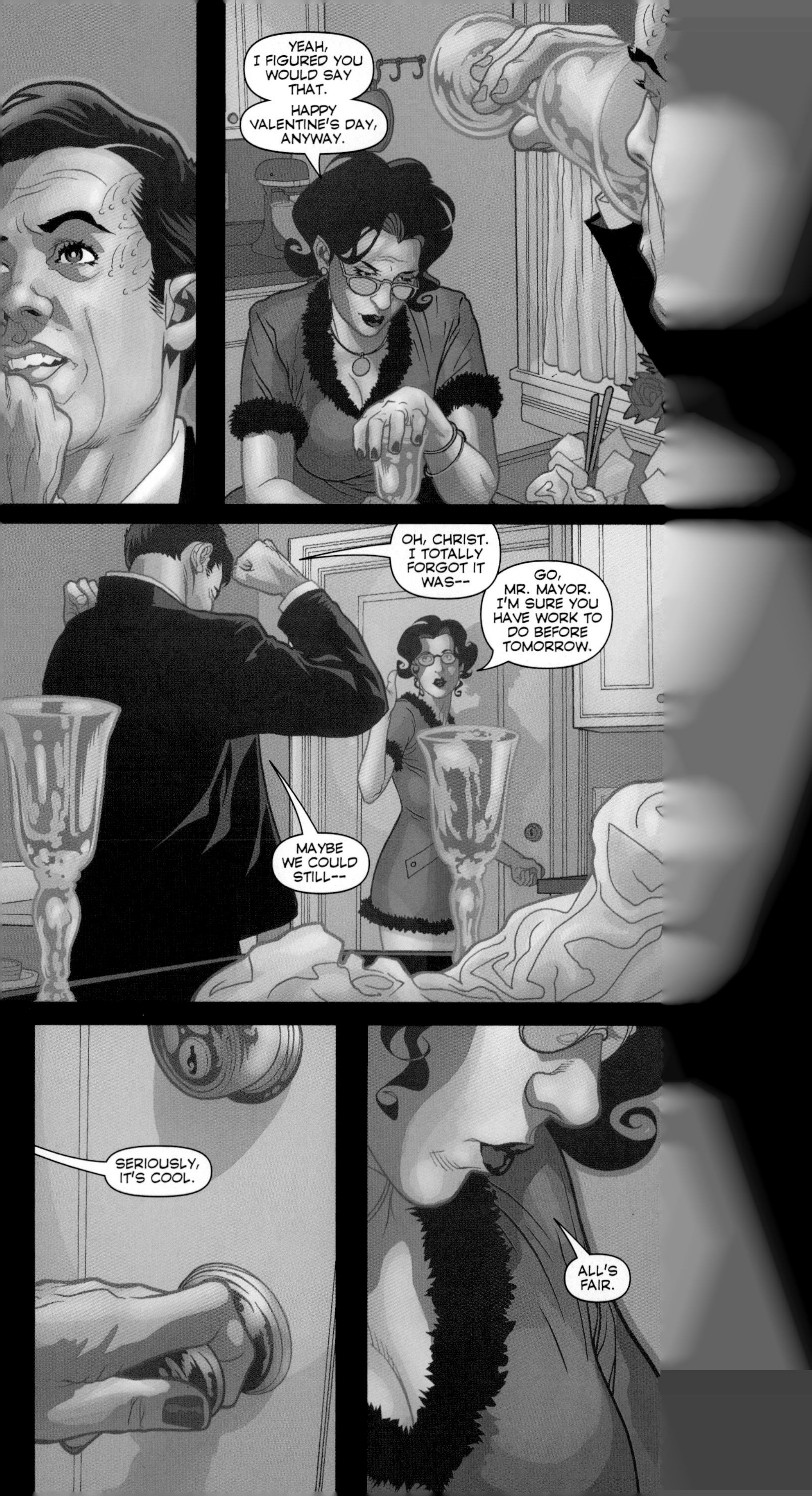
YEAH, I FIGURED YOU WOULD SAY THAT.
HAPPY VALENTINE'S DAY, ANYWAY.
OH, CHRIST. I TOTALLY FORGOT IT WAS--
GO, MR. MAYOR. I'M SURE YOU HAVE WORK TO DO BEFORE TOMORROW.
MAYBE WE COULD STILL--
SERIOUSLY, IT'S COOL.
ALL'S FAIR.

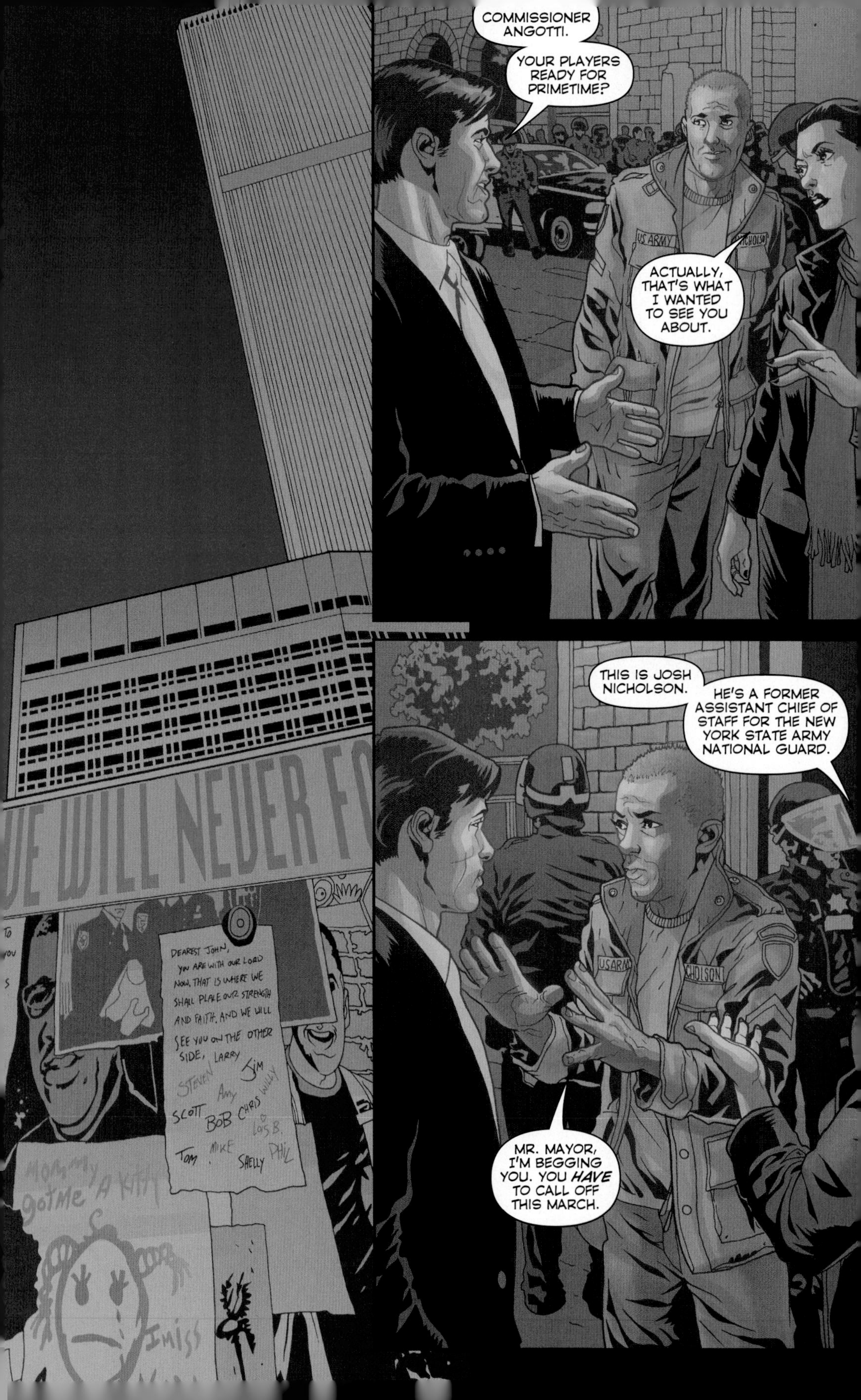
COMMISSIONER ANGOTTI.
YOUR PLAYERS READY FOR PRIMETIME?
ACTUALLY, THAT'S WHAT I WANTED TO SEE YOU ABOUT.
US ARMY
NICHOLSON
WE WILL NEVER F
DEAREST JOHN, YOU ARE WITH OUR LORD NOW, THAT IS WHERE WE SHALL PLACE OUR STRENGTH AND FAITH. AND WE WILL SEE YOU ON THE OTHER SIDE, LARRY
STEVEN JIM AMY SCOTT BOB CHRIS WILLY LOIS B. TOM MIKE SHELLY PHIL
Mommy got me A kitty
I MISS
THIS IS JOSH NICHOLSON.
HE'S A FORMER ASSISTANT CHIEF OF STAFF FOR THE NEW YORK STATE ARMY NATIONAL GUARD.
US ARMY
NICHOLSON
MR. MAYOR, I'M BEGGING YOU. YOU *HAVE* TO CALL OFF THIS MARCH.

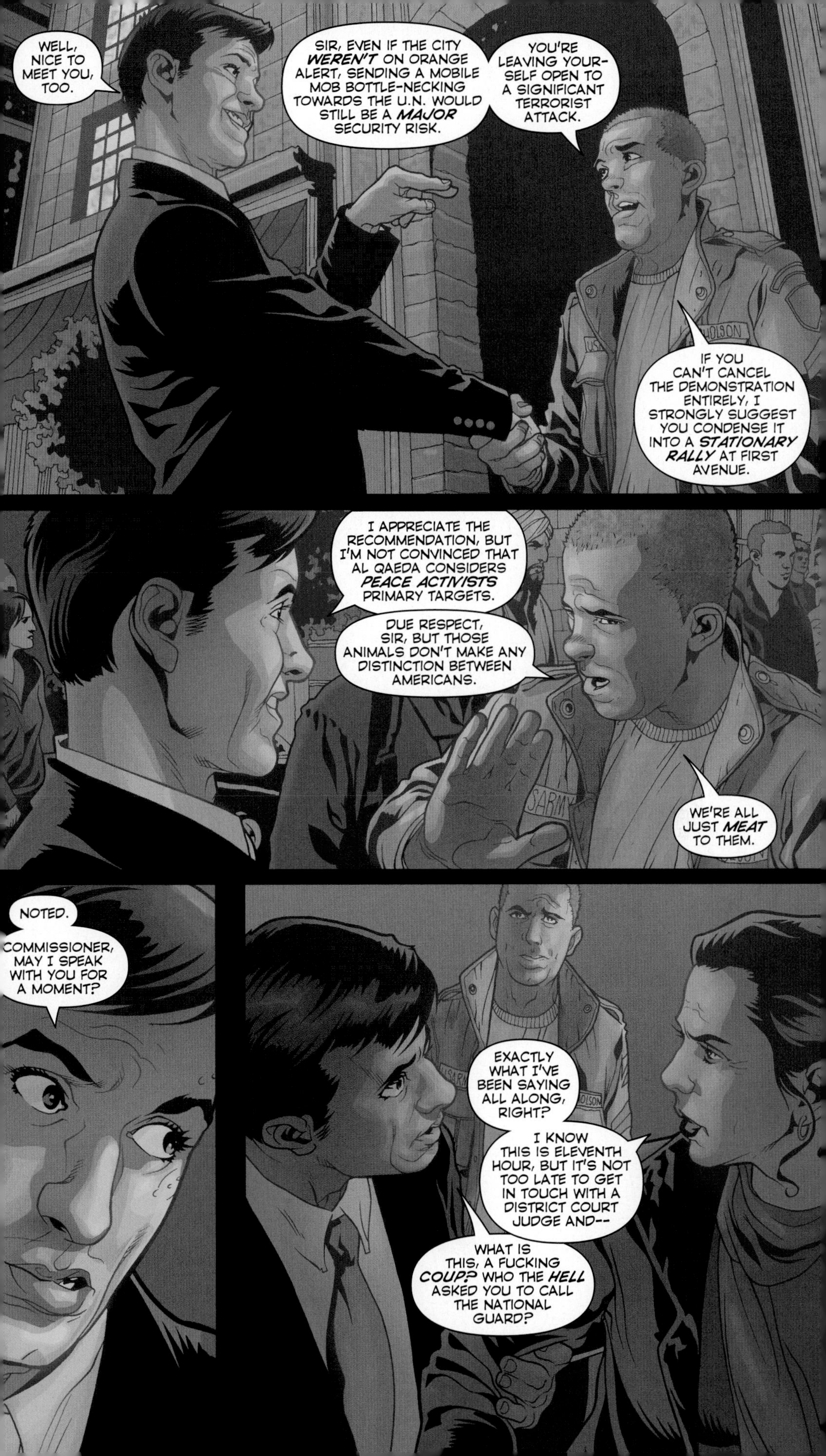
WELL, NICE TO MEET YOU, TOO.
SIR, EVEN IF THE CITY WEREN'T ON ORANGE ALERT, SENDING A MOBILE MOB BOTTLE-NECKING TOWARDS THE U.N. WOULD STILL BE A MAJOR SECURITY RISK.
YOU'RE LEAVING YOUR-SELF OPEN TO A SIGNIFICANT TERRORIST ATTACK.
IF YOU CAN'T CANCEL THE DEMONSTRATION ENTIRELY, I STRONGLY SUGGEST YOU CONDENSE IT INTO A STATIONARY RALLY AT FIRST AVENUE.
I APPRECIATE THE RECOMMENDATION, BUT I'M NOT CONVINCED THAT AL QAEDA CONSIDERS PEACE ACTIVISTS PRIMARY TARGETS.
DUE RESPECT, SIR, BUT THOSE ANIMALS DON'T MAKE ANY DISTINCTION BETWEEN AMERICANS.
WE'RE ALL JUST MEAT TO THEM.
NOTED.
COMMISSIONER, MAY I SPEAK WITH YOU FOR A MOMENT?
EXACTLY WHAT I'VE BEEN SAYING ALL ALONG, RIGHT?
I KNOW THIS IS ELEVENTH HOUR, BUT IT'S NOT TOO LATE TO GET IN TOUCH WITH A DISTRICT COURT JUDGE AND--
WHAT IS THIS, A FUCKING COUP? WHO THE HELL ASKED YOU TO CALL THE NATIONAL GUARD?

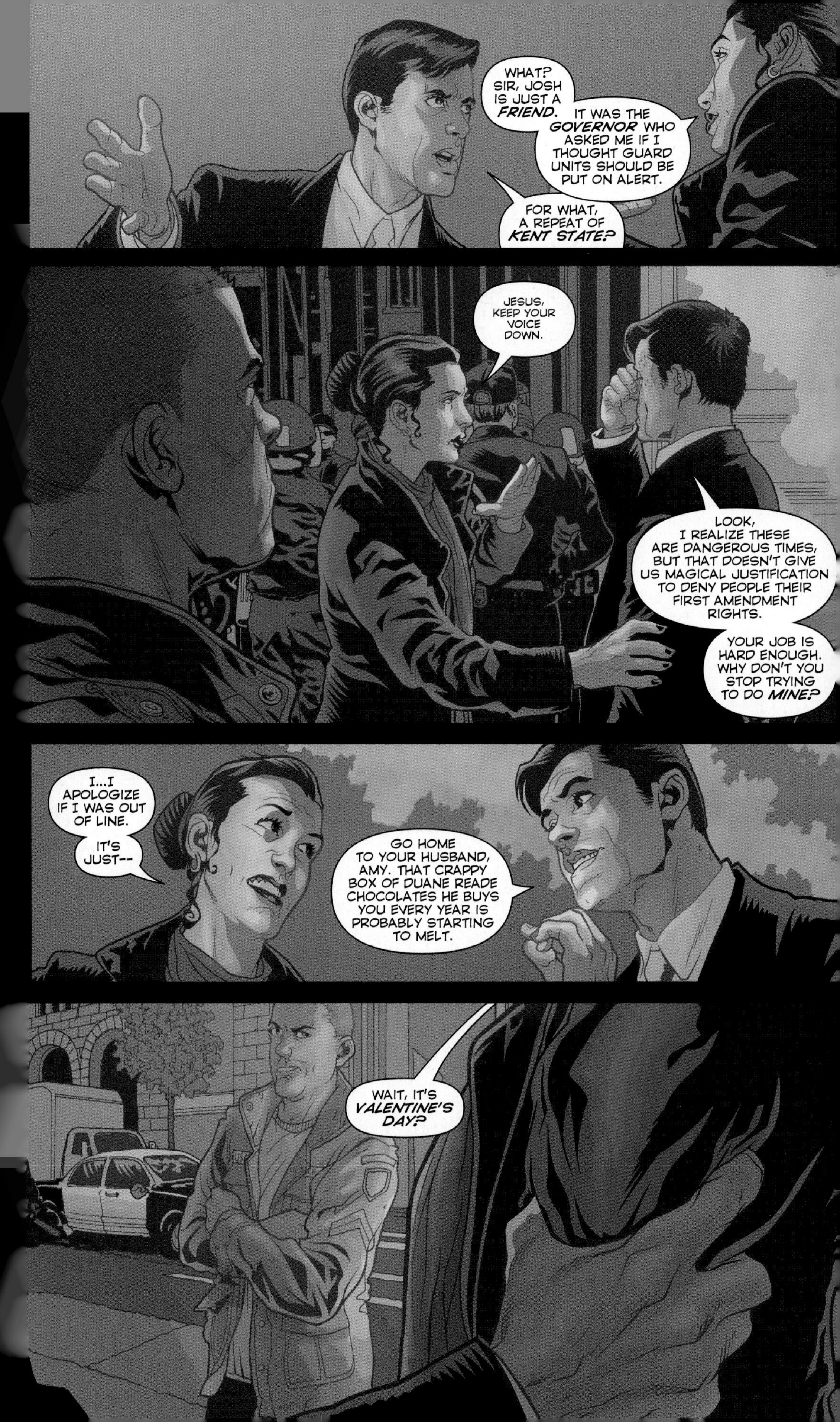
WHAT? SIR, JOSH IS JUST A FRIEND.
IT WAS THE GOVERNOR WHO ASKED ME IF I THOUGHT GUARD UNITS SHOULD BE PUT ON ALERT.
FOR WHAT, A REPEAT OF KENT STATE?
JESUS, KEEP YOUR VOICE DOWN.
LOOK, I REALIZE THESE ARE DANGEROUS TIMES, BUT THAT DOESN'T GIVE US MAGICAL JUSTIFICATION TO DENY PEOPLE THEIR FIRST AMENDMENT RIGHTS.
YOUR JOB IS HARD ENOUGH. WHY DON'T YOU STOP TRYING TO DO MINE?
I...I APOLOGIZE IF I WAS OUT OF LINE.
IT'S JUST--
GO HOME TO YOUR HUSBAND, AMY. THAT CRAPPY BOX OF DUANE READE CHOCOLATES HE BUYS YOU EVERY YEAR IS PROBABLY STARTING TO MELT.
WAIT, IT'S VALENTINE'S DAY?

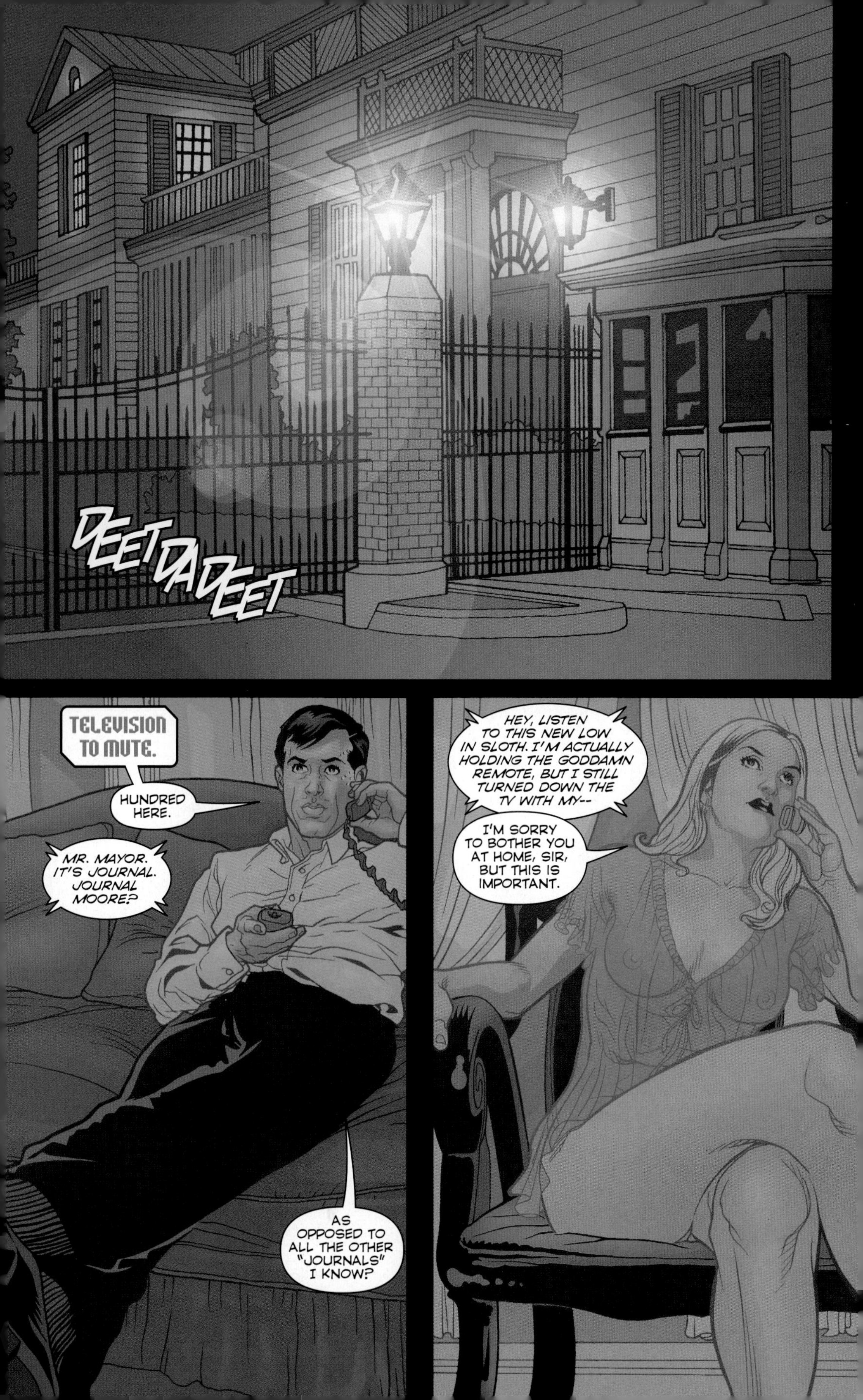
DEET DA DEET
TELEVISION TO MUTE.
HUNDRED HERE.
MR. MAYOR. IT'S JOURNAL. JOURNAL MOORE?
AS OPPOSED TO ALL THE OTHER "JOURNALS" I KNOW?
HEY, LISTEN TO THIS NEW LOW IN SLOTH. I'M ACTUALLY HOLDING THE GODDAMN REMOTE, BUT I STILL TURNED DOWN THE TV WITH MY--
I'M SORRY TO BOTHER YOU AT HOME, SIR, BUT THIS IS IMPORTANT.

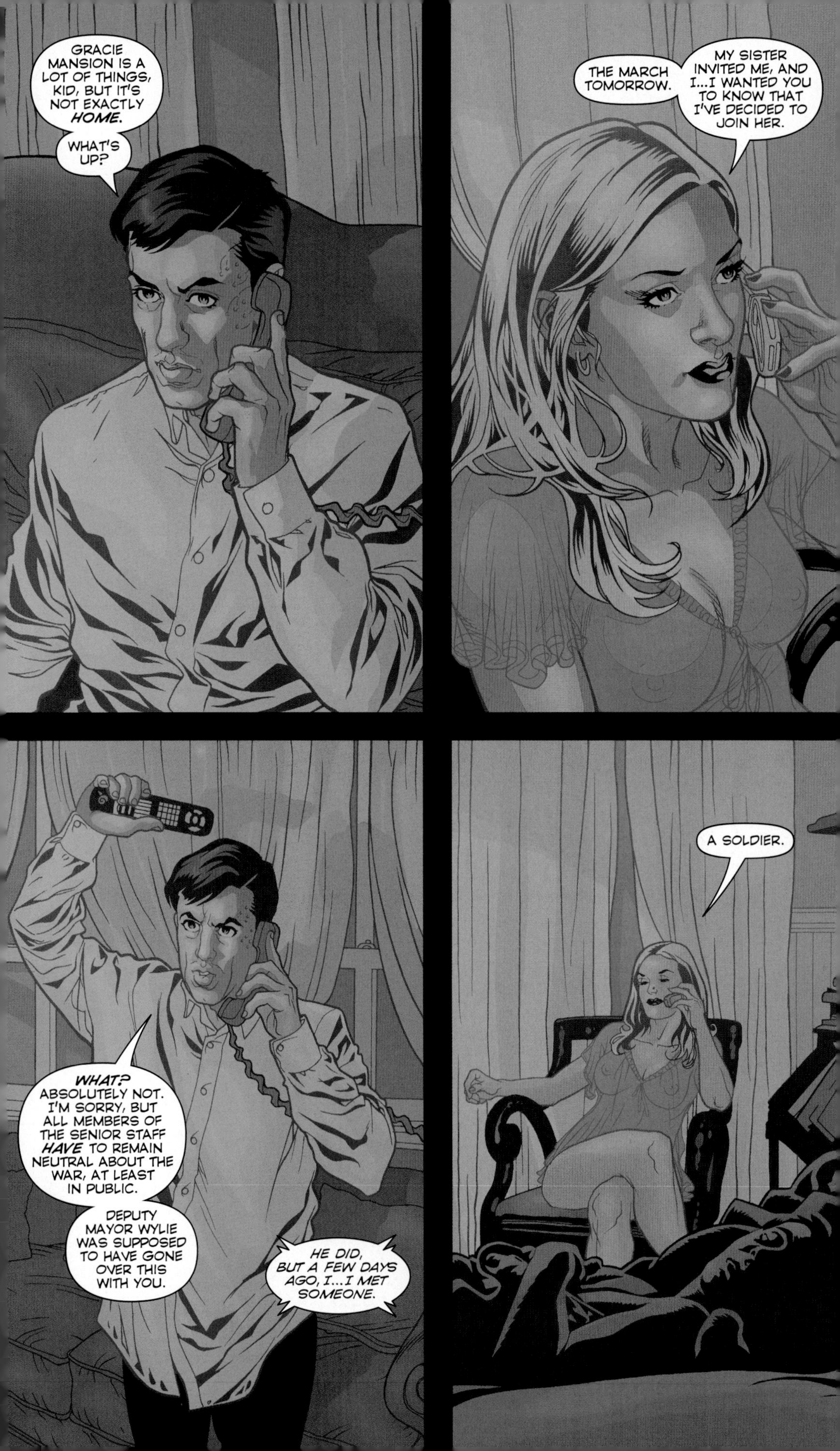
GRACIE MANSION IS A LOT OF THINGS, KID, BUT IT'S NOT EXACTLY ***HOME***.
WHAT'S UP?
THE MARCH TOMORROW.
MY SISTER INVITED ME, AND I...I WANTED YOU TO KNOW THAT I'VE DECIDED TO JOIN HER.
***WHAT?*** ABSOLUTELY NOT. I'M SORRY, BUT ALL MEMBERS OF THE SENIOR STAFF ***HAVE*** TO REMAIN NEUTRAL ABOUT THE WAR, AT LEAST IN PUBLIC.
DEPUTY MAYOR WYLIE WAS SUPPOSED TO HAVE GONE OVER THIS WITH YOU.
*HE DID, BUT A FEW DAYS AGO, I...I MET SOMEONE.*
A SOLDIER.

OH, NO.

HIS NAME IS SCOTT COOK. HE'S FROM LONG ISLAND. HE'S...HE'S IN THE RESERVES.

IF AMERICA INVADES IRAQ, HE'LL DEFINITELY GET CALLED, SIR. IT WOULD BE ONE THING IF THEY SENT HIM INTO *AFGHANISTAN*, BUT I DON'T THINK IT'S FAIR THAT--

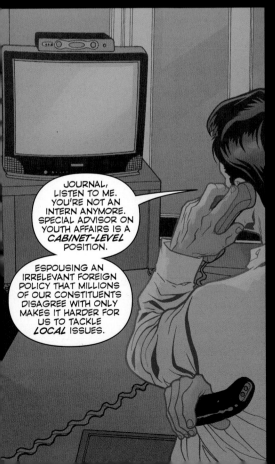

JOURNAL, LISTEN TO ME. YOU'RE NOT AN INTERN ANYMORE. SPECIAL ADVISOR ON YOUTH AFFAIRS IS A *CABINET-LEVEL* POSITION.

ESPOUSING AN IRRELEVANT FOREIGN POLICY THAT MILLIONS OF OUR CONSTITUENTS DISAGREE WITH ONLY MAKES IT HARDER FOR US TO TACKLE *LOCAL* ISSUES.

BUT *ALL* POLITICS ARE LOCAL, SIR. YOU'RE THE ONE WHO TAUGHT ME THAT.

AND WHEN RECRUITERS COME INTO *OUR* PUBLIC SCHOOLS ENCOURAGING YOUNG PEOPLE TO SIGN UP FOR THE MILITARY, HOW CAN YOU SAY THAT'S NOT RELEVANT TO WHAT WE DO?

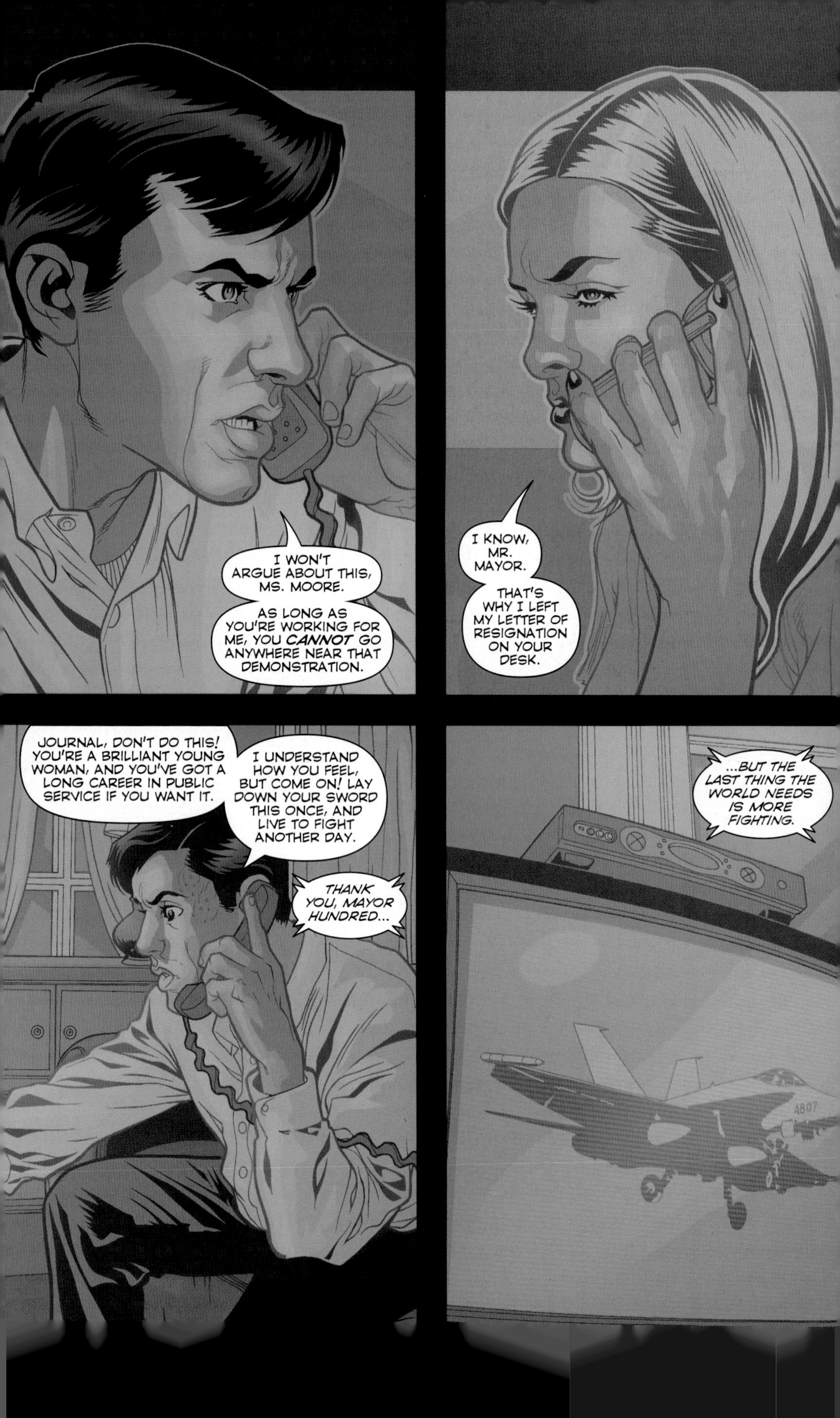
I WON'T ARGUE ABOUT THIS, MS. MOORE.
AS LONG AS YOU'RE WORKING FOR ME, YOU CANNOT GO ANYWHERE NEAR THAT DEMONSTRATION.
I KNOW, MR. MAYOR.
THAT'S WHY I LEFT MY LETTER OF RESIGNATION ON YOUR DESK.
JOURNAL, DON'T DO THIS! YOU'RE A BRILLIANT YOUNG WOMAN, AND YOU'VE GOT A LONG CAREER IN PUBLIC SERVICE IF YOU WANT IT.
I UNDERSTAND HOW YOU FEEL, BUT COME ON! LAY DOWN YOUR SWORD THIS ONCE, AND LIVE TO FIGHT ANOTHER DAY.
THANK YOU, MAYOR HUNDRED...
...BUT THE LAST THING THE WORLD NEEDS IS MORE FIGHTING.
4807

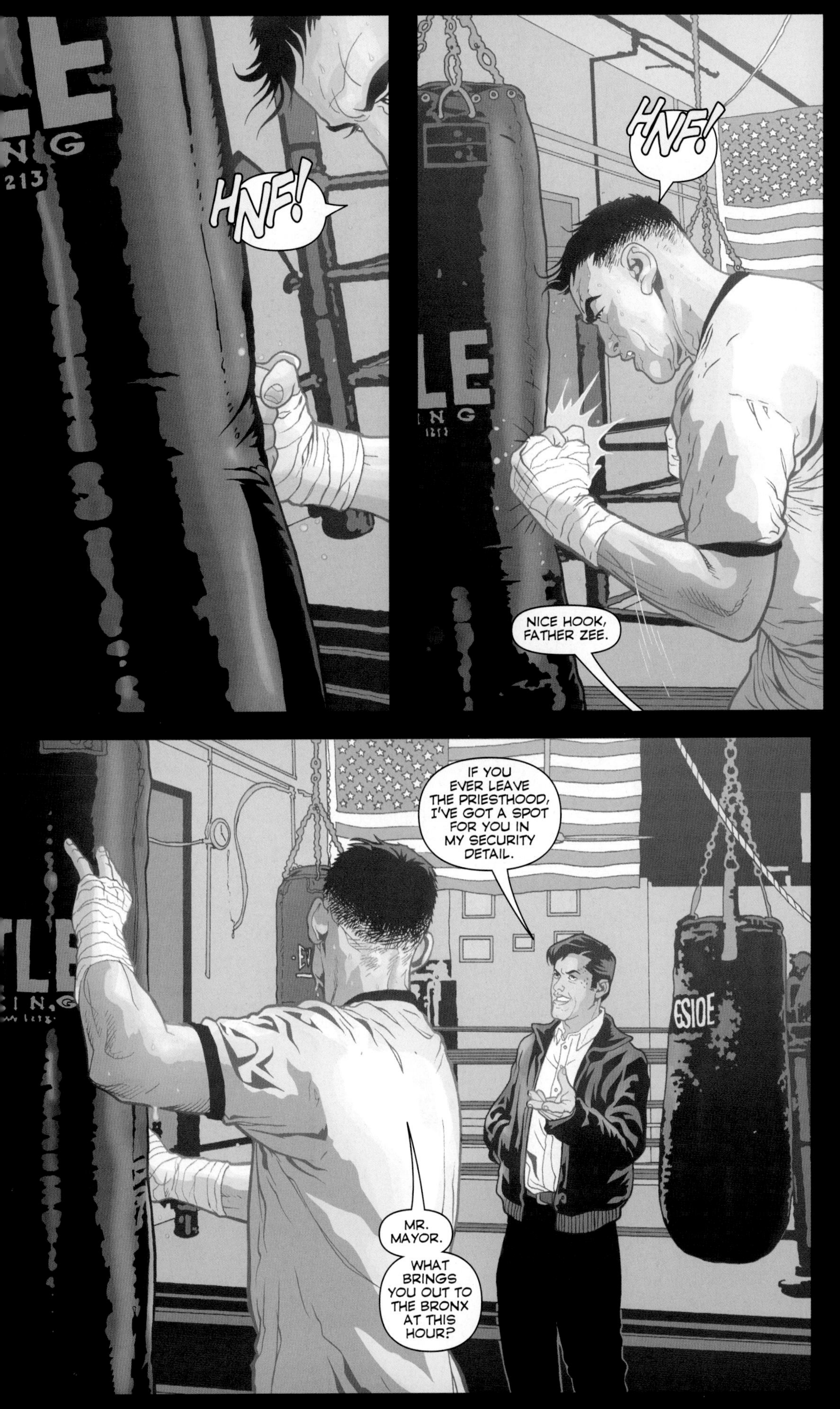

HNF!
HNF!
NICE HOOK, FATHER ZEE.
IF YOU EVER LEAVE THE PRIESTHOOD, I'VE GOT A SPOT FOR YOU IN MY SECURITY DETAIL.
MR. MAYOR.
WHAT BRINGS YOU OUT TO THE BRONX AT THIS HOUR?

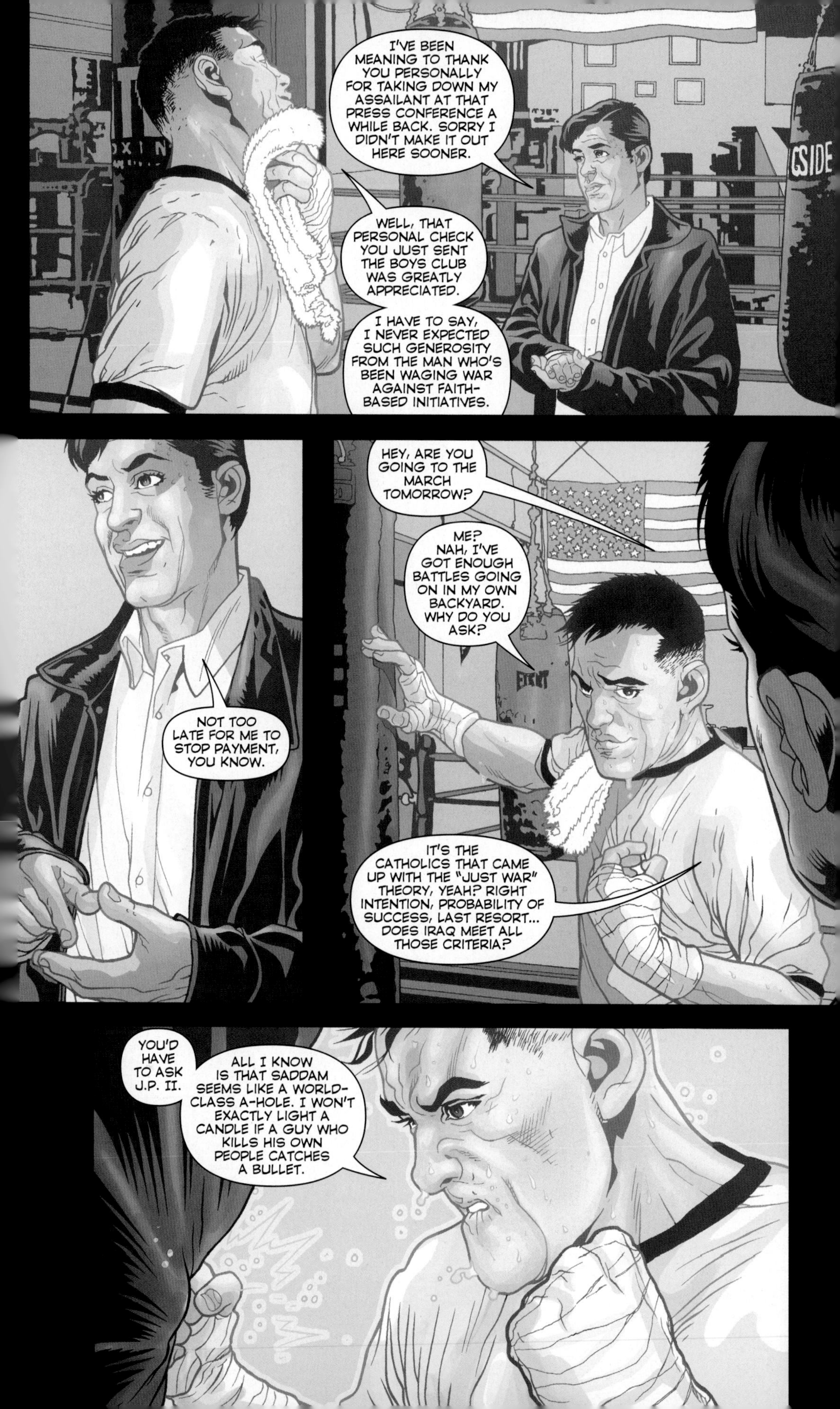
I'VE BEEN MEANING TO THANK YOU PERSONALLY FOR TAKING DOWN MY ASSAILANT AT THAT PRESS CONFERENCE A WHILE BACK. SORRY I DIDN'T MAKE IT OUT HERE SOONER.
WELL, THAT PERSONAL CHECK YOU JUST SENT THE BOYS CLUB WAS GREATLY APPRECIATED.
I HAVE TO SAY, I NEVER EXPECTED SUCH GENEROSITY FROM THE MAN WHO'S BEEN WAGING WAR AGAINST FAITH-BASED INITIATIVES.
NOT TOO LATE FOR ME TO STOP PAYMENT, YOU KNOW.
HEY, ARE YOU GOING TO THE MARCH TOMORROW?
ME? NAH, I'VE GOT ENOUGH BATTLES GOING ON IN MY OWN BACKYARD. WHY DO YOU ASK?
IT'S THE CATHOLICS THAT CAME UP WITH THE "JUST WAR" THEORY, YEAH? RIGHT INTENTION, PROBABILITY OF SUCCESS, LAST RESORT... DOES IRAQ MEET ALL THOSE CRITERIA?
YOU'D HAVE TO ASK J.P. II.
ALL I KNOW IS THAT SADDAM SEEMS LIKE A WORLD-CLASS A-HOLE. I WON'T EXACTLY LIGHT A CANDLE IF A GUY WHO KILLS HIS OWN PEOPLE CATCHES A BULLET.

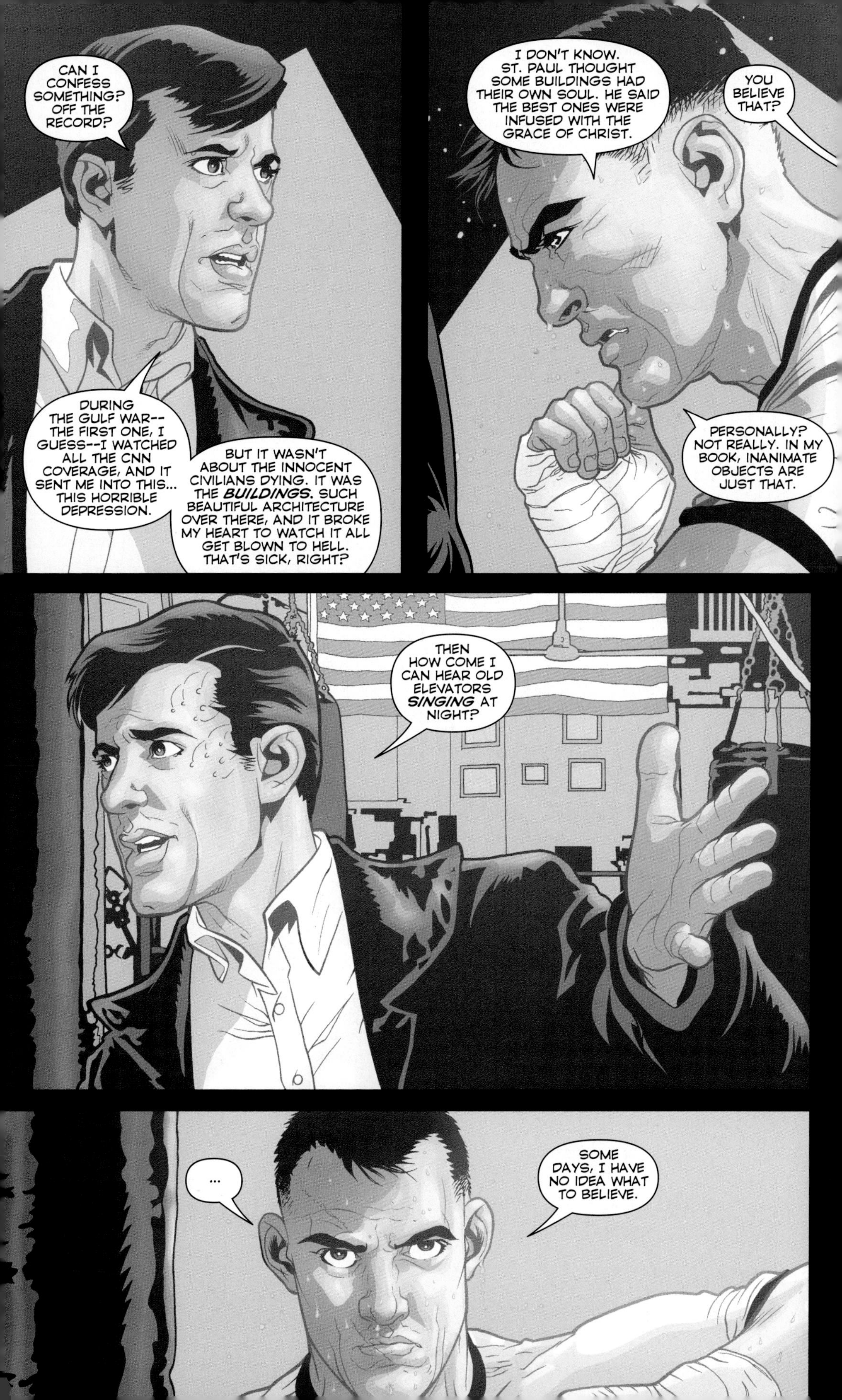
CAN I CONFESS SOMETHING? OFF THE RECORD?
DURING THE GULF WAR-- THE FIRST ONE, I GUESS--I WATCHED ALL THE CNN COVERAGE, AND IT SENT ME INTO THIS... THIS HORRIBLE DEPRESSION.
BUT IT WASN'T ABOUT THE INNOCENT CIVILIANS DYING. IT WAS THE ***BUILDINGS.*** SUCH BEAUTIFUL ARCHITECTURE OVER THERE, AND IT BROKE MY HEART TO WATCH IT ALL GET BLOWN TO HELL. THAT'S SICK, RIGHT?
I DON'T KNOW. ST. PAUL THOUGHT SOME BUILDINGS HAD THEIR OWN SOUL. HE SAID THE BEST ONES WERE INFUSED WITH THE GRACE OF CHRIST.
YOU BELIEVE THAT?
PERSONALLY? NOT REALLY. IN MY BOOK, INANIMATE OBJECTS ARE JUST THAT.
THEN HOW COME I CAN HEAR OLD ELEVATORS *SINGING* AT NIGHT?
...
SOME DAYS, I HAVE NO IDEA WHAT TO BELIEVE.

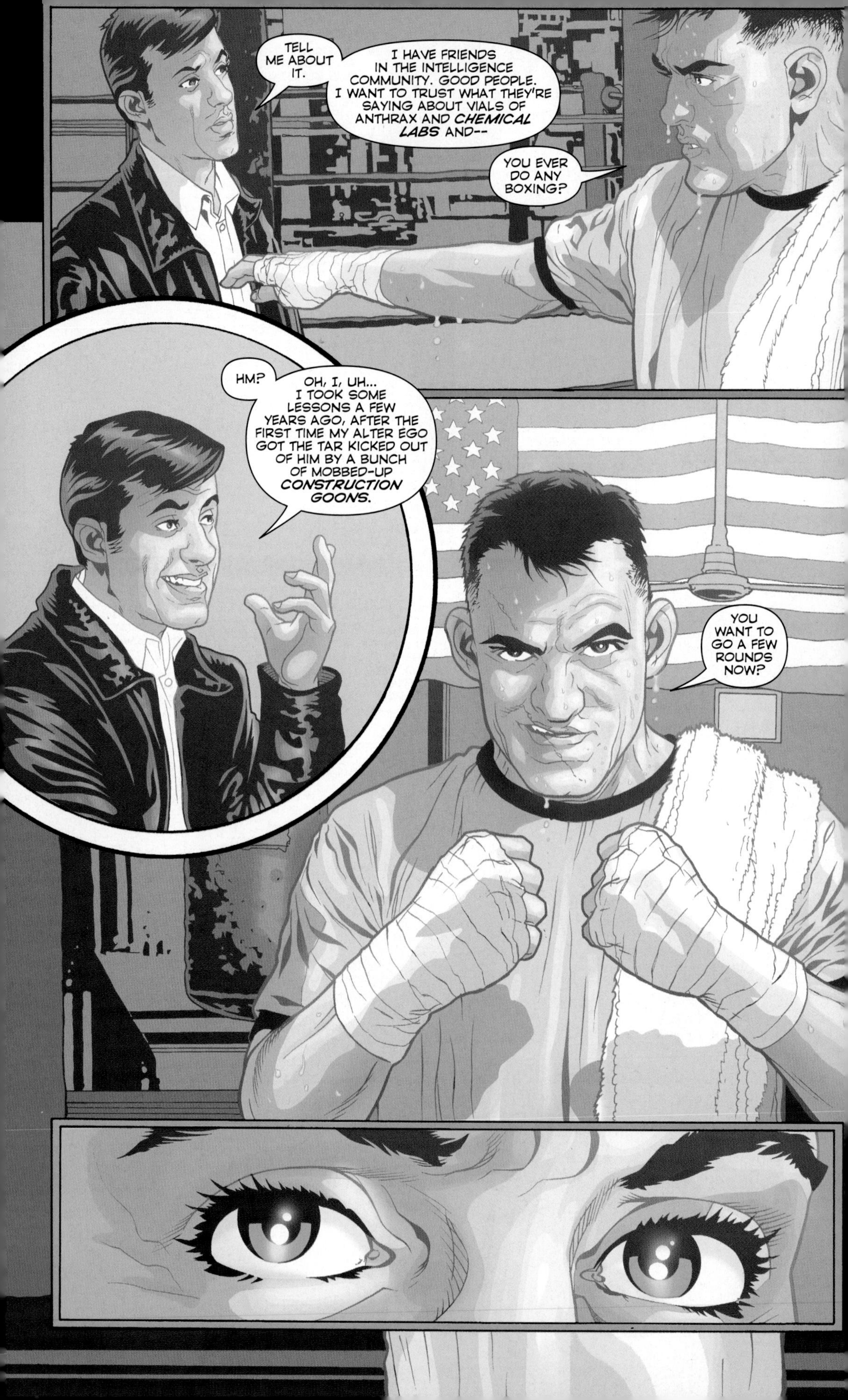
TELL ME ABOUT IT.
I HAVE FRIENDS IN THE INTELLIGENCE COMMUNITY. GOOD PEOPLE. I WANT TO TRUST WHAT THEY'RE SAYING ABOUT VIALS OF ANTHRAX AND *CHEMICAL LABS* AND--
YOU EVER DO ANY BOXING?
HM?
OH, I, UH... I TOOK SOME LESSONS A FEW YEARS AGO, AFTER THE FIRST TIME MY ALTER EGO GOT THE TAR KICKED OUT OF HIM BY A BUNCH OF MOBBED-UP *CONSTRUCTION GOONS*.
YOU WANT TO GO A FEW ROUNDS NOW?

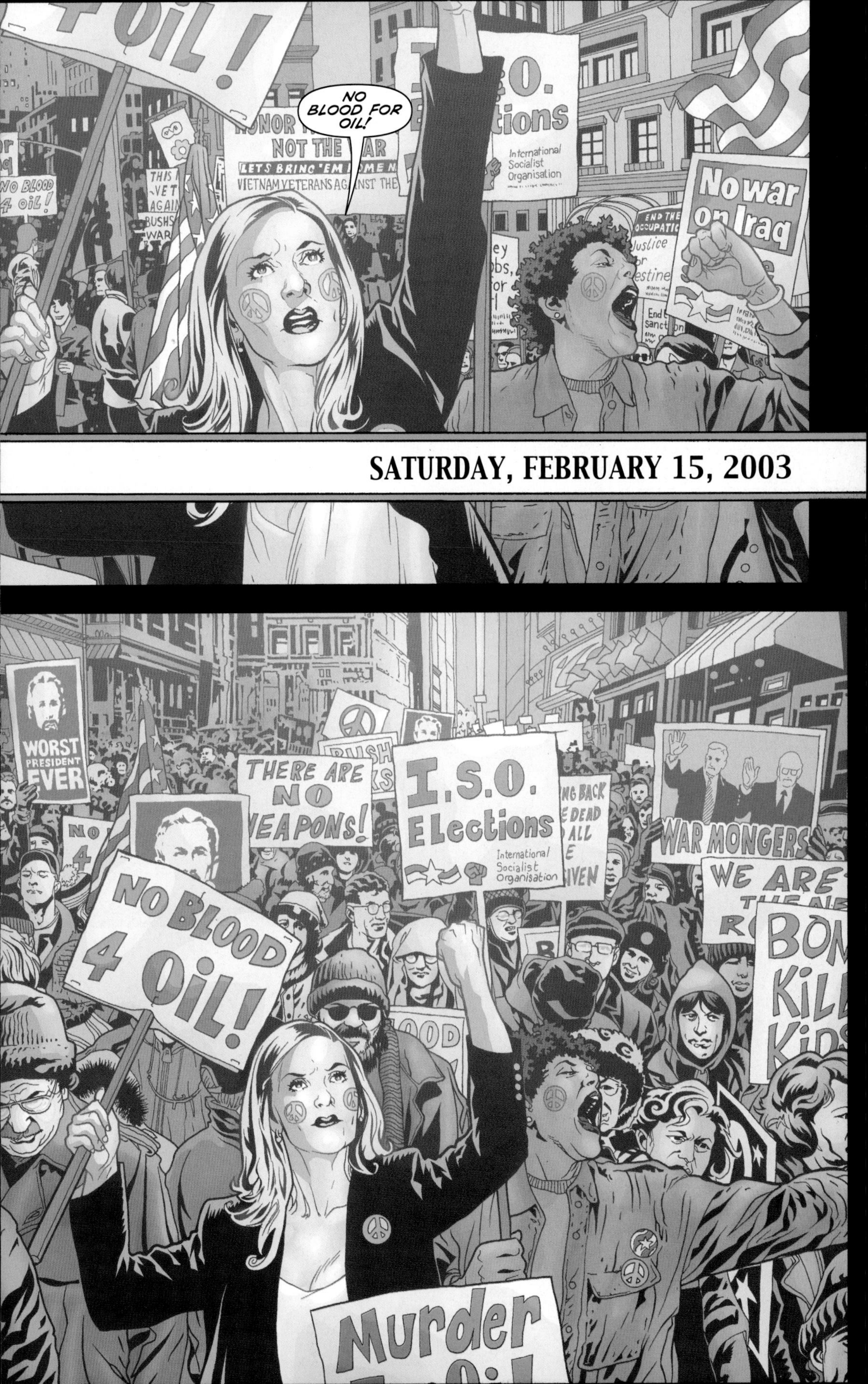

NO BLOOD FOR OIL!
SATURDAY, FEBRUARY 15, 2003
NO BLOOD 4 oiL!
VIETNAM VETERANS AGAINST THE
International Socialist Organisation
No war on Iraq
WORST PRESIDENT EVER
THERE ARE NO WEAPONS!
I.S.O. Elections
International Socialist Organisation
WAR MONGERS
NO BLOOD 4 OiL!
Murder

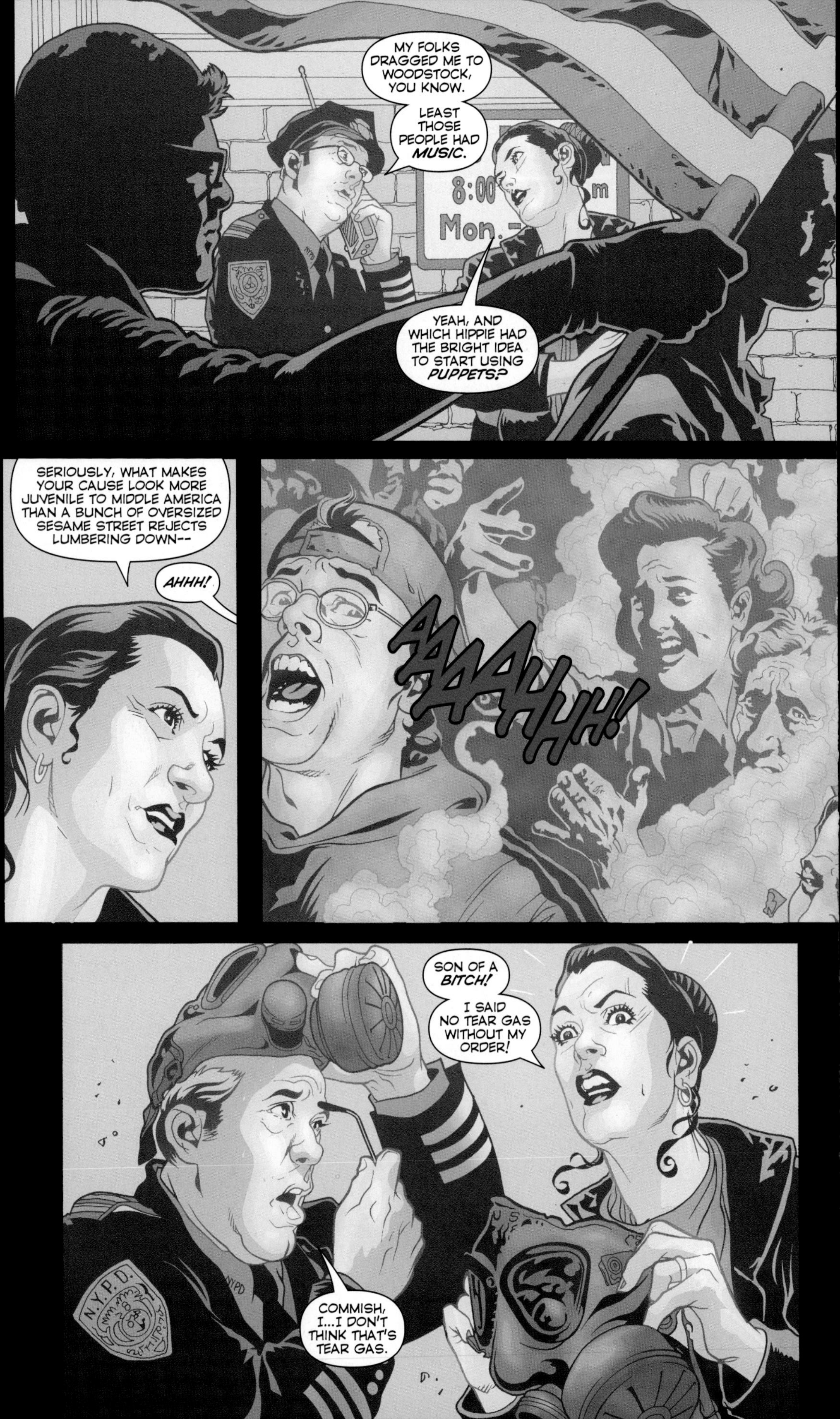
MY FOLKS DRAGGED ME TO WOODSTOCK, YOU KNOW.
LEAST THOSE PEOPLE HAD MUSIC.
8:00 m
Mon. -
YEAH, AND WHICH HIPPIE HAD THE BRIGHT IDEA TO START USING PUPPETS?
SERIOUSLY, WHAT MAKES YOUR CAUSE LOOK MORE JUVENILE TO MIDDLE AMERICA THAN A BUNCH OF OVERSIZED SESAME STREET REJECTS LUMBERING DOWN--
AHHH!
AAAAAHHHH!
SON OF A BITCH!
I SAID NO TEAR GAS WITHOUT MY ORDER!
COMMISH, I...I DON'T THINK THAT'S TEAR GAS.

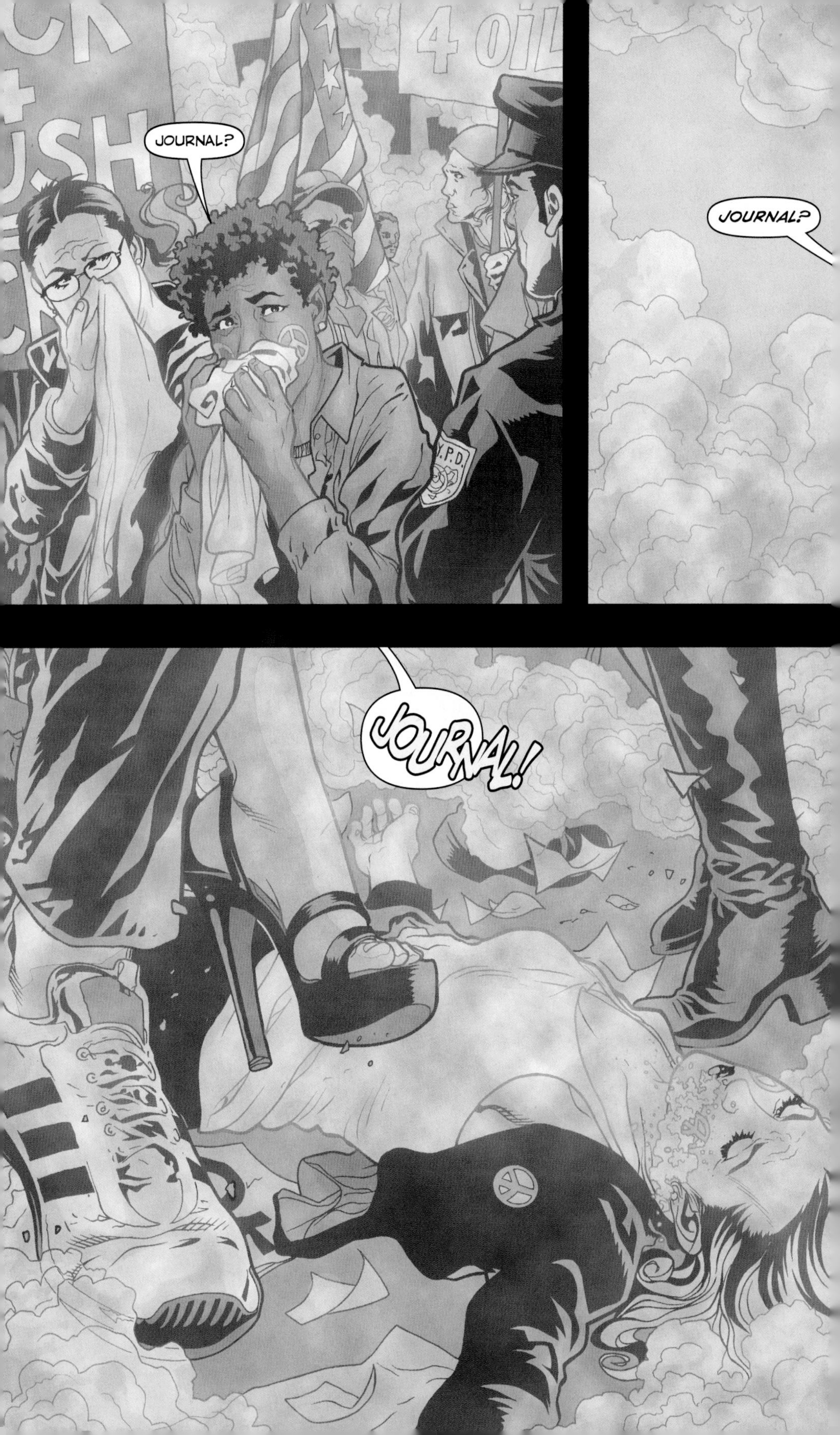
4 OiL
JOURNAL?
JOURNAL?
JOURNAL!

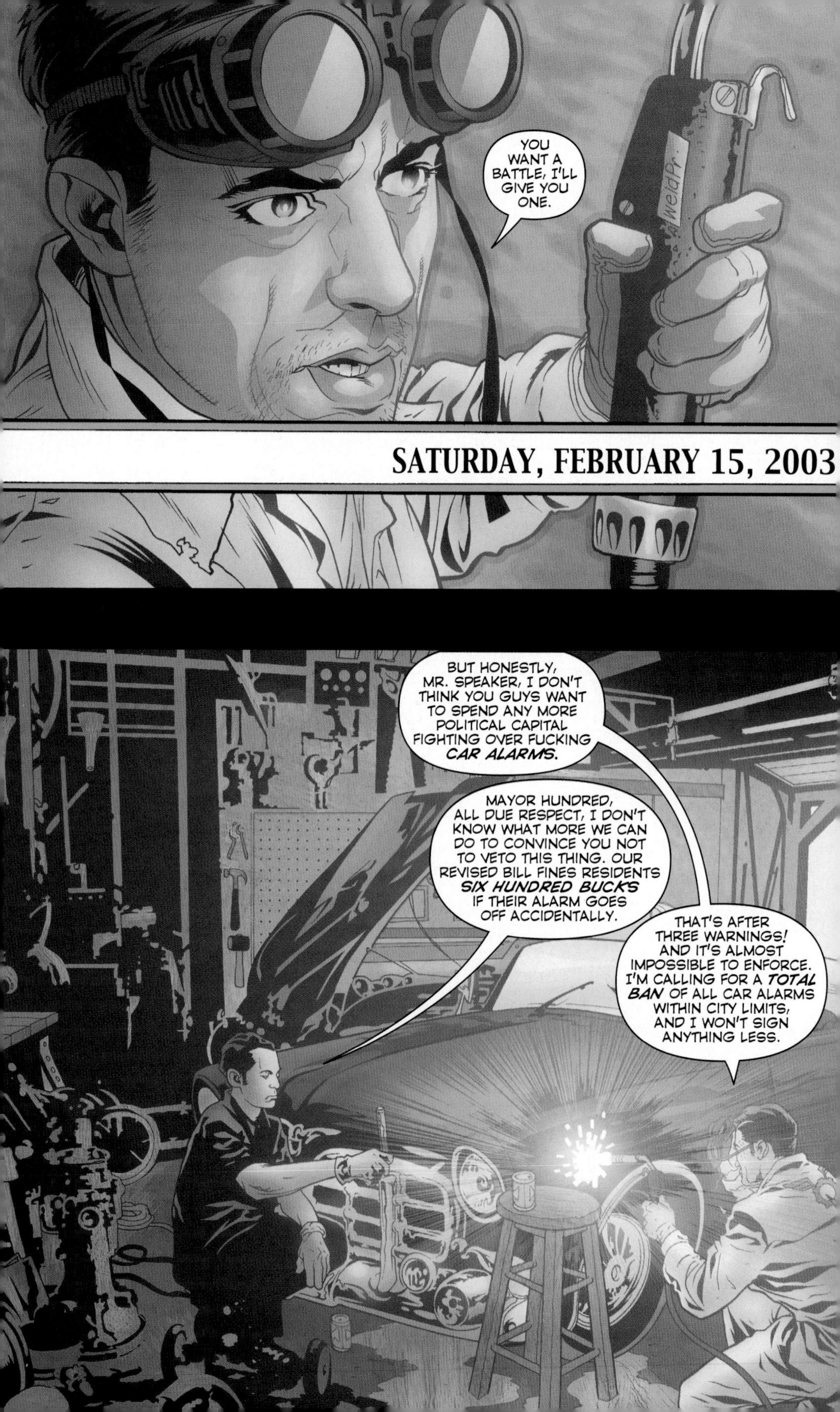
YOU WANT A BATTLE, I'LL GIVE YOU ONE.
SATURDAY, FEBRUARY 15, 2003
BUT HONESTLY, MR. SPEAKER, I DON'T THINK YOU GUYS WANT TO SPEND ANY MORE POLITICAL CAPITAL FIGHTING OVER FUCKING CAR ALARMS.
MAYOR HUNDRED, ALL DUE RESPECT, I DON'T KNOW WHAT MORE WE CAN DO TO CONVINCE YOU NOT TO VETO THIS THING. OUR REVISED BILL FINES RESIDENTS SIX HUNDRED BUCKS IF THEIR ALARM GOES OFF ACCIDENTALLY.
THAT'S AFTER THREE WARNINGS! AND IT'S ALMOST IMPOSSIBLE TO ENFORCE. I'M CALLING FOR A TOTAL BAN OF ALL CAR ALARMS WITHIN CITY LIMITS, AND I WON'T SIGN ANYTHING LESS.

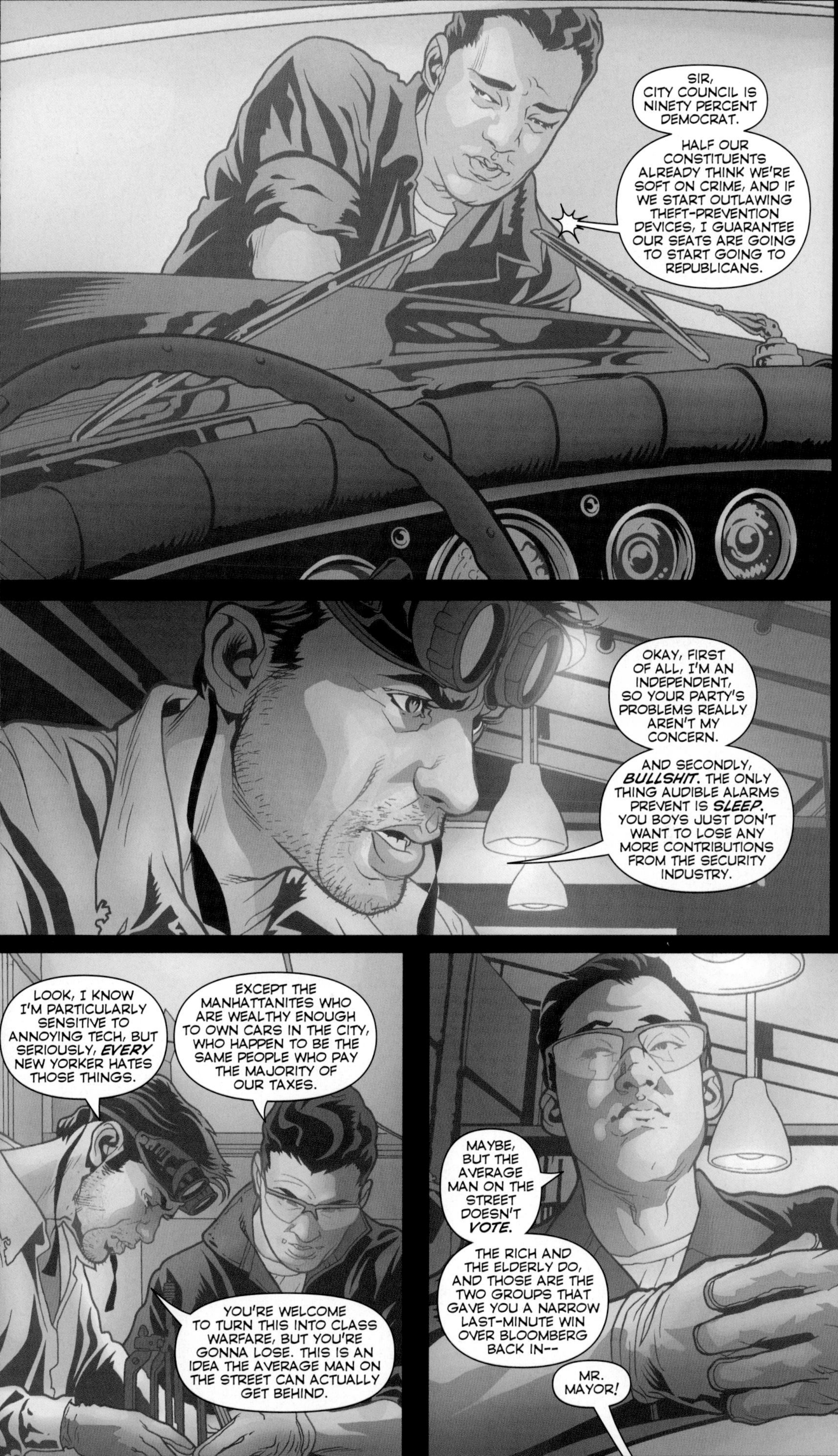
SIR, CITY COUNCIL IS NINETY PERCENT DEMOCRAT.
HALF OUR CONSTITUENTS ALREADY THINK WE'RE SOFT ON CRIME, AND IF WE START OUTLAWING THEFT-PREVENTION DEVICES, I GUARANTEE OUR SEATS ARE GOING TO START GOING TO REPUBLICANS.
OKAY, FIRST OF ALL, I'M AN INDEPENDENT, SO YOUR PARTY'S PROBLEMS REALLY AREN'T MY CONCERN.
AND SECONDLY, ***BULLSHIT***. THE ONLY THING AUDIBLE ALARMS PREVENT IS ***SLEEP***. YOU BOYS JUST DON'T WANT TO LOSE ANY MORE CONTRIBUTIONS FROM THE SECURITY INDUSTRY.
LOOK, I KNOW I'M PARTICULARLY SENSITIVE TO ANNOYING TECH, BUT SERIOUSLY, ***EVERY*** NEW YORKER HATES THOSE THINGS.
EXCEPT THE MANHATTANITES WHO ARE WEALTHY ENOUGH TO OWN CARS IN THE CITY, WHO HAPPEN TO BE THE SAME PEOPLE WHO PAY THE MAJORITY OF OUR TAXES.
YOU'RE WELCOME TO TURN THIS INTO CLASS WARFARE, BUT YOU'RE GONNA LOSE. THIS IS AN IDEA THE AVERAGE MAN ON THE STREET CAN ACTUALLY GET BEHIND.
MAYBE, BUT THE AVERAGE MAN ON THE STREET DOESN'T ***VOTE***.
THE RICH AND THE ELDERLY DO, AND THOSE ARE THE TWO GROUPS THAT GAVE YOU A NARROW LAST-MINUTE WIN OVER BLOOMBERG BACK IN--
MR. MAYOR!

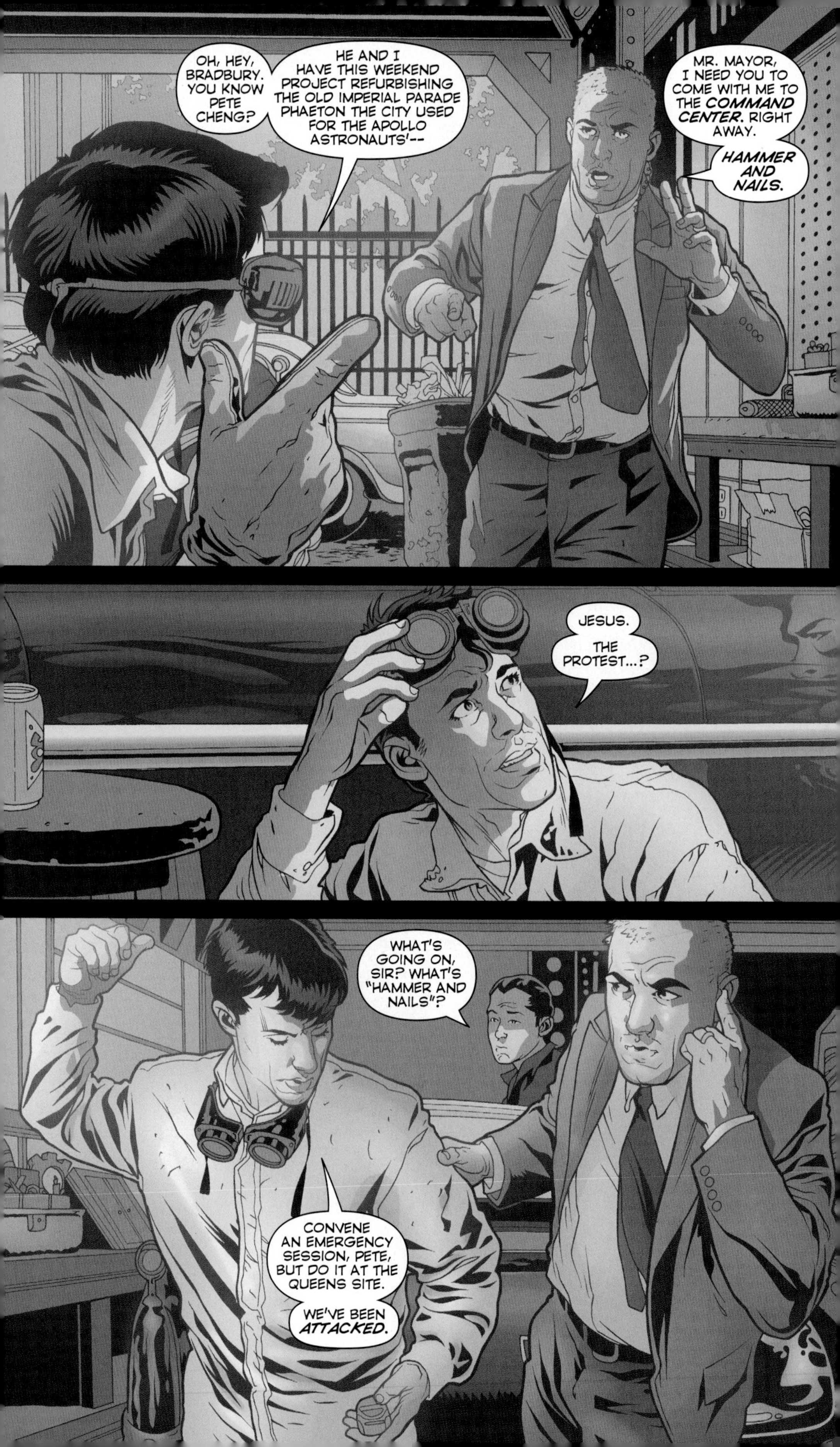
OH, HEY, BRADBURY. YOU KNOW PETE CHENG?
HE AND I HAVE THIS WEEKEND PROJECT REFURBISHING THE OLD IMPERIAL PARADE PHAETON THE CITY USED FOR THE APOLLO ASTRONAUTS'--
MR. MAYOR, I NEED YOU TO COME WITH ME TO THE COMMAND CENTER. RIGHT AWAY.
HAMMER AND NAILS.
JESUS.
THE PROTEST...?
WHAT'S GOING ON, SIR? WHAT'S "HAMMER AND NAILS"?
CONVENE AN EMERGENCY SESSION, PETE, BUT DO IT AT THE QUEENS SITE.
WE'VE BEEN ATTACKED.

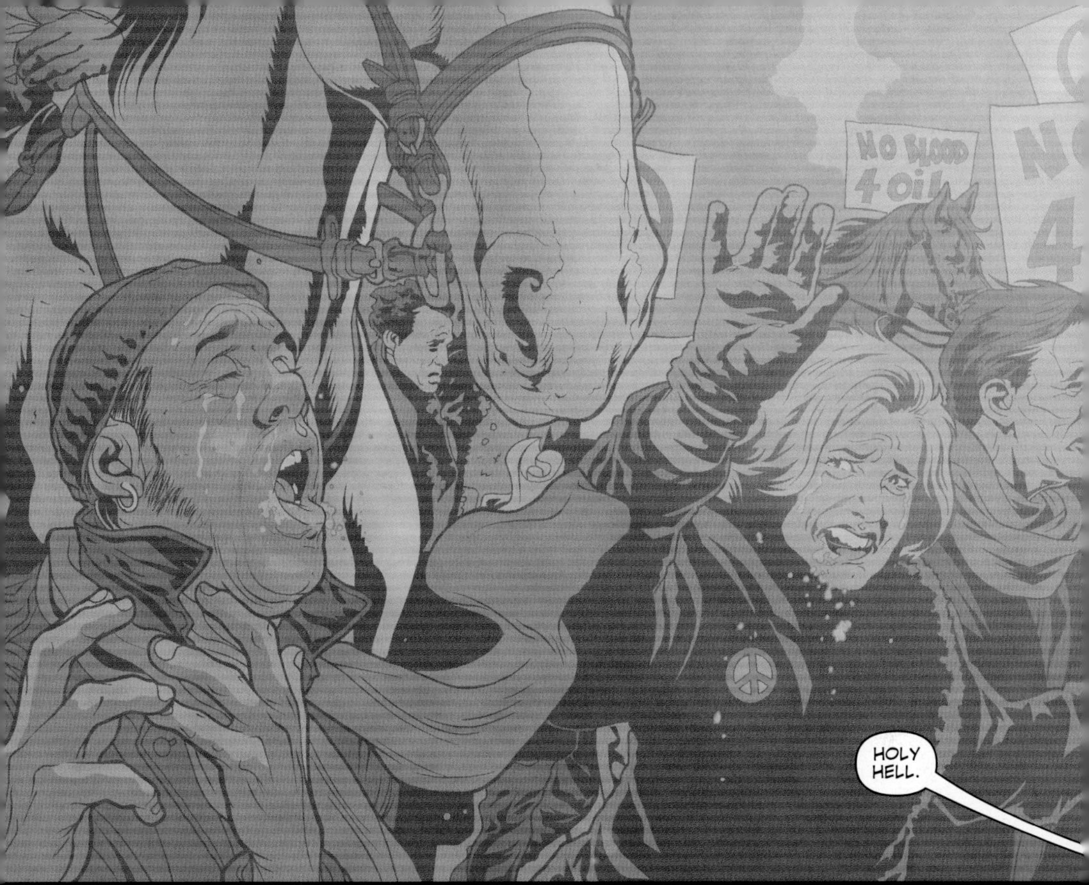
NO BLOOD 4 OIL
HOLY HELL.

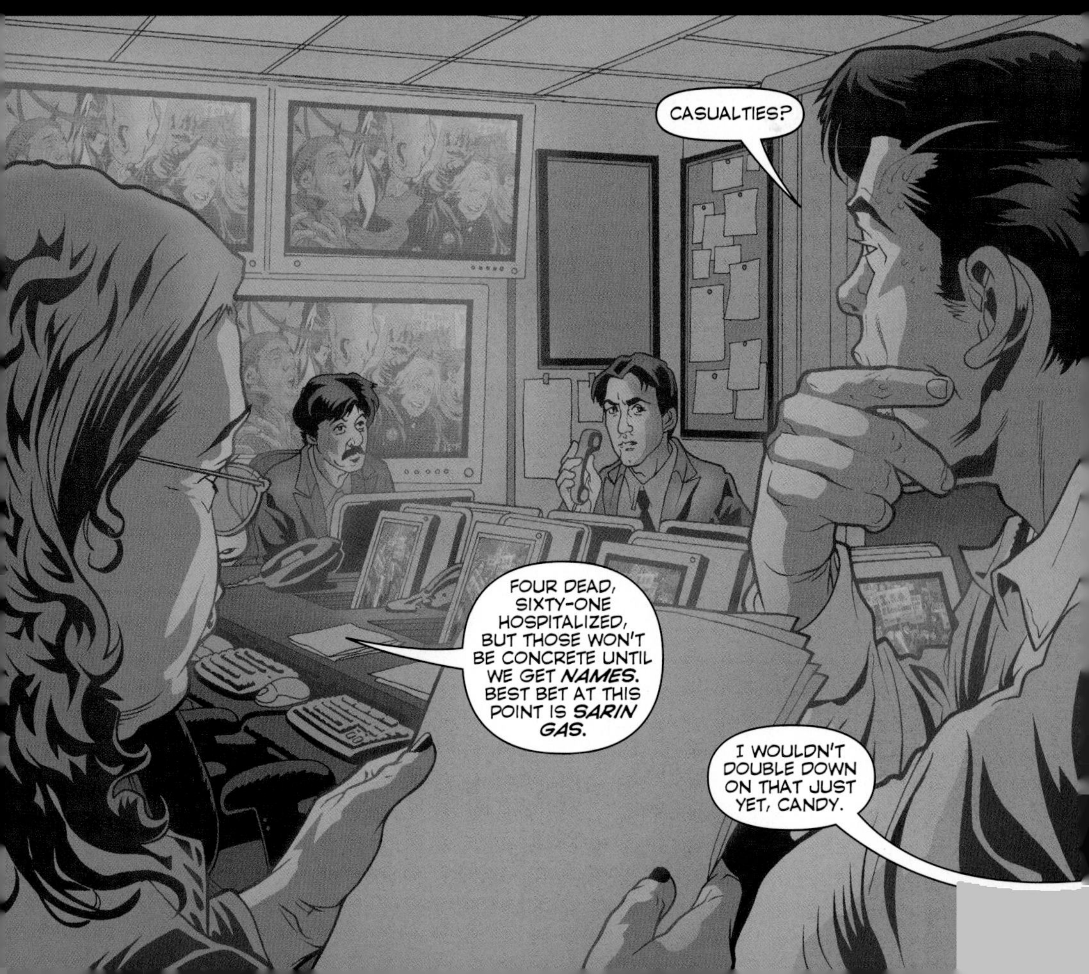
CASUALTIES?
FOUR DEAD, SIXTY-ONE HOSPITALIZED, BUT THOSE WON'T BE CONCRETE UNTIL WE GET *NAMES*. BEST BET AT THIS POINT IS *SARIN GAS*.
I WOULDN'T DOUBLE DOWN ON THAT JUST YET, CANDY.

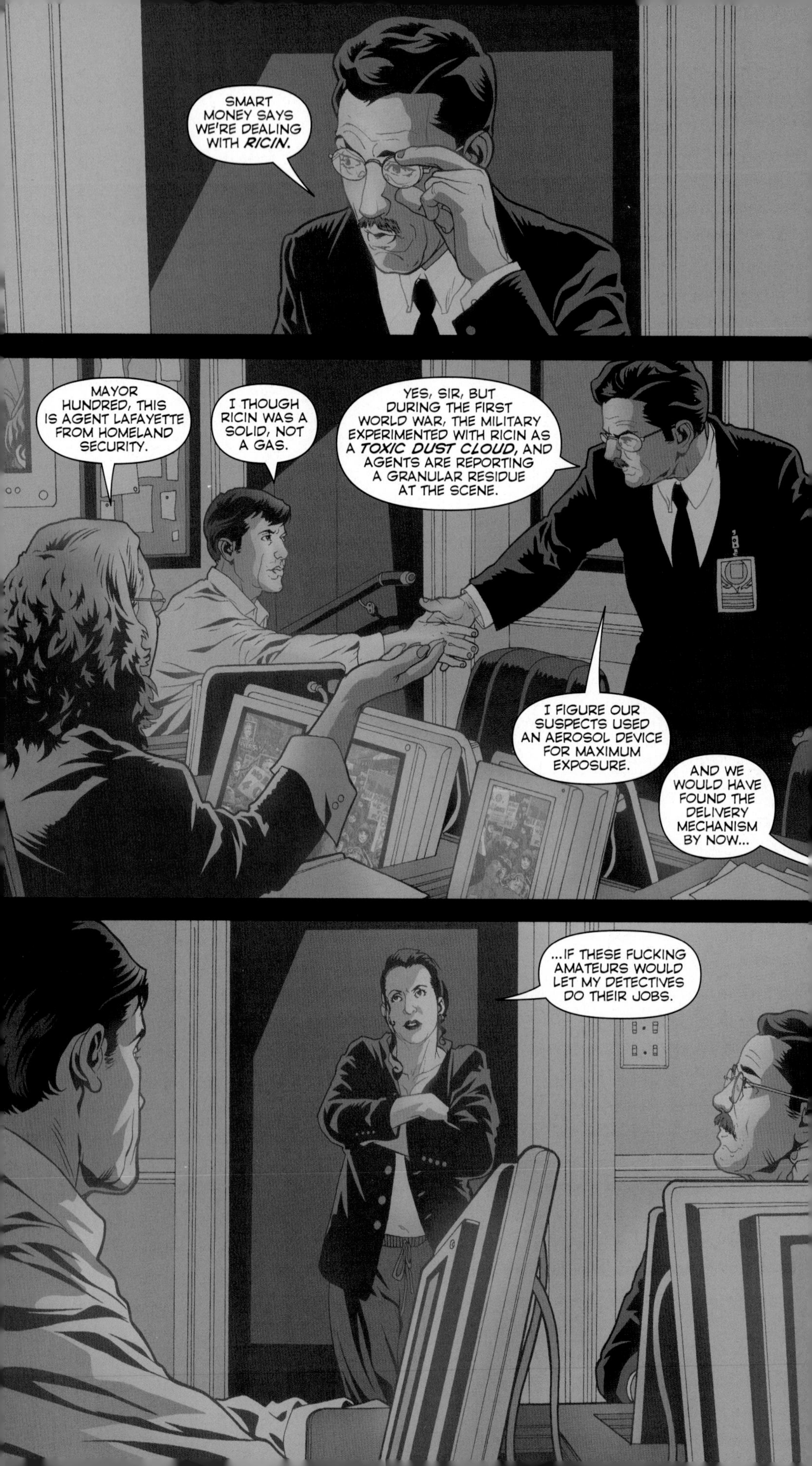
SMART MONEY SAYS WE'RE DEALING WITH RICIN.
MAYOR HUNDRED, THIS IS AGENT LAFAYETTE FROM HOMELAND SECURITY.
I THOUGH RICIN WAS A SOLID, NOT A GAS.
YES, SIR, BUT DURING THE FIRST WORLD WAR, THE MILITARY EXPERIMENTED WITH RICIN AS A TOXIC DUST CLOUD, AND AGENTS ARE REPORTING A GRANULAR RESIDUE AT THE SCENE.
I FIGURE OUR SUSPECTS USED AN AEROSOL DEVICE FOR MAXIMUM EXPOSURE.
AND WE WOULD HAVE FOUND THE DELIVERY MECHANISM BY NOW...
...IF THESE FUCKING AMATEURS WOULD LET MY DETECTIVES DO THEIR JOBS.

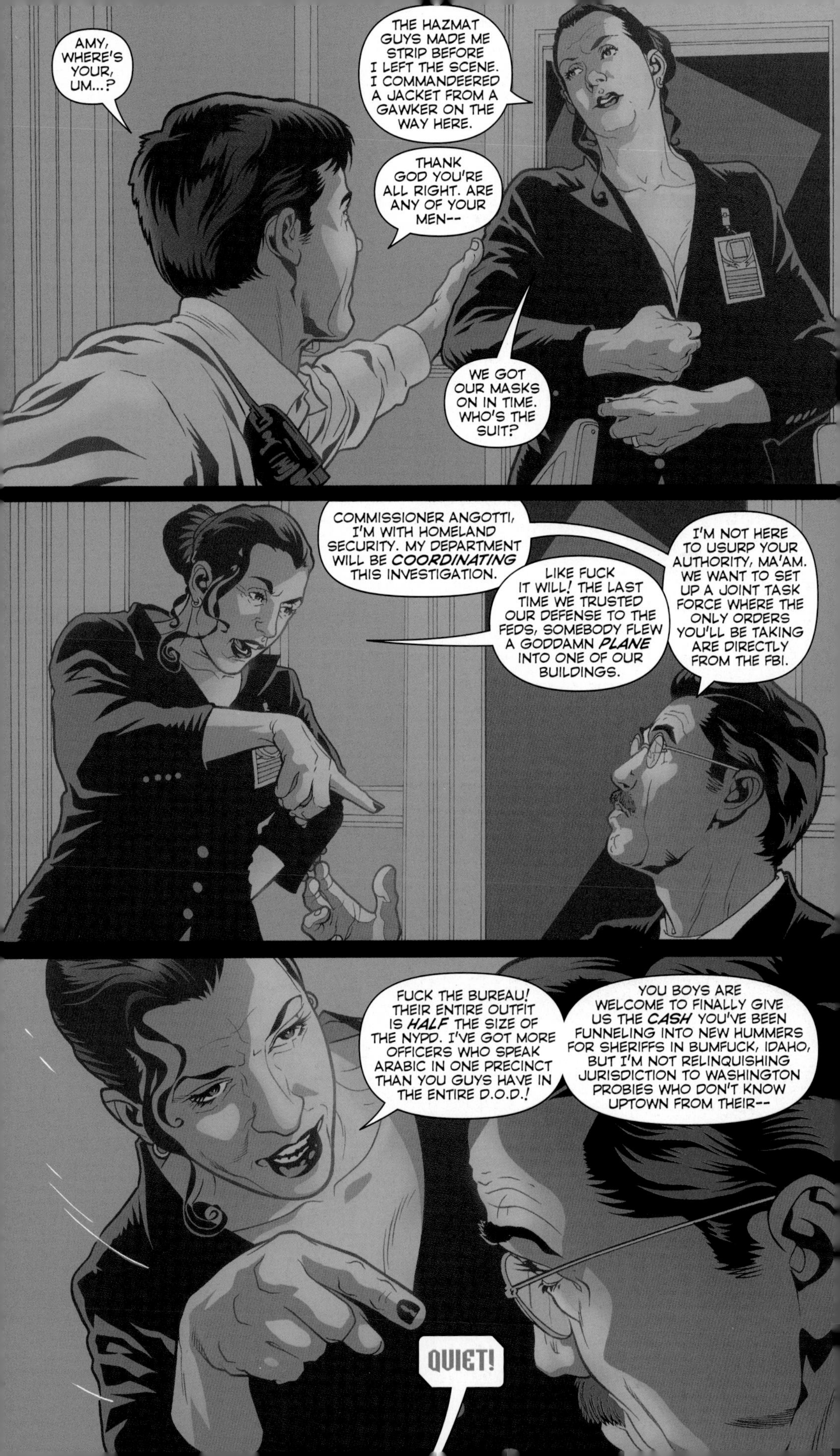
AMY, WHERE'S YOUR, UM...?
THE HAZMAT GUYS MADE ME STRIP BEFORE I LEFT THE SCENE. I COMMANDEERED A JACKET FROM A GAWKER ON THE WAY HERE.
THANK GOD YOU'RE ALL RIGHT. ARE ANY OF YOUR MEN--
WE GOT OUR MASKS ON IN TIME. WHO'S THE SUIT?
COMMISSIONER ANGOTTI, I'M WITH HOMELAND SECURITY. MY DEPARTMENT WILL BE *COORDINATING* THIS INVESTIGATION.
LIKE FUCK IT WILL! THE LAST TIME WE TRUSTED OUR DEFENSE TO THE FEDS, SOMEBODY FLEW A GODDAMN *PLANE* INTO ONE OF OUR BUILDINGS.
I'M NOT HERE TO USURP YOUR AUTHORITY, MA'AM. WE WANT TO SET UP A JOINT TASK FORCE WHERE THE ONLY ORDERS YOU'LL BE TAKING ARE DIRECTLY FROM THE FBI.
FUCK THE BUREAU! THEIR ENTIRE OUTFIT IS *HALF* THE SIZE OF THE NYPD. I'VE GOT MORE OFFICERS WHO SPEAK ARABIC IN ONE PRECINCT THAN YOU GUYS HAVE IN THE ENTIRE D.O.D.!
YOU BOYS ARE WELCOME TO FINALLY GIVE US THE *CASH* YOU'VE BEEN FUNNELING INTO NEW HUMMERS FOR SHERIFFS IN BUMFUCK, IDAHO, BUT I'M NOT RELINQUISHING JURISDICTION TO WASHINGTON PROBIES WHO DON'T KNOW UPTOWN FROM THEIR--
QUIET!

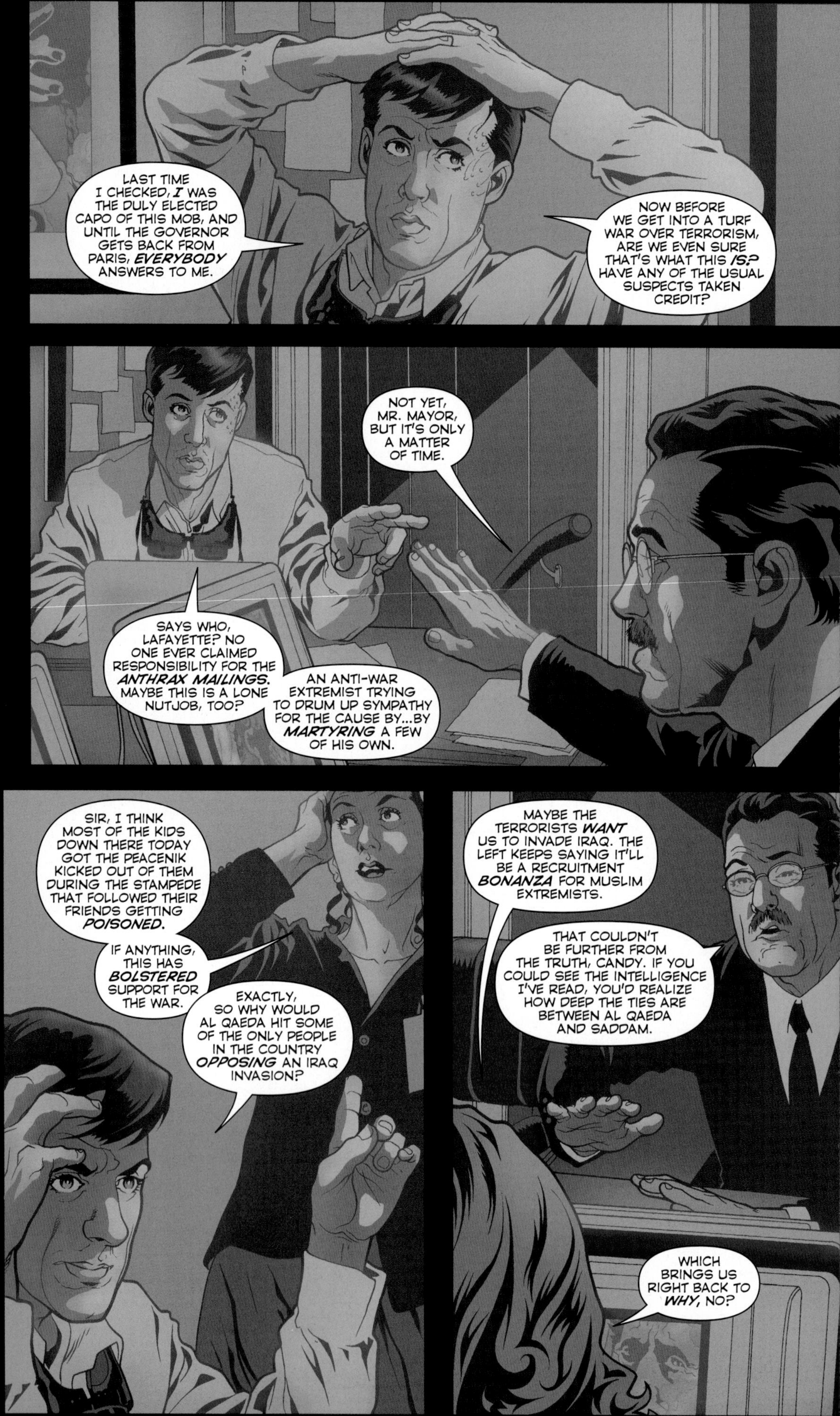
LAST TIME I CHECKED, *I* WAS THE DULY ELECTED CAPO OF THIS MOB, AND UNTIL THE GOVERNOR GETS BACK FROM PARIS, *EVERYBODY* ANSWERS TO ME.
NOW BEFORE WE GET INTO A TURF WAR OVER TERRORISM, ARE WE EVEN SURE THAT'S WHAT THIS *IS?* HAVE ANY OF THE USUAL SUSPECTS TAKEN CREDIT?
NOT YET, MR. MAYOR, BUT IT'S ONLY A MATTER OF TIME.
SAYS WHO, LAFAYETTE? NO ONE EVER CLAIMED RESPONSIBILITY FOR THE *ANTHRAX MAILINGS.* MAYBE THIS IS A LONE NUTJOB, TOO?
AN ANTI-WAR EXTREMIST TRYING TO DRUM UP SYMPATHY FOR THE CAUSE BY...BY *MARTYRING* A FEW OF HIS OWN.
SIR, I THINK MOST OF THE KIDS DOWN THERE TODAY GOT THE PEACENIK KICKED OUT OF THEM DURING THE STAMPEDE THAT FOLLOWED THEIR FRIENDS GETTING *POISONED.*
IF ANYTHING, THIS HAS *BOLSTERED* SUPPORT FOR THE WAR.
EXACTLY, SO WHY WOULD AL QAEDA HIT SOME OF THE ONLY PEOPLE IN THE COUNTRY *OPPOSING* AN IRAQ INVASION?
MAYBE THE TERRORISTS *WANT* US TO INVADE IRAQ. THE LEFT KEEPS SAYING IT'LL BE A RECRUITMENT *BONANZA* FOR MUSLIM EXTREMISTS.
THAT COULDN'T BE FURTHER FROM THE TRUTH, CANDY. IF YOU COULD SEE THE INTELLIGENCE I'VE READ, YOU'D REALIZE HOW DEEP THE TIES ARE BETWEEN AL QAEDA AND SADDAM.
WHICH BRINGS US RIGHT BACK TO *WHY,* NO?

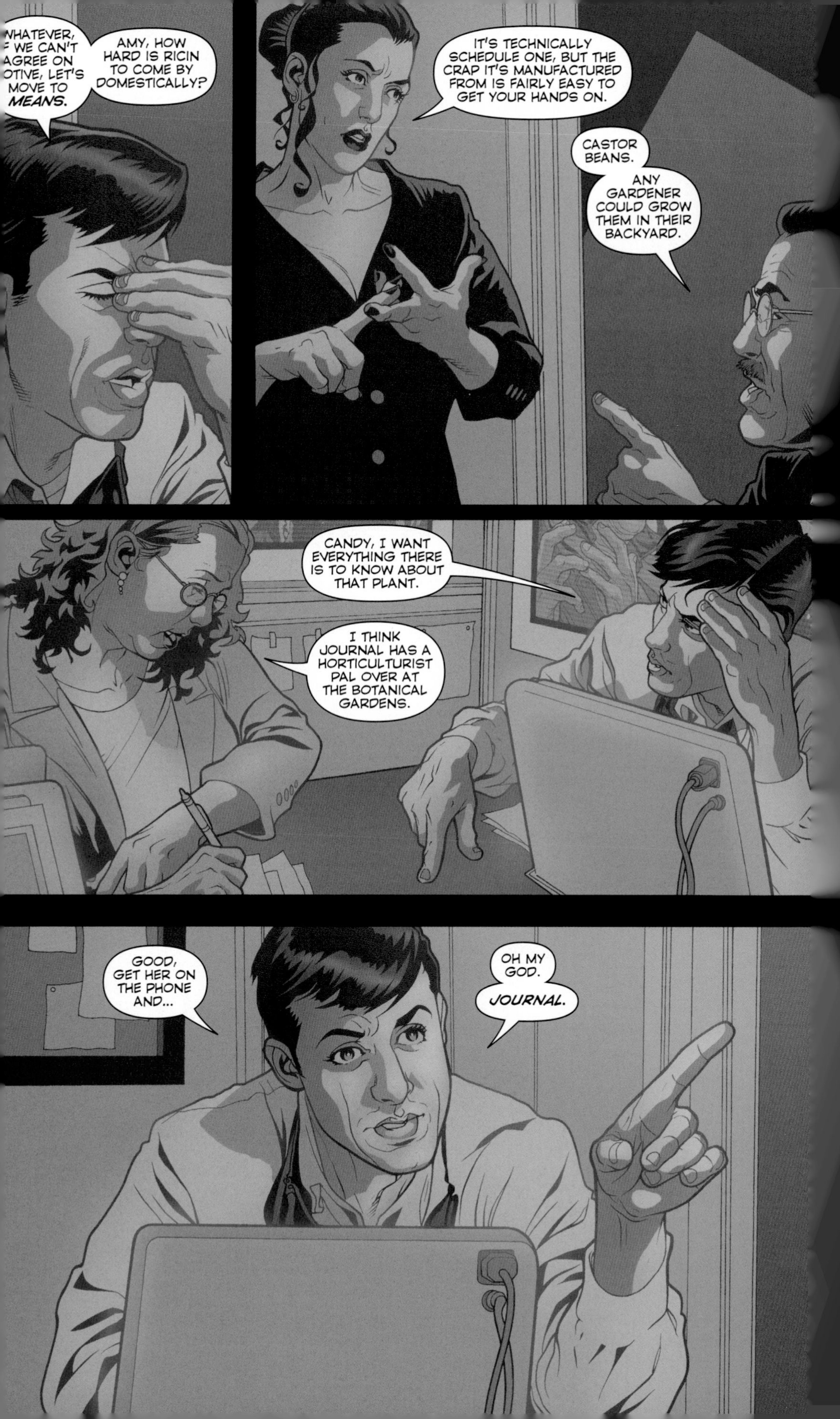
WHATEVER, IF WE CAN'T AGREE ON MOTIVE, LET'S MOVE TO *MEANS*.
AMY, HOW HARD IS RICIN TO COME BY DOMESTICALLY?
IT'S TECHNICALLY SCHEDULE ONE, BUT THE CRAP IT'S MANUFACTURED FROM IS FAIRLY EASY TO GET YOUR HANDS ON.
CASTOR BEANS.
ANY GARDENER COULD GROW THEM IN THEIR BACKYARD.
CANDY, I WANT EVERYTHING THERE IS TO KNOW ABOUT THAT PLANT.
I THINK JOURNAL HAS A HORTICULTURIST PAL OVER AT THE BOTANICAL GARDENS.
GOOD, GET HER ON THE PHONE AND...
OH MY GOD.
*JOURNAL*.

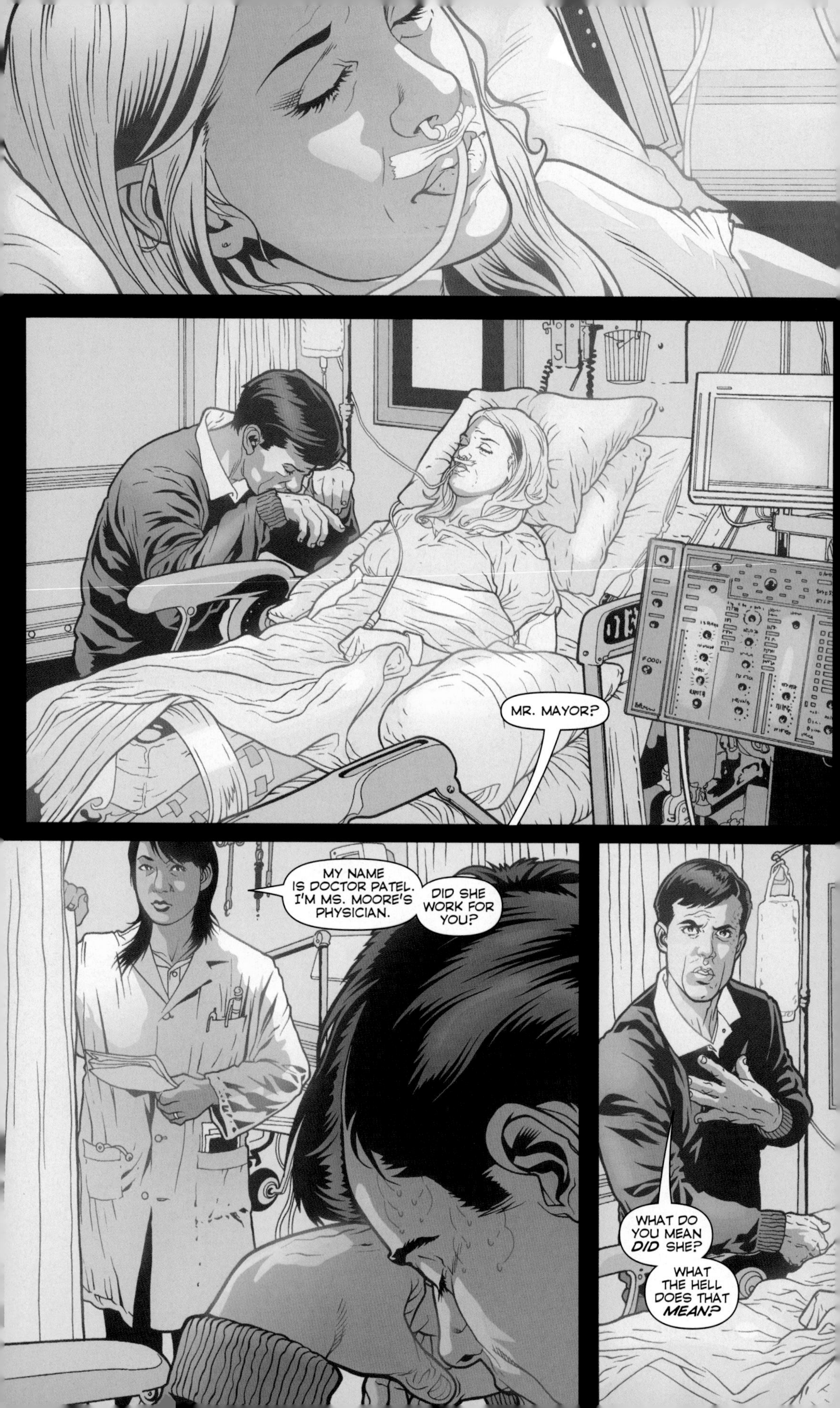
MR. MAYOR?
MY NAME IS DOCTOR PATEL. I'M MS. MOORE'S PHYSICIAN.
DID SHE WORK FOR YOU?
WHAT DO YOU MEAN *DID* SHE?
WHAT THE HELL DOES THAT *MEAN?*

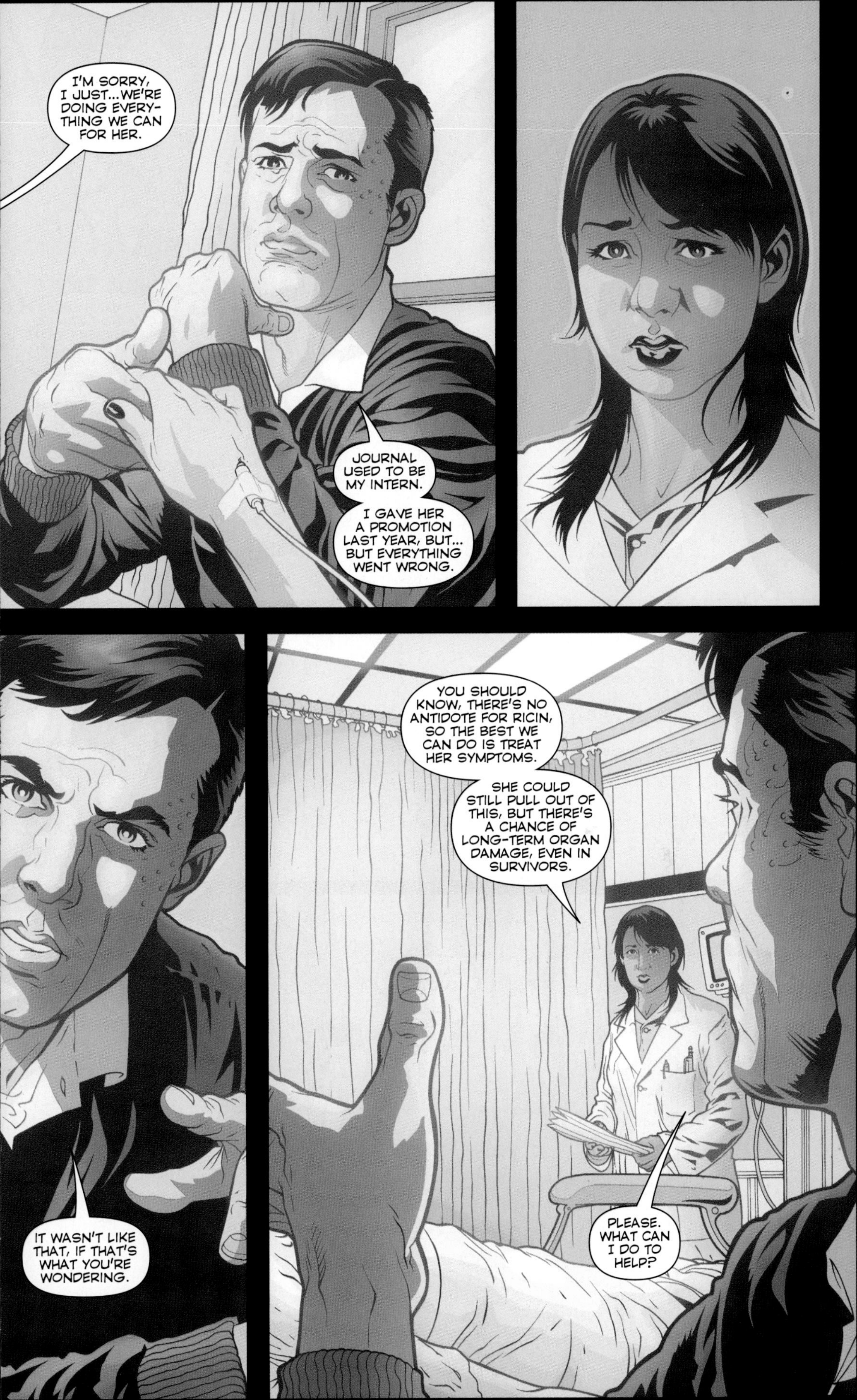
I'M SORRY, I JUST...WE'RE DOING EVERY-THING WE CAN FOR HER.
JOURNAL USED TO BE MY INTERN.
I GAVE HER A PROMOTION LAST YEAR, BUT... BUT EVERYTHING WENT WRONG.
IT WASN'T LIKE THAT, IF THAT'S WHAT YOU'RE WONDERING.
YOU SHOULD KNOW, THERE'S NO ANTIDOTE FOR RICIN, SO THE BEST WE CAN DO IS TREAT HER SYMPTOMS.
SHE COULD STILL PULL OUT OF THIS, BUT THERE'S A CHANCE OF LONG-TERM ORGAN DAMAGE, EVEN IN SURVIVORS.
PLEASE. WHAT CAN I DO TO HELP?

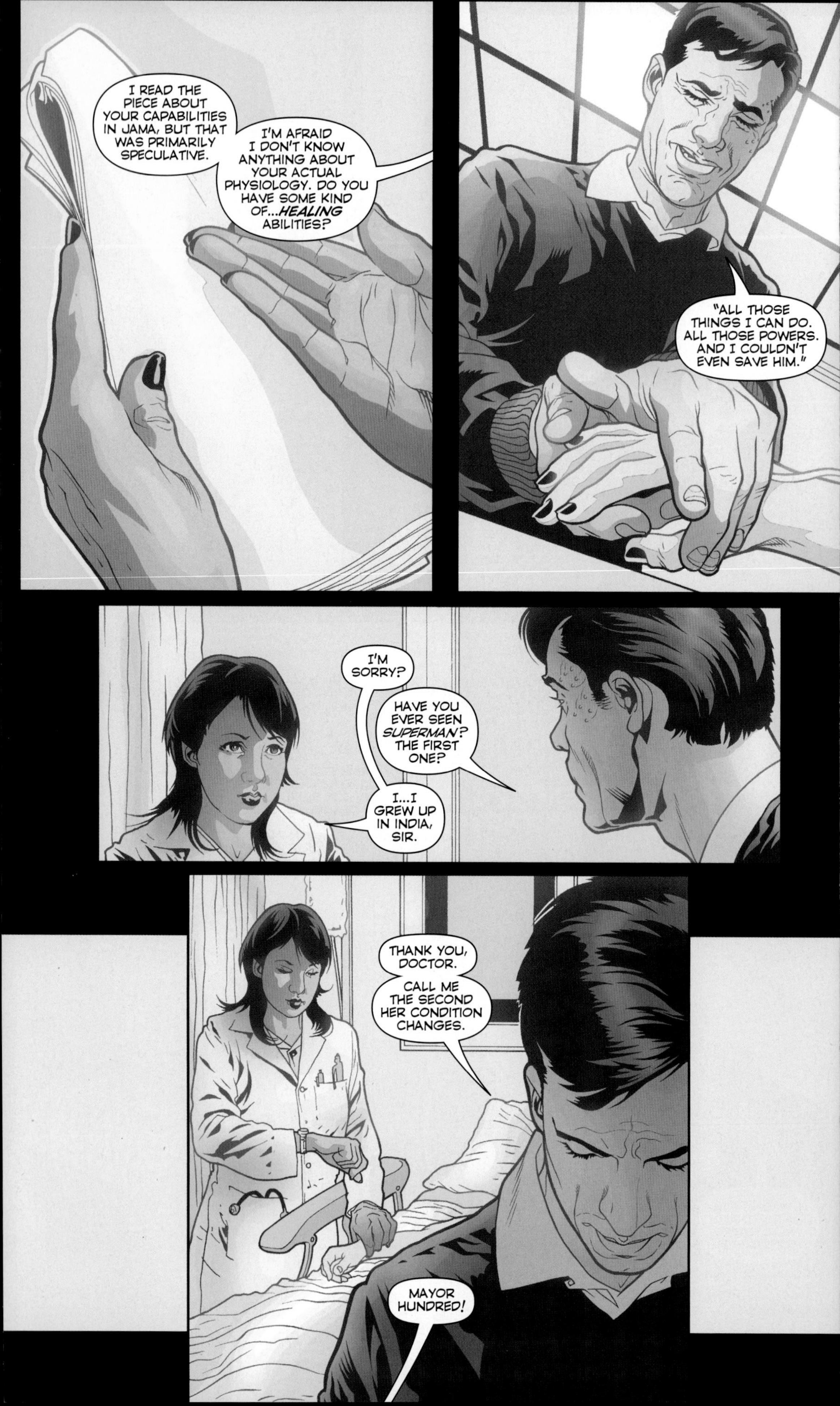
I READ THE PIECE ABOUT YOUR CAPABILITIES IN JAMA, BUT THAT WAS PRIMARILY SPECULATIVE.
I'M AFRAID I DON'T KNOW ANYTHING ABOUT YOUR ACTUAL PHYSIOLOGY. DO YOU HAVE SOME KIND OF...*HEALING* ABILITIES?
"ALL THOSE THINGS I CAN DO. ALL THOSE POWERS. AND I COULDN'T EVEN SAVE HIM."
I'M SORRY?
HAVE YOU EVER SEEN *SUPERMAN*? THE FIRST ONE?
I...I GREW UP IN INDIA, SIR.
THANK YOU, DOCTOR.
CALL ME THE SECOND HER CONDITION CHANGES.
MAYOR HUNDRED!

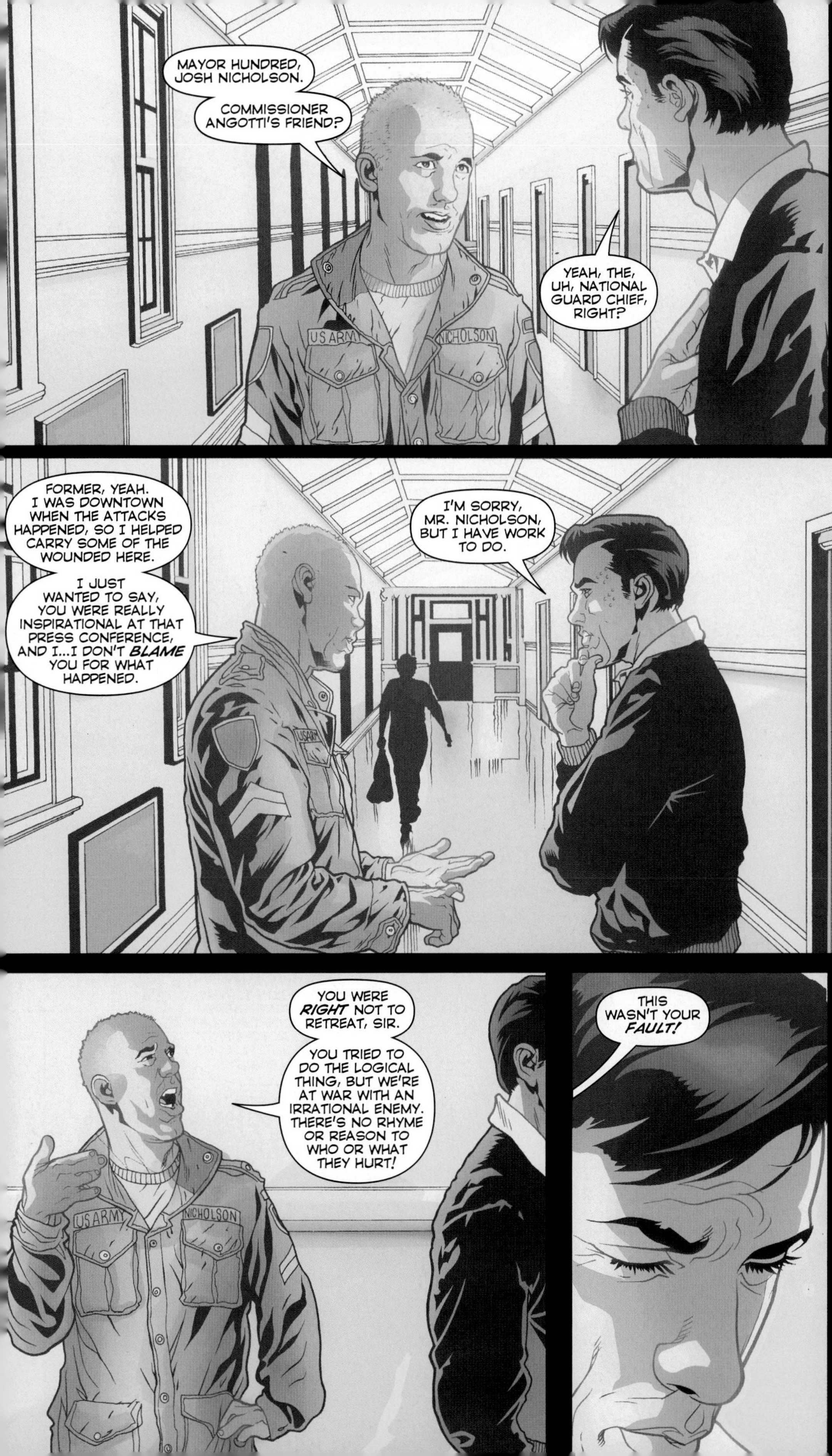
MAYOR HUNDRED, JOSH NICHOLSON.
COMMISSIONER ANGOTTI'S FRIEND?
YEAH, THE, UH, NATIONAL GUARD CHIEF, RIGHT?
US ARMY
NICHOLSON
FORMER, YEAH. I WAS DOWNTOWN WHEN THE ATTACKS HAPPENED, SO I HELPED CARRY SOME OF THE WOUNDED HERE.
I JUST WANTED TO SAY, YOU WERE REALLY INSPIRATIONAL AT THAT PRESS CONFERENCE, AND I...I DON'T *BLAME* YOU FOR WHAT HAPPENED.
I'M SORRY, MR. NICHOLSON, BUT I HAVE WORK TO DO.
YOU WERE *RIGHT* NOT TO RETREAT, SIR.
YOU TRIED TO DO THE LOGICAL THING, BUT WE'RE AT WAR WITH AN IRRATIONAL ENEMY. THERE'S NO RHYME OR REASON TO WHO OR WHAT THEY HURT!
US ARMY
NICHOLSON
THIS WASN'T YOUR *FAULT!*

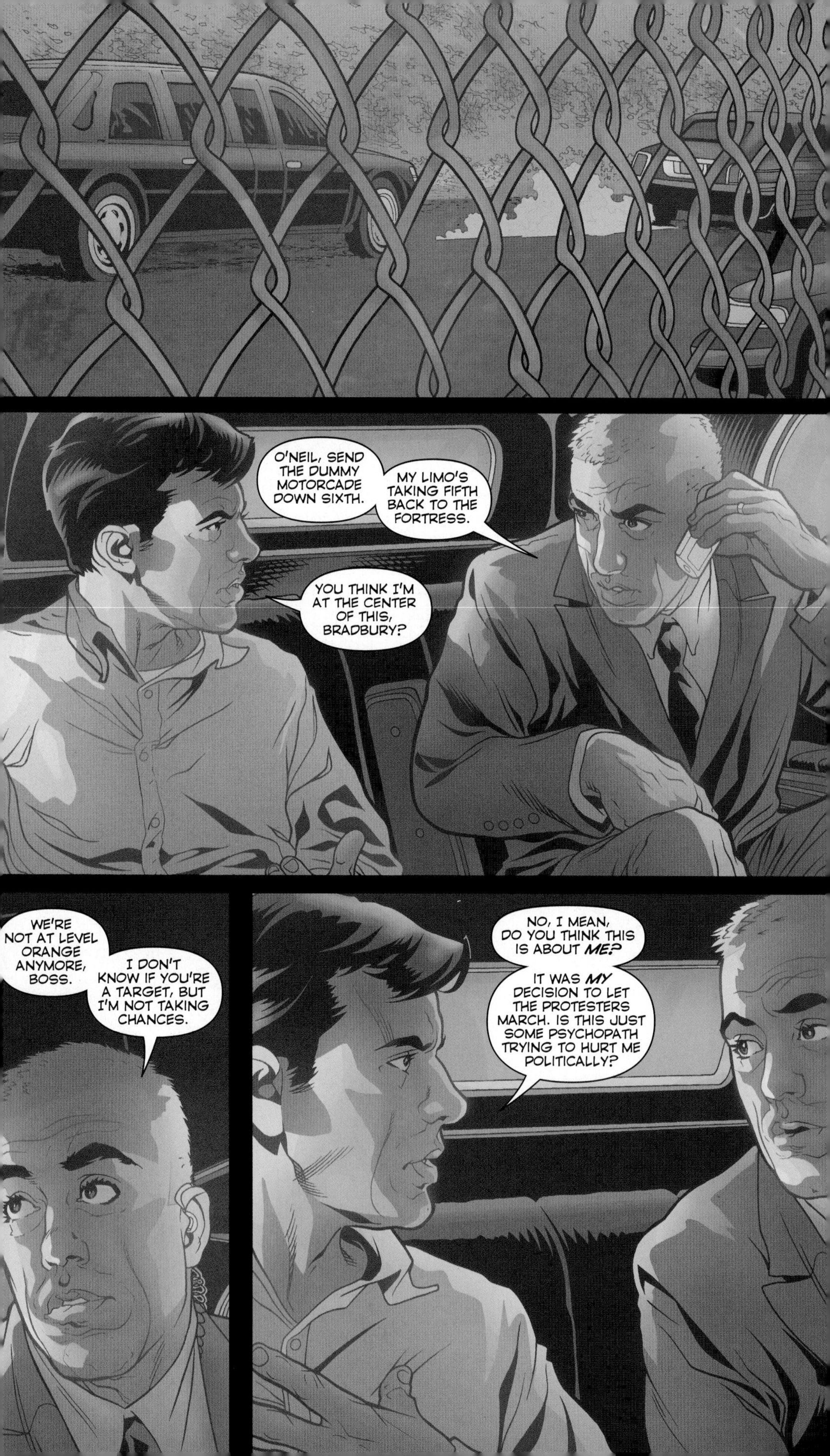
O'NEIL, SEND THE DUMMY MOTORCADE DOWN SIXTH.
MY LIMO'S TAKING FIFTH BACK TO THE FORTRESS.
YOU THINK I'M AT THE CENTER OF THIS, BRADBURY?
WE'RE NOT AT LEVEL ORANGE ANYMORE, BOSS.
I DON'T KNOW IF YOU'RE A TARGET, BUT I'M NOT TAKING CHANCES.
NO, I MEAN, DO YOU THINK THIS IS ABOUT *ME?*
IT WAS *MY* DECISION TO LET THE PROTESTERS MARCH. IS THIS JUST SOME PSYCHOPATH TRYING TO HURT ME POLITICALLY?

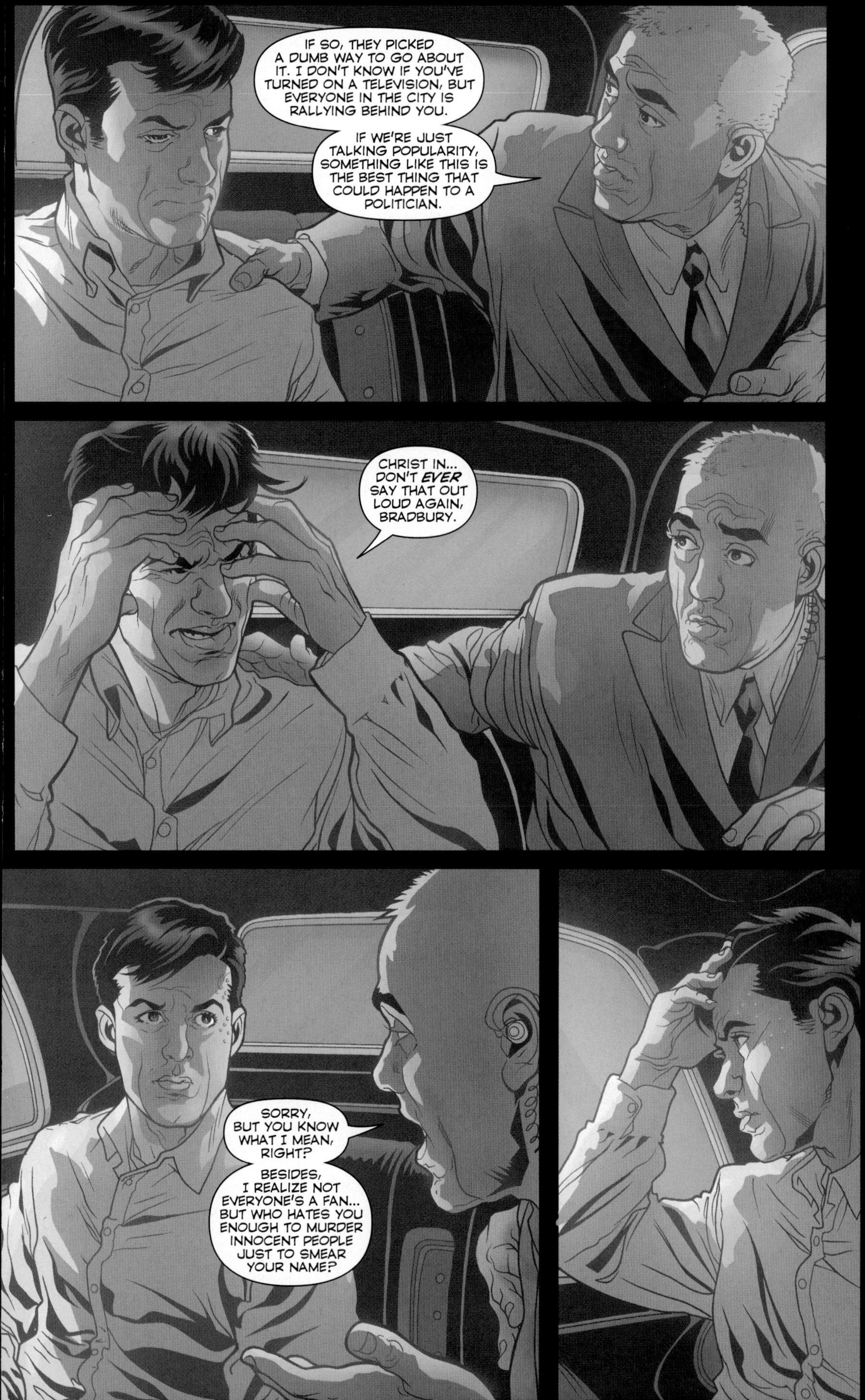
IF SO, THEY PICKED A DUMB WAY TO GO ABOUT IT. I DON'T KNOW IF YOU'VE TURNED ON A TELEVISION, BUT EVERYONE IN THE CITY IS RALLYING BEHIND YOU.
IF WE'RE JUST TALKING POPULARITY, SOMETHING LIKE THIS IS THE BEST THING THAT COULD HAPPEN TO A POLITICIAN.
CHRIST IN... DON'T *EVER* SAY THAT OUT LOUD AGAIN, BRADBURY.
SORRY, BUT YOU KNOW WHAT I MEAN, RIGHT?
BESIDES, I REALIZE NOT EVERYONE'S A FAN... BUT WHO HATES YOU ENOUGH TO MURDER INNOCENT PEOPLE JUST TO SMEAR YOUR NAME?

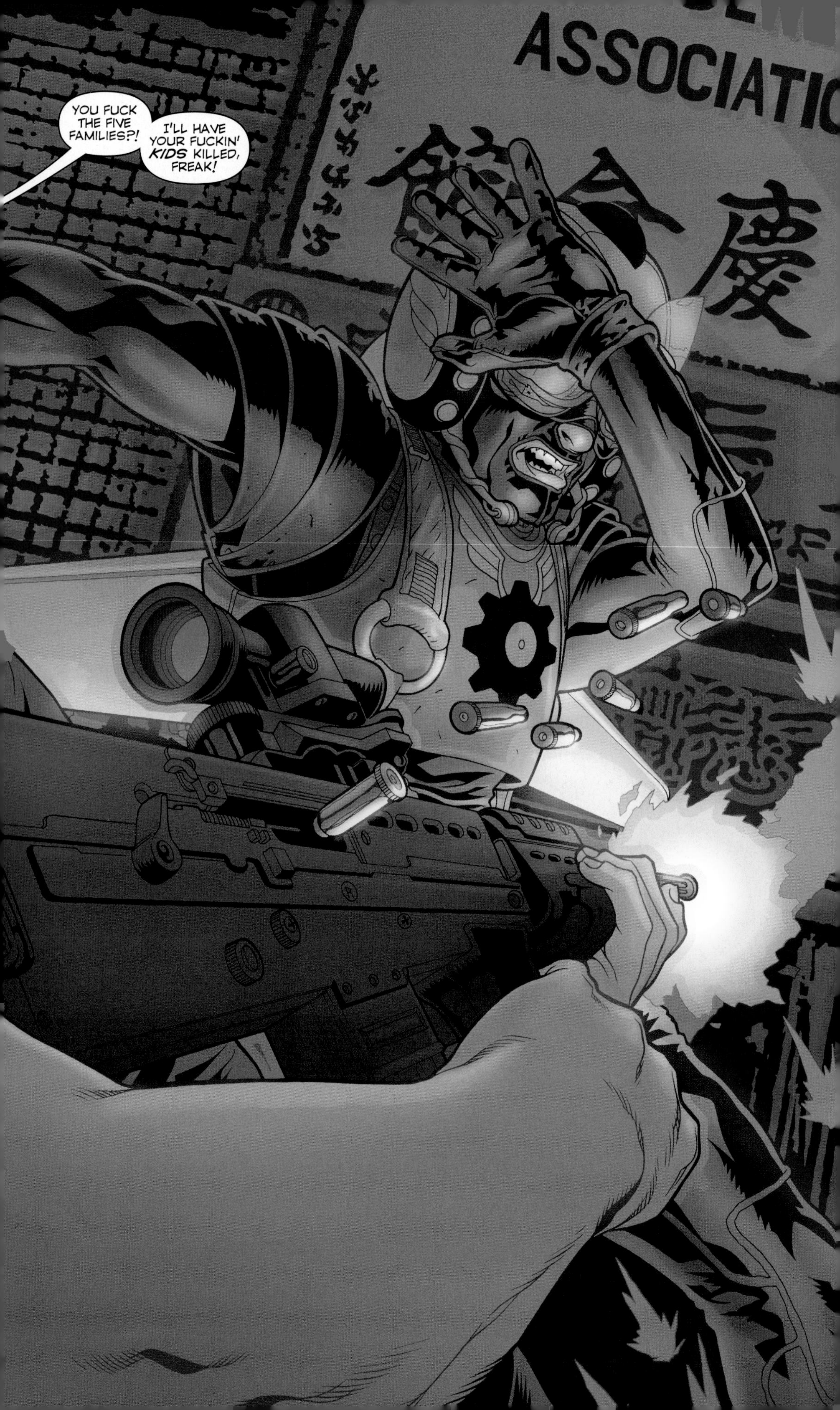
YOU FUCK THE FIVE FAMILIES?!
I'LL HAVE YOUR FUCKIN' KIDS KILLED, FREAK!
ASSOCIATIO

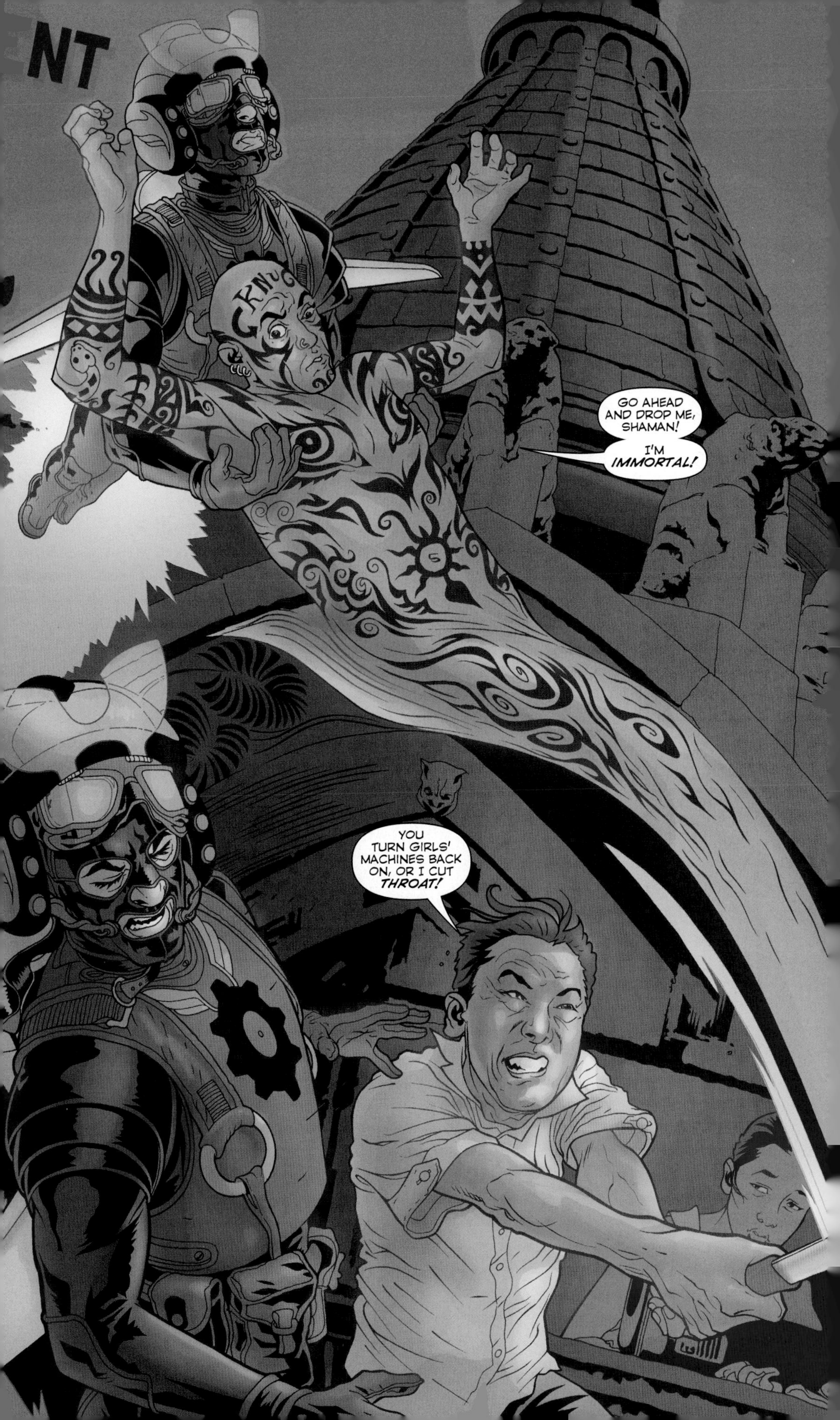
NT
GO AHEAD AND DROP ME, SHAMAN!
I'M IMMORTAL!
YOU TURN GIRLS' MACHINES BACK ON, OR I CUT THROAT!

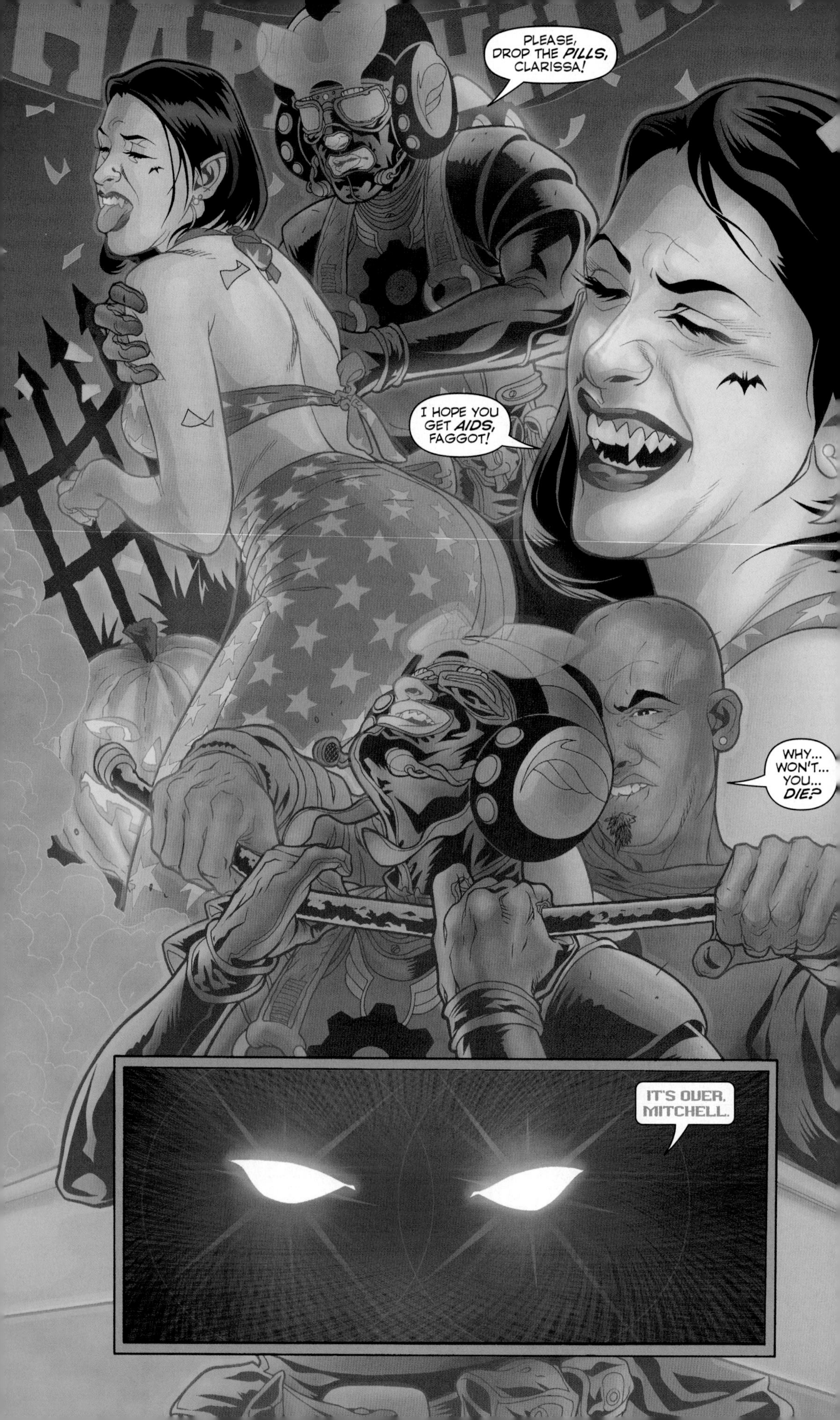

PLEASE, DROP THE PILLS, CLARISSA!
I HOPE YOU GET AIDS, FAGGOT!
WHY... WON'T... YOU... DIE?
IT'S OVER, MITCHELL.

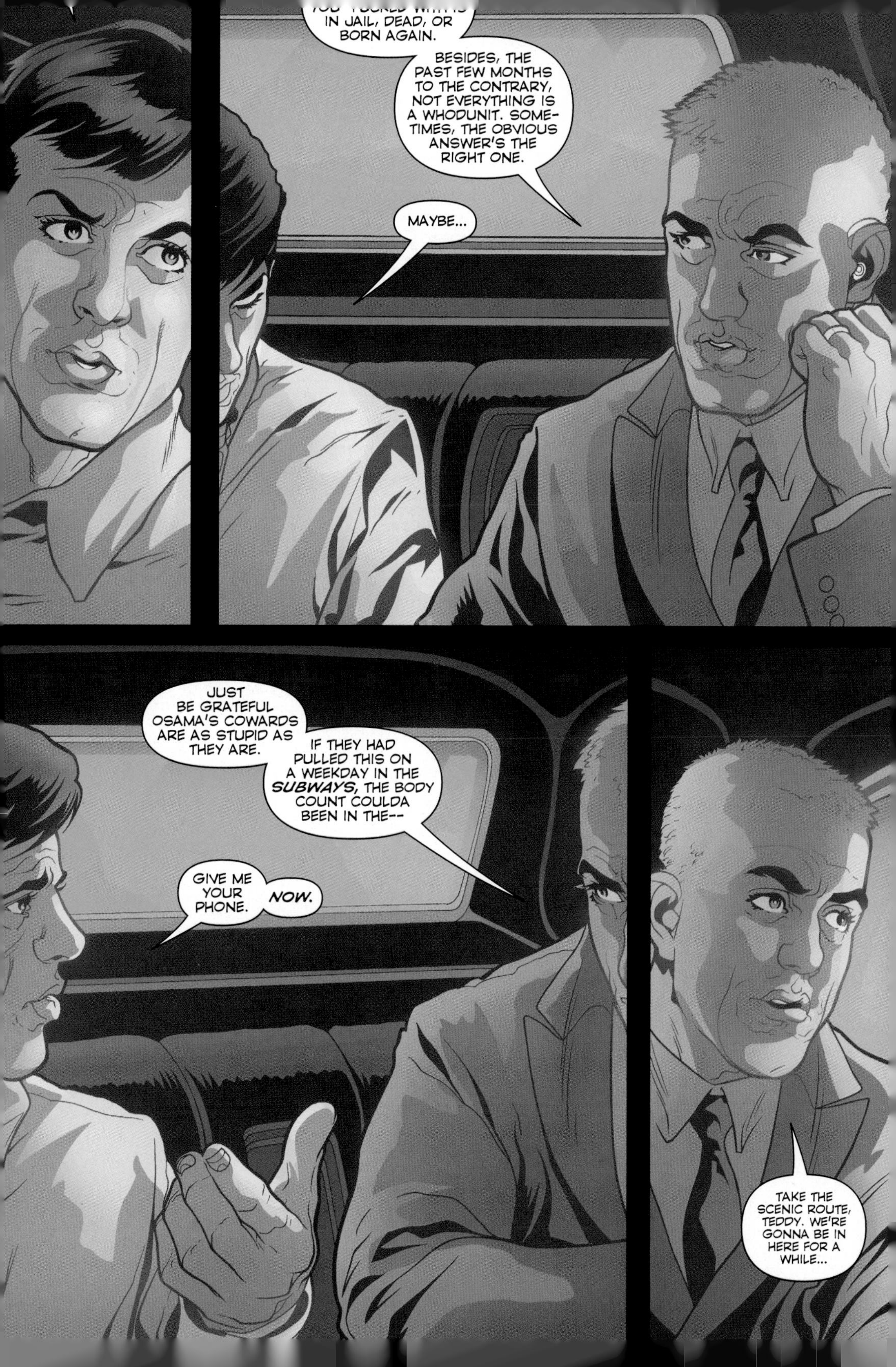
IN JAIL, DEAD, OR BORN AGAIN.
BESIDES, THE PAST FEW MONTHS TO THE CONTRARY, NOT EVERYTHING IS A WHODUNIT. SOMETIMES, THE OBVIOUS ANSWER'S THE RIGHT ONE.
MAYBE...
JUST BE GRATEFUL OSAMA'S COWARDS ARE AS STUPID AS THEY ARE.
IF THEY HAD PULLED THIS ON A WEEKDAY IN THE *SUBWAYS,* THE BODY COUNT COULDA BEEN IN THE--
GIVE ME YOUR PHONE.
*NOW.*
TAKE THE SCENIC ROUTE, TEDDY. WE'RE GONNA BE IN HERE FOR A WHILE...

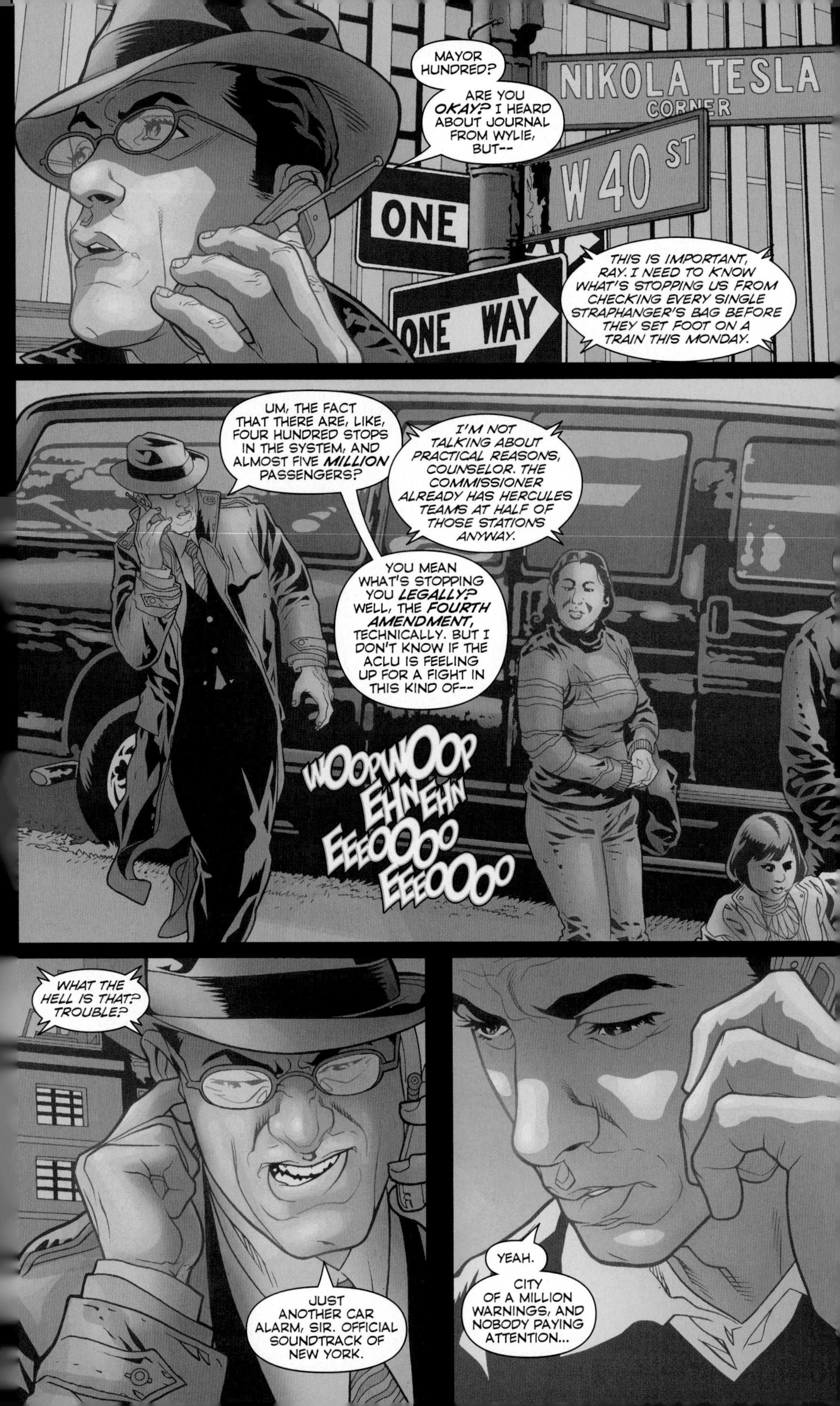
NIKOLA TESLA
CORNER
W 40 ST
ONE
ONE WAY
MAYOR HUNDRED?
ARE YOU *OKAY?* I HEARD ABOUT JOURNAL FROM WYLIE, BUT--
*THIS IS IMPORTANT, RAY. I NEED TO KNOW WHAT'S STOPPING US FROM CHECKING EVERY SINGLE STRAPHANGER'S BAG BEFORE THEY SET FOOT ON A TRAIN THIS MONDAY.*
UM, THE FACT THAT THERE ARE, LIKE, FOUR HUNDRED STOPS IN THE SYSTEM, AND ALMOST FIVE ***MILLION*** PASSENGERS?
*I'M NOT TALKING ABOUT PRACTICAL REASONS, COUNSELOR. THE COMMISSIONER ALREADY HAS HERCULES TEAMS AT HALF OF THOSE STATIONS ANYWAY.*
YOU MEAN WHAT'S STOPPING YOU ***LEGALLY?*** WELL, THE ***FOURTH AMENDMENT,*** TECHNICALLY. BUT I DON'T KNOW IF THE ACLU IS FEELING UP FOR A FIGHT IN THIS KIND OF--
WOOPWOOP
EHNEHN
EEEOOOo
EEEOOOo
*WHAT THE HELL IS THAT? TROUBLE?*
JUST ANOTHER CAR ALARM, SIR. OFFICIAL SOUNDTRACK OF NEW YORK.
YEAH.
CITY OF A MILLION WARNINGS, AND NOBODY PAYING ATTENTION...

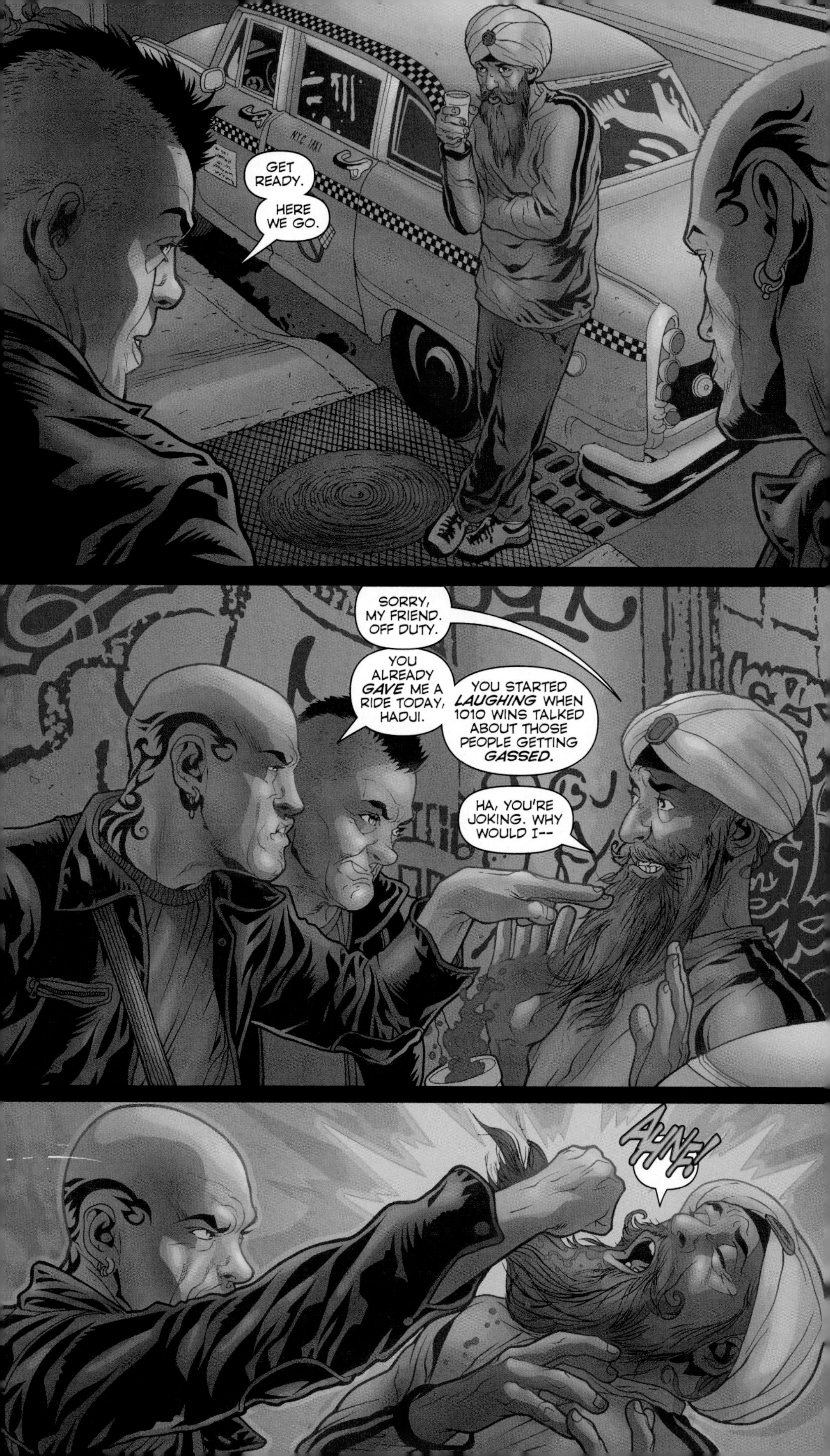
GET READY.
HERE WE GO.
SORRY, MY FRIEND. OFF DUTY.
YOU ALREADY *GAVE* ME A RIDE TODAY, HADJI.
YOU STARTED *LAUGHING* WHEN 1010 WINS TALKED ABOUT THOSE PEOPLE GETTING *GASSED*.
HA, YOU'RE JOKING. WHY WOULD I--

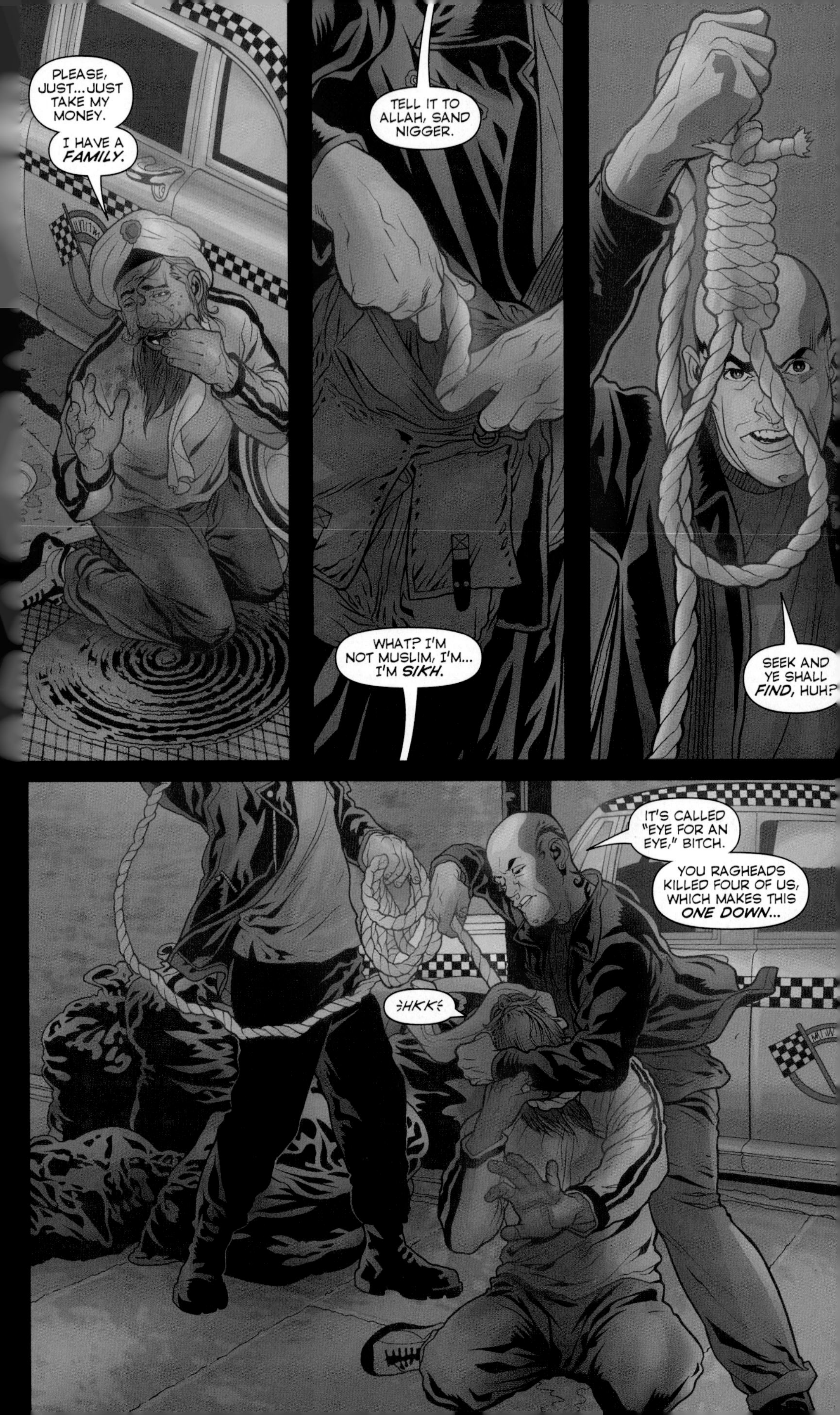
PLEASE, JUST...JUST TAKE MY MONEY.
I HAVE A *FAMILY.*
TELL IT TO ALLAH, SAND NIGGER.
WHAT? I'M NOT MUSLIM, I'M... I'M *SIKH.*
SEEK AND YE SHALL *FIND,* HUH?
IT'S CALLED "EYE FOR AN EYE," BITCH.
YOU RAGHEADS KILLED FOUR OF US, WHICH MAKES THIS *ONE DOWN...*
HKK

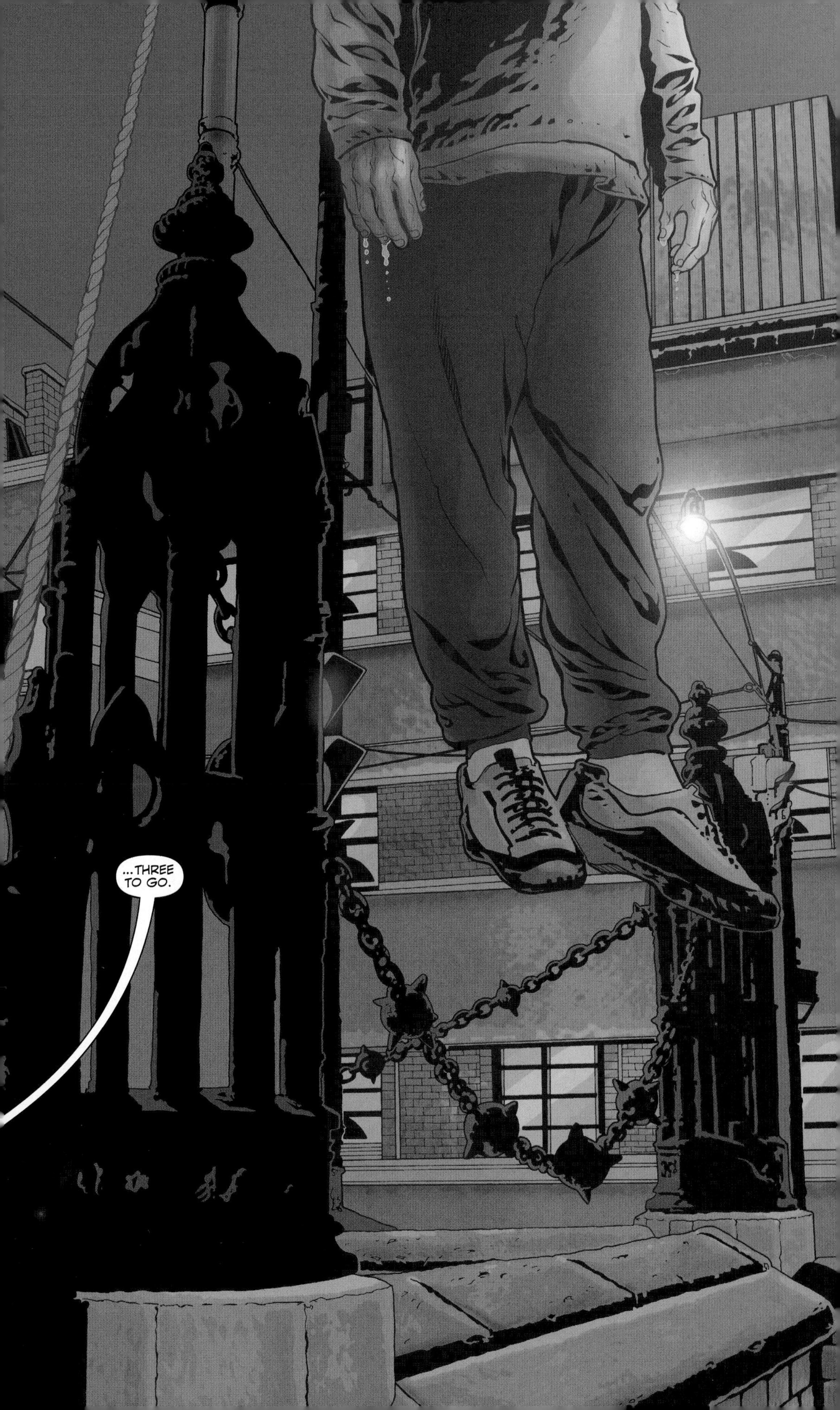
...THREE TO GO.

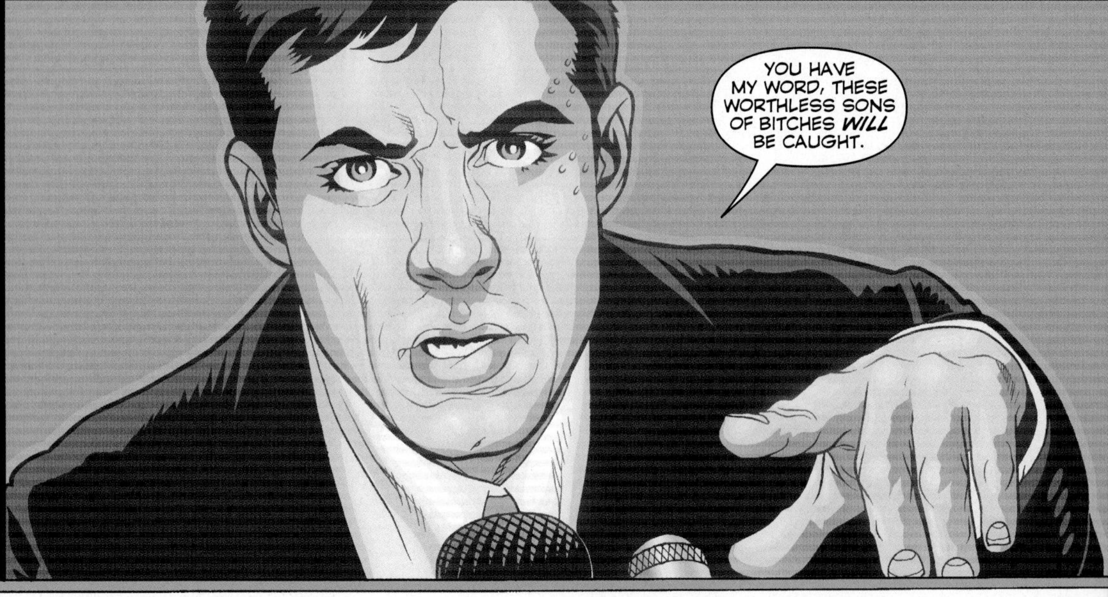
YOU HAVE MY WORD, THESE WORTHLESS SONS OF BITCHES *WILL* BE CAUGHT.

MONDAY, FEBRUARY 17, 2003

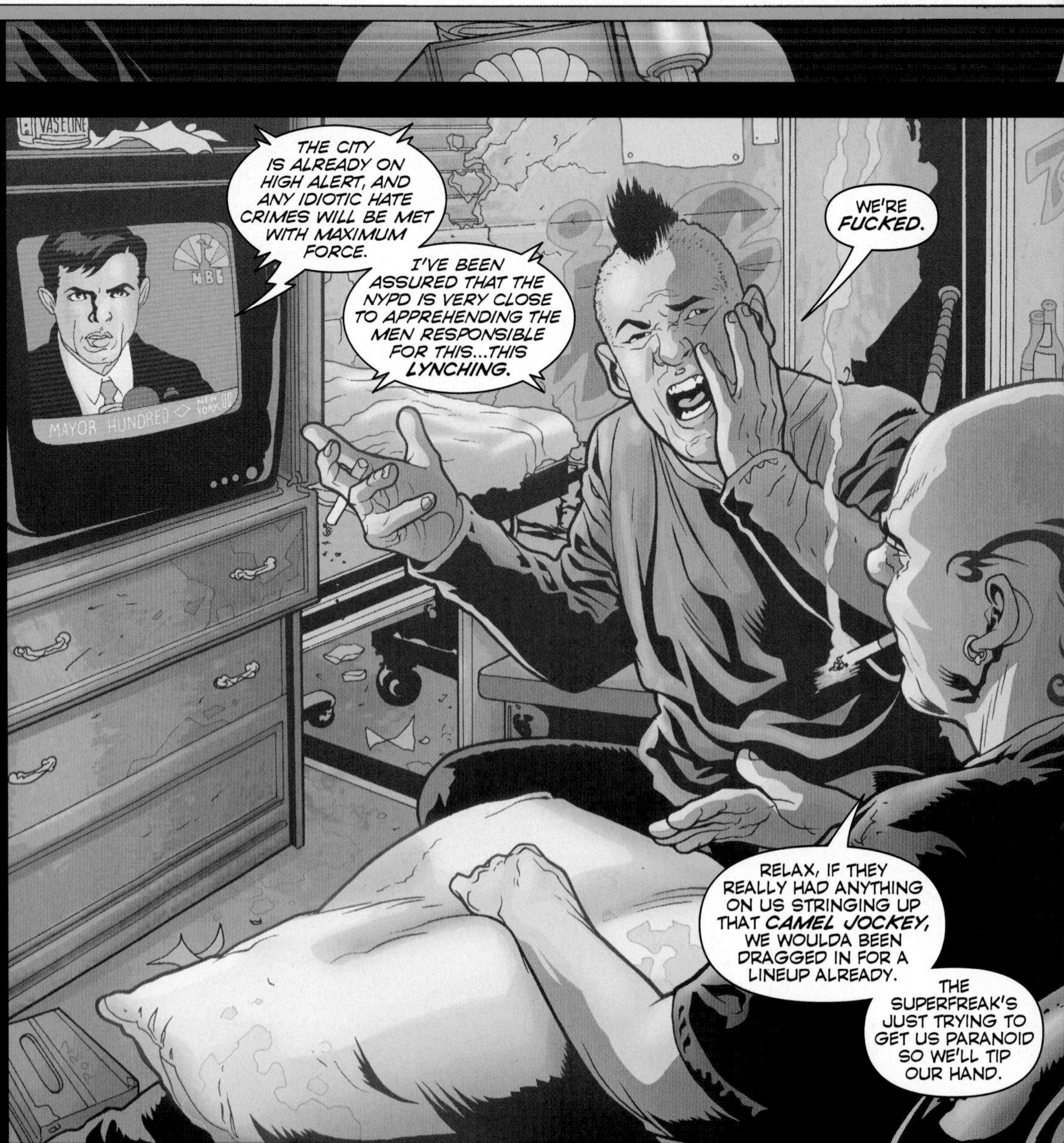
VASELINE
NBC
MAYOR HUNDRED
NEW YORK
THE CITY IS ALREADY ON HIGH ALERT, AND ANY IDIOTIC HATE CRIMES WILL BE MET WITH MAXIMUM FORCE.
I'VE BEEN ASSURED THAT THE NYPD IS VERY CLOSE TO APPREHENDING THE MEN RESPONSIBLE FOR THIS...THIS *LYNCHING.*
WE'RE *FUCKED.*
RELAX, IF THEY REALLY HAD ANYTHING ON US STRINGING UP THAT *CAMEL JOCKEY,* WE WOULDA BEEN DRAGGED IN FOR A LINEUP ALREADY.
THE SUPERFREAK'S JUST TRYING TO GET US PARANOID SO WE'LL TIP OUR HAND.

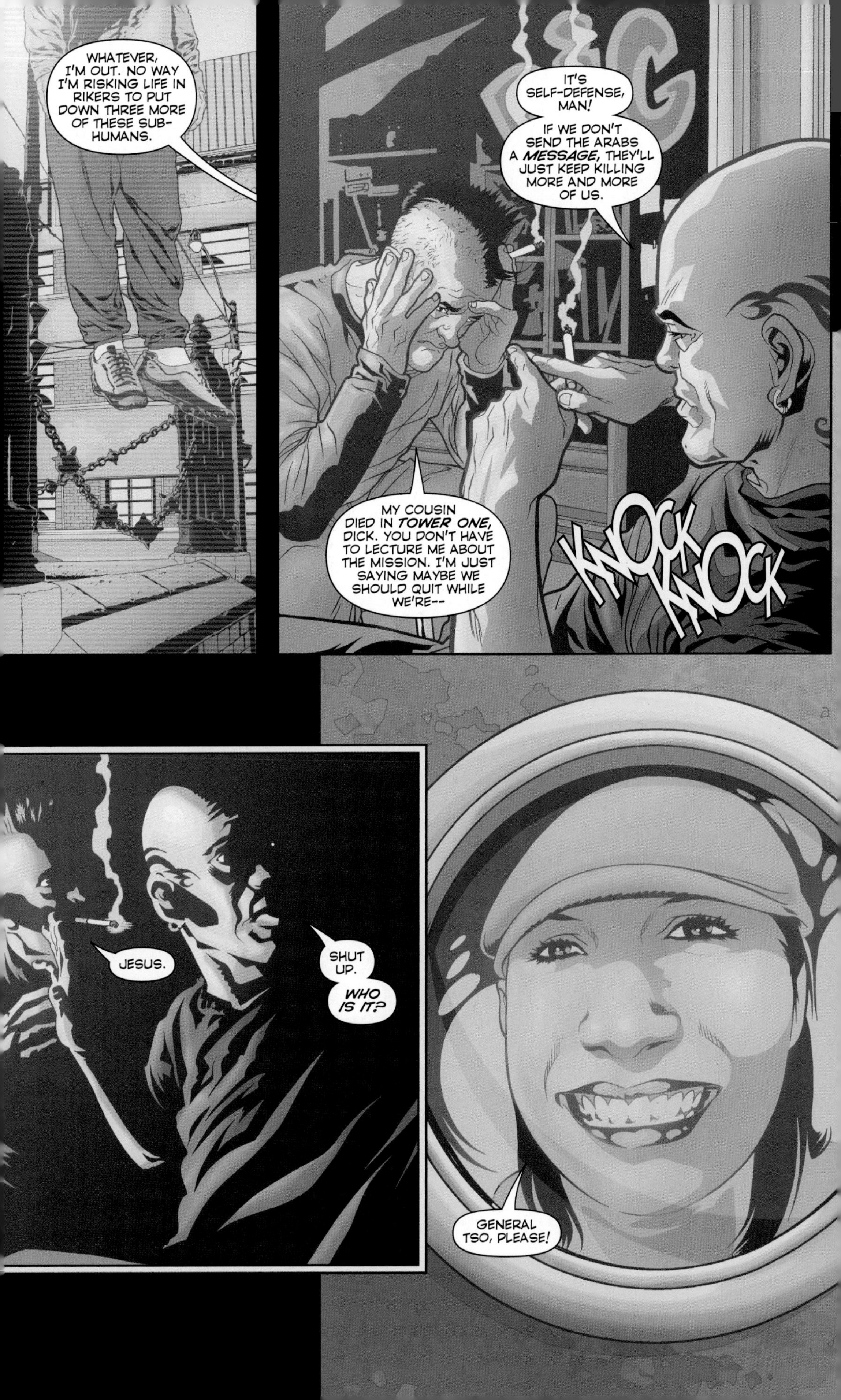
WHATEVER, I'M OUT. NO WAY I'M RISKING LIFE IN RIKERS TO PUT DOWN THREE MORE OF THESE SUB-HUMANS.
IT'S SELF-DEFENSE, MAN!
IF WE DON'T SEND THE ARABS A MESSAGE, THEY'LL JUST KEEP KILLING MORE AND MORE OF US.
MY COUSIN DIED IN TOWER ONE, DICK. YOU DON'T HAVE TO LECTURE ME ABOUT THE MISSION. I'M JUST SAYING MAYBE WE SHOULD QUIT WHILE WE'RE--
KNOCK KNOCK
JESUS.
SHUT UP.
WHO IS IT?
GENERAL TSO, PLEASE!

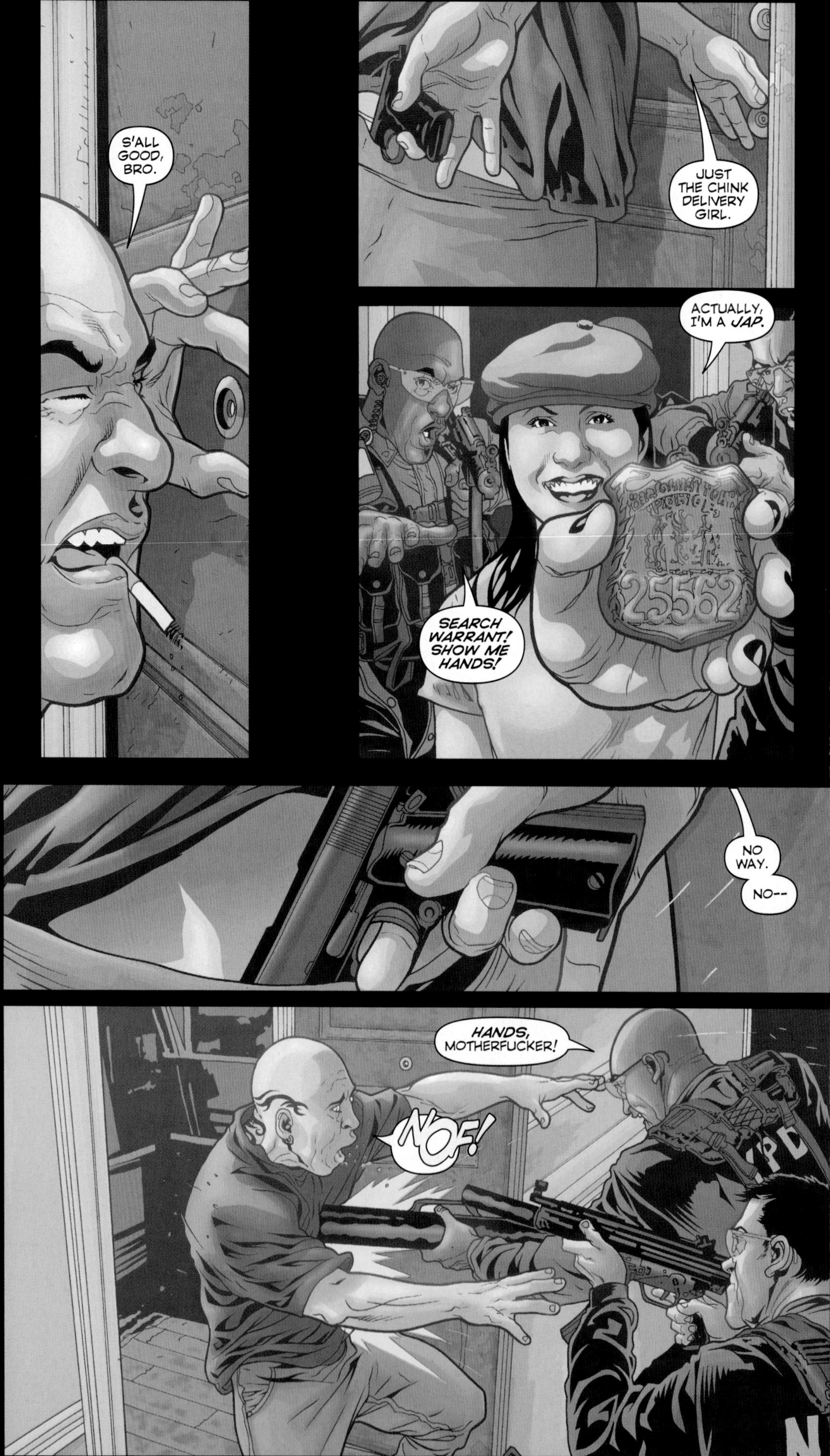
S'ALL GOOD, BRO.
JUST THE CHINK DELIVERY GIRL.
ACTUALLY, I'M A *JAP.*
*SEARCH WARRANT! SHOW ME HANDS!*
25562
NO WAY.
NO--
*HANDS,* MOTHERFUCKER!
NOF!
PD

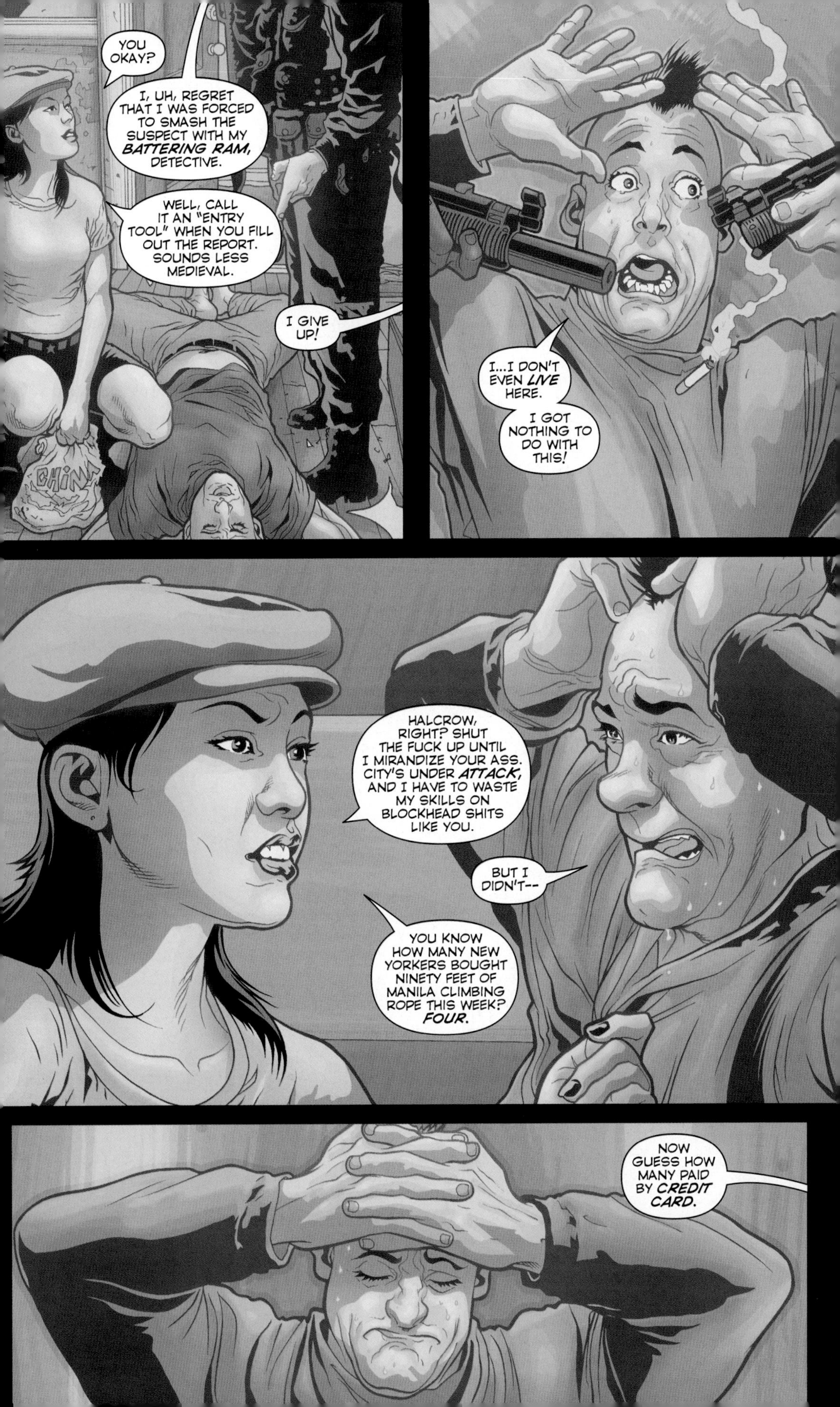
YOU OKAY?
I, UH, REGRET THAT I WAS FORCED TO SMASH THE SUSPECT WITH MY BATTERING RAM, DETECTIVE.
WELL, CALL IT AN "ENTRY TOOL" WHEN YOU FILL OUT THE REPORT. SOUNDS LESS MEDIEVAL.
I GIVE UP!
I...I DON'T EVEN LIVE HERE.
I GOT NOTHING TO DO WITH THIS!
HALCROW, RIGHT? SHUT THE FUCK UP UNTIL I MIRANDIZE YOUR ASS. CITY'S UNDER ATTACK, AND I HAVE TO WASTE MY SKILLS ON BLOCKHEAD SHITS LIKE YOU.
BUT I DIDN'T--
YOU KNOW HOW MANY NEW YORKERS BOUGHT NINETY FEET OF MANILA CLIMBING ROPE THIS WEEK? FOUR.
NOW GUESS HOW MANY PAID BY CREDIT CARD.

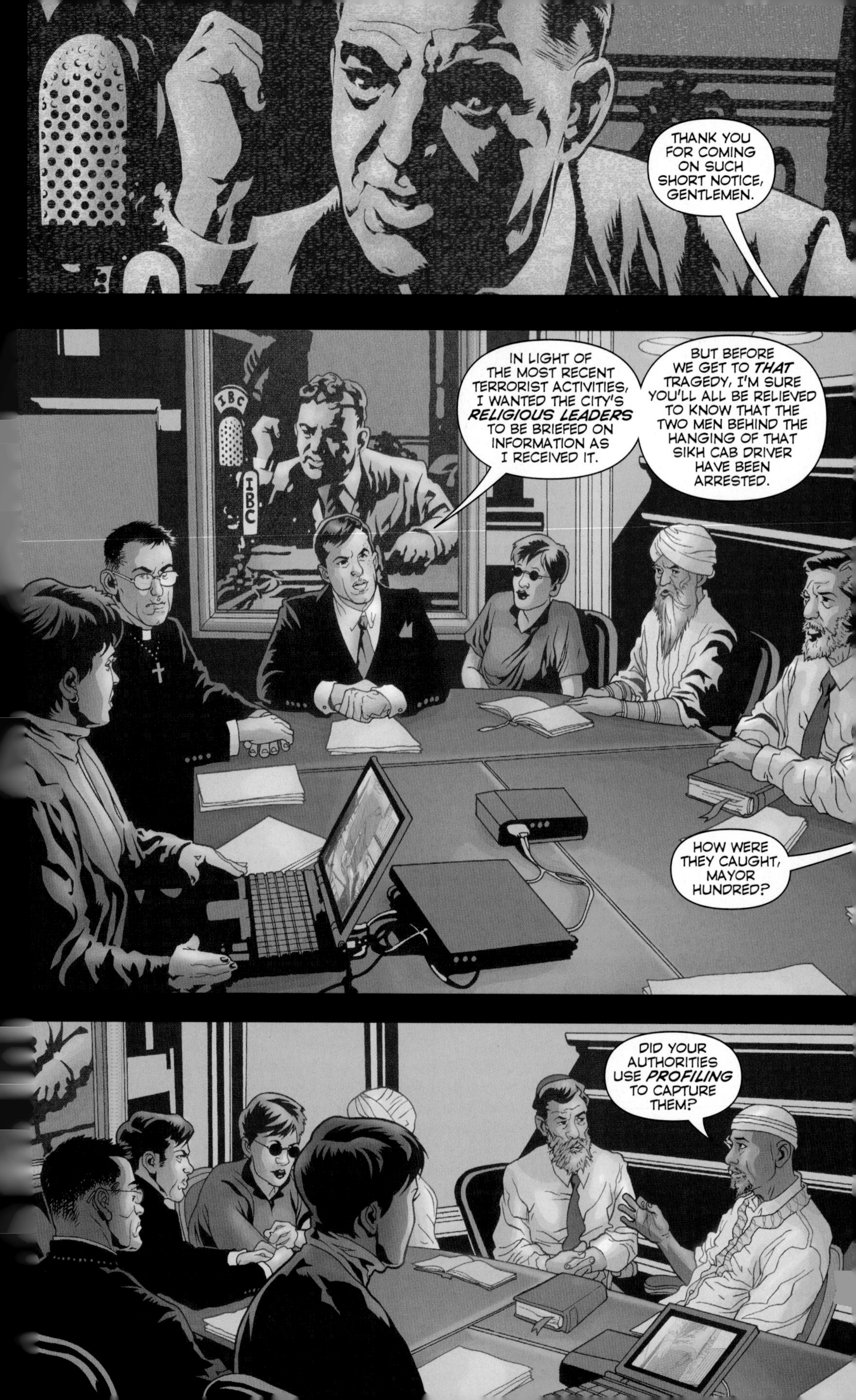
THANK YOU FOR COMING ON SUCH SHORT NOTICE, GENTLEMEN.
IBC
IBC
IN LIGHT OF THE MOST RECENT TERRORIST ACTIVITIES, I WANTED THE CITY'S RELIGIOUS LEADERS TO BE BRIEFED ON INFORMATION AS I RECEIVED IT.
BUT BEFORE WE GET TO THAT TRAGEDY, I'M SURE YOU'LL ALL BE RELIEVED TO KNOW THAT THE TWO MEN BEHIND THE HANGING OF THAT SIKH CAB DRIVER HAVE BEEN ARRESTED.
HOW WERE THEY CAUGHT, MAYOR HUNDRED?
DID YOUR AUTHORITIES USE PROFILING TO CAPTURE THEM?

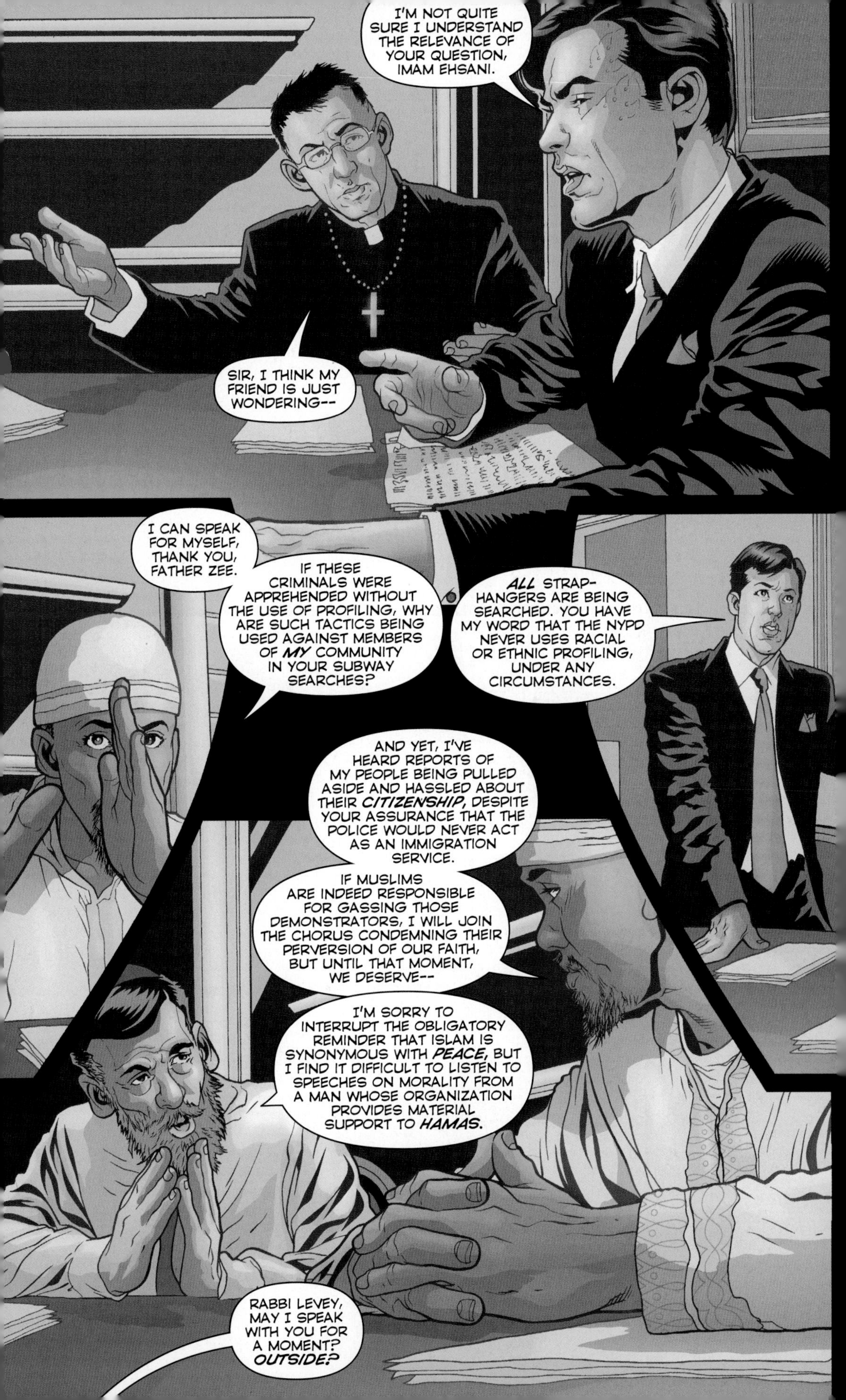
I'M NOT QUITE SURE I UNDERSTAND THE RELEVANCE OF YOUR QUESTION, IMAM EHSANI.
SIR, I THINK MY FRIEND IS JUST WONDERING--
I CAN SPEAK FOR MYSELF, THANK YOU, FATHER ZEE.
IF THESE CRIMINALS WERE APPREHENDED WITHOUT THE USE OF PROFILING, WHY ARE SUCH TACTICS BEING USED AGAINST MEMBERS OF MY COMMUNITY IN YOUR SUBWAY SEARCHES?
ALL STRAP-HANGERS ARE BEING SEARCHED. YOU HAVE MY WORD THAT THE NYPD NEVER USES RACIAL OR ETHNIC PROFILING, UNDER ANY CIRCUMSTANCES.
AND YET, I'VE HEARD REPORTS OF MY PEOPLE BEING PULLED ASIDE AND HASSLED ABOUT THEIR CITIZENSHIP, DESPITE YOUR ASSURANCE THAT THE POLICE WOULD NEVER ACT AS AN IMMIGRATION SERVICE.
IF MUSLIMS ARE INDEED RESPONSIBLE FOR GASSING THOSE DEMONSTRATORS, I WILL JOIN THE CHORUS CONDEMNING THEIR PERVERSION OF OUR FAITH, BUT UNTIL THAT MOMENT, WE DESERVE--
I'M SORRY TO INTERRUPT THE OBLIGATORY REMINDER THAT ISLAM IS SYNONYMOUS WITH PEACE, BUT I FIND IT DIFFICULT TO LISTEN TO SPEECHES ON MORALITY FROM A MAN WHOSE ORGANIZATION PROVIDES MATERIAL SUPPORT TO HAMAS.
RABBI LEVEY, MAY I SPEAK WITH YOU FOR A MOMENT? OUTSIDE?

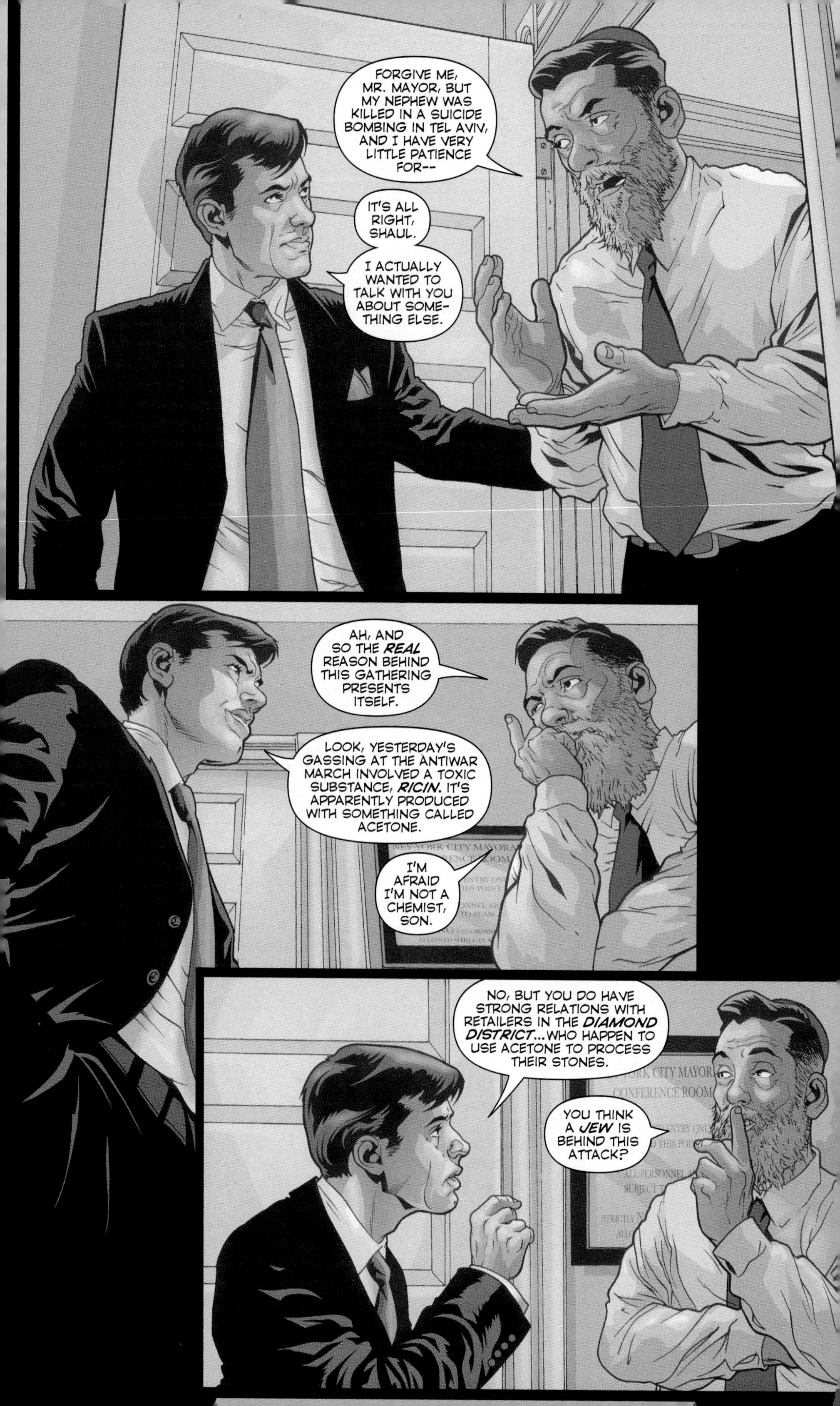
FORGIVE ME, MR. MAYOR, BUT MY NEPHEW WAS KILLED IN A SUICIDE BOMBING IN TEL AVIV, AND I HAVE VERY LITTLE PATIENCE FOR--
IT'S ALL RIGHT, SHAUL.
I ACTUALLY WANTED TO TALK WITH YOU ABOUT SOME-THING ELSE.
AH, AND SO THE *REAL* REASON BEHIND THIS GATHERING PRESENTS ITSELF.
LOOK, YESTERDAY'S GASSING AT THE ANTIWAR MARCH INVOLVED A TOXIC SUBSTANCE, *RICIN*. IT'S APPARENTLY PRODUCED WITH SOMETHING CALLED ACETONE.
I'M AFRAID I'M NOT A CHEMIST, SON.
NO, BUT YOU DO HAVE STRONG RELATIONS WITH RETAILERS IN THE *DIAMOND DISTRICT*...WHO HAPPEN TO USE ACETONE TO PROCESS THEIR STONES.
YOU THINK A *JEW* IS BEHIND THIS ATTACK?

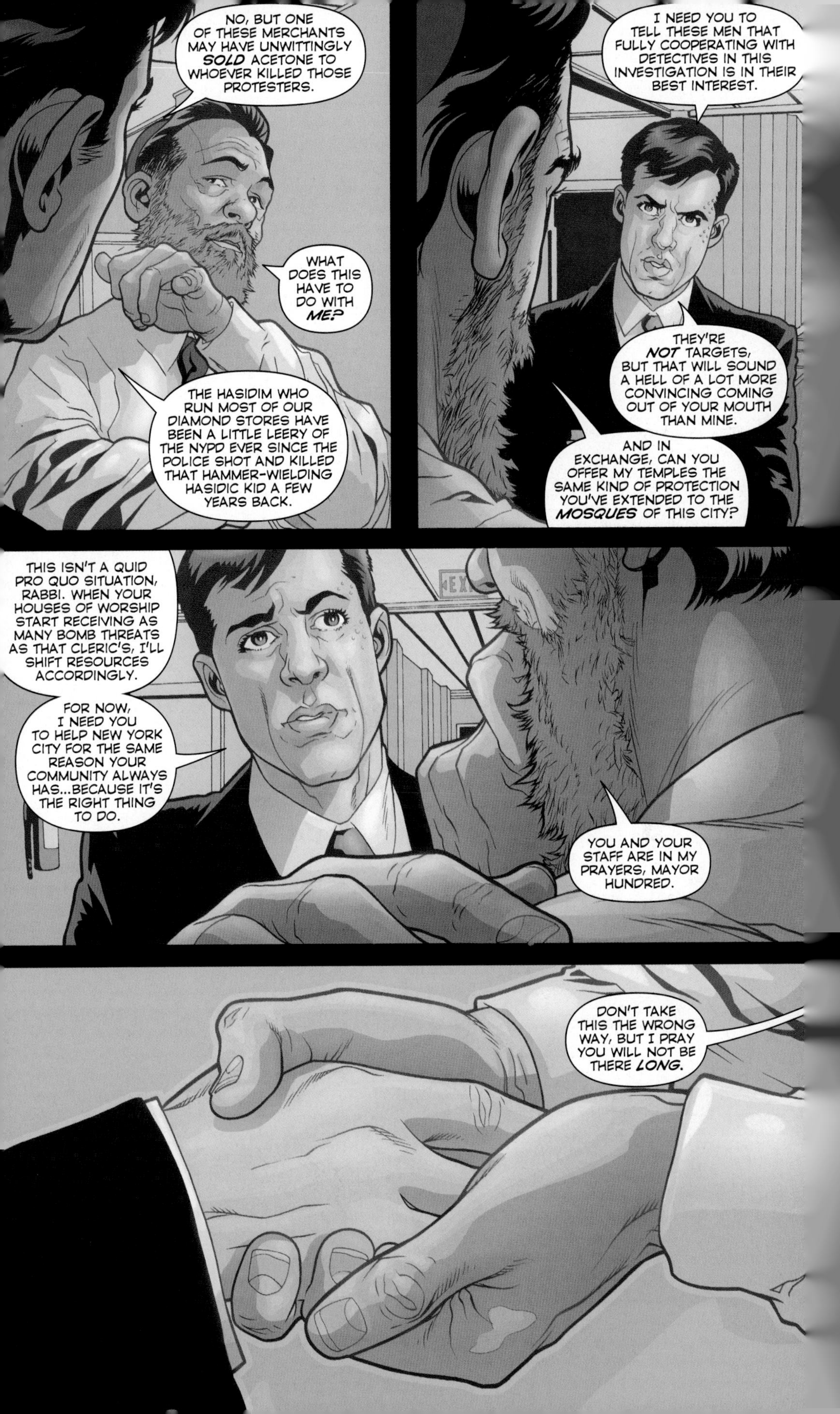
NO, BUT ONE OF THESE MERCHANTS MAY HAVE UNWITTINGLY SOLD ACETONE TO WHOEVER KILLED THOSE PROTESTERS.
WHAT DOES THIS HAVE TO DO WITH ME?
THE HASIDIM WHO RUN MOST OF OUR DIAMOND STORES HAVE BEEN A LITTLE LEERY OF THE NYPD EVER SINCE THE POLICE SHOT AND KILLED THAT HAMMER-WIELDING HASIDIC KID A FEW YEARS BACK.
I NEED YOU TO TELL THESE MEN THAT FULLY COOPERATING WITH DETECTIVES IN THIS INVESTIGATION IS IN THEIR BEST INTEREST.
THEY'RE NOT TARGETS, BUT THAT WILL SOUND A HELL OF A LOT MORE CONVINCING COMING OUT OF YOUR MOUTH THAN MINE.
AND IN EXCHANGE, CAN YOU OFFER MY TEMPLES THE SAME KIND OF PROTECTION YOU'VE EXTENDED TO THE MOSQUES OF THIS CITY?
THIS ISN'T A QUID PRO QUO SITUATION, RABBI. WHEN YOUR HOUSES OF WORSHIP START RECEIVING AS MANY BOMB THREATS AS THAT CLERIC'S, I'LL SHIFT RESOURCES ACCORDINGLY.
FOR NOW, I NEED YOU TO HELP NEW YORK CITY FOR THE SAME REASON YOUR COMMUNITY ALWAYS HAS...BECAUSE IT'S THE RIGHT THING TO DO.
YOU AND YOUR STAFF ARE IN MY PRAYERS, MAYOR HUNDRED.
DON'T TAKE THIS THE WRONG WAY, BUT I PRAY YOU WILL NOT BE THERE LONG.

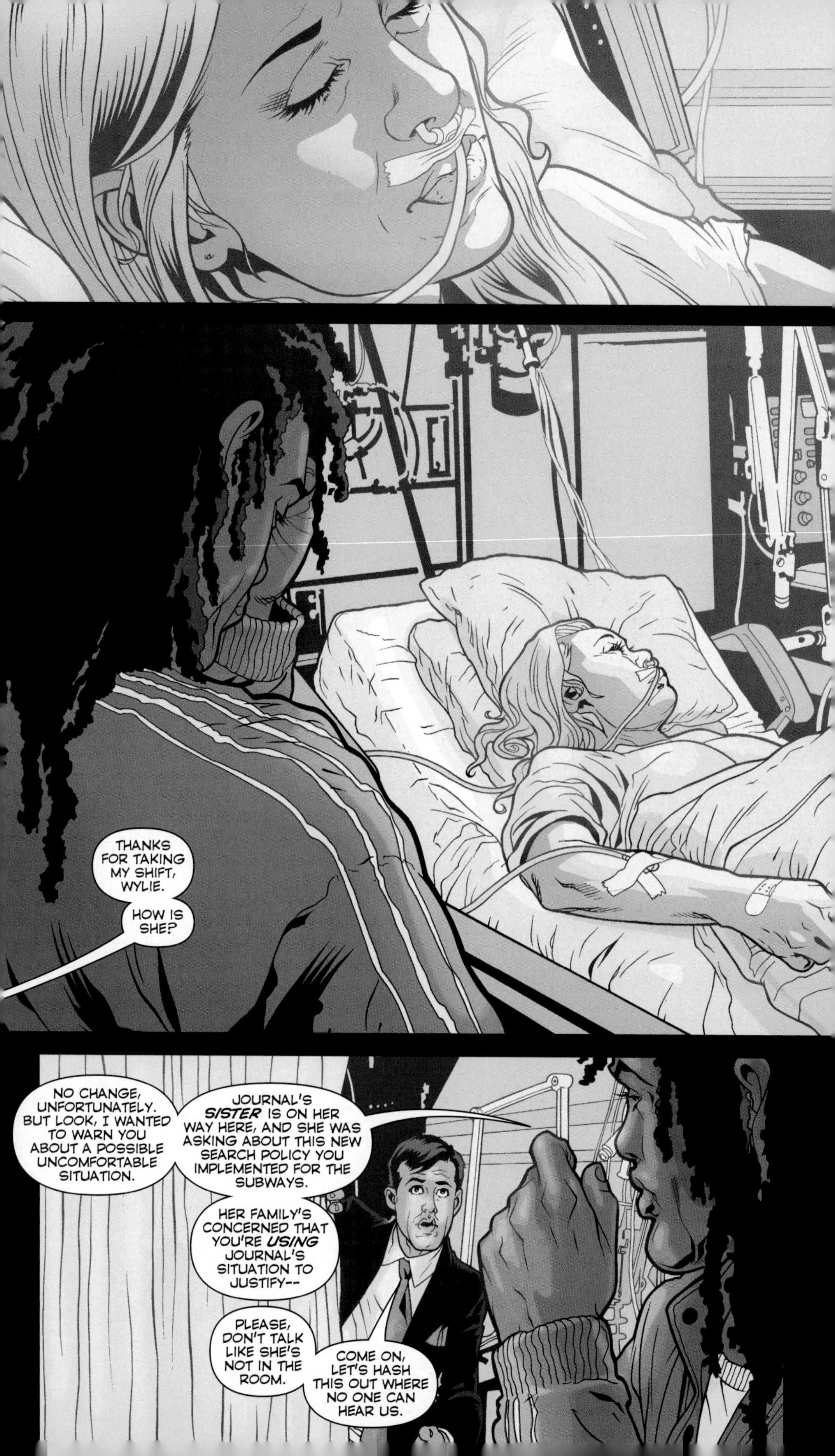
THANKS FOR TAKING MY SHIFT, WYLIE.
HOW IS SHE?
NO CHANGE, UNFORTUNATELY. BUT LOOK, I WANTED TO WARN YOU ABOUT A POSSIBLE UNCOMFORTABLE SITUATION.
JOURNAL'S SISTER IS ON HER WAY HERE, AND SHE WAS ASKING ABOUT THIS NEW SEARCH POLICY YOU IMPLEMENTED FOR THE SUBWAYS.
HER FAMILY'S CONCERNED THAT YOU'RE USING JOURNAL'S SITUATION TO JUSTIFY--
PLEASE, DON'T TALK LIKE SHE'S NOT IN THE ROOM.
COME ON, LET'S HASH THIS OUT WHERE NO ONE CAN HEAR US.

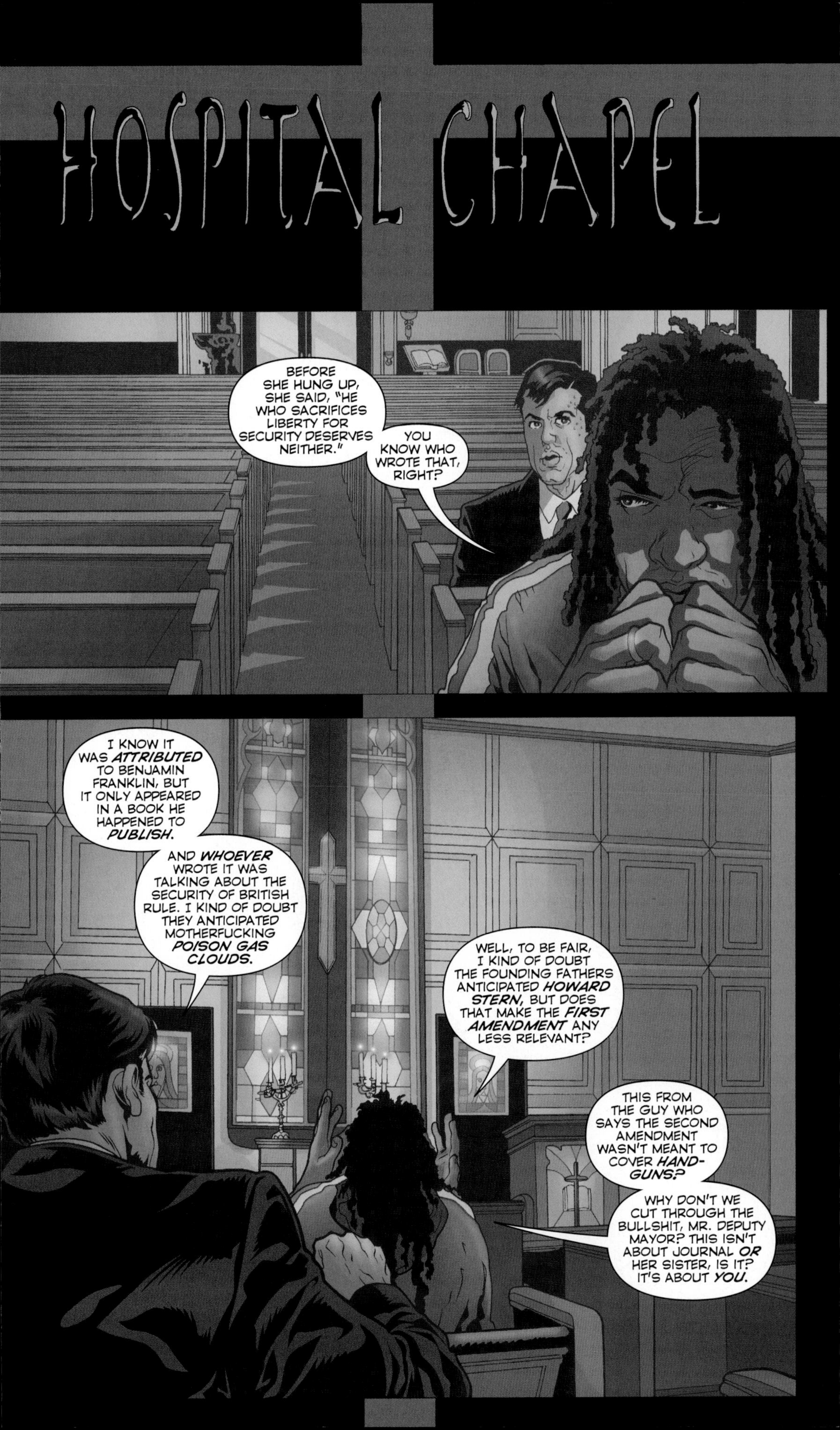
HOSPITAL CHAPEL
BEFORE SHE HUNG UP, SHE SAID, "HE WHO SACRIFICES LIBERTY FOR SECURITY DESERVES NEITHER."
YOU KNOW WHO WROTE THAT, RIGHT?
I KNOW IT WAS ATTRIBUTED TO BENJAMIN FRANKLIN, BUT IT ONLY APPEARED IN A BOOK HE HAPPENED TO PUBLISH.
AND WHOEVER WROTE IT WAS TALKING ABOUT THE SECURITY OF BRITISH RULE. I KIND OF DOUBT THEY ANTICIPATED MOTHERFUCKING POISON GAS CLOUDS.
WELL, TO BE FAIR, I KIND OF DOUBT THE FOUNDING FATHERS ANTICIPATED HOWARD STERN, BUT DOES THAT MAKE THE FIRST AMENDMENT ANY LESS RELEVANT?
THIS FROM THE GUY WHO SAYS THE SECOND AMENDMENT WASN'T MEANT TO COVER HAND-GUNS?
WHY DON'T WE CUT THROUGH THE BULLSHIT, MR. DEPUTY MAYOR? THIS ISN'T ABOUT JOURNAL OR HER SISTER, IS IT? IT'S ABOUT YOU.

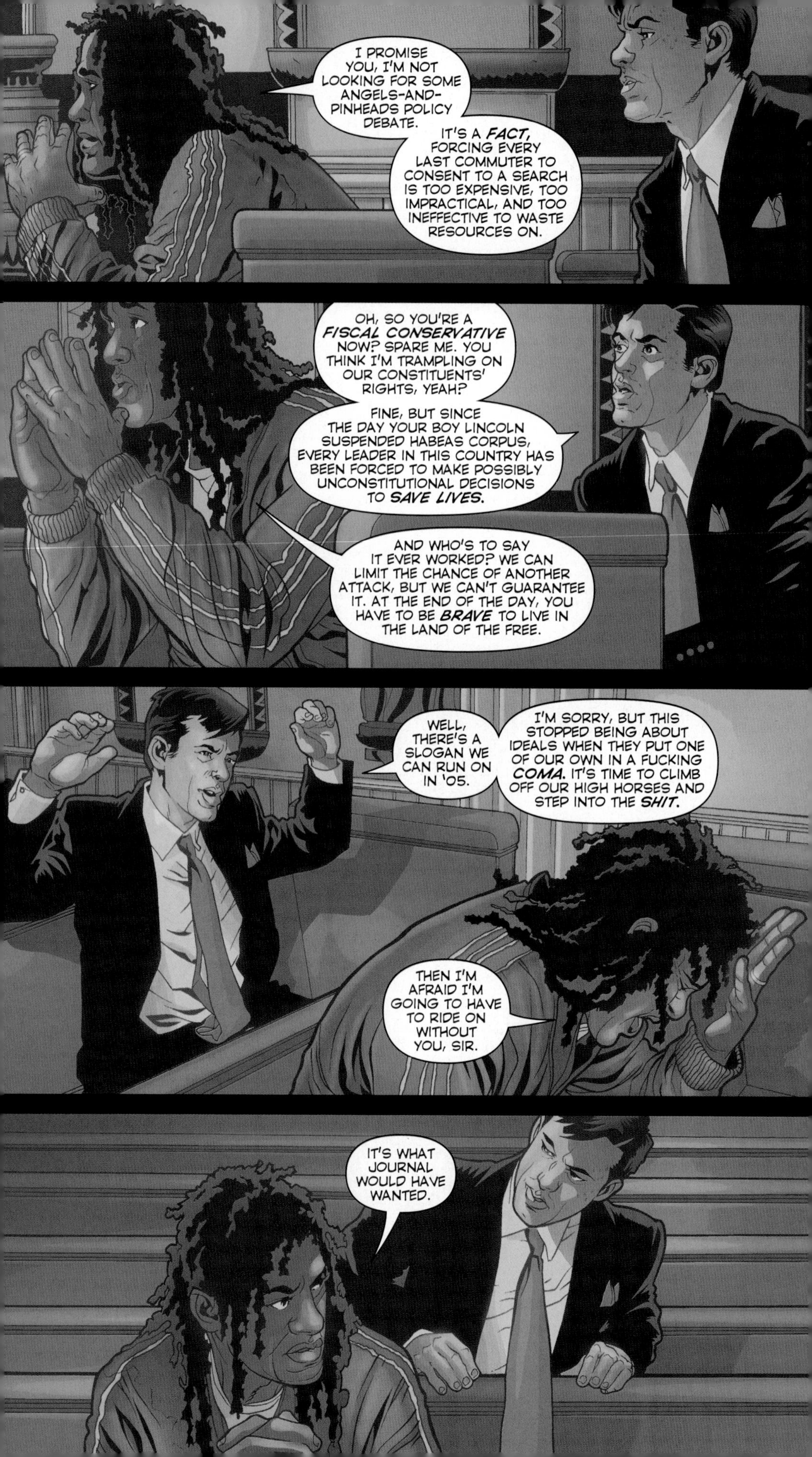
I PROMISE YOU, I'M NOT LOOKING FOR SOME ANGELS-AND-PINHEADS POLICY DEBATE.
IT'S A FACT, FORCING EVERY LAST COMMUTER TO CONSENT TO A SEARCH IS TOO EXPENSIVE, TOO IMPRACTICAL, AND TOO INEFFECTIVE TO WASTE RESOURCES ON.
OH, SO YOU'RE A FISCAL CONSERVATIVE NOW? SPARE ME. YOU THINK I'M TRAMPLING ON OUR CONSTITUENTS' RIGHTS, YEAH?
FINE, BUT SINCE THE DAY YOUR BOY LINCOLN SUSPENDED HABEAS CORPUS, EVERY LEADER IN THIS COUNTRY HAS BEEN FORCED TO MAKE POSSIBLY UNCONSTITUTIONAL DECISIONS TO SAVE LIVES.
AND WHO'S TO SAY IT EVER WORKED? WE CAN LIMIT THE CHANCE OF ANOTHER ATTACK, BUT WE CAN'T GUARANTEE IT. AT THE END OF THE DAY, YOU HAVE TO BE BRAVE TO LIVE IN THE LAND OF THE FREE.
WELL, THERE'S A SLOGAN WE CAN RUN ON IN '05.
I'M SORRY, BUT THIS STOPPED BEING ABOUT IDEALS WHEN THEY PUT ONE OF OUR OWN IN A FUCKING COMA. IT'S TIME TO CLIMB OFF OUR HIGH HORSES AND STEP INTO THE SHIT.
THEN I'M AFRAID I'M GOING TO HAVE TO RIDE ON WITHOUT YOU, SIR.
IT'S WHAT JOURNAL WOULD HAVE WANTED.

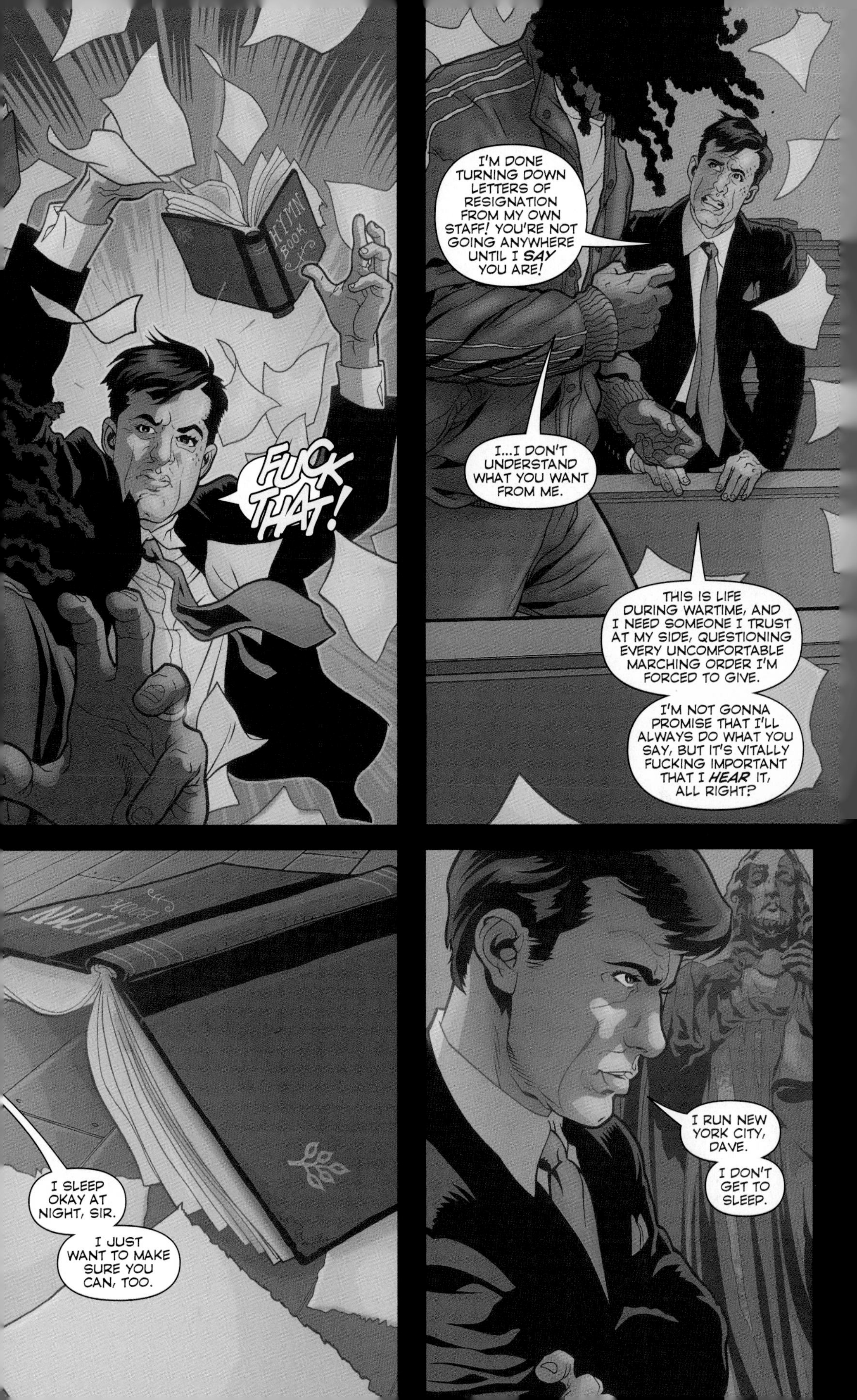
HYMN BOOK
FUCK THAT!
I'M DONE TURNING DOWN LETTERS OF RESIGNATION FROM MY OWN STAFF! YOU'RE NOT GOING ANYWHERE UNTIL I SAY YOU ARE!
I...I DON'T UNDERSTAND WHAT YOU WANT FROM ME.
THIS IS LIFE DURING WARTIME, AND I NEED SOMEONE I TRUST AT MY SIDE, QUESTIONING EVERY UNCOMFORTABLE MARCHING ORDER I'M FORCED TO GIVE.
I'M NOT GONNA PROMISE THAT I'LL ALWAYS DO WHAT YOU SAY, BUT IT'S VITALLY FUCKING IMPORTANT THAT I HEAR IT, ALL RIGHT?
I SLEEP OKAY AT NIGHT, SIR.
I JUST WANT TO MAKE SURE YOU CAN, TOO.
I RUN NEW YORK CITY, DAVE.
I DON'T GET TO SLEEP.

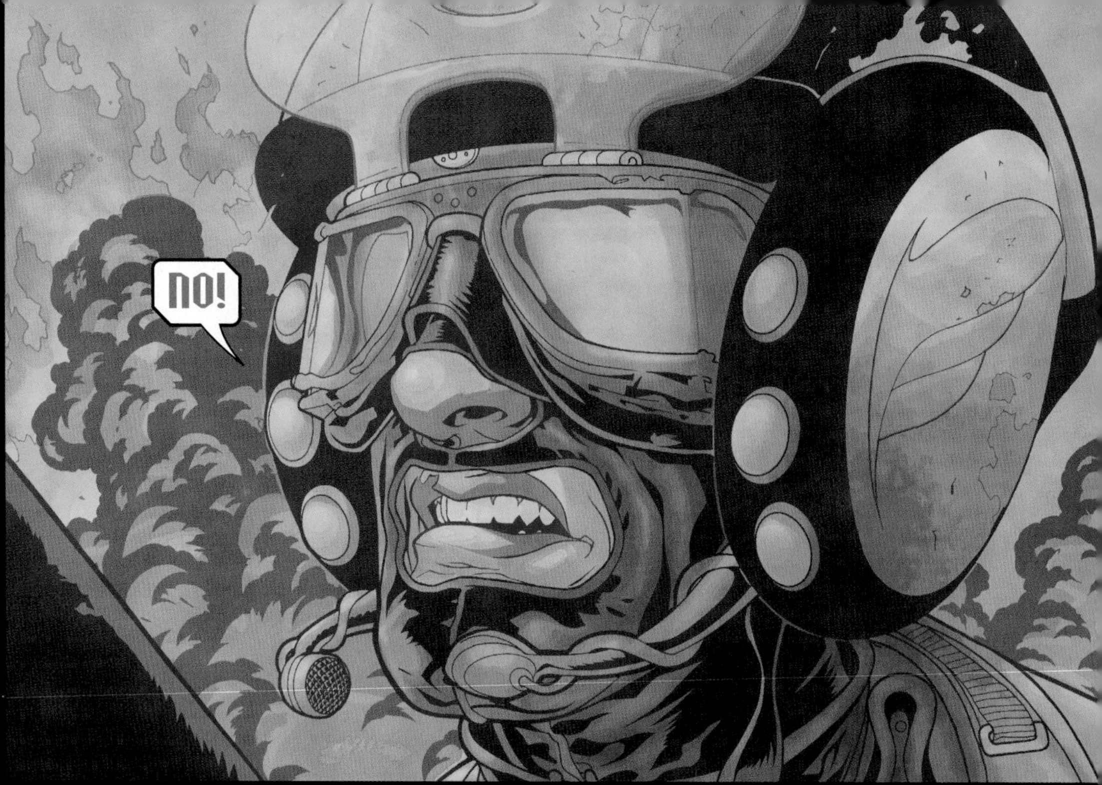
NO!

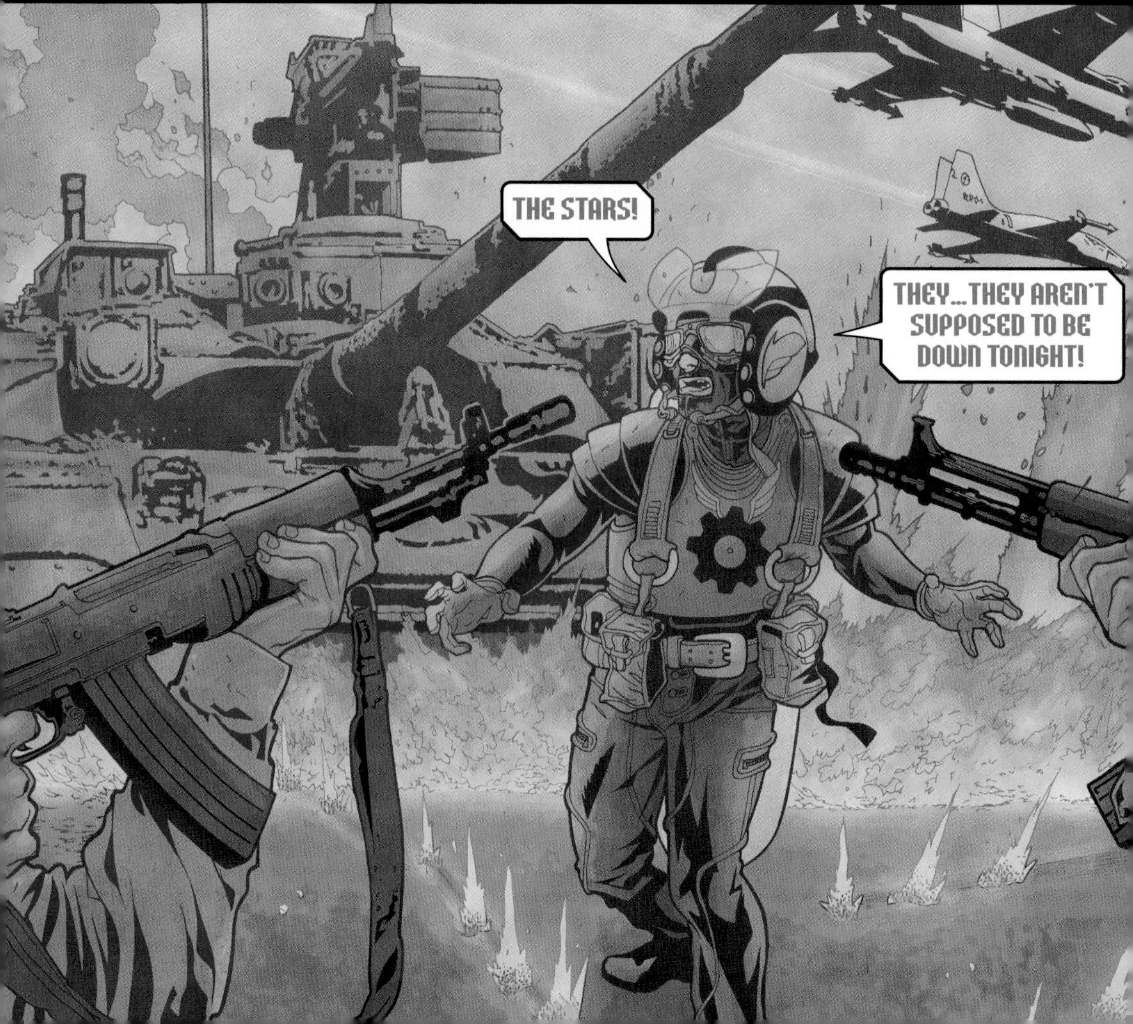
THE STARS!
THEY...THEY AREN'T SUPPOSED TO BE DOWN TONIGHT!

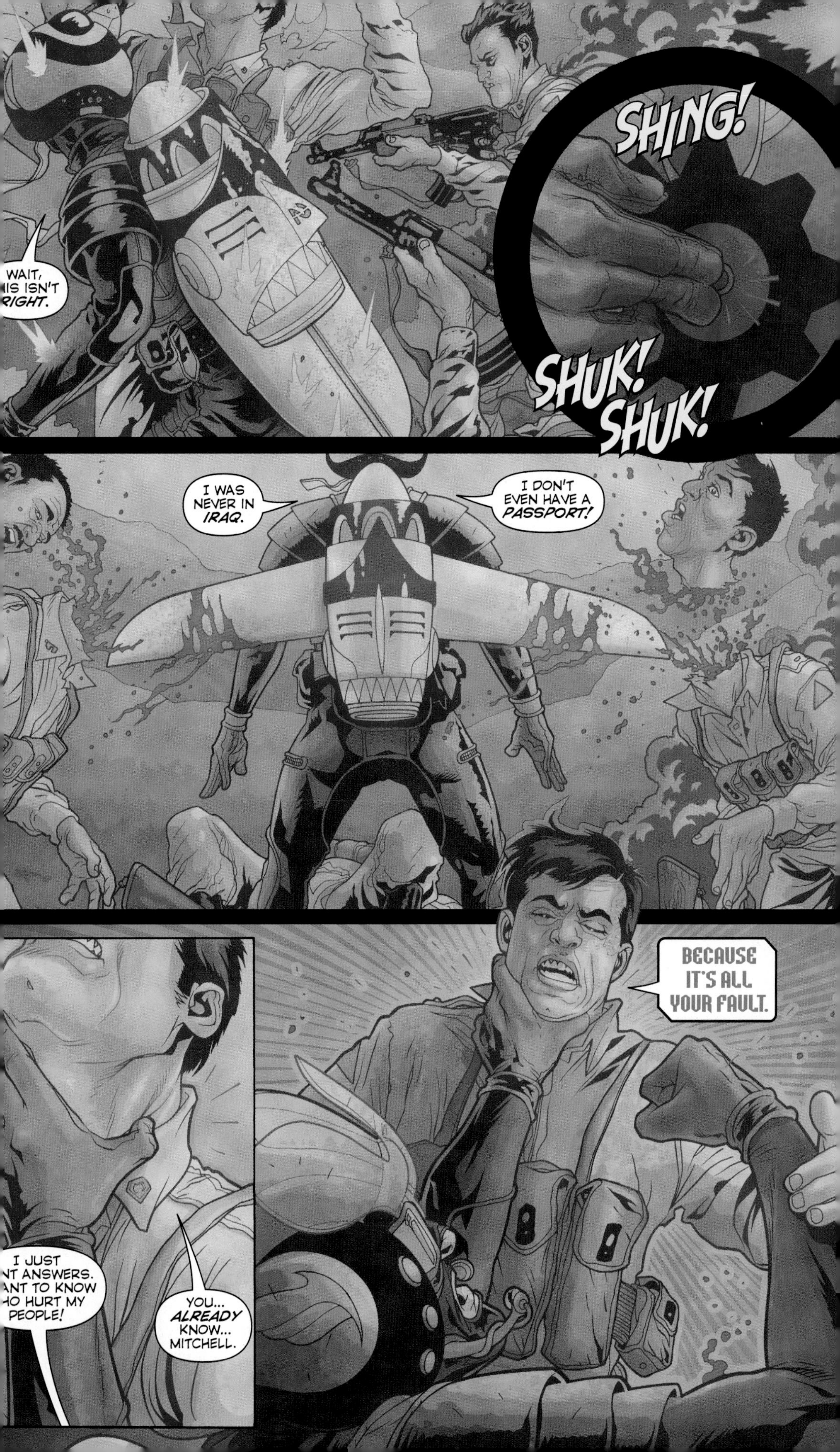
WAIT, IS ISN'T RIGHT.
SHING!
SHUK! SHUK!
I WAS NEVER IN IRAQ.
I DON'T EVEN HAVE A PASSPORT!
BECAUSE IT'S ALL YOUR FAULT.
I JUST NT ANSWERS. ANT TO KNOW HO HURT MY PEOPLE!
YOU... ALREADY KNOW... MITCHELL.

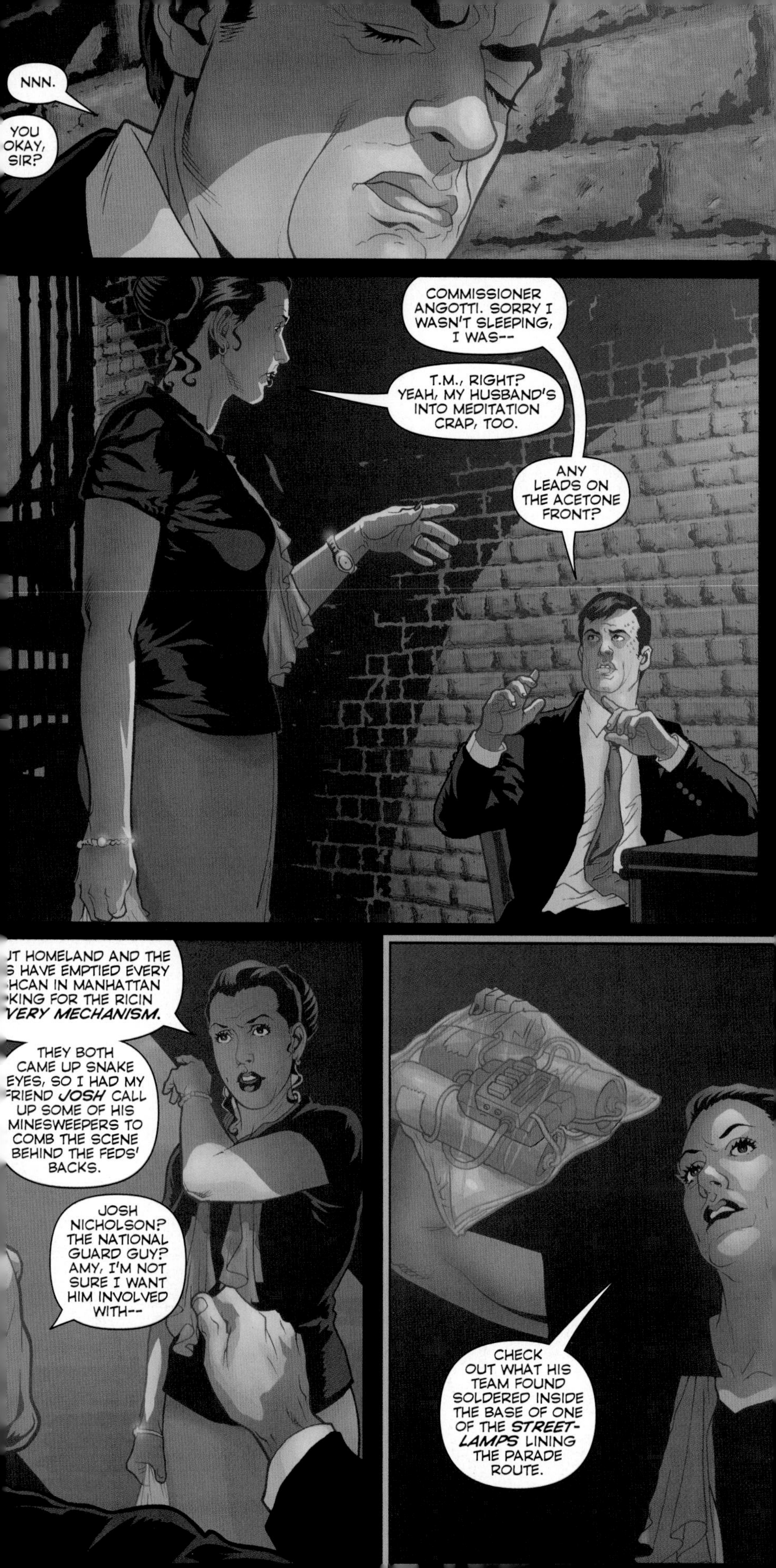
NNN.
YOU OKAY, SIR?
COMMISSIONER ANGOTTI. SORRY I WASN'T SLEEPING, I WAS--
T.M., RIGHT? YEAH, MY HUSBAND'S INTO MEDITATION CRAP, TOO.
ANY LEADS ON THE ACETONE FRONT?
UT HOMELAND AND THE S HAVE EMPTIED EVERY HCAN IN MANHATTAN KING FOR THE RICIN VERY MECHANISM.
THEY BOTH CAME UP SNAKE EYES, SO I HAD MY FRIEND JOSH CALL UP SOME OF HIS MINESWEEPERS TO COMB THE SCENE BEHIND THE FEDS' BACKS.
JOSH NICHOLSON? THE NATIONAL GUARD GUY? AMY, I'M NOT SURE I WANT HIM INVOLVED WITH--
CHECK OUT WHAT HIS TEAM FOUND SOLDERED INSIDE THE BASE OF ONE OF THE STREET-LAMPS LINING THE PARADE ROUTE.

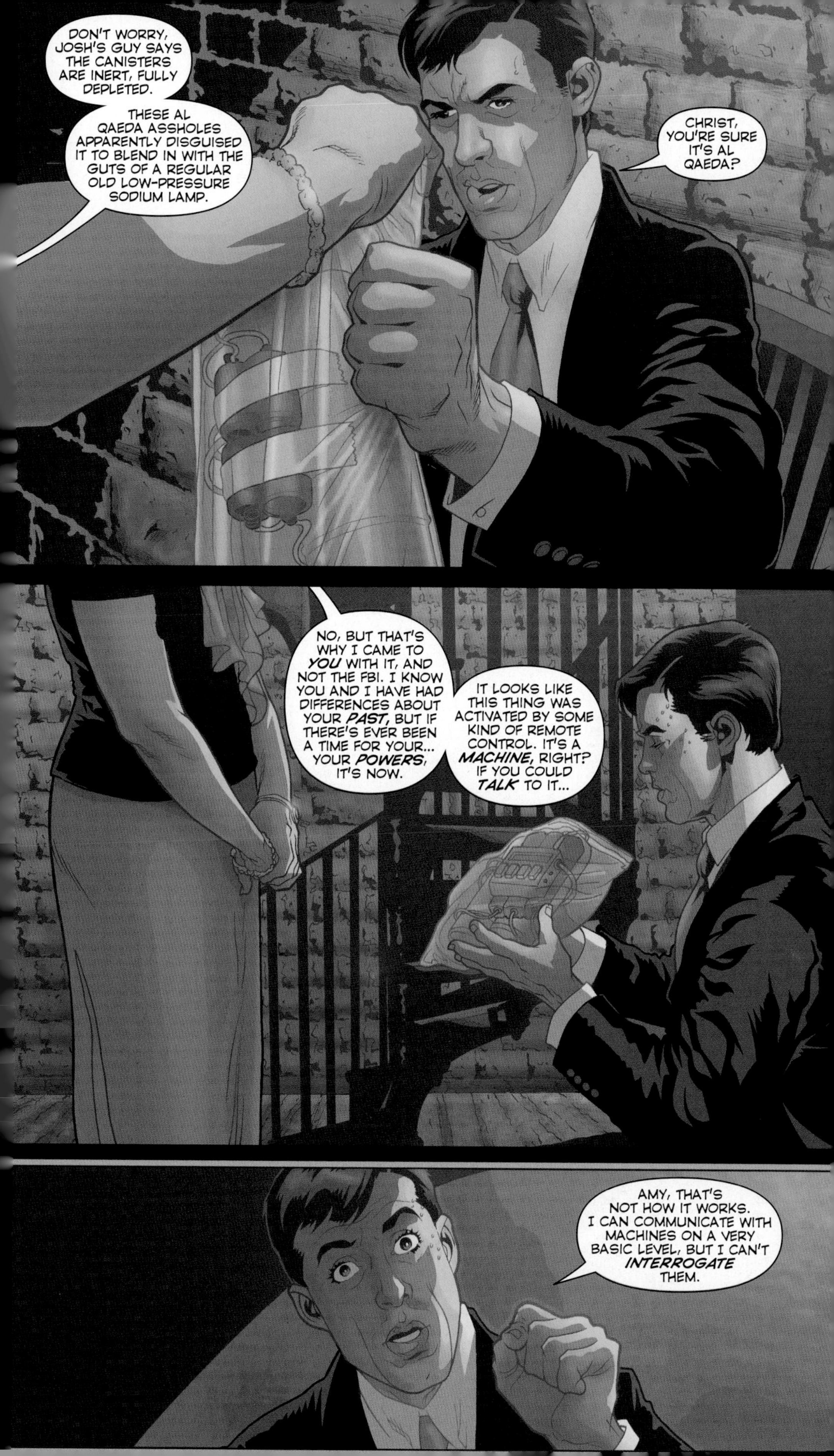
DON'T WORRY, JOSH'S GUY SAYS THE CANISTERS ARE INERT, FULLY DEPLETED.
THESE AL QAEDA ASSHOLES APPARENTLY DISGUISED IT TO BLEND IN WITH THE GUTS OF A REGULAR OLD LOW-PRESSURE SODIUM LAMP.
CHRIST, YOU'RE SURE IT'S AL QAEDA?
NO, BUT THAT'S WHY I CAME TO *YOU* WITH IT, AND NOT THE FBI. I KNOW YOU AND I HAVE HAD DIFFERENCES ABOUT YOUR *PAST*, BUT IF THERE'S EVER BEEN A TIME FOR YOUR... YOUR *POWERS*, IT'S NOW.
IT LOOKS LIKE THIS THING WAS ACTIVATED BY SOME KIND OF REMOTE CONTROL. IT'S A *MACHINE*, RIGHT? IF YOU COULD *TALK* TO IT...
AMY, THAT'S NOT HOW IT WORKS. I CAN COMMUNICATE WITH MACHINES ON A VERY BASIC LEVEL, BUT I CAN'T *INTERROGATE* THEM.

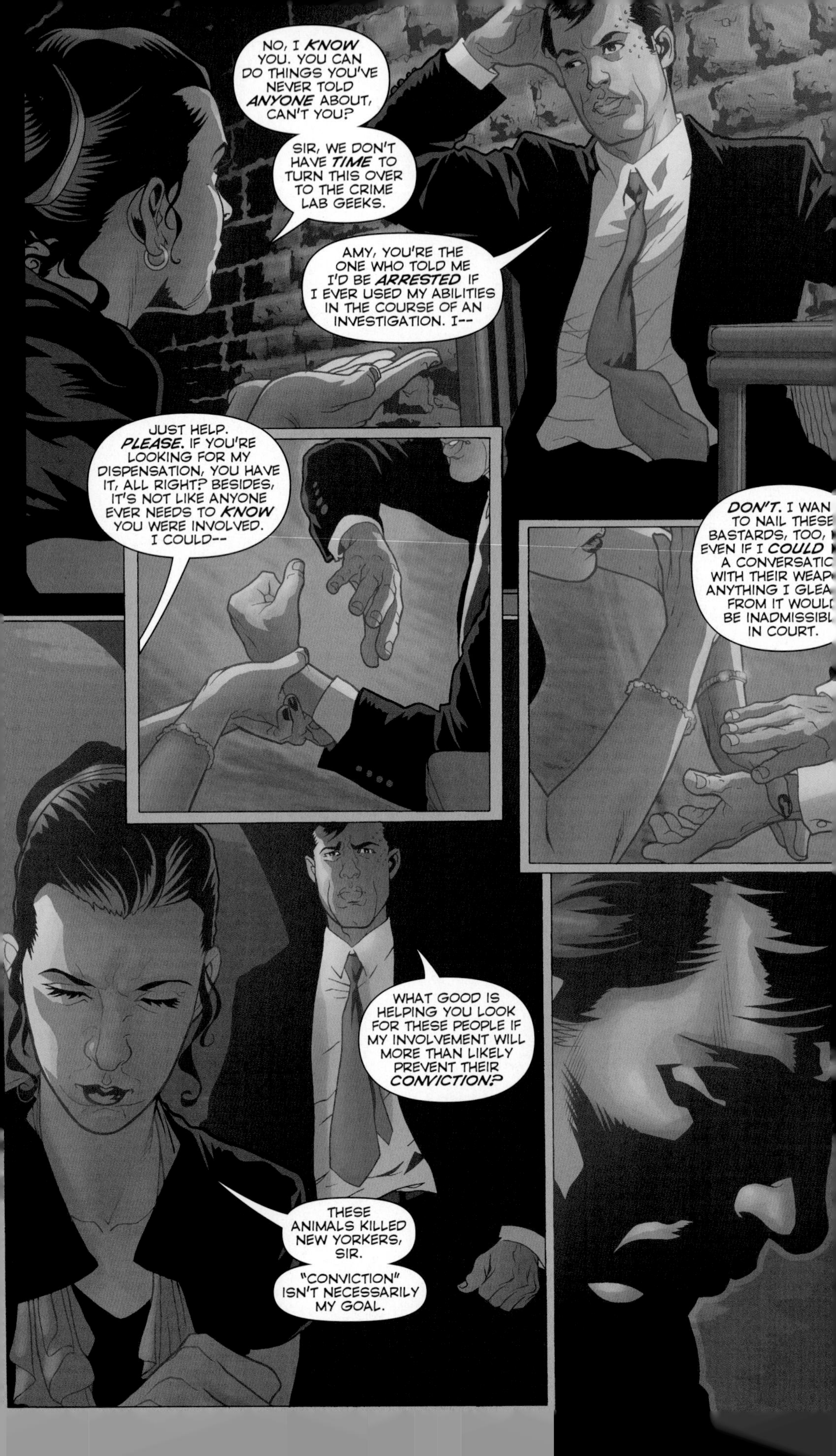
NO, I KNOW YOU. YOU CAN DO THINGS YOU'VE NEVER TOLD ANYONE ABOUT, CAN'T YOU?
SIR, WE DON'T HAVE TIME TO TURN THIS OVER TO THE CRIME LAB GEEKS.
AMY, YOU'RE THE ONE WHO TOLD ME I'D BE ARRESTED IF I EVER USED MY ABILITIES IN THE COURSE OF AN INVESTIGATION. I--
JUST HELP. PLEASE. IF YOU'RE LOOKING FOR MY DISPENSATION, YOU HAVE IT, ALL RIGHT? BESIDES, IT'S NOT LIKE ANYONE EVER NEEDS TO KNOW YOU WERE INVOLVED. I COULD--
DON'T. I WAN TO NAIL THESE BASTARDS, TOO, EVEN IF I COULD A CONVERSATIC WITH THEIR WEAP ANYTHING I GLEA FROM IT WOULI BE INADMISSIBI IN COURT.
WHAT GOOD IS HELPING YOU LOOK FOR THESE PEOPLE IF MY INVOLVEMENT WILL MORE THAN LIKELY PREVENT THEIR CONVICTION?
THESE ANIMALS KILLED NEW YORKERS, SIR.
"CONVICTION" ISN'T NECESSARILY MY GOAL.

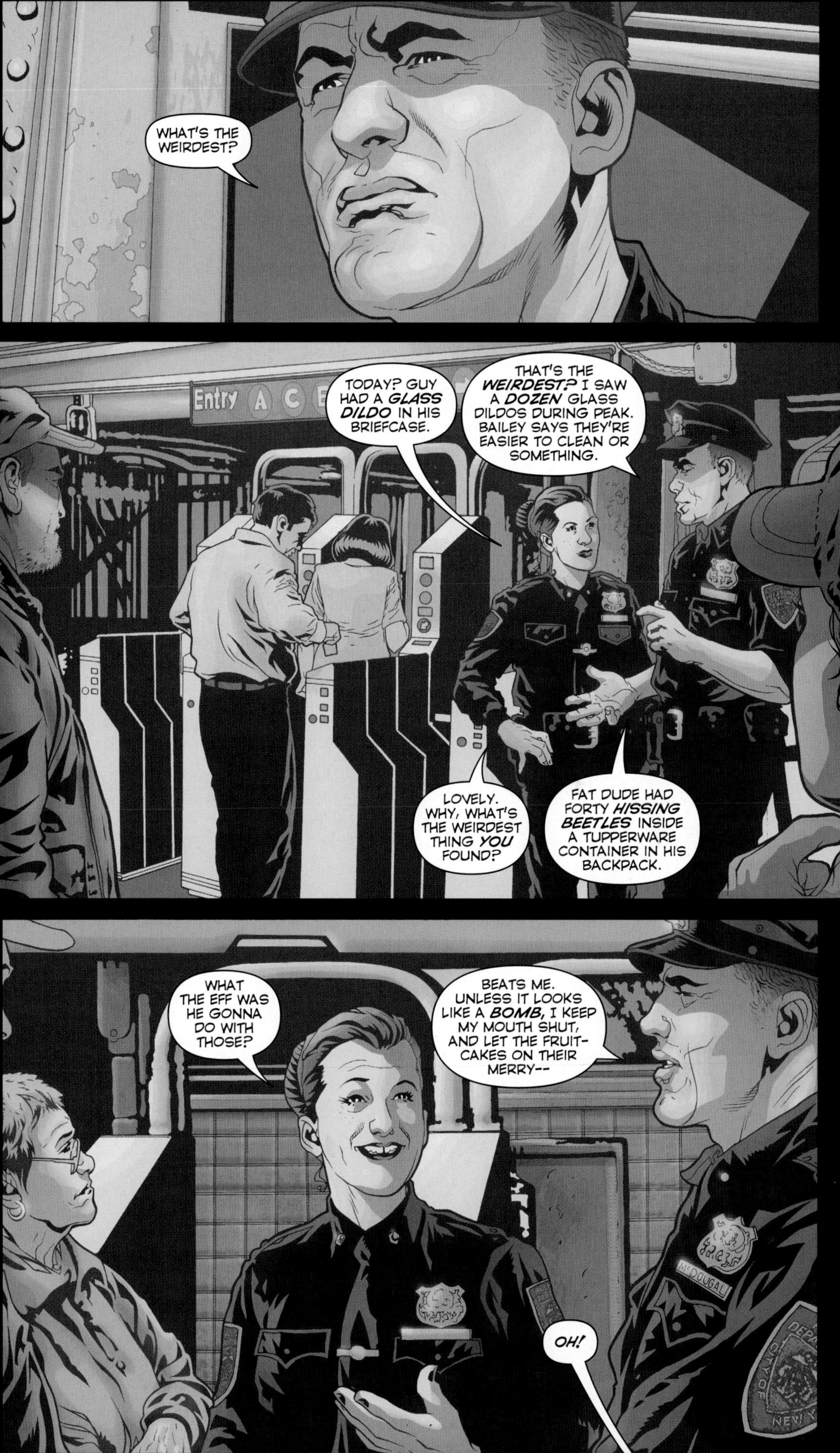
WHAT'S THE WEIRDEST?
Entry A C
TODAY? GUY HAD A ***GLASS DILDO*** IN HIS BRIEFCASE.
THAT'S THE ***WEIRDEST?*** I SAW A ***DOZEN*** GLASS DILDOS DURING PEAK. BAILEY SAYS THEY'RE EASIER TO CLEAN OR SOMETHING.
LOVELY. WHY, WHAT'S THE WEIRDEST THING ***YOU*** FOUND?
FAT DUDE HAD FORTY ***HISSING BEETLES*** INSIDE A TUPPERWARE CONTAINER IN HIS BACKPACK.
WHAT THE EFF WAS HE GONNA DO WITH THOSE?
BEATS ME. UNLESS IT LOOKS LIKE A ***BOMB,*** I KEEP MY MOUTH SHUT, AND LET THE FRUIT-CAKES ON THEIR MERRY--
McDOUGAL
***OH!***

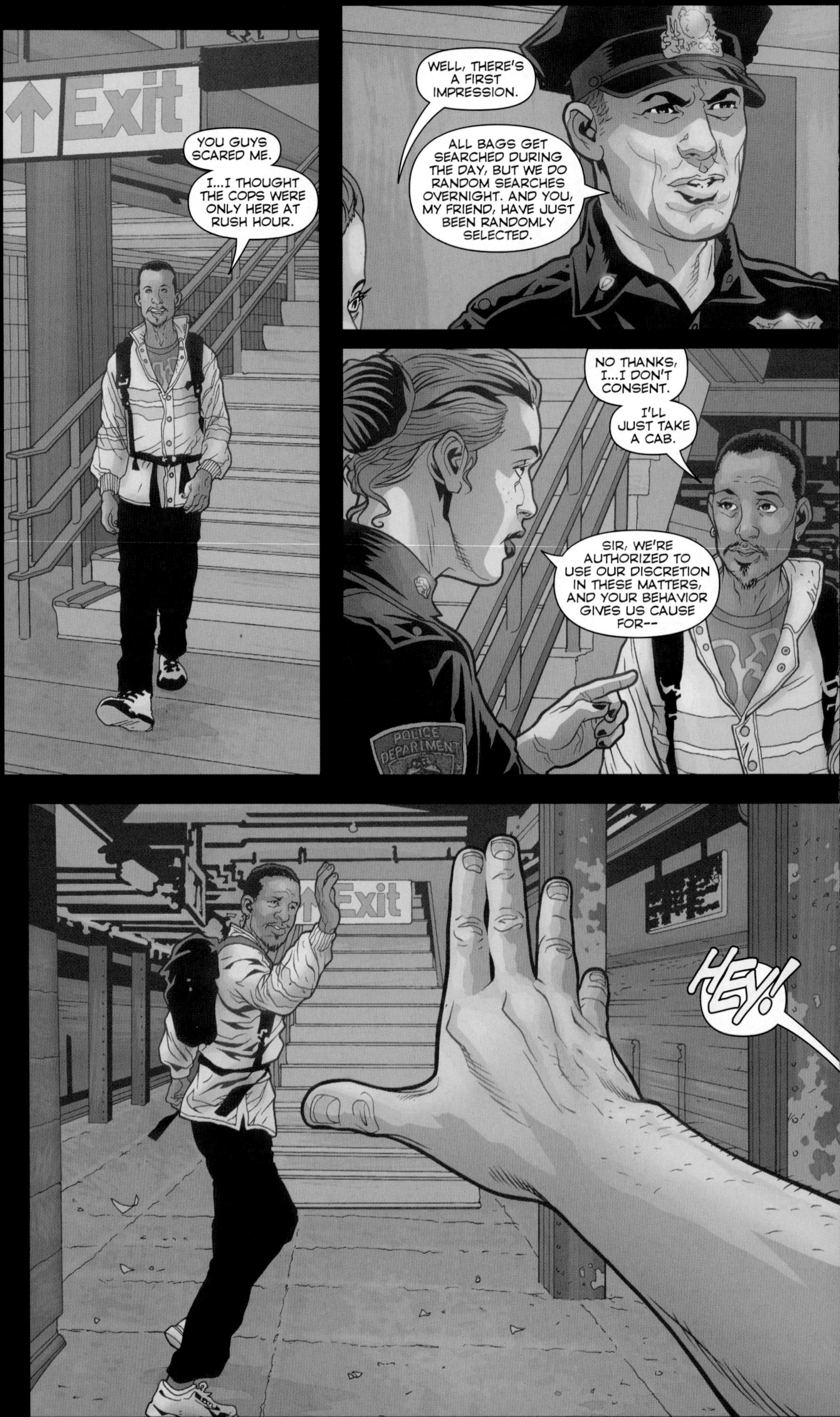
Exit
YOU GUYS SCARED ME.
I...I THOUGHT THE COPS WERE ONLY HERE AT RUSH HOUR.
WELL, THERE'S A FIRST IMPRESSION.
ALL BAGS GET SEARCHED DURING THE DAY, BUT WE DO RANDOM SEARCHES OVERNIGHT. AND YOU, MY FRIEND, HAVE JUST BEEN RANDOMLY SELECTED.
NO THANKS, I...I DON'T CONSENT.
I'LL JUST TAKE A CAB.
SIR, WE'RE AUTHORIZED TO USE OUR DISCRETION IN THESE MATTERS, AND YOUR BEHAVIOR GIVES US CAUSE FOR--
POLICE DEPARTMENT
Exit
HEY!

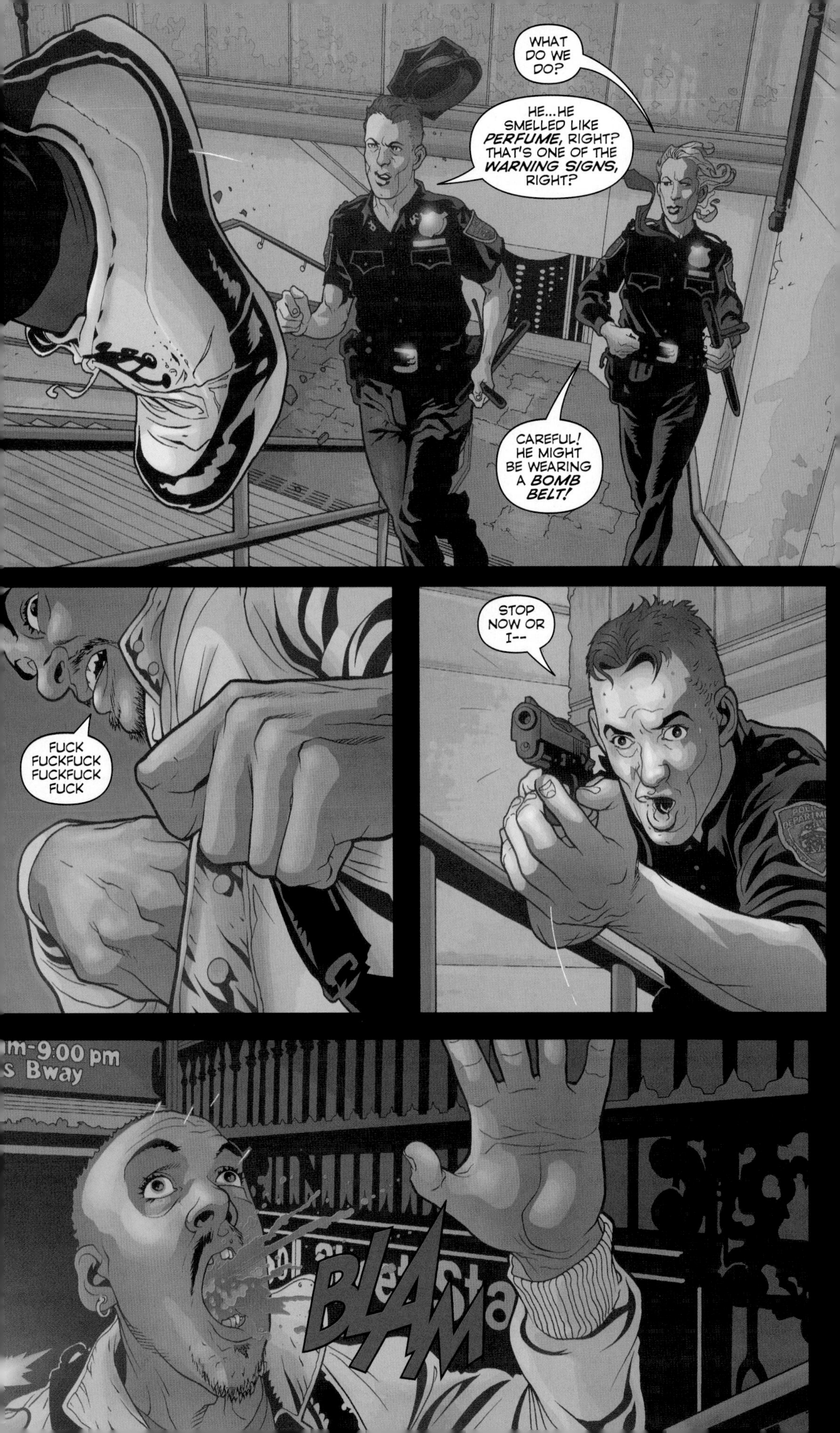
WHAT DO WE DO?
HE...HE SMELLED LIKE PERFUME, RIGHT? THAT'S ONE OF THE WARNING SIGNS, RIGHT?
CAREFUL! HE MIGHT BE WEARING A BOMB BELT!
FUCK FUCKFUCK FUCKFUCK FUCK
STOP NOW OR I--
m-9:00 pm
s Bway
BLAM

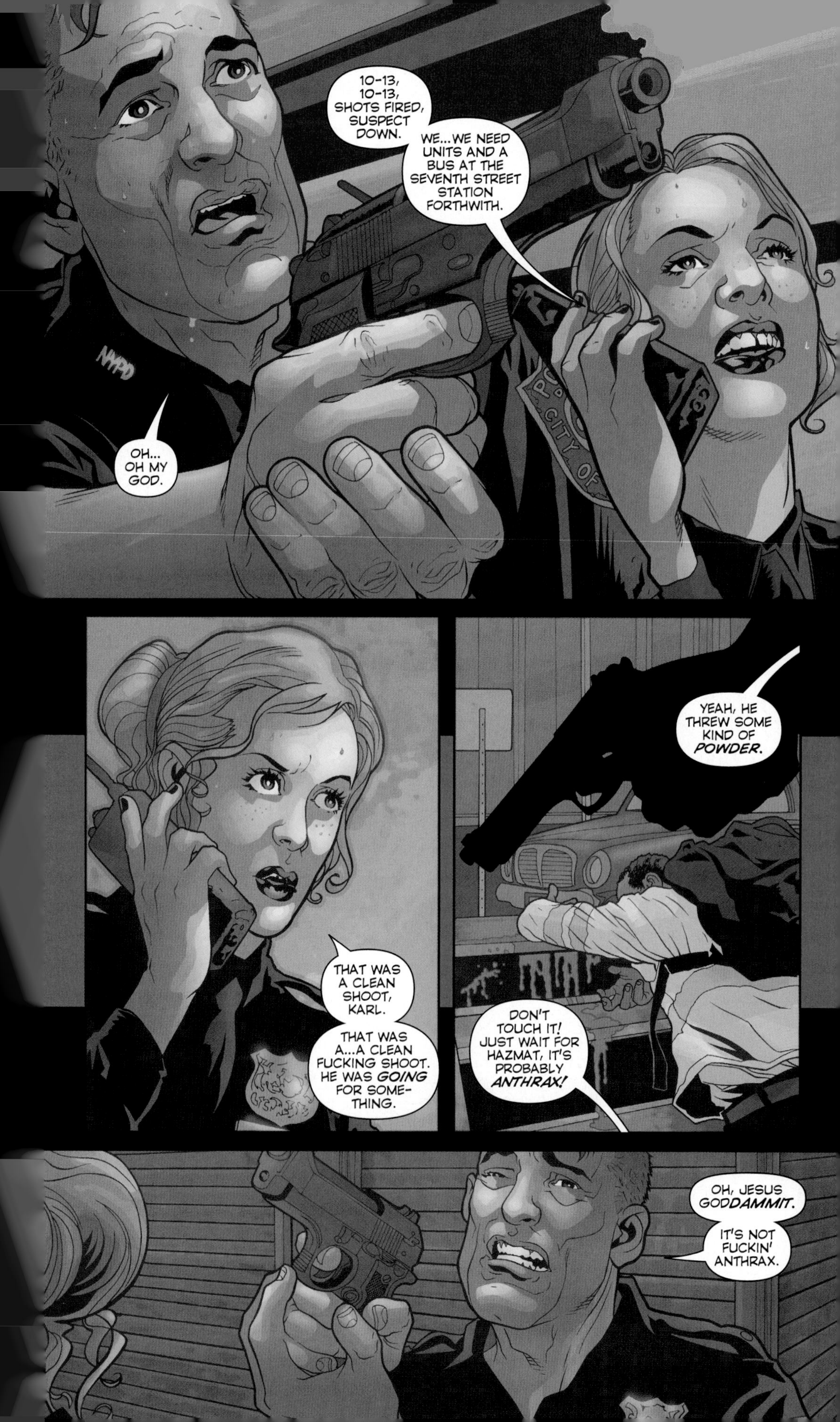
10-13, 10-13, SHOTS FIRED, SUSPECT DOWN.
WE...WE NEED UNITS AND A BUS AT THE SEVENTH STREET STATION FORTHWITH.
OH... OH MY GOD.
NYPD
THAT WAS A CLEAN SHOOT, KARL.
THAT WAS A...A CLEAN FUCKING SHOOT. HE WAS *GOING* FOR SOME-THING.
YEAH, HE THREW SOME KIND OF *POWDER*.
DON'T TOUCH IT! JUST WAIT FOR HAZMAT, IT'S PROBABLY *ANTHRAX!*
OH, JESUS GOD*DAMMIT*.
IT'S NOT FUCKIN' ANTHRAX.

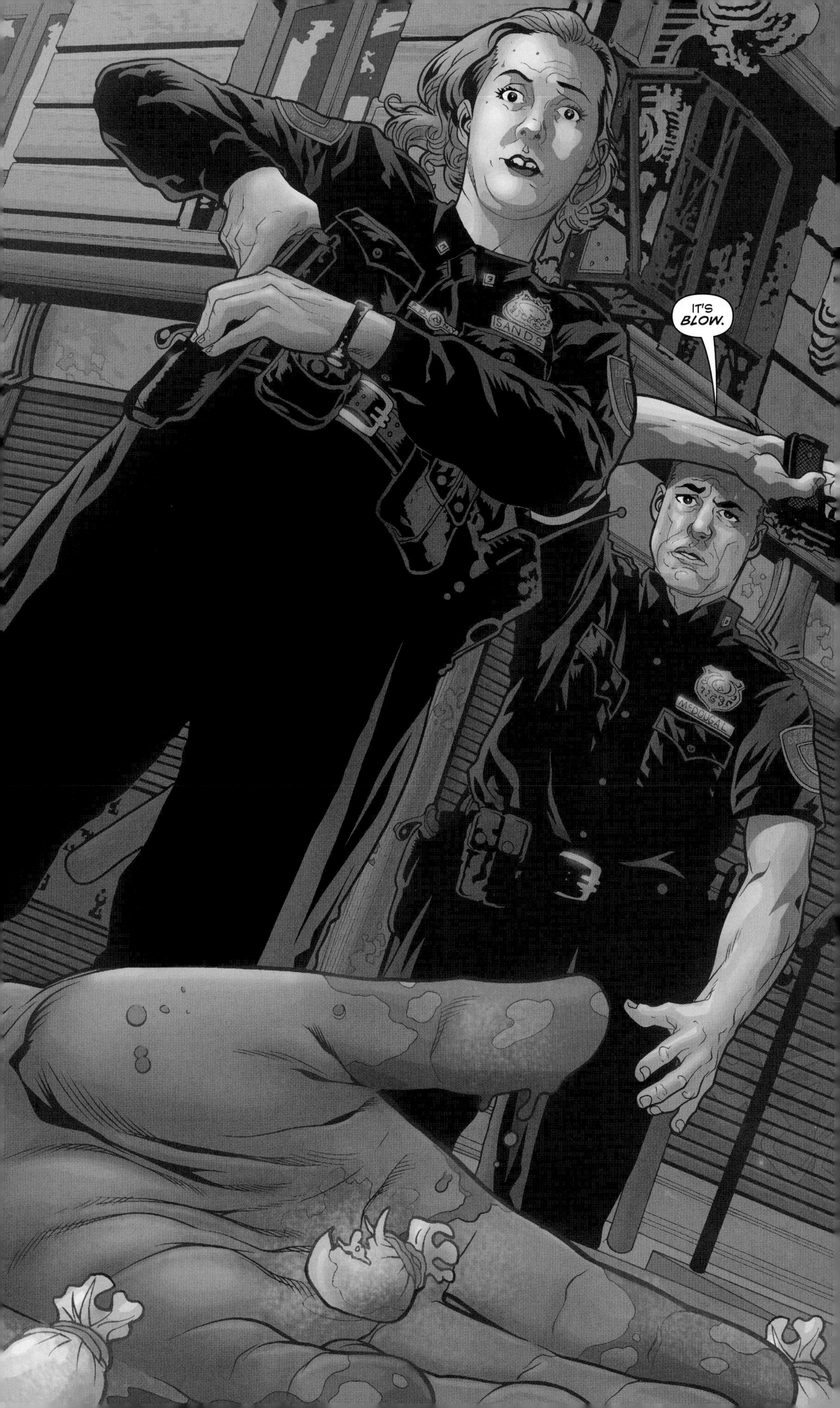
IT'S BLOW.

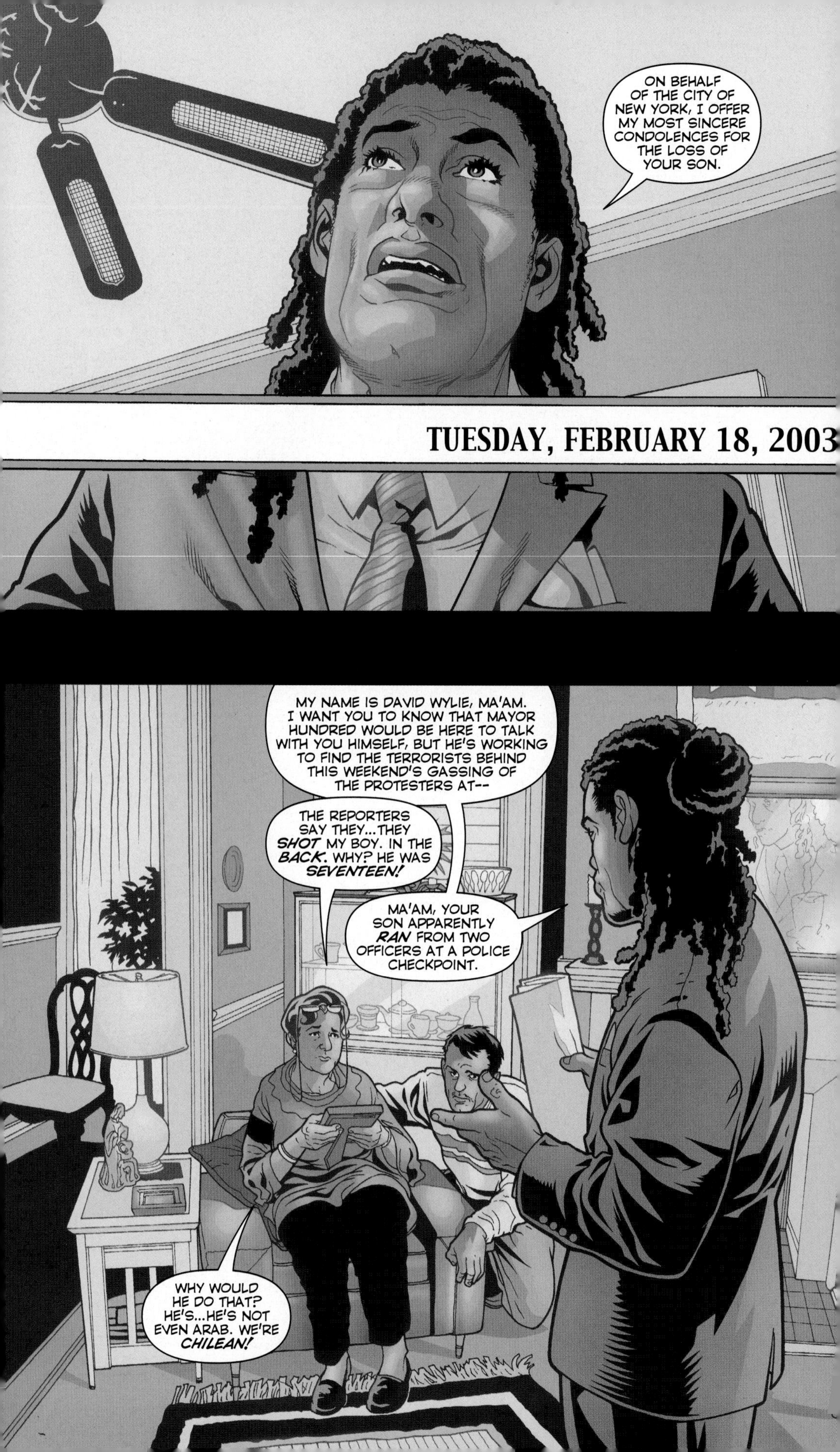
ON BEHALF OF THE CITY OF NEW YORK, I OFFER MY MOST SINCERE CONDOLENCES FOR THE LOSS OF YOUR SON.
TUESDAY, FEBRUARY 18, 2003
MY NAME IS DAVID WYLIE, MA'AM. I WANT YOU TO KNOW THAT MAYOR HUNDRED WOULD BE HERE TO TALK WITH YOU HIMSELF, BUT HE'S WORKING TO FIND THE TERRORISTS BEHIND THIS WEEKEND'S GASSING OF THE PROTESTERS AT--
THE REPORTERS SAY THEY...THEY *SHOT* MY BOY. IN THE *BACK*. WHY? HE WAS *SEVENTEEN!*
MA'AM, YOUR SON APPARENTLY *RAN* FROM TWO OFFICERS AT A POLICE CHECKPOINT.
WHY WOULD HE DO THAT? HE'S...HE'S NOT EVEN ARAB. WE'RE *CHILEAN!*

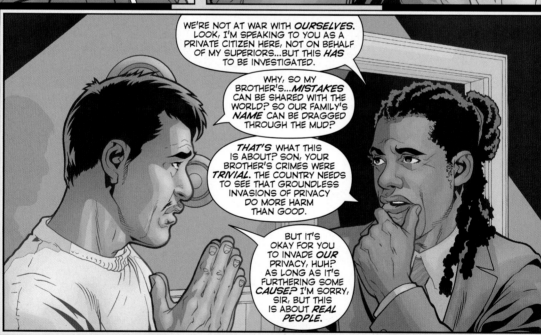

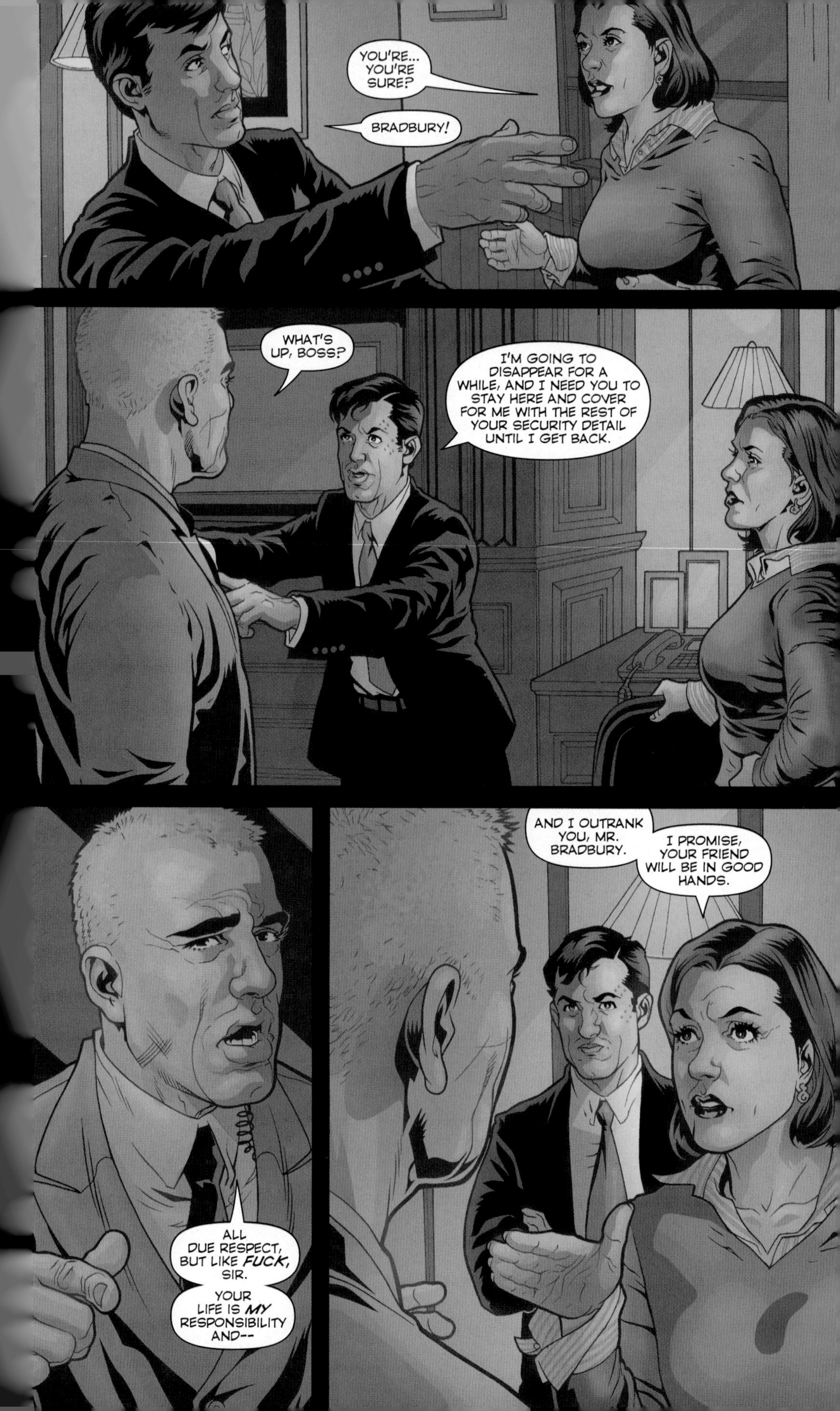
YOU'RE... YOU'RE SURE?
BRADBURY!
WHAT'S UP, BOSS?
I'M GOING TO DISAPPEAR FOR A WHILE, AND I NEED YOU TO STAY HERE AND COVER FOR ME WITH THE REST OF YOUR SECURITY DETAIL UNTIL I GET BACK.
ALL DUE RESPECT, BUT LIKE FUCK, SIR.
YOUR LIFE IS MY RESPONSIBILITY AND--
AND I OUTRANK YOU, MR. BRADBURY.
I PROMISE, YOUR FRIEND WILL BE IN GOOD HANDS.

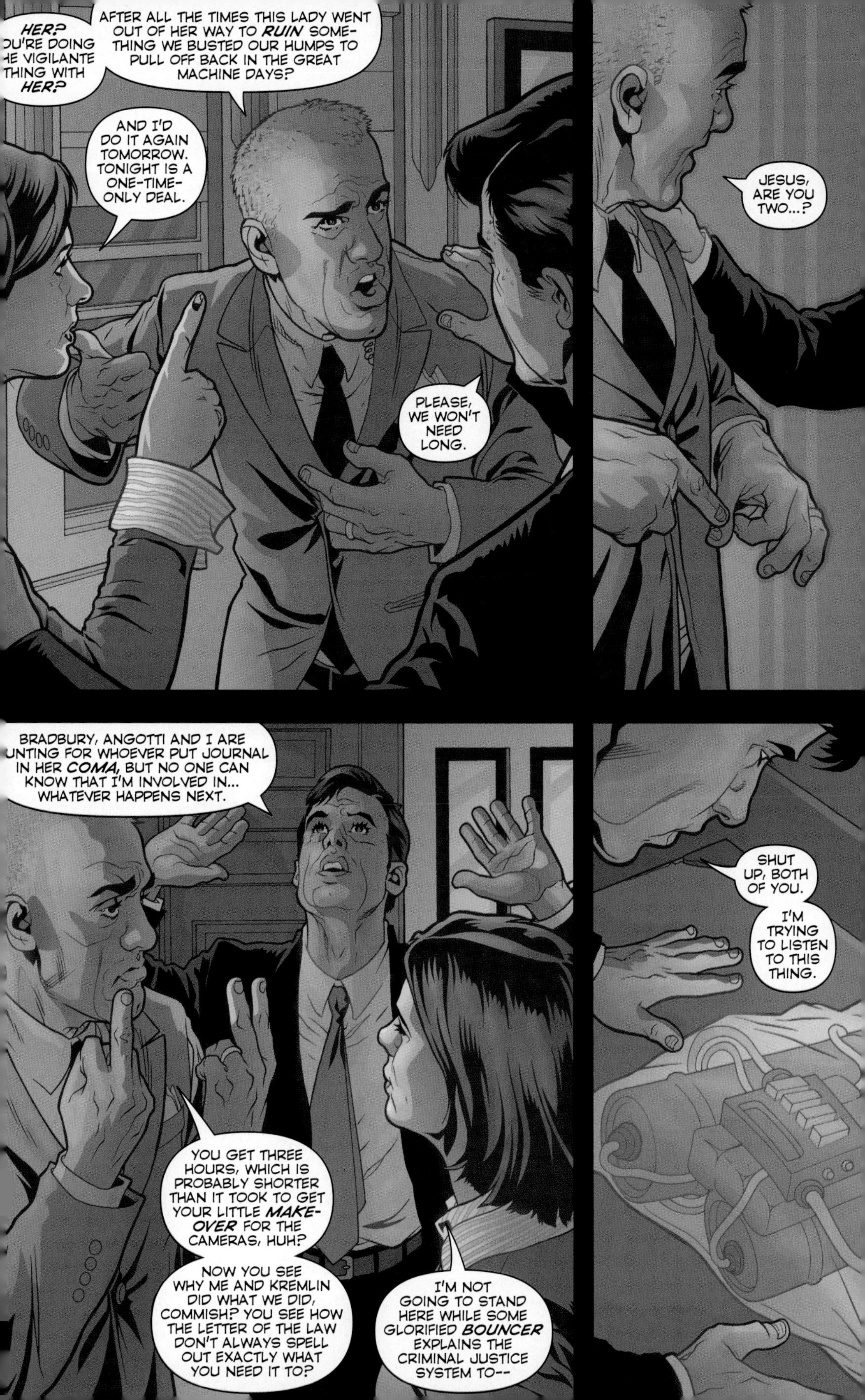

HER? OU'RE DOING HE VIGILANTE THING WITH HER?
AFTER ALL THE TIMES THIS LADY WENT OUT OF HER WAY TO RUIN SOME-THING WE BUSTED OUR HUMPS TO PULL OFF BACK IN THE GREAT MACHINE DAYS?
AND I'D DO IT AGAIN TOMORROW. TONIGHT IS A ONE-TIME-ONLY DEAL.
PLEASE, WE WON'T NEED LONG.
JESUS, ARE YOU TWO...?
BRADBURY, ANGOTTI AND I ARE UNTING FOR WHOEVER PUT JOURNAL IN HER COMA, BUT NO ONE CAN KNOW THAT I'M INVOLVED IN... WHATEVER HAPPENS NEXT.
YOU GET THREE HOURS, WHICH IS PROBABLY SHORTER THAN IT TOOK TO GET YOUR LITTLE MAKE-OVER FOR THE CAMERAS, HUH?
NOW YOU SEE WHY ME AND KREMLIN DID WHAT WE DID, COMMISH? YOU SEE HOW THE LETTER OF THE LAW DON'T ALWAYS SPELL OUT EXACTLY WHAT YOU NEED IT TO?
I'M NOT GOING TO STAND HERE WHILE SOME GLORIFIED BOUNCER EXPLAINS THE CRIMINAL JUSTICE SYSTEM TO--
SHUT UP, BOTH OF YOU.
I'M TRYING TO LISTEN TO THIS THING.

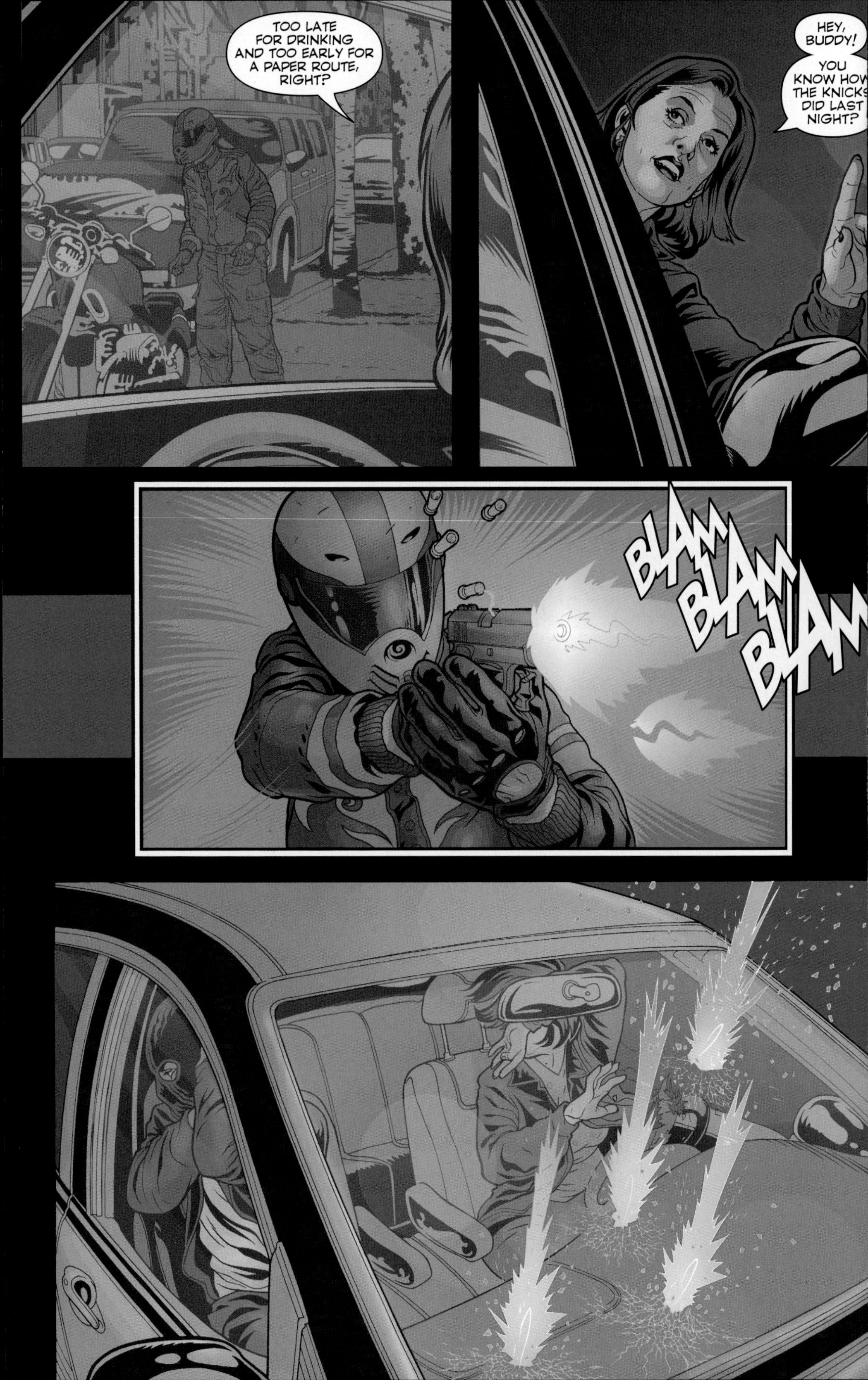
TOO LATE FOR DRINKING AND TOO EARLY FOR A PAPER ROUTE, RIGHT?
HEY, BUDDY!
YOU KNOW HOW THE KNICKS DID LAST NIGHT?
BLAM BLAM BLAM

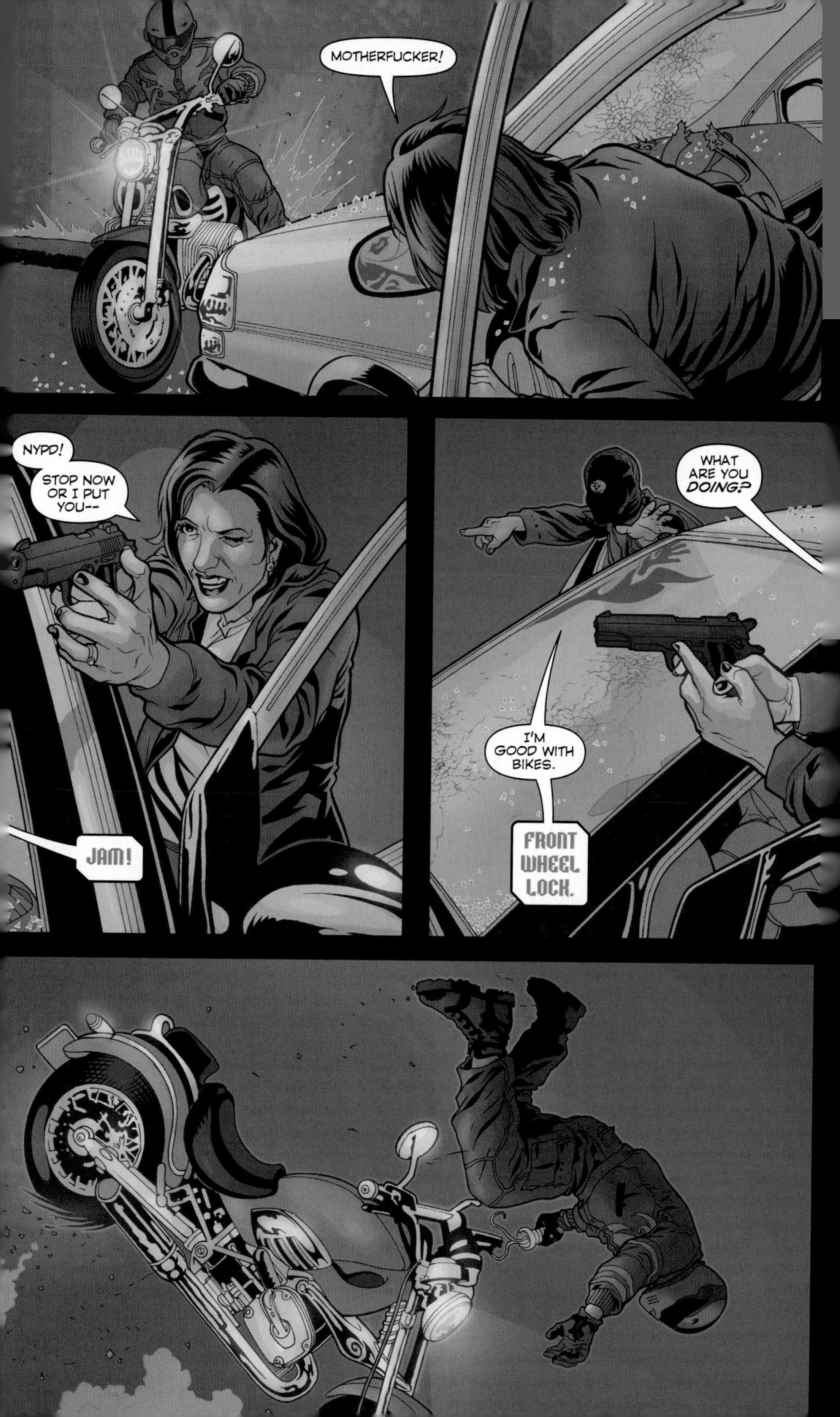
MOTHERFUCKER!
NYPD!
STOP NOW OR I PUT YOU--
JAM!
WHAT ARE YOU *DOING?*
I'M GOOD WITH BIKES.
FRONT WHEEL LOCK.

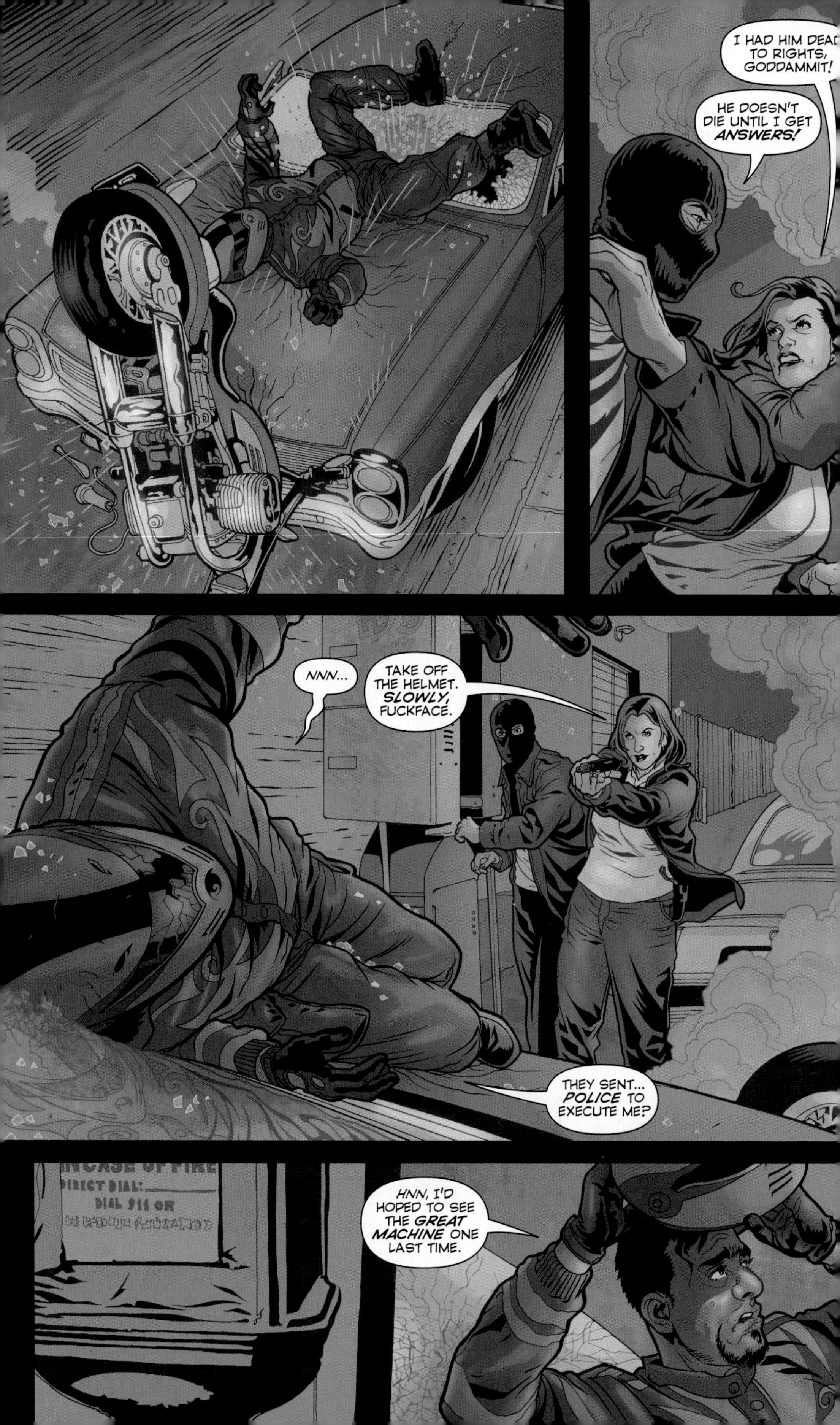

I HAD HIM DEAD TO RIGHTS, GODDAMMIT!
HE DOESN'T DIE UNTIL I GET ANSWERS!
NNN...
TAKE OFF THE HELMET. SLOWLY, FUCKFACE.
THEY SENT... POLICE TO EXECUTE ME?
DIRECT DIAL:
DIAL 911 OR
HNN, I'D HOPED TO SEE THE GREAT MACHINE ONE LAST TIME.

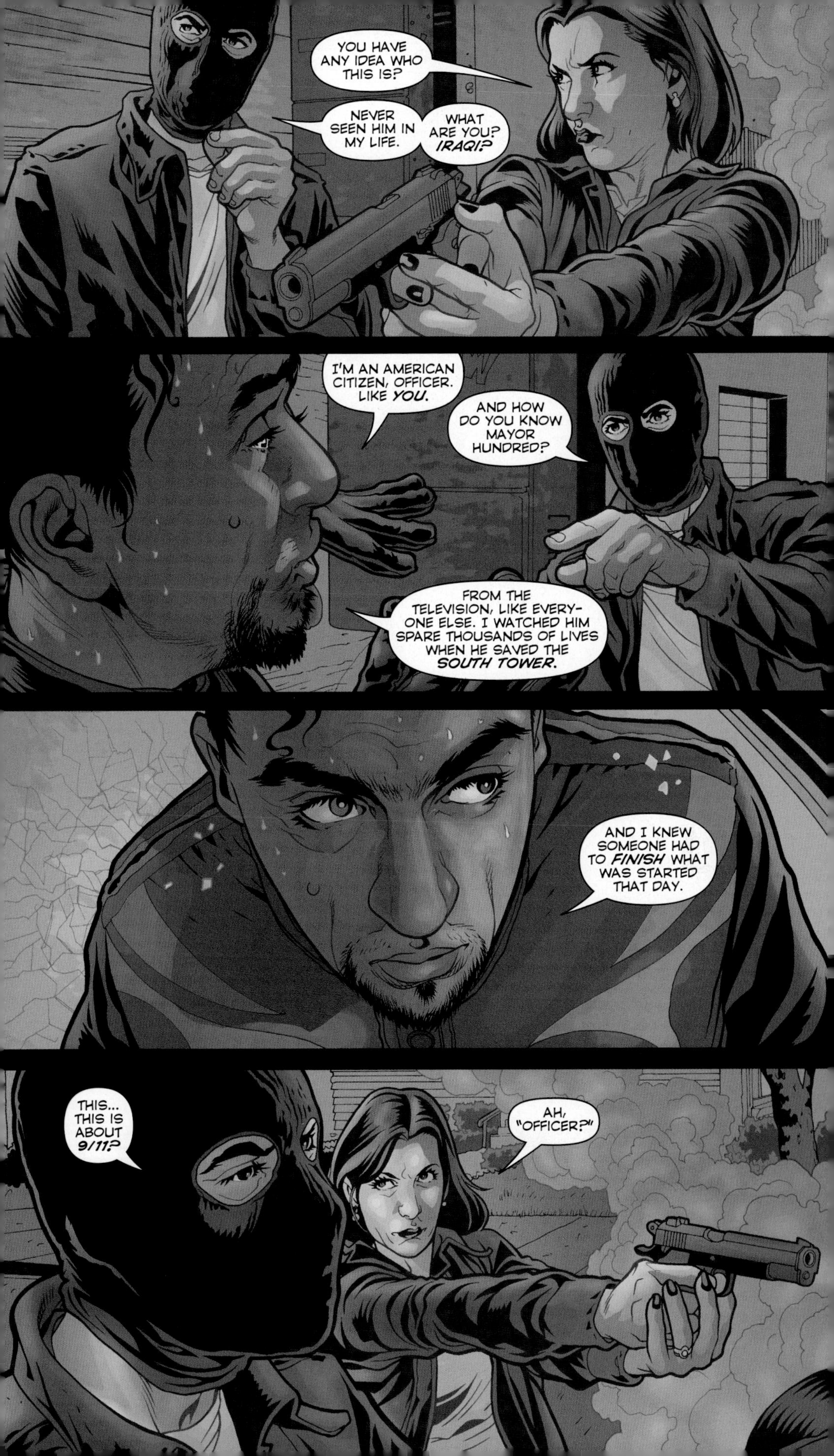
YOU HAVE ANY IDEA WHO THIS IS?
NEVER SEEN HIM IN MY LIFE.
WHAT ARE YOU? *IRAQI?*
I'M AN AMERICAN CITIZEN, OFFICER. LIKE *YOU*.
AND HOW DO YOU KNOW MAYOR HUNDRED?
FROM THE TELEVISION, LIKE EVERY-ONE ELSE. I WATCHED HIM SPARE THOUSANDS OF LIVES WHEN HE SAVED THE *SOUTH TOWER*.
AND I KNEW SOMEONE HAD TO *FINISH* WHAT WAS STARTED THAT DAY.
THIS... THIS IS ABOUT *9/11?*
AH, "OFFICER?"

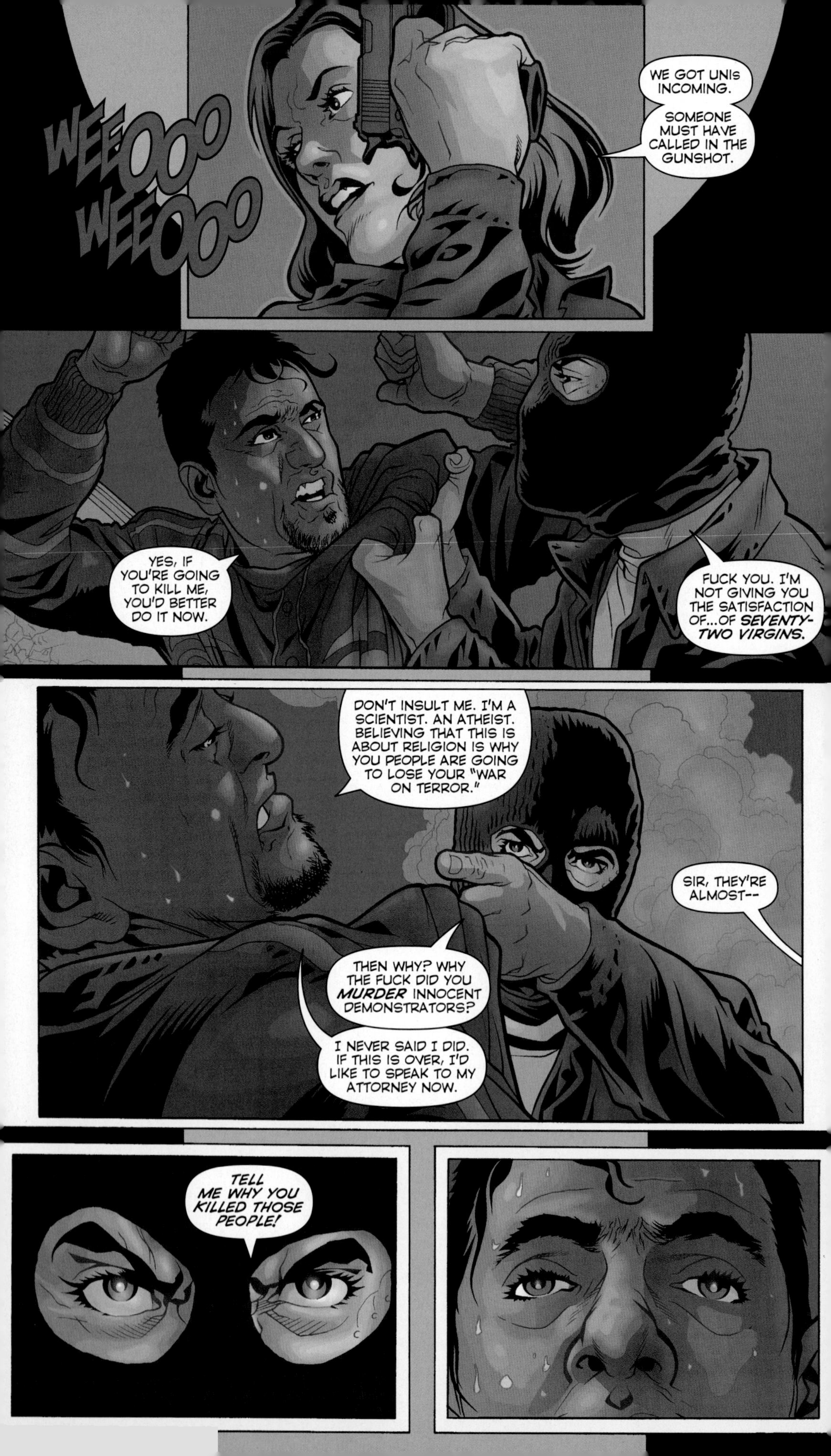
WEEOOO WEEOOO
WE GOT UNIS INCOMING.
SOMEONE MUST HAVE CALLED IN THE GUNSHOT.
YES, IF YOU'RE GOING TO KILL ME, YOU'D BETTER DO IT NOW.
FUCK YOU. I'M NOT GIVING YOU THE SATISFACTION OF...OF SEVENTY-TWO VIRGINS.
DON'T INSULT ME. I'M A SCIENTIST. AN ATHEIST. BELIEVING THAT THIS IS ABOUT RELIGION IS WHY YOU PEOPLE ARE GOING TO LOSE YOUR "WAR ON TERROR."
SIR, THEY'RE ALMOST--
THEN WHY? WHY THE FUCK DID YOU MURDER INNOCENT DEMONSTRATORS?
I NEVER SAID I DID. IF THIS IS OVER, I'D LIKE TO SPEAK TO MY ATTORNEY NOW.
TELL ME WHY YOU KILLED THOSE PEOPLE!

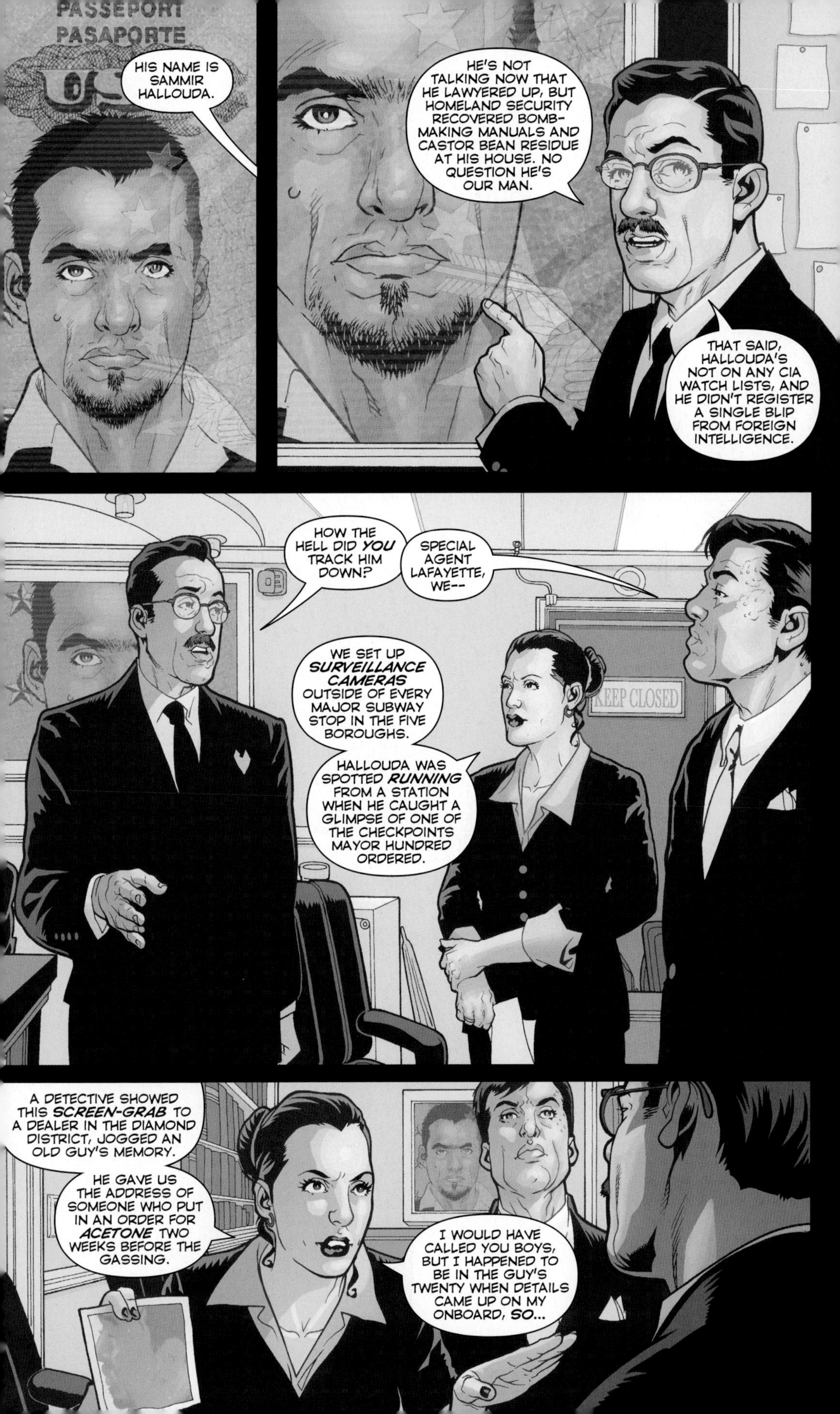
PASSEPORT
PASAPORTE
HIS NAME IS SAMMIR HALLOUDA.
HE'S NOT TALKING NOW THAT HE LAWYERED UP, BUT HOMELAND SECURITY RECOVERED BOMB-MAKING MANUALS AND CASTOR BEAN RESIDUE AT HIS HOUSE. NO QUESTION HE'S OUR MAN.
THAT SAID, HALLOUDA'S NOT ON ANY CIA WATCH LISTS, AND HE DIDN'T REGISTER A SINGLE BLIP FROM FOREIGN INTELLIGENCE.
HOW THE HELL DID *YOU* TRACK HIM DOWN?
SPECIAL AGENT LAFAYETTE, WE--
WE SET UP ***SURVEILLANCE CAMERAS*** OUTSIDE OF EVERY MAJOR SUBWAY STOP IN THE FIVE BOROUGHS.
HALLOUDA WAS SPOTTED ***RUNNING*** FROM A STATION WHEN HE CAUGHT A GLIMPSE OF ONE OF THE CHECKPOINTS MAYOR HUNDRED ORDERED.
KEEP CLOSED
A DETECTIVE SHOWED THIS ***SCREEN-GRAB*** TO A DEALER IN THE DIAMOND DISTRICT, JOGGED AN OLD GUY'S MEMORY.
HE GAVE US THE ADDRESS OF SOMEONE WHO PUT IN AN ORDER FOR ***ACETONE*** TWO WEEKS BEFORE THE GASSING.
I WOULD HAVE CALLED YOU BOYS, BUT I HAPPENED TO BE IN THE GUY'S TWENTY WHEN DETAILS CAME UP ON MY ONBOARD, **SO...**

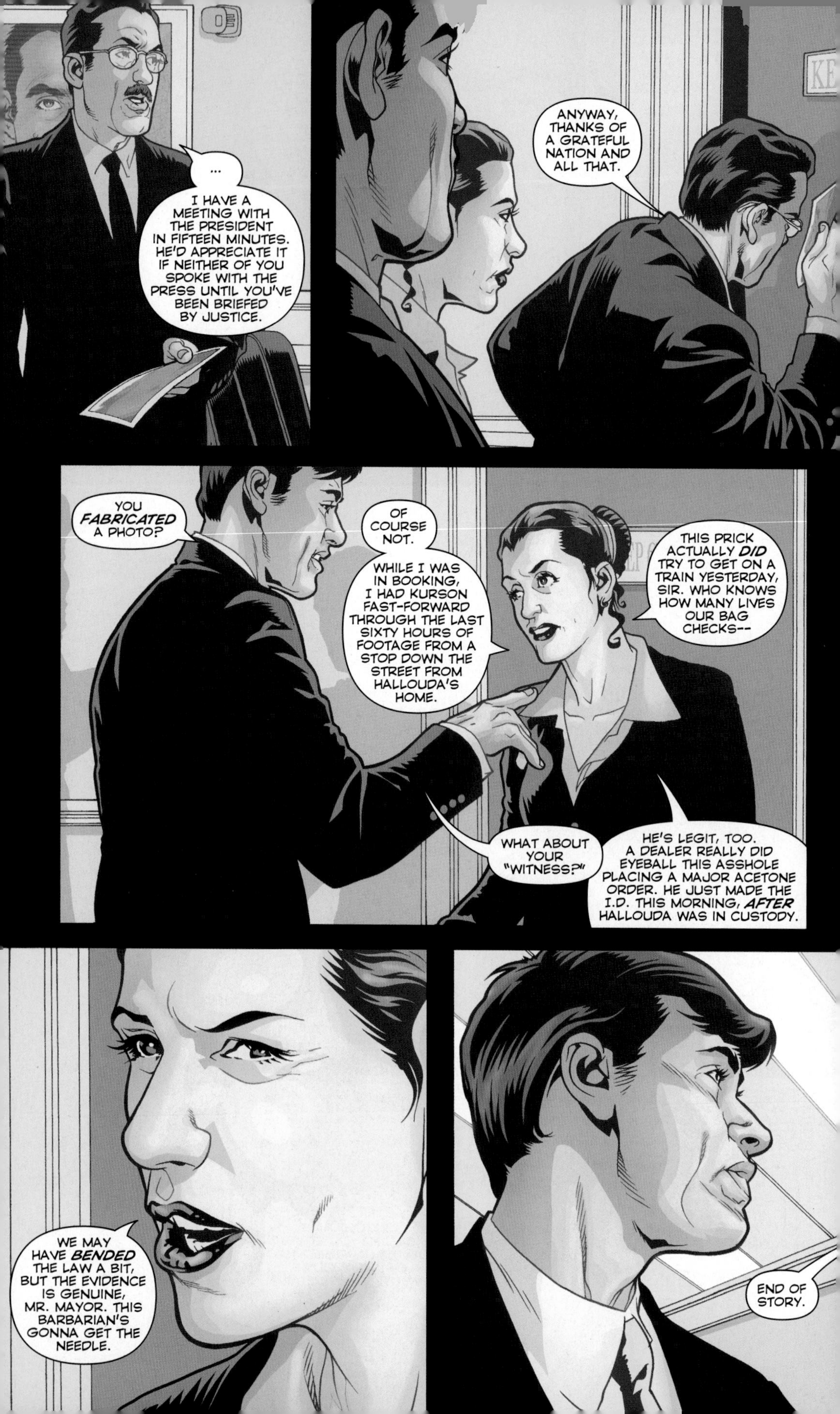
...
I HAVE A MEETING WITH THE PRESIDENT IN FIFTEEN MINUTES. HE'D APPRECIATE IT IF NEITHER OF YOU SPOKE WITH THE PRESS UNTIL YOU'VE BEEN BRIEFED BY JUSTICE.
ANYWAY, THANKS OF A GRATEFUL NATION AND ALL THAT.
YOU *FABRICATED* A PHOTO?
OF COURSE NOT.
WHILE I WAS IN BOOKING, I HAD KURSON FAST-FORWARD THROUGH THE LAST SIXTY HOURS OF FOOTAGE FROM A STOP DOWN THE STREET FROM HALLOUDA'S HOME.
THIS PRICK ACTUALLY *DID* TRY TO GET ON A TRAIN YESTERDAY, SIR. WHO KNOWS HOW MANY LIVES OUR BAG CHECKS--
WHAT ABOUT YOUR "WITNESS?"
HE'S LEGIT, TOO. A DEALER REALLY DID EYEBALL THIS ASSHOLE PLACING A MAJOR ACETONE ORDER. HE JUST MADE THE I.D. THIS MORNING, *AFTER* HALLOUDA WAS IN CUSTODY.
WE MAY HAVE *BENDED* THE LAW A BIT, BUT THE EVIDENCE IS GENUINE, MR. MAYOR. THIS BARBARIAN'S GONNA GET THE NEEDLE.
END OF STORY.

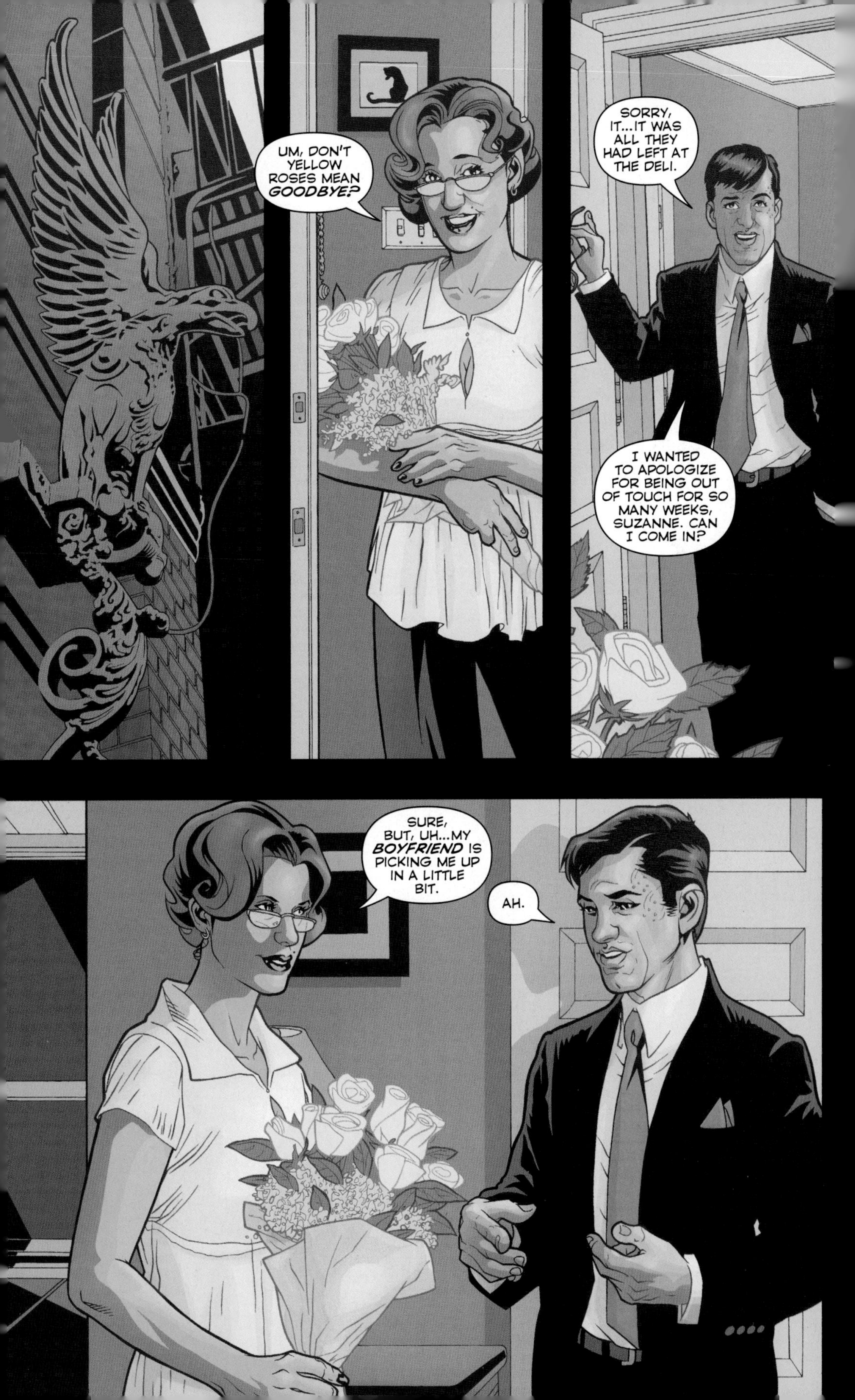
UM, DON'T YELLOW ROSES MEAN GOODBYE?
SORRY, IT...IT WAS ALL THEY HAD LEFT AT THE DELI.
I WANTED TO APOLOGIZE FOR BEING OUT OF TOUCH FOR SO MANY WEEKS, SUZANNE. CAN I COME IN?
SURE, BUT, UH...MY BOYFRIEND IS PICKING ME UP IN A LITTLE BIT.
AH.

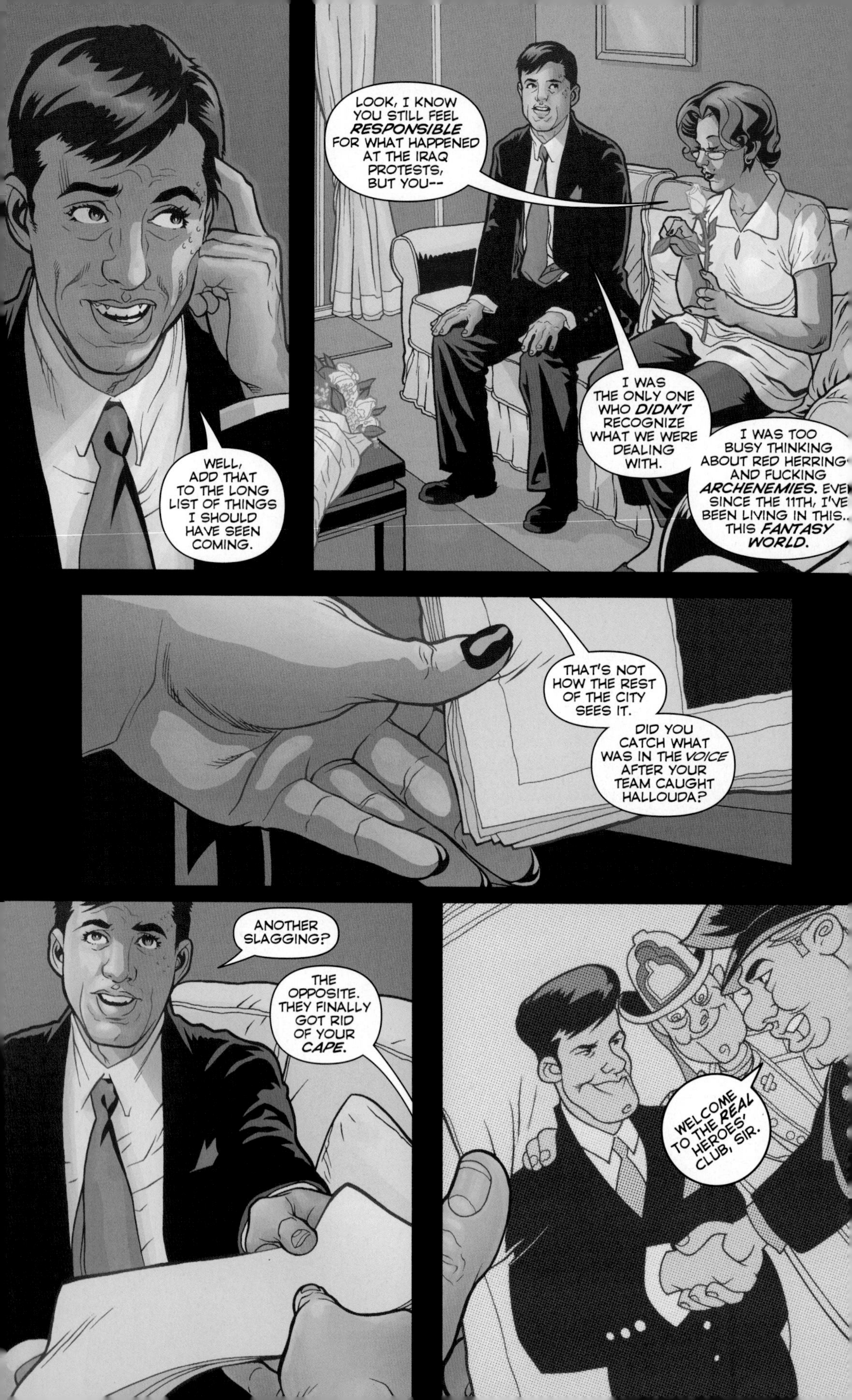

LOOK, I KNOW YOU STILL FEEL *RESPONSIBLE* FOR WHAT HAPPENED AT THE IRAQ PROTESTS, BUT YOU--
WELL, ADD THAT TO THE LONG LIST OF THINGS I SHOULD HAVE SEEN COMING.
I WAS THE ONLY ONE WHO *DIDN'T* RECOGNIZE WHAT WE WERE DEALING WITH.
I WAS TOO BUSY THINKING ABOUT RED HERRING AND FUCKING *ARCHENEMIES.* EVE SINCE THE 11TH, I'VE BEEN LIVING IN THIS.. THIS *FANTASY WORLD.*
THAT'S NOT HOW THE REST OF THE CITY SEES IT.
DID YOU CATCH WHAT WAS IN THE *VOICE* AFTER YOUR TEAM CAUGHT HALLOUDA?
ANOTHER SLAGGING?
THE OPPOSITE. THEY FINALLY GOT RID OF YOUR *CAPE.*
WELCOME TO THE *REAL* HEROES' CLUB, SIR.

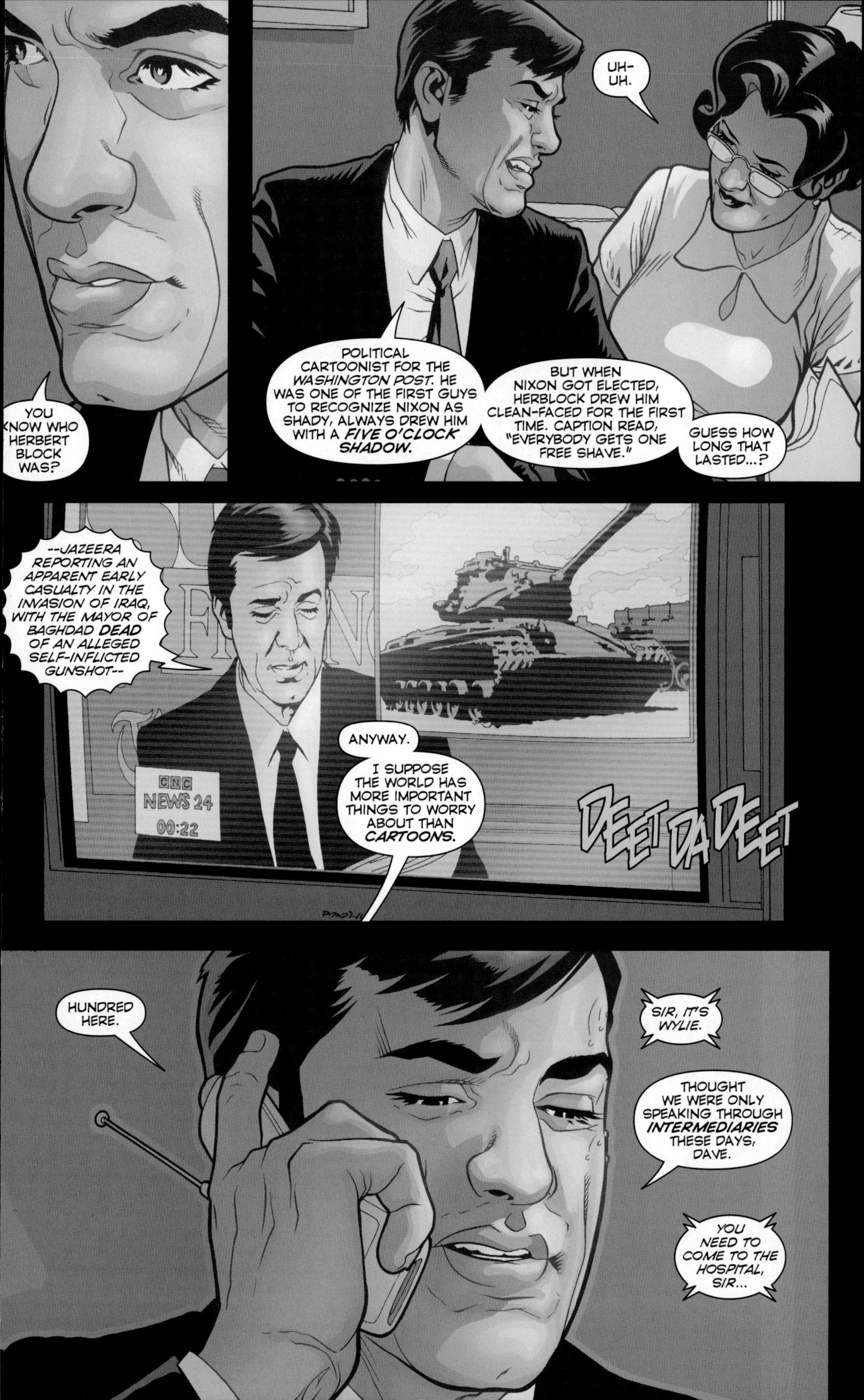
UH-UH.
YOU KNOW WHO HERBERT BLOCK WAS?
POLITICAL CARTOONIST FOR THE *WASHINGTON POST*. HE WAS ONE OF THE FIRST GUYS TO RECOGNIZE NIXON AS SHADY, ALWAYS DREW HIM WITH A ***FIVE O'CLOCK SHADOW.***
BUT WHEN NIXON GOT ELECTED, HERBLOCK DREW HIM CLEAN-FACED FOR THE FIRST TIME. CAPTION READ, "EVERYBODY GETS ONE FREE SHAVE."
GUESS HOW LONG THAT LASTED...?
*--JAZEERA REPORTING AN APPARENT EARLY CASUALTY IN THE INVASION OF IRAQ, WITH THE MAYOR OF BAGHDAD* ***DEAD*** *OF AN ALLEGED SELF-INFLICTED GUNSHOT--*
CNC
NEWS 24
00:22
ANYWAY.
I SUPPOSE THE WORLD HAS MORE IMPORTANT THINGS TO WORRY ABOUT THAN ***CARTOONS.***
DEET DA DEET
HUNDRED HERE.
*SIR, IT'S WYLIE.*
THOUGHT WE WERE ONLY SPEAKING THROUGH ***INTERMEDIARIES*** THESE DAYS, DAVE.
*YOU NEED TO COME TO THE HOSPITAL, SIR...*

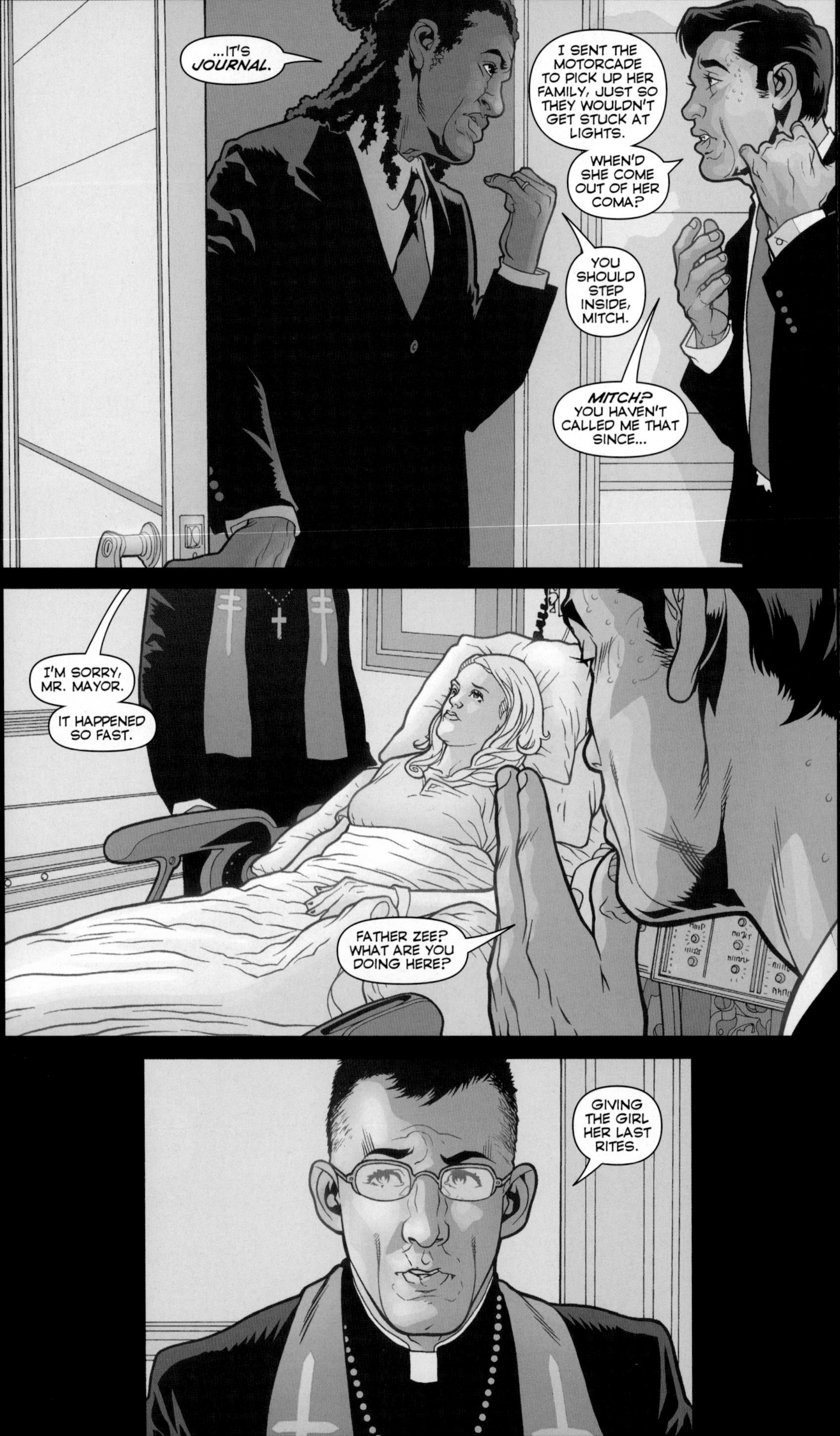
...IT'S JOURNAL.
I SENT THE MOTORCADE TO PICK UP HER FAMILY, JUST SO THEY WOULDN'T GET STUCK AT LIGHTS.
WHEN'D SHE COME OUT OF HER COMA?
YOU SHOULD STEP INSIDE, MITCH.
MITCH? YOU HAVEN'T CALLED ME THAT SINCE...
I'M SORRY, MR. MAYOR.
IT HAPPENED SO FAST.
FATHER ZEE? WHAT ARE YOU DOING HERE?
GIVING THE GIRL HER LAST RITES.

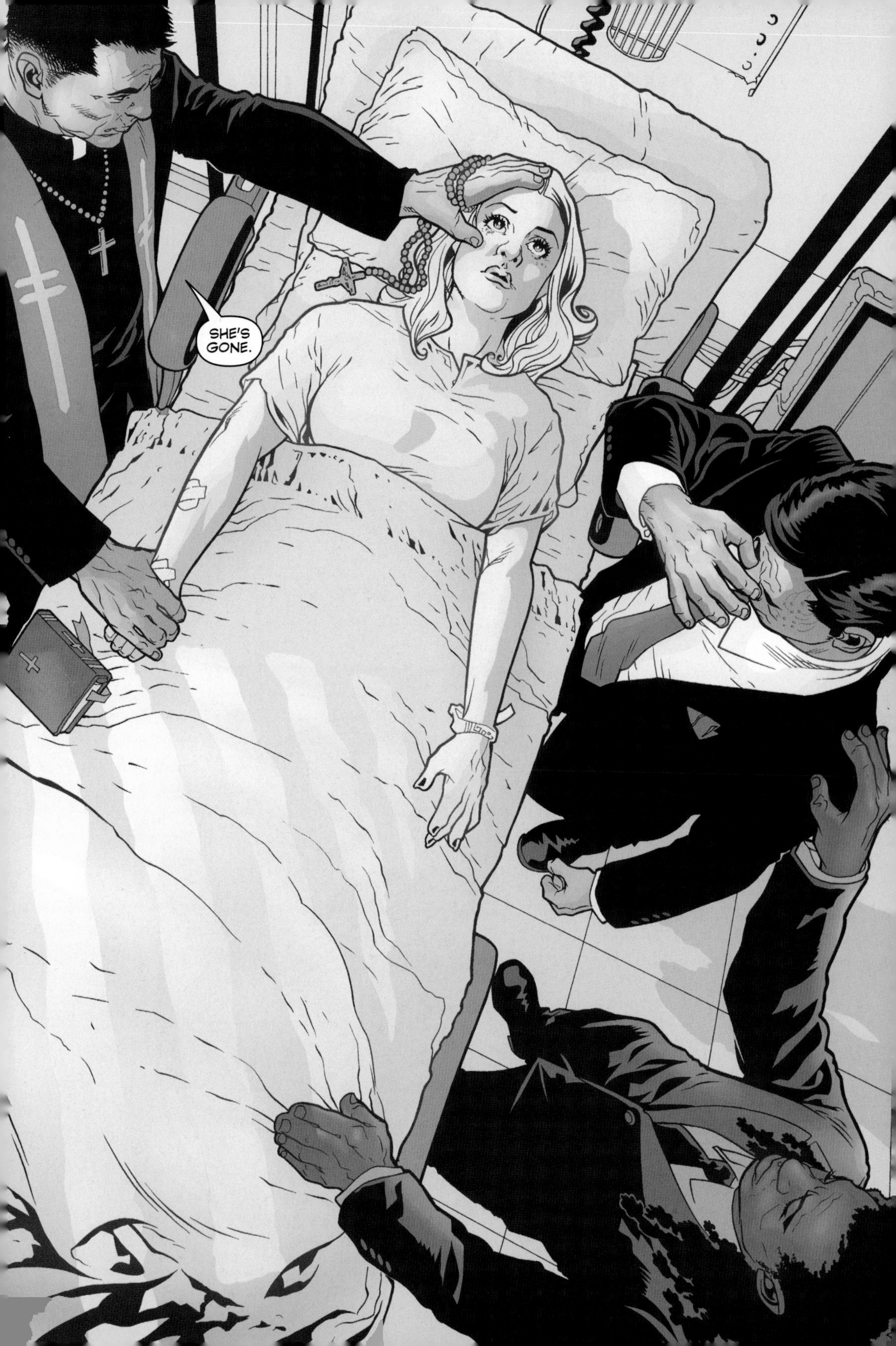
SHE'S GONE.

# CHAPTER 4 LIFE & DEATH

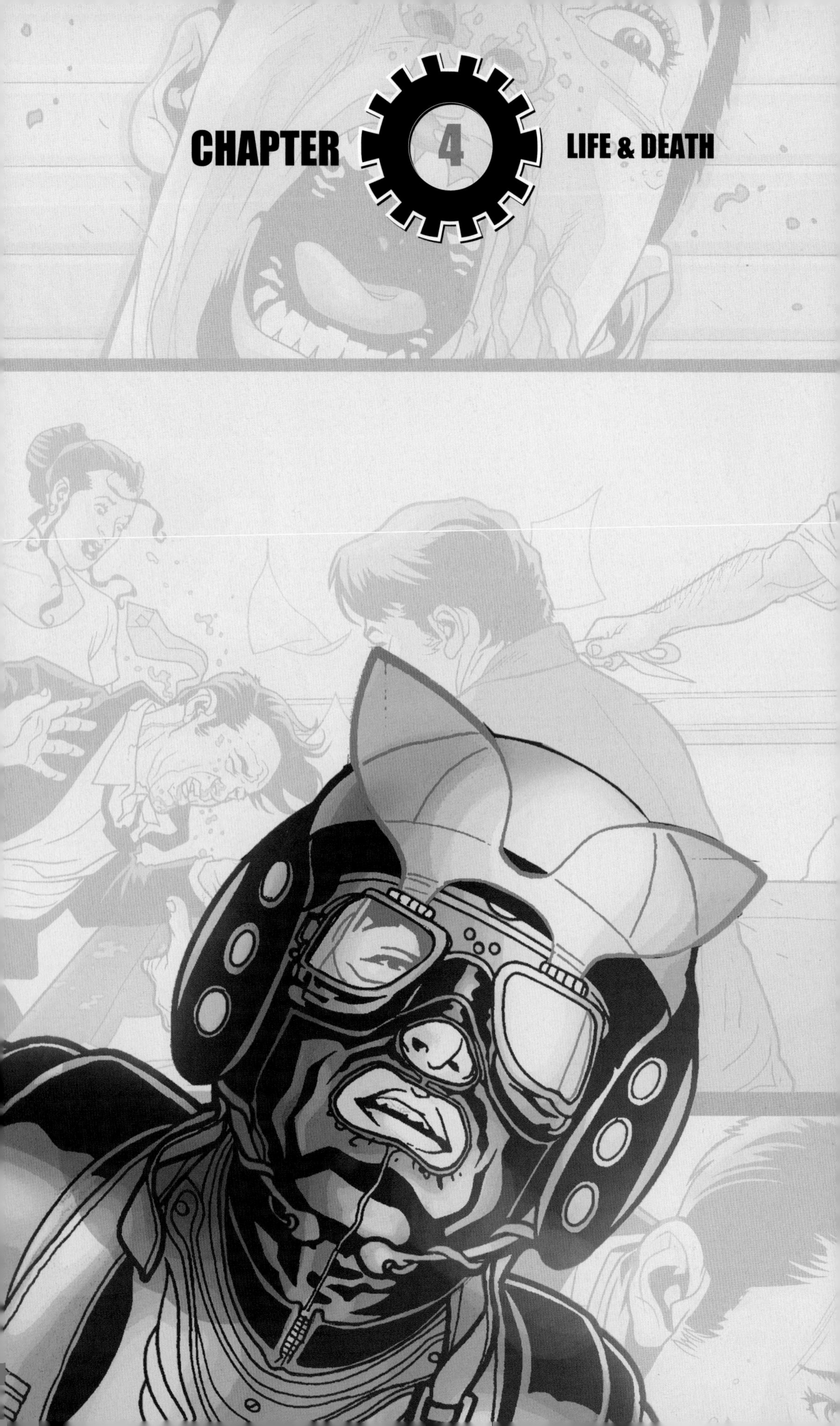

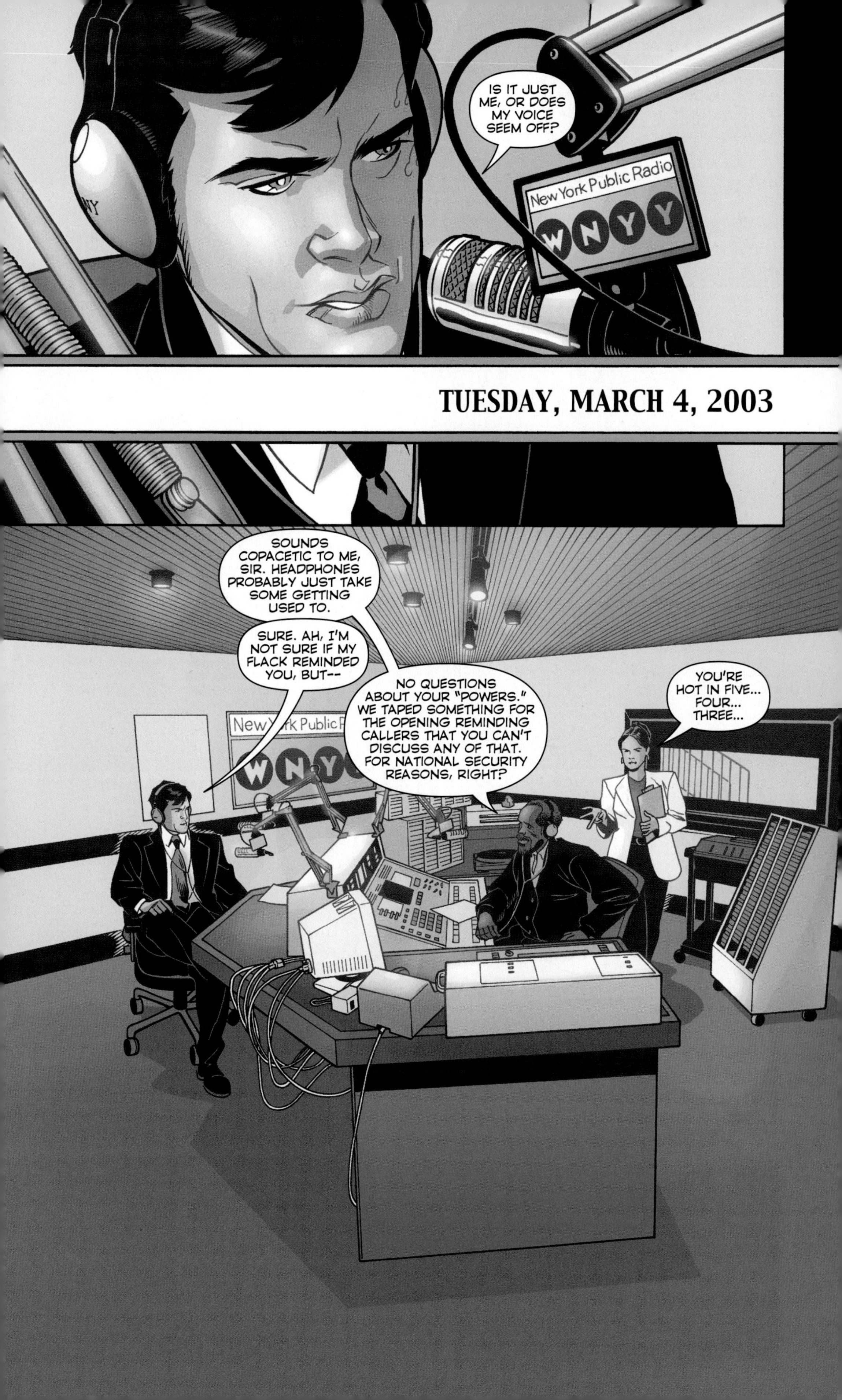
IS IT JUST ME, OR DOES MY VOICE SEEM OFF?
New York Public Radio
WNYY
TUESDAY, MARCH 4, 2003
SOUNDS COPACETIC TO ME, SIR. HEADPHONES PROBABLY JUST TAKE SOME GETTING USED TO.
SURE. AH, I'M NOT SURE IF MY FLACK REMINDED YOU, BUT--
NO QUESTIONS ABOUT YOUR "POWERS." WE TAPED SOMETHING FOR THE OPENING REMINDING CALLERS THAT YOU CAN'T DISCUSS ANY OF THAT. FOR NATIONAL SECURITY REASONS, RIGHT?
YOU'RE HOT IN FIVE... FOUR... THREE...

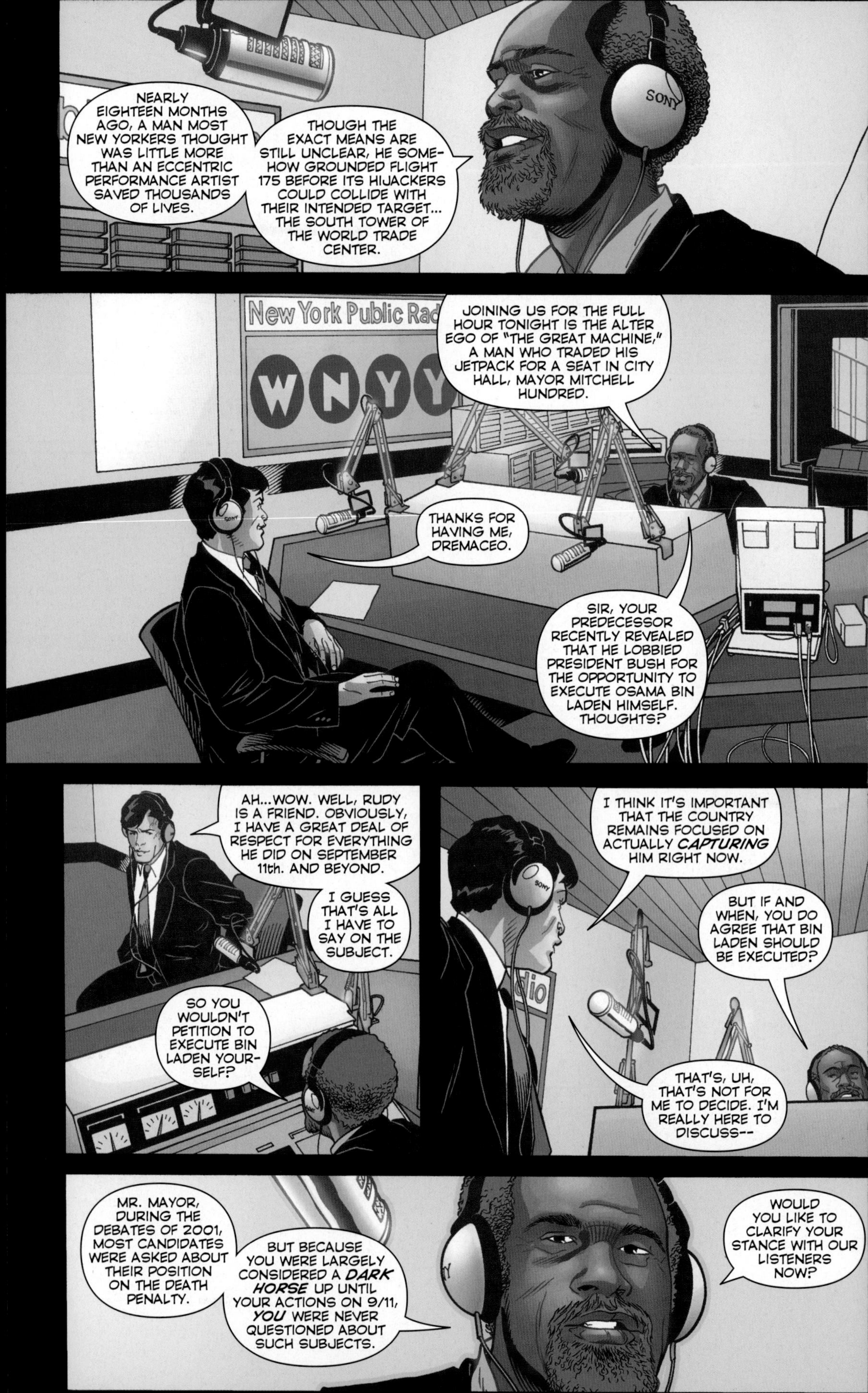
NEARLY EIGHTEEN MONTHS AGO, A MAN MOST NEW YORKERS THOUGHT WAS LITTLE MORE THAN AN ECCENTRIC PERFORMANCE ARTIST SAVED THOUSANDS OF LIVES.
THOUGH THE EXACT MEANS ARE STILL UNCLEAR, HE SOMEHOW GROUNDED FLIGHT 175 BEFORE ITS HIJACKERS COULD COLLIDE WITH THEIR INTENDED TARGET... THE SOUTH TOWER OF THE WORLD TRADE CENTER.
SONY
New York Public Rad
WNYY
JOINING US FOR THE FULL HOUR TONIGHT IS THE ALTER EGO OF "THE GREAT MACHINE," A MAN WHO TRADED HIS JETPACK FOR A SEAT IN CITY HALL, MAYOR MITCHELL HUNDRED.
THANKS FOR HAVING ME, DREMACEO.
SIR, YOUR PREDECESSOR RECENTLY REVEALED THAT HE LOBBIED PRESIDENT BUSH FOR THE OPPORTUNITY TO EXECUTE OSAMA BIN LADEN HIMSELF. THOUGHTS?
AH...WOW. WELL, RUDY IS A FRIEND. OBVIOUSLY, I HAVE A GREAT DEAL OF RESPECT FOR EVERYTHING HE DID ON SEPTEMBER 11th. AND BEYOND.
I GUESS THAT'S ALL I HAVE TO SAY ON THE SUBJECT.
SO YOU WOULDN'T PETITION TO EXECUTE BIN LADEN YOURSELF?
I THINK IT'S IMPORTANT THAT THE COUNTRY REMAINS FOCUSED ON ACTUALLY *CAPTURING* HIM RIGHT NOW.
BUT IF AND WHEN, YOU DO AGREE THAT BIN LADEN SHOULD BE EXECUTED?
THAT'S, UH, THAT'S NOT FOR ME TO DECIDE. I'M REALLY HERE TO DISCUSS--
MR. MAYOR, DURING THE DEBATES OF 2001, MOST CANDIDATES WERE ASKED ABOUT THEIR POSITION ON THE DEATH PENALTY.
BUT BECAUSE YOU WERE LARGELY CONSIDERED A *DARK HORSE* UP UNTIL YOUR ACTIONS ON 9/11, *YOU* WERE NEVER QUESTIONED ABOUT SUCH SUBJECTS.
WOULD YOU LIKE TO CLARIFY YOUR STANCE WITH OUR LISTENERS NOW?

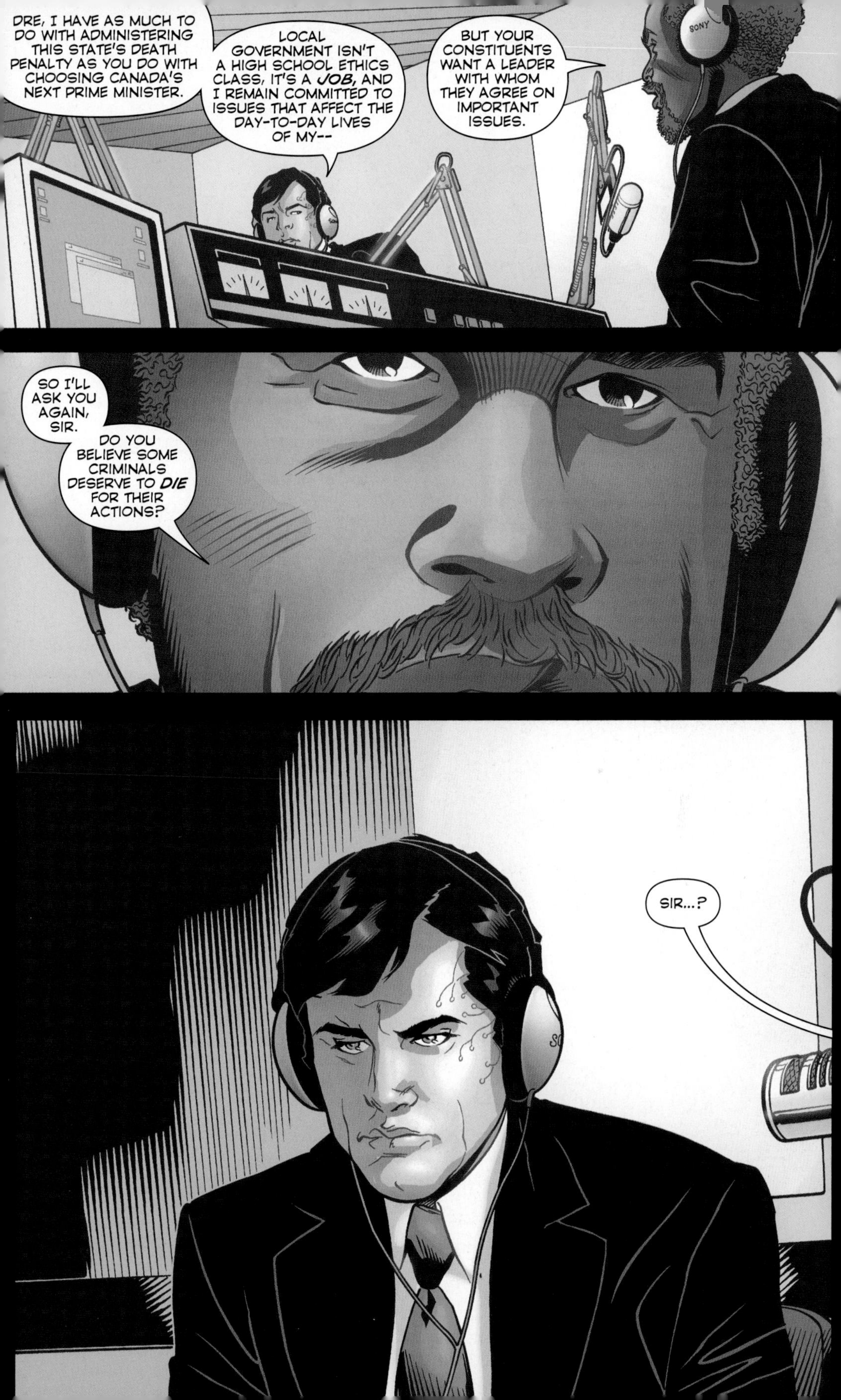
DRE, I HAVE AS MUCH TO DO WITH ADMINISTERING THIS STATE'S DEATH PENALTY AS YOU DO WITH CHOOSING CANADA'S NEXT PRIME MINISTER.
LOCAL GOVERNMENT ISN'T A HIGH SCHOOL ETHICS CLASS, IT'S A *JOB,* AND I REMAIN COMMITTED TO ISSUES THAT AFFECT THE DAY-TO-DAY LIVES OF MY--
BUT YOUR CONSTITUENTS WANT A LEADER WITH WHOM THEY AGREE ON IMPORTANT ISSUES.
SONY
SO I'LL ASK YOU AGAIN, SIR.
DO YOU BELIEVE SOME CRIMINALS DESERVE TO *DIE* FOR THEIR ACTIONS?
SIR...?

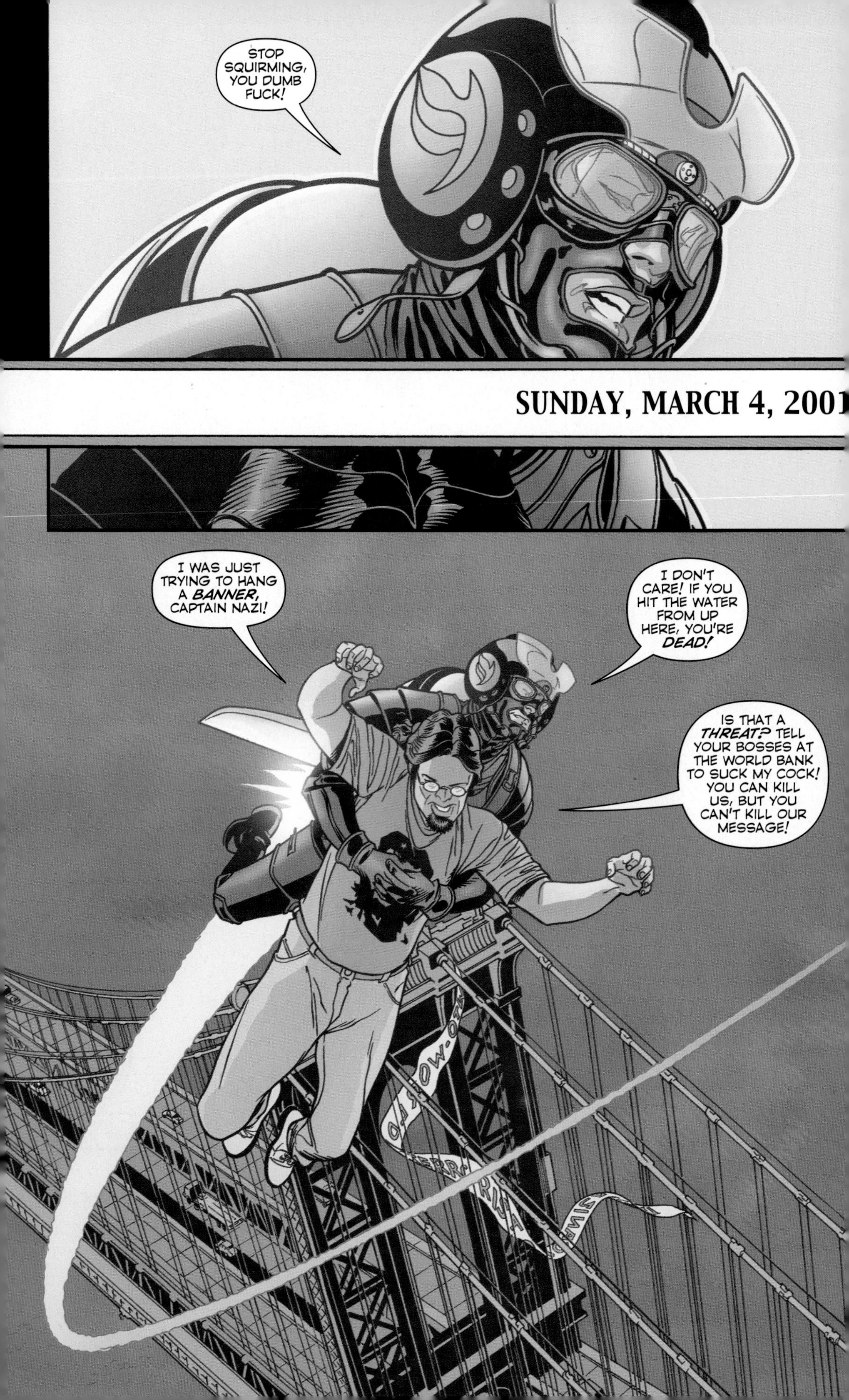
STOP SQUIRMING, YOU DUMB FUCK!
SUNDAY, MARCH 4, 2001
I WAS JUST TRYING TO HANG A BANNER, CAPTAIN NAZI!
I DON'T CARE! IF YOU HIT THE WATER FROM UP HERE, YOU'RE DEAD!
IS THAT A THREAT? TELL YOUR BOSSES AT THE WORLD BANK TO SUCK MY COCK! YOU CAN KILL US, BUT YOU CAN'T KILL OUR MESSAGE!

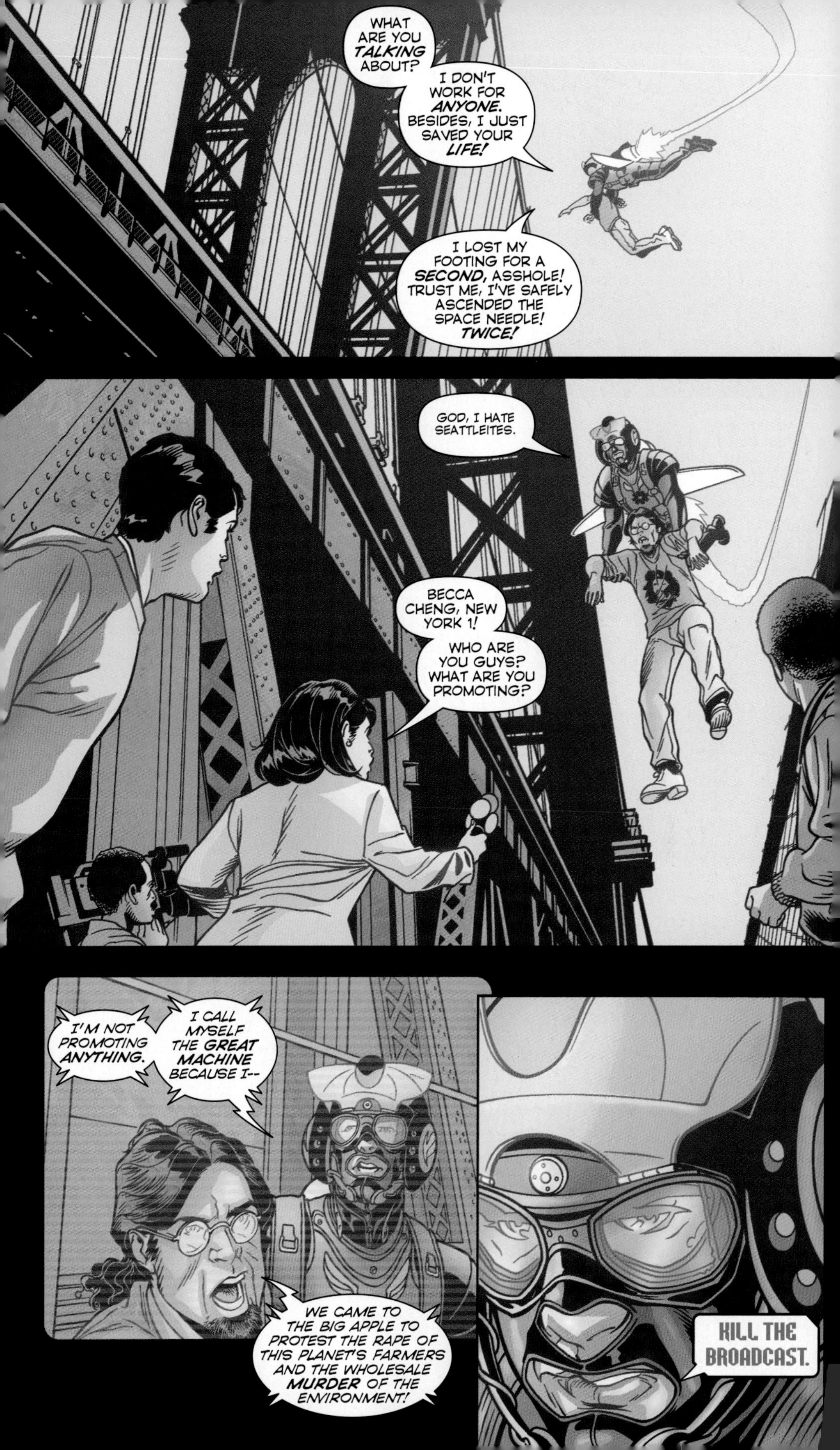
WHAT ARE YOU TALKING ABOUT?
I DON'T WORK FOR ANYONE. BESIDES, I JUST SAVED YOUR LIFE!
I LOST MY FOOTING FOR A SECOND, ASSHOLE! TRUST ME, I'VE SAFELY ASCENDED THE SPACE NEEDLE! TWICE!
GOD, I HATE SEATTLEITES.
BECCA CHENG, NEW YORK 1!
WHO ARE YOU GUYS? WHAT ARE YOU PROMOTING?
I'M NOT PROMOTING ANYTHING.
I CALL MYSELF THE GREAT MACHINE BECAUSE I--
WE CAME TO THE BIG APPLE TO PROTEST THE RAPE OF THIS PLANET'S FARMERS AND THE WHOLESALE MURDER OF THE ENVIRONMENT!
KILL THE BROADCAST.

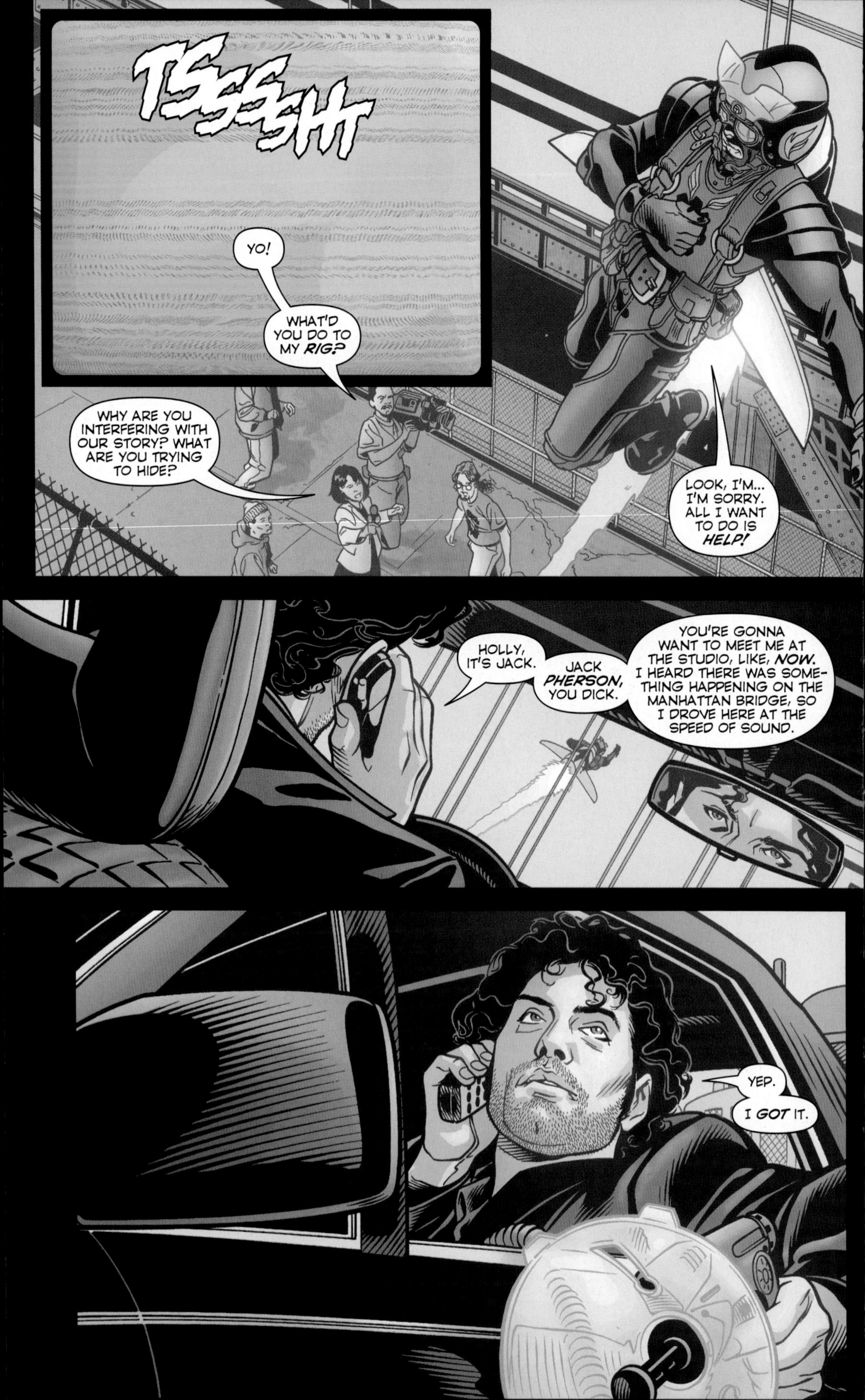
TSSSSHT
YO!
WHAT'D YOU DO TO MY RIG?
WHY ARE YOU INTERFERING WITH OUR STORY? WHAT ARE YOU TRYING TO HIDE?
LOOK, I'M... I'M SORRY. ALL I WANT TO DO IS HELP!
HOLLY, IT'S JACK.
JACK PHERSON, YOU DICK.
YOU'RE GONNA WANT TO MEET ME AT THE STUDIO, LIKE, NOW. I HEARD THERE WAS SOMETHING HAPPENING ON THE MANHATTAN BRIDGE, SO I DROVE HERE AT THE SPEED OF SOUND.
YEP.
I GOT IT.

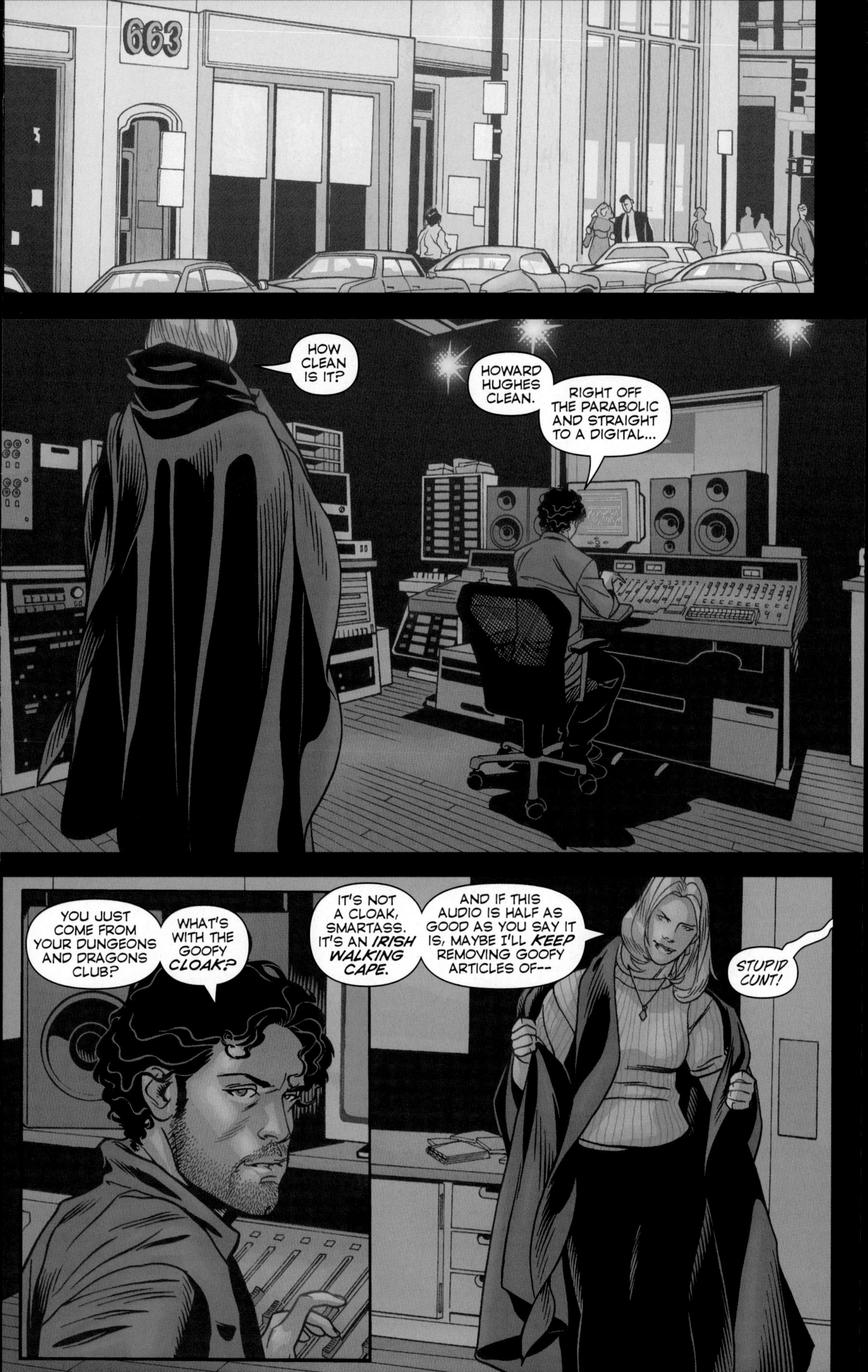
663
HOW CLEAN IS IT?
HOWARD HUGHES CLEAN.
RIGHT OFF THE PARABOLIC AND STRAIGHT TO A DIGITAL...
YOU JUST COME FROM YOUR DUNGEONS AND DRAGONS CLUB?
WHAT'S WITH THE GOOFY CLOAK?
IT'S NOT A CLOAK, SMARTASS. IT'S AN IRISH WALKING CAPE.
AND IF THIS AUDIO IS HALF AS GOOD AS YOU SAY IT IS, MAYBE I'LL KEEP REMOVING GOOFY ARTICLES OF--
STUPID CUNT!

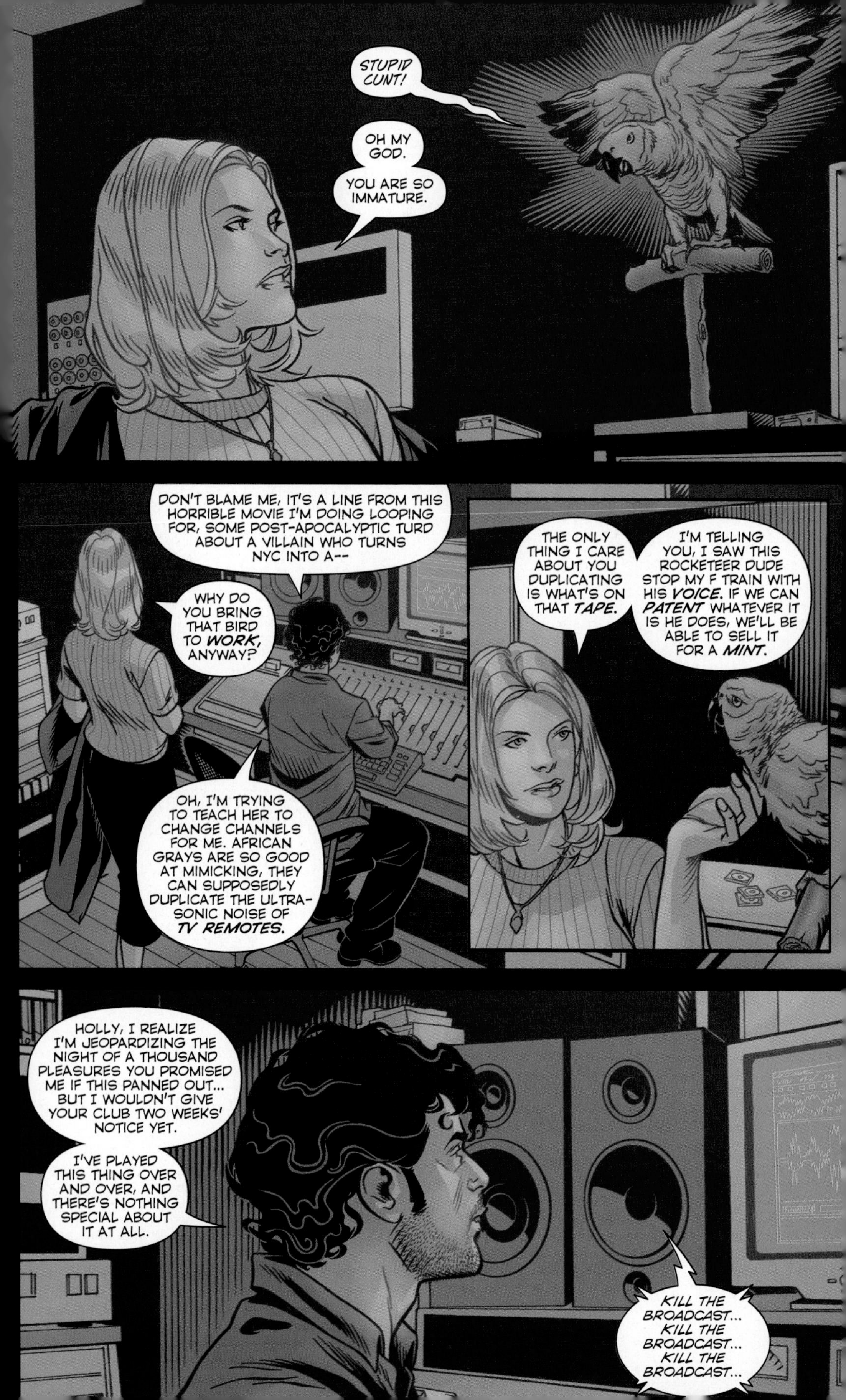
STUPID CUNT!
OH MY GOD.
YOU ARE SO IMMATURE.
DON'T BLAME ME, IT'S A LINE FROM THIS HORRIBLE MOVIE I'M DOING LOOPING FOR, SOME POST-APOCALYPTIC TURD ABOUT A VILLAIN WHO TURNS NYC INTO A--
WHY DO YOU BRING THAT BIRD TO WORK, ANYWAY?
OH, I'M TRYING TO TEACH HER TO CHANGE CHANNELS FOR ME. AFRICAN GRAYS ARE SO GOOD AT MIMICKING, THEY CAN SUPPOSEDLY DUPLICATE THE ULTRA-SONIC NOISE OF TV REMOTES.
THE ONLY THING I CARE ABOUT YOU DUPLICATING IS WHAT'S ON THAT TAPE.
I'M TELLING YOU, I SAW THIS ROCKETEER DUDE STOP MY F TRAIN WITH HIS VOICE. IF WE CAN PATENT WHATEVER IT IS HE DOES, WE'LL BE ABLE TO SELL IT FOR A MINT.
HOLLY, I REALIZE I'M JEOPARDIZING THE NIGHT OF A THOUSAND PLEASURES YOU PROMISED ME IF THIS PANNED OUT... BUT I WOULDN'T GIVE YOUR CLUB TWO WEEKS' NOTICE YET.
I'VE PLAYED THIS THING OVER AND OVER, AND THERE'S NOTHING SPECIAL ABOUT IT AT ALL.
KILL THE BROADCAST... KILL THE BROADCAST... KILL THE BROADCAST...

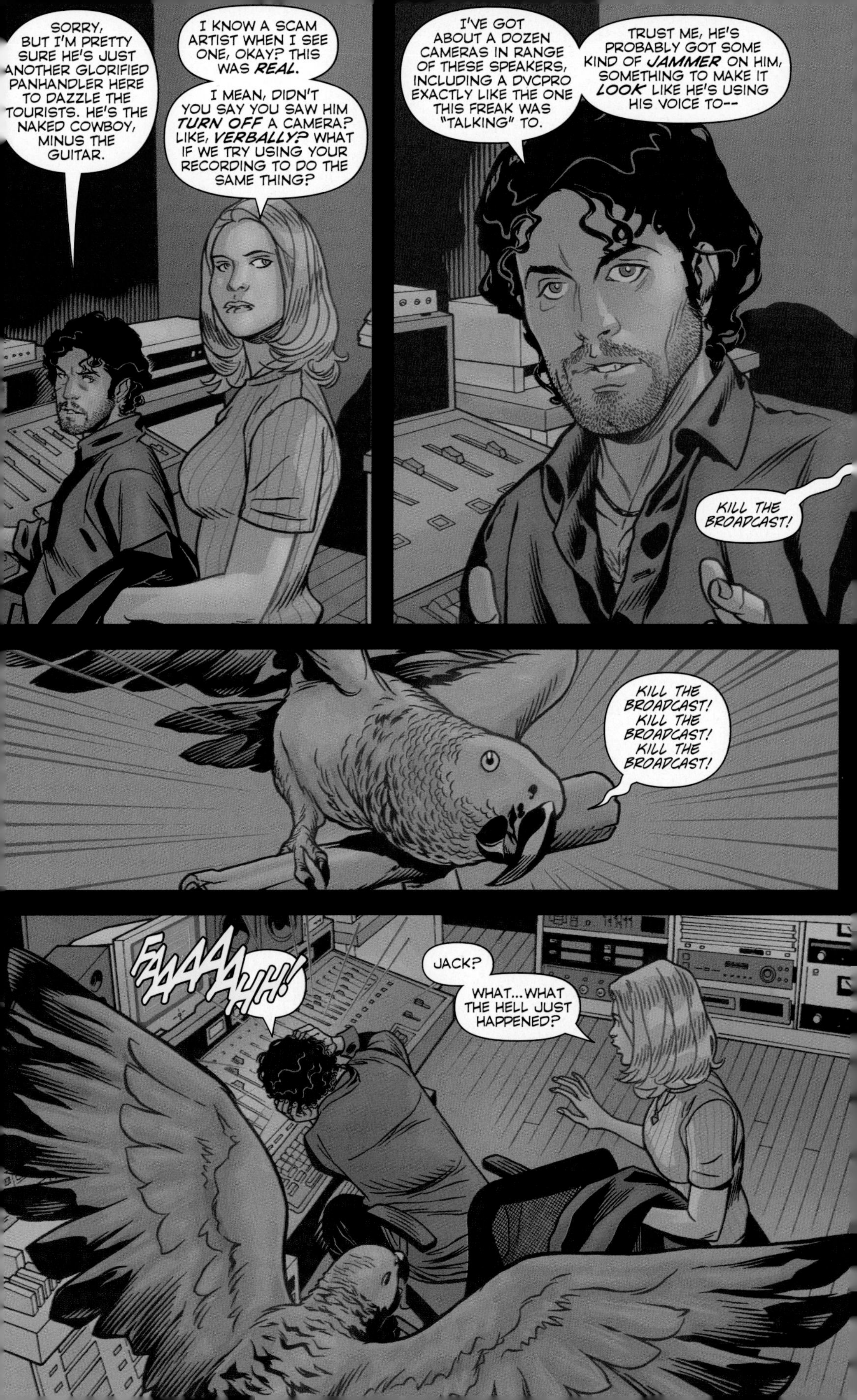
SORRY, BUT I'M PRETTY SURE HE'S JUST ANOTHER GLORIFIED PANHANDLER HERE TO DAZZLE THE TOURISTS. HE'S THE NAKED COWBOY, MINUS THE GUITAR.
I KNOW A SCAM ARTIST WHEN I SEE ONE, OKAY? THIS WAS REAL.
I MEAN, DIDN'T YOU SAY YOU SAW HIM TURN OFF A CAMERA? LIKE, VERBALLY? WHAT IF WE TRY USING YOUR RECORDING TO DO THE SAME THING?
I'VE GOT ABOUT A DOZEN CAMERAS IN RANGE OF THESE SPEAKERS, INCLUDING A DVCPRO EXACTLY LIKE THE ONE THIS FREAK WAS "TALKING" TO.
TRUST ME, HE'S PROBABLY GOT SOME KIND OF JAMMER ON HIM, SOMETHING TO MAKE IT LOOK LIKE HE'S USING HIS VOICE TO--
KILL THE BROADCAST!
KILL THE BROADCAST! KILL THE BROADCAST! KILL THE BROADCAST!
FAAAAAHH!
JACK?
WHAT...WHAT THE HELL JUST HAPPENED?

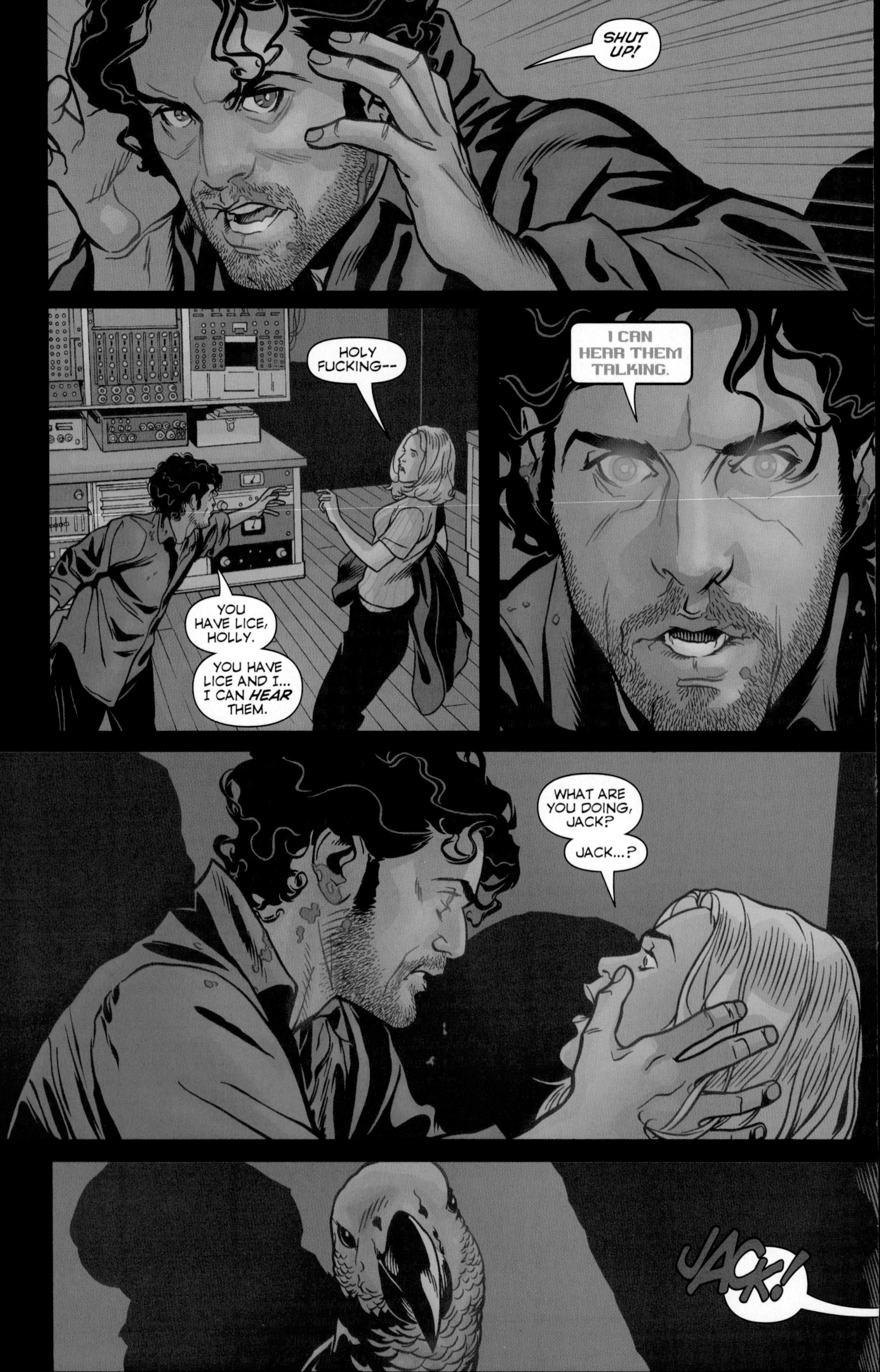
SHUT UP!
HOLY FUCKING--
YOU HAVE LICE, HOLLY.
YOU HAVE LICE AND I... I CAN *HEAR* THEM.
I CAN HEAR THEM TALKING.
WHAT ARE YOU DOING, JACK?
JACK...?
JACK!

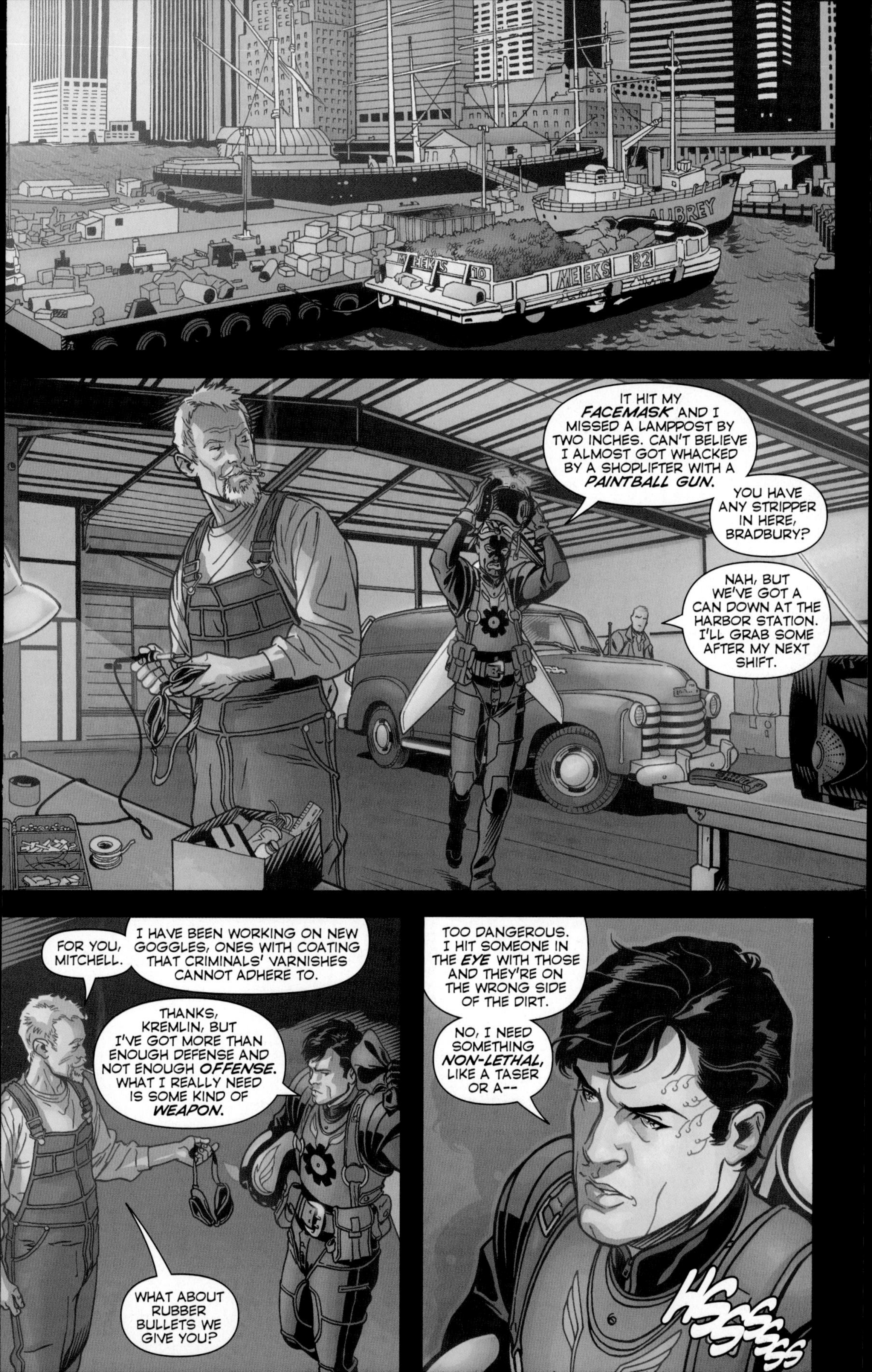

AUBREY
MEEKS 10
MEEKS 32
IT HIT MY FACEMASK AND I MISSED A LAMPPOST BY TWO INCHES. CAN'T BELIEVE I ALMOST GOT WHACKED BY A SHOPLIFTER WITH A PAINTBALL GUN.
YOU HAVE ANY STRIPPER IN HERE, BRADBURY?
NAH, BUT WE'VE GOT A CAN DOWN AT THE HARBOR STATION. I'LL GRAB SOME AFTER MY NEXT SHIFT.
FOR YOU, MITCHELL.
I HAVE BEEN WORKING ON NEW GOGGLES, ONES WITH COATING THAT CRIMINALS' VARNISHES CANNOT ADHERE TO.
THANKS, KREMLIN, BUT I'VE GOT MORE THAN ENOUGH DEFENSE AND NOT ENOUGH OFFENSE. WHAT I REALLY NEED IS SOME KIND OF WEAPON.
WHAT ABOUT RUBBER BULLETS WE GIVE YOU?
TOO DANGEROUS. I HIT SOMEONE IN THE EYE WITH THOSE AND THEY'RE ON THE WRONG SIDE OF THE DIRT.
NO, I NEED SOMETHING NON-LETHAL, LIKE A TASER OR A--
HSSSSSS

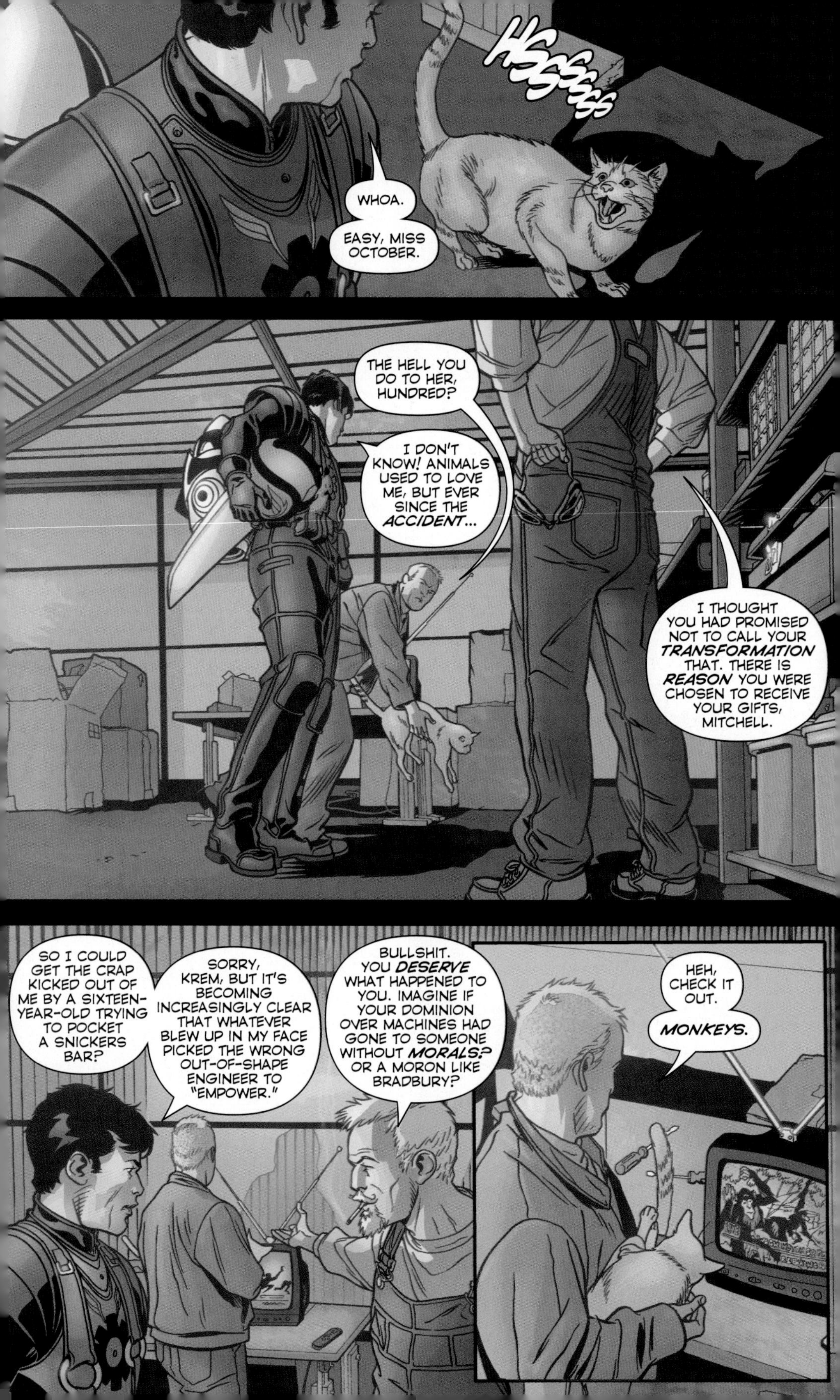
HSSSSSS
WHOA.
EASY, MISS OCTOBER.
THE HELL YOU DO TO HER, HUNDRED?
I DON'T KNOW! ANIMALS USED TO LOVE ME, BUT EVER SINCE THE ACCIDENT...
I THOUGHT YOU HAD PROMISED NOT TO CALL YOUR TRANSFORMATION THAT. THERE IS REASON YOU WERE CHOSEN TO RECEIVE YOUR GIFTS, MITCHELL.
SO I COULD GET THE CRAP KICKED OUT OF ME BY A SIXTEEN-YEAR-OLD TRYING TO POCKET A SNICKERS BAR?
SORRY, KREM, BUT IT'S BECOMING INCREASINGLY CLEAR THAT WHATEVER BLEW UP IN MY FACE PICKED THE WRONG OUT-OF-SHAPE ENGINEER TO "EMPOWER."
BULLSHIT. YOU DESERVE WHAT HAPPENED TO YOU. IMAGINE IF YOUR DOMINION OVER MACHINES HAD GONE TO SOMEONE WITHOUT MORALS? OR A MORON LIKE BRADBURY?
HEH, CHECK IT OUT.
MONKEYS.

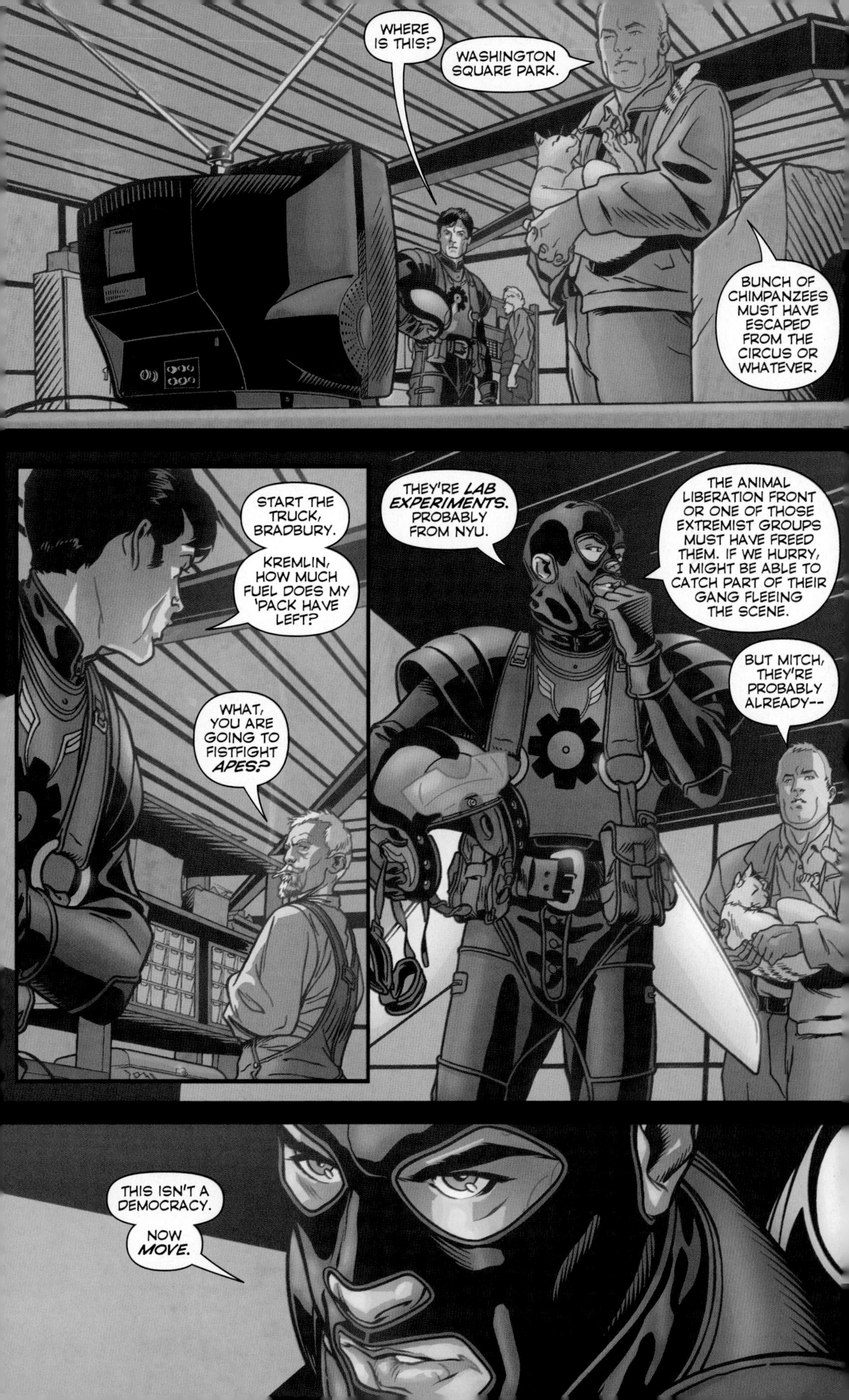
WHERE IS THIS?
WASHINGTON SQUARE PARK.
BUNCH OF CHIMPANZEES MUST HAVE ESCAPED FROM THE CIRCUS OR WHATEVER.
THEY'RE *LAB EXPERIMENTS*. PROBABLY FROM NYU.
THE ANIMAL LIBERATION FRONT OR ONE OF THOSE EXTREMIST GROUPS MUST HAVE FREED THEM. IF WE HURRY, I MIGHT BE ABLE TO CATCH PART OF THEIR GANG FLEEING THE SCENE.
BUT MITCH, THEY'RE PROBABLY ALREADY--
START THE TRUCK, BRADBURY.
KREMLIN, HOW MUCH FUEL DOES MY 'PACK HAVE LEFT?
WHAT, YOU ARE GOING TO FISTFIGHT *APES?*
THIS ISN'T A DEMOCRACY.
NOW *MOVE*.

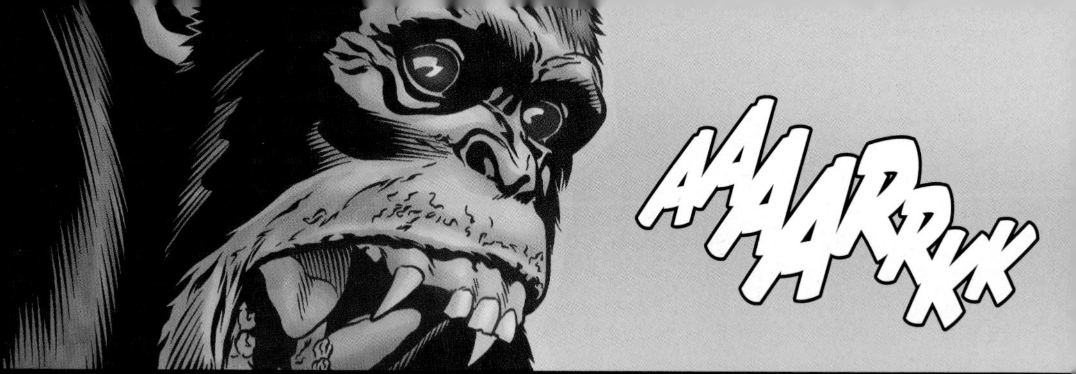
AAAAARRRKK

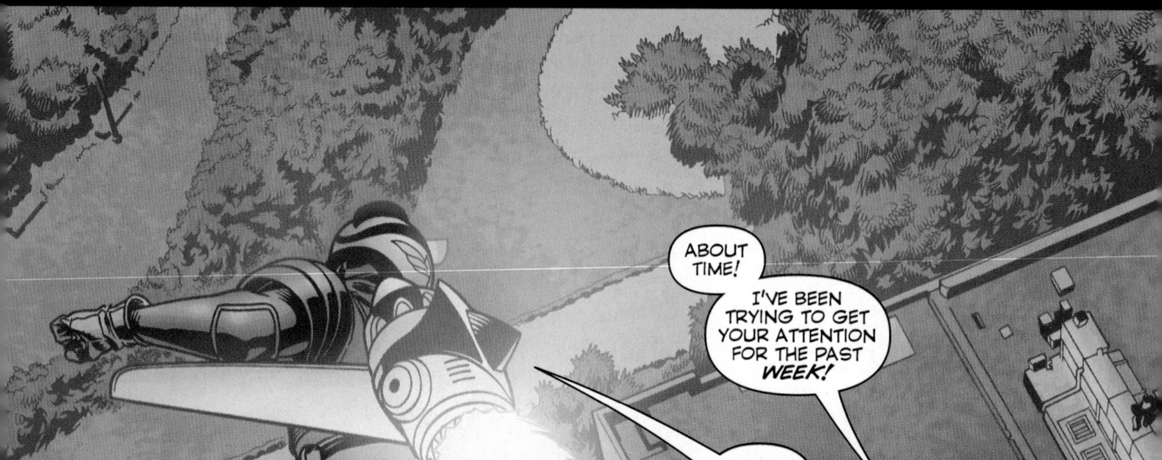
ABOUT TIME!
I'VE BEEN TRYING TO GET YOUR ATTENTION FOR THE PAST WEEK!
SORRY, DO...DO I KNOW YOU?

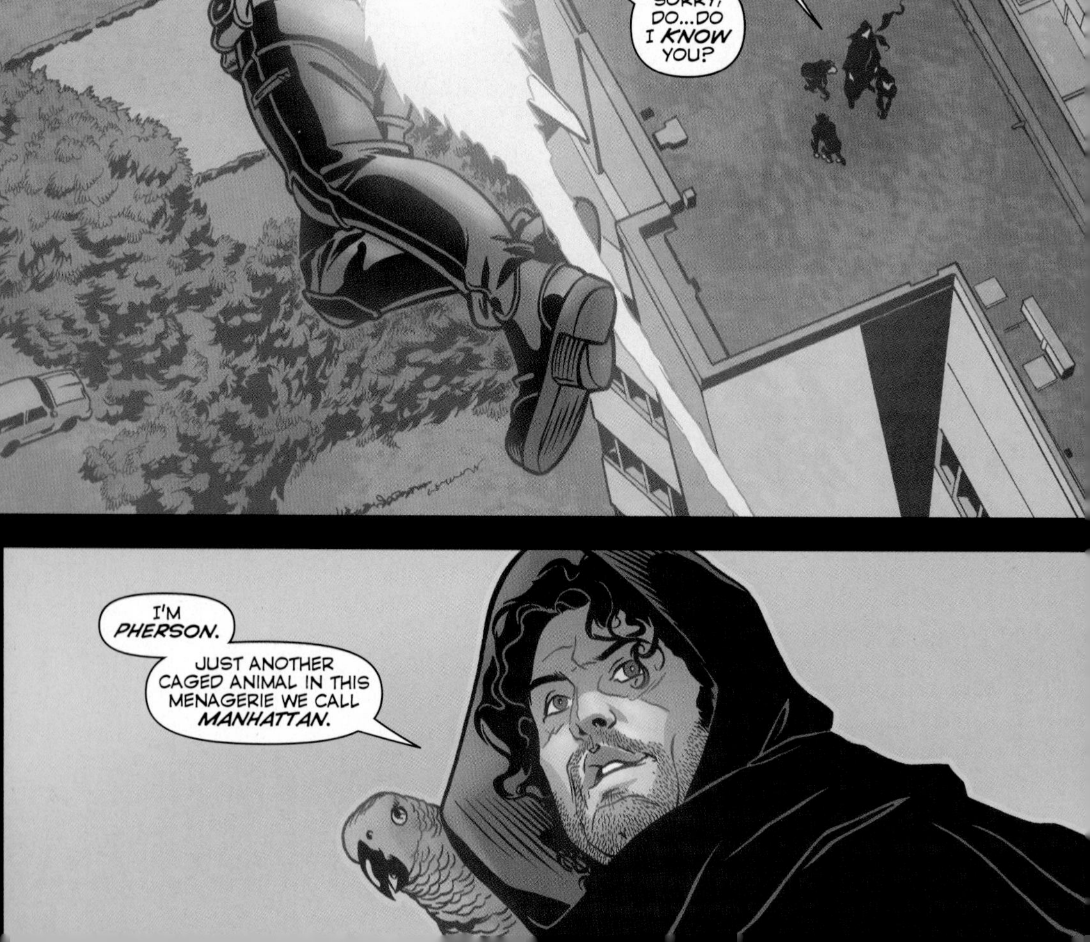
I'M PHERSON.
JUST ANOTHER CAGED ANIMAL IN THIS MENAGERIE WE CALL MANHATTAN.

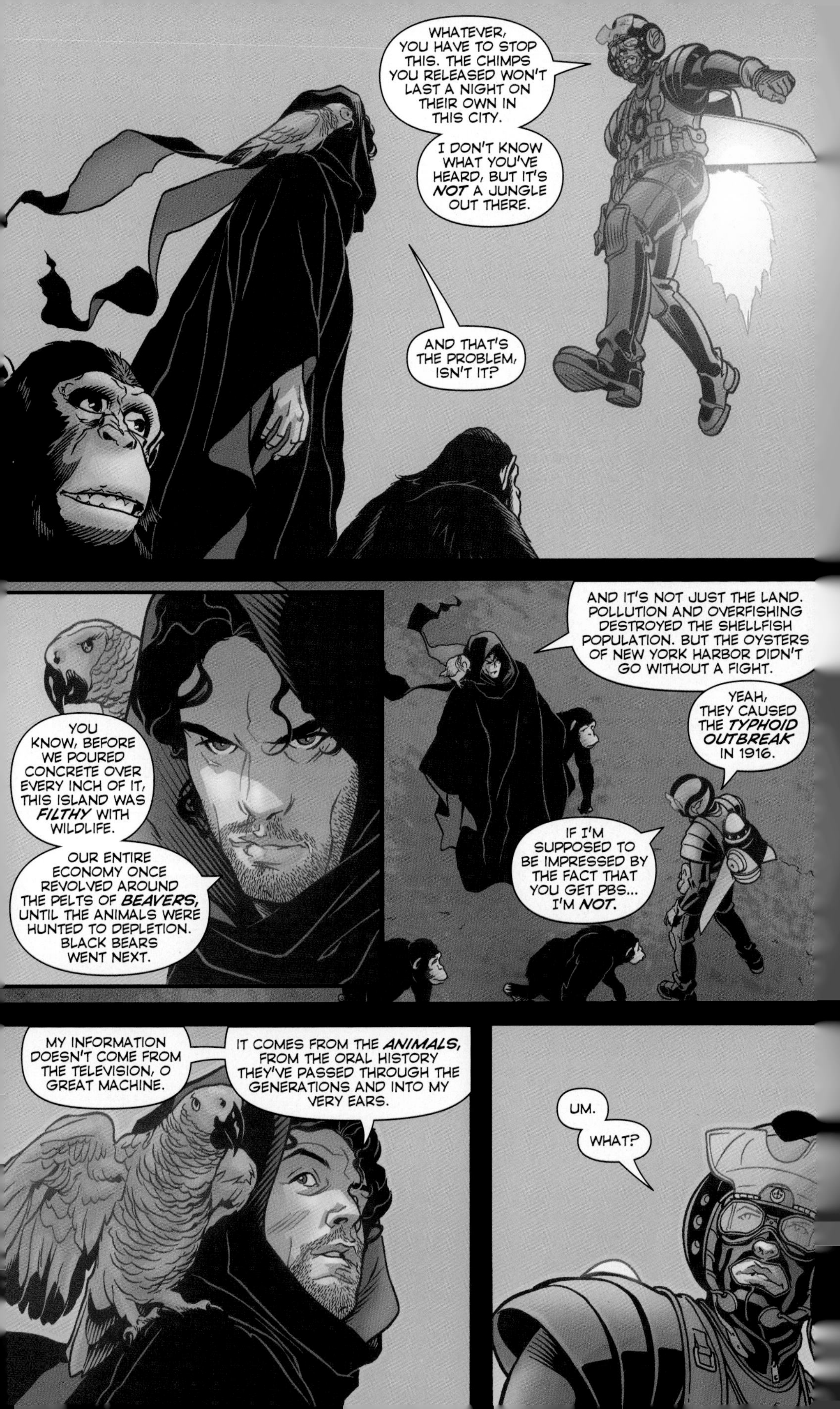
WHATEVER, YOU HAVE TO STOP THIS. THE CHIMPS YOU RELEASED WON'T LAST A NIGHT ON THEIR OWN IN THIS CITY.
I DON'T KNOW WHAT YOU'VE HEARD, BUT IT'S *NOT* A JUNGLE OUT THERE.
AND THAT'S THE PROBLEM, ISN'T IT?
YOU KNOW, BEFORE WE POURED CONCRETE OVER EVERY INCH OF IT, THIS ISLAND WAS *FILTHY* WITH WILDLIFE.
OUR ENTIRE ECONOMY ONCE REVOLVED AROUND THE PELTS OF *BEAVERS,* UNTIL THE ANIMALS WERE HUNTED TO DEPLETION. BLACK BEARS WENT NEXT.
AND IT'S NOT JUST THE LAND. POLLUTION AND OVERFISHING DESTROYED THE SHELLFISH POPULATION. BUT THE OYSTERS OF NEW YORK HARBOR DIDN'T GO WITHOUT A FIGHT.
YEAH, THEY CAUSED THE *TYPHOID OUTBREAK* IN 1916.
IF I'M SUPPOSED TO BE IMPRESSED BY THE FACT THAT YOU GET PBS... I'M *NOT*.
MY INFORMATION DOESN'T COME FROM THE TELEVISION, O GREAT MACHINE.
IT COMES FROM THE *ANIMALS,* FROM THE ORAL HISTORY THEY'VE PASSED THROUGH THE GENERATIONS AND INTO MY VERY EARS.
UM.
WHAT?

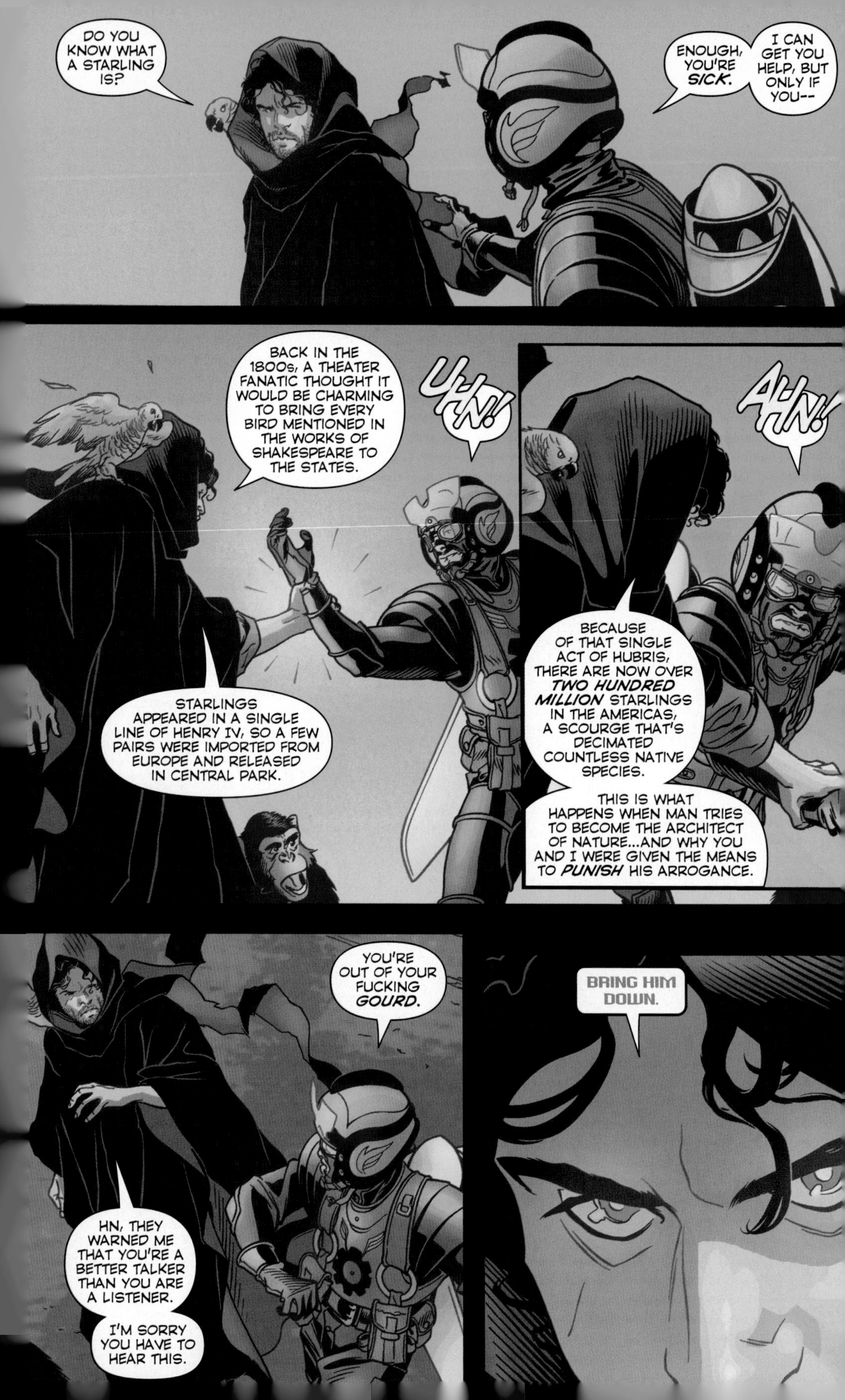
DO YOU KNOW WHAT A STARLING IS?
ENOUGH, YOU'RE *SICK*.
I CAN GET YOU HELP, BUT ONLY IF YOU--
BACK IN THE 1800s, A THEATER FANATIC THOUGHT IT WOULD BE CHARMING TO BRING EVERY BIRD MENTIONED IN THE WORKS OF SHAKESPEARE TO THE STATES.
UHN!
STARLINGS APPEARED IN A SINGLE LINE OF HENRY IV, SO A FEW PAIRS WERE IMPORTED FROM EUROPE AND RELEASED IN CENTRAL PARK.
AHN!
BECAUSE OF THAT SINGLE ACT OF HUBRIS, THERE ARE NOW OVER ***TWO HUNDRED MILLION*** STARLINGS IN THE AMERICAS, A SCOURGE THAT'S DECIMATED COUNTLESS NATIVE SPECIES.
THIS IS WHAT HAPPENS WHEN MAN TRIES TO BECOME THE ARCHITECT OF NATURE...AND WHY YOU AND I WERE GIVEN THE MEANS TO ***PUNISH*** HIS ARROGANCE.
YOU'RE OUT OF YOUR FUCKING ***GOURD***.
HN, THEY WARNED ME THAT YOU'RE A BETTER TALKER THAN YOU ARE A LISTENER.
I'M SORRY YOU HAVE TO HEAR THIS.
BRING HIM DOWN.

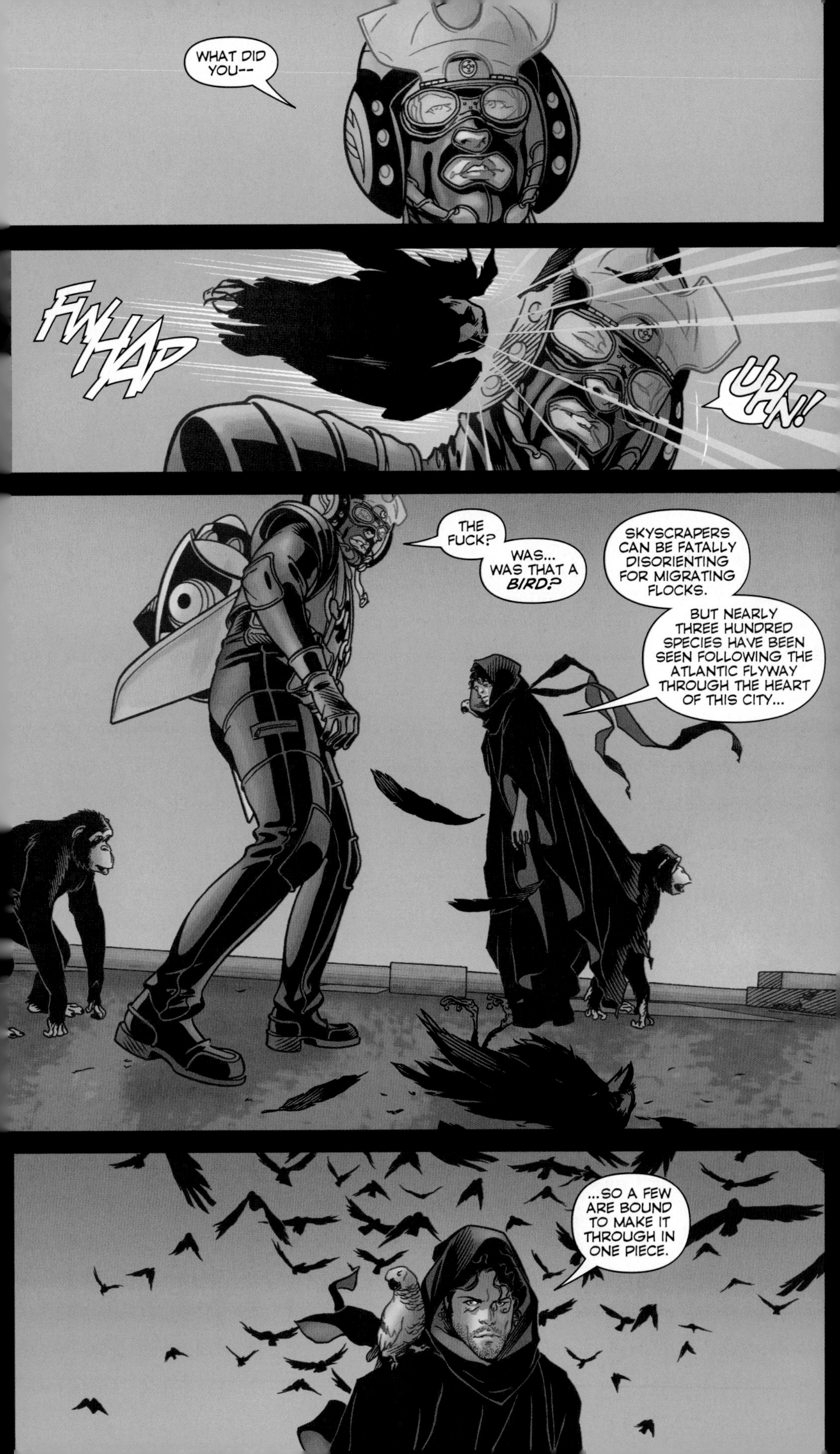
WHAT DID YOU--
FWHAP
UHN!
THE FUCK?
WAS... WAS THAT A *BIRD?*
SKYSCRAPERS CAN BE FATALLY DISORIENTING FOR MIGRATING FLOCKS.
BUT NEARLY THREE HUNDRED SPECIES HAVE BEEN SEEN FOLLOWING THE ATLANTIC FLYWAY THROUGH THE HEART OF THIS CITY...
...SO A FEW ARE BOUND TO MAKE IT THROUGH IN ONE PIECE.

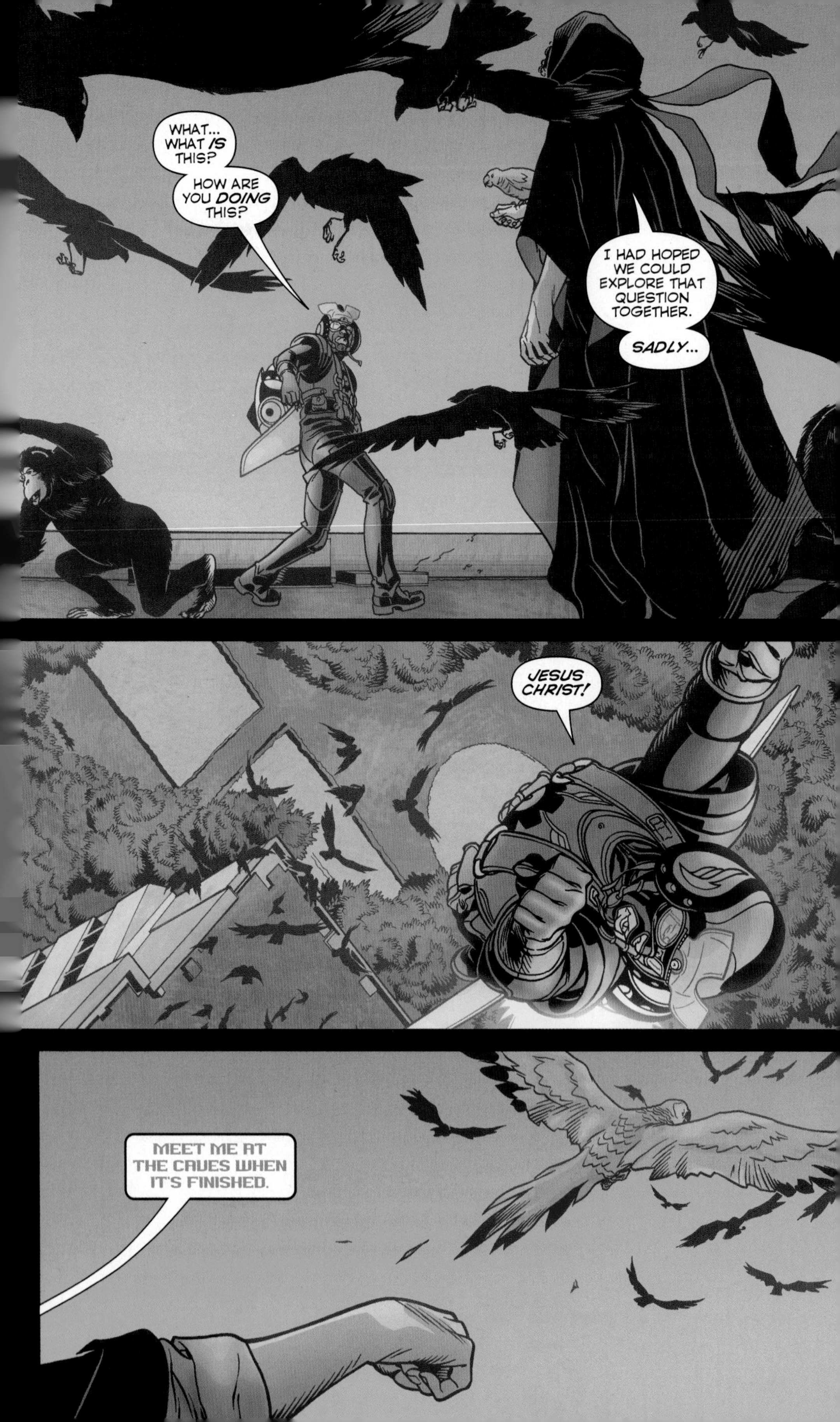
WHAT... WHAT *IS* THIS?
HOW ARE YOU *DOING* THIS?
I HAD HOPED WE COULD EXPLORE THAT QUESTION TOGETHER.
*SADLY...*
*JESUS CHRIST!*
MEET ME AT THE CAVES WHEN IT'S FINISHED.

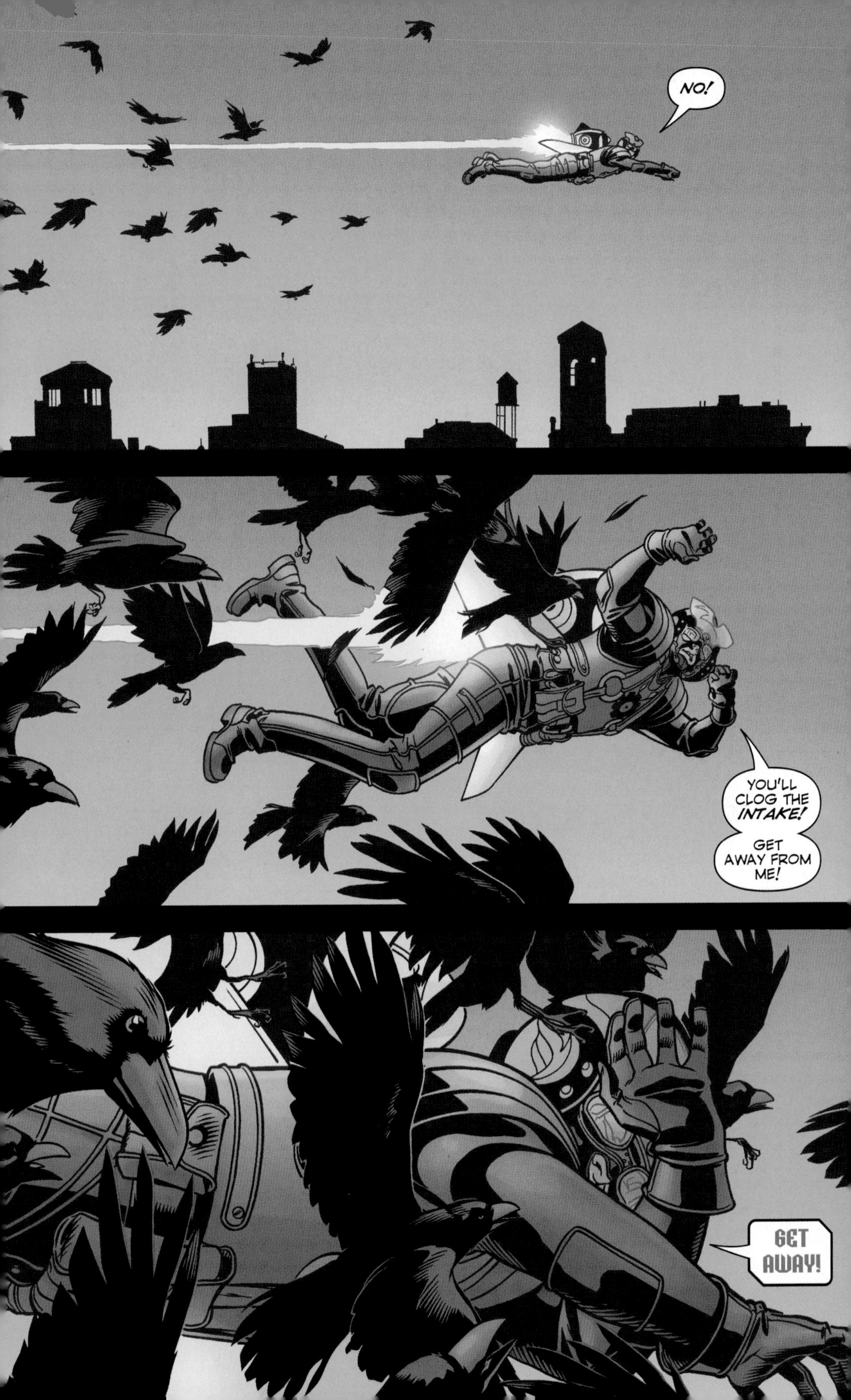
NO!
YOU'LL CLOG THE INTAKE!
GET AWAY FROM ME!
GET AWAY!

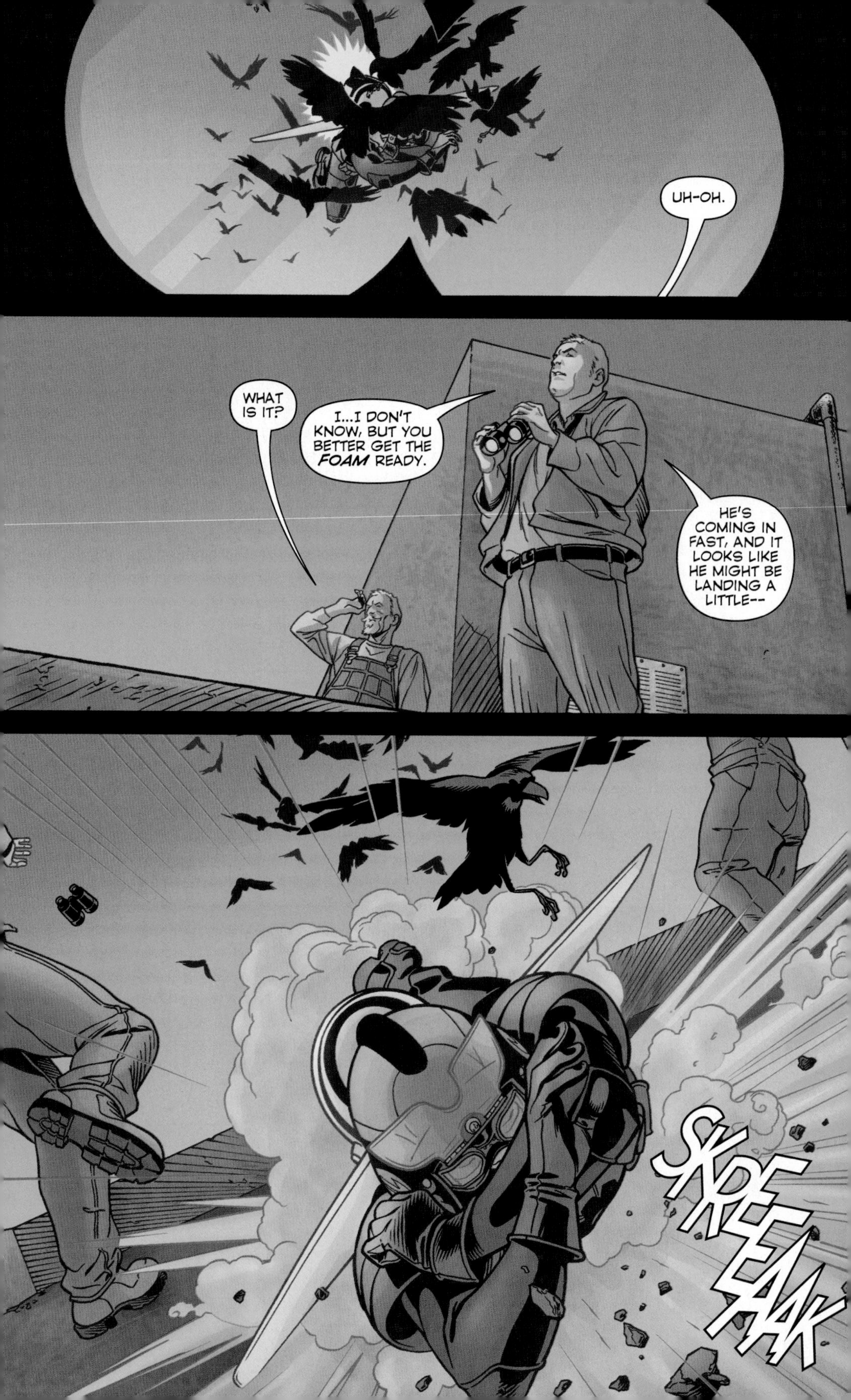
UH-OH.
WHAT IS IT?
I...I DON'T KNOW, BUT YOU BETTER GET THE *FOAM* READY.
HE'S COMING IN FAST, AND IT LOOKS LIKE HE MIGHT BE LANDING A LITTLE--
SKREEEAAK

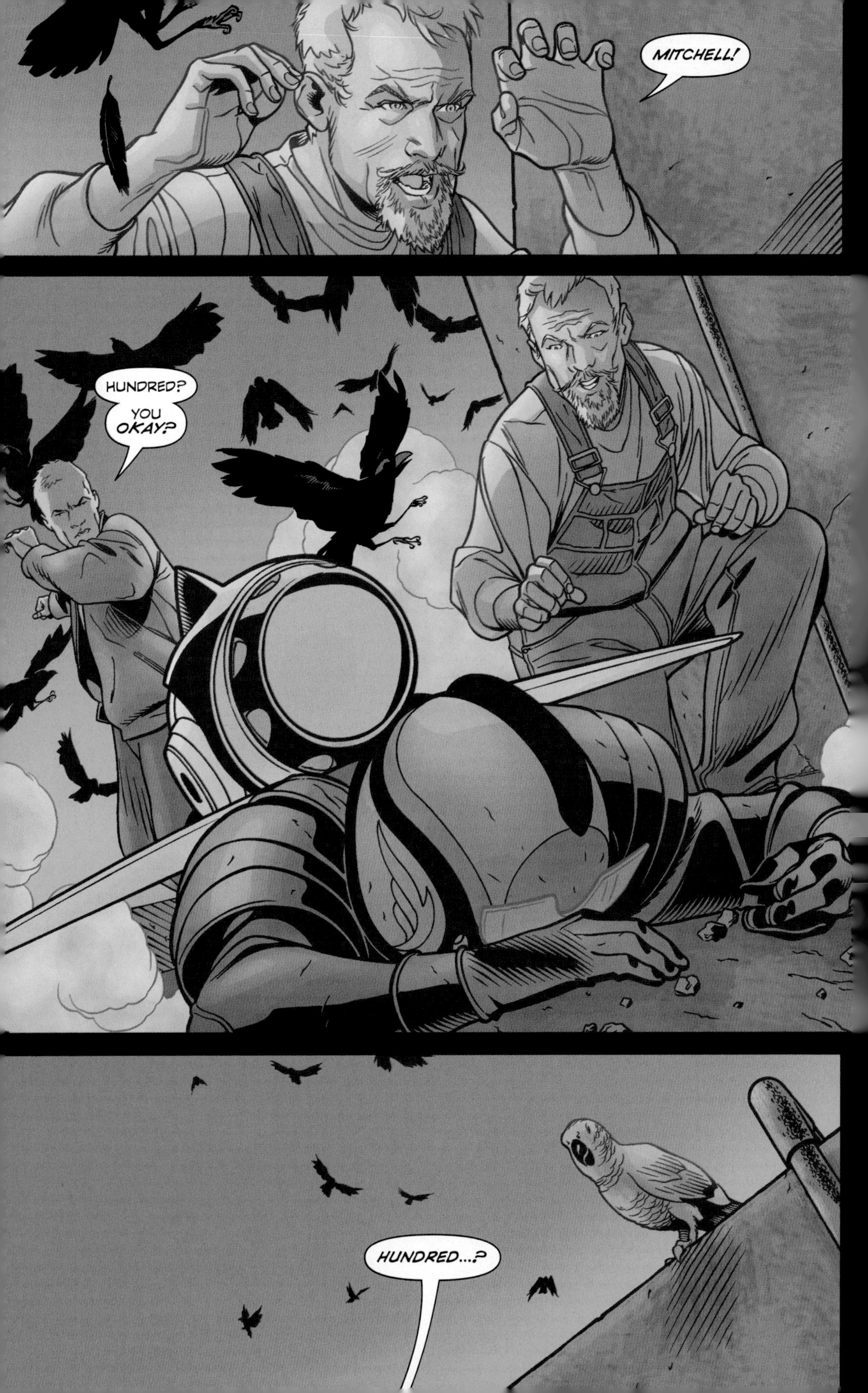
MITCHELL!
HUNDRED? YOU OKAY?
HUNDRED...?

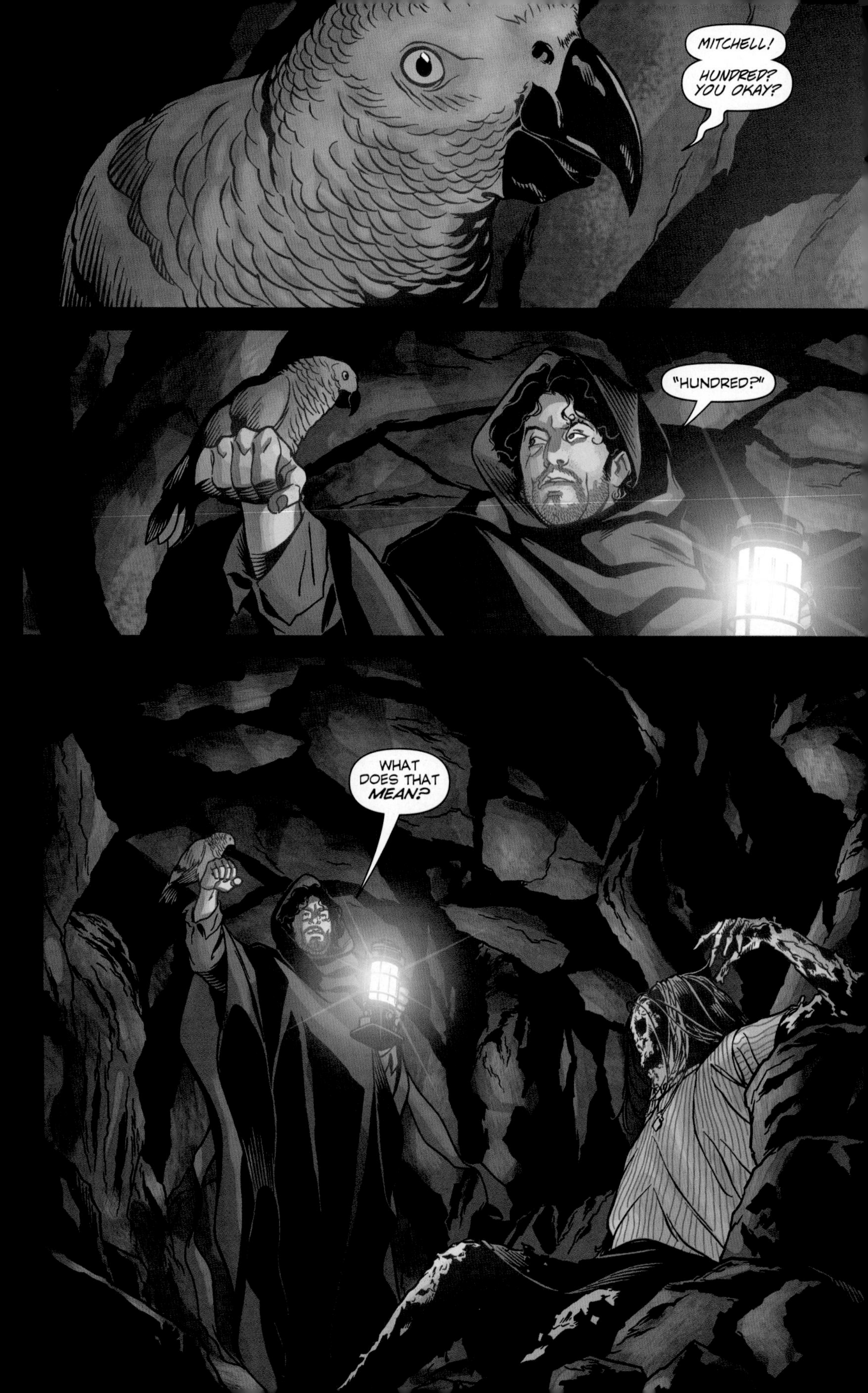
MITCHELL!
HUNDRED? YOU OKAY?
"HUNDRED?"
WHAT DOES THAT MEAN?

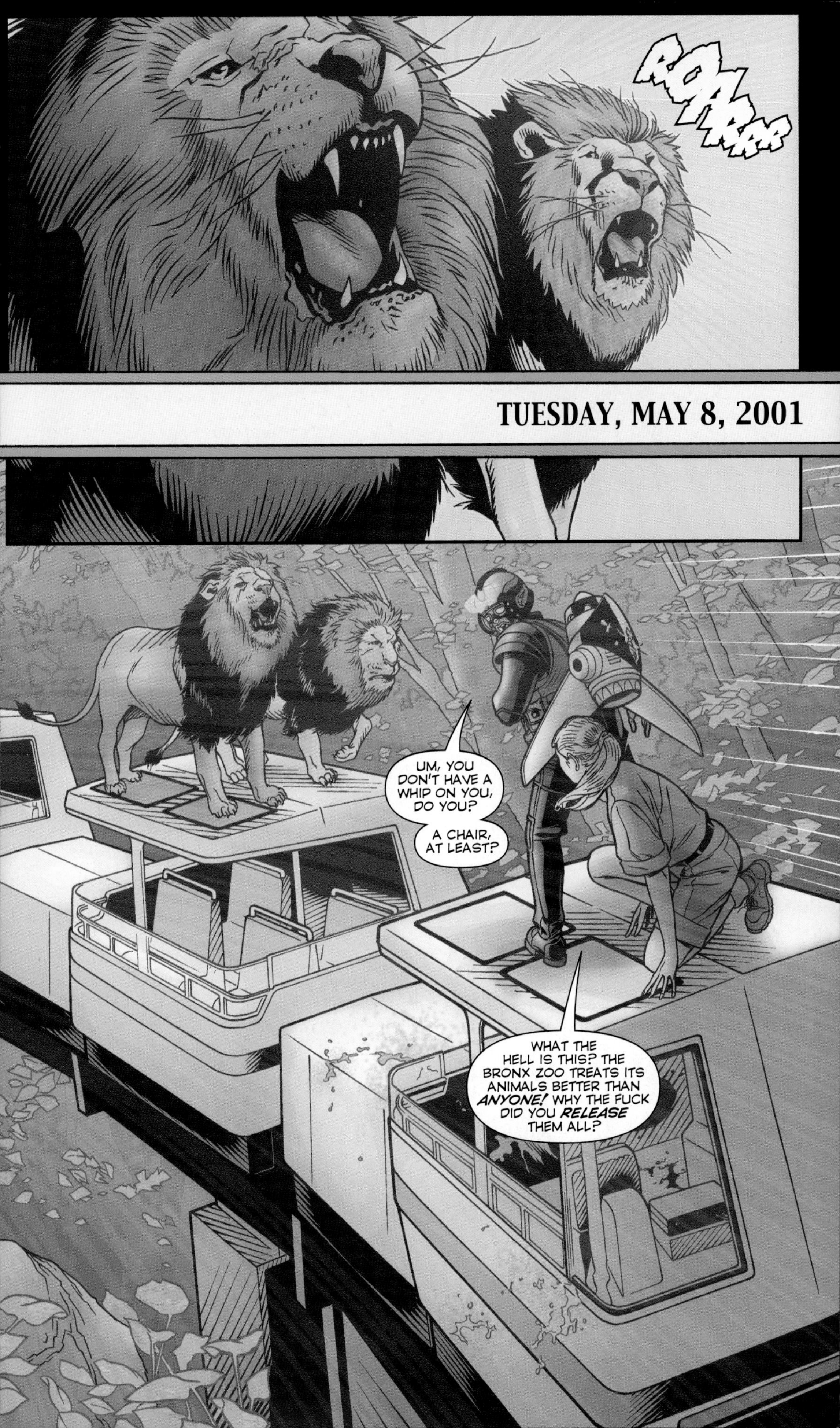
ROARRR
TUESDAY, MAY 8, 2001
UM, YOU DON'T HAVE A WHIP ON YOU, DO YOU?
A CHAIR, AT LEAST?
WHAT THE HELL IS THIS? THE BRONX ZOO TREATS ITS ANIMALS BETTER THAN ANYONE! WHY THE FUCK DID YOU RELEASE THEM ALL?

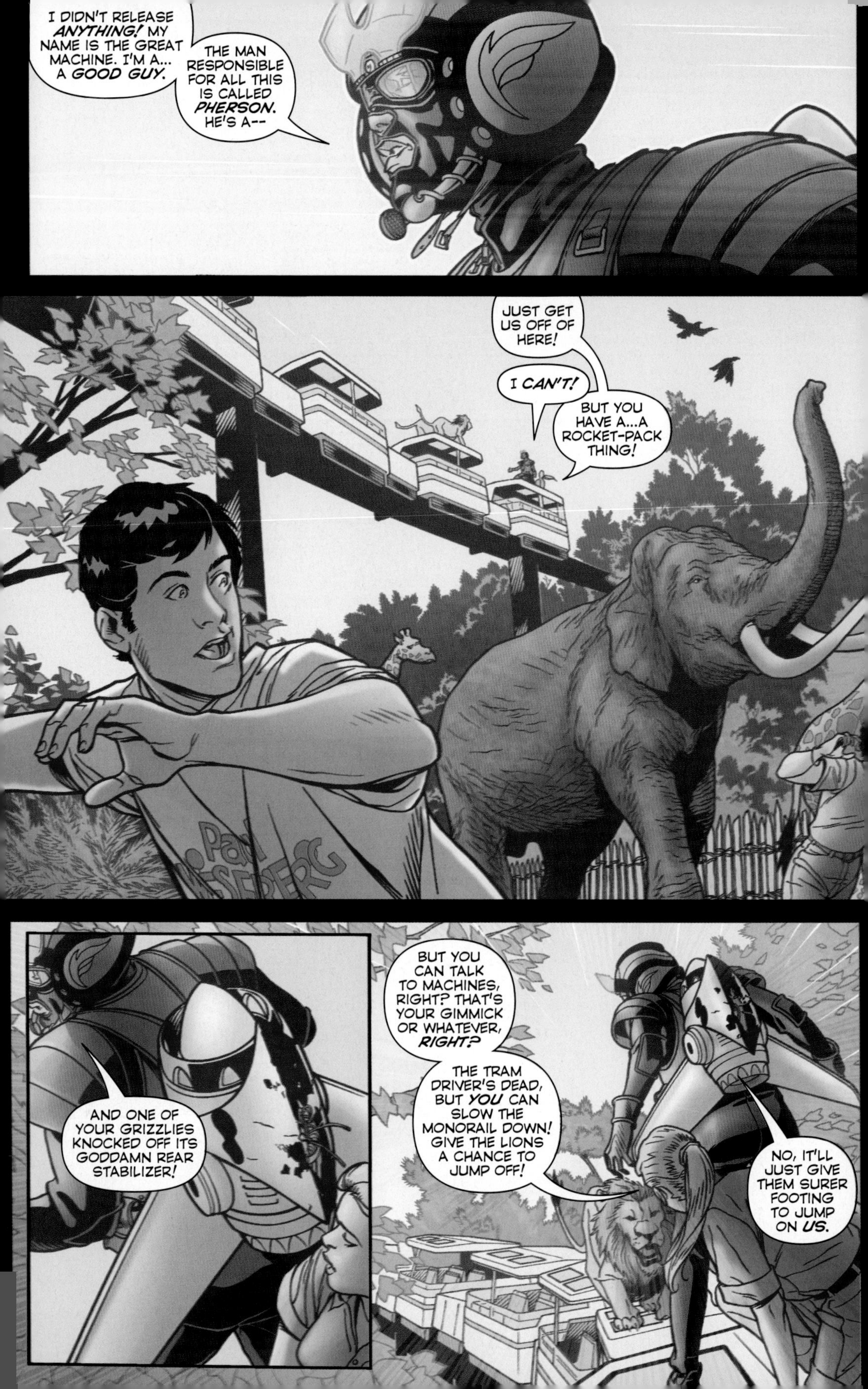
I DIDN'T RELEASE *ANYTHING!* MY NAME IS THE GREAT MACHINE. I'M A... A *GOOD GUY*.
THE MAN RESPONSIBLE FOR ALL THIS IS CALLED *PHERSON*. HE'S A--
JUST GET US OFF OF HERE!
I *CAN'T!*
BUT YOU HAVE A...A ROCKET-PACK THING!
AND ONE OF YOUR GRIZZLIES KNOCKED OFF ITS GODDAMN REAR STABILIZER!
BUT YOU CAN TALK TO MACHINES, RIGHT? THAT'S YOUR GIMMICK OR WHATEVER, *RIGHT?*
THE TRAM DRIVER'S DEAD, BUT *YOU* CAN SLOW THE MONORAIL DOWN! GIVE THE LIONS A CHANCE TO JUMP OFF!
NO, IT'LL JUST GIVE THEM SURER FOOTING TO JUMP ON *US*.

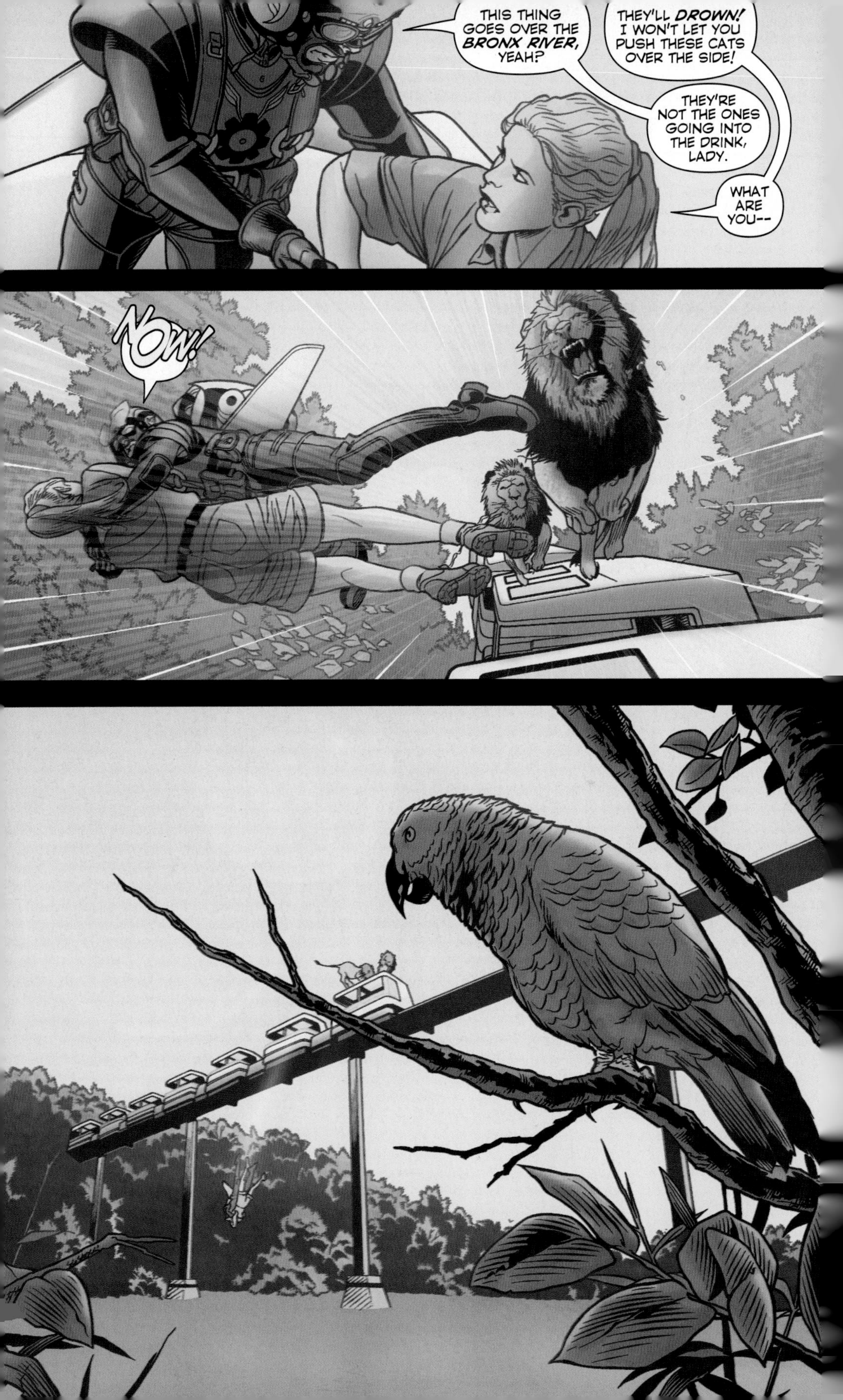
THIS THING GOES OVER THE BRONX RIVER, YEAH?
THEY'LL DROWN! I WON'T LET YOU PUSH THESE CATS OVER THE SIDE!
THEY'RE NOT THE ONES GOING INTO THE DRINK, LADY.
WHAT ARE YOU--
NOW!

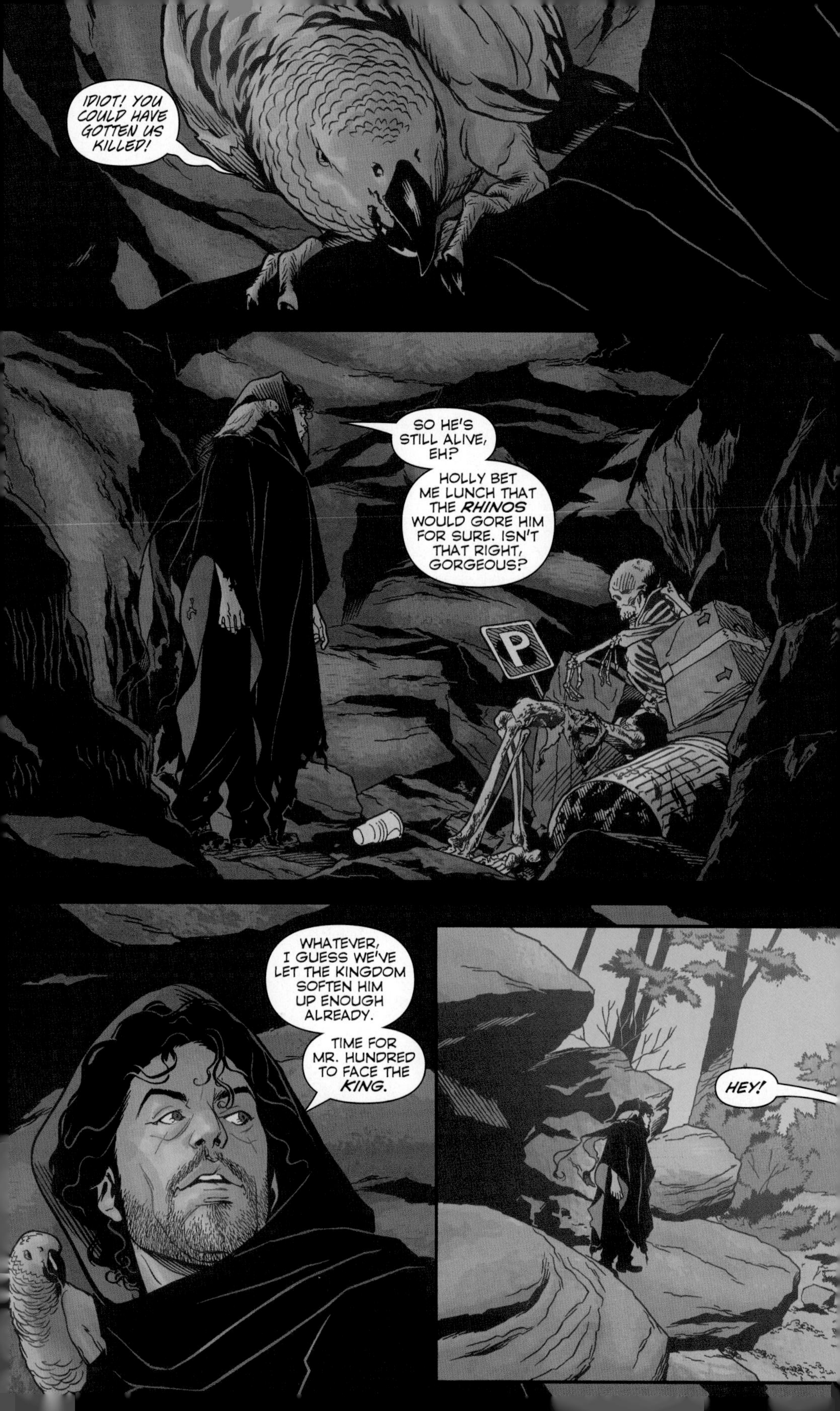
IDIOT! YOU COULD HAVE GOTTEN US KILLED!
SO HE'S STILL ALIVE, EH?
HOLLY BET ME LUNCH THAT THE RHINOS WOULD GORE HIM FOR SURE. ISN'T THAT RIGHT, GORGEOUS?
P
WHATEVER, I GUESS WE'VE LET THE KINGDOM SOFTEN HIM UP ENOUGH ALREADY.
TIME FOR MR. HUNDRED TO FACE THE KING.
HEY!

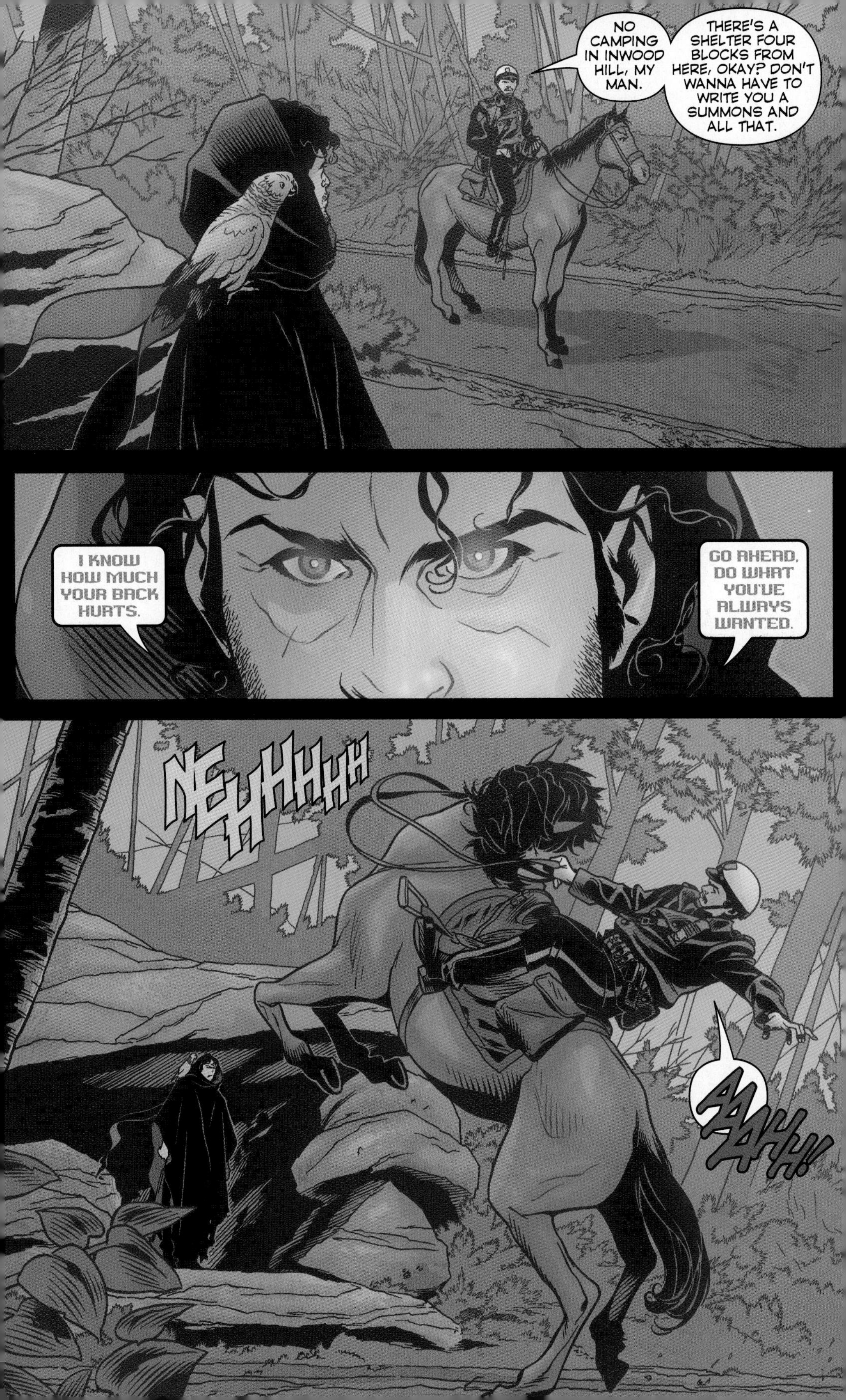
NO CAMPING IN INWOOD HILL, MY MAN.
THERE'S A SHELTER FOUR BLOCKS FROM HERE, OKAY? DON'T WANNA HAVE TO WRITE YOU A SUMMONS AND ALL THAT.
I KNOW HOW MUCH YOUR BACK HURTS.
GO AHEAD, DO WHAT YOU'VE ALWAYS WANTED.
NEHHHHHH
AAAHH!

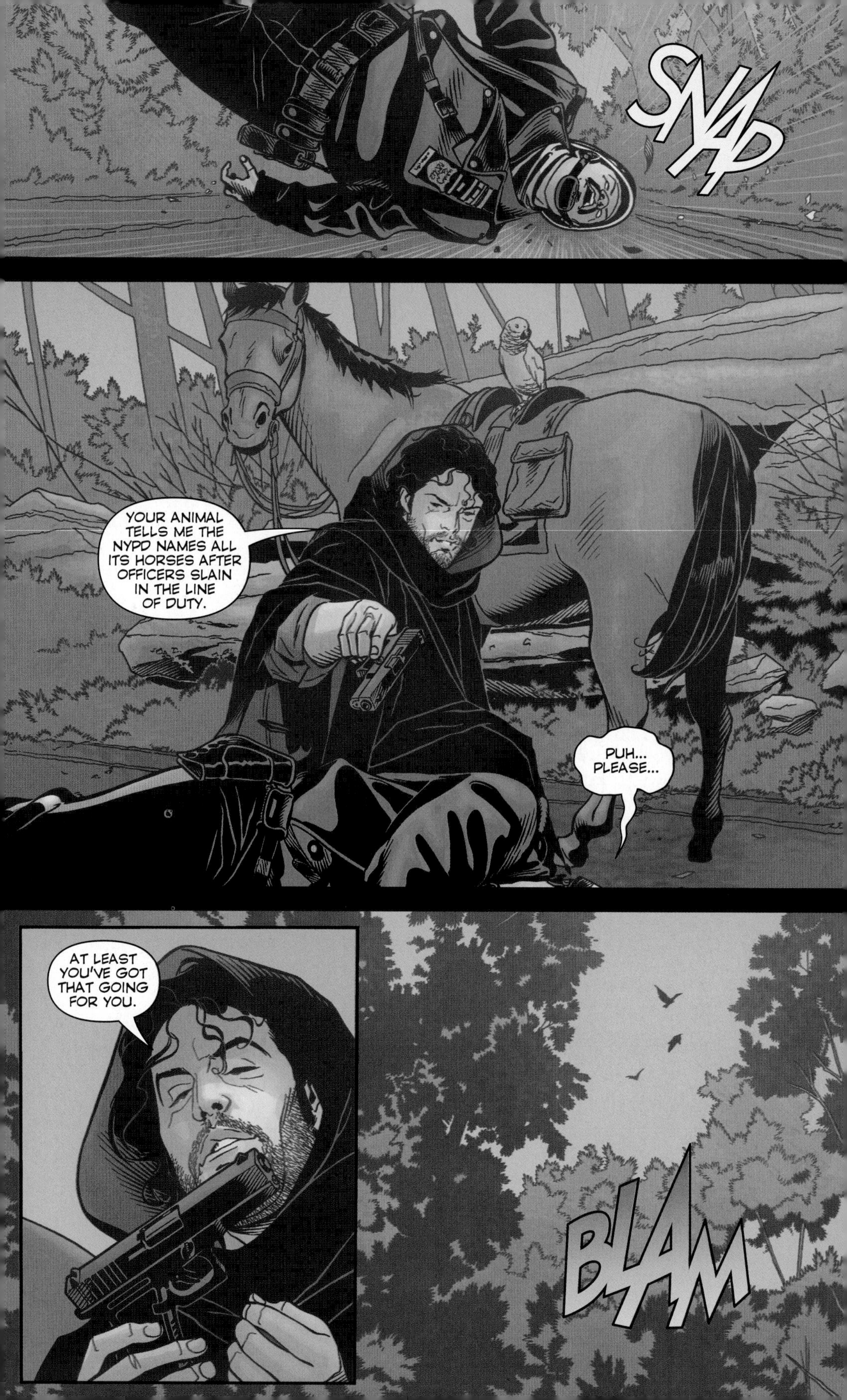
SNAP
YOUR ANIMAL TELLS ME THE NYPD NAMES ALL ITS HORSES AFTER OFFICERS SLAIN IN THE LINE OF DUTY.
PUH... PLEASE...
AT LEAST YOU'VE GOT THAT GOING FOR YOU.
BLAM

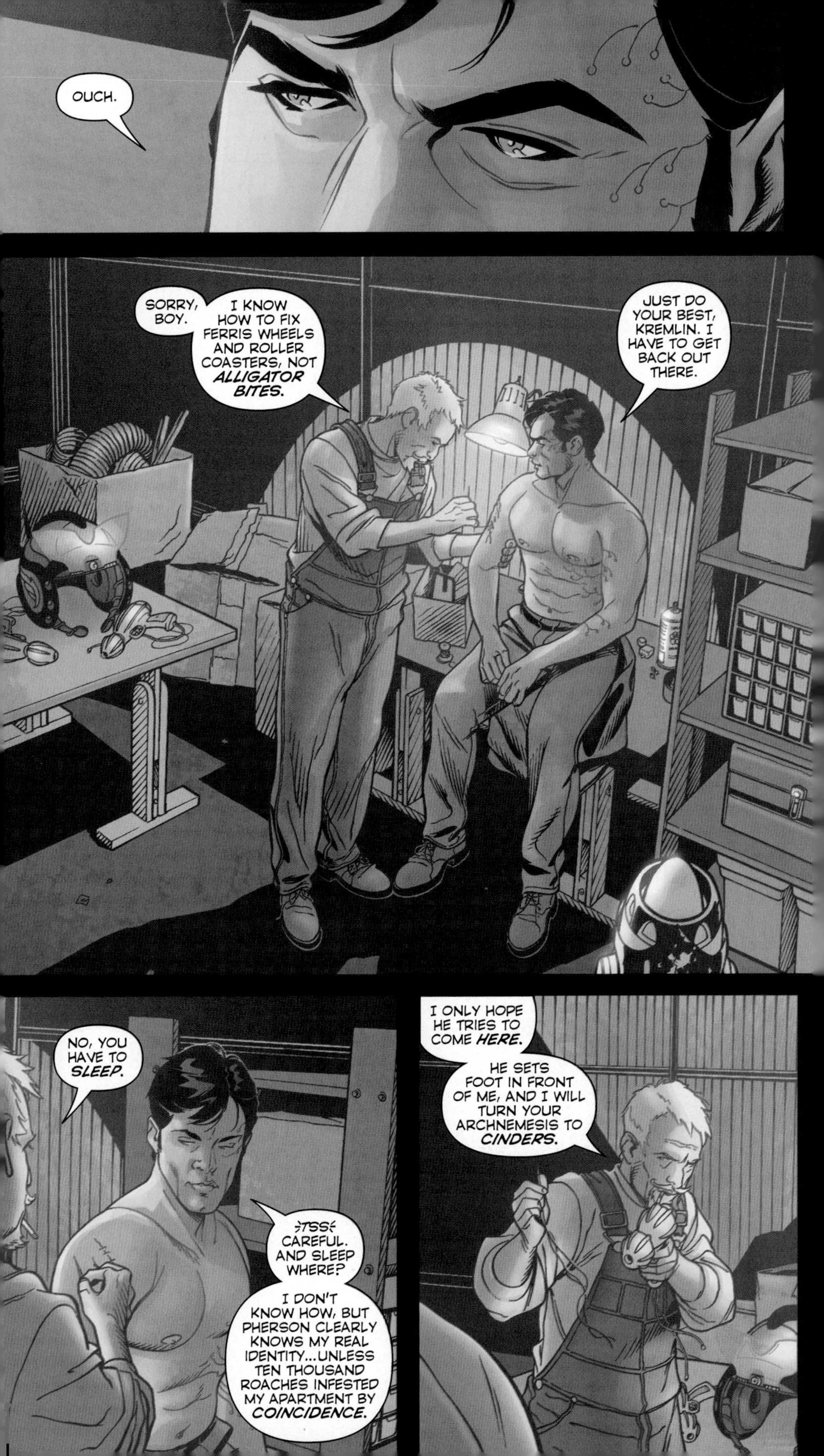
OUCH.
SORRY, BOY.
I KNOW HOW TO FIX FERRIS WHEELS AND ROLLER COASTERS, NOT ALLIGATOR BITES.
JUST DO YOUR BEST, KREMLIN. I HAVE TO GET BACK OUT THERE.
NO, YOU HAVE TO SLEEP.
TSS
CAREFUL. AND SLEEP WHERE?
I DON'T KNOW HOW, BUT PHERSON CLEARLY KNOWS MY REAL IDENTITY...UNLESS TEN THOUSAND ROACHES INFESTED MY APARTMENT BY COINCIDENCE.
I ONLY HOPE HE TRIES TO COME HERE.
HE SETS FOOT IN FRONT OF ME, AND I WILL TURN YOUR ARCHNEMESIS TO CINDERS.

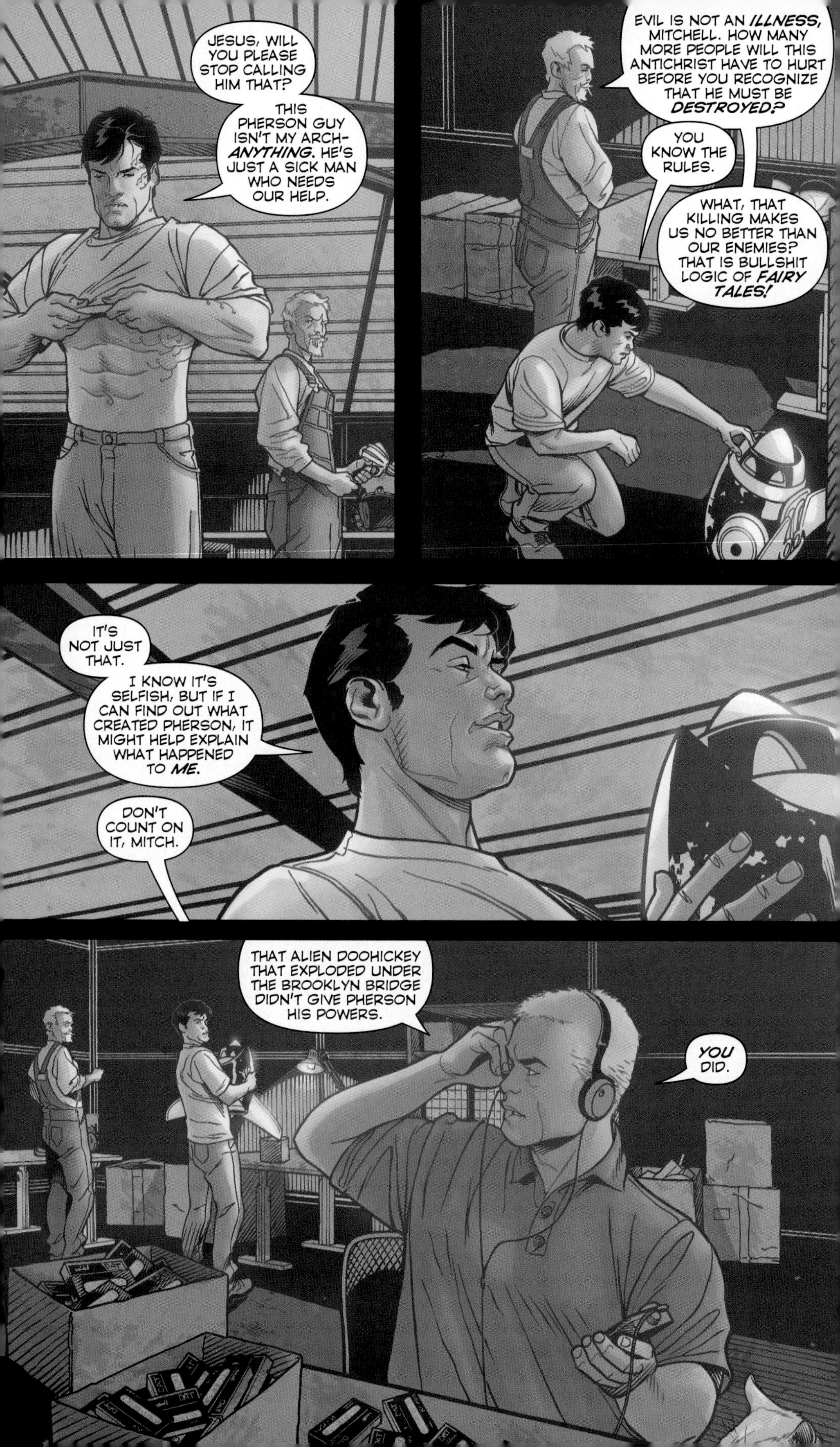
JESUS, WILL YOU PLEASE STOP CALLING HIM THAT?
THIS PHERSON GUY ISN'T MY ARCH-ANYTHING. HE'S JUST A SICK MAN WHO NEEDS OUR HELP.
EVIL IS NOT AN ILLNESS, MITCHELL. HOW MANY MORE PEOPLE WILL THIS ANTICHRIST HAVE TO HURT BEFORE YOU RECOGNIZE THAT HE MUST BE DESTROYED?
YOU KNOW THE RULES.
WHAT, THAT KILLING MAKES US NO BETTER THAN OUR ENEMIES? THAT IS BULLSHIT LOGIC OF FAIRY TALES!
IT'S NOT JUST THAT.
I KNOW IT'S SELFISH, BUT IF I CAN FIND OUT WHAT CREATED PHERSON, IT MIGHT HELP EXPLAIN WHAT HAPPENED TO ME.
DON'T COUNT ON IT, MITCH.
THAT ALIEN DOOHICKEY THAT EXPLODED UNDER THE BROOKLYN BRIDGE DIDN'T GIVE PHERSON HIS POWERS.
YOU DID.

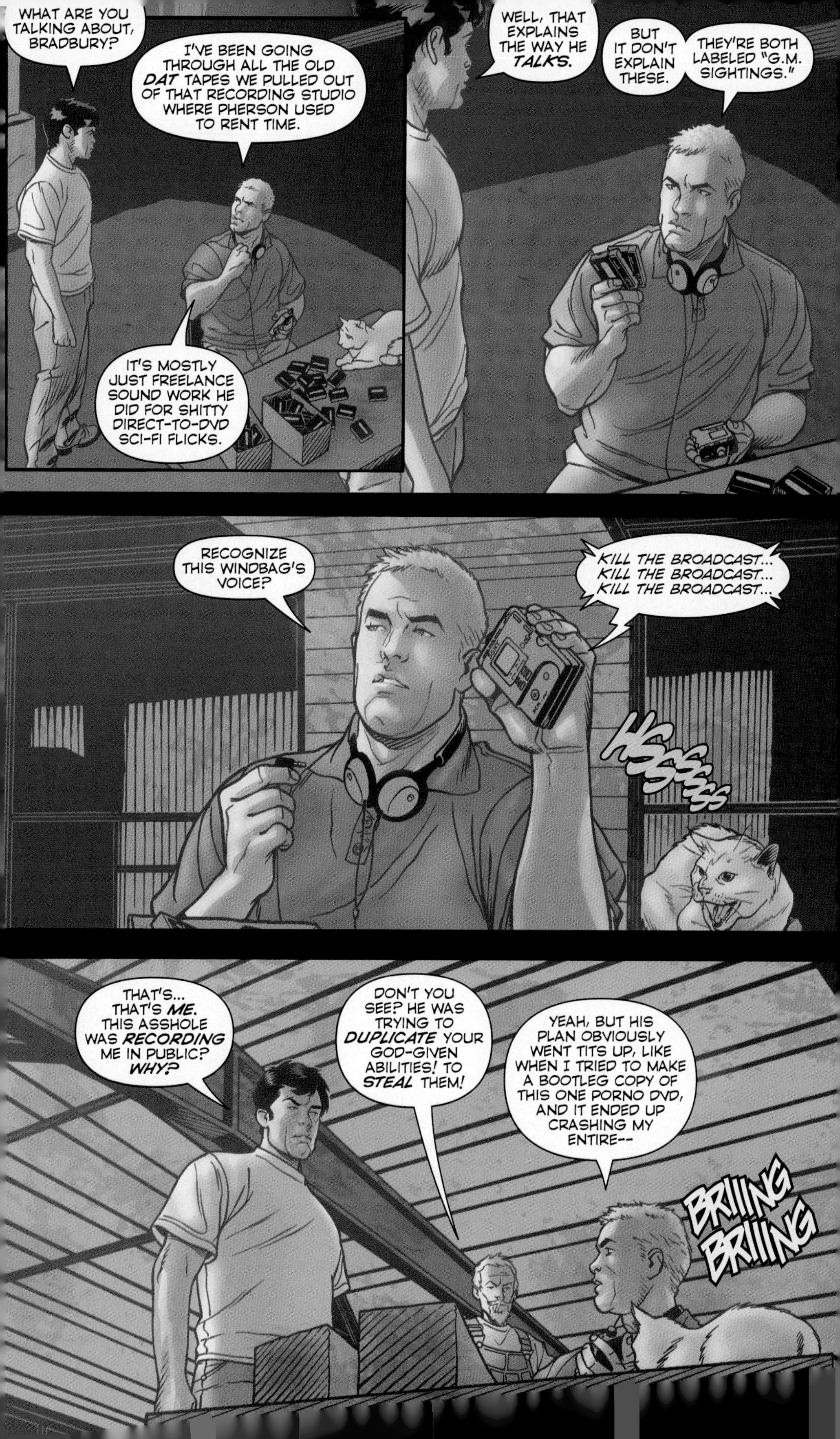
WHAT ARE YOU TALKING ABOUT, BRADBURY?
I'VE BEEN GOING THROUGH ALL THE OLD DAT TAPES WE PULLED OUT OF THAT RECORDING STUDIO WHERE PHERSON USED TO RENT TIME.
IT'S MOSTLY JUST FREELANCE SOUND WORK HE DID FOR SHITTY DIRECT-TO-DVD SCI-FI FLICKS.
WELL, THAT EXPLAINS THE WAY HE TALKS.
BUT IT DON'T EXPLAIN THESE.
THEY'RE BOTH LABELED "G.M. SIGHTINGS."
RECOGNIZE THIS WINDBAG'S VOICE?
KILL THE BROADCAST... KILL THE BROADCAST... KILL THE BROADCAST...
HSSSSSS
THAT'S... THAT'S ME. THIS ASSHOLE WAS RECORDING ME IN PUBLIC? WHY?
DON'T YOU SEE? HE WAS TRYING TO DUPLICATE YOUR GOD-GIVEN ABILITIES! TO STEAL THEM!
YEAH, BUT HIS PLAN OBVIOUSLY WENT TITS UP, LIKE WHEN I TRIED TO MAKE A BOOTLEG COPY OF THIS ONE PORNO DVD, AND IT ENDED UP CRASHING MY ENTIRE--
BRIIING BRIIING

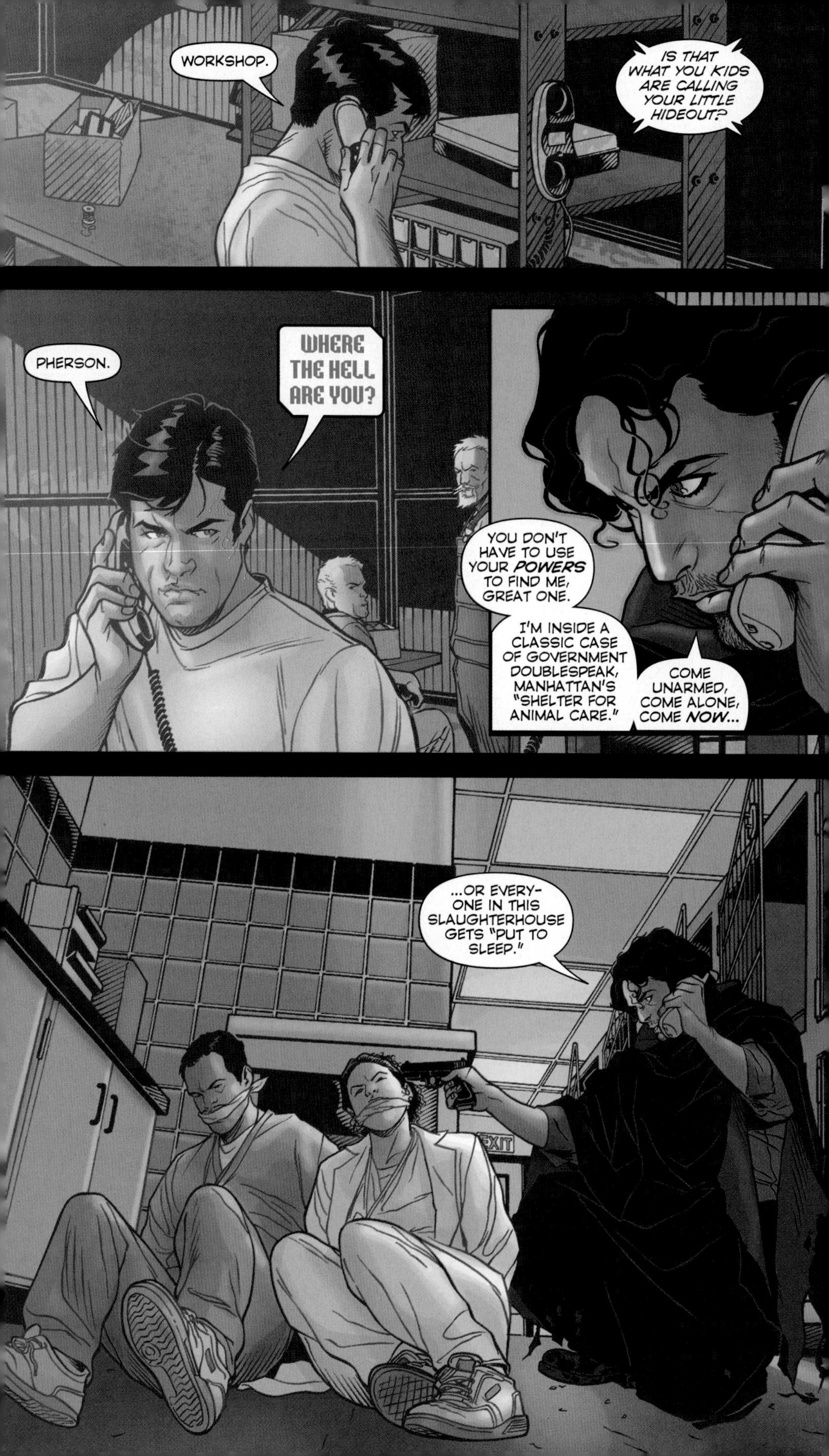

WORKSHOP.
IS THAT WHAT YOU KIDS ARE CALLING YOUR LITTLE HIDEOUT?
PHERSON.
WHERE THE HELL ARE YOU?
YOU DON'T HAVE TO USE YOUR POWERS TO FIND ME, GREAT ONE.
I'M INSIDE A CLASSIC CASE OF GOVERNMENT DOUBLESPEAK, MANHATTAN'S "SHELTER FOR ANIMAL CARE."
COME UNARMED, COME ALONE, COME NOW...
...OR EVERY-ONE IN THIS SLAUGHTERHOUSE GETS "PUT TO SLEEP."
EXIT

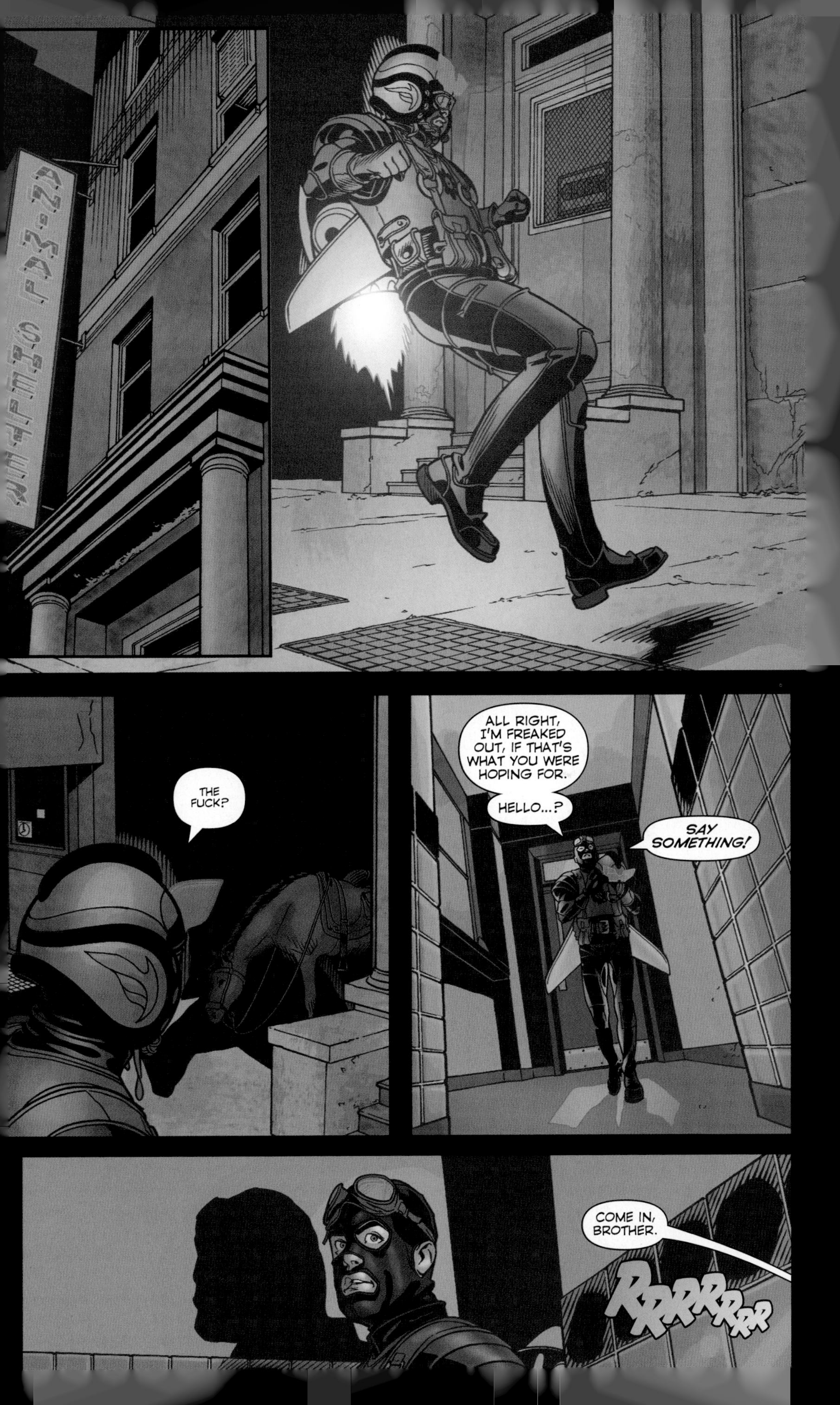
ANIMAL SHELTER
THE FUCK?
ALL RIGHT, I'M FREAKED OUT, IF THAT'S WHAT YOU WERE HOPING FOR.
HELLO...?
SAY SOMETHING!
COME IN, BROTHER.
RRRRRRRR

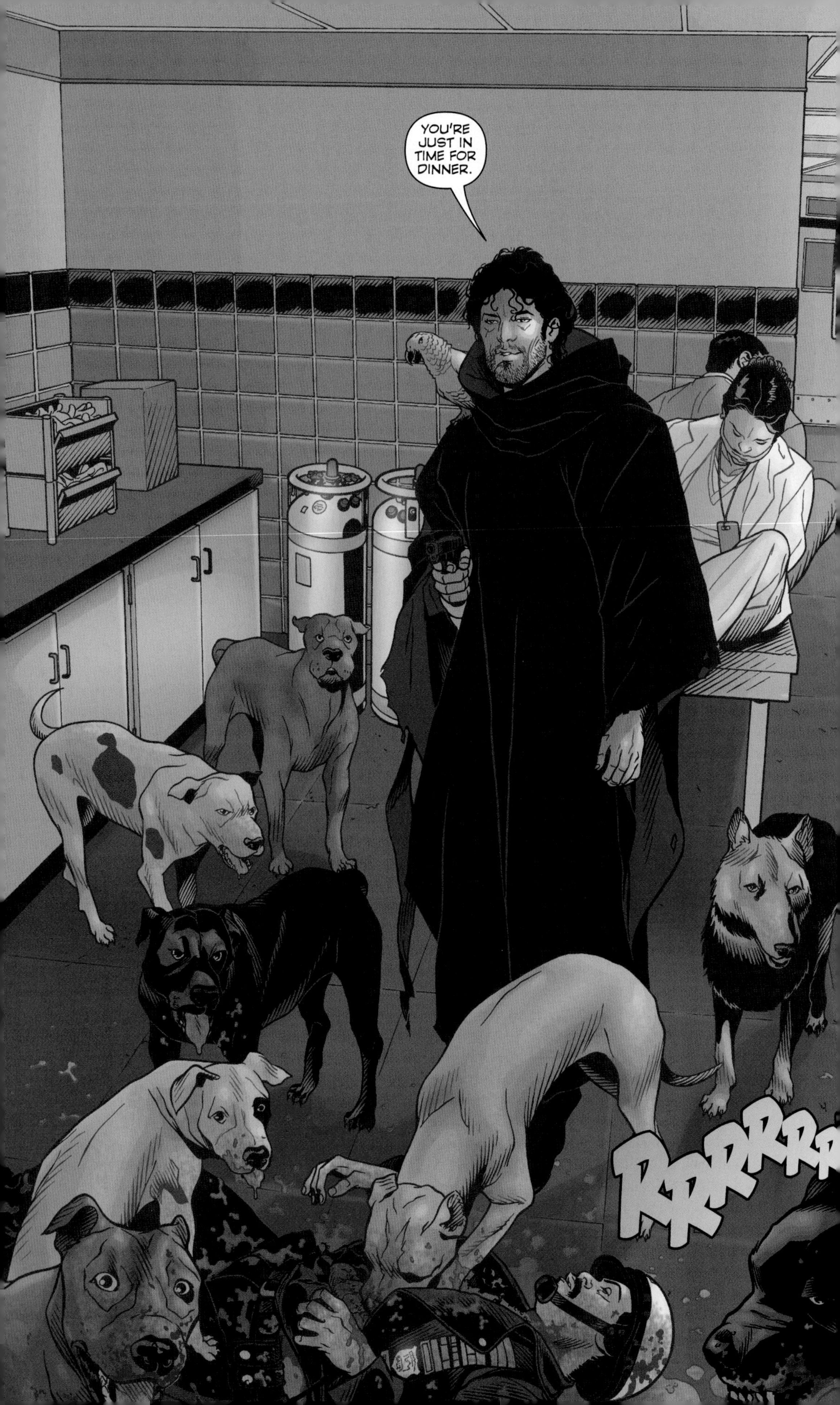
YOU'RE JUST IN TIME FOR DINNER.
RRRRRR

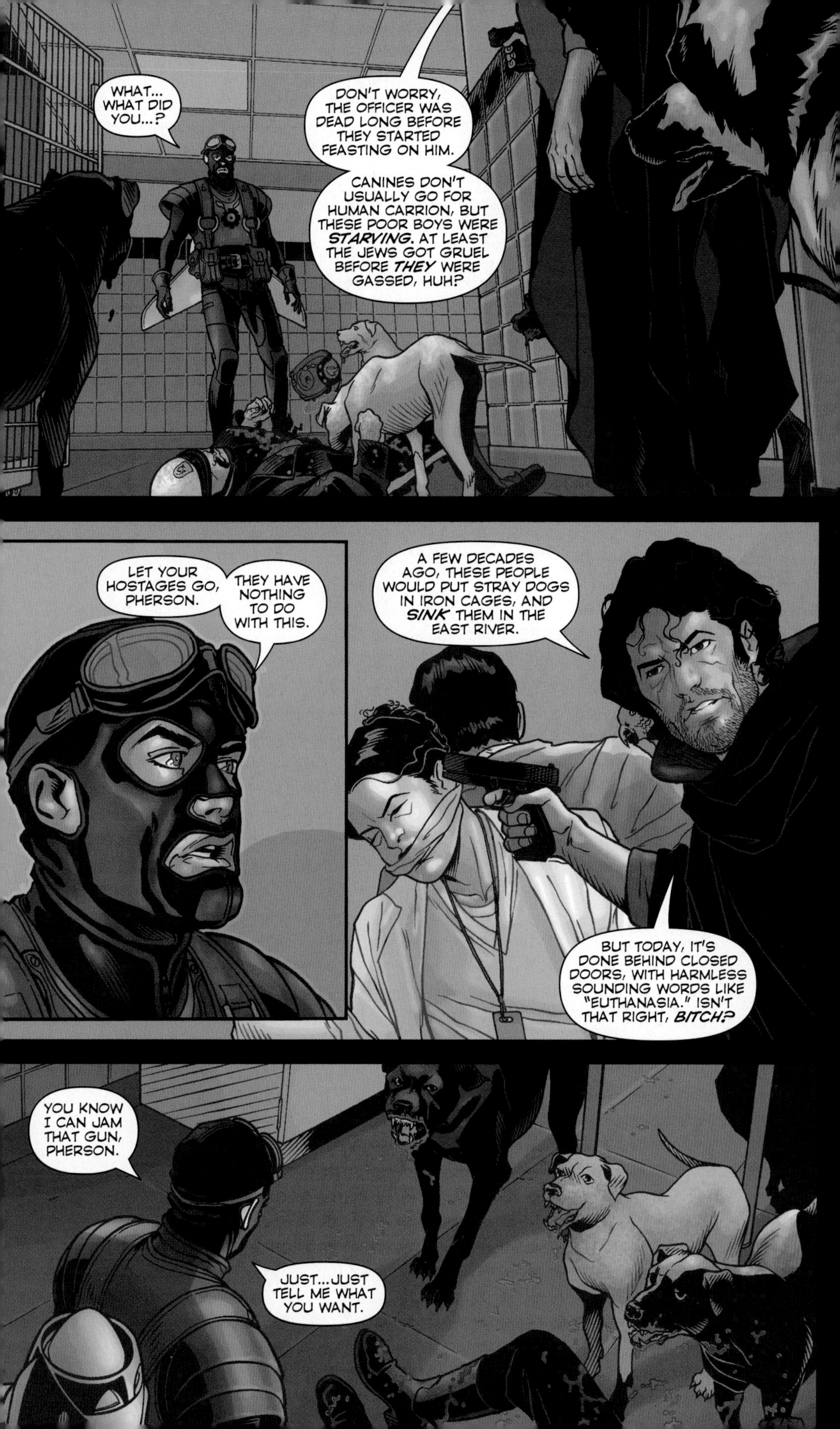
WHAT... WHAT DID YOU...?
DON'T WORRY, THE OFFICER WAS DEAD LONG BEFORE THEY STARTED FEASTING ON HIM.
CANINES DON'T USUALLY GO FOR HUMAN CARRION, BUT THESE POOR BOYS WERE STARVING. AT LEAST THE JEWS GOT GRUEL BEFORE THEY WERE GASSED, HUH?
LET YOUR HOSTAGES GO, PHERSON.
THEY HAVE NOTHING TO DO WITH THIS.
A FEW DECADES AGO, THESE PEOPLE WOULD PUT STRAY DOGS IN IRON CAGES, AND SINK THEM IN THE EAST RIVER.
BUT TODAY, IT'S DONE BEHIND CLOSED DOORS, WITH HARMLESS SOUNDING WORDS LIKE "EUTHANASIA." ISN'T THAT RIGHT, BITCH?
YOU KNOW I CAN JAM THAT GUN, PHERSON.
JUST...JUST TELL ME WHAT YOU WANT.

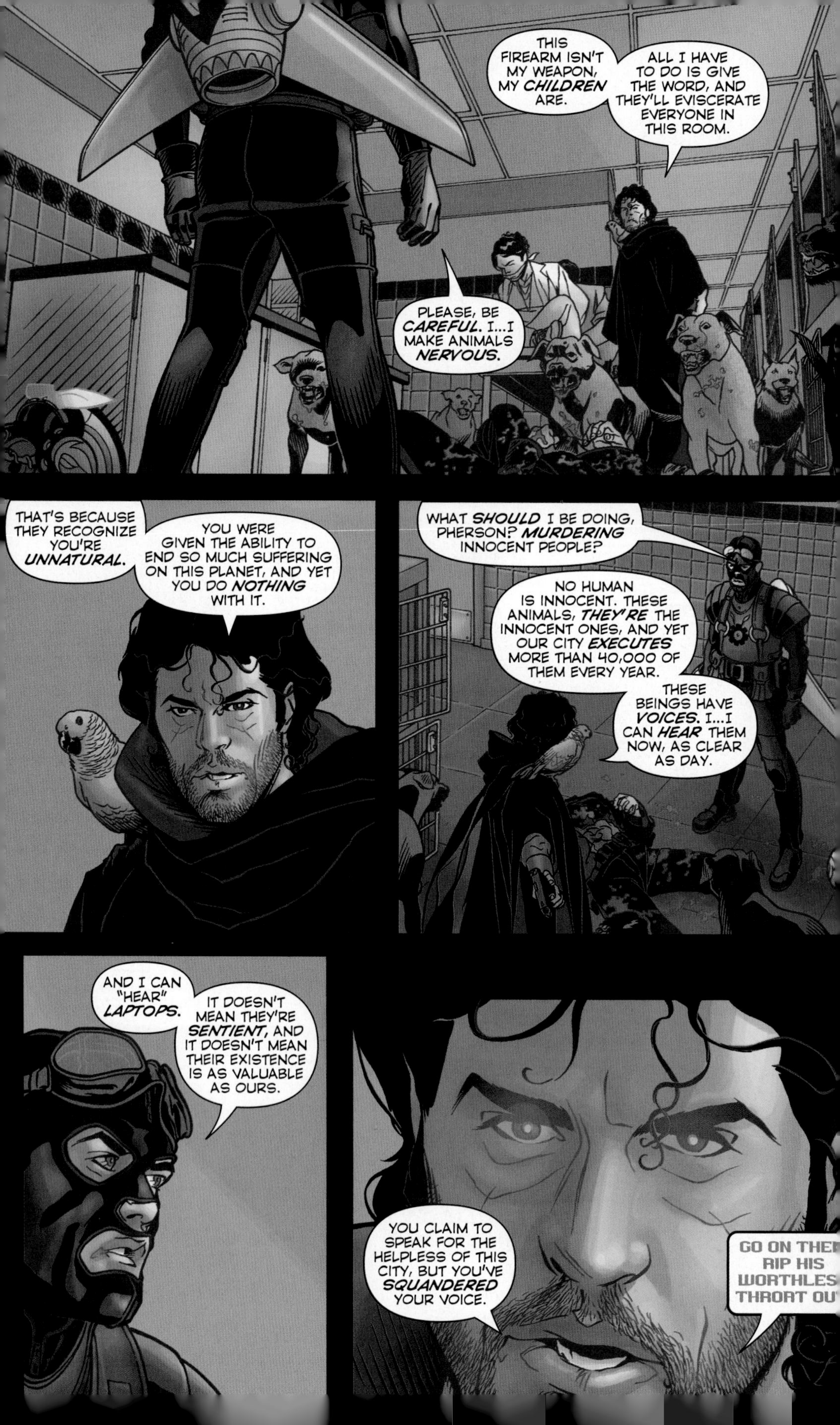

THIS FIREARM ISN'T MY WEAPON, MY *CHILDREN* ARE.
ALL I HAVE TO DO IS GIVE THE WORD, AND THEY'LL EVISCERATE EVERYONE IN THIS ROOM.
PLEASE, BE *CAREFUL*. I...I MAKE ANIMALS *NERVOUS*.
THAT'S BECAUSE THEY RECOGNIZE YOU'RE *UNNATURAL*.
YOU WERE GIVEN THE ABILITY TO END SO MUCH SUFFERING ON THIS PLANET, AND YET YOU DO *NOTHING* WITH IT.
WHAT *SHOULD* I BE DOING, PHERSON? *MURDERING* INNOCENT PEOPLE?
NO HUMAN IS INNOCENT. THESE ANIMALS, *THEY'RE* THE INNOCENT ONES, AND YET OUR CITY *EXECUTES* MORE THAN 40,000 OF THEM EVERY YEAR.
THESE BEINGS HAVE *VOICES*. I...I CAN *HEAR* THEM NOW, AS CLEAR AS DAY.
AND I CAN "HEAR" *LAPTOPS*.
IT DOESN'T MEAN THEY'RE *SENTIENT*, AND IT DOESN'T MEAN THEIR EXISTENCE IS AS VALUABLE AS OURS.
YOU CLAIM TO SPEAK FOR THE HELPLESS OF THIS CITY, BUT YOU'VE *SQUANDERED* YOUR VOICE.

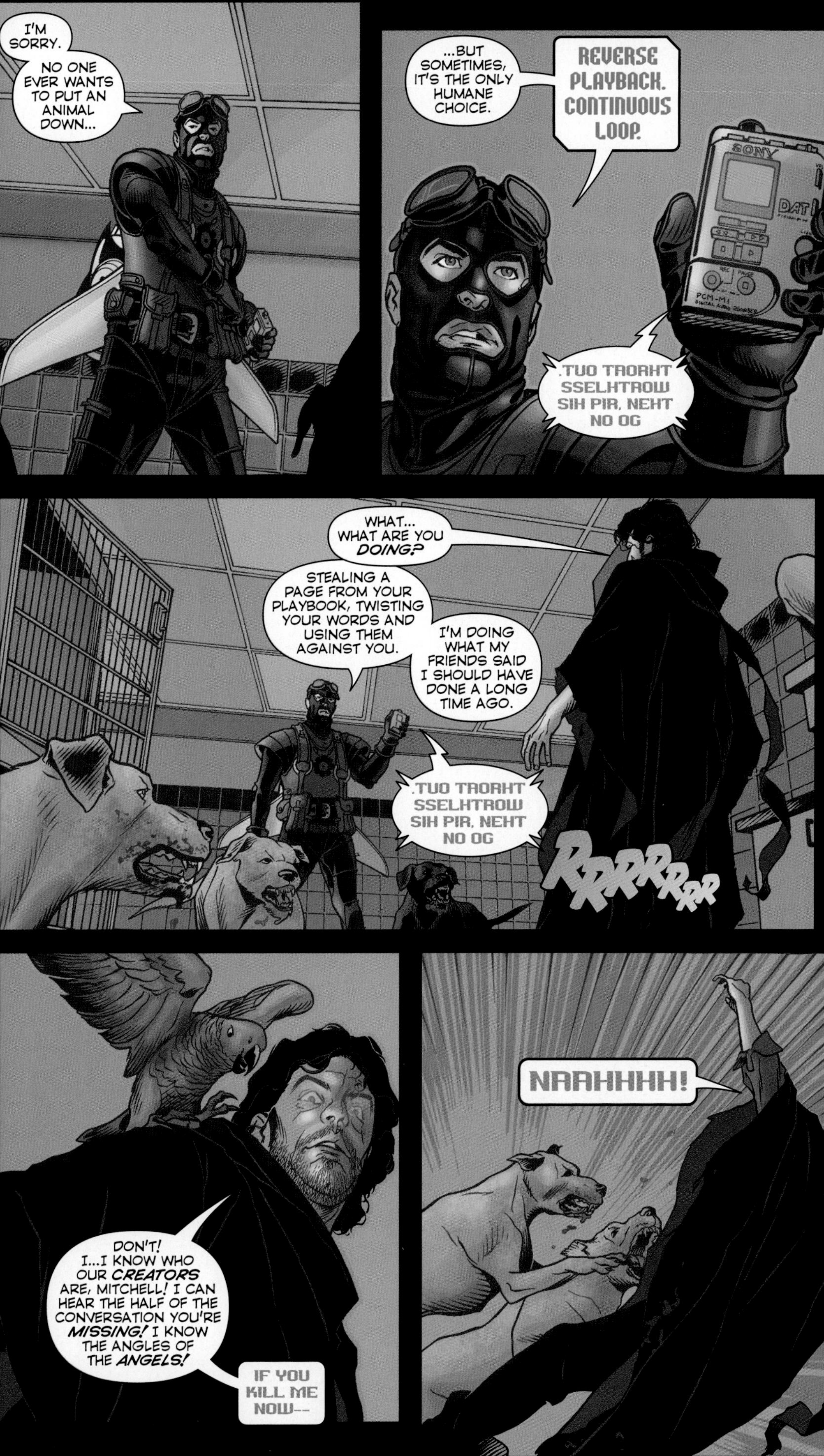
I'M SORRY.
NO ONE EVER WANTS TO PUT AN ANIMAL DOWN...
...BUT SOMETIMES, IT'S THE ONLY HUMANE CHOICE.
REVERSE PLAYBACK. CONTINUOUS LOOP.
SONY
DAT
PCM-M1
.TUO TRORHT SSELHTROW SIH PIR, NEHT NO OG
WHAT... WHAT ARE YOU DOING?
STEALING A PAGE FROM YOUR PLAYBOOK, TWISTING YOUR WORDS AND USING THEM AGAINST YOU.
I'M DOING WHAT MY FRIENDS SAID I SHOULD HAVE DONE A LONG TIME AGO.
.TUO TRORHT SSELHTROW SIH PIR, NEHT NO OG
RRRRRRRR
DON'T! I...I KNOW WHO OUR CREATORS ARE, MITCHELL! I CAN HEAR THE HALF OF THE CONVERSATION YOU'RE MISSING! I KNOW THE ANGLES OF THE ANGELS!
IF YOU KILL ME NOW--
NAAHHHH!

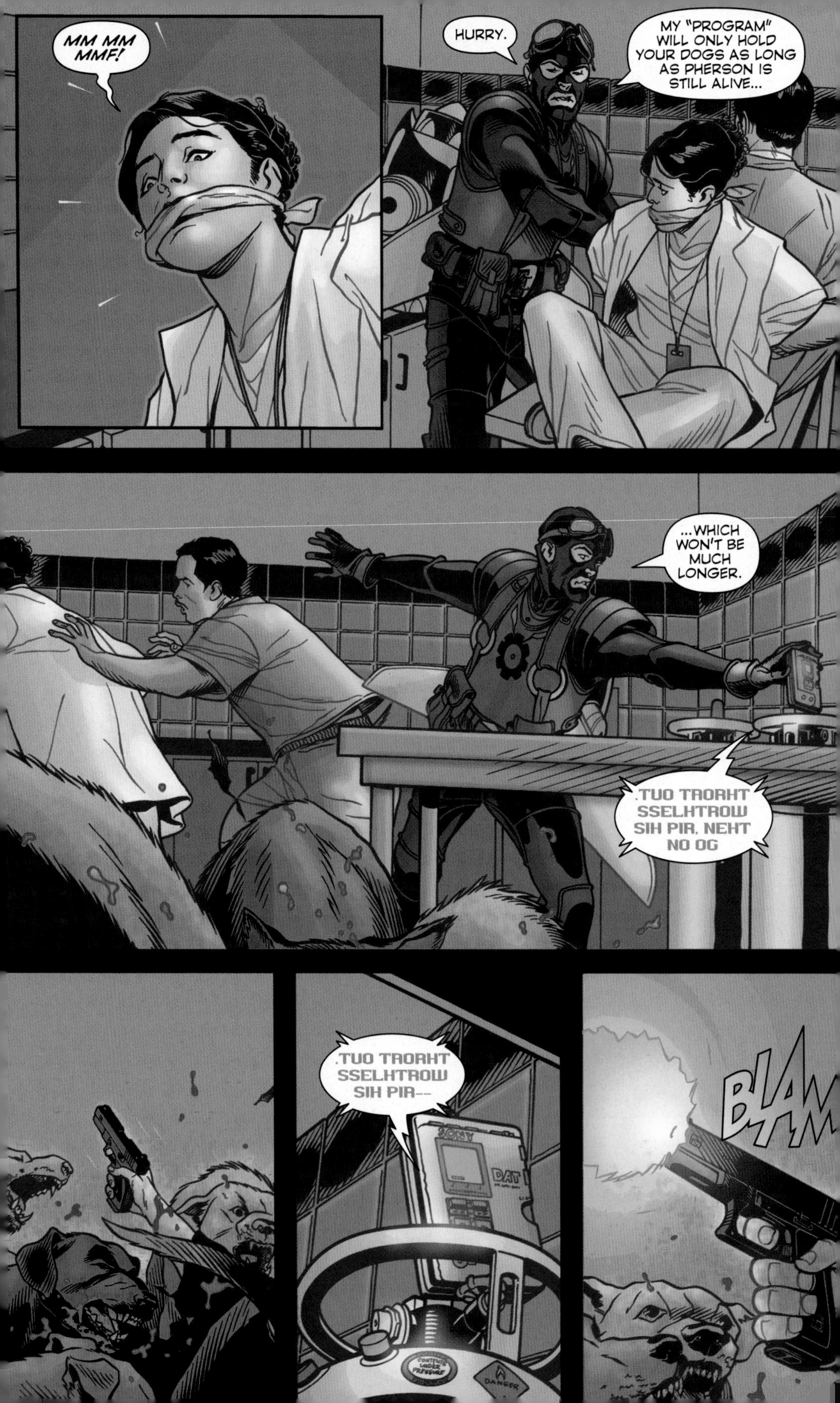
MM MM MMF!
HURRY.
MY "PROGRAM" WILL ONLY HOLD YOUR DOGS AS LONG AS PHERSON IS STILL ALIVE...
...WHICH WON'T BE MUCH LONGER.
.TUO TRORHT SSELHTROW SIH PIR, NEHT NO OG
.TUO TRORHT SSELHTROW SIH PIR--
SONY
DAT
BLAM

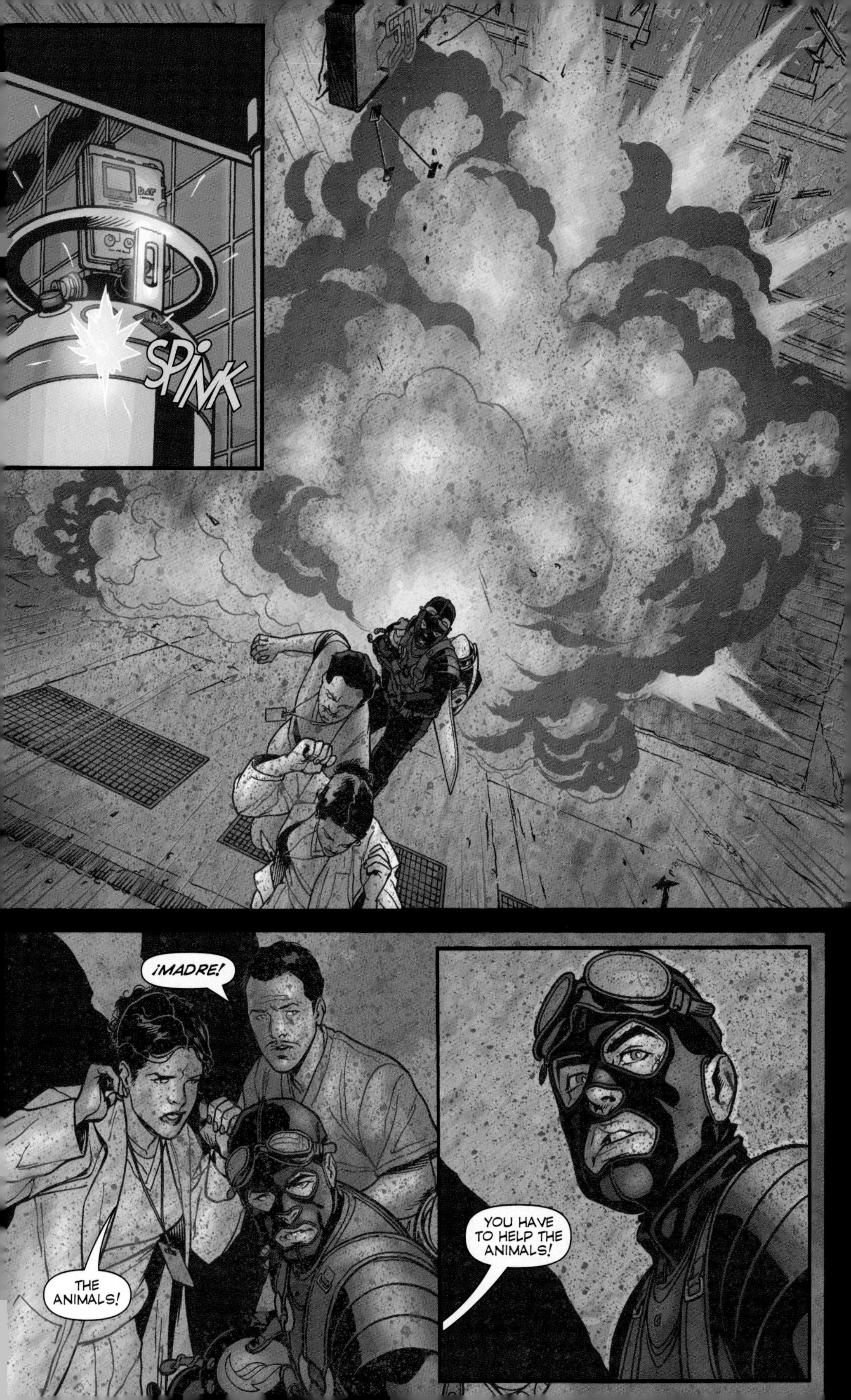
SPINK
¡MADRE!
THE ANIMALS!
YOU HAVE TO HELP THE ANIMALS!

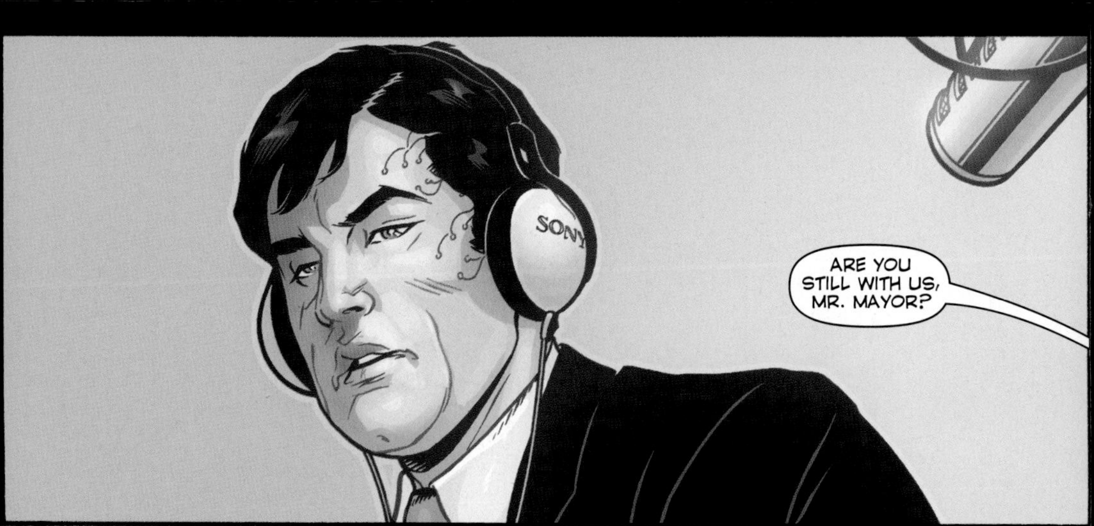
SONY
ARE YOU STILL WITH US, MR. MAYOR?

TUESDAY, MARCH 4, 2003

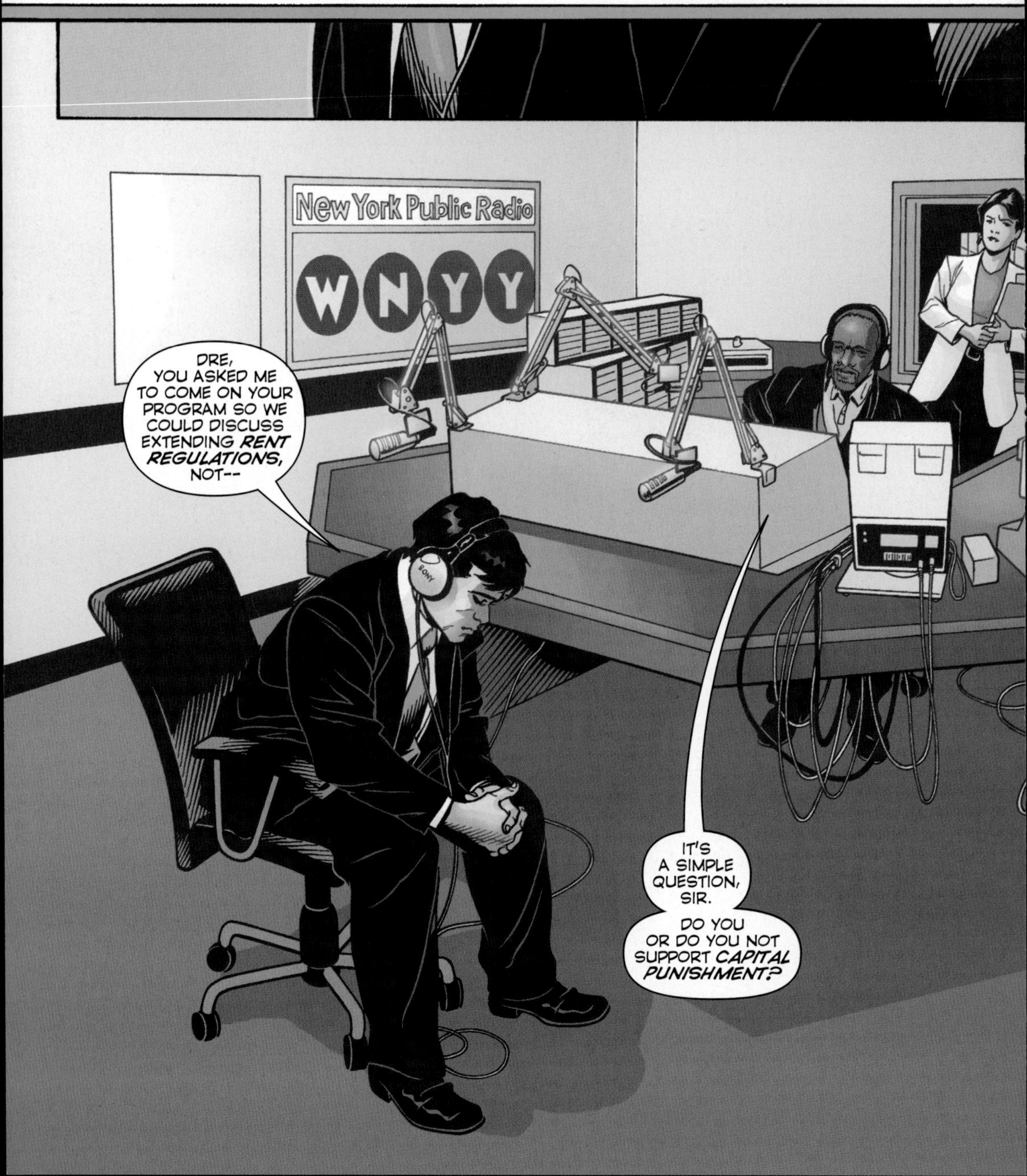
New York Public Radio
WNYY
DRE, YOU ASKED ME TO COME ON YOUR PROGRAM SO WE COULD DISCUSS EXTENDING *RENT REGULATIONS,* NOT--
SONY
IT'S A SIMPLE QUESTION, SIR.
DO YOU OR DO YOU NOT SUPPORT *CAPITAL PUNISHMENT?*

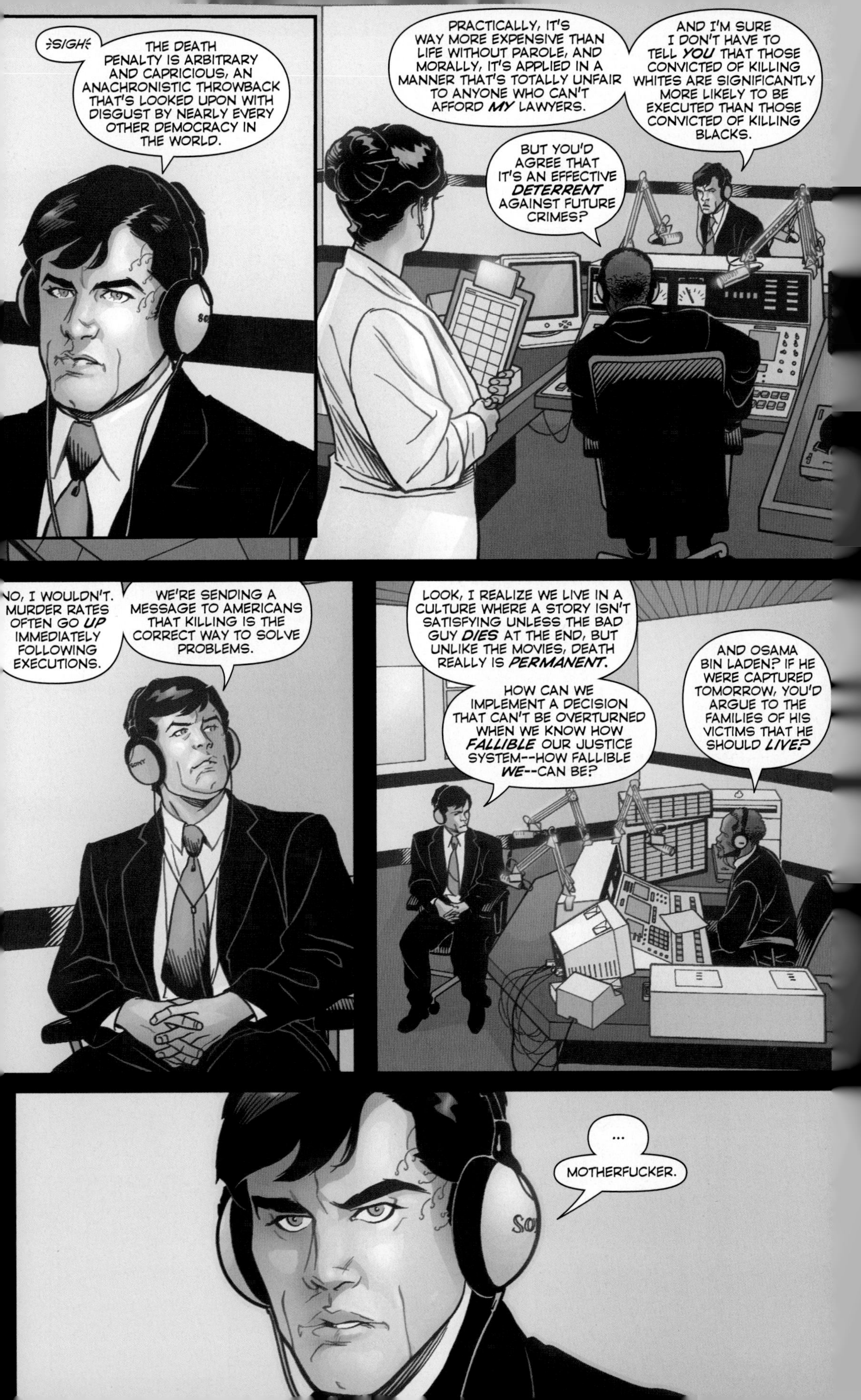

SIGH
THE DEATH PENALTY IS ARBITRARY AND CAPRICIOUS, AN ANACHRONISTIC THROWBACK THAT'S LOOKED UPON WITH DISGUST BY NEARLY EVERY OTHER DEMOCRACY IN THE WORLD.
PRACTICALLY, IT'S WAY MORE EXPENSIVE THAN LIFE WITHOUT PAROLE, AND MORALLY, IT'S APPLIED IN A MANNER THAT'S TOTALLY UNFAIR TO ANYONE WHO CAN'T AFFORD *MY* LAWYERS.
AND I'M SURE I DON'T HAVE TO TELL ***YOU*** THAT THOSE CONVICTED OF KILLING WHITES ARE SIGNIFICANTLY MORE LIKELY TO BE EXECUTED THAN THOSE CONVICTED OF KILLING BLACKS.
BUT YOU'D AGREE THAT IT'S AN EFFECTIVE ***DETERRENT*** AGAINST FUTURE CRIMES?
NO, I WOULDN'T. MURDER RATES OFTEN GO *UP* IMMEDIATELY FOLLOWING EXECUTIONS.
WE'RE SENDING A MESSAGE TO AMERICANS THAT KILLING IS THE CORRECT WAY TO SOLVE PROBLEMS.
LOOK, I REALIZE WE LIVE IN A CULTURE WHERE A STORY ISN'T SATISFYING UNLESS THE BAD GUY *DIES* AT THE END, BUT UNLIKE THE MOVIES, DEATH REALLY IS *PERMANENT*.
HOW CAN WE IMPLEMENT A DECISION THAT CAN'T BE OVERTURNED WHEN WE KNOW HOW *FALLIBLE* OUR JUSTICE SYSTEM--HOW FALLIBLE *WE*--CAN BE?
AND OSAMA BIN LADEN? IF HE WERE CAPTURED TOMORROW, YOU'D ARGUE TO THE FAMILIES OF HIS VICTIMS THAT HE SHOULD *LIVE?*
...
MOTHERFUCKER.

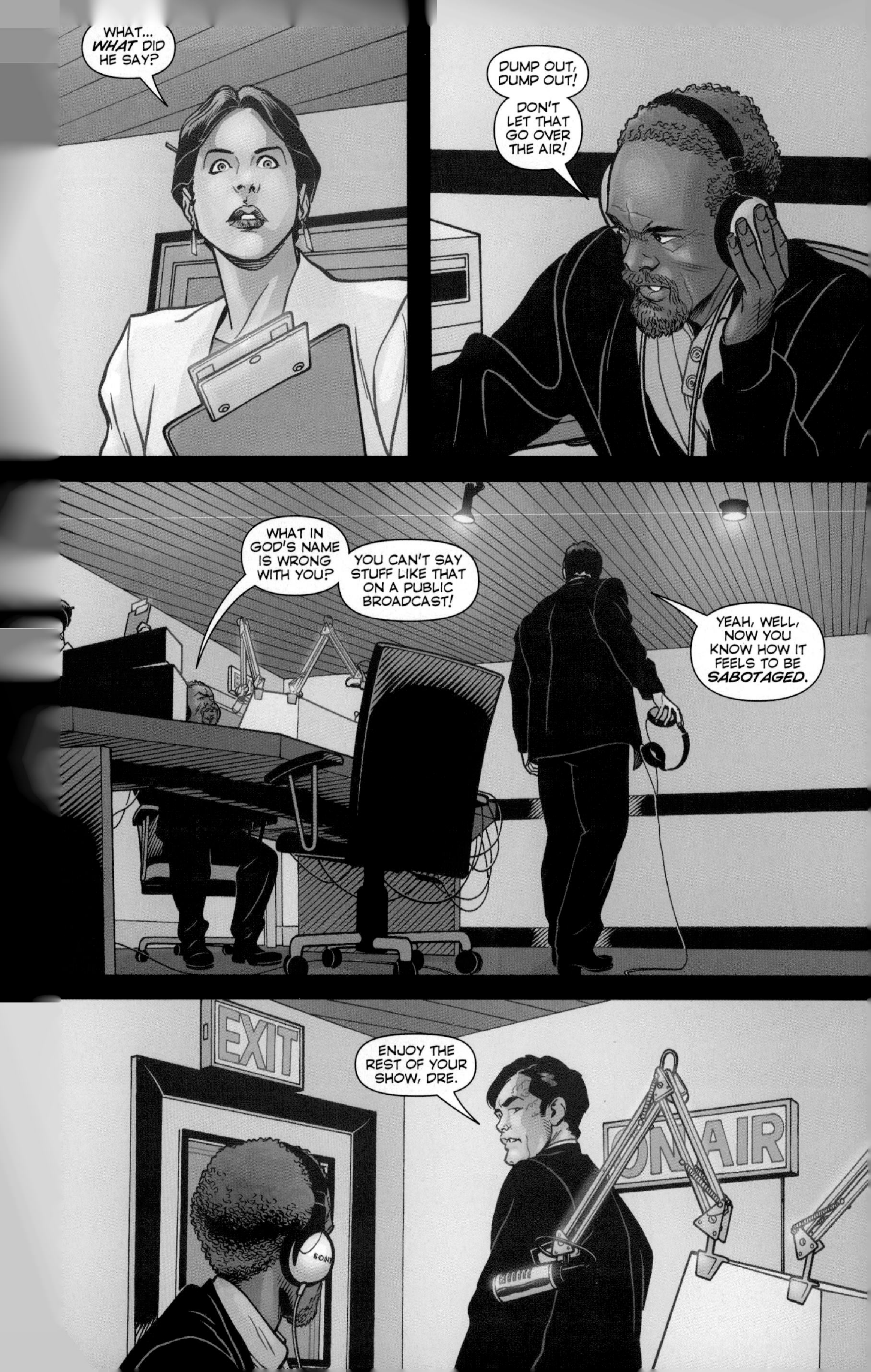
WHAT... WHAT DID HE SAY?
DUMP OUT, DUMP OUT!
DON'T LET THAT GO OVER THE AIR!
WHAT IN GOD'S NAME IS WRONG WITH YOU?
YOU CAN'T SAY STUFF LIKE THAT ON A PUBLIC BROADCAST!
YEAH, WELL, NOW YOU KNOW HOW IT FEELS TO BE SABOTAGED.
EXIT
ENJOY THE REST OF YOUR SHOW, DRE.
ON AIR
SONY

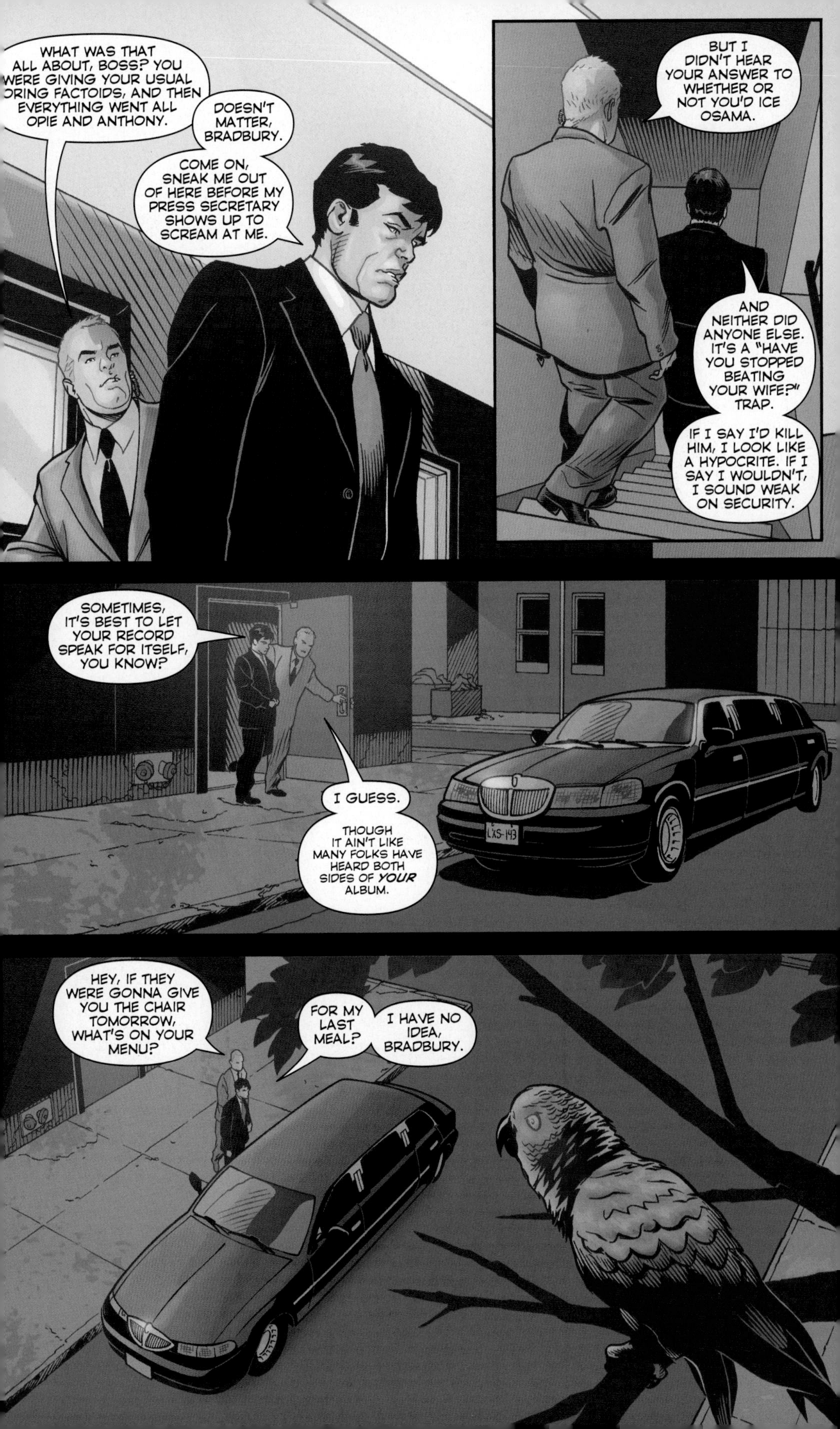
WHAT WAS THAT ALL ABOUT, BOSS? YOU WERE GIVING YOUR USUAL ORING FACTOIDS, AND THEN EVERYTHING WENT ALL OPIE AND ANTHONY.
DOESN'T MATTER, BRADBURY.
COME ON, SNEAK ME OUT OF HERE BEFORE MY PRESS SECRETARY SHOWS UP TO SCREAM AT ME.
BUT I DIDN'T HEAR YOUR ANSWER TO WHETHER OR NOT YOU'D ICE OSAMA.
AND NEITHER DID ANYONE ELSE. IT'S A "HAVE YOU STOPPED BEATING YOUR WIFE?" TRAP.
IF I SAY I'D KILL HIM, I LOOK LIKE A HYPOCRITE. IF I SAY I WOULDN'T, I SOUND WEAK ON SECURITY.
SOMETIMES, IT'S BEST TO LET YOUR RECORD SPEAK FOR ITSELF, YOU KNOW?
I GUESS.
THOUGH IT AIN'T LIKE MANY FOLKS HAVE HEARD BOTH SIDES OF *YOUR* ALBUM.
HEY, IF THEY WERE GONNA GIVE YOU THE CHAIR TOMORROW, WHAT'S ON YOUR MENU?
FOR MY LAST MEAL?
I HAVE NO IDEA, BRADBURY.

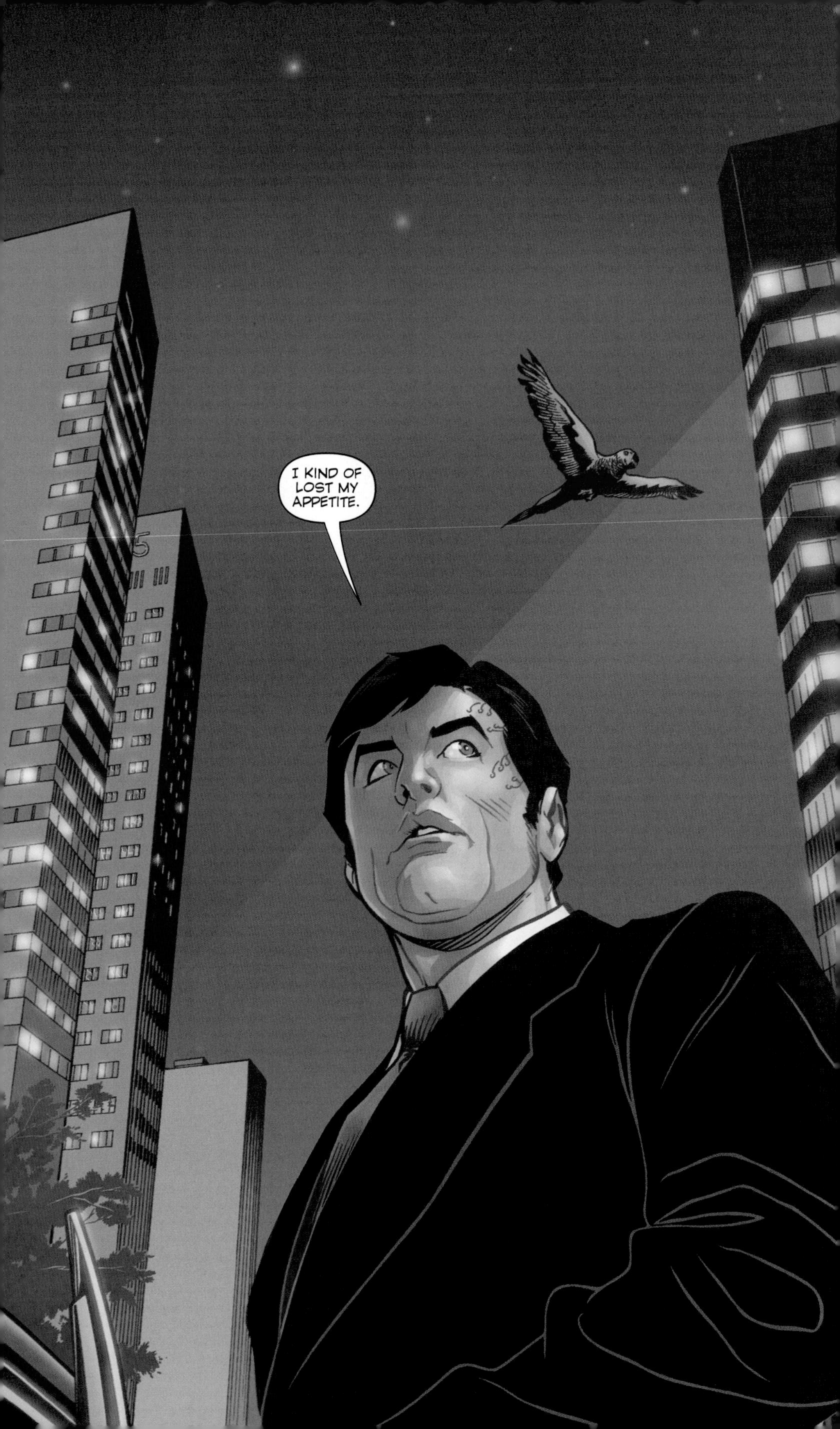
I KIND OF LOST MY APPETITE.

## A NOTE FROM THE EDITOR:

**In Book One, we showed you Brian's original proposal for this series. This time, we've got the full script to issue #20, presented with Tony's pencils. Enjoy!**

The Full Script for
EX MACHINA #20
Prepared for Tony Harris
and WildStorm
February 18, 2006

### Page One

**Page One, Panel One**
Okay, we open with this close-up of DEPUTY MAYOR WYLIE, looking sincerely apologetic.

1) Wylie: On behalf of the City of New York, I offer my most sincere condolences for the loss of your son.

**Page One, Panel Two**
One of these things, same as always:

2) Date (in the style of a right-justified newspaper heading): **Tuesday, February 18, 2003**

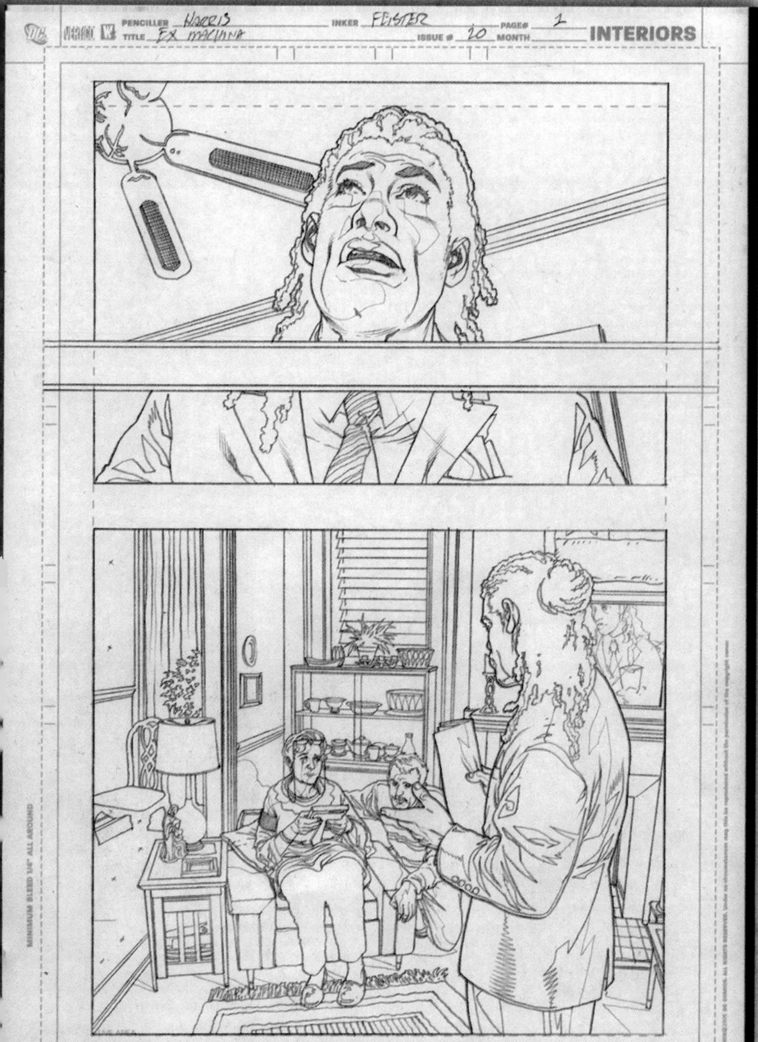

PENCILLER HARRIS
TITLE EX MACHINA
INKER FEISTER
ISSUE # 20
PAGE# 1
MONTH
INTERIORS
DOUBLE PAGE SPREAD: CUT AS SHOWN, ABUT PAGE EDGES, TAPE ON BACK, DO NOT OVERLAP


**Page One, Panel Three**
Pull out to the largest panel of the page, as we reveal that we're inside of a modestly decorated Brooklyn living room of an OLDER CHILEAN WOMAN and her TWENTY-SOMETHING SON, who has a military-style flattop haircut (this is the family of the kid shot by police last issue). It's the middle of the night, and the frightened and confused woman is seated in a chair. Her son is standing behind her. Wylie is also standing as he solemnly addresses the two.

3) Wylie: My name is David Wylie, ma'am.

4) Wylie: I want you to know that Mayor Hundred would be here to talk with you himself, but he's working to find the terrorists behind this weekend's gassing of the protesters at--

5) Woman: The reporters say they… they shot our boy. In the back. Why? He was seventeen!

## Page Two

**Page Two, Panel One**
Change angles on the three characters, as the young man silently listens to his mother argue with Wylie.

1) Wylie: Ma'am, your son apparently ran from two officers at a police checkpoint.

2) Woman: Why would he do that? He's… he's not even Arab. We're Chilean!

3) Wylie: I promise you that race had nothing to do with this.

4) Woman: And we're supposed to believe that because you're black? That's why they sent you here, right?

**Page Two, Panel Two**
Push in on Wylie, as he sheepishly says:

5) Wylie: I'm very sorry to have to tell you this, but Patricio was found carrying several ounces of cocaine.
6) Wylie: We think that's why he--

**Page Two, Panel Three**
Pull out to the largest panel of the page for a shot of Wylie and the woman, as the horrified woman LEAPS out of her chair at the startled Deputy Mayor.

7) Woman: LIAR!

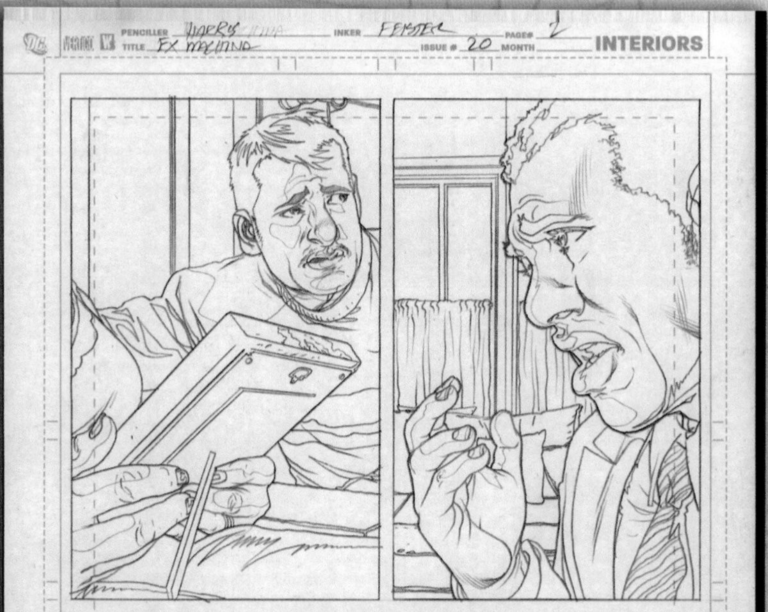

INTERIORS
DOUBLE PAGE SPREAD: CUT AS SHOWN, ABUT PAGE EDGES, TAPE ON BACK, DO NOT OVERLAP

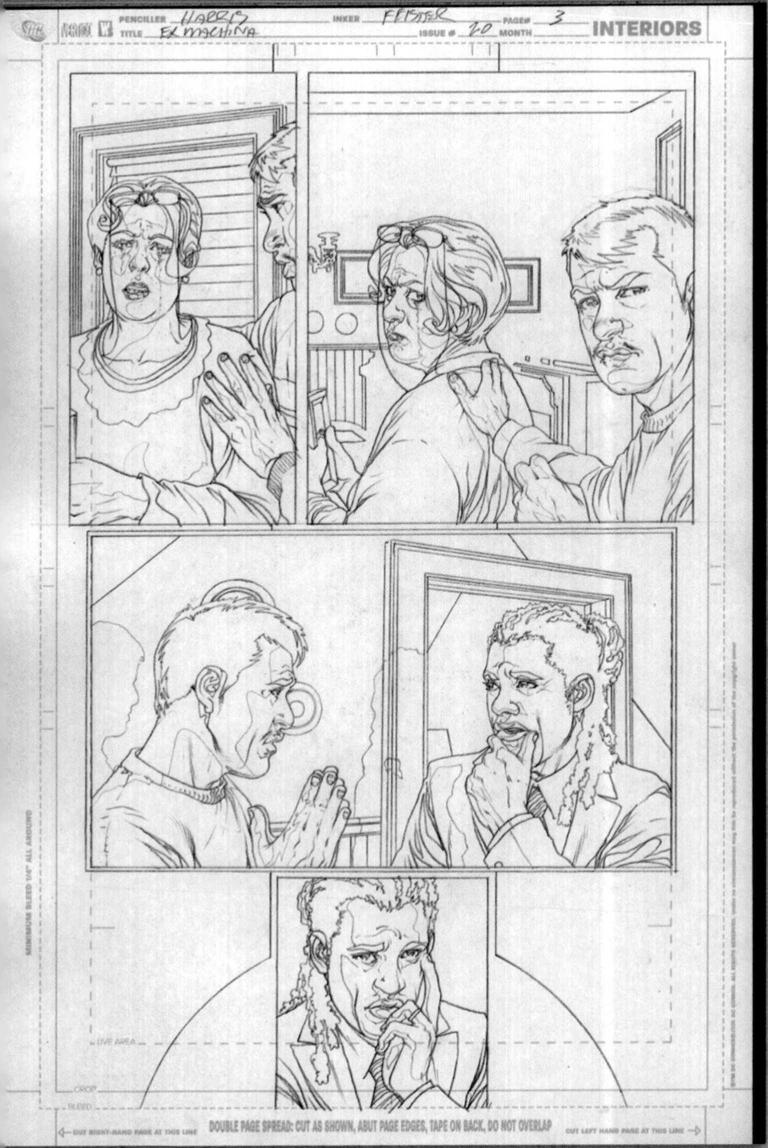
PENCILLER HARRIS
INKER PFISTER
PAGE# 3
TITLE EX MACHINA
ISSUE # 20
MONTH
INTERIORS
DOUBLE PAGE SPREAD: CUT AS SHOWN, ABUT PAGE EDGES, TAPE ON BACK, DO NOT OVERLAP

## Page Three

### Page Three, Panel One

Pull out to a shot of all three characters for this largest panel of the page, as the young man PULLS his cursing mother off of Wylie.

1) Man: Mom, enough!

2) Woman: ¡Vaya al infierno!

### Page Three, Panel Two

Change angles on the three, as the woman storms off into another part of the house. Wylie brushes himself off as he talks with the dead kid's brother.

3) Wylie: I know past administrations have automatically sided with the NYPD in incidents like this, but I swear to you that there will be a full and vigorous investigation.

4) Man: We don't want one, Mr. Deputy Mayor. My family has no intention of taking action against the city.

5) Man: I graduated West Point. I… I understand that honest mistakes happen in the fog of war.

### Page Three, Panel Three

Push in closer on the two, as Wylie pulls the young man close to confide his personal feelings with him. Please leave room for the talky-talk, Tony.

6) Wylie: We're not at war with ourselves. Look, I'm speaking to you as a private citizen here, not on behalf of my superiors… but this has to be investigated.

7) Man: Why, so my brother's… mistakes can be shared with the world? So our family's name can be dragged through the mud?

8) Wylie: That's what this is about? Son, your brother's crimes were trivial. The country needs to see that groundless invasions of privacy do more harm than good.

9) Man: But it's okay for you to invade our privacy, huh? As long as it's furthering some cause? I'm sorry, sir, but this is about real people.

### Page Three, Panel Four

Push in on Wylie, looking hurt and tired.

10) Man (from off): Why can't the folks in charge ever understand that?

## Page Four

### Page Four, Panel One

Smash cut to later that late night for this image on a FLATSCREEN TELEVISION. We're at the crime scene from last issue, and a news camera is showing several DETECTIVES standing over the sheet-covered BODY of the kid killed by the NYPD.

No Copy

### Page Four, Panel Two

Pull out to the largest panel of the page, as we reveal that we're in the upstairs City Hall office of MAYOR HUNDRED, who is watching this flatscreen television with COMMISSIONER AMY ANGOTTI. The evidence-bagged GAS CANISTERS Amy had at the end of last issue are now on Mitch's desk.

1) Mitchell: How's the officer who did the shooting, Commissioner?

2) Amy: Tried to kill himself with his service weapon about an hour ago.
3) Amy: His partner stopped him, thank Christ. He's on suicide watch at the psych ward now.

### Page Four, Panel Three

Push in on Amy, calmly pleading her case.

4) Amy: This is what terrorism is, Mr. Mayor.

5) Amy: All it takes is that first spark of violence, and the wildfire will just keep taking more and more lives, until the source of the inferno is extinguished.

6) Amy: I understand why you're reluctant to use your… communication skills, but without your help, I'm worried we'll never find the bastards behind--

### Page Four, Panel Four

Cut back to Mitch, as he suddenly says:

7) Mitchell: I'm in.

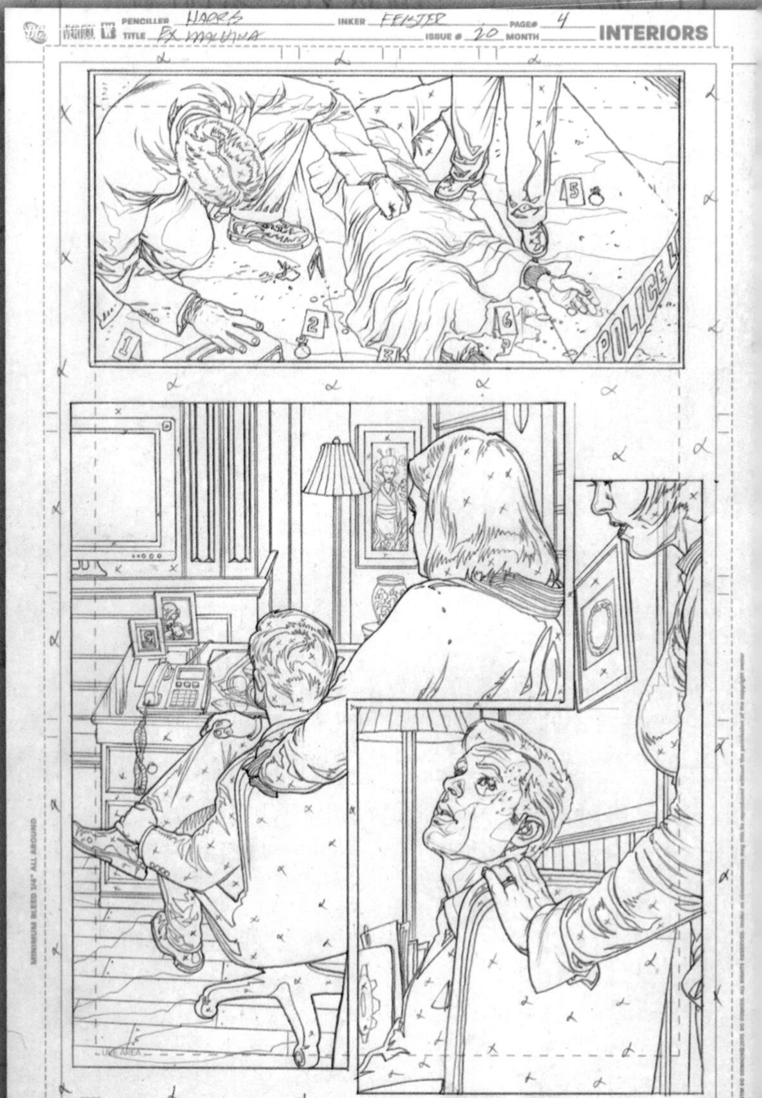

INTERIORS
POLICE
DOUBLE PAGE SPREAD: CUT AS SHOWN, ABUT PAGE EDGES, TAPE ON BACK, DO NOT OVERLAP

PENCILLER HARRIS
INKER FEISTER
PAGE# 5
INTERIORS
TITLE EX MACHINA
ISSUE # 20 MONTH
DOUBLE PAGE SPREAD: CUT AS SHOWN, ABUT PAGE EDGES, TAPE ON BACK, DO NOT OVERLAP

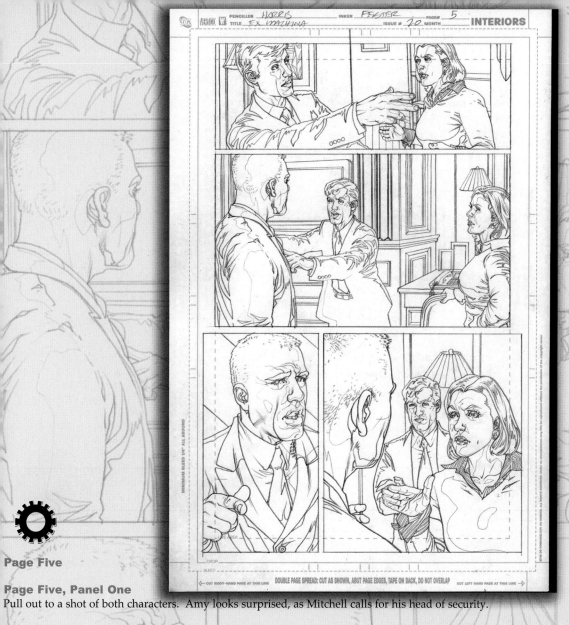

## Page Five

### Page Five, Panel One

Pull out to a shot of both characters. Amy looks surprised, as Mitchell calls for his head of security.

1) Amy: You're… you're sure?

2) Mitchell: Bradbury!

### Page Five, Panel Two

Pull out to the largest panel of the page for this shot of Mitchell and BRADBURY, as Bradbury enters the room and talks with his boss.

3) Bradbury: What's up, boss?

4) Mitchell: I'm going to disappear for a while, and I need you to stay here and cover for me with the rest of your security detail until I get back.

### Page Five, Panel Three

Push in on Bradbury, who obviously thinks this is an awful idea.

5) Bradbury: All due respect, but like fuck, sir.
6) Bradbury: Your life is my responsibility and--

### Page Five, Panel Four

Cut over to Amy, as she sternly says:
7) Amy: And I outrank you, Mr. Bradbury.
8) Amy: I promise, your friend will be in good hands.

## Page Six

### Page Six, Panel One

Change angles for this largest panel of the page, a shot of Bradbury and Amy, as the two old enemies have a showdown.

1) Bradbury: Her? You're doing the vigilante thing with her?
2) Bradbury: After all the times this lady went out of her way to ruin something we busted our humps to pull off back in the Great Machine days?

3) Amy: And I'd do it again tomorrow. Tonight is a one-time-only deal.

PENCILLER HARRIS
TITLE EX MACHINA
INKER PFISTER
ISSUE # 20
PAGE# 6
MONTH
INTERIORS
DOUBLE PAGE SPREAD: CUT AS SHOWN, ABUT PAGE EDGES, TAPE ON BACK, DO NOT OVERLAP

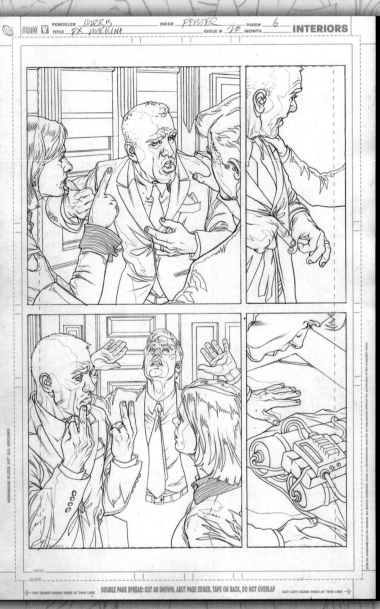

### Page Six, Panel Two

Change angles for this shot of Mitchell and a confused Bradbury.

4) Mitchell: Please, we won't need long.

5) Bradbury: Jesus, are you sleeping with her?

6) Mitchell: Bradbury, Angotti and I are hunting for whoever put Journal in her coma, but no one can know that I'm involved in… whatever happens next. Understood?

### Page Six, Panel Three

Change angles for another shot of Bradbury and Amy.

7) Bradbury: You get three hours.
8) Bradbury: Now you see why me and Kremlin did what we did, Commish? You see how the letter of the law don't always spell out exactly what you need it to?

9) Amy: I'm not going to stand here while some glorified bouncer explains the criminal justice system to--

10) Mitchell (from off): Shut up, both of you.

### Page Six, Panel Four

Finally, cut back to Mitchell, who's now holding up the bagged device that was on his desk.

11) Mitchell: I'm trying to listen to this thing.

## Page Seven

### Page Seven, Panel One

Cut to later than night for this establishing shot of the lit-up UNISPHERE sculpture in Queens:
http://www.playle.com/KDL/64689.jpg
http://www.bjwhalen.com/pics/globe1.jpg

No Copy

### Page Seven, Panel Two

Cut inside an UNMARKED CAR for this largest panel of the page, a shot of Amy (in the driver's seat) and Mitch (holding the bagged terrorist device while sitting in the car's passenger side). As a kind of disguise, Mitch is now wearing an NYPD S.W.A.T. JACKET and a black WATCH CAP like this one:http://www.heatreliefdepot.com/catalog/images/mfg_hotrods_1073.gif

1) Amy: Wait, how do you know this contraption Josh found was built in Queens?

2) Mitchell: Take the next left.
3) Mitchell: Sorry, it's probably a federal offense for you to know any more than you already do.

4) Amy: Yeah, well, in for a penny…

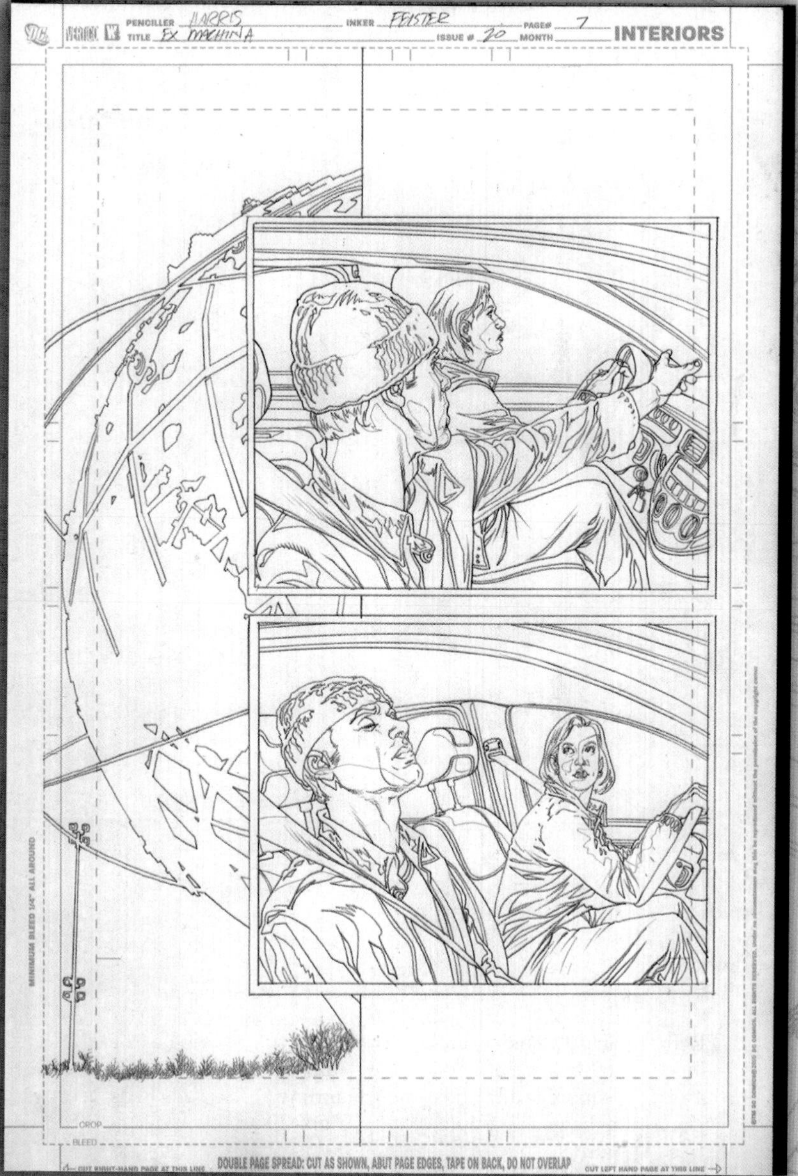
PENCILLER HARRIS
TITLE EX MACHINA
INKER FEISTER
PAGE# 7
ISSUE # 20
MONTH
INTERIORS
CROP
BLEED
DOUBLE PAGE SPREAD: CUT AS SHOWN, ABUT PAGE EDGES, TAPE ON BACK, DO NOT OVERLAP

### Page Seven, Panel Three

Push in on Mitch, as he closes his eyes and MEDITATES.

5) Mitchell: The night that I first… changed, I experienced a kind of sensory overload, blacked out half of Manhattan. After that, my abilities re-presented
themselves slowly, like a stroke patient learning to talk again.
6) Mitchell: At first, I could only "hear" machines that I was holding. Over time, I discovered the ability to "talk back" to them. And with practice, I extended my reach to any machine that I could see…

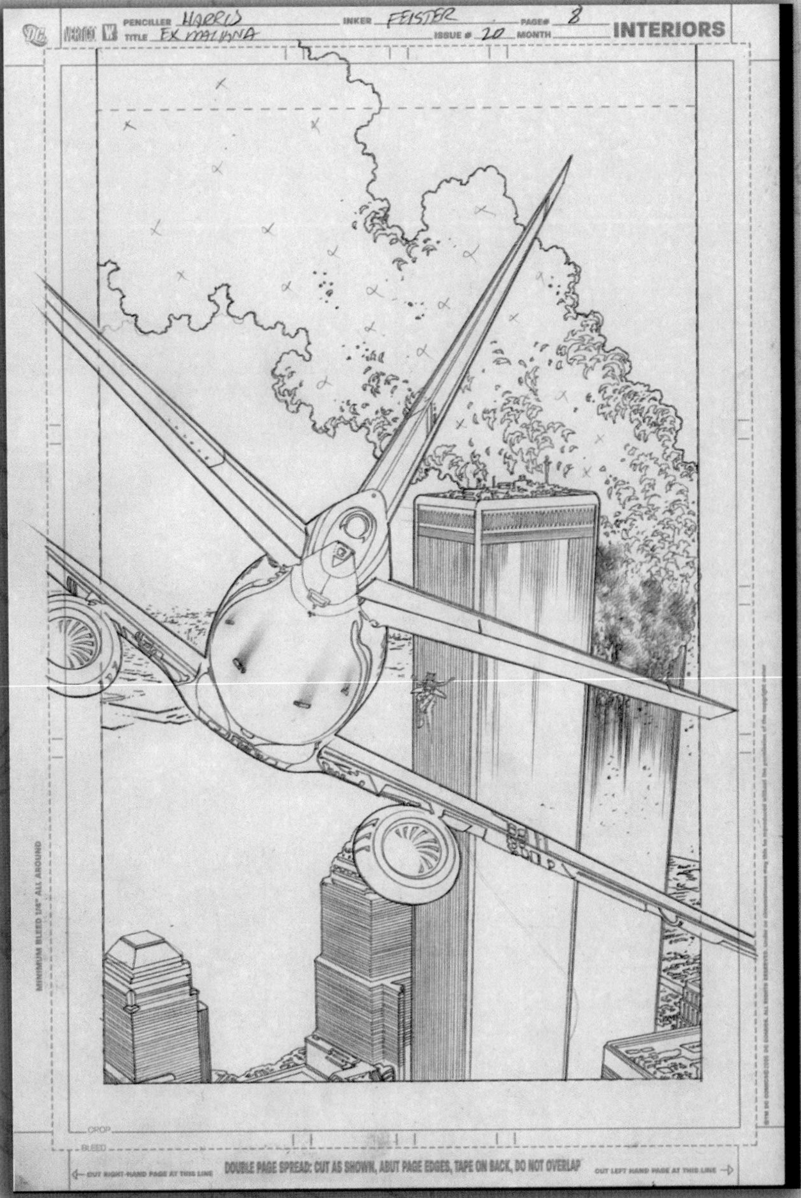
PENCILLER HARRIS
INKER FEISTER
PAGE# 8
TITLE EX MACHINA
ISSUE # 20
MONTH
INTERIORS
DOUBLE PAGE SPREAD: CUT AS SHOWN, ABUT PAGE EDGES, TAPE ON BACK, DO NOT OVERLAP

## Page Eight

### Page Eight, SPLASH

Okay, for this horrific SPLASH, we're going to look at the events of 9/11 from an angle we haven't yet seen. In the foreground of this shot, we're just behind the nose of a BOEING 767 (though we can't see inside the cockpit, or see ANY markings on this aircraft):

http://www.aerospaceweb.org/aircraft/jetliner/b767/b767_01.jpg
http://www.postcardpost.com/lt4.jpg

This plane is flying right at the GREAT MACHINE, who is hovering in the middle-ground of this shot, in front of the WORLD TRADE CENTER'S SOUTH TOWER, which is in front of the NORTH TOWER (the one with the big radio antenna), whose upper floors are BURNING in the background of this shot: http://news.bbc.co.uk/furniture/in_depth/americas/2001/day_of_terror/in_pictures/1.jpg

1) Tailless Balloon: Thankfully, I guess.

## Page Nine

### Page Nine, Panel One

Cut back to Mitchell, whose scars GLOW as he opens his eyes. Feel free to get extra design-y with this page, Tony, as Mitchell uses his powers to "telepathically" search for a machine somewhere out there. Maybe this can be in a similar style to your cellular phone "call-tracing scene" from the issue with Mitch's mom?

1) Mitchell: Anyway, by the time I retired, I was just learning to have a dialogue with devices beyond even my field of vision.

2) Mitchell: Hopefully, that's how I'm going to find this thing's master.

### Page Nine, Panel Two

Pull out to the largest panel of the page for another shot of Mitch and Amy, as Mitch holds up the bagged device.
3) Amy: Master?

4) Mitchell: Oh, "master/slave" is just an engineering term, but that's how my brain interprets the relationship--for lack of a better word--that some machines share.

5) Mitchell: See, this device was triggered by what looks like an engine from a radio-controlled car. That means it "misses" the remote that used to give it its orders. It's still calling out for it now.

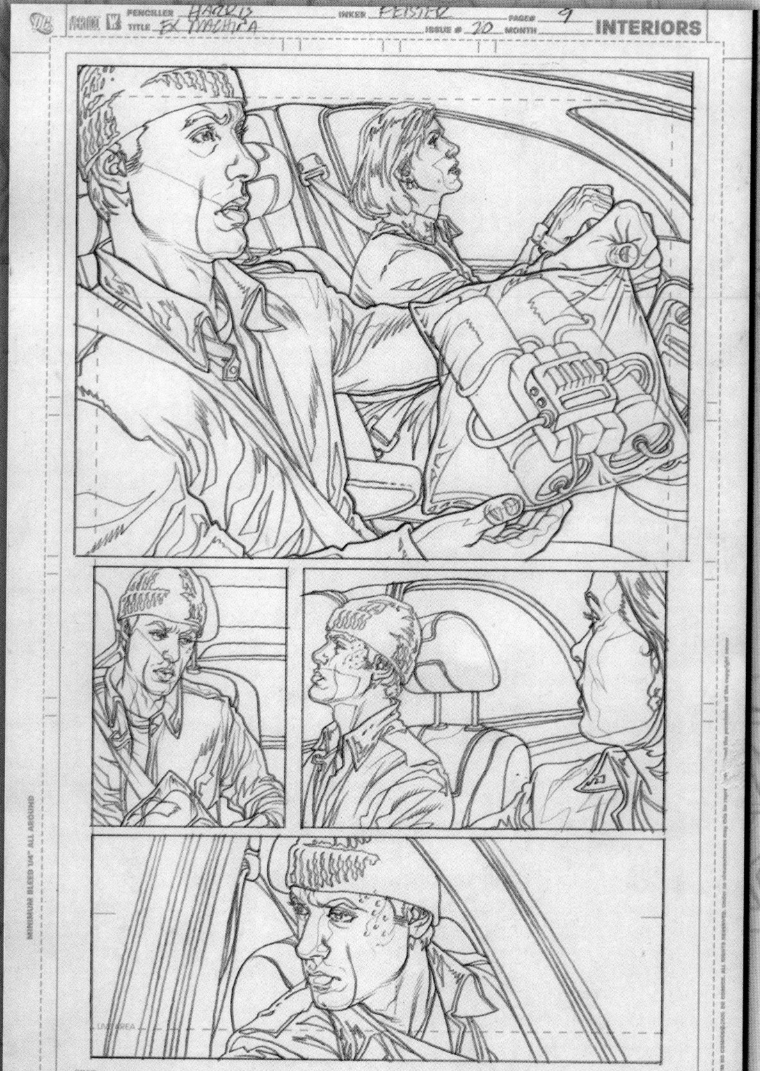
PENCILLER HARRIS
INKER FEISTER
PAGE# 9
TITLE EX MACHINA
ISSUE # 20 MONTH
INTERIORS
MINIMUM BLEED 1/4" ALL AROUND
DOUBLE PAGE SPREAD: CUT AS SHOWN, ABUT PAGE EDGES, TAPE ON BACK, DO NOT OVERLAP

### Page Nine, Panel Three

Push in on Amy and Mitch.

6) Amy: So you're eaves–dropping on a lonely piece of… sadomasochistic electronics?

7) Mitchell: I don't understand myself either most days.

8) Amy: But, whoever we're dealing with isn't an idiot. Odds are they ditched the remote right after they gassed those kids.

### Page Nine, Panel Four

Push in on Mitchell, as he looks out his window at the dark little houses in this Queens neighborhood.

9) Mitchell: Right, but I'm hoping this thing might point me in the direction of other devices that interfered with its past conversations. Cordless phones, high voltage transformers, shit like that.

10) Mitchell: They all work on pretty much the same frequency, but each wavelength is like a language to me. Even when everyone's speaking English, I can still pick out individual voices.

11) Mitchell: And one of them is getting louder…

**Page Ten**

**Page Ten, Panel One**

Cut outside this unmarked car, as it comes to a stop in a sleeping Queens neighborhood. There are a bunch of ROW HOUSES like these: http://www.bridgeandtunnelclub.com/bigmap/queens/flushing/boothmemorialave/

There's a MOTORCYCLE parked on the street in front of one of these houses. Your call what kind of bike, Tony.

1) From Car: Yeah, it's deafening now.

**Page Ten, Panel Two**

Cut inside the car for this largest panel of the page, a shot of Amy and Mitch, as Mitch pulls down his watch cap, which we can now see is actually a BLACK SKI MASK that hides most of his face.

2) Amy: So this is it? You're positive?

3) Mitchell: Well, this thing was activated somewhere nearby. It recognizes a microwave oven that used to interrupt its master's "sessions."

4) Mitchell: I can't guarantee the builder is still here, but it's worth us canvassing the block.

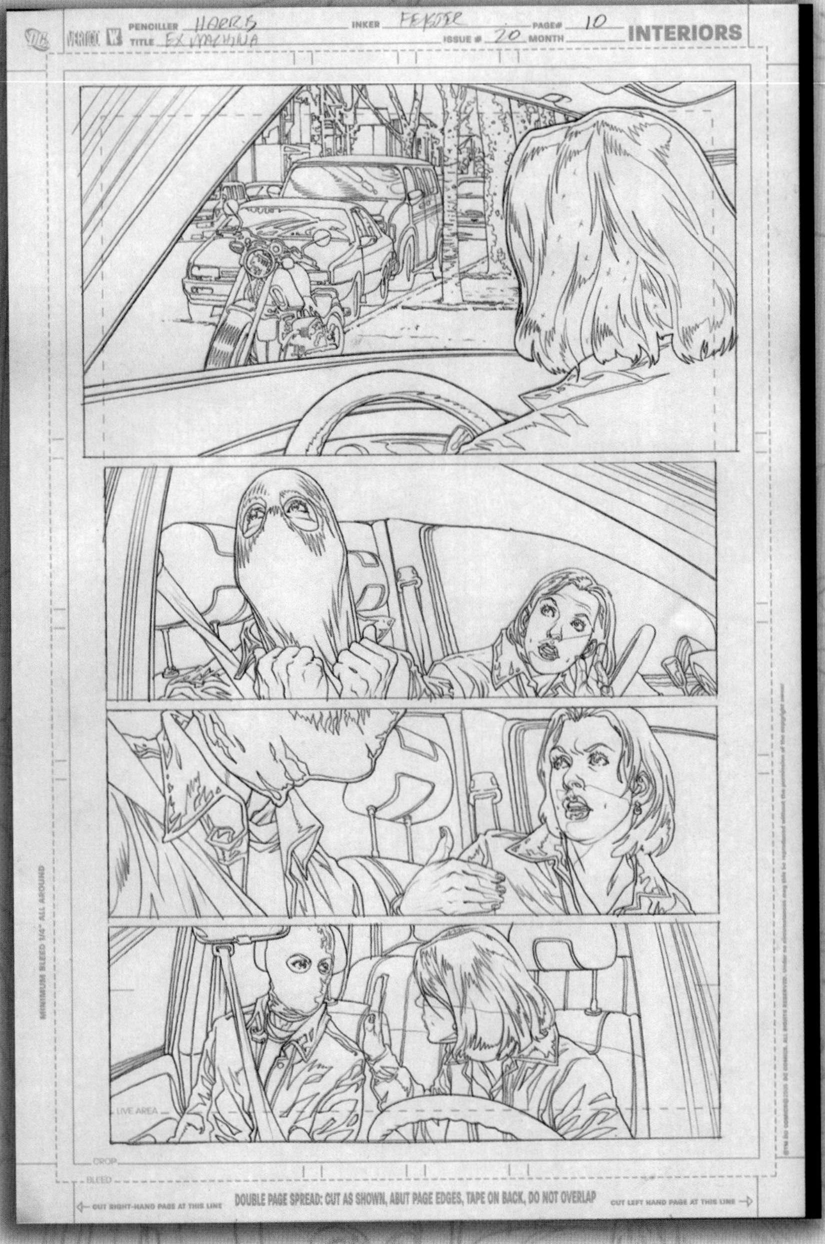

PENCILLER
INKER
PAGE# 10
INTERIORS
TITLE EX MACHINA
ISSUE # 20
MONTH
LIVE AREA
DROP
BLEED
MINIMUM BLEED 1/4" ALL AROUND
CUT RIGHT-HAND PAGE AT THIS LINE
DOUBLE PAGE SPREAD: CUT AS SHOWN, ABUT PAGE EDGES, TAPE ON BACK, DO NOT OVERLAP
CUT LEFT HAND PAGE AT THIS LINE


**Page Ten, Panel Three**

Change angles on Amy and the masked Mitchell.

5) Amy: No, it's not. You did your job, Mayor Hundred. I'm calling the feds to take it from here.

6) Mitchell: But… what are you going to tell them?

7) Amy: Anonymous tip? I don't know, but I'm not gonna risk sending my cops--especially pretend ones--into some terrorist's biological hot zone.

**Page Ten, Panel Four**

Push in on the masked Mitchell.

8) Mitchell: Amy, please. I'm afraid this… this isn't terrorism. I think whoever gassed those people has something to do with me.

9) Mitchell: I can't let anyone else get hurt because of some disgruntled hood I wronged in my past life. Just let me--

10) Amy (from off): Wait a second.

## Page Eleven

### Page Eleven, Panel One

We're looking over Amy's shoulder in the foreground of this shot, as she sees a MAN IN A MOTORCYCLE HELMET (the kind that totally obscures his face) stepping out of one of the row houses across the street.

1) Amy: Too late for drinking and too early for a paper route, right?

### Page Eleven, Panel Two

Change angles, as Amy sticks her head out the window, and yells at the off-panel dude with the motorcycle helmet.

2) Amy: Hey, buddy!
3) Amy: You know how the Knicks did last night?

### Page Eleven, Panel Three

Cut back to the guy with the motorcycle helmet for this largest panel of the page, as he suddenly pulls out a handgun and FIRES it at the off-panel car!

4) SFX: BLAM

### Page Eleven, Panel Four

Cut back to the car, as Amy and the masked Mitchell FLINCH as the bullet SMASHES through the middle of their windshield.

5) SFX: KARACK

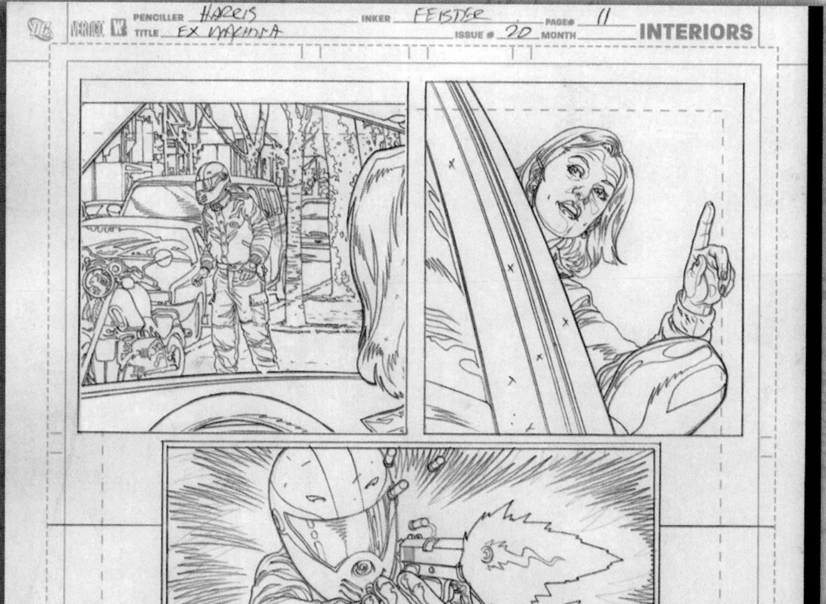

PENCILLER Harris
INKER Feister
PAGE# 11
TITLE Ex Machina
ISSUE # 20
MONTH
INTERIORS
DOUBLE PAGE SPREAD: CUT AS SHOWN, ABUT PAGE EDGES, TAPE ON BACK, DO NOT OVERLAP

**Page Twelve**

**Page Twelve, Panel One**
Cut behind Amy, as she hops out of the car and watches this guy JUMP on his motorcycle in the background of this shot.

1) Amy: Motherfucker…!

**Page Twelve, Panel Two**
Change angles on Amy, as she draws her GLOCK and aims it at the off-panel motorcycle guy.

2) Amy: NYPD!
3) Amy: Stop now or I put you--

4) Mitchell (from off, GREEN FONT): JAM!

**Page Twelve, Panel Three**
Pull out for this shot of Amy and Mitchell, as the masked Mitchell jumps out of his door. His scars GLOW under his ski mask. Amy looks pissed that he ruined her shot.
5) Amy: What are you doing?

6) Mitchell: I'm good with bikes.
7) Mitchell (GREEN FONT): Front wheel lock.

**Page Twelve, Panel Four**
For this largest panel of the page, cut to the guy speeding away on the motorcycle, as his front wheel suddenly LOCKS UP. The guy goes FLYING over the handlebars of his bike, forcing him to DROP his gun.

No Copy

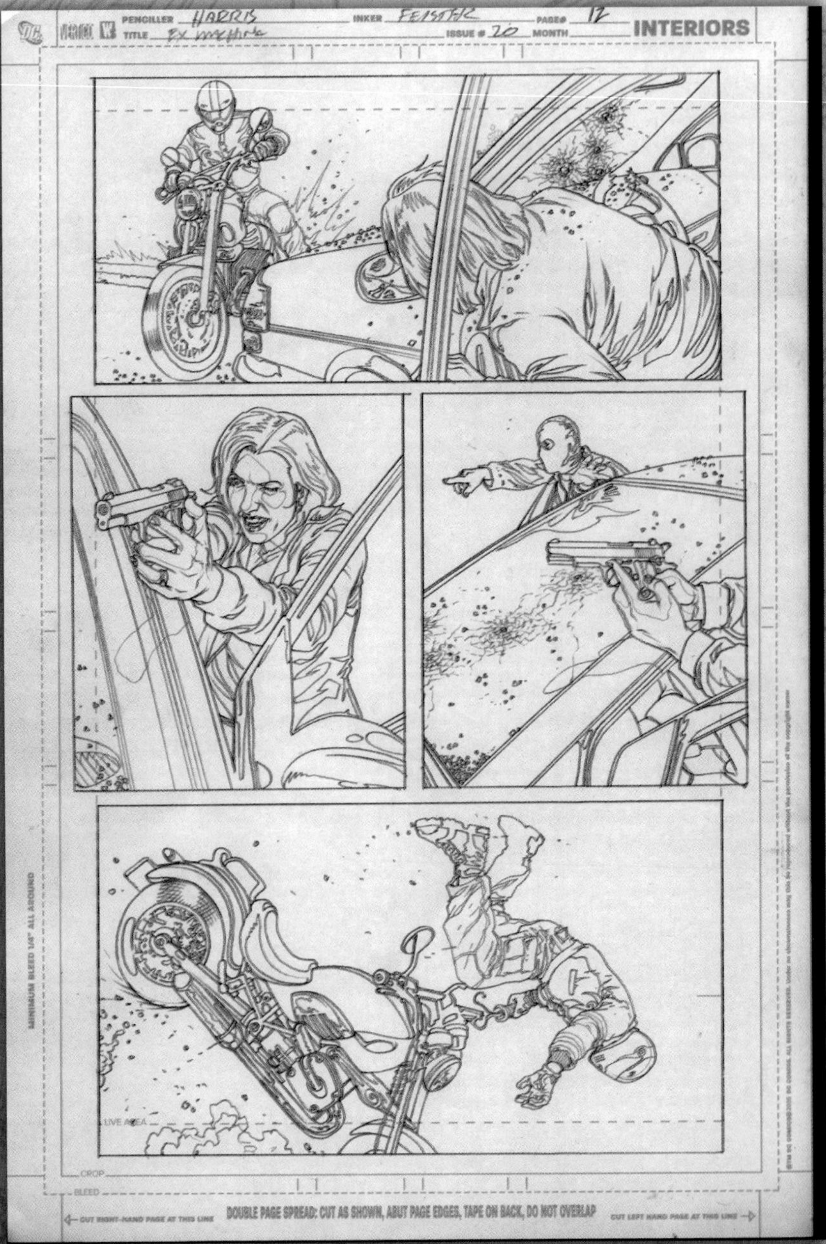

PENCILLER HARRIS
INKER FEISTER
PAGE# 12
INTERIORS
ISSUE # 20
MONTH
DOUBLE PAGE SPREAD: CUT AS SHOWN, ABUT PAGE EDGES, TAPE ON BACK, DO NOT OVERLAP

## Page Thirteen

### Page Thirteen, Panel One
Change angles for the largest panel of the page, as the guy SMASHES into the windshield of someone's empty parked car down the street.

No Copy

### Page Thirteen, Panel Two
Cut back to Amy and the disguised Mitchell, as they RACE for the off-panel Biker.

1) Amy: I had him dead to rights, goddammit!
2) Mitchell: He doesn't die until I get answers!

### Page Thirteen, Panel Three
Pull out for a shot of all three characters, as Amy aims her gun at the Biker, who's writhing in pain on the hood of a beat-up old car. Mitch is watching this tense standoff nervously.

3) Biker: Nnn…

4) Amy: Take off the helmet. Slowly, fuckface.

5) Biker: They sent… police to execute me?

### Page Thirteen, Panel Four
Push in on the Biker, as he removes his helmet, and we see his face for the first time. He's a THIRTY-SOMETHING ARABIC MAN, a new character we've never met before. Feel free to take inspiration from any of these infamous mugshots, Tony, though our final character should look totally unique:

http://www.danzfamily.com/pictures/pictures02/hijackers.jpg

6) Biker: Hn, I'd hoped to see the Great Machine one last time.

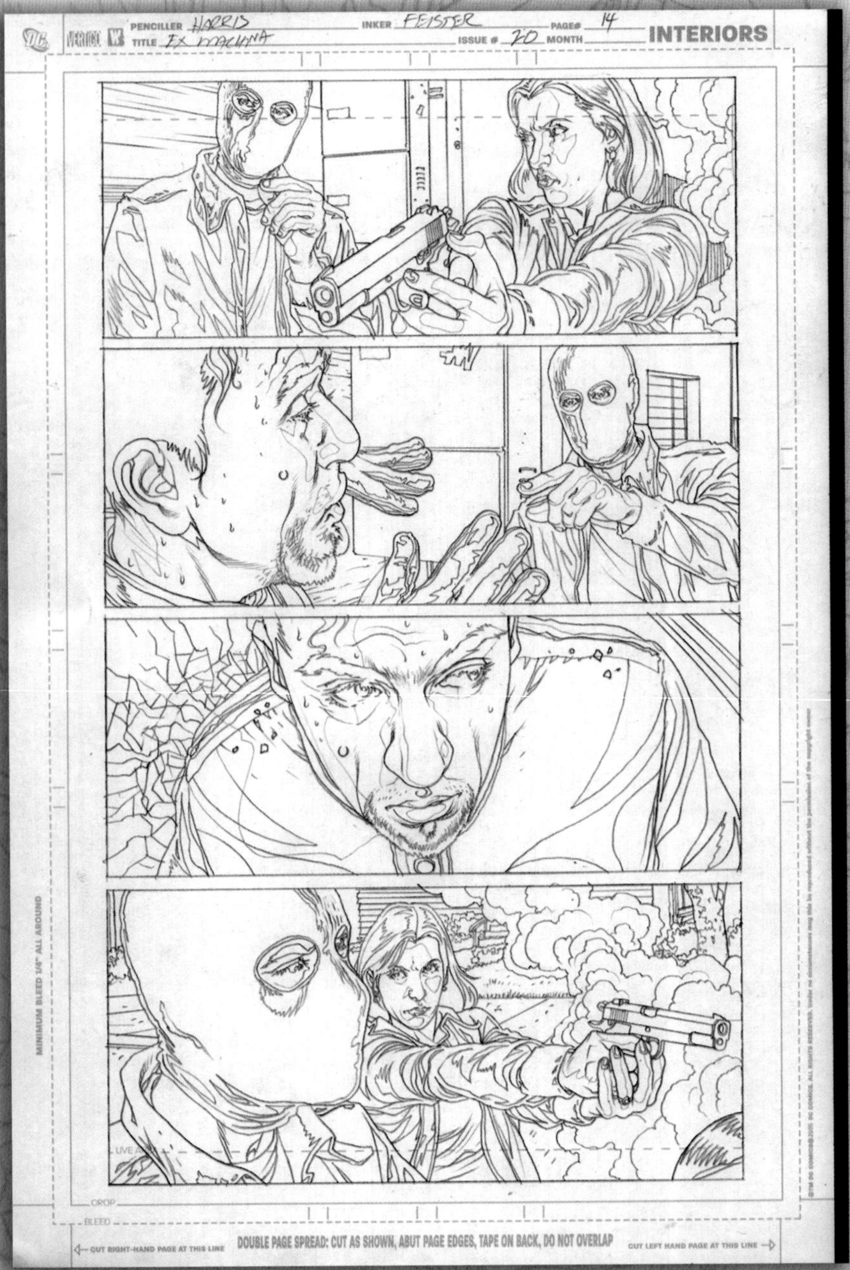
PENCILLER HARRIS
TITLE EX MACHINA
INKER FEISTER
ISSUE # 20
PAGE# 14
MONTH
INTERIORS
DOUBLE PAGE SPREAD: CUT AS SHOWN, ABUT PAGE EDGES, TAPE ON BACK, DO NOT OVERLAP

## Page Fourteen

### Page Fourteen, Panel One

Cut over to Amy and the masked Mitchell, both of whom look confused.

1) Amy: You have any idea who this is?

2) Mitchell: Never seen him in my life.
3) Mitchell: What are you? Iraqi?

### Page Fourteen, Panel Two

Pull out to the largest panel of the page, as the masked Mitchell angrily approaches this wounded man.

4) Biker: I'm an American citizen, officer. Like you.

5) Mitchell: And how do you know Mayor Hundred?

6) Biker: From the television, like everyone else. I watched him spare thousands of lives when he saved the South Tower.

### Page Fourteen, Panel Three

Push in on the biker for this extreme close-up, as he calmly says:

7) Biker: And I knew someone had to finish what was started that day.

### Page Fourteen, Panel Four

Cut back to Mitchell, completely stunned.

8) Mitchell: This… this is about 9/11?

9) Amy (from off): Ah, "Officer?"

## Page Fifteen

### Page Fifteen, Panel One

Cut over to Amy, as she sees the lights of two POLICE CARS approaching far down the street. They're about a minute away.

1) Amy: We got unis incoming.
2) Amy: Someone must have called in the gunshot.

### Page Fifteen, Panel Two

Cut back to Mitchell for this largest panel of the page, as he GRABS the biker by the front of his jacket (or whatever) and PULLS him up to his eye level.

3) Biker: Yes, if you're going to kill me, you'd better do it now.

4) Mitchell: Fuck you. I'm not giving you the satisfaction of… of seventy-two virgins.

5) Biker: Don't insult me. I'm a scientist. An atheist. Believing that this is about religion is why you people are going to lose your "war on terror."

### Page Fifteen, Panel Three

Push in closer on the two men.

6) Mitchell: Then why? Why the fuck did you murder innocent demonstrators?

7) Biker: I never said I did.
8) Biker: If this is over, I'd like to speak to my attorney now.

9) Amy (from off): Sir, they're almost--

### Page Fifteen, Panel Four

This is just a tight shot of Mitch (from the biker's P.O.V.) as he SCREAMS right in our face.

10) Mitchell: Tell me why you killed those people!

### Page Fifteen, Panel Five

And finally (sorry to give you a fifth panel here, Tony, but this is important!), this is just a close-up of the biker, staring at us silently, without a hint of an emotion. He's not giving us the satisfaction of an answer.

No Copy

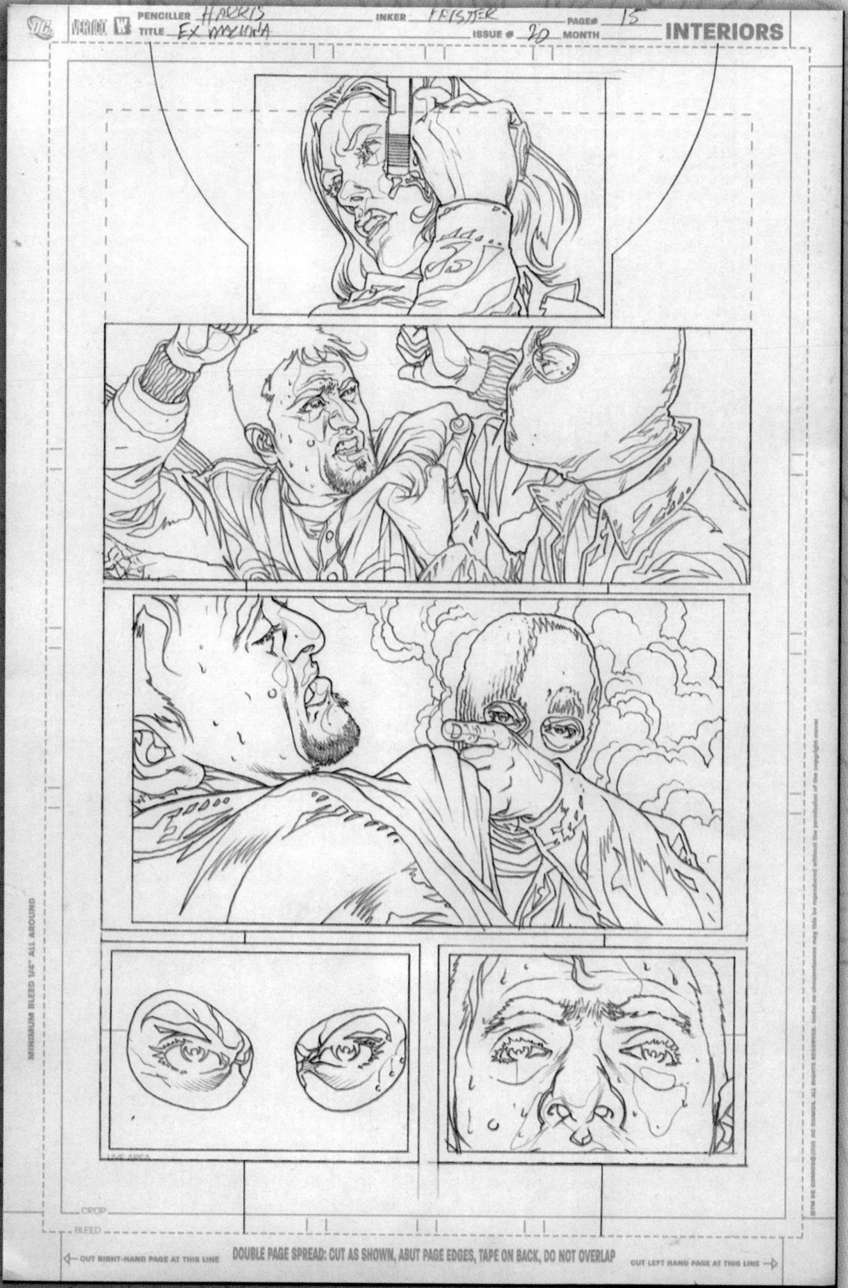
PENCILLER HARRIS
INKER FEISTER
PAGE# 15
TITLE EX MACHINA
ISSUE # 20
MONTH
INTERIORS
MINIMUM BLEED 1/4" ALL AROUND
CROP
BLEED
CUT RIGHT-HAND PAGE AT THIS LINE
DOUBLE PAGE SPREAD: CUT AS SHOWN, ABUT PAGE EDGES, TAPE ON BACK, DO NOT OVERLAP
CUT LEFT HAND PAGE AT THIS LINE

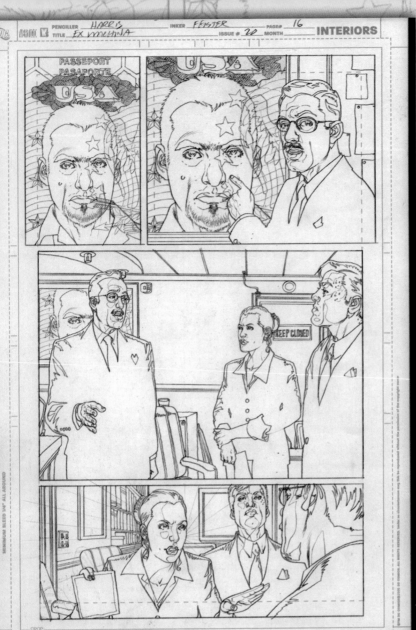

PENCILLER HARRIS
INKER FEISTER
PAGE# 16
INTERIORS
TITLE EX MACHINA
ISSUE # 20
MONTH
PASSPORT
PASAPORTE
USA
KEEP CLOSED
CROP
BLEED
MINIMUM BLEED 1/4" ALL AROUND
DOUBLE PAGE SPREAD: CUT AS SHOWN, ABUT PAGE EDGES, TAPE ON BACK, DO NOT OVERLAP

## Page Sixteen

### Page Sixteen, Panel One

Smash cut to the next morning for this shot of a color PASSPORT PHOTO of the biker (who we'll soon learn is named SAMMIR HALLOUDA), taken from two or so years ago.

1) Lafayette (from off): His name is Sammir Hallouda.

### Page Sixteen, Panel Two

Pull out to the largest panel of the page to reveal that we're back in the SITUATION ROOM from two issues ago. Homeland Security SPECIAL AGENT LAFAYETTE is standing in front of a large projected picture of Hallouda's passport photo.

2) Lafayette: He's not talking now that he lawyered up, but Homeland Security recovered bomb-making manuals and castor bean residue at his house. No question he's our man.
3) Lafayette: That said, Hallouda's not on any CIA watch lists, and he didn't register a single blip from foreign intelligence. How the hell did you track him down?

### Page Sixteen, Panel Three

Cut over to Mitchell (wearing his standard suit and tie) and Amy Angotti, the only other two people in this room. Mitchell starts to confess what happened, but Amy interrupts him.

4) Mitchell: Special Agent Lafayette, we--

5) Amy: We set up surveillance cameras outside of every major subway stop in the five boroughs.
6) Amy: Hallouda was spotted running from a station when he caught a glimpse of one of the checkpoints Mayor Hundred ordered

### Page Sixteen, Panel Four

Push in on Amy, as she holds up a black-and-white print-out of a screen grab from a grainy surveillance video. This photo clearly shows Hallouda nervously exiting a subway entrance in Queens like this one: http://www.mylife2live.com/mt/subway.jpg

7) Amy: A detective showed this screen-grab to a dealer in the Diamond District, jogged an old guy's memory.
8) Amy: He gave us the address of someone who put in an order for acetone two weeks before the gassing. I would have called you boys, but I happened to be in the guy's twenty when details came up on my onboard, so…

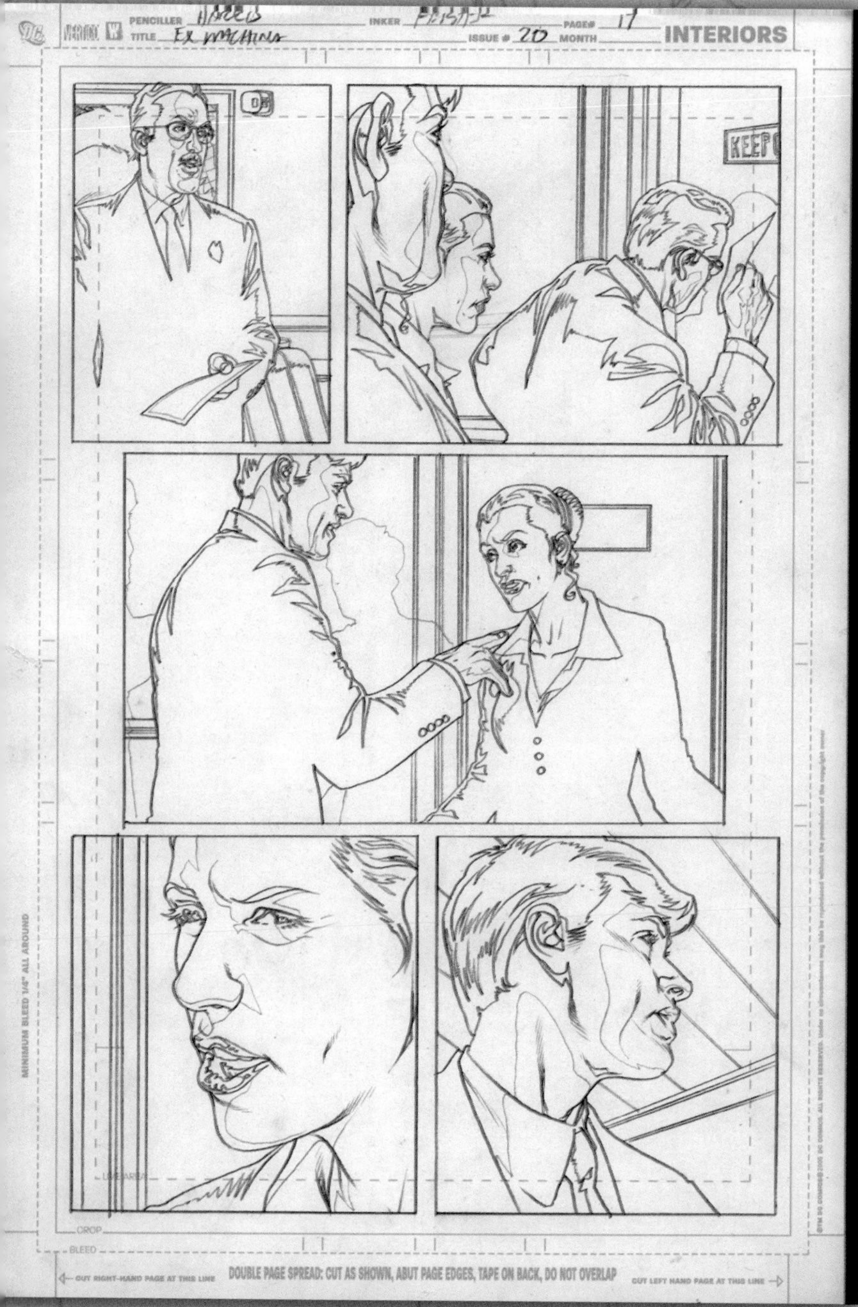
PENCILLER
INKER
PAGE# 17
TITLE Ex Machina
ISSUE # 20
MONTH
INTERIORS
KEEP
DOUBLE PAGE SPREAD: CUT AS SHOWN, ABUT PAGE EDGES, TAPE ON BACK, DO NOT OVERLAP

## Page Seventeen

### Page Seventeen, Panel One

Cut over to Lafayette, as he takes the printout Amy just handed him. He's not quite sure what to believe.

1) Lafayette: …
2) Lafayette: I have a meeting with the President in twenty minutes. He'd appreciate it if neither of you spoke with the press until you've been briefed by Justice.

### Page Seventeen, Panel Two

Pull out to the largest panel of the page for a shot of all three characters, as Lafayette coldly walks out of the situation room, leaving Mitchell and Amy alone.

3) Lafayette: Anyway, thanks of a grateful nation and all that.

### Page Seventeen, Panel Three

Push in on Mitchell and Amy, as they whisper to each other. Mitch can't believe what Amy apparently did.

4) Mitchell: You fabricated a photo?
5) Amy: Of course not. While I was in booking, I had Kurson fast-forward through the last sixty hours of footage from a stop down the street from Hallouda's home.
6) Amy: This prick actually did try to get on a train yesterday, sir. Who knows how many lives our bag checks--

7) Mitchell: What about your "witness?"

### Page Seventeen, Panel Four

This is just a small shot of Amy.

8) Amy: He's legit, too. A dealer really did eyeball this asshole placing a major acetone order. He just made the I.D. this morning, after Hallouda was in custody.
9) Amy: We may have bended the law a bit, but the evidence is genuine, Mr. Mayor. This barbarian's gonna get the needle.

### Page Seventeen, Panel Five

Finally (sorry, but this fifth panel's important, too!), this is just a small shot of Mitch, not looking particularly satisfied about this finale.

10) Amy (from off): End of story.

**Page Eighteen**

**Page Eighteen, Panel One**

I know these big establishing shots are a pain in the ass, Tony, but this one is important to show that a lot of time has passed. Anyway, this is a sunny early morning shot of a poorly maintained EAST VILLAGE GARDEN. It's early spring now, and the trees are green again: http://www.cgpix.com/images/East_Village/East_Village_Garden.jpg

No Copy

**Page Eighteen, Panel Two**

Cut inside one of those East Village apartments for this shot of reporter SUZANNE PADILLA, wearing conservative work attire. She's standing at the open door of her apartment, holding a big BOUQUET OF YELLOW ROSES.

1) Suzanne: Don't yellow roses mean goodbye?

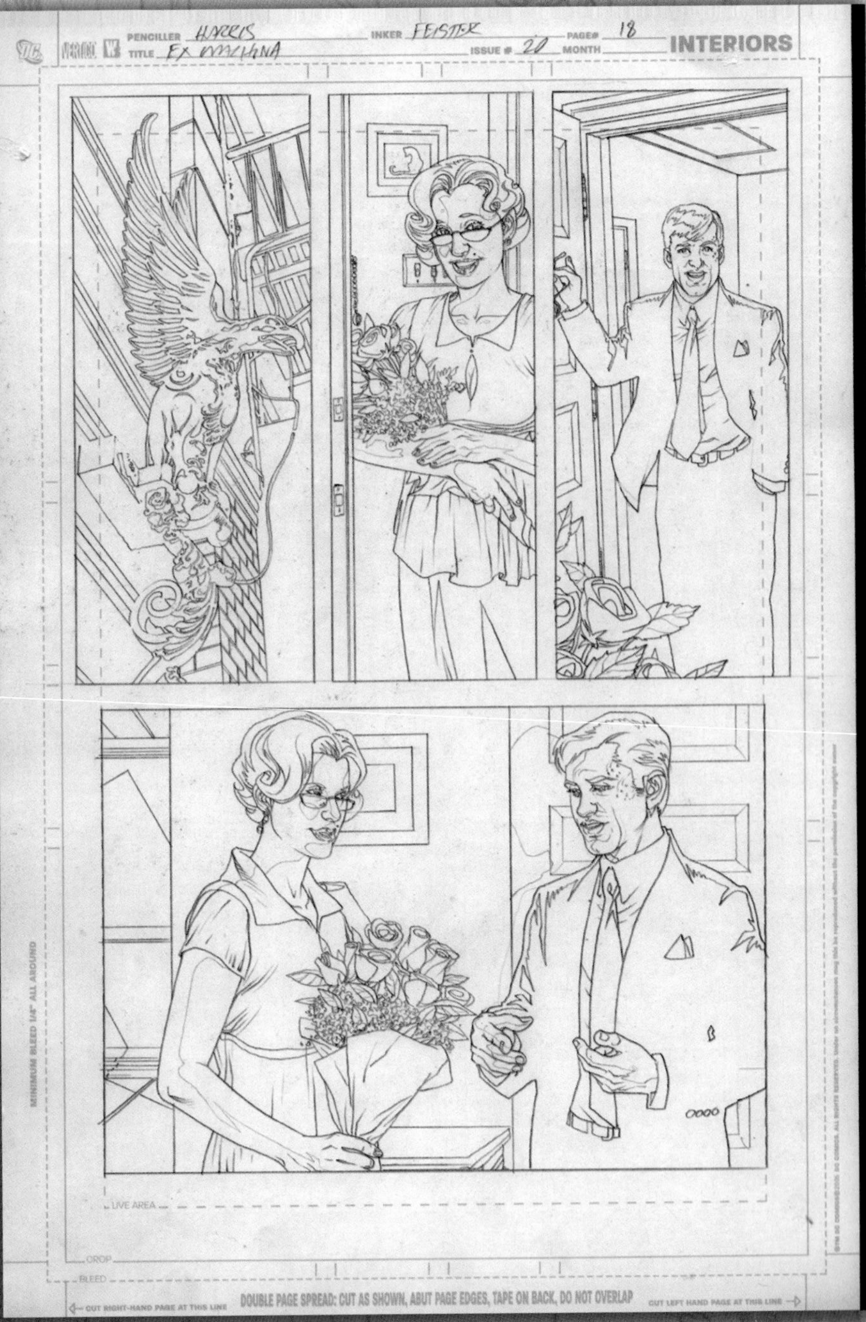
PENCILLER HARRIS
INKER FEISTER
PAGE# 18
TITLE EX MACHINA
ISSUE # 20
MONTH
INTERIORS
LIVE AREA
CROP
BLEED
MINIMUM BLEED 1/4" ALL AROUND
DOUBLE PAGE SPREAD: CUT AS SHOWN, ABUT PAGE EDGES, TAPE ON BACK, DO NOT OVERLAP

**Page Eighteen, Panel Three**

Change angles for this shot of an apologetic Mitchell, standing in Suzanne's hallway. It's early morning now, so he's in his regular attire, on his way to work.

2) Mitchell: Sorry, it… it was all they had left at the deli.

3) Mitchell: I wanted to apologize for being out of touch for so many weeks, Suzanne. Can I come in?

**Page Eighteen, Panel Four**

Push in on Suzanne, as she opens the door, and sheepishly admits:

4) Suzanne: Sure, but, uh… my boyfriend is picking me up in a little bit.

## Page Nineteen

### Page Nineteen, Panel One

Cut to Mitchell as he walks inside.

1) Mitchell: Ah.
2) Mitchell: Well, add that to the long list of things I should have seen coming.

### Page Nineteen, Panel Two

Pull out to a shot of both characters, as Mitchell sits down on Suzanne's couch. Suzanne is reaching for something here.

3) Suzanne: Look, I know you still feel responsible for what happened at the Iraq protests, but you--

4) Mitchell: I was the only one who didn't recognize what we were dealing with.
5) Mitchell: I was too busy looking at red herrings and fucking archenemies. Ever since the 11th, I've been living in this… this fantasy world.

### Page Nineteen, Panel Three

Push in on Suzanne, as she hands a newspaper to the off-panel Mitchell. We can't see what's in it yet.

6) Suzanne: That's not how the rest of the city sees it.
7) Suzanne: Did you catch what was in the Voice after your team caught Hallouda?

### Page Nineteen, Panel Four

This largest panel of the page is just a shot of the newspaper now in Mitch's hand. We're tight on a CARTOON drawn in the same style as the one from the first chapter of this story. It's a caricature of Mitchell Hundred (in regular clothes, no cape) shaking hands with a CARTOON POLICE OFFICER, who's joined by a CARTOON FIREFIGHTER and a CARTOON PARAMEDIC. The tone of the cartoon is respectful this time. The city really has been celebrating Mitchell, even the cartoonists.

8) Suzanne (from off): They finally got rid of your cape.

9) Cartoon Police Officer: "Welcome to the real heroes' club, sir."

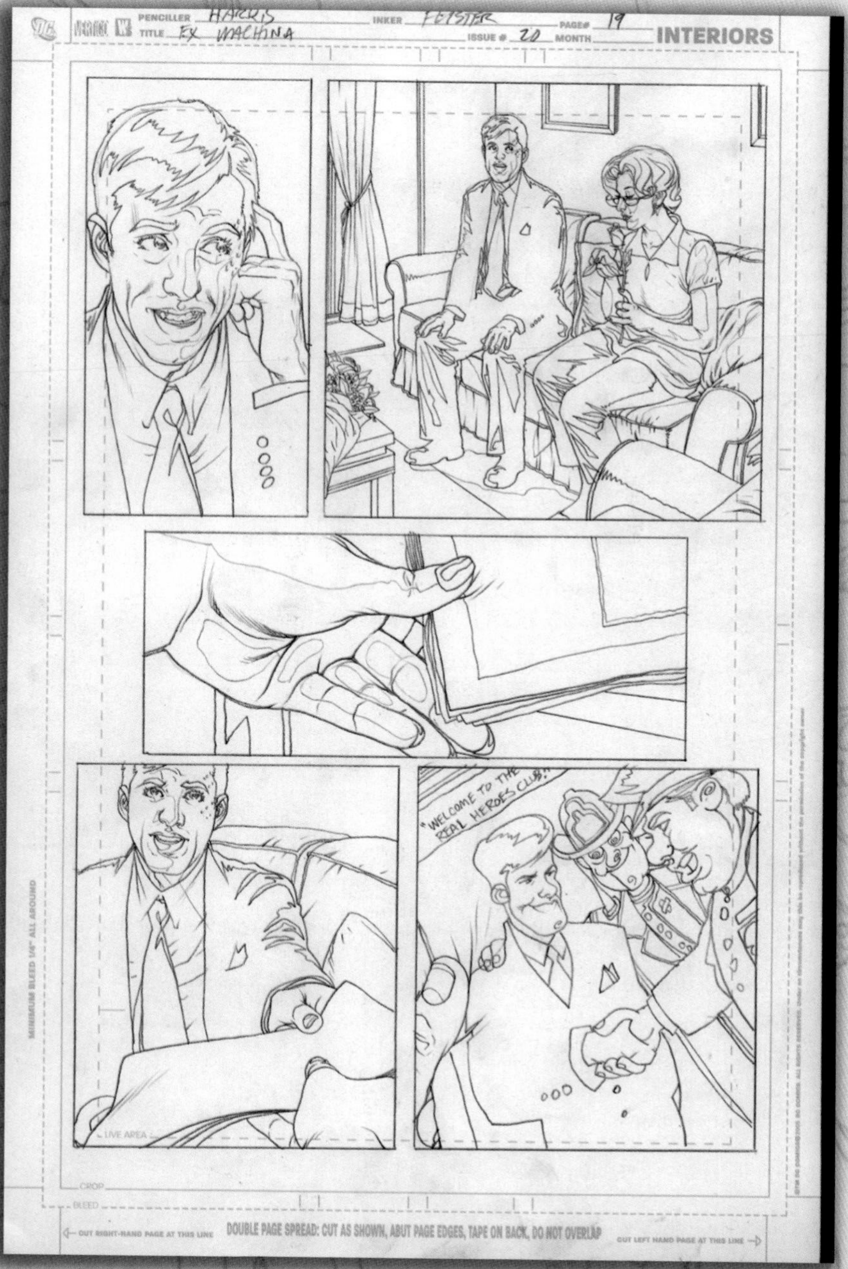

PENCILLER HARRIS
INKER FEISTER
PAGE# 19
TITLE EX MACHINA
ISSUE # 20 MONTH
INTERIORS
"WELCOME TO THE REAL HEROES CLUB!"
DOUBLE PAGE SPREAD: CUT AS SHOWN, ABUT PAGE EDGES, TAPE ON BACK, DO NOT OVERLAP

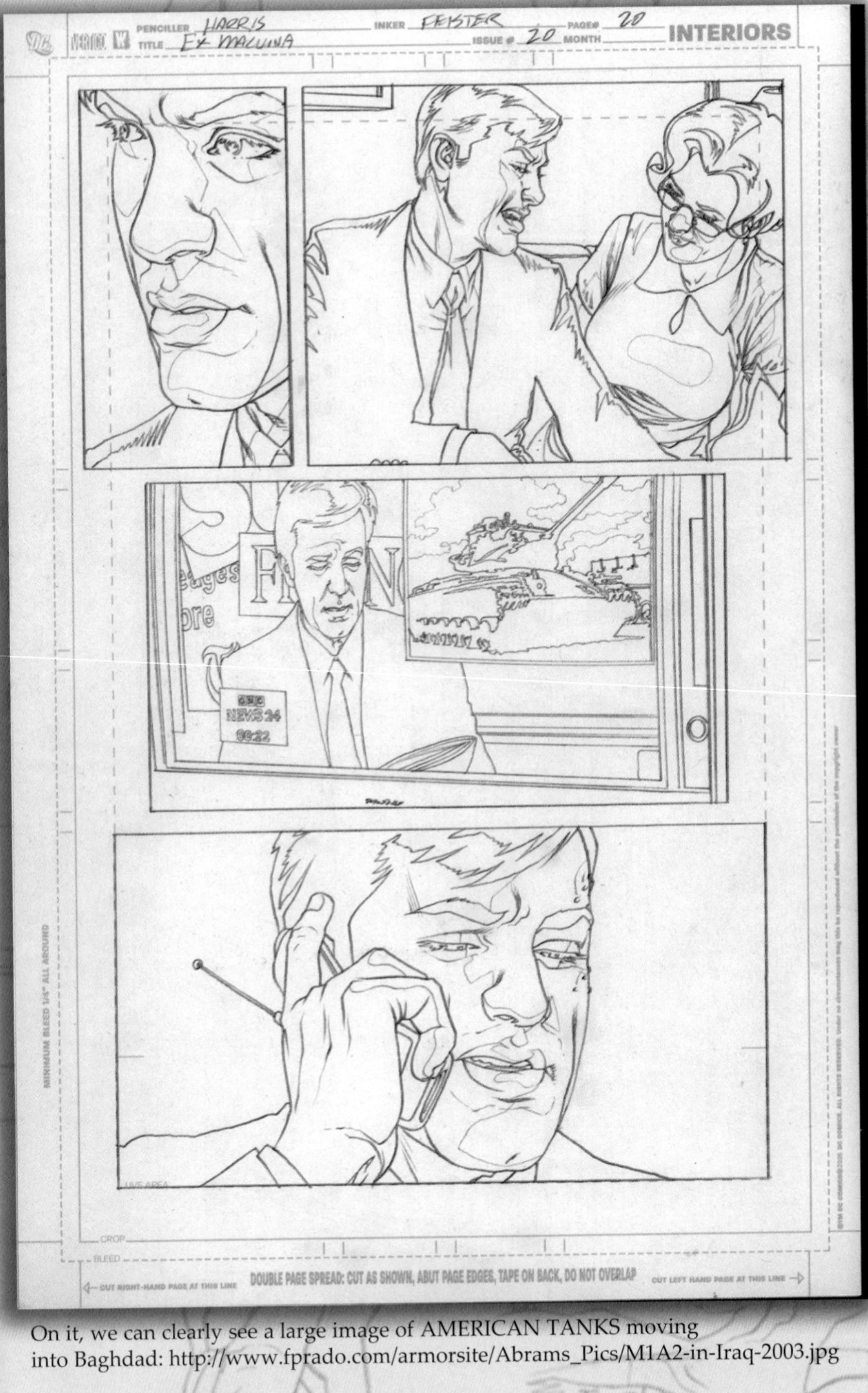
PENCILLER HARRIS
INKER FEISTER
PAGE# 20
TITLE EX MACHINA
ISSUE # 20
MONTH
INTERIORS
NEWS 24
CROP
BLEED
MINIMUM BLEED 1/4" ALL AROUND
DOUBLE PAGE SPREAD: CUT AS SHOWN, ABUT PAGE EDGES, TAPE ON BACK, DO NOT OVERLAP

## Page Twenty

### Page Twenty, Panel One

Change angles for this shot of a somber Mitchell, still looking down at the cartoon.

1) Mitchell: You know who Herbert Block was?

### Page Twenty, Panel Two

Pull out for this shot of Suzanne and Mitchell, as he tosses the old paper aside.

2) Suzanne: Uh-uh.

3) Mitchell: Political cartoonist for the Washington Post. He was one of the first guys to recognize Nixon as shady, so he always drew him with a five o' clock shadow.

4) Mitchell: But when Nixon got elected, Herblock drew him clean-faced for the first time. Caption read, "Everybody gets one free shave."

5) Mitchell: Guess how long that lasted…?

### Page Twenty, Panel Three

Change angles for this largest panel of the page, a shot of Mitchell, as he turns to look at a big-screen television in Suzanne's house. On it, we can clearly see a large image of AMERICAN TANKS moving into Baghdad: http://www.fprado.com/armorsite/Abrams_Pics/M1A2-in-Iraq-2003.jpg

6) Mitchell: Anyway.

7) Mitchell: I suppose the world has more important things to worry about than cartoons.

8) SFX (from off): vrrr vrrr

### Page Twenty, Panel Four

Push in on Mitch, as he suddenly answers his CELL PHONE.

9) Mitchell: Hundred here.

10) Electronic (tailless): Sir, it's Wylie.

11) Mitchell: Thought we were only speaking through intermediaries these days, Dave.

12) Electronic (tailless): You need to come to the hospital, sir. It's Journal.

**Page Twenty-one**

**Page Twenty-one, Panel One**

Cut to later that day for this close-up of the flashing SIRENS on the top of Mitchell's motorcade.

No Copy

**Page Twenty-one, Panel Two**

Cut into the hospital for this shot of an excited Mitchell, as he approaches a suddenly despondent Wylie, who's standing guard outside of an open hospital room.

1) Mitchell: I sent the motorcade to pick up her family, just so they wouldn't get stuck at lights. When'd Journal come out of her coma?

2) Wylie: You should step inside, Mitch.

3) Mitchell: Mitch? You haven't called me that since…

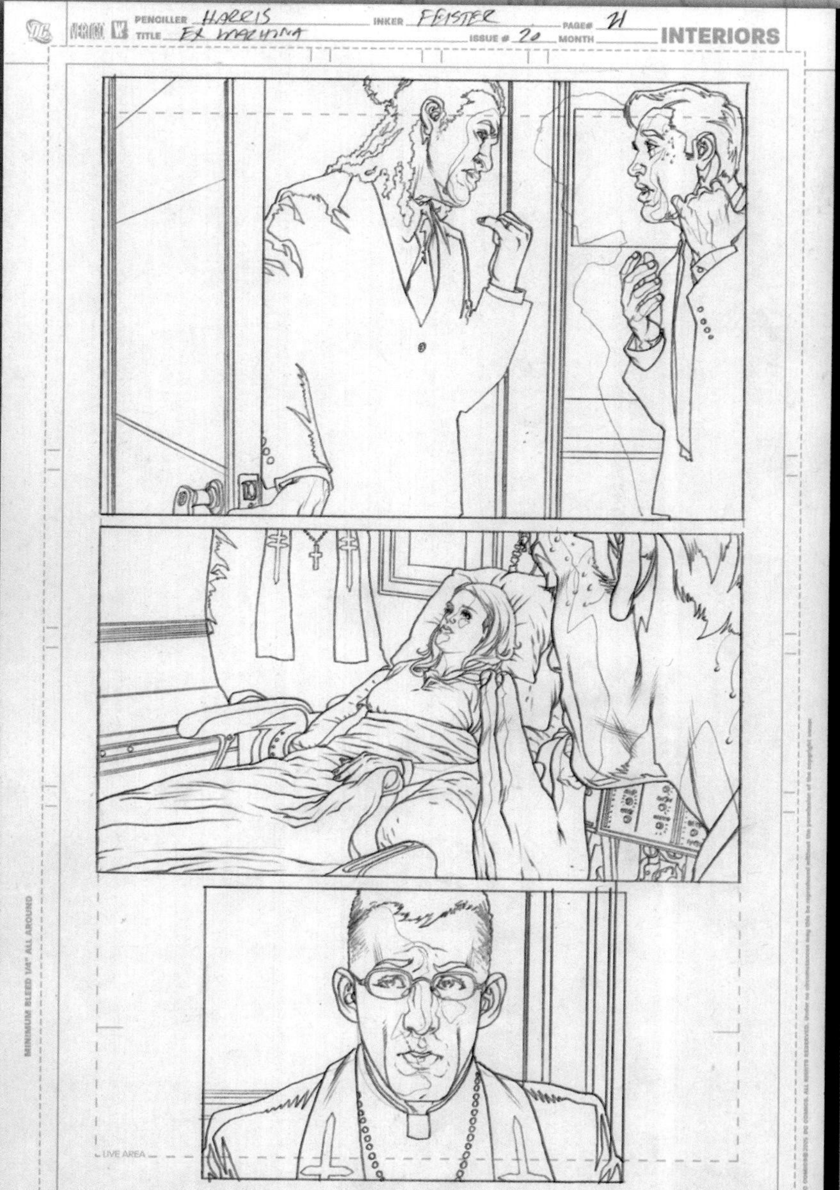
PENCILLER HARRIS
INKER FEISTER
PAGE# 21
TITLE EX MACHINA
ISSUE # 20
MONTH
INTERIORS
MINIMUM BLEED 1/4" ALL AROUND
LIVE AREA
CROP
BLEED
DOUBLE PAGE SPREAD: CUT AS SHOWN, ABUT PAGE EDGES, TAPE ON BACK, DO NOT OVERLAP

**Page Twenty-one, Panel Three**

Pull out to the largest panel of the page. As Wylie escorts Mitchell into the room of a sleeping (?) JOURNAL MOORE, he's greeted by FATHER ZEE, who is standing over the girl.

4) Wylie: I'm sorry. It happened so fast.

5) Priest: Good morning, Mr. Mayor.

6) Mitchell: Father Zee? What are you doing here?

**Page Twenty-one, Panel Four**

Push in on Zee, as he looks up at us, and reluctantly says:

7) Priest: Giving the girl her last rites.

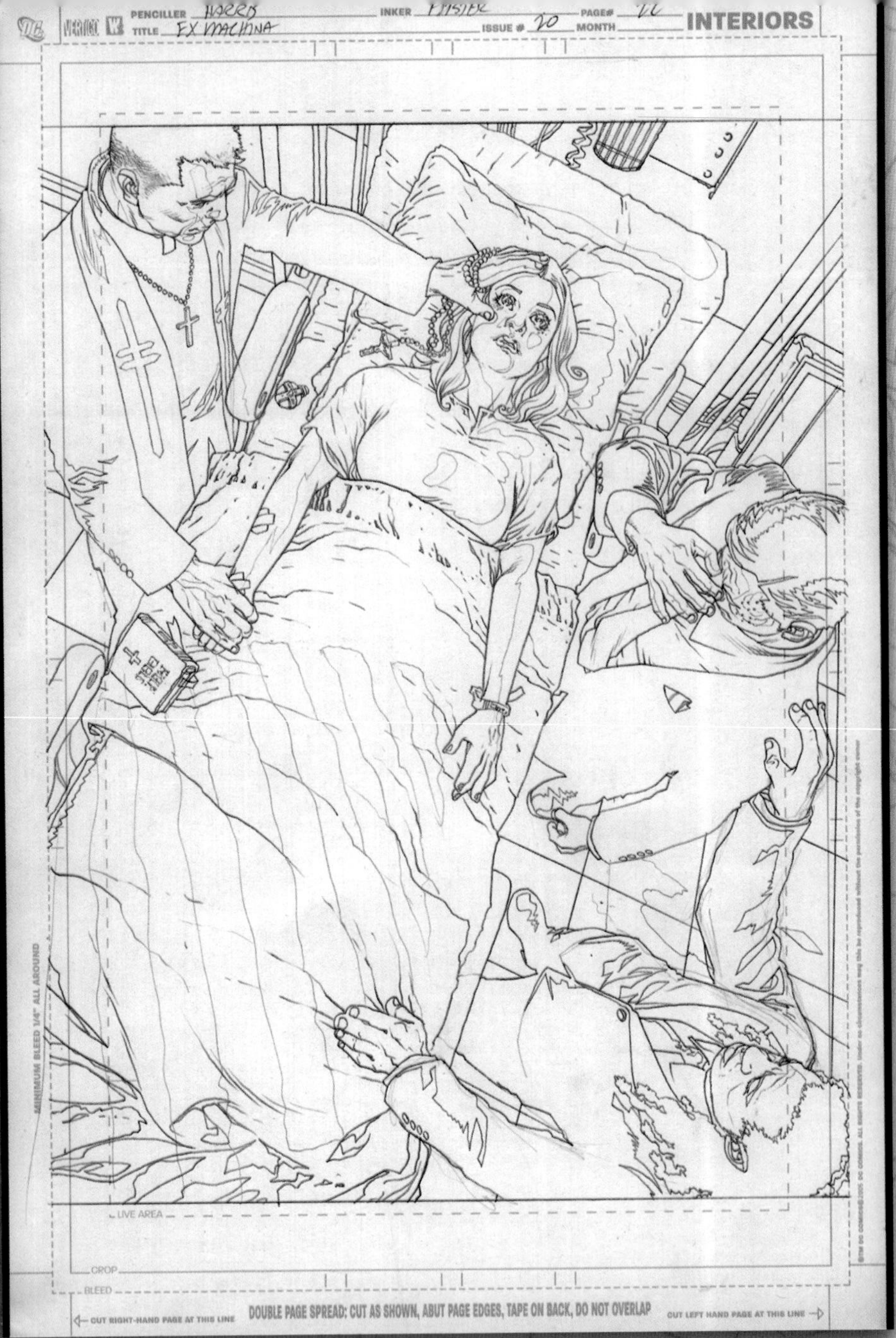
PENCILLER
INKER
PAGE#
TITLE
ISSUE #
MONTH
INTERIORS
LIVE AREA
CROP
BLEED
MINIMUM BLEED 1/4" ALL AROUND
CUT RIGHT-HAND PAGE AT THIS LINE
DOUBLE PAGE SPREAD: CUT AS SHOWN, ABUT PAGE EDGES, TAPE ON BACK, DO NOT OVERLAP
CUT LEFT HAND PAGE AT THIS LINE

## Page Twenty-two

## Page Twenty-two, SPLASH

This final SPLASH is actually an OVERHEAD SHOT, looking directly down at a full-figure, head-to-toe image of Journal, lying peacefully in her deathbed with her arms at her side. We can see just the tops of the heads of Father Zee, Wylie, and Mitchell, since I think it's more sad to show them standing at the girl's bedside than letting us actually see their grieving emotions. Maybe Wylie is putting a hand on Mitch's shoulder here? Either way, this is the last we're ever going to see of Journal, Tony, so please make this closing splash count!
Oh, and don't forget to leave a little room for our closing credits at the very bottom of this page.

1) Priest: She's gone.
2) Title:

## MARCH TO WAR conclusion

3) Credits:
Brian K. Vaughan - Writer Tony Harris - Penciller Tom Feister - Inker JD Mettler - Colorist
Jared K Fletcher - Letterer Kristy Quinn - Assistant Editor Ben Abernathy - Editor
Ex Machina created by Vaughan & Harris